On the following pages, many ideas are explored that show how teachers can build quality in the writing of children.

Creative Teaching

Literature can be used as a base for creative teaching in a variety of ways. Creative teaching is a unique kind of teaching. To teach creatively in the area of children's literature requires: (1) a knowledge of what creativity is; (2) a knowledge of children's literature; (3) a knowledge of the basic principles in the development of creativity in children; and (4) an understanding of the growth patterns and preferences of children. These themes are developed in the chapters that follow.

Literature as a Base for School Curriculum

Because of its diverse content and endless subject matter, literature serves two very important functions in the elementary school: (1) as a tool to teach subject matter, and (2) as enrichment for all areas of the curriculum.

Some teachers and librarians differ in their concept of the place of literature in the reading program. For instance, some feel strongly that the main purpose for teaching reading is to enable children to read the literature written for them, while others would separate the reading and literature programs completely. These differing viewpoints need to be resolved in terms of changes in modern society and scrutinized from the viewpoint of the child within that society.

Children's librarians often say that a good piece of literature or a good poem will stand by itself; it needs no embellishment or no elaboration. They generally concede that a good storyteller may help to put across the author's message. They will note, however, that very few children "hear" good literature anymore and that most of their contact with good literature comes from the books supplied in the reading program or in the school library, or from comic books, television shows, or moving picture cartoons. Because of this, many librarians and teachers sometimes frown upon any activity that detracts from the story or poem being read to the children.

While the basic criterion for using any piece of literature is that it communicate effectively and beautifully, much can be done to develop children's taste in literature. Today's children are exposed to much cheap, yet often impressive, writing. They become confused when no attempt is made to help them distinguish between good and poor literature.

Through literature the child develops his tastes in reading for pleasure. If he experiences satisfaction in the stories the teacher reads, he will seek out this satisfaction in other stories. Satisfaction, happiness, contentment, fun, joy, positive release, pleasure—all these feelings should accompany the literature period in the classroom.

Literature fulfills a need in the modern school. It touches on every aspect of living and therefore should become an integral part of the entire school program. At least once every day, and in some instances many more times than this, a teacher should read a poem or story to the children regardless of age range or grade placement. The wealth of available material gives her resources for every occasion.

FIGURE 1–4. A classroom reading center for five- and six-year-olds.

Although literature is often classified among the fine arts, in the elementary school it can be combined with any area of the school curriculum. Social studies textbooks can only be, at best, a summary of facts about a country or a period in history. They cannot consume space to give children the feeling for the way of life in any given country or any period of time. Without the "feeling" element, facts cannot help children understand life in a time or place different from their own. Reading about Switzerland in a social studies book is one thing, and reading *Heidi* is another. Facts about the Revolutionary War cannot impart to children the terror, the suspense, the fear, the bravery, the compassion, or the hatred which war arouses in the hearts of men, but reading Marian Boyd Havighurst's *Strange Island* or Betty Cavanna's *Ruffles and Drums* can. Social studies books reach the minds of children, but literature reaches their hearts. Because literature is, in a sense, a recording of the experiences and feelings of the human race, it, in turn, provides a vicarious experience for its readers.

Good literature recaptures the *mood* rather than the *facts* of life. The life of a bygone period of time is reconstructed, a strange place comes alive, or a feeling or mood saturates the listener to the extent that the author is able to communicate in an imaginative manner. It is not the story of Tom and Huck Finn that makes *Tom Sawyer* a delightful book—it is the author's unique ability to make every boy today feel a kinship with Tom. Tom makes fires glow in the hearts of fathers, bringing back the carefree adventurous feeling of their own boyhoods. Twain evokes nostalgic memories through the magic grouping of words. So literature can transplant us to another

Word Music
and Word Magic

A book is made to dream by.

Word Music and Word Magic:

Children's Literature Methods

James A. Smith
Dorothy M. Park
State University of New York, Oswego

Allyn and Bacon, Inc.
Boston   London   Sydney   Toronto

To
Emilio Chamberlain Marianelli
Esther Stinson Marianelli and
Lillian Edith Smith

Who originally put
music
and
magic
in our
words . . .

Library of Congress Cataloging in Publication Data

Smith, James A.
    Word music and word magic.

    Includes bibliographies and index.
    1.   Language arts (Elementary).   2.   Children's
literature—History and criticism.   3.   Books and
reading for children.   I.   Park, Dorothy M., joint
author.   II.   Title.
LB1576.S622   372.6'4   76-41861

ISBN 0-205-05587-7

Material on pages 236–241 used with the permission of Mr. Tony Chen
Material on pages 100–101 from James A. Smith, *Creative Teaching of Reading in the Elementary School,* 2nd edition
(Boston: Allyn and Bacon, Inc., 1975), pages 31–34.
Photos courtesy of Saisuke Ieno, Chris Savas, and Courtenay Wilson

Contents

Preface

This book deals directly with developing an understanding of children's literature for the student in training and for the classroom teacher. It promotes the idea that literature in the space age can rightfully be the core of the elementary school curriculum.

We have written this book with a specific philosophy in mind. First of all, we believe that literature must be experienced as well as "heard" in order to be enjoyed. We believe that experiences can be turned into adventures that will motivate children to create their own literature. We feel that adventures with literature develop the creative characteristics of the child and ensure an appreciation of the creative writing of others. Appreciation and taste for literature are elusive qualities at best, but they *can* be developed in children through strategies presented here, and not discussed in other books on children's literature. We also believe that appreciation and taste in children can be developed through certain types of adventuring, if the teacher will respect the child's values, will try to understand what is relevant to each child, and will allow each child's individuality to be a guide.

This is also a book about creative teachers in action, teachers who have been inspired by the concepts promoted in this book. They adventure with children's literature differently than most teachers in that they do not rely on manuals of predetermined strategies, modules, systems, or gimmicks. They are creative enough to invent their own techniques. Their methodology is sound; it is based on tried-and-proven principles of child development, learning, and creativity, which produce different, unusual, and unique results. These teachers have provided this text with many "verbal observations" by allowing us into their classrooms to see them adventuring creatively with children and literature.

This is also a book about children and about the kinds of classroom organizations in which they learn best—ranging from the structured classroom to the open school. It shows children in humane situations in which they rate above books and materials and are individuals who count—individuals loved and respected by their teachers.

As a result of reading this book, we hope that teachers will take a hard look at the place that children's literature plays in the school program and will set about to revamp their programs in order to elevate literature to its rightful place in the priorities of learnings.

To teach literature according to the philosophy of this book, teachers must prepare themselves in five areas:

1. They must establish a philosophy about teaching children's literature.
2. They must know about the nature of children.
3. They must know about children's literature and the people who write it.
4. They must know ways in which it can be used in the classroom.
5. They must know about the available resources.

This book is presented in sections that reflect these areas of necessary preparation. Part I deals with establishing a philosophy about literature and the nature of children. Part II deals with children's literature and the people who write it. Part III deals with ways literature can be used in the classroom, and Part IV provides selected resource lists that will be of immediate help in the classroom. The appendixes, which contain bibliographies and lists of publishers and distributers of all types of media that relate to children's literature, provide a permanent reference for the teacher.

The book titles chosen for "verbal observations" of classroom projects in this volume are the most popular with boys and girls today. We were guided in selecting them by *Best Selling Children's Books* by Jean Spealman Kujoth (Metuchen, New Jersey: Scarecrow Press, 1973). Ms. Kujoth's book is a survey of the best-selling books in print today. According to her text, a best-selling book is one that has sold 100,000 copies or more since it was first published. To these titles, we have added many others that have not been in print long enough to reach the criteria established by Ms. Kujoth.

Our visits to many schools supported the fact that best-selling books are those most popular with children. As we photographed the literature projects of children, we found that many of the old classics still play as important a part in the life of the child today as do the newer books. *The Adventures of Robin Hood* and *Little Women* were being used as often as Judy Blume's stories of realistic fiction.

Some of our readers will dislike the use of the personal pronoun "she," which we have used throughout the book in referring to teachers. The majority of the observations reported here are of women teachers, and we justify the use of "she" in referring to them simply because it was more comfortable writing that way.

We are indebted to many teachers for new materials presented in this edition. Many of the "verbal observations" are accounts of adventures with the children we have taught, but others are of those sent to us by teachers who were students in our graduate courses or with whom we worked in classrooms, experimenting with new ideas and observing results. We owe a debt of gratitude to our student teachers who dared to be adventurous, to the children who worked so responsively in our classes, and to the parents who allowed us to use materials in this volume. Thanks also must go to the school principals and superintendents who made us welcome and willingly offered their school resources.

Special acknowledgments must be made to the following people: John Ritson for the use of some of the material in *The Creative Teaching of Art;* Dorothy Hickock for material previously printed in *The Creative Teaching of Music;* David Furman for some of the beautiful writing by children;

Rosalind Kimmich, children's librarian of the Campus School at State University College at Oswego for her help and patience; Judy Blume, author, for her delightful interview and reactions; Cecelia Linder for her charming pictures; and Helen E. Buckley for the use of her files and personal materials and for her advice and encouragement.

We would be remiss if we did not extend a special thanks to the following people for inviting us to their schools to observe children and to take pictures: Holly Weller of the Palmer School in Baldwinsville, New York; Jan Greco and Paul Anderson of the Alden Elementary School in Baldwinsville, New York; Floyd Wallace, principal of the Lanigan School and his teachers; Blaine Webb, principal of the Volney School and his teachers; and George McDonald, elementary supervisor, all of Fulton, New York; Joseph Pittarelli and his colleague Maureen Davison of the Brewerton Elementary School. A special thanks must go to Kathleen Brown and her sixth graders at Brewerton Elementary School who wrote beautiful letters, drew lovely illustrations, and helped develop the story "The Day of the Bubble."

We are grateful to Alexander Park for typing and for judicious criticism, to Roswell Park, Jr., for important leg work and helpful research, to Roswell Park, Sr., who calmly tolerated many inconveniences; and to the following people for a number of reasons: Susan Harmon, Miss Patricia Smith and Mr. John Roloff of the McNamara Elementary School in Baldwinsville, New York; Courtenay Wilson for taking some beautiful pictures for us; and young Scott Andrew Harmon, our frontispiece boy.

Last of all, we owe gratitude to a talented, delightful, and inspiring person, Tony Chen, for his interview and for sharing with us his beautiful philosophy of life.

James A. Smith
Dorothy M. Park

PART
I

Introduction to Books and Children

CHAPTER 1

Word Music and Word Magic:
A Viewpoint

A NAME IS BORN

"I think," said Miss Baxter, "that Charlene has a poem to read. What did you name your poem, Charlene?"

"I call it *Just Imagine*," said Charlene as she moved to the front of the group. "And I like the way it turned out." She began to read:

JUST IMAGINE

Just imagine snowmen could talk.
Just imagine that trees could walk.
Just imagine a lot of things
Like if you had fairy wings.
Just imagine that rain is dry,
That beautiful flowers never die,
That rainbows come down from the skies
To be a shawl for butterflies
And puddles make a silver coat
On which a chickadee can float.
There is so much I never see
Imagination makes for me!

CHARLENE
Age 11

A thoughtful silence filled the room when Charlene finished. Finally Jimmy said, "Boy, was that good!"

"Indeed, it was good," said Miss Baxter. "It was beautiful, Charlene. And why did you like it so much, Jimmy?"

"She really put her words together so that we could see beautiful pictures," said Jimmy, "like when she said rainbows came down from the skies to be a shawl for butterflies."

"And when she said that puddles make a silver coat," said Sara.

"I liked the rest of that too," added Judy, "especially the part about the chickadees floating."

"Do you remember what we call it when people use words that paint pictures in our minds—when they compare two different things in the way that Charlene compared the rainbow to a shawl and puddles to a silver coat?"

"Yes," said Tom, "we call it a metaphor. Miss Baxter, can we have her read it again? Man, that's a real neat poem!"

So Charlene read her poem again.

Sara raised her hand. "Miss Baxter," she said, "poems are really *word music*. You can't just read them. You almost have to *sing them*."

"What you just said is poetic," said Miss Baxter. "I like calling poetry *word music*. You are right. Good poems like Charlene's do sing. Let's use that title on the bulletin board where we share our poems. Word music! Very good!"

So the children named this book for us. After a few days of writing word music, another bulletin board for class stories and essays appeared with the words WORD MAGIC over it. *Word Music and Word Magic*—poetry and prose—the children's own name for their literature!

CHILDREN'S LITERATURE AS CREATIVE COMMUNICATION

Literature is one of the most creative forms of communication.[1] Webster defines it as "the writings of a period or a country, especially those kept alive by their beauty of style or thought." Literature can take the form of a book, a poem, a story, an essay, a saying, or a thought.

Exposure to creative forms of communication places before children the beauty of the written word. One of the major objectives of the elementary school in the space age is to develop *effective* as well as "correct" communication skills among children.

Developing effective communication in children means helping them to become aware of the importance of style in writing and helping them to establish a style of their own. Children develop their own style as soon as they begin to use speech, and individual differences intensify as

---

1. Because over 2,000 references are made to the titles of children's books in this volume, the authors have taken the liberty of saving space by annotating only those books which play an important part in developing the theme of any one section. Public school teachers assure us that they rarely send individually to a publisher for a book. Rather, they are likely to consult the school librarian for a particular book and its publisher. We have, therefore, referred to most books by title and author.

Also, the thrust of this book is not to use specific strategies with specific pieces; we intend, instead, to show how a teacher may use many creative ideas to accomplish many objectives through the use of children's literature. Hopefully, she will use any worthy books at her immediate disposal.

they grow older. Their uniqueness of style can be developed into effective speech. The current pattern in most schools, however, is to attempt to make all children alike in their thinking and in their speech patterns.

When a three-year-old asks, "Are those pansies growing by your door?" he is asking a simple question. But when he says, "Why are you growing all the faces?" he is effectively communicating a unique idea, and demonstrating his own ability to create literature. Such statements could be the basis of a style of writing. The question requires only a simple answer, but it evokes an emotional response; my heart melts, my eyes twinkle, my lips curve at the corners because I have been able to empathize with the child's feelings. The ability to empathize is a necessary quality of a writer.

This book is based on the specific philosophy of developing in children a love of literature and a talent for creating literature. Such a philosophy is grounded on the following assumptions:

- To develop effective communication skills in children, the teacher must expose children continually to effective forms of communication, such as the children's literature of the world.
- An appreciation and understanding of children's literature is best developed by "adventuring" with children in literature, rather than by simply reading literature.
- Children develop a love and taste for literature when they experience the varying styles of many authors while they are involved in the process of forming their own styles of writing.
- Children develop a taste for and an appreciation of literature from two specific types of adventures: (1) exposure to many forms of literature, as mentioned above; and (2) direct confrontations with style and form, and a study of both.
- To be of value to children, their adventures with literature must be relevant.
- Children's literature can motivate the development of creativity in children.
- The ability of children to write creatively correlates directly with their own ambitions to create a distinct style and with their encounters with the styles of creative writers.
- Ways to activate creativity in children are to develop their ability to use simile, metaphor, and analogy, and to expand their powers of perception and empathy.
- Literature can become meaningful and beautiful to all children when creative teaching strategies are used in the classroom.
- Literature can be the base for teaching most subjects in the elementary school curriculum.
- Children's literature is the rightful heritage of all children, rather than a chosen few in any one classroom.
- Literature can be taught, but taste and appreciation cannot really be "taught." Teachers can set conditions for literature to be read, experienced, and enjoyed, but appreciation and taste are highly individual matters, and each child will develop his own tastes and his own appreciations as a result of his own adventures with literature. A teacher cannot cultivate taste and appreciation by imposing his or her own preconceived values on the child's thinking.

Exposure to Literature

The most likely way to develop a love of good literature in children is to expose them to it. But exposure in itself is not enough. Most of the exposure that children in American schools receive is limited to books selected by librarians and teachers, who have weeded out books they feel are inappropriate or unsuitable for children.

Exposure to a wide variety of books will accommodate individual interests, personal taste, and variation in reading ability. If children are introduced to a variety of writing styles, they will be made aware of story line, style, and the effectiveness of the printed word.

Adventures and Experiences

The children in Miss Baxter's classroom were having an adventure in children's literature. What is an adventure? How do adventures differ from experiences?

Webster says that an *experience* is "the actual living through an event or events; actual enjoyment or suffering; hence the effect upon the judgment or feelings produced by personal and direct impressions; as, to know by experience." Another definition given by Webster is "the sum total of the conscious events which compose an individual's life."

Webster defines an *adventure* as "a bold undertaking, in which hazards are to be met and the issue hangs upon unforeseen events; a daring feat; a remarkable experience; to venture or hazard oneself, as adventuring upon paths unknown; to take the risk."

A sign faces you: "Robin Hood Rides Again." What do you predict? An experience or an adventure? Which is more motivating: "Today we will write poems," or "Today is Just Imagine Day"? A workbook experience or a clean sheet of paper with crayons? A chance to "do your thing" or the chance to follow the teacher's instructions to the letter? A chance to take risks or to be perpetually guided?

According to Webster, almost anything is an experience. Going to school is an experience; so is going to the circus. Eating lunch is an experience, but so is eating a Mexican lunch. Doing a workbook exercise is an experience, but so is seeing a flannel board magic story. Eating a bagel from the bakery is an experience, but so is baking and icing a cake all by yourself! Riding in a snowmobile is an experience, but so is building a soap box car for the derby! All are experiences, but certainly all are not the same level of experience! Some are more than experiences: they are adventures! Experiences can be enjoyable, like eating dinner; or miserable, like doing a workbook exercise. Experiences may be lived through, but do not necessarily require involvement. Experiences may produce impressions the individual may want to remember—or forget!

An adventure is different. Adventures, like experiences, are enjoyable or unenjoyable, but, according to our definition, they must also be remarkable—a *remarkable* experience. Adventures cannot just be lived through; they require personal involvement and risk, and consequently keen personal reaction. One must be willing to take risks—to venture onto paths of the unknown. When one has a remarkable experience, one learns in an involved and dramatic way.

FIGURE 1–1. An adventure with puppets: John and David prepare a play of The Painted Pig.

John Dewey said, "We learn by doing!" He believed experience to be the basis of all learning. We would like to substitute the word "adventure" for "experience." We learn by adventuring, by having *remarkable* experiences that deal with both the cognitive and the affective domain.

Adventures help boys and girls develop their creativity because they force them to play roles in which creative characteristics are brought into play. These include the willingness to experience something new or different; the willingness to take risks (there comes a time when the teacher withdraws and leaves the children to face the unknown, something unusual, or original results), to largely assume the responsibility for their own learning, and to use open-ended situations.

The creative teacher provides remarkable experiences (adventures) for her students. The children in Miss Baxter's classroom were having an adventure with poetry. It grew out of reading many of Dr. Seuss's books and a long, provocative discussion on imagination, which followed. The children concluded that imagination could put words into patterns that made them funny—and that imagination could also put words into patterns that made the words beautiful. They decided to try writing their own funny or beautiful poems. The class situation described above was one of the resulting "adventure" sessions with word music.

Style

To develop an appreciation of style in writing, the problem of style must be confronted head on, and not left to chance. Reading many kinds of literature does not necessarily make children aware of the reasons *why* one piece of writing appeals to them more than another. This is not to suggest that teachers should spend time analyzing and dissecting forms of literature with children; however, encounters with literature will take on new dimensions because of the type of questions teachers ask during the discussion that follows the reading of any passage in a story or poem. The teacher must train herself to know *what* questions to ask. Questions of the following type are commonly used at present:

"Did you like the story?"
"Why did you like this story?"
"Who was the main character in this story?"
"What was the idea of the story?"

They should be changed to such questions as:

"How did this author make you feel about Anna?"
"Where did he put words together in such a beautiful way that you saw a picture immediately?"
"How did the author make you feel you knew Jed?"
"Did he make you feel like Jed?"
"Where in the story did you want to laugh? To cry? To help Jed?"
"Inasmuch as these are only words on this page, how did the author put these words together so that they made you have such deep feelings?"
"How does the style of this story compare to the story we read yesterday? Could this author have told this story as effectively in poetry?"
"Let's find a place in the story where the author used two or more words together to create a new or beautiful idea."
"The author paints pictures by comparing things and places to other things, like here on page 10 where he says, 'The clouds were torn lace across the sky.' Can we find other beautiful descriptions?"

Taste and Appreciation

A taste or appreciation for literature develops as a result of personal experience. A child's taste for a particular type of literature is largely imposed on him by adults, since teachers, parents, and librarians generally choose the literature a child reads. Children who enjoy the selections made by adults tend to look for more books of the same sort. Children may be learning what good books are in this process, but can we say that, left on their own in a corner bookstore, they will continue to choose only the excellent books? Much has been done to expose children to good books, but little is done to actually develop their appreciation and taste to the point where they can consciously say *why* they like one book better than another, or *why* a certain book appeals to them.

Selections of books for children should not betray a prejudice against certain forms of literature or deprive children of encounters with some forms of literature. Adult tastes and children's tastes are not the same. Consequently, adult criteria for the selection of literature are not likely to be the same as children's. Appreciation and taste are personal feelings and must develop inside each human being.

One aspect related to the development in children of "taste" for literature is the sentiment and snobbery that often appear when students, teachers, and librarians reach the point where they feel that no literature is good literature unless it complies specifically with pre-established criteria. This attitude inhibits the ability to appreciate, to accept new styles and types of literature, and to rediscover some of the literature of the past, unknown because it is not in vogue, but nevertheless highly creative.

Much adult literature today makes its claim to fame because it deals with controversial issues or with topics not dealt with in the past, or uses language that was formerly taboo. Yet none of these criteria necessarily make good literature. Writing about sex, abortion, violence, crime, and venereal disease does not make literature: it is *how* the words are put together that counts. Books written about contemporary social issues can be as skillfully and beautifully written as books on other themes, when the skill of the author is developed through a unique writing style.

In the long run, what is a "good" piece of literature for a child at a given age is highly dubious. The answer probably lies in the response of the child to the piece. If he loves the piece, identifies with it, reads it over and over, or asks that it be read to him, it has value for him at that point in his life, whether or not the teacher or librarian thinks it is a good book. A wise teacher will use these criteria to evaluate the child's growth in appreciation and will plan his next contacts with literature from this point.

How does a teacher measure the development of appreciation in children? What is taste in literature?

APPRECIATION. When we talk of appreciation here, it is in terms of some or all of the following observable behaviors:

Children accept all books for what they are. They demonstrate this acceptance by:

The careful manner in which they handle books

The frequency with which they pick up books and thumb through them or study the pictures

The number of times they pick up a book to read when they have finished other work before others in the class

The frequency with which they borrow books from the library

The degree to which they talk about books during class discussion times

Their attitude of complete absorption when reading a book

The degree to which they bring books from home or from the library to share with others

The manner in which they study bulletin boards in the classroom and/or the library that tell about books

The number of times they ask for a story or a poem to be read

Their reaction of joy when the teacher asks if they would like a story read to them

Their absorption in adventures with books in the classroom

Their response to commercially prepared artifacts and paraphernalia about books (such as the toy plastic characters of Dr. Seuss)

Their own unsolicited comments of enthusiasm or joy after reading a book.

WHAT IS TASTE? "Taste," as we define it here, is a step above appreciation. It means that from his respect for all books, the child has developed preferences of his own. These preferences may result from any number of combinations of factors within the individual. They may come from a strong interest, as children who love dogs will love *Ginger Pye*. They may be due to a writing style that appeals to the child or to a book's involvement with people of his own life style. A book may have psychological appeal because it copes with the same problems he has, or it may serve as an *escape* from his life style into adventure and fantasy. It may appeal to his taste not because of the content at all but because of the type of book or because of the author.

Taste is used in this volume in terms of the following observable behaviors in children:

- A child repeatedly seeks a *specific* type of book even though he likes many books.
- He reacts lovingly to this kind of book—may drop everything else when he sees a book of this type.
- He clutches these books to him, carries them around, treats them like his friends.
- He returns to these books again and again and reads them or asks to have them read repeatedly.
- He may or may not share a book of his taste with others. Some children will talk endlessly about it, describing it as "cool" and "neat." Others seem to feel they have a secret with the author. Their eyes twinkle when

FIGURE 1–2. *Behavior indicates love for a book: Everyone wants to play a part in* Mr. Popper's Penguins.

the book is mentioned, they may hug themselves or comment briefly as they read it, but, on the whole, they do not seem inclined to talk with others about it.

- He reacts most enthusiastically to bulletin boards and exhibits about books of his taste.
- He is completely absorbed in his book when reading it. After calling Billy three times while he was reading Lloyd Alexander's *The High King,* one teacher gently rapped on his forehead with her knuckles and smilingly said, "Yoo-hoo, Billy, are you in there?"
- He reacts to artifacts and paraphernalia about his specific tastes and may collect some.
- He responds enthusiastically and joyously after reading such books.
- He is a key person in working on adventures in the classroom built around his type of book.

When someone has a special taste for or appreciation of something, it is easily discernible in his conversation or by his behavior. Yet conscious attempts to develop appreciative behavior in our elementary classrooms have been meager. In most modern texts, authors suggest exposure to good books and experiences with children's literature as the basic strategies for developing appreciation and taste. Both appreciation and taste, however, are treated as mystic, elusive qualities that cannot really be instilled in children. To a degree this may be true, but we feel that attitudes can be changed through planned educational experiences and that appreciation and taste are also subject to educational methods.

Relevancy

To be worthy of use in the classroom, the writing must be relevant to the child. Many of the cherished customs and ideas of the past have fallen by the wayside because of changes in our way of living. Many of the concepts of the past are still relevant to modern life, but have not been presented to children in a relevant or meaningful manner, so that students have failed to see their importance and have not learned them. One of the major problems of teachers from nursery school through college is how to present material in a manner so relevant to students that they understand its worth from the moment of presentation. The prime answer to the problem is to use creative methods of teaching—methods never before employed but methods which motivate children, which use the techniques and hardware of their generation and get the students so involved that their values are developed, their skills and knowledge expanded, and their behavior changed.

Every planned unit and lesson, every book selected, should contain an answer to the question, "How relevant is this to the child of the space age?" or "How can I make this relevant to children living today?"

Relevancy is rarely measured by the tests given at the close of a study. One guide for relevancy is behavior change. Relevancy deals with the affective domain as well as the cognitive. It can best be measured by observing behavior of the students during the learning process; by careful observation on the part of the teacher on how well each student enters into the study—the ideas generated by the students, the materials they bring to the school, their willingness to spend time outside of school, the books they select, the books they discuss, the pictures they share.

Adults generally choose the books placed before children in school, in the library, and even at home. Much of the research that claims to indicate children's preferences in books is already biased by this fact and, consequently, does not actually show what it claims to show. Even noting the number of times a book is withdrawn from a library does not indicate free choices in books; it indicates the most popular books of those chosen by the librarian. True, when these adult-selected books are read to or by children, they are generally well received. But the fact remains that the child's reading material is contaminated with adult opinion.

Books and pictures are sometimes sentimental residue of what some adult *thinks* an ideal childhood is like. Most of Disney's films are built around this concept. As many adults as children often make up the lines waiting for admission to a Disney film.

Adult selection of children's reading material and setting up criteria for the selection of children's books by adults helps the teacher and parent select excellent literature for children, but it *can* also have negative results. Authors who must sell their books to make a living may be limited in their excursions into creative writing and in the creative use of books by the fact that they feel they must meet the preconceived criteria and consequently limit their creative output.

Rarely, if ever, do pop-up books and novelty books that have folds and gadgets on the pages make the selected book lists. Yet we find some of these books highly artistic, beautifully written, creatively engineered, and dearly loved by all children.

Such books are often criticized as being lacking in durability. Durability criteria were established years ago when good children's books were very expensive compared to toys and other materials. Now the costs are moderate, especially of total reproductions in paperback editions, and an educated public has come to appreciate their value. One questions whether durability of this nature is any longer a relevant criterion. When children love books, they can be taught to care for them.

One of the most loved books of one of the authors' children was a copy of *A Visit From St. Nicholas*, from which an enormous Santa Claus popped out of the chimney when the book was opened. His daughter cherished this book to the point where she now shares it with her own three-year-old.

Many little books that parents find in chain stores appear to meet the criteria for good literature and are highly relevant to children, but do not make the book list selections. One author found such a book while browsing over a rack in Woolworth's lately. It was a little thing called *A Quiet Place* and was written by Lynn Wheeling, published by the Western Publishing Company of Racine, Wisconsin. In it a little girl searches for a quiet place to be alone and eventually finds it—"the quiet place was in her heart." The book is simple and sincere. It carries a direct theme: peace with yourself is lasting peace. The illustrations are charming. The emotional reaction is one of delight and warmheartedness. It is a gem. Yet Miss Wheeling's little book is not found on any book list, which brings up another point: children never really get to see many books because they are not reviewed by the experts and consequently do not appear on book lists used by librarians, teachers, and parents.

Although much of the literature in books found in the chain store and supermarket is trash, some is also very good; this is also true of the literature being written for children. We need some sort of universal review system whereby good books are not overlooked, whether they appear in the library or the supermarket.

In selecting books for children, adults should remember that the main criteria are that the children must enjoy the story or book and that it must be sincere. Relevance is a prime factor in this enjoyment.

The Creative Development of Children

Literature is the creative product of the minds of creative people. Just as a painting can fire the imagination, so can a fine story, a well-composed poem, or a good book. As paint and brushes serve the skill of the artist, as notes serve the skill of the musician, as stone and mortar serve the skill of the architect, so do words serve the skill of the writer.

Children's literature is no exception. Many of the books written for children are masterpieces in writing by any standard. Children's literature makes definite contributions toward creative development in boys and girls and offers many opportunities for creative teaching.

Because there is a great need to develop the creativity of children in the world today, Chapter 4 is devoted to a review of the research in cre-

FIGURE 1–3. Creativity is brought into play when children love books enough to type and share their own.

ativity, and Chapters 13 and 14 deal with creative methods of adventuring in children's literature, so that the creative thinking powers of children are developed. Taste, as described above, is developed in children largely through creative adventuring in the classroom. In Chapter 4 special attention is given to the help afforded the creative child through the use of literature. In Chapter 3 we also discuss the nature of children and what is currently known about their choices in literature. In the development of children, creativeness begets creativeness.

Creative Writing

One of the chief values of using children's literature was demonstrated with the opening story of this chapter. Children's literature gently persuades children to try their own hands at writing and recording in a beautiful and creative manner. Children who create their own literature are generally eager and anxious to read the literature of others. And children who read the literature of others are anxious to try their hands at writing.

Observe the following poem composed by Donald, a fifth-grade boy, after reading *A Tree Is Nice* by Janice Udry.

TREES
Weeping willows dipping in the wind
  Bow down to the grazing cattle,
While the oak stands sturdy in the breeze
  As if making a bold speech.

DONALD MYERS
Grade 5

Much of the writing of children is inspired because they come to love the books they read or have read to them.

Developing Literary Abilities

The quality of writing and appreciation of writing can be improved in children, but not by trying to make children conform to the adult's values and standards. Only a sensitive and understanding teacher is able to develop quality in children's writing and in their appreciation of the writing of others. The teacher needs to continually remind herself that, should a particular child in her classroom be gifted at writing, he will become a great writer only if he creates a style of his own.

Literary abilities *can* be effectively developed in children. One fourth-grade teacher, Mr. Bell, formed a literary group to encourage his children to write creatively. Any class member could become a member of the literary group by submitting some creative writing each week. But this was not all. The group discussed various forms and types of literature, shared good writings of various authors, and were taught about writing by their teacher. In this way, *quality* in writing was developed in the children. Many of the excellent poems and stories in this book were sent to us by members of Mr. Bell's literary group.

world or another period of time; it can create an emotional situation, a mood or tone, a feeling. We experience sadness, love, joy, disgust, hatred, sympathy. This we do through empathy, our ability to project ourselves into the situation and live within the consciousness of the characters created by the author. The ability to empathize is what gives us our power to understand imagery, to develop compassion for others, and to create. Because literature is written communication at its best, it can become an integral part of the language arts program.

The therapeutic value of literature must be recognized. Creative writing provides emotional release, and, in reading the writings of others, many children are able to project themselves so that they receive help with their own problems. They come to understand human nature by learning that their problems are not unique.

The field of literature, then, belongs in the area of the creative arts for the aesthetic values it has; it belongs to the field of language arts because it is the most perfected use of symbolic communicative tools; it belongs to the area of the social sciences for the knowledge and understanding it develops. More intimately than any other subject-matter area, literature, as children read and write it, goes hand-in-hand with the goals of the modern school. It *is* communication through creative experiences.

Literature For All Children

As classroom teachers, we were always bewildered by the assumptions in most books written about children's literature. These assumptions seemed to say that: (1) in order for children to fully enjoy literature, they must be able to read, and (2) that adults select for children what literature is worthy of being read. Now, neither of us was ever lucky enough to have a classroom in our entire teaching careers where every child could read well enough to read all the books we thought they would enjoy. Nor did we teach in but one school where we had access to all the library books of our choice.

The teacher who feels that children become acquainted with good literature through their reading program is giving little or no consideration to the children who cannot read at all or who do not read well, so find little enjoyment in reading. These children need not be deprived of good literature if programs such as those described in this book are developed. The children hear the stories as their teachers or classmates read them and come to know the power and beauty of words. By role-playing or "experiencing" stories and selections, they come to know and understand them. Certainly a fringe benefit of such a program to these children is the development of a *desire* to read, so that they may read other stories by themselves. The teacher will also need to remember that many children's books are written with the *intent* that they should be read aloud. This is especially true of most poetry.

Literature should be read and enjoyed as it is written, rather than taught through dissection and analysis. The teacher's job in sharing a story or a poem with children is a simple one: she is an intermediary between the author and his audience, and her major duty is to try to put across the author's ideas as though she were a substitute for him. She may find literature helpful, however, in teaching many other things. And by teaching directly many of the components of literature, she may greatly increase its enjoyment by her children.

Setting Conditions for "Teaching" Literature

In the teaching of literature, conditions must be set for adventuring with it in a manner that will help develop some of the concepts mentioned in this chapter. Lessons can be given to develop certain aspects of literature, such as metaphor, simile, perceptual abilities, but, for the most part, it is the psychological and social situation in the classroom that builds appreciation and taste for literature in children. If exposure to books is an important element in carrying out a worthy program, as suggested above, physical and intellectual conditions must also be considered.

Specific references are made throughout this volume to the special settings created for adventuring in literature, such as the school library, the development of a book fair, and the use of the total school program (see Chapters 5, 13, 14, 15, and 16).

SUMMARY

Literature is the epitome of creative communication. In the elementary school it serves to identify an area of study often neglected, that of *effective* communication rather than *correct* communication, which appears to be the chief target for instruction. Literature is effective because of style, that is, *how* a story is told rather than the story itself.

This book is written with a specific philosophy about the teaching of literature to children. We feel that children must be continually exposed to effective forms of communication in order to learn to communicate effectively themselves. We believe that appreciations and tastes are developed in children through adventuring with children's literature and focusing attention on style of writing rather than on content. We also feel that the literature used with children must be relevant to them and that literature can play a substantial part in developing the child's own creativity, especially in guiding his own creative writing. Finally, we believe that literature can become the core of the curriculum, and creative strategies for adventuring with it can be devised so that all children can really appreciate it and learn from it.

This philosophy is translated into action through: (1) exposing children to many styles of writing, (2) planning regular adventures in literature in the classroom, (3) studying various styles of writing directly, (4) developing skills in using metaphor, simile, analogy, perception, empathy, and other elements necessary for literate reading, (5) making literature relevant to *all* children through careful motivation, (6) focusing on the development of the creative powers of children through creative teaching, (7) providing many opportunities for creative writing in the classroom, and (8) deliberately attempting to improve the quality of children's writing.

TO THE COLLEGE STUDENT

1. Recall all the facts you have been taught about poetry. For what purpose were you taught these facts? Did they teach you how to write poetry? Did they teach you to better appreciate poetry? Now consider the poem written by Charlene at the beginning of this chapter. Does this little girl know how to write poetry? Does she understand it? Appreciate it? How do you account for the fact that a child who has not studied poetry has learned so much about it and likes it so much?

2. Think of all the drill you experienced in your elementary schooling in grammar. This was supposed to help you to communicate correctly. Do you remember any instances when you were taught to use metaphor, simile, perception, analogy, and empathy to help you to write effectively? Discuss this concept of *correct writing* and *effective writing*, and suggest ways the ele-

mentary school program should be changed to develop the latter.

3. Often it is difficult to determine whether or not an act is creative because only the product is viewed and not the process. Discuss this statement as it applies to children, and suggest classroom behaviors that will prevent the teacher from passing judgment on children's products.

4. Which of the topics discussed in this chapter had the greatest effect on developing your appreciation for children's literature: exposure to it, adventures with it, its style, its relevancy, your own environment, the development of your own literary abilities, or the teaching of some memorable teacher?

5. Try writing and illustrating a children's story. Read it before a group of children and note their reactions.

TO THE CLASSROOM TEACHER

1. Obtain a copy of the report of the American Library Association's Annual Conference and look for these facts:
a. How many children's titles were published in the past year?
b. How many children's titles were published in 1940?
c. Note what books were the most popular with children. How many of them do you remember as being translated into television shows?
d. From these observations, can you tell whether children are reading more or less than they did twenty years ago, and can you draw some conclusions about the effect of television on children's reading? Consider the fact that population growth may have had some influence on these changes.

2. How much time do you allot for poetry in your schedule? Do you have delightful adventures with poetry such as those described in this chapter? Why or why not? Do you think Miss Baxter worked on developing quality in writing? How do you think she did this?

3. Think through all the ways you could teach some phase of your social studies program as well or better by using children's literature.

4. Is it possible to teach science more effectively through the use of children's literature?

5. Think of all the ways you could make an old classic such as *Uncle Tom's Cabin* relevant to a group of middle school children today.

TO THE COLLEGE STUDENT
AND THE CLASSROOM TEACHER

1. Which of the concepts listed on pages 5–8 are new to you? Try to recall an incident within the past six months that illustrates each of these concepts. Share them with other teachers or students as a base for a discussion about creativity.

2. Assign some members of the class to select passages from current literature, both good and poor. Have each member read a selection of his choice, but do not tell the origin of the writing. Ask the class members to rate the passages on the following basis:

a. Excellent piece of writing (good literature)
b. Good piece of writing (fair as literature)
c. Fair piece of writing
d. Poor piece of writing (poor literature)

After all the passages have been read and rated, expose the origins. Can you identify good literature?

3. Discuss these problems and statements together:

a. To what degree should a teacher impose her standards for good literature on children?
b. By what techniques can a teacher develop good taste for literature in children?

c. The filming of children's classics often destroys the joy of reading the classic by children.
d. The violence on television is no greater than that to which children have been exposed in such stories as *The Red Shoes, Hansel and Gretel, Grimm's Fairy Tales,* and *Little Red Riding Hood.*
e. Children today do not seem to have much use for poetry. Boys, in particular, regard the reading of poetry as "sissy." How might this specific characteristic be identified with creativity?
f. The lack of an appreciation of poetry by elementary school children is caused by the fact that poetry is not a part of the general school curriculum in most schools today.

4. Collect specific stories from children's literature that lend themselves to interpretation through puppetry, dramatizations, dance, pantomime, shadow plays, and music.

SELECTED BIBLIOGRAPHY

Allen, Arthur T. "Literature for Children: An Engagement with Life," *The Horn Book Magazine* (December 1967): 732–737.

Anderson, W., and P. Groff. *A New Look at Children's Literature.* Belmont, Calif.: Wadsworth, 1972.

Arbuthnot, May Hill, et al. *The Arbuthnot Anthology.* Glenview, Ill.: Scott, Foresman, 1971.

Bechtel, Louise. *Books in Search of Children: Essays and Speeches.* New York: Macmillan, 1969.

Butler, F., ed. *The Great Excluded: Critical Essays on Children's Literature.* vols. I and II. Storrs: University of Connecticut, 1973.

Cameron, Eleanor. *The Green and Burning Tree: On the Writing and Enjoyment of Children's Books.* Boston: Little, Brown, 1969.

Carlson, Ruth Kearney. *Literature for Children: Enrichment Ideas.* Dubuque, Iowa: Wm. C. Brown Company, 1970.

Clark, Margaret. *Keeping Up with Children and Books, 1963–1965.* Glencoe, Ill.: Scott, Foresman, 1966.

Colby, Jean Poindexter. *Writing, Illustrat-ing and Editing Children's Books.* New York: Hastings House, 1967.

Cullinan, Bernice E. *Literature for Children: Its Discipline and Content.* Dubuque, Iowa: Wm. C. Brown Company, 1971.

Duff, Annis. *Bequest of Wings: A Family's Pleasure with Books.* New York: Viking Press, 1961.

Duff, Annis. *Longer Flight.* New York: Viking Press, 1965.

Eaton, Anne Thaxter. *Treasure for the Taking.* New York: Viking Press, 1957.

Fenwick, Sara Innis, ed. *A Critical Approach to Children's Literature.* Chicago: University of Chicago Press, 1967.

Georgiou, Constantine. *Children and Their Literature.* Englewood Cliffs, N.J.: Prentice-Hall, 1969.

Haviland, Virginia. *Children and Literature: Views and Reviews.* Glenview, Ill.: Scott, Foresman, 1973.

Jacobs, Leland B., ed. *Using Literature with Young Children.* New York: Teachers College Press, 1965.

Jan, Isabelle. *On Children's Literature.* New York: Schocken Books, 1974.

Lanes, Selma. *Down the Rabbit Hole: Adventures and Misadventures in the Realm of Children's Literature.* New York: Atheneum Press, 1971.

Lonsdale, Bernard, and Helen K. Mackintosh. *Children Experience Literature.* New York: Random House, 1972.

Lukens, Rebecca. *A Critical Handbook of Children's Literature.* Chicago: Scott, Foresman, 1976.

Pratt-Butler, Grace K. *Let Them Write Creatively.* Columbus: Charles E. Merrill, 1973.

Reasoner, Charles F. *Releasing Children to Literature: A Teacher's Guide to Yearling Books.* New York: Dell, 1968.

Robinson, Evelyn Rose. *Readings About Children's Literature.* New York: David McKay, 1966.

Root, Sheldon Camp, ed. *Adventuring With Books: 2,400 Titles for Pre-Kindergarten–Grade 8.* New York: Citation Press, 1973.

Sayers, Frances Clarke. *Summoned by Books.* New York: Viking Press, 1965.

Sebesta, Sam Leaton, and William J. Iverson. *Literature for Thursday's Child.* Chicago: Science Research Associates, 1975.

Smith, James Steel. *A Critical Approach to Children's Literature.* New York: McGraw-Hill, 1967.

Smith, Lillian H. *The Unreluctant Years: A Critical Approach to Children's Literature.* Chicago: American Library Association, 1953.

Townsend, John Rowe. *Written For Children: An Outline of English Children's Literature,* rev. ed. Philadelphia: J. B. Lippincott, 1975.

Walsh, Frances, ed. *That Eager Zest: First Discoveries in the Magic World of Books: An Anthology.* New York: J. B. Lippincott, 1961.

Wheeler, Sarah H. *Literature for Children.* Chicago: Field Enterprises, 1965.

CHAPTER 2

The Nature of
Children's Literature

ADVENTURE WITH HALIBUT BONES

The front of the room, which was covered with two sheets, turned —
green. Soft music swelled from the back of a small stage constructed there.
A child's voice spoke above the music:

"Green, green, what is green?"

And another voice answered:

*"Green is the grass
And the leaves of trees
Green is the smell
Of a country breeze."*[1]

The color changed to yellow. Now the child's voice said, "Yellow,
yellow, what is yellow?"
And another voice answered, "Yellow is the color of the sun."
A large cardboard sun came out of the wings into the yellow light
and climbed to the top of the stage.

*"Yellow, yellow, what is yellow?
The feeling of fun."*

Four children danced out on the stage. The music changed to "Here
We Go Round the Mulberry Bush" and they joined hands and danced in a
circle. The soft music swelled forth; the children sat on the floor, and the
voices backstage resumed:

---

1. Mary O'Neill, *Hailstones and Halibut Bones* (New York: Doubleday, 1961),
p. 51.

FIGURE 2–1.   *A dramatization of* Hailstones and Halibut Bones *by Mary O'Neill leads to some creative writing by the children.*

> *"Yellow, yellow, what is yellow?*
> *The yolk of an egg*
> *A duck's bill*
> *A canary bird*
> *And a daffodil."*[2]

On the yellow-tinted sheets the shadow of an egg appeared, broke open, and the yellow yolk dropped out. Then a little duck silhouette entered on one side of the "stage" and quacked his way to the other side. A yellow canary flew across the stage and then a large daffodil face covered the screen.

As the voices backstage continued, different objects appeared in silhouette on the yellow sheets. At times, different children appeared on the stage dressed in crepe paper costumes. A few performed for some of the lines such as:

> *"Yellow, yellow, what is yellow?*
> *Yellow blinks*
> *On summer nights*
> *In the off-and-on of*
> *Firefly lights."*[3]

---

2. *Ibid.*, p. 55.
3. *Ibid.*

A group of four girls with streamers of yellow crepe paper hanging from their shoulders danced in to the tune of the "Sugar Plum Fairy." They carried a daisy chain in which was concealed a string of Christmas tree lights with yellow bulbs. During their dance, which consisted of many up and down fluttery movements to make allowance for the extension wire on the floor, the Christmas tree lights were turned on and the yellow lights blinked on and off, giving the illusion of fireflies flickering among the dancers.

This adventuring into colored lighting was prompted by the reading together in Miss Sawyer's fourth-grade class of Mary O'Neill's *Hailstones and Halibut Bones*. The book intrigued the children. They began to make lists and collect objects of a specific chosen color. Many of the children wrote poems entitled "Gray, Gray, What Is Gray?" or "Blue, Blue, What Is Blue?" They studied color in science and learned how it came to be. Miss Sawyer brought in colored cellophane and encouraged them to experiment with color effects on sheets strung in the front of the room by using the cellophane on an overhead projector. This was the technique they used to color the front of the room. By moving the projector far back from the sheets, they could cover an area any size they liked with any particular color. When the daffodil and the duck appeared on the sheet, they were simply a small flower and duck cut from light cardboard, laid on the overhead projector, and brought into focus. The children had thought of these many ways to present O'Neill's *Hailstones and Halibut Bones* in a charming, appropriate manner.

In this situation we again witness an adventure in literature. Literature plays a very real and important part in children's learning. It should be included in the modern school program to fulfill many objectives, most of which are currently neglected. From our discussion to this point, we can conclude that the use of literature in the elementary classroom can fulfill the following objectives:

1. It can stimulate children to write.
2. It can provide a means of therapy for troubled children, and meet many of their psychological needs.
3. It can serve as the core for teaching the elementary school subjects, especially those areas designed to develop affective learning and understanding of mankind and the world.
4. It can widen horizons for children in all aspects of life through vicarious experiences.
5. It can help to develop sound social insights in children.
6. It can contribute extensively to the fun, merriment, and joy of living.
7. It can serve as a basis for deepening an appreciation of beauty.
8. It can help children build skills in expression, in defining, and in elaboration.
9. Literature can help build a colorful vocabulary that will assist each child to express himself better.
10. It can serve as a basis for constructive daydreaming and complete identification with a problem (a necessary process in creative problem solving).
11. It can make children more discreet in passing judgment and making choices, especially in the use of words.
12. It can be a perpetual source of creative stimulation for every child.

13. It can develop a sensitivity to places, sights, sounds, words, life problems, and people.
14. It serves as a basis for the building of a set of standards and values regarding creative writing.
15. It serves as a basis for developing tastes and appreciation in reading.
16. It provides a record of the history of mankind and brings alive the tales and ballads of times long past and places far away.

In Chapter 1 it was mentioned that a teacher must understand what creativity is and how it is developed, what literature is, and the nature of children, before she can teach literature creatively in order to accomplish the above objectives. This chapter introduces the teacher and the college student to the commonly used classifications of children's literature, as employed by teachers and children themselves.

CLASSIFICATIONS OF CHILDREN'S LITERATURE

All literature is classified into two broad divisions: fiction and nonfiction. Fiction is imaginative writing through which an author creates a story. The story may be based on facts about real people and/or real events. Fictional literature includes poetry and drama as well as narrative prose. It takes the form of short stories, novels, tales, fables, myths, legends, ballads, fairy tales, and so forth.

Nonfiction is factual writing about people, events, information, and opinion, running the gamut from science to literary criticism. Nonfiction appears in the form of history, biography, autobiography, factual presentations, concept books, journals, diaries, critiques, and other non-story forms.

Literature for children cannot be simply divided into the two broad divisions of fiction and nonfiction. Such a division is too cumbersome and too general to be of much use as a classification scheme.

Thus, children's literature is generally classified by two processes: (1) according to the oral, audial, and reading development of the child, and (2) according to the subject matter, such as animal stories, fairy tales, or biography, largely because this is the way children themselves describe and request books. We are dealing with category 2 in this chapter.

Adults who work with children often classify children's books by many systems: (1) according to the "approach" of the author (for example, realistic fiction, modern fantasy, or humor); (2) by genre or type (such as folklore, which includes myths, legends, fables, epics); (3) as fiction (fantasy, mystery, realistic stories, stories of peoples of different races, ethnic groups, and countries), and nonfiction; (4) as poetry (Mother Goose rhymes, nonsense verse, and ballads); and (5) as informational books (biography and subjects as varied as technology, science, travel, and art). Information books constitute the largest, broadest, and most diverse of all genres.

Regardless of the system utilized for the classification of children's books, the categories are bound to be overlapping, mixed, and inexact. For example, a particular children's book may be a folktale of India whose characters are animals, the animals have exciting adventures, magic is involved in overcoming the obstacles of the plot, and the entire tale is told in a humorous style. How would a teacher classify such a book? Is it an animal story, a folktale, an adventure tale, a tale of India, a story of magic, or a humorous story? If the book happens to be one with many pictures or illustrations, might it also be classed as a story-picture book? Actually, the book may be legitimately placed in each classification.

Why, then, try to classify children's books at all? Mainly because, in dealing with children's literature and in utilizing it as a core for curriculum building, some frame of reference is needed. We have tried to cull from the material available those classifications most commonly used among writers of children's literature. Our main guide, however, has been to heed the labels that children and teachers have attached to various types of books when they were using them daily in the classroom.

A description of the categories we have selected follows, with frequent illustrations of how each has been used in an elementary school classroom, and why each category seems to appeal to children.

> Picture Books
> > Picture-story books
> > Books with illustrations
> Mother Goose Nursery Rhymes
> > Alphabet books
> > Counting books
> > Concept books
> Animal Books
> Humor Books
> Poetry
> Folklore
> > Fables, myths, legends, epics
> > Ballads and story poems
> > Fairy tales
> Adventure Tales
> Mystery
> Romance
> Fantasy
> > Tales of high imagination
> > Science fiction
> Realistic Fiction
> > Social awareness
> > Character development
> Nonfiction Books
> > Biography
> > Information books
> > Other times and places
> > References and handbooks

Certain conditions influence the classification of children's literature. Every book reflects the life of a particular author because it represents his reaction to the culture in which he lives or from which he emerges. Always, in each generation, however, there are authors who dare to break away from accepted mores, morals, and styles of writing, and who set a new style or a new classification of literature. These daring individuals are often the most creative of the lot and truly bring new thinking into the world.

The bulk of authors, however, while loyal to their own unique style, write within the accepted styles and mores of their culture because they must have their work accepted in order to earn a living. The slow changes of life style over the decades, however, eventually create changes in all literary style.

Consequently, the time in history in which an author writes affects the classification of books. Fantasy and realistic fiction are two examples. The fantasy written by Hans Christian Andersen is very different from the modern fantasy of Madeline L'Engle's *A Wrinkle in Time*. Science fiction written by Jules Verne is very different from that of Isaac Asimov. Realistic fiction written by Louisa May Alcott is different from that of Judy Blume.

In establishing criteria for each genre of children's literature, historical setting also bears consideration. Stories concerning minority literature (racial, religious, and economic) must be viewed from a historical perspective. To fully appreciate the work of an author, it is helpful to know about his life and the time in which he lived. To aid the reader in understanding our classifications, we have included five later chapters that tell about authors and illustrators and about the time and circumstances that influenced their work. (*See* Chapters 6 through 10.)

One other point needs to be made. Too often literature is considered solely as material written down in some form of the printed word. From the beginning of time, nonliterate people have depended on oral literature. Since

FIGURE 2–2. The clown puppet that lived in the laundry bag.

much of the world's population is still illiterate, the oral tradition of literature remains alive and provides the same pleasure for many ethnic groups
that books do for literate peoples. The large body of oral literature is called
folk literature. At one time all literature was folk literature, and in many
places in the world today, children and adults still rely on oral folk literature
for entertainment.

Picture Books, Picture-Story Books, and Illustrated Books

Picture books are children's first books. When a child is very young and
unable to read, he enjoys looking at the pictures; consequently, the illustrations play a primary role in the enjoyment a child receives from the book.
The books that illustrators produce for children from infancy up through
sixth grade fall into three categories.

First is the so-called pure picture book with little or no text. In these
books children learn to identify animals, letters, numbers, and objects.
Excellent examples of imaginative wordless picture books are Bruno Minori's
ABC, Frank Asch's *The Blue Balloon*, Lilo Fromm's *Muffel and Plums*, Brian
Wildsmith's *Circus, Birds, Fishes,* and *Wild Animals*, Ruth Carroll's *What
Whiskers Did*, Jan Wahl's *Push Kitty*, and a book by Françoise called *The
Things I Like*.

Second is the picture-story book in which the pictures and text are
equal partners; ideally neither should upstage the other. When a child is
very young and unable to read, he looks at the pictures and "reads" the
story through the illustrations. The child enjoys hearing an adult read the
story to him, and he follows the text, aided by the pictures. As the book is
read over and over by an adult, the child is able to memorize the text. It is a
pleasant experience to "read" by oneself. An example is Paul Galdone's *The
Three Bears*, which Galdone both wrote and illustrated. The story, familiar
and simple to memorize, is able to be "read" by a pre-school child because
each sentence has an accompanying illustration. When the text says, "First
she tasted the porridge of the Great Big Bear. But it was too hot," there is
an illustration of a saucy-looking Goldilocks holding a very large spoon and
tasting the porridge. The next two sentences: "Then she tasted the porridge
of the Middle-Sized Bear. But it was too cold." Goldilocks's spoon is obviously middle-sized in the illustration, compared with the big spoon she is
holding in the illustration above. The third illustration shows Goldilocks
licking her lips happily as she holds a small spoon. And the accompanying
text reads, "Then she tasted the porridge of the Little Wee Bear." Children
are very literal about wanting the illustrations and the text to synchronize
precisely.

Marjorie Flack's *Angus Lost* (as well as her other Angus books) are
examples of older picture-story books. More recent examples include *Rain
Makes Applesauce* by Julian Scheer, *The Lion in the Box* by Marguerite de
Angeli, *Why Couldn't I Be An Only Kid Like You, Wigger?* by Barbara
Shook Hazen, and *The Sad Story of the Little Hungry Cat* by Edna Mitchell
Preston.

The third kind of picture book is the illustrated book in which the
text becomes longer, the story is more complicated, and hence the illustrations appear less frequently and often take less space on the pages.

Examples are Garth Williams's sketches for E. B. White's *Charlotte's Web* and Maurice Sendak's sketches for *Higglety, Pigglety Pop!* Older children enjoy seeing illustrations. Even when children have become more proficient at reading, they nevertheless delight in viewing an illustration of a scene, an episode, or one line from the text. Today's children are fortunate. They are introduced to good literature at the same time that they are introduced to examples of outstanding art through the media of picture books.

Although many children learn to read through the use of picture-story books, this is not their main purpose. Such books often use words beyond the child's reading ability because many of them are designed to be read to children to enrich their vocabularies while watching the pictures and hearing the words.

The basic concepts of learning to read are acquired through the use of picture-story books, however. Exposure to them helps children almost intuitively to identify those elements which make a good story. Through picture-story books, children learn about organizing ideas in a logical sequence; they are introduced to the concept of printed symbolism, and they encounter their first adventures with *style* of writing.

Picture-story books have been adapted to the individualized reading program of many schools. The concept of the picture book has been used in pre-primers, primers, and "easy" reading books for beginning readers. As might be expected, some of these imitations have deserted literature as such, in that they have little or no style. Many, however, have maintained a definite style which, along with beautiful or humorous illustrations, has served as a double delight to children when they found they could read not only the pictures but the word symbols as well! The books of Dr. Seuss (*The Cat In the Hat* and *The Cat In the Hat Comes Back*) and Else Holmelund Minarik's Little Bear series are examples of early books that can be read, but have not abandoned literary qualities.

It is true that these books are of uneven quality and each must be evaluated individually. The main criterion for selecting picture-story books for beginning reading purposes is that *they contain a printed vocabulary that reflects the oral vocabulary of the children who will read them.*

OTHER CRITERIA. First of all, picture-story books must have all the earmarks of good literature. The book *Where the Wild Things Are,* for instance, is a picture-story book. Maurice Sendak uses only 300 words to tell the story of Max and his visit to the land of the Wild Things, but his pictures tell a multitude of stories that make more words unnecessary. Pictures and story together create a style that appears in no other type of book.

There are many picture-story books that are not classics like Sendak's creation. Children need exposure to some of these books in order to come to recognize, by comparison, the skills of artists such as Sendak. But the major standards for selecting picture-story books for use in the classroom, according to scholars of children's literature, reflect the following:

• Children want the pictures to be synchronized precisely with the text.
• Children have no specific preference for color—they appear to like all colors if they are in keeping with the style of the author and the mood of the text. Even black and white pictures are acceptable if they are fitting to the story.

- They accept and delight in the unusual when the book is a fairy tale or another type of fantasy book.
- Children appear to like action pictures just as they appear to like action plots.
- Contrary to many opinions, children are fascinated by tiny details in pictures—a three-year-old will sit and seek out the little and unexpected things.
- Young children like a sturdy book that has tough paper and a strong binding. They have not always learned to use books respectfully when they come to school, and they are often heartbroken if a book is torn or defaced. They can be taught later to care for fragile books. The advent of paperback picture books and picture-story books at minimal prices lessens the importance of binding.
- Children will accept the unusual in pictures—unusual or different clothes, hairstyles, scenery, and trappings—but the teacher must be prepared to answer many questions about the pictures.
- Picture-story books are not solely the property of the world of children. Many adult picture-story books accomplish the same objectives as children's picture books, and do it in a manner that is unique, forceful, and relevant. Two superb examples of this art are the following:

    CULLUM, ALBERT. *The Geranium On the Window Sill Just Died But Teacher You Went Right On.* British Commonwealth: Harlin Quest, Inc. (distributed by Franklin Watts, New York), 1971.

    SILVERSTEIN, SHEL. *Uncle Shelby's ABZ Book.* New York: Simon and Schuster, 1961.

    Picture books and picture-story books of great charm and value on almost every subject can be found currently on the commercial market.
- Picture books should not use pictures merely for their illustrative value, but to develop the tone, mood, and theme of the book.

Mother Goose Rhymes

Although Mother Goose rhymes are rightfully classified in many volumes as folklore and as picture books, we choose to place them here in a category by themselves, for many reasons.[4]

Mother Goose rhymes provide an introduction to literature for many children. Just as all literature was once oral, so does literature for children begin orally today. A parent or adult sings, chants, or fingerplays Mother Goose rhymes to a young child. Most children begin their visual experiences with literature by seeing these simple, happy rhymes in picture books.

Mother Goose rhymes also play a special part in the development of appreciations and skills in the elementary school curriculum. They furnish a bond that has linked the hearts of children throughout the ages. They appeal to children because of the unique way in which the words are put together and the delightful way they roll off the tongue. Mother Goose rhymes often do not make much sense. Children seem to understand this and delight in saying the words, whether or not they know what they mean.

The name *Mother Goose* was first associated with eight folk tales recorded by the Frenchman, Charles Perrault, for his son Pierre Perrault

---

4. The main source of the classification material below is May Hill Arbuthnot, *Children and Books,* 3rd ed. (Glenview, Ill.: Scott, Foresman, 1964).

d'Armancour around 1697. Among these stories were *The Sleeping Beauty, Little Red Riding Hood, Bluebeard, Puss in Boots, Diamonds and Toads, Cinderella,* and *Little Thumb.* This publication was called *Tales of Mother Goose* and marked the beginning of the publication of literature for children. There were no verses in the original book. Later the name became so associated with the charming verses that it is no longer used in connection with the above stories.

Legend has it that the original Mother Goose was a Dame Goose of Boston, whose remains lie in the Old Granary Burying Grounds. The French think Mother Goose was originally Goose-footed Bertha, wife of Robert II. The English link Mother Goose with Robert Powell and his clever puppet shows, which were originally played in London between 1709 and 1711. One of these plays was entitled *Mother Goose.*

John Newbery published a collection of nursery rhymes called *Mother Goose's Melody* or *Sonnets for the Cradle.* In America, Isaiah Thomas published the first *Mother Goose* in Worcester, Massachusetts, in 1889. This was a book of rhymes much like the Mother Goose rhymes known today except they were disguised under strange titles, and each was followed by morals and wise sayings. Other American editions appeared from time to time and are still being published.

Throughout the long history of publishing, the Mother Goose rhymes have created discussion and controversy as to their meaning. As they were told and reprinted from generation to generation, they changed. Comparisons of early original editions and modern editions show these changes clearly. Many people believe that Mother Goose rhymes always were nonsense rhymes and that is all they were intended to be. Some students of literature, however, feel that each rhyme bears significance and is related to some important personage or some historical event.

One of the authors remembers a story told to him many years ago by an Englishman who assured him that each Mother Goose rhyme bore a special significance to some person or event, or even might be a secret way of telling news or passing a message in code from one person to a group. This was done, he assured me, in the pubs of England during the years when spies for the king were all about and no one dared speak against the crown for fear of being beheaded. These spies filled the pubs and reported on the rebels, so that secret messages and items of gossip were often sung or recited in the course of the evening and passed along among the common folk. *Banbury Cross* was one nursery rhyme he used as a case in point. It communicated a secret message to the people that Queen Elizabeth I was to leave the castle, which was, in itself, an unusual event. What is more, she would travel on a mission to meet in a secluded place with the king of Spain for secret negotiations. Because she was unaware of the proper way to travel secretly, she was taking her entire entourage, creating great excitement, and being very conspicuous wherever she went.

"Ride a Cock Horse to Banbury Cross" told them that they should go to the hamlet of Banbury Cross to see this great phenomenon, and that because the distance was great and the time was short, they would need a horse—preferably a strong one—to get there. "To see a fine lady ride on a fine horse, With rings on her fingers and bells on her toes" signified, of course, that they would see the queen. Who else but the queen would wear rings on her fingers or could afford little bells on her shoes? "She shall have music wherever she goes" indicated that she had with her her ladies in waiting, her musicians, and so on.

Other stories have it that Humpty Dumpty was really Richard III toppling off his throne.

Although a great deal of research has been done to link people and events with the nursery rhymes, there is still little proof that these beliefs are true. Children are fascinated by this concept, however, often as much so by the possible stories about the nursery rhymes as by the verses themselves. Older children who are studying peoples and places can have their interest renewed in Mother Goose rhymes by linking them with their current studies. This should be done in an honest way, telling the children that some people believe these stories to be true, but that there is actually little proof for many of them.

Many scholars have tried to identify the great appeal of Mother Goose rhymes for children year after year, generation after generation. Arbuthnot and Sutherland[5] identify the following qualities as those most appealing to children:

Variety: The verses range from sheer nonsense to clever little stories and cover almost every topic of interest to children.

Musical quality: All the rhymes throw the voice into a musical pattern almost like a chant. One almost sings when he recites a nursery rhyme— the rhythms are so definite and the vowel sounds so flowing that they seem as much a natural part of bodily rhythm as the act of walking.

Action: In all the Mother Goose rhymes something happens!

Humor: Children love many of them simply because they are delightful fun. The humor is simple and on the level of understanding of the children, although adults may see a different type of humor than children.

Illustrations: From the beginning of the publication of Mother Goose rhymes, artists appeared to be challenged by Mother Goose, and books have appeared with pictures of fantasy, realism, humor, and decoration. These beautiful pictures have generally enhanced the verses, adding great appeal to the books themselves.

Mother Goose starts children on their way to literature, to poetry, and to music. Unfortunately, school programs tend to drop Mother Goose like a hot potato after the nursery school and kindergarten years. Actually, the use of these rhymes can be extended into the grade school years and used in a multitude of ways. They can become an introduction to formal music. In the middle school grades one author has used them as motivation for units on history, especially the history of England, as related above. They also form an excellent basis for beginning work in choral speaking.

They can serve well as beginning stories in the teaching of reading. Mother Goose rhymes can also be a splendid base for the improvement of speech among children who have speech problems. In some school programs, the transition from a native language to English has been made easily and comfortably by foreign-born children when nursery rhymes were used as the transition strategy.

---

5. May Hill Arbuthnot and Zena Sutherland, *Children and Books*, 4th ed. (Glenview, Ill.: Scott, Foresman, 1972), pp. 114–117.

The rhymes provide excellent situations for dramatizations, role-playing, and as incentives for children to make up their own creative sounds.

Many classic versions of Mother Goose nursery rhymes, such as Leslie Brook's *Ring O' Roses*, Kate Greenaway's *Mother Goose*, and Ray Wood's *The American Mother Goose*, still remain popular with children. Modern versions appear on the market yearly. A few of the popular ones are Beni Montresor's *I Saw a Ship A Sailing*, Margaret Taylor Burrough's *Did You Feed My Cow? Street Games, Chants and Rhymes*, Nonny Hogrogian's *One I Love, Two I Love: And Other Loving Mother Goose Rhymes*, Nicholas Tucker's *Mother Goose Lost*, Brian Wildsmith's *Mother Goose*, Raymond Brigg's *Mother Goose Treasury*, and Frederick Winsor's *The Space Child's Mother Goose*. A recent (1975) book of children's nursery rhymes, *Cakes and Custard* written by Brian Alderson and illustrated by Helen Oxenbury, presents many less familiar nursery rhymes to modern youngsters.

Alphabet and Counting Books

Alphabet books (commonly called ABC books) that teach the alphabet and counting books that teach numbers are extensions of Mother Goose books. It follows logically that once a child has been introduced to the sounds and the pictures of Mother Goose, he is developmentally ready to recognize the sounds and the letters he is speaking and the numbers he has memorized. Therefore, counting and number books are a special kind of book for young children. Again the categories overlap, since, as an extension of nursery rhymes, these alphabet and counting books often rhyme. Each generation of writers has produced its variants of Mother Goose. Excellent examples of different treatment of this theme are found in comparing Edward Lear's *A Apple Pie*, a nonsense rhyming book; Fritz Eichenberg's *Ape in a Cape: An Alphabet of Odd Animals;* Bruno Minari's *ABC*, a colorful picture book that emphasizes the phonetic sound of letters; Leonard Baskin's *Hosie's Alphabet*, a "joke"-type alphabet book; Beni Montresor's *A for Angel;* Lucy Floyd and Kathryn Lasky's *Agatha's Alphabet;* Helen Oxenbury's *ABC of Things;* and Remy Charlip and Jerry Joyner's *Thirteen*, all of which present the alphabet in a creative and unusual way.

One recent interesting counting book is Richard Scarry's *Best Counting Book Ever*. Popular with youngsters are Tomi Ungerer's *One, Two, Three* and *One, Two, Where's My Shoe?*

Concept Books

The term *concept books* is used in this volume to classify those books, for both younger and older children, which present one concept that not only identifies objects, such as numbers and the alphabet, but that also presents a concept about environment, ecology, race, or life style. Examples of concept books in this framework are Jeanne Bendick's *Names, Sets and Numbers*, Ann McGovern's *Black is Beautiful*, and A. Harris Stone's *The Last Free Bird*. Colorful illustrations and a skilled writing style are wedded in these books to develop a concept with children. Many nonfiction books fall into the category of concept books, for example, George Fichter's *The Animal Kingdom* and Ruth Kraus's *A Hole Is To Dig*.

Animal Stories

Animal stories may be categorized into three types, independent of whether they are written for young or older children: (1) animals that behave like human beings (often called "ourselves in fur"); (2) animals that act like animals but talk, and (3) animals that act like animals behaving true to their scientific nature. Examples of the first type of animal story are found in the *Babar* series by Jean and Laurent de Brunhoff and Russell Hoban's stories about Frances, a female badger, including *Bedtime for Frances* and *A Babysitter for Frances*. Anna Sewell's *Black Beauty* and Felix Salten's *Bambi* behave as animals scientifically true to their nature, but are able to think and/or talk as if they were human. Sterling North's *Rascal* and Marjorie Flack's *The Story About Ping* depict animals as animals, scientifically true and objectively presented.

Stories about animals written in the first and second categories often may be more fantasy than fact inasmuch as the main characters are more like humans than animals. They may well be the author's subtle way of pointing out the fallacies and strengths of humans—actually a satire on human life.

Reactions to animal stories in all categories have been mixed as to their value to children. This is probably due to the fact that the children's book market has been flooded with many books in which animals talk and are endowed with other human characteristics, books that tend to be trite and oversentimentalize the animal hero. These are criticized for many reasons, one being the fact that they give children false impressions of animal life. Illustrations for these books generally add to the false illusion, often by showing animals standing on their hind legs, wearing glasses, and living in surroundings similar to those inhabited by human beings.

Criticisms of such books may appear to be valid until one remembers A. A. Milne's *Winnie the Pooh,* Felix Salten's *Bambi,* and Beatrix Potter's *The Tale of Peter Rabbit*. The delight which these books and others like them have brought to thousands of children and adults indicates that such books have a special place in the area of children's literature. The evaluation of these books cannot lie in a set of preconceived standards dealing with concepts, but in the writing itself. Some authors seem to be able to take animal subjects and to capture the essence of their characteristics in conversation and illustrations. Dorothy Lathrop, author of *Who Goes There?* and *Hide and Seek*, is one such artist. When these authors write, great books result.

The Story of Ferdinand by Munro Leaf illustrates another kind of animal story: one in which the author deliberately reverses the accepted characteristics of an animal and makes him unique. As one fourth grader put it, "Ferdinand is a sissy bull." But Ferdinand has become a classical character in children's literature. Ferdinand does not speak but he thinks like a human and he acts like one.

Another book in which the actions of the animal are described, but where the animal does not talk, is Virginia Lee Burton's charming tale of

Calico, the Wonder Horse. C. W. Anderson's story of *Billy and Blaze* and his subsequent books are reminiscent of Sewell's *Black Beauty,* and have won a place in the hearts of children everywhere.

Animal stories told by a skilled artist seem to run the gamut of content of all stories written about humans. They provide delightful fantasy, as in Elizabeth Coatsworth's *The Cat Who Went to Heaven.* They deal with fables (James Henry Daugherty's *Andy and the Lion*); they are beautifully humorous (R. and F. Atwater's *Mr. Popper's Penguins* and Barbara Williams's *Albert's Toothache*); with adventure (Margot Austin's *Growl Bear*); with character development (Nathaniel Benchley's *Feldman Fieldmouse*); with topics of other times and other places (Lloyd Alexander's *Time Cat*); with biography (Robert Lawson's *Ben and Me*); and with realism as in Joan Heilbroner's *Robert the Rose Horse.*

Animal stories continue to be a subject for modern writers, as indicated by Mercer Mayer's *What Do You Do With A Kangaroo?* William Armstrong, Newbery Award winner, wrote *My Animals* in 1974, a book presenting seventeen short tales about favorite animals. Alice Schick has recently written *Kongo and Kumba,* a story of the growing years of two young primates, one in the field and one in the zoo. It is a fascinating study of animal behavior and won a Junior Literary Guild award.

Oswald, the Silly Goose, a recent title by K. R. Whittington, is a book for primary children that contains seven hilarious tales about a silly but personable goose. Beatrice Schenk de Regnier's *May I Bring a Friend?* is already a favorite among children and is a fantasy of people and animals who talk together.

Joan Aiken's *The Kingdom and the Cave* is the story about Mickie, a palace cat, who discovers that the Under people are coming above ground, and he searches for them with the help of Prince Michael and Minerva, the mare. The animal friends teach the prince how to become invisible and how to speak Universal Animal Language and thus overcome the forces that threaten the kingdom. Ms. Aiken's *Arabel's Raven* is a book recounting three episodes in the life of a family that adopts a raven.

Other prize-winning authors continue to write appealing animal stories. The past few years have produced *The Greentail Mouse* by Leo Lionni; *The Mills of God,* a story about a boy and his dog in a lonely Appalachian village by William Armstrong; *Psst! Doggie!,* a primary book by Ezra Jack Keats; *What Did You Bring Me?,* a story of a spoiled, pampered mouse by Karla Kuskin; *The Little Wood Duck* by Brian Wildsmith; *The Silver Pony* by Lynd Ward; a cumulative tale *Rolling Downhill* by Ruth Carroll; fun stories such as *Shaggy Dogs and Spotty Dogs and Shaggy and Spotty Dogs* by Seymour Leichman; *The Crocodile in the Tree* by Roger Duvoisin; and a new book originally written in 1906, *The Sly Old Cat,* by Beatrix Potter, but never before published as a book, to name a few.

Also classified as animal stories are those about insects. One of the most beautiful pieces of writing to come from the field of children's literature is E. B. White's charming book about a spider and a pig, *Charlotte's Web.*

One recent book by Norma Farber, *As I Was Crossing Boston Common* (1975), shows how categories overlap. It is a bestiary alphabet book.

Animal stories appeal to children for many reasons: (1) Children are fascinated by and love animals and are eager to learn about them or to identify with them; (2) the animal stories that parody people promote a closer identification of the child with the animals; (3) many animal stories appeal to children because of their play on emotions, especially humor; (4) they help children understand animals, often inducing them gently into the hardships of animal life; (5) they help children understand such qualities as courage, loyalty, love, faithfulness, a zest for and an appreciation of life; and (6) because of the wide coverage of topics in animal stories, they continually place children in new places where exciting things happen and where they learn about life.

Humor

While many books are purposely written for the purpose of provoking laughter in children, humor is found in all the classifications of children's literature listed here. It is obvious in the nonsense of the nursery rhymes such as *Simple Simon* and *Peter Piper*. It appears in the droll, dry writing of Krasilovsky's *The Man Who Didn't Wash His Dishes* and Wanda Gag's *Millions of Cats*. It appears in regional fiction (such as Twain's *Tom Sawyer*) and fantasy (Astrid Lindgren's *Pippi Longstocking*). It is predominant in modern fiction for children, as in Harry Allard's *The Tutti Frutti Case* and Pat Hutchin's *The House That Sailed Away*.

Humor is written for children of all ages and takes all forms. Raskin's *Nothing Ever Happens on My Block* is written for primary grades and has a dry humor that primary children appear to understand. Barbara Williams's *Kevin's Grandma* and H. A. Rey's *Curious George* and *Cecily G. and the Nine Monkeys* are humorous books for young children. Many of these books help children understand accepted behaviors but do it in a fun way, such as Joslin Sesyle's *What Do You Say, Dear? Caps for Sale* by Esphyr Slobodkina is a simple adventure story for young children peppered with laughable situations.

Dr. Seuss's books have common appeal to children of all ages. The humor of these books lies largely in the unusual situations in which the characters find themselves, the clever manipulation of the words that rhyme, and the imaginative and creative illustrations in each book. The prose books by Dr. Seuss, such as *The Five Hundred Hats of Bartholomew Cubbins* and *The King's Stilts,* are also appealing to young and old and can be read by third and fourth graders.

Favorites on the intermediate level are *Homer Price* and *Centerburg Tales* by Robert McCloskey, tales about the Huckabuck family from *Rootabaga Stories* by Carl Sandburg, and *Curious George* by H. A. Rey.

Because many juvenile authors are now writing books of humor, they deserve a special subcategory. Their books may fall into more than one classification but when the basic intent of the book is to make children laugh, it should be classed as a book of *humor*. Humor books can often be a step away from comic books into the realm of good literature.

Children love to laugh, and this, of course, is the main appeal of books of humor. The writer of books of humor must be well aware of the kind of humor that appeals to each age level, since humor is a developmental characteristic.

To the young child who is learning to recognize and accept a multitude of shapes in his environment, anything out of its natural shape is funny. Falling down the stairs may not be funny for the person who is doing the falling, but it can send a seven-year-old into hysterical laughter. Words spoken out of order or in an unusual way bring a smile to the face of the primary child, which accounts for his laughter at the mention of an unusual name such as *Amelia Bedelia*. He delights, too, in the singing words —those that rhyme and form jingles.

As a child grows older, his sense of humor takes on many forms and he is capable of appreciating much of the humor of adults. He likes best, in the middle grades, stories with well-drawn characters in which one or two characters are in contrast to the others, causing awkward and hilarious situations wherein unusual things happen, as in the story of *Homer Price and the Super Duper* from the book *Homer Price*. Children identify strongly with these characters and situations and sense their absurdity. Some humor comes through because of the style of writing in Harve Zemach's *The Judge;* Alvin Schwartz's *Cross Your Fingers, Spit In Your Hat;* and Robert Tallon's *Rhoda's Restaurant*.

Books of humor have therapeutic value for children. Nothing can return a class to equilibrium faster after a classroom catastrophe or a schoolroom misfortune than the reading of a good book liberally treated with humor. Children who arrive at school unhappy because of some home situation can be helped to start their day in a good frame of mind if they can hear a story or section from one of these delightful books.

FIGURE 2–3. Children exhibit their good sense of humor in a mural made after reading Ezra Jack Keats's Snowy Day.

Poetry

Poetry deserves a great deal of attention as a teaching and learning tool in the elementary classroom. To allow for more complete coverage, the authors have devoted all of Chapter 11 to a discussion of it.

Folklore

Folklore is part of the verbal and recorded life and imagination of the simple, common people of all times. It includes games, songs, festivals, dances, rituals, old tales, superstitions, and verses. In this volume it embraces the types of children's literature identified as folktales, fables, myths, legends and epics, fairy tales (tales of wonder), magic tales (tales of trickery), cumulative tales, droll tales, and hero tales (including ballads).

The term "folklore" serves as an umbrella phrase that covers many types of literature. Each type, however, has certain unique characteristics, which will be described on the following pages. We have referred to specific types as folktales, implying that folk stories are not solely accounts of rituals, superstitions, games, or songs, although these elements may be woven into the fabric of a folktale.

Folktales served specific purposes for the time in which they were created. They attempted to give logic and reason to the behavior of human beings in times when much behavior did not appear to be logical. These tales were told in a raw, unsophisticated form. Emotions were often re-

FIGURE 2–4.   Like folklore, folk music is an exciting part of literature.

garded as natural reasons for committing great acts of violence and performing great deeds of love. Folktales have been found in all countries of the world.

Folktales grew out of an oral tradition. Before the invention of the printing press, writing and reading were not universal skills. Tales were passed along by word of mouth, from parents to children, from adults to adults, from minstrels to audiences, from the court jester to the court, and from child to child.

Many scholars believe folktales to be the remnant of a "single-origin" myth, wherein the similarities of the folkstories of various peoples are explained by their belief that a superior race of people traveled the ancient lands and established colonies, and that the folktales from these lands are familiar in plot because they reflect the nature myths of these people. Some students believe that folktales are remnants of nature myths, and interpret every story in terms of some common or unusual event in nature. Other students believe folktales to be the remnants of religious myths and rituals.

In contrast to the "single-origin" myth, some scholars believe the similarity in folktales comes from the fact that all human beings are moved by the same emotions: love and pity, fear and anguish, jealousy and hatred. They believe that everyone can observe the results of selfish ambitions, greed, quiet courage, and kindliness. Every culture on earth has witnessed character types such as the wicked stepmother, the gallant prince-charming, the underdog, the aggressive child, and the submissive child. Because these characteristics and types are common to all Man, it is only natural that the stories emerging from these cultures should have similar characters in similar situations.

Psychologists tend to interpret folktales and fairy tales as symbols of emotional fantasies experienced by all people; these include such universal feelings as unconscious sexual love for the parent, hatred of paternal or maternal authority, love and jealousy among brothers and sisters.[6]

Another psychological explanation of folktale origin is that the people who created them found in fancy the satisfaction of unconscious frustrations or drives. The imaginative tales they concocted provided wish fulfillment—and consequently temporary relief from their wretched state of life, hope in the midst of despair.

Anthropologists in recent years have attempted to study folklore in detail. Arbuthnot[7] reports that "their conclusion may be summed up in one sentence: *folk tales are the cement of society.* They not only express but codify, sanction and reinforce the way people think, feel, believe and behave."

There is probably a great deal of truth in all these beliefs regarding the origins of folktales, enough to warrant consideration. We do know that these origins are imbedded in the early history of man and that they do contain elements of past religions, rituals, superstitions, and history. They have also served this purpose of meeting man's basic emotional needs.

---

6. May Hill Arbuthnot and Zena Sutherland, *Children and Books,* 4th ed. (Glenview, Ill.: Scott, Foresman, 1972), p. 140.
7. *Ibid.,* p. 142.

Arbuthnot and Sutherland[8] classify folktales into the following types: (1) Cumulative Tales (in which the opening of a story is repeated and something new is added with each repetition, such as *Three Billy Goats Gruff*); (2) Talking Beasts (where the animals talk, as in *The Three Little Pigs*); (3) Droll or Humorous Stories (which are fun and nonsense, generally about sillies or numbskulls, such as *Clever Elsie*); (4) Realistic Stories (in which the happenings could be the real thing but are unlikely and the characters are highly unlikely also, such as *The Boy Who Would Do Anything*. Realistic in this sense means that the events *could* happen but not as they are related in the story); (5) Religious Tales such as *Samson and Delilah;* (6) Romance (where the lovers are impersonal and what happens to them to achieve romantic relationships is of more importance than the romance itself, such as *Cinderella*); (7) Magic (where the impossible happens naturally. Magic is the heart of all folktales, such as that of *King Arthur and the Knights of the Round Table.*).

Folktales offer splendid opportunities for creative teaching. Here the teacher can legitimately encourage the children to allow their imaginations to take flight. Encouraging children to write stories of magic and to create myths of their own can become a highly creative activity.

Certainly the life of people is captured and displayed like a Cinerama moving picture by the folklore of the past. *Robin Hood of Sherwood Forest* (McGovern) and *King Arthur and His Knights* give children a feeling and longing for times long past and an appreciation of fragments of life in the present when they see a film or television show such as *Camelot*. Children can empathize and become a peasant or a knight or a king when they read *Sir Gawain and the Green Knight*. They can readily imagine themselves in any country of the world and in any period of history when they read the folktales of other peoples. In reading folktales, it is as if the children of today find a bond with the children of all time all over the world, and that bond is creativity at its best.

American Folktales

Folktales are generally thought of as coming from the "old country," but every country in the world has developed folktales of its own. The United States has been especially fortunate in developing a stock of folk literature. As immigrants from every country flooded the shores of America, they brought with them the ballads and folktales of their own countries. In settling the vastness of a new land, they adapted old folktales to their new lives and created new stories to fit life in the new land. Certainly there was a minstrel or two in every covered wagon train that went west who created or shared stories with the group, as they sat around the fire and danced and sang after the evening meal. Thus were born the legend of Paul Bunyan, the adventures of Johnny Appleseed, and the story of Casey Jones. America has, indeed, a heritage of folk literature that is rich and abundant.

Mr. Arnold, a fifth-grade teacher, in establishing a time-line sequence of events in American history, had his children collect folklore of America.

---

8. *Ibid.,* pp. 143–145.

The stories and ballads were read or sung and often dramatized. Then Mr. Arnold helped the children arrange the stories and ballads as nearly as possible in chronological order by making a time line of heavy string stretched diagonally across the ceiling of the room and representing each tale by a symbol: an apple for Johnny Appleseed, an axe for Paul Bunyan, an engine for Casey Jones, a covered wagon for Sweet Betsy from Pike, a tar baby for Uncle Remus, a teepee for Hiawatha, etc. Then Mr. Arnold helped the children trace the history of the United States by researching the origin and meaning of the songs.

The children found that folklore in the United States fell basically into five categories, and they made charts on which they placed cards with the stories they had read:

Folktales of the American Indian

Folktales of the American Negro

Tall Tales

Folktales Adapted from Other Countries

Tales of Appalachia—often termed "Hillbilly Tales"

Folktales hold an appeal for children for the following reasons:

- They stimulate the imagination of the child because they are good stories.
- They generally contain a subtle humor that children understand and enjoy.
- They provide escape for children and reassure them that there are forces at work that will reward compassionate behavior.
- They give children hope that all problems are solvable.
- They present and/or reinforce the basic values of a culture.
- They help meet the emotional needs of children in a vicarious, if not in a direct, way.
- They present children with a style, form, and character portrayal that are different from the stories of modern-day writing and that appeal to children.
- They emphasize plot over characterizations. The characters in all folk tales are stereotyped, although memorable for some unique feature; e.g., Paul Bunyan differs from the giant in *Jack and the Beanstalk.*
- There is great variety among folktales: a teacher can find a folktale to suit almost any topic or mood. Modern versions of folktales are published each year, such as Paul Galdone's *The History of Mother Twaddle and the Marvelous Achievements of Her Son Jack,* a new rhymed version of *Jack and the Beanstalk;* his 1972 *The Three Bears;* his 1973 *The Three Billy Goats Gruff,* beautifully illustrated; and his new *The Little Red Hen.* Bradbury Press has recently reissued Charles Perrault's *Cinderella* with vibrant, jewellike pictures that provide a visual treat for readers. And Evaline Ness has written and illustrated *Tom Tit Tot* in a delightful recapitulation of the old English folktale.
- Folktales always contain a great deal of action, which begins early in the story. Children are drawn into the story immediately.
- Because they were originally conceived by those who could not read or write, the language is direct and simple.

Fables

Fables have made a comeback in appeal in recent years as they appear in various new guises, often beautifully illustrated. James Daugherty's *Andy and the Lion* is a newer version of *The Lion and the Mouse*. Kenneth Mc-Leish's *Chicken Licken* is a retelling of *Chicken Little*.

The spirit of fables is recaptured in Mercer Mayer's recent book, *Two Moral Tales: Bird's New Hat and Bear's New Clothes*. Modern editions of fables include *Three Aesop Fox Fables*, written and illustrated by Paul Galdone; *Aesop's Fables*, selected and illustrated by Gaynor Chapman; *Aesop: Lions and Lobsters and Foxes and Frogs* by Edward Gorey, illustrated by Ennis Rees; Lee Cooper's *Five Fables from France*, illustrated by Charles Keeping; *Tales From India* by Asha Upadhyay; and *The Blue Jackal*, collected and illustrated by Mehlli Gobhai.

Fables have influenced the attitudes of a culture toward moral and ethical problems. They have one characteristic that differentiates them from other folklore: they seek to teach or illustrate a moral. The ever-popular *Aesop's Fables* were used at one time for the purpose of teaching Sunday School–type lessons to children.

Children almost intuitively seem to resent stories that moralize. Consequently, fables have never been as popular as other types of folklore. Modern versions of the fables are more palatable. In *Andy and the Lion* by Daugherty, the fable is told straightforwardly and without emphasis on the

FIGURE 2–5. *After reading Marcia Brown's fable, one child created this delightful scene. The mouse and the tiger are made of painted stones.*

moral. The child is left to interpret the story for himself if he feels it necessary. The fables seem to come off better this way, especially as far as modern youth is concerned, provided, of course, that the teacher in reading the modern version is not too contaminated by the influence of her childhood and does not do verbally what the author has carefully avoided in his writing.

Some modern children's writers have used the theme of the old fables but changed their emphasis. John Ciardi's *John J. Plenty and Fiddler Dan* is such a story. Written in verse, it retells the story of the grasshopper and the ants in a charming, realistic way, and the grasshopper, Fiddler Dan, does not come out the loser. Ciardi promotes the concept that there are toilers in the world, and workers, and artists, and that we all need each other. "There must be music," says Ciardi, "and that's what John J. never knew!"

Barbara Cooney's *Chanticleer and the Fox,* adapted from Chaucer's *Canterbury Tales,* is a book that won the Caldecott Medal in 1958.

Because of their simplicity and their appeal to human nature and to the building of values, fables continue to remain popular—to some degree—both to children, who seem to return to them, and to authors, who continue to rewrite and revise them.

Those fables which children do enjoy make excellent material for dramatizations. They are simple and short and provide a large variety of characters that young children like to pretend to be.

Myths

As a follow-up on the list of topics suggested by the children, Mr. Arnold's class decided to write their own myths to explain natural phenomena in an unscientific way, much the same as people living years ago might explain it. Here is one result:

WHY IT SNOWS

> *Once upon a time there lived a Goddess named*
> *Mother Goose and I think that you have heard of*
> *her and her nursery rhymes.*
> *One day she flew up to the sky and went into*
> *her house. She started to clean and finally she*
> *came to her feather bed, and it was so dusty she*
> *said to herself, "I think I will shake it out the*
> *window," and she did so.*
> *But what do you think happened? All the feathers*
> *flew all over and that's why people believe it snows.*

> RAY
> *Grade 3*

Basically, this child has captured the essence of the myth. Myths are very old and very complicated in plot and in their development. They have no known authors and, like all folktales, were passed along by word of mouth until they were eventually written down. Myths deal with gods and goddesses and are focused around a heroic character. They tell about life in the world that preceded the present life and describe the origins of things.

Myths seem to be common to all countries. They contain man's attempt to explain his gods and their place in nature. They deal with sacred themes and the heroes and heroines are semi-divine. In myths the problems are always solved with the aid of a god or goddess.

These gods and goddesses have become rightfully classified among the legendary heroes of children's literature: Apollo, Zeus, Aphrodite, Sigurd, Thor, and Brynhild have taken their place in the child's fancy, along with Robin Hood, King Arthur, and Paul Bunyan.

Children can well understand myths when they are introduced to them as part of the culture of the ancient people they study and when they write their own myths to explain natural phenomena, as Mr. Arnold had them do. Mr. Arnold felt that his students enjoyed their creative writing so much that he had them list questions of unexplained phenomena in *their* society today and, lacking scientific explanations, he asked the children to write fictitious explanations for these phenomena. This is actually the essence of myths.

Some of the questions asked and later used as topics for myths were:

What is electricity?
Why does a light bulb give light?
What is cancer?
What makes seeds grow to be different things?
Are there people on Mars?
What are flying saucers?
Why are dogs afraid of cats?

Myths have great appeal to children because: (1) they always contain a great deal of action and children like this; (2) they are excellent

FIGURE 2–6. *These children wrote myths, made character masks, and dramatized them in the fashion of the Ancient Greeks.*

"escape" material full of fantasy, magic, and imagination; (3) they comfort children in that virtue is rewarded and evil is punished; (4) the stories are straightforward and of high dramatic quality; (5) the emotional needs of children are satisfied; and (6) myths stimulate the imagination.

Legends

Legends are similar to myths in that they are fictitious accounts of great happenings. However, they are less concerned with origins and more concerned with human heroism. They are more complicated in plot than the simpler folktales, and therefore more suitable to the middle grades than to the primary grades. Legends, like myths, go back in their origins to great antiquity but to far less primitive conditions than some folktales. Legends, like myths and other hero tales, were recorded after being handed down orally for hundreds of years, so they have no known authors. They are generally based on historical facts, but are elaborated to the point where the facts are no longer verifiable. Names associated with them are generally those of people who first recorded the legend, someone who has revised or rewritten a particular version of a legend, or someone who has made an adaptation of it.

Intermediate-grade children commonly associate with contemporary heroes or identify with professions and/or occupations dedicated to humanistic causes, such as medicine, nursing, teaching, etc. Many scholars believe that these children identify with the great heroes of legends at this age for the same reason—they dream about their own contributions to mankind through their heroes. Sloo Foot Sue is a heroine to these children, and a very human one. Robin Hood and King Arthur are known by every true-blooded American boy and are recreated in his dramatic play. Odysseus is a hero to both boys and girls, and every girl hopes that some day she will be Helen of Troy and will control the world by her own beauty.

The legendary heroes of the past are probably akin to the modern child's version of Superman. To children who have not become acquainted with the great legendary heroes of the past, Superman has become a substitute.

Legends seem to please children for the same reasons that other folklore appeals to them, with the added element of an unusual or gifted hero or heroine with whom children can identify.

Epics

An epic is a sustained narrative that combines the elements of myths and legends into a unified story about one country and its gods and heroes. Epics are often told in poetic form. In the epic, the heroes achieve some extraordinary feat of great value to the future of mankind. Perhaps the best known examples of an epic are found in Homer's *Iliad* and *Odyssey*.

All countries have their epics. In India, *Ramayana* is popular with all children. The story of the Ramayana was told in 1954 in Joseph Gaer's *The Adventures of Rama*. In 1969 Elizabeth Seeger wrote a memorable and beautiful book, *The Ramayana,* for children. Another of her books, *The Five Sons of King Pandu* (1967), tells of another Indian epic.

From Babylonia comes one of the oldest epics in the world, *Gilgamesh*. From Norway comes the epic *Volsunga Saga*.

Only a few authors have written the old epics into versions for children to read today. Olivia Coolidge's books, *Greek Myths* and *Trojan War*, are two examples of such writings. Although published in 1949 and 1952, they are still read by children interested in epics. From England comes Sidney Lanier's *The Boy's King Arthur*.

Among the most popular writings of the past several years are Dorothy Hosford's *Sons of the Volsungs* (1932) and *Thunder of the Gods* (1952), and Barbara Leonie Picard's *Tales of the Norse Gods and Heroes* (1953). A picture book edition by Ingri and Edgar Parin D'Aulaire, entitled *Norse Gods and Giants* (1955), is probably one of the most popular of today's epic books. Barbara Louise Picard's *Stories of King Arthur and His Knights*, illustrated by Roy Morgan (1967), is a current popular epic story. Constance Hieatt's books, *Sir Gawain and the Green Knight* (1967), *The Sword and the Grail* (1972), and *The Castle of Ladies* (1973), are all popular editions of King Arthur epics.

From Japan comes the epic *Warlord of the Genji* by Dale Carlson (1970), from Mexico *The Creation of the Sun and the Moon* by B. Traven (1968), from China *Chinese Myths and Fantasies* by Cyril Birch (1961).

Epics also include ballads such as *Beowulf* and bible stories told in epic style.

Ballads and Story-Poems

A ballad is a poem that tells a story. Often it is called a story-poem. A classical ballad is *Beowulf*, and a classical story-poem often classified as a ballad is Robert Browning's *The Pied Piper of Hamelin*.

Ballads are truly the songs of the ages. Long before there were newspapers, minstrels traveled from town to town bearing the news to the country folk who gathered in a hamlet, or to royalty who gathered in the halls of a feudal castle. These men often supported themselves by singing the songs of the time while they strummed a musical instrument. The people, rich and poor alike, loved to sit by the hour around a roaring fire and hear stories told by these men. Of course, the stories changed often in the telling as a minstrel's memory grew faulty or as he noted what elements caused the greatest reaction among the members of his audience.

After the invention of the printing press, ballads were recorded and became more stable. They also became less creative because they were less subject to adaptiveness and change. The creative modern narrative poems grew out of the ballad concept.

Ballads were sung in some countries by professional singers. In Denmark these singers were known as *scalds*. In England they were called *scops* or *bards*. These men were the poets of the times. The *scop* later became known as a minstrel. It was common for a king to maintain a minstrel as a member of his household. Even monasteries maintained a minstrel.

As the minstrel became more important, he assumed the role of professional entertainer. He wrote his own ballads and stories and created his own tunes. The content of many of these stories, which were recorded with the invention of printing, would indicate that these men were largely associated with the nobility since most of the ballads are about kings and queens and take place in castles. The content also indicates that these were men of some education and above-average intelligence because of the choice of words in the ballads and their scholarly manipulation. There is also some historical evidence to support the belief that ballads may have begun with the clergy; this argument is plausible because from the clergy of this time came the carols, the lyrics, and the miracle plays.

Some scholars believe that ballads are the result of the meeting of a group of simple people to celebrate an event such as a religious holiday, a wedding, or a burial. These people danced and sang together and were led by a talented leader who began to tell a story to which the group of listeners sang a refrain in choral response. The refrain was believed to allow the leader to think about the next verse and to give him time to create a new story.

Ballads maintain their appeal to children because of the following characteristics:

The fast movement of the verse.

The swift movement of the story.

The great variety of content available in ballads, ranging from nonsense rhymes such as *The Owl and the Pussycat* to the epic ballads such as Edna St. Vincent Millay's *The Ballad of the Harp-Weaver*. Ballads embrace such classifications as romance, tragedy, humor, nonsense, autobiography, mystery, and adventure.

The action, which is fast-moving with a minimum of words.

The musical quality of the writing.

The high, almost primitive, dramatic quality of the story. Most ballad plots are tragic rather than humorous.

The abrupt beginnings and endings, which children appear to enjoy.

The lack of detailed description. It is a unique feature of the ballad to plunge the reader into the plot and to get on with it.

Real ballads are not written by known authors (although story-poems are). The anonymity of the writing has made it everyone's fare—people through the ages have contributed to its effectiveness until it now seems to appeal to everyone.

The amount of repetition in a ballad makes it musically and narratively appealing to children. A common pattern in ballads is for each verse to repeat the form of the preceding verse with a new element added that advances the story.

Ballads and story-poems are especially appealing to the children of the middle grades. For the most part, they should be read to children in order to maintain the beauty of the rhythm and the dramatic flow of words. Besides, many of the old ballads are loaded with dialect, abbreviations, and obsolete words too difficult for the average child to read.

Ballads are an excellent departure for teaching history and social studies, but not in poetic form. Mr. Carr uses the ballad of Robin Hood for this purpose in his middle school classroom in Chapter 5. Ballads can also furnish a basis for creative writing, for the teaching of certain aspects of word structure, and for vocabulary building. Smith[9] tells of a group of nine-

---

9. James A. Smith, *Adventures in Communication: Language Arts Methods* (Boston: Allyn and Bacon, 1972), pp. 443–444.

and ten-year-olds who were studying ballads and dinosaurs. Miss Allen, the teacher, felt the children were highly motivated over dinosaurs and ballads and decided to use the dinosaur unit as the basis of teaching rhyming words to help the children write some original narrative poems ("ballads").

On the top of a piece of construction paper, Miss Allen printed words such as dinosaur, ago, tree, breaks, etc. She then talked to the children about rhyming words. Placing the children in pairs, she gave each pair a sheet of paper on which was written one key word. They were asked to write, in a five-minute time limit, all the words they could think of that rhymed with the key word.

When time was called, all the papers were posted along the chalk tray, and each pair of children read the words they had put on their chart. In some instances, the class suggested additional words. In others, a few obvious misfits were crossed out.

Miss Allen then placed a strip of paper on the bulletin board which contained this line:

In the forest lived Denny, the dinosaur

"Now look at our chart of words that rhyme with dinosaur," said Miss Allen, "and see if anyone can pick a word that can be put at the end of this sentence, but with words filled in so it will make sense."

And on the bulletin board, below the first sentence, she added:

He ate_____ _____ _____ _____ _____ _____.

Finally Charlie volunteered, "He ate all the time and wanted more." The children were delighted, so Miss Allen put up another line.

He lived on the earth many years ago.

And she said, "Now finish this with a word that rhymes with ago."

Which was_____ _____ _____ _____ _____ _____.

Soon Debby raised her hand and said, "Which was long before the ice and snow!"

They were off. The following poem resulted. Italicized words indicate those supplied by the children.

THE BALLAD OF DENNY THE DINOSAUR

In the forest lived Denny, the dinosaur
He ate *all the time and wanted more,*
He lived on the earth many years ago
Which was *long before the ice and snow*
He loved to lie in the cool, cool shade
He ate *little beasts and drank lemonade*
He walked very clumsy like a big old man
And he never *never never ran.*
One day he went to a mountain top
To get some *air and a new rag mop*
But he slipped and fell with every step
Until he *lost all his pep*
He lay in the mud and there he died
And *dust and dirt soon covered his hide*
Three billion years later he came to the top
Denny, the dinosaur *carrying a mop!*

The children wrote many poems after this kickoff. Many were illustrated and bound into individual books. Miss Allen had made word usage and vocabulary building a relevant activity for her pupils.

Also, these children were constructing ballads through the concept of group contributions and group spontaneity. Later they put their ballad to music. Christine could play a guitar, so she worked out simple chords, and the children sang the lines by using two groups, each singing alternate lines. They received the opportunity to evaluate their work when Miss Allen taped the ballad, and they heard the playback over the school's speaker system. The principal, who always opened the day with a short program, heard Christine practicing one day and found out about the children's work. He immediately suggested they use it for an opening exercise some day so all the children could enjoy it.

Fairy Tales (Tales of Wonder)

Fairy tales were originated long ago by common, humble people who had little to eat or to keep them warm. These people were often enslaved, victims of a life that offered them little or no chance to resolve their dilemma. So they invented stories that were really dreams. In their dreams they became rich, generally in two ways: either they were virtuous as they were taught to be and were rewarded for their virtue by a benevolent benefactor (often a rich prince or king), or they were favored by a miracle of some sort. The plots of the stories were contrived, unreal visions of striving to gain security in life, to be loved, to be comfortable, to be safe, to be happy. Fairy tales were highly symbolic of the struggles of man against his environment and reflected his eternal hope for Shangri-la. They always contain symbols of the ultimate in comfort: roaring fires, sumptuous feasts, sparkling jewels, gorgeous palaces, strong virtues, and often a supernatural means of protection.

Fairy tales are part of the culture of the world, and as such belong to folk literature. They receive their name from the French word *fee*, which was the name given to a kind of supernatural creature who inhabited a world known as *faiere*. Each country of the world has stories about supernatural little people. Generally they live in secret places such as tree trunks or underground palaces. They possess supernatural powers and can perform great acts of magic.

Fairy tales include many types of people with magical power: gnomes, elves, jinns, genies, leprechauns, little people, fairy godmothers, giants, ogres, witches, wisemen, wizards, magicians, trolls, wee folk, good people, pixies. They also include fairy animals who talk or possess unusual powers, and objects that are enchanted or have magical power, such as wands, fountains, rivers, or even clothes.

Fairy tales appeal to children, as they do to all who have listened to them throughout history:

They provide escape from the realities of life and, in the imagination, make all life beautiful. They release people temporarily from the problems and negative aspects of life.

- They provide hope for mankind, children included. Just as an adult dreams of the miracle of winning a lottery ticket, so do children dream of the miracle that will bring them a new sled, or riches, or freedom from a nagging older sister.
- They reinforce the teachings of adults to children and are, therefore, comforting. If one remains good, virtuous, and honest, he will ultimately be rewarded.
- They help to instill values in children, because the righteous person always does the right thing and is rewarded, while evil is always punished.

Adventure Tales

Adventure stories cannot be classified as belonging to any one period of time or to any one place. They are tales about a hero or heroine or a group of people who find themselves in a predicament requiring skill, daring, courage, and fortitude to overcome. Often in adventure stories several such predicaments succeeded each other, and each must be solved by the hero, as in *Treasure Island* by Stevenson, *The Slave Dancer* by Paula Fox, and *The Boy Who Sailed Around the World Alone* by Robin Lee Graham and Derek L. T. Gill. As indicated by these selections, adventure stories may be fictional or true adventure.

Adventure stories are loved by both children and adults. They are probably the most popular of all writing. They can cover the entire range of classifications of children's literature presented in this book. Fairy tales, myths, and folk stories are all generally adventure stories.

Tales of adventure have been written to cover all reading ability levels and to appeal to all ages. They are available from all over the world and from all periods of history. Their heroes and heroines can be animals, humans, or inanimate objects. Many biographies can legitimately be called adventure stories.

One type of adventure story is Mollie Hunter's *The Thirteenth Member*, the narrative of Gilly Duncan, a witch and a kitchen maid. The story is set in sixteenth-century Scotland and is based on records of a plot to kill King James I. Witchcraft is the method chosen by the conspirators. Adam Lowrie, a young servant, saves Gilly and the king from death.

Another fascinating adventure story dealing with witchcraft is Elizabeth George Speare's *The Witch of Blackbird Pond*. It is a story of Kit Tyler who comes from Barbados to live in a bleak puritanical Connecticut town with Aunt Rachael, Uncle Matthew, and her two cousins, Judy and Mercy. Written for juveniles, it is an excellent book for advanced middle graders.

Many adventure stories are actually historical fiction, for example, Rose Wilder Lane's *Let the Hurricane Roar*, the adventure of Charles and Caroline, young homesteaders beset with the problems of settling the West: hurricanes, grasshoppers, fires, and snow. Laura Ingalls Wilder's *Little House* books also fall into this category.

Other types of adventure stories written in historical settings are such books as *The Bright and Morning Star* by Rosemary Harris, one of a series of books that dramatically portray life in ancient Egypt. This particular book, exciting and beautifully written, tells the story of Reuben, Prince of Canaan, and his wife Thamar who return to the capital city of

FIGURE 2–7. Bright and Morning Star *by Rosemary Harris provided the motivation for Mr. John's unit on Ancient Egypt in his middle grades.*

Kemi to seek help for their second son, Sadhi, who has been left deaf and dumb after an illness.

Still another type of adventure story is Eleanor Clymer's *Take Tarts As Tarts Is Passing.* It is about brothers Jeremiah and Obadiah who have been sent into the world to seek their fortunes and who have opposite reactions to the advice of Aunt Hattie, the village wise woman. Their adventures delight children in the primary grades.

Another modern adventure story for the primary grades, *Ralph and the Queen's Bathtub* by Kay Chorao, is a story of a boy proud to be old enough to walk to school alone but afraid to walk by the house called *Queen's Bathtub* which, it is rumored, is inhabited by a giant witch. One day Ralph winds up inside the house, and his adventures are astonishing. This story combines adventure and fantasy very successfully.

In Bruce Clement's *I Tell A Lie Every So Often,* the hero finds that a lie he tells takes him 500 miles away from home and results in some strange adventures. This book is written for middle graders and juveniles and combines humor with adventure.

One recent, unusual, adventure story for primary children is *Bush Walkabout* by Alex Poignant, an outstanding photo-picture story of the adventures of two aborigine children who find themselves lost in the Australian bush.

Many children's books that have become classics are adventure stories. Carol Brink's *Caddie Woodlawn,* the story of a pioneer girl and her encounter with the Indians; C. W. Anderson's animal stories of *Salute;* Stevenson's *Treasure Island;* Virginia Lee Burton's *Katy and the Big Snow;* Robert McCloskey's *Homer Price;* Jean L. Latham's *Carry On, Mr. Bowditch;* and James Boyd's *Drums* are all classic adventure stories.

The popularity of adventure stories is emphasized in the flood of reissues of the classics on the current market. Heritage Press has recently republished *Treasure Island* by Stevenson, and *Tom Sawyer* and *Huckleberry Finn* by Mark Twain. Harcourt, Brace and Jovanovich has recently republished *Robinson Crusoe: My Journal and Sketches.*

Tomi Ungerer has written a new book called *A Storybook: A Collection of Stories Old and New,* which contains six old classics retold, among them adaptations of *The Husband Who Was To Mind the House* by Bernard Garfinkel, *The Tinder Box* by Hans Christian Andersen, and *Little Red Riding Hood* by Ungerer.

Adventure stories appeal to children for obvious reasons, but primarily they are an escape device. Inasmuch as they cover all the categories listed in this chapter, they appeal to children for most of the reasons listed at the end of each category. They encompass a variety of literary styles and provide that wealth of material needed for a rich reading program in the elementary school. Adventure tales are examples of the ability of men and women to use their imagination to shape realism or fantasy into creative experiences for boys and girls.

Mystery Stories

Mystery stories directly develop the divergent thinking qualities of children and are, therefore, very closely associated with creative thought. In the mystery story, the reader is presented with a body of facts and clues which he keeps reshuffling in his own mind in order to solve the crime or to resolve a mysterious situation. The farther he reads and the more the clues are introduced, the narrower is his choice of solutions, but perhaps this choice is more challenging.

Even before the days of Edgar Allan Poe, mystery stories were popular with children. There is something spellbinding about the unknown, the horrible, and the violent which grips children and adults. Many adult fiction stories capitalize (as do some modern moving pictures) on this primitive characteristic in man, using violence, brutality, horror, and disfigurement, and write novels solely for their shock value. Many "comic" strips have also used this technique.

Modern writers for children have been challenged to use this awe of the unknown, along with violence and horror, in such a manner that children can cope with it, and it will not be damaging to their own value development. Critics of educational practices have pointed out that there never have been stories written that portrayed violence, bloodshed, horror, and inhumanity more viciously than the early fairy tales and folktales such as *Bluebeard* and *Hansel and Gretel.* They make a good point, because most of the fairy tales and many of the folktales have been altered through the years to make them more palatable to adults as well as to children.

One of us recently took a college class to see a revival of *The Red Shoes.* None of the college students had read this beautiful old fairy tale. The students felt the ending of the film would be too sticky to explain to children. A committee was sent to the library to find an old copy of *The Red Shoes.* The students found one in a volume written in 1914. When it was read to the class, one student protested after a while and was actually ill. The malice, inhumanity, and cold-blooded treatment toward individuals in this version was so callously told as to be unbelievable to this college group. Today's television violence was mild beside it.

Fortunately, modern authors of children's books have recognized both the need and the dangers for good mystery stories and have done something about it. Current book lists contain beautifully written mystery stories.

Perhaps the best remembered of all mystery books are some of the Nancy Drew series written under the name of Carolyn Keene (and others). Although there was no Carolyn Keene as such, these books became very popular a generation or two ago and are still being printed. Even if these books lack literary quality, they have pointed up the love of juveniles for mystery stories and were perhaps responsible, to a large degree, for the writing of more mystery stories for children.

One of the most famous of all children's mystery stories is Henry Winterfield's *Detectives in Togas*, which is not only an excellent story of suspense but also an outstanding picture of ancient Rome.

Joan Aiken's *Night Fall* is a very adult mystery that uses all the techniques of the modern melodrama in a well-developed piece of fiction. The book includes an exciting and suspenseful chase. It is well written, with scenes and places beautifully described and the story realistically developed. There is even romance in the book—on a level very understandable to girls and boys in the fifth and sixth grades. We have found this book to be very popular with advanced sixth graders.

Eleanor Cameron's delightful story, *The Room Made of Windows*, revolves around the mystery of what goes on in an old house next door. It, too, deals with the development of the character of a rebellious and exciting girl who lives in a small town and wants to be a writer. The story is well developed, the characters are realistic, and the mystery is logically explained.

Humor and mystery are beautifully combined in Sesyle Joslin's clever book, *The Spy Lady and the Muffin Man*, and in her more recent book, *Last Summer's Smugglers*. Scott Corbett makes an exciting mystery story in *The Case of the Silver Skull*, an adventure about Roger, who investigates the theft of silver from old Mrs. Hargrove's house. These books are written for middle graders.

In *The Truth About Stone Hollow* by Zilpha Keatley Snyder, Amy and Jason explore haunted Stone Hollow with some spine-tingling results. Car nuts and mystery buffs are especially fond of the combined mystery and adventure story, *The Gunshot Grand Prix* by Douglas Rutherford. Both books are written for middle graders. *The Devil's Storybook* by Natalie Babbitt is a collection of ten original stories (some funny and some serious) about Old Scratch and his battle for souls.

Erich Kastner's book, *Emil and the Detectives*, is another book that is well written and enchanting to children. A timely book about three children who try desperately to keep a wild and beautiful spot from being developed by commercial enterprises is *The Dark Tower Mystery* by Mary C. Jane, written for ages 9–11. Elizabeth Honness's *Mystery of the Pirate's Ghost* is a somewhat typical story for the same age group. It is about a sister and brother who find a mystery in a "haunted" New England house and find the explanation more natural than any ghost.

Mystery stories are not restricted, as we can see, to middle-grade ages. Clyde Bulla's *Ghost Town Treasure* is written for the primary grader. Steven Kellogg has written a book for pre-school and primary children, *The*

Mystery of the Missing Red Mitten, in which Annie, the main character, reaches a funny and surprising solution to the mystery.

Modern authors have written mystery stories in all types of settings. Witness, for instance, Betsy Haynes's *Spies on the Devil's Belt,* an espionage story of conflict between the colonists on the Connecticut coast and British-held Long Island; and *Strange Island,* a story of the traitor Aaron Burr, by Marian Boyd Havighurst. Another popular contemporary mystery story is Esther Allan's *The Night Wind.*

A word must be said about ghost stories and tales of the occult, which seem to be very popular, especially with middle school children. A recent book, *Witch, Witch: Stories and Poems of Sorcery, Spells and Hocus-Pocus,* selected by Richard Shaw and illustrated by Clinton Arrowood, is a compilation of over twenty-five spooky pieces from around the world for ages 9 and up. Many such books are sought by children. Because of their mysterious qualities, we have placed them under "mystery," but they could be comfortably classified as magic or fantasy.

Mystery stories appeal to children because (1) they excite the child's primitive sense of facing the unknown and the terrible, yet in a cloak of safety; (2) they promote his divergent thinking abilities; (3) they contain action, excitement, and drama; (4) they stimulate imagination; and (5) they satisfy certain human emotional needs not met in other types of stories.

Romance

Children are exposed to the glib advertisement of paperback books, night club reviews, and pornographic movies in the newspapers and magazines that come into their homes. Discussions on sex are held in many elementary schools as part of the health courses. Unfortunately, in the public exploitation of sex, children see more of the seamy side of love than they do the uplifting, beautiful side.

The need for stories about love and sex is indicated by the way young girls consume the trash published in current magazines. The need for books that show love and sex as part of man's normal, needed behavior is great. Many of today's authors have accepted the challenge and have written books that are essentially love stories. Others, to make their characters real and true, have them falling in love.

In *Up a Road Slowly* by Irene Hunt, Julie Trelling, the heroine, as part of her growing up, thinks she is in love with Danny, an aggressive, somewhat conceited high school boy. Danny has a great effect on Julie's emotional development and on the establishment of her values.

In Joan Aiken's *Night Fall,* the heroine thinks she is in love with a boy, only to find later the difference between a girlish "crush" and true love.

Many of the old classics contained a love story for the heroine. Jo's love story in *Little Women* is well known to all girls. More modern examples of good romance stories can be found in Florence Crannell Mean's *Knock at the Door, Emmy,* and *Tolliver.*

Boys of middle school age are generally not as developed as girls nor as mature in their tastes. Their preference for books of adventure, mystery, legendary heroes, and realism is stronger at this age than their need for romance. Most of the children's books written with a love theme for this age are definitely directed toward girls. There are books boys enjoy, however, that have a minor love theme. An excellent example is *Johnny Tremain* by Esther Forbes.

Fantasy

Tales of Imagination

Imagination seems to be a quality all children possess almost from birth. It is the basis of all creative thinking, a vital part of the divergent thinking process. Without imagination, great literature could not exist. Walter Loban[10] says:

> Usually we agree on at least three goals: self-understanding, extension of experience, and a balanced perspective on life. All of these depend upon imagination and the insight it bestows. Imagination is a mental activity which—because it is relatively free from realistic demands—enables one to summon up images, feelings, memories, sensations, and intuitions. Free from immediate practicality, the imaginative thinker rearranges and recombines these mosaics of perception in fluid fashion, to create new delightful or useful relationships.

All literature is born of imagination, even when the writing is based on fact. Some types of literature, however, are purely imagination in that the writer begins with an idea and develops every succeeding idea and description from his own reservoir of thought. The characters in these fanciful tales may perform acts and have experiences like all people, but by no stretch of the imagination could these stories ever be true. These imaginative stories contain the same elements found in folktales that make them favorites with children.

Folktales are, of course, stories of imagination and form the basis for the pattern of imaginative and fanciful tales that are still being written. Hans Christian Andersen's works are stories of imagination, many adapted from the folktales of his own and other countries. He is probably the inventor of stories about inanimate objects such as *The Fir Tree* and *The Steadfast Tin Soldier*. Andersen also used stories of talking beasts, such as *The Ugly Duckling*, which may be classified as a fanciful tale.

Fantasy has always been popular in children's literature. Many of these stories of the past were adaptations of Andersen's tales. Each generation has contributed to the backlog of material classified as fantasy or tales of imagination.

Lewis Carroll's *Alice's Adventures in Wonderland* is a popular fantasy book of the nineteenth century. Charles Kingsley's *The Water-Babies* is another example of an older fantasy book. The list of such books may include Sir James Barrie's *Peter Pan*, Mary Norton's *The Borrowers*, Carolyn Sherwin Bailey's *Miss Hickory*, and William Pene Du Bois's *Twenty-One Balloons*.

---

10. Walter Loban, "Balancing the Literature Program," *Elementary English* 43 (November 1966): 746–747.

FIGURE 2–8. A Shower of Books *is the theme for this April Literature-mobile. As children read a book, they drew a picture in a raindrop shape and attached it to the decorated umbrella.*

Fantasies are very popular among boys and girls today, and modern authors are writing some of the best fantasy ever produced. The world is ripe for it. Fantasy books exist for all age levels. Pat Ross has written a primary-grade fantasy in *Hi Fly*. It is a story of a girl who becomes the size of a fly and sees her home from a fly's point of view. *Hi Fly* is a wordless picture book with illustrations by John Wallner. Mercer Mayer's *What Do You Do With A Kangaroo?* is a delightful fantasy of how a beleaguered little girl copes with some unexpected and hard-to-please animal guests. It is a fun book for all ages.

The old classic fantasies still hold their appeal for the young generation. Heritage Press recently reissued Kenneth Grahame's *The Wind in the Willows,* first published in 1908.

Science Fiction

Because of the ever-developing interest in the physical and behavioral sciences, science fiction has become a major category in children's books. Science fiction in years past was classified largely as "escape" literature, such as the Jules Verne books, or "fantasy," such as the work of H. G. Wells. Whereas these older books were really flights of the imagination into unknown places and times, modern science fiction has a more serious purpose: that of hypothesizing what is or can be from facts already known. In reading modern science fiction, the child will come across enough true information (commonly published in magazines, textbooks, and newspapers) to have the feeling that all that is happening is possible. Robert Heinlein's books are excellent examples of modern science fiction. His *Have Space Suit—Will Travel* is loaded with imagination, but the imagination is built on fact.

Another recent change in science fiction stories is in the *attitude* of the writing. Almost all older science fiction stories were about people of this planet taking over those of other worlds or planets—other worlds and outer space were inhabited by strange creatures, all less worthy and less intelligent than the humans of civilized earth. New explorations in outer space, new discoveries and theories in archeology, and new insights into the human mind have changed this attitude into a curiosity about the universe. Modern science fiction tends to depict life as the writers feel it might be or could be, with less emphasis on plots in which earth men know what is best for all.

Louis Slobodkin's *The Space Ship under the Apple Tree* was one of the first science fiction books written especially for children. Ray Bradbury's books, especially *Fahrenheit 451*, have long been popular. Another early science fiction book was Ellen MacGregor's *Miss Pickerell Goes to Mars*, published in 1951.

Isaac Asimov's *David Starr: Space Ranger, Lucky Starr and the Pirates of the Asteroids*, and *Lucky Starr and the Oceans of Venus* (1952–1954) are excellent examples of science fiction books which began to exploit the new "attitude."

Madeline L'Engle's books *A Wrinkle in Time* and *A Wind in the Door* are classic examples of modern explorations of the human mind.

John Christopher's *White Mountains*, Robert C. O'Brien's *Mrs. Frisby and the Rats of Nimh*, Ben Bova's *Flight of Exiles*, Peter Dickinson's *Heartsease* and *The Devil's Children*, and A. M. Lightner's *The Day of the Drones* are all excellent examples of modern science fiction.

Realistic Fiction

Although children today have a great devotion to folktales, fairy tales, tales of fantasy and imagination, they also need and want realistic books: books which deal with life as it is today and which present problems common to them, with plausible solutions, free from the contamination of magic or make-believe. As children grow older, the appeal for this kind of book increases.

Realistic tales serve many purposes to a child. They help him to see how people solve problems. Often the problems of the main character are those of the child reader and he receives a great deal of confidence and self-concept by coming to realize that most problems can be solved—and that he, too, may be able to solve his.

Realistic tales help a child prepare for the differences in the world in which he does not live by recognizing the similarities between it and his own world. They help him to better understand people and places. They appeal to his creative drives and can help him stretch his imagination. Realistic stories help him to face reality and to cope with social problems on his own level of thinking. They help him to empathize and understand the feelings and predicaments of others, and to identify problems in himself.

Realistic tales have appealed to children over the generations. *Little Women* and *The Adventures of Tom Sawyer* were probably two of the first classic realistic tales. *Hans Brinker or The Silver Skates* and *Heidi* are others. Many modern writers of children's books are writing realistic tales for the middle grades. Telling about life as it really is, with all the hardships as well as the pleasures, can do many of the things the old stories also do for children. Boys and girls who read Robert McCloskey's *Time of Wonder* are enthralled with the vivid descriptions of the coming of the great blow as the hurricane hits the Maine coast. They sit taller in their seats and their eyes sparkle when Mother breaks out in song during the heart of the storm. Surely they are experiencing courage and are identifying with their roles as mothers or fathers, the protectors of all children.

"Do people really live like that?" asks a wealthy suburban boy after hearing Neville's *It's Like This Cat*. They want to know what other books she has written. We go to the library to find *The Seventeenth-Street Gang*. They like it as much as *Cat*, and a whole new way of life has been opened to them. It is a credit to the skill of the author when Gerry says, "I'd like to live there!"

The beauty and the heartaches of all mankind are reflected in the sea of faces turned up to the teacher when she reads Marjorie Rawlings's *The Yearling*. Some of them wipe a tear away. But they ask for the book over and over. In the primary grades the children particularly enjoy a very direct, honest little book by Eleanor Schick, *City in the Winter*. It appeals very much to suburban children because it shows them another way of life —with familiar characters in unfamiliar guises. Grandmother in *City in the Winter* wears an old sweater, sneakers, and bobby socks, quite unlike the sophisticated cigarette-smoking grandmothers of some children. The little boy in the story has no father. Mother goes to work. School is closed because of the great snowstorm that cripples the city. The sketches by Eleanor Schick are a story in themselves, showing how small creative acts may enrich the lives of poor children.

P. A. Engebrecht's *Under the Haystack* deals with the problem of desertion. When her mother and stepfather do not come home for dinner, Sandy has a sense of foreboding. Haystacks are a security place where children go to hide and work out their problems, and there Sandy takes refuge to figure out how she will keep her family—her two sisters and herself—together. This is a beautiful but sad story, with the haystacks serving as symbols for Sandy's growing up, and as she solves her problems, the pile of haystacks becomes smaller.

A very realistic book by Sharon Bell Mathis, *Teacup Full of Roses*, is written for juveniles (junior high school), but one of us found it a very effective book to use in a middle school in a disadvantaged urban area. It is a poignant story of the life of a black family in the ghetto. Like all humans, the members of Joe's family have their dreams, most of which turn out to be a teacup full of roses to be shattered before the story ends.

Paul, the younger brother, can paint but is near death because of drug addiction. Davey, the middle boy, is brilliant in school and skilled as a basketball star. Joe himself loves to tell stories. Because Joe loves his brothers, he leaves school to go to work so he can earn money to help them realize their dreams. For two long years he works days and goes to school nights in order to earn his high school diploma. He receives little help from his mother, who always babies Paul, the family weakling, or from his father, who is an invalid. Finally, on the day of his graduation, he realizes that Davey is the only one who is going to be able to make his dream come true, so he withdraws his money from the bank and gives it to Davey. But Paul finds where it is hidden and steals it to buy drugs. Davey is killed trying to find and save Paul.

All of this very melodramatic material, but Miss Mathis writes with authority from experience and knowledge and states that her book is "a salute to black kids."

A modern author primarily noted for her realistic stories is Judy Blume. An interview with Mrs. Blume is included in Chapter 10. Her books deal openly with children's conflicts about divorce, religion, puberty, changes in socioeconomic status, handicapped children, and children's cruelty to each other. These books help children realize that other children face problems similar to theirs, and consequently they seem to find comfort in reading them.

Other books, such as Lee Wyndham's *Candy Stripers*, help children identify their roles in society. These books do not talk down nor preach to children. They simply incorporate the problems of today's child into the stories.

Sam Cornish has written a realistic story in *Grandmother's Pictures,* the story of a black boy in a black community in New England who visits his Grandmother Keyes and sees her album of snapshots, each of which holds an interesting story.

Some realistic stories deal comfortably with problems such as death. Charlotte Zolotow and William P. DuBois have done a magnificent job in touching the human emotions that surround a mother and son in *My Grandson Lew*. Such books make a definite attempt to help children feel and share honest emotion.

Another popular realistic tale for young children is Judith Viorst's *Alexander and the Terrible, Horrible, No Good, Very Bad Day*, which shows children that everyone, everywhere, has his bad days, "even in Australia." Children can see the humorous side of a problem of their own from reading books like *Alexander*.

These realistic books appeal to children because they help them to identify with their world as it is, to understand that roles may be played in many ways, and that there are many life styles by which to live. They show children that man's emotions are common and basic to his life, but that he uses them in different ways and for different purposes.

Realistic tales build a sense of empathy in children. Every child is enraged over the treatment of the boy in *Sounder,* and every child knows better the meaning of civil rights because of that beautiful book. Realistic tales help children see why the adoption of one moral code is preferable to some others in certain life situations. They help children to build realistic values for their time, and to recognize acceptable and profitable behavior. Such books are not generally escape literature: they hit too near home for that.

FIGURE 2–9. Role-playing a story in the classroom often provides psychological securities for children.

Social Awareness

One particular type of realistic tale that is becoming more and more popular among children is the book on *social awareness*. These books are written in prose beautiful enough to qualify as good literature. They reflect a type of living with all its beauty and hardships in a manner that helps children understand the life styles of other people and other times. *Sounder* by William Armstrong, mentioned above, is one such book. It has been made into a film that has already received many awards.

Social awareness books are not new to the field of children's literature. *Gulliver's Travels* and *Robinson Crusoe*, two of the first popular children's books, were originally designed for adults. They harbored political implications and gave insight into political crises at a time when citizens were afraid to write against their government for fear of being beheaded. Consequently, they couched their objections to and criticisms of the government in these stories. Adults reading these books understood what they were trying to say, but to children they were simply delightful stories. As such they became classics.

Charles Dickens's *David Copperfield* was a treatise on the mistreatment of children of his time. Because the message was imbedded in beautiful writing, it became an immortal record of one of the social political problems of the nineteenth century. Many great books have been written with social injustice, political intrigue, and man's inhumanity to man as basic themes.

Some modern social awareness books are done in simple, picture book style and give children a realistic perspective of the elements of living common to all life styles. Rose Blue's book *A Quiet Place* is one such book. It tells of the love of one little black boy for his quiet place—a chair in the public library where he is free from the noise of his household and the arguments of his family. A crisis results when he learns the library is to be replaced by a newer building and will be torn down. He is heartbroken and despairs at losing his quiet place until he has a long talk with the librarian on the last day the library is open.

A Quiet Place depicts a problem any child of any race could have. The book develops a social awareness of the value of public institutions such as the library in a clever and realistic way. The blurred, dreamylike illustrations of Tom Feelings make possible the projection of any child into the pictures so he himself may take an active part in the story.

Social awareness books deal with all modern problems: drugs, communication, transportation, human rights, the plight of ethnic cultural groups and minority groups, and the many "isms" of our times: racism, nationalism, sexism, etc.

They appeal to a child because: (1) they tell stories that are or could be true; (2) they are of infinite variety; (3) they generally contain action and adventure; (4) they often contain humor; (5) they help him understand and establish accepted behavior patterns in situations known and unknown to him; (6) they may help him psychologically if he identifies closely enough with the problems presented in the story; (7) they always contain many dramatic situations; and (8) they stimulate imagination and problem-solving thinking.

Character Development

Many current realistic children's books are developed around strong, recognizable characters. Although there is an excellent plot, the main appeal of the story seems to be the development of the main character himself. Passages are devoted to the actions and descriptions of the characters, who become so familiar to the reader that their behavior is almost predictable. It is the influence of these strong, stable characters on the hero or heroine that makes possible the resolution of some problem in his life.

The characters in these books are like people we have known. The hero (or heroine) has his faults and emotional outbursts, but he learns from experience, and generally, by the time the book ends, he has formulated his own values and ideals and has come to understand how to live with people around him, thus adjusting to his world less passionately and becoming more appreciative of people unlike himself. Some of the prose in these books is of the highest quality found in any modern writing.

No one who has read *Up a Road Slowly* by Irene Hunt can ever forget the strong, forceful character of Aunt Cordelia or the weak character of Uncle Haskell. Uncle Haskell's message to the heroine, Julie, on the day before he dies is perhaps one of the most beautiful bits of prose ever written to explain life to a growing child. Julie emerges in the story as an intelligent, level-headed young woman, tolerant and understanding because of the people who have shared her life.

And Now Miguel by Joseph Krumgold is another unforgettable piece of writing, showing the development of the character of Miguel, a Spanish boy, as he strives to become a man. Full of the passions and tenderness of growing up, the script leads any twelve-year-old boy to see himself trying to become a part of manhood. There is no writing to surpass the simplicity and beauty of this book. Children are completely absorbed by it.

Character development books deal effectively with history as well as with current problems. *Johnny Tremain* by Esther Forbes is the story of a boy of Revolutionary War days who is apprenticed to a silversmith, Mr. Lapham. Johnny burns his hand seriously and is turned out into the world as a handicapped person. Hot-headed and a rebel, it is easy to see why he becomes a participant in the Boston Tea Party. Johnny's experiences during the Revolutionary period eventually give him perspective and mellow his outlook. His character development throughout the story is logical and real. Johnny grows up in hard and trying times and learns that the world is largely a reflection of oneself.

Miss Forbes weaves her story in a series of bold, believable experiences, and Johnny Tremain becomes a man of stature against odds greater than those faced by most youngsters of today. But the story rings true, and Johnny Tremain has become one of the memorable characters of all literature.

Character development books are not written solely for the middle-grade student. Many years ago Louis Slobodkin wrote *Magic Michael,* which has helped children to be aware of the differences between pretense and reality. Lorraine and Jerrold Beim's books such as *Two Is A Team* help children build values that develop character.

The "security" books by Helen Buckley, *Grandmother and I, Grandfather and I, Michael is Brave,* and others, are sensitively written story-picture books which help three- to five-year-olds identify real characters and often provide a sense of security and guidance to their own behavior.

Robert Lawson's *They Were Strong and Good* is about character. Books of this nature help children to realize that all people's characters are different, and that character is something that develops in children as a result of experiences in life. In this category fall such books as *Clara Barton* by Mildred Master Pace, obviously a book written about the development of the character of a great personality.

Modern authors are presenting stories about character development that are couched in a larger plot. *The Vandals of Treason House* by Nancy Veglahn is one such book. Four young people are caught vandalizing an abandoned house and are each sentenced to one hundred hours of work, cleaning up the property. One of the group becomes interested in the history of the mansion and in the legends surrounding it. Adventures follow and attitudes change as a result of the summer at Treason House. The book shows how knowledge and sharing viewpoints can change attitudes and alter character.

Eleanor Estes's recent book, *The Coat-Hanger Christmas Tree,* is a story wherein Marianna and Kenny make a coat-hanger Christmas tree because their mother will not allow them to have a real one. In her subtle telling, the author evokes empathy for all the characters in the story.

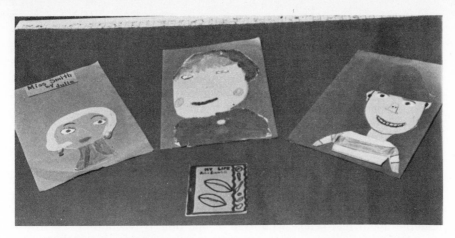

FIGURE 2–10. *Primary children work their own autobiographies and draw self-portraits to go with them.*

A story for primary children told with a minimum of words is Byron Barton's *Harry Is a Scaredy-Cat*. It deals with a little boy who gains courage after being carried aloft by some balloons.

Carol Carrick's book *Sleep Out* is a story of a city boy who gets a sleeping bag for his birthday and masters the fears of his first sleep-out.

Paige Dixon's recent book about a boy dying of a muscular disease, *May I Cross Your Golden River?* is a study in character as the hero faces inevitable death.

Character development is often successfully demonstrated in animal stories, as in Robert O'Brien's Newbery Award book, *Mrs. Frisby and the Rats of Nimh*.

Character development books appeal to children because: (1) they are written about real people, or people who *could* be real and with whom children clearly identify; (2) these people are faced with real (not fantasy) problems that are logically or realistically solved; (3) they present children with situations demanding examination of their own set of values; (4) they help to reinforce the moral code of children; and (5) they enable many children, through empathy, to meet their emotional needs.

Nonfiction

Biography

"Reading about all these people is stuffy," said Jimmy. Then I gave him a copy of *Ben and Me* and five minutes later I heard him chuckling in the reading corner.

"I wish the guy who wrote *Johnny Tremain* would write books about people and make them as interesting," said Bill. I straightened him out by telling him that Esther Forbes was not a guy, gave him a handy copy of *Daniel Boone* by James Daugherty, and said, "Well, I don't have a book about anybody written by Esther Forbes right here, but here's a man who writes in a way I like and maybe you will too." The next day he was back from the library with other books by James Daugherty, and *America's Paul Revere* by Esther Forbes and Lynd Ward!

The essence of biography as children's literature is shown in these two illustrations. For biography to classify as literature, it must fulfill the primary criterion of all literature: it must have style. Too often, biographies written for children in the past were no more than accounts of the happenings in a person's life, presented much like the encyclopedia from which the facts were taken, or they were modified versions of a person's life with episodes selected to glorify that person, presenting them to children as too good to be human. The old story of George Washington and the Cherry Tree is a good example of this warped style of presentation.

Modern writers of biographies for children write realistically and present the person with his frailties as well as his strengths: a person who makes mistakes, has failures and successes, with whom they can identify. Material about real people who lived at one time is fascinating when it is presented with style, and when the writing reflects the feeling of the person and the time in which he lived.

Children's interest in biography is a phenomenon that has swept America in the past three decades. Excellent writers are now publishing whole sets of books of biography, and children seek them out much as they seek adventure stories.

One fine example is the "set" of writings by the team of Ingri and Edgar Parin D'Aulaire. Their *George Washington, Benjamin Franklin, Abraham Lincoln,* and *Columbus* are picture books written for primary grades and are beautifully illustrated. On the middle-grade level, the Landmark books are popular with children. These are published by Random House and contain such titles as *Daniel Boone* and *Robert E. Lee and the Road of Honor.* They are written by famous and established authors such as Quentin Reynolds, Dorothy Canfield Fisher, Samuel Hopkins Adams, and others. Each book has a literary style and quality of its own, and they are marked for reading level and interest level.

One set of biographies written by a single author is that by Clara Ingram Judson. Many books in the set are about the presidents of the United States and are beautifully and authentically written with handsome illustrations to enrich the text. Other books by Clara Ingram Judson include *Pioneer Girl: The Early Life of Frances Willard* and *Boat Builder: The Story of Robert Fulton.*

Like juvenile fiction, biographies are now available on many reading levels. The illustrations in some of these books are works of art.

In setting criteria for the selection of a biography, the following should be considered: (1) authenticity (it must be as accurate as research can make it); (2) objectivity (the author must not take sides on any issue in which his character was involved if there is no evidence to indicate how his character acted on the issue; he must present his character as he finds him. Even the conversations of these texts must have happened); (3) sources (the source used must be reliable, the documentation accurate). The author must present his characters as people, and these people must appear real.

Typed characters such as "Honest Abe" and "Washington Never Told a Lie" are not acceptable to young readers today. Vivid details from the person's life that are compatible with the character must be presented.

Children like action, and the author should include vivid, unusual details that give life and color to the events reported.

Biographies appeal to children for a variety of reasons, chief among them being that they are about real people. Children tend to identify strongly with real people, to laugh and to suffer with them. They recognize in them those qualities of character which make people great: courage, strength, the willingness to fight and die for ideals. They come to understand the meaning of fortitude, of what it means to overcome obstacles created by heredity and/or environment. They learn about compassion, suffering, tragedy, but they also learn that life contains joy, fun, and laughter.

Biographies cover all phases of life and all eras of history and are written on all ability levels. They contain humor, adventure, and action. The real essence of history can often be relived through the reading of biographies as in Elizabeth Yates's beautifully written *Amos Fortune: Free Man*, which tells the story of slavery in the United States, but also tells in a straightforward manner the part played by blacks in the founding of America.

Another biography that appeals to middle-grade children is *Fiddlestrings* by Marguerite de Angeli. It is a memoir of the childhood of her husband, who grew up to be a concert violinist. Boys will enjoy *Thank You, Jackie Robinson* by Barbara Cohen, which is the story of the friendship between a fatherless white boy and an old black man who share an enthusiasm for the Dodgers. Although not a biography in the complete sense of the word, this book will encourage children to learn more about their heroes.

Recent (1975) sports biographies include *Sports Hero Biographies* by Marshall and Sue Burchard, with wonderful action photos to tempt readers. It contains biographies of O. J. Simpson, Phil Esposito, Muhammad Ali, and Billie Jean King.

Information Books

One type of book that has become popular with children and teachers over the past decade is the information book. These books, not unlike picture books, are beautifully illustrated and the text, although basically planned to provide children with accurate and relevant information, is written in an appealing and often beautiful manner. Because of the format and language of many of these books, they are rightfully classified as children's literature. Often children can learn more about an era or a topic from books of information than they can from textbooks, which are often wordy, dull, and lacking in imagery.

Because information books are used by many teachers as a supplement to or substitute for textbooks in teaching science and social studies, they are discussed further in Chapter 15.

Tales of Other Lands and Other Times

Children's literature is rich in material about other lands and other times. These books contribute genuinely to the child's development of understandings and concepts of the world about him. They create for the child a feeling for a country or a period in history which no textbook or resource book can do. "Time and place" stories have always been popular and have contributed to the enrichment of the total school program. Because the writing of many of these books has been beautiful and truly in fine literary style, children have been able to empathize with the heroes and heroines and have found themselves living in another time or another place.

With all the historical fiction available for boys and girls these days, it is incredible that more attention has not been given to the teaching of history and social studies through the use of children's literature. Miss Galvin is a teacher who shows how it might be done. Read the account of her unit on other times and places taught through the study of famous authors, in this case Lois Lenski (*see* page 325).

Almost any part of the world can be studied through children's literature—and almost any time or event in history has been written in some form for children, often in a variety of books ranging from easy reading to young adult reading and from picture books to solid prose. Great events have been also written as ballads and poems. The value of using literature in teaching of times and places is discussed in Chapter 15. Lists of excellent children's books for other places and other times appear in Appendix J.

References and Handbooks

Among the worthy nonfiction books are beautiful books of reference and handbooks for children. These are put together with such artistry and with such beautifully expressed thoughts or concepts that they are truly of literary value.

Such books run the gamut of topics from puppet making to science and mathematics. A few contemporary titles will give the reader an idea of the range covered.

> Franklyn Branley. *A Book of Moon Rockets for you* (1970)
> Isaac Asimov. *The Noble Gases* (1966)
> Laurence Pringle. *Into the Woods: Exploring the Forest Ecosystem* (1973)
> Walter H. Gregg. *Physical Fitness Through Sports and Nutrition* (1974)
> David Macaulay. *City: A Story of Roman Planning and Construction* (1974)
> Claude J. DeRossi. *Computers: Tools for Today* (1972)
> Seymour Simon. *The Rock-Hounds Book* (1973)
> Joan Elma Rahn. *Grocery Store Botany* (1974)
> Leonard Bernstein. *The Infinite Variety of Music* (1966)

Chapter 15 of this volume deals with the use of literature as the core of the elementary school curriculum. In a school program designed around the use of children's literature, these books are indispensable.

In using information books and handbooks with the intent of promoting literature appreciation as well as knowledge, skills, attitudes, and understandings, the teacher will need to consider the following criteria:

1. Does the book have literary value, that is, a style and "atmosphere" of its own?
2. Are the illustrations artistically conceived, and do they fulfill the criteria of good illustrating of other types of children's literature?
3. Are the books accurate?
4. Are the diagrams, photos, and drawings accurate and important to developing the text?
5. Is the book written with a level of vocabulary compatible with the age level of the child who is likely to be interested in it?
6. Are the illustrations imaginative? Do they emphasize the human aspects of the subject as well as the "things" aspect?
7. Are concepts clearly developed?
8. Does the book satisfy the child's interest?

SUMMARY

The creative use of literature in the classroom can fulfill many of the objectives of teaching in the elementary school. Before the teacher can use literature creatively, however, she must have an understanding of the common classifications for children's literature. These classifications fall under the two main categories of fiction and nonfiction. Fiction includes picture books, picture-story books, Mother Goose rhymes, animal tales, books of humor, poetry, folklore (including fables, myths, legends, epics, ballads, story-poems, and fairy tales), adventure stories, mystery stories, romance, fantasy, and realistic fiction. Nonfiction books are categorized as biography, information books, books of other times and places, reference books, and handbooks.

These classifications provide a frame of reference for the material that follows.

TO THE COLLEGE STUDENT

1. Encourage members of the class to sign up for one category of literature mentioned in this chapter and to find a typical example of each category. Share them with each other. Your presentation will be more valuable if you tell a little about the author of your selection.

2. Secure a copy of *Hailstones and Halibut Bones* by Mary O'Neill and read pages of it together. Brainstorm ideas for presenting the concepts of color just as the children did in the account narrated at the beginning of this chapter. Are your ideas more creative than theirs?

3. The *New York Times* publishes a Sunday supplement of children's books twice a year. This is a very valuable resource. Watch for it and add it to your files.

4. Which are your favorite children's stories? Can you determine why they remain so dear to you after all these years? Think about the situation under which you were first introduced to these stories and of succeeding experiences with them. How much of the content of the story contributed to your liking it? The mood? The circumstances under which it was first read? Are conditions important in introducing literature to children?

5. There are many children's magazines on the market. Some are excellent, others are tawdry. Collect copies of various kinds

of children's magazines and assess them for their literary value.

6. The next time a children's classic is being shown at a local theater, call the manager and ask for an approximate attendance figure. Then call the local library and check on the circulation record of the particular book being shown in the film. Also check with your school library. Check other evidence to determine whether films encourage or discourage the reading of the book.

7. Reread your favorite children's story and compare it with a similar good story written recently. How does your story seem now, using criteria? Do you see indications of stereotyping?

TO THE CLASSROOM TEACHER

1. One way to help children become interested in literature is to afford them the opportunity to share books through creative book reports. Some ideas for such book reports are mentioned in Chapter 13. Take one reading period a week and devote it to this kind of activity rather than to skills reading. Watch to see if it pays dividends. Do children become more interested in books? Is the library visited more often? Do the children carry books home more frequently?

2. In planning your next unit, use the *Basic Book Collection for Elementary Grades*, published yearly by the American Library Association, to see how many ways literature can be used in correlation with social studies, science, arithmetic, and the creative arts.

3. Many children's stories have been made into motion pictures or cartoons. Among the many popular ones have been:

Snow White and the Seven Dwarfs, Bambi, Peter Pan, Treasure Island, Hansel and Gretel, Cinderella, Pinocchio, Lassie Come Home, Ivanhoe, Mary Poppins, Sounder, Charlotte's Web, and a host of others. In translating these classics to the screen, is the producer justified in taking liberties with the original manuscript? Do you feel his interpretation for any particular one was creative or commercial? Do you think films of great literature endear the writing to children or just make it easy for them to get the idea of the book? Discuss this.

4. Plan a project from a good piece of children's literature, such as the example from Miss Sawyer's classroom in this chapter. Allow the children in your classroom to contribute to the planning of the project. Consider all the advantages of projects of this nature in helping children develop socially and intellectually and in their taste for good literature.

TO THE COLLEGE STUDENT
AND THE CLASSROOM TEACHER

1. Following is a list of recent children's books. Have each member of your group sign up for one book, find it in the library, read it, and classify it according to the categories mentioned in this chapter.

Alexander, Martha. *No Ducks in Our Bathtub.* New York: Dial, 1973.

Bellairs, John. *The House with a Clock in Its Walls.* New York: Dial Press, 1973.

Biro, Val. *The Honest Thief.* New York: Holiday House, 1973.

Buchwald, Emilie. *Gildaen: The Heroic Adventures of a Most Unusual Rabbit.*

New York: Harcourt Brace Jovanovich, 1973.

Budney, Blossom. *After Dark.* New York: Lothrop, Lee and Shepard, 1975.

Butterworth, Oliver. *The Narrow Passage.* Boston: Atlantic–Little, Brown, 1973.

Chauncy, Nan. *Hunted in Their Own Land.* New York: Seabury, 1973.

Erdman, Loula Grace. *A Bluebird Will Do.* New York: Dodd, Mead, 1973.

Fisk, Nicholas. *Trillions.* New York: Pantheon, 1973.

Galdone, Paul. *The Moving Adventures of Old Dame Trot and Her Comical Cat.* New York: McGraw-Hill, 1973.

Gardner, John. *Dragon, Dragon and Other Tales.* New York: Alfred A. Knopf, 1975.

Goodall, John S. *Creepy Castle.* New York: Atheneum Press, 1975.

Hinton, S. E. *Rumble Fish.* New York: Delacorte Press, 1975.

Hoban, Lillian. *The Sugar Snow Spring.* New York: Harper & Row, 1973.

Hoberman, Mary Ann. *A Little Book of Little Beasts.* New York: Simon and Schuster, 1973.

Houston, John. *The Meddybemps Fair.* Reading, Mass.: Addison-Wesley, 1973.

Howells, Mildred. *The Woman Who Lived in Holland.* New York: Farrar, Straus, and Giroux, 1973.

Kahn, Joan. *Some Things Strange and Sinister.* New York: Harper & Row, 1973.

Karen, Ruth. *Kingdom of the Sun: The Inca Empire Builders of the Americas.* New York: Four Winds, 1975.

Klein, Norma. *It's Not What You Expect.* New York: Pantheon, 1973.

Leach, Christopher. *Free, Alone and Going.* New York: Crown, 1973.

Levy, Elizabeth. *The People Lobby: The SST Story.* New York: Delacorte Press, 1973.

Lofts, Norah. *Rupert Hatton's Story.* New York: Nelson, 1973.

McDermott, Gerald. *The Magic Tree: A Tale from the Congo.* New York: Holt, Rinehart and Winston, 1973.

McKinnon, Robert. *To Yellowstone.* New York: Holt, Rinehart and Winston, 1975.

Marshall, James. *Yummers!* Boston: Houghton Mifflin, 1973.

May, Julian. *Wild Turkeys.* New York: Holiday House, 1973.

Mayer, Mercer. *Bubble Bubble.* New York: Parents' Magazine Press, 1973.

Mazer, Harry. *Snowbound.* New York: Delacorte, Press, 1973.

Meeks, Esther K. *The Dog Who Took the Train.* Chicago: Follett, 1973.

Mohr, Nicholasa. *El Bronx Remembered.* New York: Harper & Row, 1975.

Moremen, Grace E. *No, No Natalie.* Chicago: Children's Press, 1973.

Myers, Bernice. *The Apple War.* New York: Parents' Magazine Press, 1973.

Zolotow, Charlotte. *When the Wind Stops.* New York: Harper & Row, 1975.

2. Observe the titles of the books listed above. Do you think they make children want to go adventuring between the covers? Which ones appeal to you? Can you determine why?

3. One of the most valuable references you can have in your teaching is a file of children's literature. Explore children's books by having each member of your class bring one to class each day to read. Have each member find out something about the author and the other books he has written. Each class member can take notes on these readings on 3 X 5 cards and can begin to build such a file.

4. Also start to collect magazine articles and pictures of children's books and build a file of these for use in your student teaching.

5. Make a list of all the children's books or stories you remember which you did *not* like as a child. Why did you *not* like them? Check them against the criteria stated in this chapter and decide whether or not they could be classified as good literature. Reread some of these stories now and see if you still feel the same.

6. Collect specific stories from children's literature that lend themselves to: (a) the building of values, (b) the solution of children's problems, (c) the development of appreciations, and (d) the development of empathy.

7. Conduct a survey in your campus school or a school that works with your college on the preferences of children in your community for books and illustrations. Design a simple sheet for children to check books they like best, and another sheet of the pictures they like best. Tabulate these to find class preferences, if any. Do the *types* of books differ from the ones suggested in this chapter? Note whether children choose colored illustrations over black and white. How much does the community environment influence children's choices, do you suppose?

Adams, Bess Porter. *About Books and Children: Historical Survey of Children's Literature.* New York: Henry Holt, 1953.

Alderson, Brian. *Looking at Picture Books.* New York: Children's Book Council, 1973.

Allen, Arthur T. "Literature for Children: An Engagement with Life," *Horn Book Magazine* (December 1967).

Anderson, William, and Patrick Groff. *A New Look at Children's Literature.* Belmont, Calif.: Wadsworth, 1972.

Arbuthnot, May Hill. *Children and Books,* 3rd ed. Glenview, Ill.: Scott, Foresman, 1964.

Arbuthnot, May Hill, and Evelyn L. Wenzel. *Time for Discovery: Informational Books.* Glenview, Ill.: Scott, Foresman, 1970.

Arbuthnot, May Hill, and Zena Sutherland. *Children and Books,* 4th ed. Glenview, Ill.: Scott, Foresman, 1972.

Bacon, Wallace A., and Robert S. Breen. *Literature as Experience.* New York: McGraw-Hill, 1959.

Blount, Margaret. *Animal Land: The Creatures of Children's Fiction.* New York: William Morrow, 1974.

Bredsdortt, Elias. *Hans Christian Andersen.* New York: Scribner and Sons, 1976.

Brooks, Peter, ed. *The Child's Part.* Boston: Beacon Press, 1972.

Bulfinch, Thomas, et al. *Age of Fable, or Stories of Gods and Heroes,* 2nd ed. New York: Heritage Press, 1958.

Chambers, Dewey W. *Children's Literature in the Curriculum.* Chicago: Rand McNally, 1971.

Chiu, Lian Hwang. "Reading Preferences of Fourth Grade Children Related to Sex and Reading Ability," *Journal of Educational Research* 66 (April 1970): 369–373.

Clark, Margaret M. *Keeping Up with Children and Books, 1963–1965.* Glenview, Ill.: Scott, Foresman, 1966.

Cullinan, Bernice. *Literature for Children: Its Discipline and Content.* Dubuque, Iowa: Wm. C. Brown Co., 1971.

Doyle, Brian. *The Who's Who of Children's Literature.* New York: Schocken Books, 1968.

Early, Margaret, and Norine Odland. "Literature in the Elementary and Secondary Schools," *Review of Educational Research* 37 (April 1967): 178–185.

Ellis, Alec. *How To Find Out about Children's Literature,* 2nd ed. New York: Pergamon, 1966.

Fisher, Margaret. *Intent upon Reading.* New York: Franklin Watts, 1961.

Fisher, Margery. *Who's Who in Children's Books: A Treasury of Familiar Animals of Children.* New York: Holt, Rinehart and Winston, 1975.

Freeman, G. L., and R. S. Freeman. *The Child and His Picture Book.* Watkins Glen, N.Y.: Century House, 1967.

Georgiou, Constantine. *Children and Their Literature.* Englewood Cliffs, N.J.: Prentice-Hall, 1969.

Gillespie, Margaret. *Literature for Children: History and Trends.* Dubuque, Iowa: Wm. C. Brown Co., 1970.

Higgins, James. *Beyond Words: Mystical Fancy In Children's Literature.* New York: Teachers' College Press, 1970.

Hollowell, Lillian. *A Book of Children's Literature,* 3rd ed. New York: Holt, Rinehart and Winston, 1966.

Hopkins, Lee Bennett. *Books Are by People: Interviews with 104 Authors and Illustrators of Books for Young Children.* New York: Citation Press, 1969.

Huck, Charlotte S., and Doris A. Kuhn. *Children's Literature in the Elementary School.* New York: Holt, Rinehart and Winston, 1968.

Hurlimann, Bettina. *Picture-Book World.* New York: World, 1969.

Johnson, Edna, Evelyn R. Sickels, and Frances Clarke Sayers. *Anthology of Children's Literature,* 4th ed. Boston: Houghton Mifflin, 1970.

Jordan, Alice Mabel, and Helen Masten. *Children's Classics,* 4th ed. Boston: Horn Book, 1967.

Larkin, David. *Fantastic Kingdom.* New York: Ballantine Books, 1974.

Loban, Walter. "Balancing the Literature Program," *Elementary English* 43 (November 1966): 146–147.

MacCann, Donnarae, and Olga Richard. *The Child's First Books: A Critical Study of Pictures and Texts.* New York: Wilson, 1973.

McKendry, John J., ed. *Aesop: Five Centuries of Illustrated Fables.* New York: Metropolitan Museum of Art, 1964.

Meigs, Cornelia, Anne Thaxter Eaton, Elizabeth Nesbitt, and Ruth Hill Viquers. *A Critical History of Children's Literature.* Rev. ed. New York: Macmillan, 1969.

Nelson, Mary Ann. *Comparative Anthology of Children's Literature.* New York: Holt, Rinehart and Winston, 1972.

Pellowski, Anne. *The World of Children's Literature.* New York: R. R. Bowker, 1968.

Perrault, Charles. *Perrault's Complete Fairy Tales.* New York: Dodd, Mead, 1961.

Pickard, P. M. *I Could a Tale Unfold: Violence, Horror and Sensationalism in Stories for Children.* New York: Barnes, 1961.

Prager, A. "The Secret of Nancy Drew, Pushing Forty and Going Strong," *Saturday Review* 52 (Jan. 25, 1969): 18–19.

Robinson, Evelyn R. *Readings about Children's Literature.* New York: David McKay, 1966.

Rosenblatt, Louise M. *Literature as Exploration,* rev. ed. New York: Noble and Noble, 1968.

Sutherland, Zena, ed. *The Arbuthnot Anthology of Children's Literature.* Glenview, Ill.: Scott, Foresman, 1976.

Wenzel, Evelyn L., and May Hill Arbuthnot. *Time for Discovery.* Glenview, Ill.: Scott, Foresman, 1970.

CHAPTER 3

The Nature of Children

One day in the fall the children took a "sensory" walk around the school. The object of the walk was to smell fall smells and feel fall textures. When they returned to the classroom, they wrote about the things that had appealed to their senses. Olga wrote about the dandelions she had blown.

FUZZIES

I took a breath and blew
A bunch of fuzzies into the air,
I saw them blowing here and there
Like frightened fairies running everywhere.

OLGA
Grade 6

Eric wrote about something he had seen and smelled:

FALL SMELLS

My eyes watered
  like tears
My nose twitched
  in smothering
My throat choked
  in gasping
My skin smarted
  in heat
Yet, I love
  a fall bonfire!

ERIC
Grade 6

Maxine saw other things:

MY WALK

I saw a piece of rainbow fall from trees.
I heard a rustle underneath my feet.
I felt a butterfly rest on my cheek.
I turned my face to catch the sun's bright heat.
My walk was only minutes long
But September sang to me her song!

Later, during a similar winter walk, Shelly wrote:

WINTER

Gracefully sparkling snowflakes flutter down
Tall trees reach icy fingers to the sky,
Silvery snow blankets the peaceful town,
Cheerful children laughingly sleigh by.

SHELLY

How beautifully and yet how differently these children have been helped to express themselves! Already, in their young years, they have developed unique styles of writing their own literature. Already they are showing their own individuality and their own uniqueness.

It is inconceivable that anyone could approach a study of children's literature without first studying children, especially from the standpoint of problems that create barriers to children's enjoyment of literature. In this chapter we will discuss common and unique growth patterns of children, the psychological needs of children that influence their choice of books, children's choices in their reading, the types of illustrations they prefer, and the award books chosen to satisfy these preferences. We will also talk about the elements of a good plot, the need for style, and the format of books. Finally, we will discuss the nature of children's learning as it relates to the teaching of reading.

COMMON AND UNIQUE GROWTH

Children exhibit common growth patterns and common likes and dislikes from the day they are born. But they also demonstrate unique and individual growth patterns and preferences. For instance, boys and girls definitely choose some of the same stories and books, such as Dr. Seuss books or fantasies or fables like Barbara Cooney's adaptation of Chaucer's *Chanticleer and the Fox*. But studies show that early in life, boys' preferences for some types of books differ from those of girls, and that preferences also vary within the sexes.

It is the uniqueness and difference in each individual that make each child a personality. These differences, which tend to become more and more noticeable as children mature, are the greatest asset of humans in our culture today. From these uniquenesses and differences in children come the ideas new to the world: the creative ideas of mankind. Consequently, these differences are not to be regarded as troublesome, but are to be coddled and developed as one of our greatest national resources. Children's literature has come into existence because of the unique ability of the authors.

Individual differences sometimes appear and mature *in spite of* the teacher rather than *because of* her. It is often a nuisance to plan many lessons for individual children rather than one lesson for an entire class. But individualized instruction must be promoted if the basic principles of a democracy are to be perpetuated and the creativity of children developed in the elementary school.

Each teacher will need to know the characteristics and interests of *each* individual child as well as of all children in general. It is hoped that once she has come to know each child personally, she will be able to provide him with material in the realm of literature that will help him meet his needs.

PHYSICAL CHARACTERISTICS OF CHILDREN

The work of the child development psychologists has helped the teacher understand the growth patterns of children and some of the psychological

FIGURE 3–1. Adventuring in literature can often satisfy many needs in children, especially the need to have a bosom buddy.

problems that accompany deviations from these growth patterns. It is an accepted concept, for instance, that girls mature physically faster than boys at the elementary school level. They are more academically oriented and this fact affects their attitude toward schoolwork. Generally, girls read better than boys, which will, of course, influence their choices in literature. Because girls mature physically faster than boys, they become more interested in stories of romance. Sixth-grade girls often ask for sentimental love stories and like best those containing an adventure element as well as a romantic interest.

Many of the old studies of child development are obviously reflections of the pressure placed on children to comply with predetermined sex roles. Other cultural pressures are reflected in the activities and choices of children. With the liberation movements in America in the late 1960s and early 1970s, changes may come about in children's choices in literature that reflect their involvement with parents who are playing different sex roles than formerly. The changes in the structure of the American family, the emergence of different systems of values, the new relaxed morality, and several other revolutions on the American scene will create changes in those behavior patterns of children that relate to environmental influences.

To date, however, the child development studies help the teacher to understand the physical growth of children and alert them to the fact that while some of the social and psychological needs of children have changed considerably under cultural pressures, others have become more intense.

PSYCHOLOGICAL NEEDS

Children, like adults, have basic human needs that must be met in order for the child to exist comfortably in his world. When certain of these psychological needs are not met directly, they may be met vicariously, largely through the element of hope. Literature (especially escape literature such as fairy tales, imaginary tales, and realistic fiction) can help children to vicariously meet these needs. It is interesting to note that one eminent psychologist believes that creativity in humans cannot emerge until certain basic human needs are met.

This psychologist, Abraham Maslow,[1] contributed greatly to our understanding of human needs and how they determine our behavior in his hierarchy-of-needs theory. It was Maslow's contention that first-level needs must be met in human beings before second-level needs can be faced, and that second-level needs must be met before third-level needs can be considered, and so on.

In his hierarchy, Maslow placed *physiological needs* as first-level needs. These are the most essential body needs: food, water, air, sexual gratification, warmth, comfort, etc.

---

1. Abraham H. Maslow, "A Theory of Human Motivation," *Psychological Review* 50 (1943): 370–396; and Abraham H. Maslow, *Motivation and Personality*, 2nd ed. (New York: Harper, 1954).

FIGURE 3–2. *Adventuring with literature can help a child feel worthy when he presents his ideas to his classmates: John prepares an exhibit for Lloyd Alexander's book,* The High King.

Second-level needs were classified as *safety needs.* Once basic physiological needs are met, humans must be assured that such comforts will continue and certain securities will be established.

Third-level needs were identified as *belongingness:* those needs related to love—to be loved, to have affection, care, attention, and emotional support. This love relationship is not necessarily a sexually based one, but it is a "trust"-based one.

After humans feel they are loved and can love, they are free to develop *esteem* needs. These are needs that relate to maintaining satisfying relationships with others—to be valued, accepted, and appreciated as a person; to be esteemed and respected; to have status; and to avoid rejection and disapproval.

Maslow's fifth level of needs included needs that relate to self-actualization—to become everything that one is capable of becoming. These needs relate to achievement and self-expression, to being creative and productive; to performing acts that are useful and valuable to others; to realizing one's potential and translating it into "actuality."

Later in his life, Maslow added two other needs to his hierarchy: the need to know and understand, and aesthetic needs. In his aesthetic needs, Maslow recognized man's need for beauty. From his research he concluded that many people have an instinctive need for beauty, and ugliness is sickening to them.

Maslow felt that children cannot *achieve* until their first three levels of needs are comfortably taken care of. Creativity functions most freely on

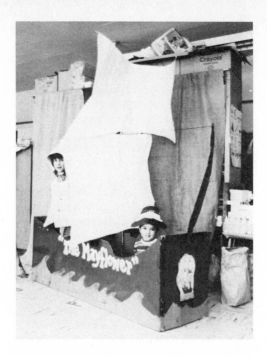

FIGURE 3–3. The need to belong, to be part of a group: Five-year-olds play out the landing of the Mayflower.

levels four and five. He felt that the full creative powers of people are released only after they have had enough physical and psychological security in life to be free of strong ego involvements. Lack of achievement, according to Maslow, may very well be due to unmet basic physical, safety, and emotional needs in children. By the same line of reasoning, it is unlikely that creativity in children can be developed until certain physical and status needs are met.

Many psychologists of late have theorized that an ongoing development of the individual's potential capacities and talents operates through opportunities for originality and inventiveness, as a supplement to the older concepts of tension reduction.

The vicarious experiences that children have in reading good literature can compensate, or at least maintain, a child's hope that certain unmet needs will eventually be fulfilled. It is also important to note that certain basic primary-level needs in children must be met before literature has *any* effect on the growing child.

Although not a psychologist, May Hill Arbuthnot[2] long ago attempted to isolate those human needs that she felt were met directly or vicariously through the use of children's literature. In light of Maslow's contributions to our thinking of needs as hierarchies, Arbuthnot's classification can well bear a new scrutiny. She identified the needs covered in the following six sections.

2. May Hill Arbuthnot and Zena Sutherland, *Children and Books,* 4th ed. (Glenview, Ill.: Scott, Foresman, 1972), p. 3.

The Need for Security: Material, Emotional, Intellectual, and Spiritual

Arbuthnot and Sutherland point out that the human animal must make himself feel safe, must have the courage to hang on, to endure hardships, to be as snug and comfortable as possible, as beloved and happy as life permits. They note that material satisfactions are often the chief symbols of security in children.[3]

The desire for material and economic security is a powerful drive in humans and of unfailing interest as a motif or leading idea for the plot of stories.

Arbuthnot defines emotional security as the rightness and stability of the affections. Stories about families and their battles against outside forces appeal to children because of these needs.[4] *Caddie Woodlawn* by Carol Brink, *The Moffats* by Eleanor Estes, and *Kirsti* by Helen Markley Miller are examples of books that fall into this category.

Intellectual security is described as the need to know accurately and surely. Children and adults have read good literature throughout history for the true and reliable knowledge it brings them. Books such as *Heidi* by Johanna Spyri, *Appleseed Farm* by Emily Douglas, Ann Nolan Clark's *My Mother's House*, Clara Ingram Judson's *City Neighbor: The Story of Jane Addams*, and Leo Politi's *Song of the Swallows* impart knowledge to children in an interesting, realistic, and often beautiful manner while telling their stories.

Spiritual security is that which "enables human beings to surmount dangers, failures and even stark tragedies." It is often the result of strong religious faith, "a belief in God and a universe in which moral law ultimately prevails.[5] Books written around this theme can give children an honest picture of religious diversity and a respect for different beliefs and traditions.

The need for security of all kinds begins with the child himself and is centered around his needs and wants. Books can help him to grow out of his egocentricity to the point where he wants security for other people too.

The Need To Belong

From an egocentric beginning, the child identifies with his family, then his gang, his school, and later with his city and country. Finally, he may identify with the world.

Some beautiful books have been written that help children satisfy this need. Eleanor Estes's award book, *The Hundred Dresses,* is one of these. In this book a child, an outcast, is the object for a touchingly sensitive lesson in human relations in a fifth-grade classroom. Other examples of such books are Rumer Godden's *The Story of Holly and Ivy,* Munro Leaf's

---

3. May Hill Arbuthnot, *Children and Books,* 3rd ed. (Glenview, Ill.: Scott, Foresman, 1964), p. 6.
4. *Ibid.,* p. 6.
5. *Ibid.,* p. 10.

Wee Gillis, Emily Neville's Newbery award book, *It's Like This, Cat,* and Kate Seredy's *The Good Master.*

Many of the classics deal with the problems of children who are different, yet who have the same driving need to belong to a group as all children. Hans Christian Andersen's *The Ugly Duckling* and *The Wild Swans* are typical of such stories. They are still loved by children of all ages.

Some stories deal with the problem of children who want to belong to groups alien to their own. Carolyn Sherman Bailey's *The Rabbit Who Wanted Red Wings* is one such classic. Recently, old and new stories of racial problems and group integration have become popular, such as DeAngeli's *Bright April,* the story of a lovely black girl and her encounter with racial prejudice and how she overcame the problem, and *Just One Indian Boy* by Elizabeth Witheridge.

Many new books deal directly with the problem of belonging, and can be comforting and helpful to children having similar problems. A few examples of such books are: Dorothy Aldis's *Dumb Stupid David,* Thomas Fall's *Eddie No-Name,* Miriam Evangeline Mason's *The Middle Sister,* Robert Kraus's book *Leo the Late Bloomer,* and Judy Blume's *Blubber.*

Many of Judy Blume's books are concerned with the child's needs to belong amid the problems of modern life. One of these needs is to be accepted by peer groups. *Then Again Maybe I Won't* is one such story. In *It's Not the End of the World,* Mrs. Blume deals with the emotional frustrations and the feelings of despair experienced by modern children in a family in which there is a divorce. Reading her books helps children feel they are not alone with their problems and that all problems are surmountable.

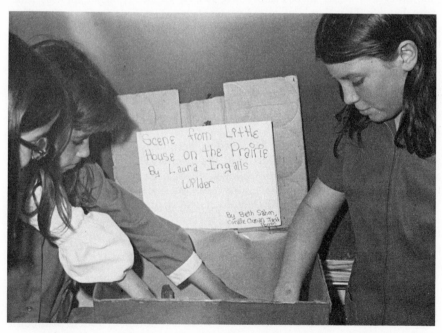

FIGURE 3–4. *Working for others makes one feel worthy. Constructing a scene from* Little House on the Prairie *by Laura Ingalls Wilder.*

The Need To Love and Be Loved

This need might well be classified under emotional security. For every human, in order to exist in a state of good mental health, must be loved and accepted, and needs to love in return. Books that dwell on family love often help children identify their sex roles. Later, books dealing with love outside the family—even boy-girl love—can help children understand the life that lies before them and can prepare them emotionally, to a degree, to meet it. Stories of love build sensitivities in children to the needs of individuals, animals, groups, nations, and the world as a whole.

Many classics have appeal because of the sense of dependable love that they pass along to children. Louisa May Alcott's *Little Men* and *Little Women* might be classified in this category. Joan Walsh Anglund's little picture book *What Color Is Love?* attempts to identify love for children, as does her *Love Is a Special Way of Feeling*. A. A. Milne's *Winnie the Pooh* is built around the love of a boy for his toy bear, which is a theme all children can understand. Evaline Ness's *Josefina February* is the story of a little Haitian girl who loves a baby burro. Mary O'Hara's *My Friend Flicka* is a book whose theme is a boy's love for his horse.

Many modern books also deal with the theme of love: Rose Blue's little book *A Quiet Place* has a calm secure sense of love in the relationship of a little black boy with his mother, and the security he finds in having a place of his own that he loves. Helen Buckley's books, *Grandfather and I, Grandmother and I, My Sister and I*, are basically stories of love and understanding among family members which give children a sense of well-being and security. Margaret Wise Brown's *The Runaway Bunny* is a simple, well-told story of mother love. Family love is expounded in books such as Marjorie Flack's *The New Pet* and Eve Garnett's *The Family from One End Street*.

Boy-girl love is recognized in such books as *Forever* by Judy Blume, *Seventeenth Summer* by Maureen Daly, and *Going on Sixteen* by Betty Cavanna, in which adolescent love is explored in a realistic and honest manner.

Love in marriage is well portrayed in such books as Adrien Stoutenburg and Laura Nelson Baker's *Dear, Dear Livy*, the story of Mrs. Mark Twain.

The need to love and be loved is best met by the love between a child and his family, his friends, and his teacher. However, many children come to school these days from homes where little love is shown. In such circumstances, a heavy responsibility falls on the school to show children what love can be like so that they do not grow up unloving and unloved. Many experiences with love in all of its forms can be obtained vicariously through the use of books.

The Need To Achieve—To Do or Be Someone Worthy of Respect

Everyone needs to do something for which he is respected and loved. All people must have status in their own world, children included. Although the heroes of the young child are people who are active and who accomplish all sorts of tasks, somewhere along the line an appreciation of emotional, intellectual, and moral achievement begins to grow. This is reflected in the child's love for biography in the middle school and early adolescent years. Achievement in the face of defeat is a life conflict that children come to admire and respect.

Books telling of the achievements of children and adults span all levels of reading and all topics. Helen Buckley's *Michael Is Brave* will help the timid preschool child understand that he is not the only one who is afraid to go down a slide for the first time. Joan Walsh Anglund's *The Brave Cowboy* cleverly gives children the impression that it is good to let your imagination run rampant when you want to achieve acts of heroism and you are not yet physically able to do so. Hardie Gramatky's *Little Toot* has become a classic demonstration of one way children learn about determination and its place in achievement. Nathaniel Benchley's delightful book, *Feldman Fieldmouse*, puts an emphasis in a humorous manner on achieving through knowledge and action. In Gunilla Norris's book *Green and Something Else*, Green, the hero, overcomes great fears because of his love for his little mouse, and in so doing achieves a place of status in the eyes of his worst enemy. *Amelia Bedelia* by Peggy Parish is another primary book built around the theme of achievement which children enjoy.

Books for children in the upper primary dealing with achievement of character and/or knowledge also run the gamut. Some are told as folktales in humorous form, such as Anita Brenner's *A Hero By Mistake* and *The Boy Who Could Do Anything*. James Boyd's story *Drums* is a fine novel of the American Revolution. Johnny Fraser, its hero, joins the freedom fighters and finds himself on the *Bonhomme Richard* with John Paul Jones. What happens is an exciting adventure in courage and the rewards obtained from it.

Upper-grade reading lists abound in books dealing with achievement. Such books as *Onion John* by Joseph Krumgold, *Call It Courage* by Armstrong Sperry, *Invincible Louisa* by Cornelia Meigs, *Waterless Mountain* by Laura Adams Armer, and *The Incredible Journey* by Sheila Burnford are all stories of great achievement by some person, persons, or animals in a situation in which many odds were overcome.

Historical novels for the reading pleasure of intermediate-grade children are plentiful. These novels are all built around people of character who achieve because of their determination and grit. In *The Great Rope* by Rosemary Nesbitt, one young boy helps the men of Oswego to carry a great rope on their shoulders to Sacketts Harbor to haul the American ships out into Lake Ontario so they may fight the British. The great feat is accomplished because of the sterling qualities of these men. In *The Matchlock Gun* by Walter Edmonds, the children of the household save themselves from the Indians during the Revolutionary War because of their dauntless courage.

Alice Dalgliesh's *The Courage of Sarah Noble* is a true story of a pioneer girl in 1707 and helps children understand that they, too, are capable of great deeds and achievements. Other books in this category are *Prairie Winter* by Elsie Kimmel Field, *Appleseed Farm* by Emily Douglas, and *Bound Girl of Cobble Hill* by Lois Lenski.

Biographies are basically stories of achievement, and there are endless numbers of well-written biographies and autobiographies available today for all age levels. Frances Cavanah's *Triumphant Adventure: The*

Story of Franklin Delano Roosevelt is a splendid portrait of a man who achieved the presidency in spite of the crippling effects of infantile paralysis. David Harbison's book *Reaching for Freedom* is the story of four black men who played active roles in various periods of America's history and is a thought-provoking document for middle-graders.

Modern authors are also writing about great achievements. In *Island of the Blue Dolphins*, Scott O'Dell tells of the trials and triumphs of an Indian girl who spent eighteen years alone (a modern Robinson Crusoe) on an island inhabited by a ferocious pack of wild dogs and susceptible to other hazards. It is an adventure of the spirit that haunts the reader. From loneliness and terror, Karana, the heroine, gains strength and serenity. Another novel of modern-day achievement is *The Seventeenth-Street Gang*, a well-written book of surprises by Emily Cheney Neville.

The young child needs stories that contain a great deal of action and that move along quickly. This love for action carries over into later childhood and adolescence when the child enjoys adventure, mystery, and career stories where tangible achievements are made by the heroes, whether they be animal, human, or imaginary.

Play: the Need for Change

Everyone needs change for mental health and to reorganize inner forces in order to continue the tasks of life. Children suffer more than we realize from the pressure of routines, adult coercion, tensions, and the necessity of conforming to a code of manners and morals whose reasonableness they do not always understand. They may use books as a means of escape from many of life's tensions and problems. In some instances this may not be healthy if the book becomes a substitute for reality. Often, however, it provides the child with sympathetic understanding because he reads about other children solving problems and he builds hope that his own problems

FIGURE 3–5. Playing at change: Preparing for a dramatization of The Coming of the Pilgrims by Brooks Smith and Robert Meredith.

are solvable. In either case, the books children read are often helping them over an extremely difficult period in their life and are affording them a means of maintaining mental balance.

Some books deal directly with change in life. They serve the purpose of making the child sensitive to life around him and more observing of it. Such a book as Joan Walsh Anglund's *Spring Is a New Beginning* is directed toward this end. Lois Lenski's *I Like Winter* and *Spring Is Here* serve a similar purpose. May Garelick's lovely book *Where Does the Butterfly Go When It Rains?*, with its beautiful illustrations by Leonard Weisgard, is a well-written document of one of nature's most beautiful phenomena.

Other books help children realize that change takes place in an orderly fashion and is a way of life. Laura Ingalls Wilder's *Little House on the Prairie* goes back in time, whereas Madeleine L'Engle's *A Wrinkle in Time* goes forward in time. In one case, the child compares his own life to that of the children in the book and is aware of the changes since the story took place. In the other, he realizes that further changes must take place before the story can happen, so he sees himself at a point along a continuum in time.

Such books help children establish a time-line concept along which they can eventually place themselves in relation to history. Excellent historical fiction can bring the child into a realistic confrontation with the changes of the past. Examples of such books are Laura Ingalls Wilder's *These Happy Golden Years*, Lois Lenski's *Prairie School* and *Strawberry Girl*, Erick Berry's *Lock 'Er Through* and *The Wavering Flame*.

FIGURE 3–6. *When Bill was kidded about wearing his new glasses, the teacher helped develop understanding through the use of Ellen Raskin's book, Spectacles.*

Some books help children adjust to change by dealing with it in terms of the H. G. Wells time machine concept. In Lloyd Alexander's *Time Cat,* Gareth the cat has nine lives and can have Jason, his master, participate in almost any one of them in a different place and at a different time in history. Virginia Lee Burton indicates the need for change in her book *The Little House,* when the growing city crowds the little house into the country.

Change in behavior is the subject of many children's books. Humorously, Sesyle Joslin helps children see the reason for certain social customs in her charming book *What Do You Say, Dear?* Michael sees a need to forsake his overly active imagination and become a boy once more in Louis Slobodkin's *Magic Michael.*

Playing at being what you are not is exemplified in Janice Udry's little book *Let's Be Enemies.* Children imitate emotions as well as people.

Role changes are also enjoyed by children in such books as *The Man Who Didn't Wash His Dishes* by Phyllis Krasilovsky.

Even messages *about* change appear in children's literature. There are some people who never see change even when it happens right under their noses. This message comes through loud and clear in Ellen Raskin's amusing picture book, *Nothing Ever Happens on My Block.*

Children can also play with language through the use of books. Remy Charlip's books such as *Arm in Arm* and *Fortunately* not only play with words but play with their placement on the page. His books are definitely a change from other books, and children enjoy them immensely.

An understanding of the need for change will help children to accept change in themselves and in others. It will also help the teacher to plan varying activities during the school day to prevent children from falling into the proverbial rut. Many types of literature are necessary to establish a good program, and a large variety of classroom adventures utilizing this literature is indicated.

The Need for Aesthetic Satisfaction

This is the need to create and to appreciate that which is created by others.

Aesthetic satisfaction is both emotional and intellectual. It is that part of all of us which strives to make our possessions not only functional but beautiful. It appears in many forms: a poor tenement room with a splash of color made by the addition of some gaudy tissue-paper flowers; a college dormitory room, practical but overcrowded, made personal with a large cuddly teddy bear on the bed, made beautiful with a montage of newsclippings, dance programs, sorority pictures, and the like; a Fifth Avenue office, stark and sterile, but softened by beautiful tapestries and an exquisite modern painting. Our clothes reflect our need for aesthetic satisfaction, as do our hair styles and our way of living.

Books can satisfy the aesthetic need to a great extent. Children's books are often so beautifully written as to compete with the great literature of the world. Children can gain aesthetic satisfaction from the beautiful way words are put together, from the rhymes, jingles, or phrases that tickle their imaginations or their funny bones. They often like a book because of the way words flow off the tongue, although they may not under-

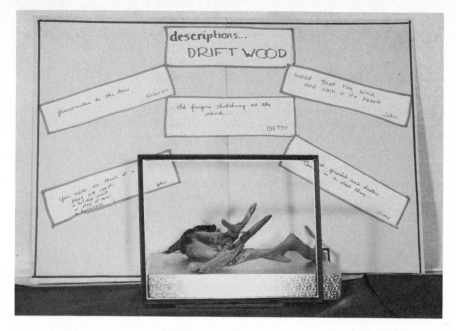

FIGURE 3–7. *A non-story bulletin board from a middle-grade room. Children wrote and posted their own beautiful sayings about a piece of driftwood.*

stand all the words. Certain books tease their imaginations into the most delightful self-created images.

In Leo Politi's *The Butterflies Come,* the mood of the story is enhanced by gentle country scenes and the flashing color of the artist. Margaret Wise Brown's *The Golden Egg Book* is certainly a visual experience never to be forgotten. The pictures by Leonard Weisgard are unsurpassed in their color appeal and content appeal. *Where the Wild Things Are* by Maurice Sendak has such fierce and wonderful monsters on the pages that no words are needed to tell a story.

Many books help children develop sensitivity to aesthetic quality, both in the style of the writing and in the illustrations. They deal directly with imagination, perception, observation, metaphor, simile, and analogy. Bertha Morris Parker's book *The Wonder of Seasons,* illustrated by Eloise Wilkin, is one such book. Margaret Wise Brown's *The Important Book, A Child's Good Night Book,* and *A Child's Good Morning* are others. Discussions dealing with the style and technique of such books can help children meet their aesthetic needs.

CHILDREN'S CHOICES OF LITERATURE

Children's needs and interests change with maturation. Using these as a basis, the appeal of some books can be predicted.

Periodically, surveys are developed to assist the teacher in the selection of appropriate literature at various age levels.[6] These surveys show that children tend to have specific interests at different ages, but that some overall ones persist. Children tend to maintain an interest in machines, nature, everyday experiences, holidays, love, fun stories and poems, and make-believe people and animals.

Young children prefer stories built around one main plot. They want to be able to anticipate the outcome of the story. They like literature that sets a mood, and they like "direct" conversation. They enjoy colorful, "tongue-tickling" words and prefer simple, natural climaxes in their stories. They like tales developed around one main character, generally an acceptable boy or girl hero, although sometimes an animal hero may be a suitable substitute. And they like literature with illustrations that also tell the story.

As children grow older, they develop a keener interest in animals, especially specific animals such as horses or cats. Older children like folk literature and stories of American folk heroes; of modern magic; of contemporary experiences; and historical, regional, and intergroup fiction. They enjoy reading about child life in other countries, and biographies and books about science. They also enjoy stories built around such themes as sports, religion, arts, humor, mystery, travel, nature; or stories about children with their own characteristics and problems.

In choosing books for children's reading or in guiding children in the selection of their own reading, teachers should keep in mind the following sources: contemporary literature, great stories and classics, realistic tales, fanciful tales, stories of fiction, stories of information, current material in periodicals, popular materials and distinctively literary reading matter, anthologies, and inexpensive books on children's literature.

Recent studies in children's preferences in literature are available to some degree. With the coming of television and other mass media, children have been subject to exposure to many kinds of vicarious experiences, both verbal and visual. This exposure has had a great effect on their interests and tastes. Also, the world of technology in which we live has introduced many new topics that were unreal or unheard of when the big surveys were last done. Recent studies are largely regional or have been conducted with ethnic groups. Some resources such as Kujoth's book indicate that children are still interested in the topics mentioned above, but have added other interests in the past several years, such as science fiction, biographies of current heroes, outer space, the universe, oceanography, ecology, nonfiction books on sports and crafts, how-to-do-it books, and fictionalized stories of famous people.

---

6. Early classic studies of children's interests that currently seem to be outdated because of changes in ethnic cultures and sex roles include *Interest and Ability in Reading* by Arthur I. Gates (New York: Macmillan, 1930); *A Comparative Study of Children's Reading Interests* by Robert L. Thorndike (New York: Bureau of Publications, Teachers College, Columbia University, 1941); *What Boys and Girls Like to Read* by George W. Nowell (New York: Silver-Burdett, 1958); Chapter 3 in *The Teaching of Reading* by Paul Witty, Alma Moore Freeland, and Edith H. Grotberg (Boston: D. C. Heath, 1966). More recent surveys of interest to the reader include the following: Robin C. Ford and J. Koplyay, *Reading Teacher* 22 (December 1968): 233–237; Sam Sebesta, Dianne L. Monson, and Frank Love, "Research Critiques," edited by Patrick Groff, *Elementary English* 48; Robert Emans, "What Do Children in the Inner City Like to Read?" *Elementary School Journal* 69 (December 1968): 118–122; Jerry L. Johns, "What Do Inner City Children Prefer to Read?" *Reading Teacher* 26 (February 1973).

Some studies have shown that the remembered favorites of adults are still being read by or to today's youth to a considerable degree.[7]

CRITERIA FOR CHOOSING LITERATURE FOR CHILDREN

What makes "good" literature for children? Experts in children's literature have set up certain criteria for evaluating individual works of literature and for selecting literature for classroom use. These criteria are best exemplified by the honors bestowed on outstanding children's books.

The Newbery Awards

Each year a committee of children's and school librarians chosen from the American Library Association honor John Newbery by awarding the best children's book of the year a gold seal in his honor. John Newbery was the first English publisher of children's books. He translated *Mother Goose* from the French version and was perhaps the first publisher to become aware of the potential of the child as a consumer of books. He is the author of *Mother Goose's Melody or Sonnets for the Cradle* (1760–1765) and is often given credit for writing *The History of Little Goody-Two-Shoes* (1765), the

FIGURE 3–8. *The Newbery Medal. Island of the Blue Dolphin* by Scott O'Dell, Houghton Mifflin Company, publisher.

7. B. Cooper and D. M. Smith, "Reactions of Sixth Grade Students to Remembered Favorite Books of Elementary School Teachers," *Elementary English* 49 (May 1972): 1010–1014.

first juvenile novel written especially for children. The Newbery award was created in 1922 by Frederic G. Melcher, a publisher. The book chosen for the Newbery Medal wears the gold seal on its jacket and is honored in all libraries and book stores. Because they are chosen, these books experience substantial sales and are popular with adults as well as children. Following is a list of the Newbery Medal books.

NEWBERY MEDAL AWARD BOOKS

Year	Title	Author	Publisher
1922	*Story of Mankind*	Van Loon	Liveright
1923	*The Voyage of Dr. Doolittle*	Lofting	Stokes
1924	*Dark Frigate*	Hawes	Little
1925	*Tales from Silver Lands*	Finger	Doubleday
1926	*Shen of the Sea*	Chrisman	Dutton
1927	*Smoky*	James	Scribner's
1928	*Gay-Neck*	Mukerji	Dutton
1929	*Trumpeter of Krakow*	Kelly	Macmillan
1930	*Hitty, Her First Hundred Years*	Field	Macmillan
1931	*The Cat Who Went to Heaven*	Coatsworth	Macmillan
1932	*Waterless Mountain*	Armer	Longmans Green
1933	*Young Fu of the Upper Yangtze*	Lewis	Holt, Rinehart & Winston
1934	*Invincible Louisa*	Meigs	Little
1935	*Dobry*	Shannon	Viking
1936	*Caddie Woodlawn*	Brink	Macmillan
1937	*Roller Skates*	Sawyer	Viking
1938	*White Stag*	Seredy	Viking
1939	*Thimble Summer*	Enright	Holt, Rinehart & Winston
1940	*Daniel Boone*	Daugherty	Viking
1941	*Call It Courage*	Sperry	Macmillan
1942	*Matchlock Gun*	Edmonds	Dodd
1943	*Adam of the Road*	Gray	Viking
1944	*Johnny Tremain*	Forbes	Houghton
1945	*Rabbit Hill*	Lawson	Viking
1946	*Strawberry Girl*	Lenski	Lippincott
1947	*Miss Hickory*	Bailey	Viking
1948	*Twenty-One Balloons*	Du Bois	Viking
1949	*King of the Wind*	Henry	Rand
1950	*Door in the Wall*	deAngeli	Doubleday
1951	*Amos Fortune, Free Man*	Yates	Dutton
1952	*Ginger Pye*	Estes	Harcourt
1953	*Secret of the Andes*	Clark	Viking
1954	*And Now Miguel*	Krumgold	Crowell
1955	*Wheel on the School*	DeJong	Harper
1956	*Carry On, Mr. Bowditch*	Latham	Houghton
1957	*Miracles on Maple Hill*	Sorenson	Harcourt
1958	*Rifles for Watie*	Keith	Crowell
1959	*Witch of Blackbird Pond*	Speare	Houghton
1960	*Onion John*	Krumgold	Crowell

Year	Title	Author	Publisher
1961	*Island of the Blue Dolphins*	O'Dell	Houghton
1962	*Bronze Bow*	Speare	Houghton
1963	*A Wrinkle in Time*	L'Engle	Farrar
1964	*It's Like This, Cat*	Neville	Harper
1965	*Shadow of a Bull*	Wojciechowska	Atheneum
1966	*I, Juan de Pareja*	de Trevino	Farrar
1967	*Up a Road Slowly*	Hunt	Follett
1968	*From the Mixed-Up Files of Mrs. Basil E. Frankweiler*	Konigsburg	Atheneum
1969	*High King*	Alexander	Holt, Rinehart & Winston
1970	*Sounder*	Armstrong	Harper
1971	*The Summer of the Swans*	Byars	Viking
1972	*Mrs. Frisby and the Rats of Nimh*	O'Brien	Atheneum
1973	*Julie and the Wolves*	George	Harper
1974	*Slave Dancer*	Fox	Bradberry
1975	*M. C. Higgins, the Great*	Hamilton	Macmillan
1976	*The Gray Prince*	Cooper	Atheneum

A survey of the books on children's literature and a reading of the Newbery Medal books reveal a remarkable agreement among experts as to what constitutes a good story and/or a good children's book. To study the criteria established by one expert is to cover them all fairly well.

Among the authorities on children's literature, May Hill Arbuthnot ranks at the top. Arbuthnot has served teachers for many years with her scholarly and detailed anthologies and articles. Her insight into the field of children's literature is deep and rich, and her writings have become a primary resource for problems and answers in the field. Her recent death has left a void yet to be filled.

Arbuthnot stated: "A book is a good book for children only when they enjoy it; a book is a poor book for children, even when adults rate it a classic, if children are unable to read it or are bored by its contents."[8]

She pointed out that although children like other types of reading, basically they search for a *good story*. She felt that children's books must be strong, written with levelness and honesty both in content and in style, "rather than little juvenile tracts designed to teach this lesson or that."[9]

Stories

What makes a good story? Arbuthnot and Sutherland[10] list four criteria:

1. An adequate theme (suitable for the interests and understanding of the age level for which it is written)
2. A lively plot
3. Memorable characters
4. A distinctive style

---

8. Arbuthnot, *op. cit.*, p. 2.
9. *Ibid.*, p. 11.
10. Arbuthnot and Sutherland, *op. cit.*, p. 34.

The theme is the most important of these criteria. Without a well-defined theme, story, characters, and style tend to appear forced and unimaginative. A strong theme will support a vigorous plot with action, suspense, and a clear-cut conclusion.

When the writing is clear, children tend to become familiar with basic plots. This does not make the stories less exciting.

One of the authors was recently visiting a first-grade classroom and the teacher was reading a story about a kitten who had lost his mother. The children were fascinated by the story and sat in rapt and concentrated attention. When the teacher paused to turn a page, she said, "Oh dear, I wonder if Peter will ever find his mother?" and a little child sitting near said reassuringly, "Oh sure, they always do!" The ability to anticipate possible endings is one of the reasons for personal involvement in a book.

Plot is the action of the story, and the skill of the writer comes into play here. The degree to which he builds his story around the theme he has selected makes for the success of the story. In plots, children want heroes who have obstacles to overcome, conflicts to settle, different goals to achieve. Children must be able to identify strongly with the characters and the situation of the plot. They like action-filled stories in which heroes and heroines realistically and vigorously attain their goals.

A good plot in a story can only be surpassed by the *characters* who develop the plot. It is interesting that many children, after a passage of time, will remember the main character of a story better than they will recall the story itself. Some books are remembered for the plot, some for both plot *and* characters, and some for the characters alone. *Millions of Cats* is one book remembered largely for the plot, and *Pinocchio* and his antics are inseparable, but Amy is often remembered well as a character long after children have forgotten the things she did in *Little Women*. Arbuthnot says this about characters:

> It is true that children go through a stage during which mere tales of action, peopled with stereotypes, satisfy them . . . But, happily, most children recover and want characters which are not merely stereotypes of bravery or beauty but real flesh-and-blood individuals, unique and memorable. The story may be realistic or fantastic, but the characters must be realistic.[11]

Who can ever forget Mary Poppins, Horton, Cinderella, Caddie Woodlawn, Jo from *Little Women,* Miguel, Scrooge, Christopher Robin, Johnny Tremain, Homer Price, the Moffats, and a host of other characters in children's literature, once one has met them? Through reading about these characters, children gain new insight into their own personal problems and also acquire understandings and skills in dealing with other people.

Style is difficult to define, yet it is conspicuous when absent. Lack of a definite writing style is often the factor that makes a story or book a poor or mediocre piece. Style is the music of the writing: that which makes it easy and enjoyable to read. It is the ability of the creator to put across his ideas so beautifully that word pictures are formed in the imagination, so

---

11. Arbuthnot, *op. cit.,* p. 25.

pleasantly or excitingly that sounds fall on the ears, so that reaction grips the reader although he may never leave his chair by the window. Style is the essence of knowing how to use the right word at the right time and in the right place. A book written with style may take the reader completely away from his physical setting for an hour or more and make him oblivious to all that is happening around him. Such a book can make a person reread lines just because he is delighted over the images he gets or the way the words are put together. Style can make shivers race up and down the back, make a reader roar with laughter, tense with anticipation, sob with heartbreak, and hug himself with well-being and contentment.

Leland Jacobs,[12] another authority on children's literature, selects six criteria for the selection of material to read to children:

1. The story must have a fresh, well-paced plot.
2. It must have unique individuality.
3. It should contain plausible, direct conversation.
4. It must have well-delineated characters.
5. The story must have authentic outcomes.
6. The story must appeal to the feelings as well as to the intellect.

Jacobs states that good children's literature must be free from obvious sentimentality while being rich in honest sentiment; free from direct moralizing but rooted in genuine spiritual and moral values; free from cuteness and triteness but vigorously unhackneyed and distinctive; free from talking down or misunderstanding of children's abilities. He feels good literature has "memory value"—there is a residue of meaning after time lapses. To meet these criteria, books must obviously have emotional appeal.

There is some danger in selecting books if the "memory value" of a book is the only criterion on which it is selected. Many books today sustain their popularity because the teacher or parent has a "memory value" about them. Such books may have little appeal or meaning to the child of today. The evaluator of children's books must remain objective in applying criteria to his selections or he may find himself choosing books for the wrong kind of "memory value." In looking at books that were classics in her childhood, the teacher will note that many no longer seem to have the literary value they once enjoyed. Fashions change in writing. Many books, once popular, consequently fall out of favor. Another criterion must therefore be added to those listed above: The story must be relevant to the child.

One final criterion we would add to the above list: The style of the book should influence the child in his reading and his interpretation of the material, as discussed above.

The use of words in children's books should be creative to the extent that the child "catches on" to the style and reads the material as the author intended. The awareness of style should not detract from the reading but should add to it. It should help children realize that telling stories requires a style. A three-year-old does not tell a story as a list of events strung to-

---

12. Leland Jacobs, "Children's Experiences in Literature," in *Children and the Language Arts,* edited by Virgil E. Herrick and Leland B. Jacobs (Englewood Cliffs, N.J.: Prentice-Hall, 1955), p. 194.

gether by "ands" and "thens." He begins with "Once upon a time there was a boy named Scott. He had a mother named Sue." And he is off. He is aware of style.

Awareness of the creative aspects of communication should encourage and inspire children themselves to write with style.

The Non-Story

A multitude of books greatly enjoyed by children are not stories. What is their appeal to children? Do the criteria that make story books interesting to children also make the non-story books appealing? What draws children to Ruth Krauss's *A Hole Is to Dig*, to Margaret Wise Brown's *The Golden Egg Book,* and to Joan Walsh Anglund's *Spring Is a New Beginning.*

Basically, these books are popular because they are good writing even though there is no plot. Literature, according to our definition, is the ability to put words together with beauty and style. It can assume the form of an essay, a poem, a written speech, a description, a critique, an incident, or the simple expression of a thought. Literature leaves the reader with deep thoughts.

Non-story books for children do that: they are really "concept" books which leave the reader chuckling, sighing, smiling, crying, or experiencing a sense of well-being. *A Hole Is to Dig* is a series of thoughts built around one concept, beautifully expressed and so childlike and honest that they bring back to the adult the thoughts of childhood and help the child classify his own feelings into new understandings. Like much nonfiction, non-story books can be written with style and beauty.

Spring Is a New Beginning causes the adult to experience waves of beauty, sadness, and joyousness almost at the same time. To children this book brings together a multitude of concepts they have had about spring, in a new and beautiful way. The simplicity of the presentations, the concentration on one thought, and the appeal to the emotions of the reader make these books rightfully take their place among the sophisticated children's literature of our time.

Non-story books are generally accompanied by excellent illustrations. They often appear in the form of picture books. A few are books of poetry. These books are short and read quickly although they are not always easy reading material. Some have no words at all.

It is probably a fact that non-story books appeal as much to adults as to children, though for totally different reasons.

A check against the criteria for story books shows that non-story books appeal to children when they fulfill the following criteria:

1. There is an adequate theme, though little or no plot.
2. An important concept is developed simply and well.
3. There is a distinctive style.
4. They are generally well illustrated.
5. They are relevant to the child and his life.
6. They are unique, original, and creative.

These criteria can be applied to popular books such as Joan Walsh Anglund's *Childhood Is a Time of Innocence,* Margaret Wise Brown's *The*

Golden Egg Book, Garelick's *Where Does the Butterfly Go When It Rains?,* and Ruth Krauss and Crockett Johnson's *Is This You?*

When the vocabulary is suitable, non-story books are often the first trade books many children learn to read.

The Caldecott Medal

In 1938, Frederic G. Melcher sponsored a second award. This was to be a medal for the most distinguished picture book for children published each year in the United States. The Caldecott Medal was named after Randolph Caldecott, an artist who gained fame for his illustrations of children's books. Like the Newbery Medal books, the Caldecott books are awarded a gold medal which they wear on their book jackets. These books serve as a fitting memorial to great artists for children. The Caldecott Medal books follow:

CALDECOTT MEDAL AWARD BOOKS

Year	Title	Author	Publisher	Artist
1938	*Animals of the Bible*	Lathrop	Stokes	Lathrop
1939	*Mei Li*	Handforth	Doubleday	Handforth
1940	*Abraham Lincoln*	d'Aulaire	Doubleday	d'Aulaire
1941	*They Were Strong and Good*	Lawson	Viking	Lawson
1942	*Make Way for Ducklings*	McCloskey	Viking	McCloskey

FIGURE 3–9. *The Caldecott Medal. The Biggest Bear* by Lynd Ward, Houghton Mifflin Company, publisher.

Year	Title	Author	Publisher	Artist
1943	*Little House*	Burton	Houghton	Burton
1944	*Many Moons*	Thurber	Harcourt	Slobodkin
1945	*Prayer for a Child*	Field	Macmillan	Jones
1946	*Rooster Crows*	Petersham	Macmillan	Petersham
1947	*The Little Island*	MacDonald	Doubleday	Weisgard
1948	*White Snow, Bright Snow*	Tresselt	Lothrop	Duvuisin
1949	*The Big Show*	Hader	Macmillan	Hader
1950	*Song of the Swallows*	Politi	Scribner	Politi
1951	*The Egg Tree*	Milhous	Scribner	Milhous
1952	*Finders Keepers*	Will & Nicolas	Harcourt	Morduinoff
1953	*Biggest Bear*	Ward	Houghton	Ward
1954	*Madeline's Rescue*	Bemelmans	Viking	Bemelmans
1955	*Cinderella*	Perrault	Scribner	Brown
1956	*Frog Went A-Courtin*	Langstaff	Harcourt	Rojankovsky
1957	*A Tree Is Nice*	Simont	Harper	Simont
1958	*Time of Wonder*	McCloskey	Viking	McCloskey
1959	*Chanticleer and the Fox*	Cooney	Crowell	Cooney
1960	*Nine Days to Christmas*	Etts and Labastida	Viking	Etts
1961	*Baboushka and the Three Kings*	Robbins	Parnassus	Sidjakov
1962	*Once a Mouse*	Brown	Scribner	Brown
1963	*Snowy Day*	Keats	Viking	Keats
1964	*Where the Wild Things Are*	Sendak	Harper	Sendak
1965	*May I Bring a Friend?*	de Regniers	Atheneum	Montresor
1966	*Always Room for One More*	Leodhas	Holt	Hogrogian
1967	*Sam, Bangs, & Moonshine*	Ness	Holt	Ness
1968	*Drummer Hoff*	Emberley	Prentice-Hall	Emberley
1969	*The Fool of the World and the Flying Ship*	Ransome	Farrar	Shulevitz
1970	*Sylvester and the Magic Pebble*	Steig	Simon	Steig
1971	*A Story a Story*	Haley	Atheneum	Haley
1972	*One Fine Day*	Hogrogian	Macmillan	Hogrogian
1973	*The Funny Little Woman*	Mosel	Dutton	Lent
1974	*Duffy and the Devil*	Zemach	Farrar	Zemach
1975	*Arrow in the Sun: A Pueblo Indian Tale*	McDermott	Viking	McDermott
1976	*Why Mosquitos Buzz in People's Ears*	Aardema	Dial	Dillon and Dillon

Arbuthnot suggests the following as criteria for good illustrations in children's books:

1. The pictures must be a truthful interpretation of the text.
2. In fantasy books, children abandon their literalness and accept almost any quirk of the artist's imagination.
3. Pictures must be synchronized with the text.
4. Children like action pictures as much as they enjoy action plots.
5. Children like bright colors but they also like muted colors and black and white when they are well done.
6. Even small children see many details in the pictures and seem to enjoy hunting them out.

To pass the test of an illustrator of children's books in the space age, one must first of all be a true artist. The exposure children receive to good art through the use of children's books is, indeed, comparable to a succession of trips to a museum. The dazzling, colored illustrations of Maurice Sendak in *Where the Wild Things Are* and Tony Chen in *Run Zebra, Run,* the moody black and white pictures drawn by James Barkley for *Sounder,* the simple, colorful drawings by Uri Shulevitz in *The Fool of the World and the Flying Ship,* the black and white sketches in *From the Mixed-Up Files of Mrs. Basil E. Frankweiler,* are, first of all, works of art. An experience with these books is an experience with some of the greatest artists of the country.

Because of the emphasis and interest placed on the illustrations in children's books, illustrators find themselves in the unique situation of being forced to please an adult audience as well as a child audience. This leads to problems in the development of taste in children. Times and environments change, and what is accepted in one generation may be rejected in the next, be it good or bad. We would add to the criteria stated above that criterion we added to the selection of good literature: *For the illustrations of a book to be acceptable to the child reader, they must be relevant.* We have seen many young adult students reject books such as *Finders Keepers* by William Lipkind and Nicolas Mordvinoff because the illustrations were not in keeping with the reader's concept of dogs in their environment, consequently not relevant to them.

It has been stated that the imposition of "taste" in illustrations is not the same as the development of taste. Even the experts are sometimes guilty of becoming sentimental about children's pictures. Uses of the phrase "quaint, old-fashioned" and "charming little portraits" show a particular person's prejudices and likes, and do not necessarily reflect the preferences of children in a particular stage of their development. Exposure to beautiful pictures is one way to help children develop their tastes, but if the criteria for excellence in illustrations are to be valid at all, they must all be subordinate to the overall criterion: that children enjoy the material. One popular writer of "children's" books illustrates her books with little old-fashioned pictures. Experimenting with children in our nursery school (the age for which these books are supposedly written) disclosed the fact that these children almost never chose these books to look at alone, and many wandered away from the group when the books were read. Yet the bookstore cannot keep these books in stock. Investigation of the purchasers of these books shows that they are immensely popular with college-age students, who give them as gifts to each other or start whole collections of them. The question arises: Are we judging these as children's books because they are about children, when actually they are adult books that appeal to adults because they afford a "charming" record of the best parts of childhood?

More research is needed to find out what a child demands in the illustrations in his books. There is, for instance, some recognition given to the exciting and beautiful photographs in children's books, but little recognition to photographic "art" currently used to illustrate many commercial books. Yet children identify very closely with these beautiful art photographs. A case in point is Jane Ellen Dwyer's *I See a Poem,* which uses lovely colored photographs to illustrate popular children's poems, and *Beyond the High Hills: A Book of Eskimo Poems* with exquisite photographs by Guy Mary-Rousseliere. Perhaps the lack of photographic art in the so-called good books has been discouraged because there is no "Eastman Award" or its counterpart to encourage experimentation with this medium in the field of children's literature. If this is the case, then setting limits for creating illustrations for children's books with predetermined criteria may be discouraging to the creativity of photographic artists and those who wish to express their interpretation of a book through the use of a new or different medium. One final criterion needs to be added, then, for judging illustrations in children's books: The illustrators of children's books should be creative to the degree that *they continually invent new, unique, and challenging media and techniques to express their interpretations of the book.* Remy Charlip is one illustrator who has dared to change the accepted styles of children's books in his new illustration techniques.

If creative illustrating is to flourish, teachers, librarians, and parents must come to realize that the only way an illustrator can survive is to illustrate, and that although all have the right to evaluate, accept, or reject any book published, we do not have the right to determine how any book shall be illustrated before it is published. Rigid predetermined criteria can create unrealistic limitations on an artist's work.

FORMAT OF THE BOOK

A cliché from the past is that in order for a book to be a "good" book, it must be sturdy and durable, as mentioned earlier. Since the introduction of paperbacks to the child's world, these two criteria are not as valid as they once were. It is not durability and sturdiness that determine the life of a book: it is love. Love for books and a wholesome attitude towards their care must become a part of the literature program of a school, or no book will endure for long. Too much emphasis on sturdiness and durability may deprive children of some of the lovely, fragile, and exquisite books that are highly creative and that children can come to love. We are thinking particularly of a little book called *Love* by Lowell Siff.

When books like these are first introduced to children, a discussion on how they should be cared for and where they should be kept will help each child come to realize the value of such books and his responsibility for preserving them.

Of course, books for very young children must be sturdy in order to survive—but sturdy in stitching and in stout covers more than anything else.

In the past a great deal of emphasis has been put on the size of the book. It was advocated that books for pre-schoolers be light enough for them to handle comfortably. However, size in inches actually seems to have little or no bearing on children's book choices. Children love the pictures in *The Big Book of Real Fire Engines* by George Zaffo even though they must set it on a table to turn the large pages one by one. And they also love tiny books such as *The Brave Cowboy* by Joan Walsh Anglund, which they can clutch in one hand and carry about. They seem to enjoy the sense of possession they acquire when they can easily transport a small book. Maurice Sendak's *Nutshell Library*, a collection of tiny books, is a very treasured collection for most children.

The matter of print in children's books has been given considerable attention in past years. Many children's books are printed in large boldface type like their beginning reading textbooks. This makes the book suitable for reading by the child, provided, of course, that the vocabulary is not too difficult. Books for older children may be printed in smaller print. Co-ordinating the print in the literature books with the reading books makes possible the use of literature as a base for the reading program. Such concepts as the individualized reading program have emerged because of the quantity of children's books now available in appropriate type.

Some children's books are printed in script writing or capital letters throughout. This almost forces the teacher to read these books aloud, because children rarely can read script printing at an early age. A child must reach a certain age before his eyes can focus on the print of a book. He learns many of his words in the beginning stages simply by memorizing their shape. Laymen do not realize that the printed word for horse and the written word for horse, or the capitalized word for horse, have shapes as different from each other as two different words such as *horse* and *chair*. To try to make a child learn three types of print can slow down his reading process to the point where he is so frustrated trying to figure out words that he never does understand or enjoy the content of the story—which is the only reason for reading it in the first place.

Some teachers have been unhappy about the fact that all books do not follow this simple rule of printing. One of us makes this statement: "My children fell in love with the *Babar* books. Many of my good readers could have read them if they had been in print and not in script. It is true that a few did figure them out, but, for the most part, they remained 'reading-aloud' books."

In the selection of children's books, the size of type and the spacing of the words is important. Large type may be resented by older children, but type that is too small turns them off and often causes eyestrain.

VOCABULARY IN CHILDREN'S BOOKS

We cannot leave our discussion on the nature of children without exploring how it relates to reading and a full experience with literature.

A great deal has been written about the vocabulary used in children's books and the problem of the teaching of reading as it relates to children's literature. Criticism has been leveled at teachers and educators because they have "watered down" the children's books in their frenzy to find material for children to read. The methods of teaching reading and children's lack of interest in books have also been criticized. Many laymen feel that the inability of children to read books of great literature has been the result of the sight method of teaching, of the push of the publishers to market their products, and a host of other obscure reasons. Critics bewail the state of children's reading ability, and some boast of the fact that by the time *they* had completed first grade, they had finished *David Copperfield, Little Women,* and the *Bible.*

Frances Clark Sayers poses some of the criticisms in an essay called "Lose Not the Nightingale." Mrs. Sayers says:

> The concern of modern education with reading has had an influence upon the reading done by children and upon the production of children's books, which is somewhat detrimental. In an effort to enliven and enrich the business of teaching reading, the mechanics of reading has encroached upon the ultimate purpose of reading, the art of reading, if you will, and the result is confusion. "The poor fisherman said (of the mechanical nightingale): 'It sounds very nice, and it is very like the real one, but there is something wanting, we don't know what.'"
>
> There are two theories of modern education which have done much to rob reading of its challenge to the mind and the imagination of the child. The first is the emphasis of modern education upon actual experience as the chief instrument of teaching. The child must be submitted to nothing beyond his experience. I question the infallibility of this emphasis on actual experience. It leads to an exaggerated effort to create, artificially, the experience which is presumed to be "meaningful" to the children. It leads to an activity program which results in an overstimulation of the children, and a loss of ability to respond. It tends to rob children of their natural sense of wonder....
>
> The second attitude of modern education which has had a detrimental influence upon children's reading is the insistence upon measuring reading ability: defining what words the child should know at a certain age. This practice, together with the emphasis upon the technical reading difficulties of the non-reader, or slow reader, has again resulted in encroaching upon the goals of the art of reading.[13]

While there is always truth in criticism, there are generally also many misunderstandings. Some of these need to be cleared before teachers and parents select books for children.

One criticism often heard about modern education is that children no longer read as well or as much as they used to. This statement has little evidence to support it, and considerable evidence to negate it. For instance, more children's books are now printed in the United States than adult books (about 3,000 per year). Books are printed to be sold. They are sold because people read them; the people in this case are children. The circulation of

13. Sayers, Frances Clark, *Summoned by Books: Essays and Speeches,* Marjeanne J. Blinn, ed. (New York: Viking Press, 1965).

children's books continues to skyrocket. More and more schools in America have their own school libraries and learning resource center personnel each passing year.

Records of selective populations taken over a span of years show the reading ability of children is slowly growing year by year, and this in spite of the fact that back in the early 1900s very slow children were not tested, and consequently not included in the reports, exceptional children were not taught in the regular classroom even if they were physically present, and the range of scores on tests were therefore skewed to a normal and above normal population. In today's schools, provision is made for *all* children, and reading ability is measured for *all*. The low scores of slow readers balance the higher ends of the normal curve.

Adults who remember reading *Little Women* at the age of six or eight are perhaps guilty of a faulty memory or were unusually gifted intellectually, for there is a high correlation between intelligence and the ability to read well.

It is not possible for most children to be able to read at a very early age for many reasons. For one thing, children aged five or six have simply not lived long enough to get meaning from most of the words. The public school, by its very definition, is responsible for teaching *all* children to read to their ability levels. Children who were brilliant and could read well in one of the authors' classrooms of forty years ago were supplied with the classics and other books to read even though it meant he had to drive nineteen miles every two weeks to get books for them. Good teachers we observe today do the same thing for their students. Even slow learners these days have more contact with good children's literature than our children did because the reading books are full of good stories, many with the original writing intact.

FIGURE 3–10. Thanksgiving Story *by Alice Dalgliesh prompted this middle-grade bulletin board.*

The concept of *experience* in reading has been greatly misunderstood. We would like to reprint here a passage from a book by Smith that we hope will show the reader the meaning of the experience concept.

What Is Reading?

Reading is the ability to recognize and understand the printed symbols of the child's spoken vocabulary. Printed words, as well as spoken ones, are meaningful to the young child only insofar as his field of experience overlaps that of the author of the printed text. The old cliché, "You can take from a book only what you bring to it," is, in essence, true. The reader learns from a book only if he is able to understand the printed symbols and rearrange them into vicarious experiences in his mind. His ability to think, to reason, and to conceptualize makes it possible for him to receive new ideas from a printed page without actually experiencing the new idea, *but he must have experienced each symbol that helps make up the new idea!*

This is illustrated by an incident in a typical first-grade room. A city child told of a trip he took in the summer to an animal farm, where, among other things, he saw a kangaroo. Ideally, the teacher would show a picture of a kangaroo and, through discussion, build the understandings necessary to give children a correct visual image of a kangaroo. But there was no picture available at the moment, so the teacher resorted to the use of word symbols. She printed the idea on the board:

Tommy went to the game farm.
He saw a kangaroo.

Because of the unusual shape of the word "kangaroo," children memorized it quickly, but they learned nothing until the word took on meaning. The teacher gave the word meaning by using the children's past experiences. Every child in the room had experienced size and variances in height, so when Tommy said, "The kangaroo is as tall as my Daddy," an image formed in each child's mind. If the children did not know Tommy's daddy, this image varied among them as they compared it to their own daddies. In the early part of the year, a rabbit had been brought to the classroom, so each child had experienced "hopping," "softness," and various concepts about the rabbit. Consequently, when the teacher added, "The kangaroo is soft. He hops. His back legs are much bigger than his forelegs," the children projected their past experiences into the new experience and gradually the blurred image of the kangaroo became more clear. Experience combined with the power of imagery made it possible for the children to gain new understandings, concepts, and learnings from their reading of the new word.

The sentence below may or may not communicate meaning:

"John drove into the megalopolis each Saturday and took a class in origami."

Immediately we know that John went somewhere and took a course in something. But only those who have experienced and labeled a city or chain of cities as a megalopolis, and only those who have seen the art of Japanese paper-folding and have used the label "origami" to define it, will know the entire meaning of the sentence.

Read the sentences below:

1. The sentinent walked down the street with a pogo.
2. The coult walked down the street with a jeliet in his hand. Along came a magpiet.
3. The sentinent barep denred his oastes.

In each of these situations, you can probably read each sentence perfectly. But can you? Can you read or can you simply figure out sounds and words? Your knowledge of phonics and the skills in attacking new words, which you learned in grade school, have all been summoned up and put to use—but to what avail? Do you yet know the meaning of the sentences? You may be able to guess the meaning of numbers 1 and 2, but with number 3 you are completely lost because it contains so many words unrelated to your field of experience that all your reading skills are still not adequate to give meaning to the sentence. It is beyond your reading level because it is beyond your experience level (both direct and symbolic).

Think back on how you read these sentences. Here are some of the things you probably did:

1. You sounded out the unfamiliar words and said them two or three different ways, trying to associate them with some spoken symbol within your own experience. *Children learning to read do this also. They try to apply phonics skills to new words and then associate them with some word in their oral vocabulary.*

2. You probably then associated the word *sentinent* with the word *sentinel* because they look alike and the sentence makes sense when you use this particular word. *In learning to read, children, too, associate words with other, familiar words in their visual vocabulary if they make sense.*

3. You probably then related the word *pogo* to a *pogo stick* because it, too, looks like the word "pogo" and it, too, makes some sense. *Children, in learning to read, learn meanings of words by the way they are used in context.*

In sentence 2 you probably thought of *coult* as a young horse because you associated it with the word *colt*. The word *jeliet* was probably difficult because, even though you could pronounce it, you could associate it with no word looking like it that could be effectively substituted in this particular context to give it meaning. Then you came to the word *hand,* and the meaning you had been able to build up in the sentence to this point was immediately shattered because young horses do not have hands. You hastened on to try to find a context clue but did not get much help. You probably read the last sentence as "Along came a bird," associating *magpiet* with *magpie.*

Sentence 3 is completely lost to you; it is no more than jargon. Can you, then, read the sentence? No, you can not. Because reading is not word-calling; it is the ability to recognize, say, and understand the printed symbols on a page. The teaching of reading means simply helping children acquire the skills needed to do this. But we have seen that the acquisition of all the skills is of little or no value without the ingredient basic to all reading—experience with the words to make them meaningful.

Reading is a skill or tool that helps an author communicate with the reader. Children read because they want to know what is on the page. The reading itself is not sacred. It is what the reading *tells* the child that is important. Reading is an important means of communication, but it is not the only one, nor is it the best. To insure the development of a good primary reading program, children must have: (1) a large background of experiences, (2) the ability to listen well, and (3) a good oral vocabulary to label their experiences meaningfully. With this background, almost every child can be taught to read, provided, of course, he also has the required intelligence and has no serious physical, social, or emotional problems.

Because of the variations among children in ability to learn, in interests, and in attitudes, one basic truth remains dominant: If all children are to become literate in the area of children's literature, the literature program cannot be built on reading ability. It is the rightful heritage of all children to share in the stories and songs of the past. Adults have no compunctions about reading to pre-schoolers and should realize that many children are not mentally equipped to read books even on their interest level. No matter how concentrated or how talented the reading instruction, half the children in any normal class will be below grade level in reading. For grade level norms are averages, and an average is the point above which falls half of any group of scores and below which we find the other half. For the half of the children who fall below the norm, the teacher will need to provide many adventures with literature because they will get it in no other way. Most of all, like the pre-schooler, they will need to be read to frequently. It is hoped that reading to these children will provide one technique for motivation that will keep them performing at their peak level and will insure their continued love for reading.

It is not the intent of any reading program to limit the experiences, real or vicarious (and reading is a vicarious experience), but rather to *expand* them so children can read more and more words with meaning. With all the criticism leveled against television, one glaring fact remains: the constant barrage of words a child faces when he witnesses a fantastic number of vicarious experiences on the tube each day has equipped him with a multitude of new words in his oral vocabulary which he can now recognize in print, thus increasing his reading ability.

Testing children's reading abilities is the only way a teacher can tell if the child is making progress; it also serves as a means of diagnosing reading problems. The word lists that children should know at various ages are only for the slow, retarded, underprivileged, and deprived child. They have no bearing on the vocabulary development of any child who is reading well. Testing a child is one way to reach an understanding of why his vocabulary may not develop as well as he is capable of developing it.

In choosing the proper book for the specific child, one *must* consider vocabulary, or the frustrations that abound within the child who wants to get on with the story and cannot may cause him to abandon reading for television or some other more direct means of communication. Children who read well may have the classics. A sixth-grade girl recently gave us an exquisite summary of *Gone with the Wind,* which she was inspired to read after seeing a rerun of the movie. But there was one child in the same classroom whose intelligence and home background were such that he was enjoying Claire H. Bishop's *The Five Chinese Brothers!*

In choosing a book for any child to read, the teacher should consider the following:

1. Is the vocabulary suitable for the child's experience level, that is, will he know what it is about?
2. Are the new words those he has the skill to decipher, that is, can he recognize these words as part of his oral vocabulary once he has "sounded them out"? Or can he gain meaning from a new word by the way it is used in the text?
3. Is the topic of interest to him, so he will sustain his reading in spite of barriers?

The important fact to remember is that *each* child needs books chosen especially for him. In this way, he progresses on his own initiative and at his own speed.

SUMMARY

The first criterion for selecting books for a child should be the child himself. Each child may, because of his own needs, background, and interests, be reading material different from that of other children. A teacher may be aware of the basic needs of children at all age levels as defined in this chapter, but she must also be aware of the unique needs and interests of each child.

All children need books that will widen their horizons and deepen their understandings of places, people, and life around them. They also need material that will help them understand themselves and that will provide sound social insights.

Children need books that help them to develop an appreciation of beauty, mainly beautiful writing and beautiful images created by that writing; books of heroism to help them become aware of and develop such traits as courage, loyalty, and independence; fantasy books as an escape medium; and also books dealing with down-to-earth realism. They need books to help them understand when conformity is necessary and when they may remain individuals. Finally, through books they can be helped to understand right from wrong.

"Good" literature for all children is exemplified by the awards given to honor the best in children's books. The most coveted of all awards are the Newbery Medal for the best-written book and the Caldecott Medal for the book with the best illustrations.

Another criterion for selecting books is the quality of good writing that distinguishes it as literature for any age group or group of people. Mentioned in this section are the following:

1. An adequate theme.
2. A lively well-paced plot (with authentic outcomes).
3. Memorable characters (well-delineated).
4. A distinctive style (a unique individuality and plausible direct conversation).
5. Good design and attractive illustrations.

6. Evoking of a feeling response as well as an intellectual response.
7. Relevance to the child.
8. Uniqueness, individuality, difference, creativity, and provocation of thinking in the child.

The illustrations in children's books play a large part in telling the story. Illustrating children's books has become a high-level art form. Illustrations enhance a book when they: (1) provoke a truthful interpretation of the text; (2) are synchronized with the text; (3) depict action; (4) have bright colors or well-done black and white drawings; (5) are relevant to the child; and (6) evoke a creative response from the child.

To be effective, children's books must be put together well, must be sensitive to the reader's oral vocabulary limits, and must be within the realm of the child's experience in terms of understandings and concepts, though not necessarily in terms of specific details or facts. Teachers need to know what reading is, the place of *experience* in the reading process, and the value of norms before they can successfully select books for individual children.

TO THE COLLEGE STUDENT

1. Using the criteria stated in this chapter for good children's literature, bring a collection of children's books to class and evaluate them. Which books do you feel are especially creative or contribute to children's creative development?

2. If you have designed and made a book, evaluate it by using the criteria from this chapter.

3. Plan a social studies unit that you could teach entirely through children's literature.

4. Discuss the following problems in class:

a. What part do picture books play in a literature program? Are picture books good literature?
b. How does television contribute to an appreciation of good literature in children?
c. What makes a classic in children's literature?
d. What authors do you remember from your childhood? What authors do children currently enjoy?

5. If you have access to groups of children from different environmental cultures, choose a book mentioned in this chapter and try reading it to a group of children in each of these cultures. Take *Johnny Tremain,* for instance: read it to a group of children in a typical middle-class suburban community, to a group in an inner-city school of the same age, and to a group of the same age in a rural central school. Also try books such as *It's Like This, Cat; A Quiet Place; Spring Is a New Beginning;* and others. Note the reactions of the children. Do they react the same in each group? Would you say that some books have appeal for all groups? Which ones are popular in some groups and not in others? Does this activity violate, to a degree, the philosophy expounded in this chapter?

6. Read some of the children's books mentioned in this chapter and categorize them under the following headings, showing what needs the book might meet:

a. security need—general
b. spiritual security need
c. need to belong
d. need to love and be loved
e. need to achieve, to be respected
f. need for change
g. need for aesthetic satisfaction

7. Use your library to see if any studies have been conducted to indicate children's preferences for films. For TV programs? Is there any link between the *types* of films and TV shows the children prefer and their book choices as indicated here?

8. Choose a child's book from this chapter that you like a great deal and use it as a basis for a puppet show, a colored light show, a rock concert, or some other presentation. Make your project as creative as possible and present it to the remainder of the class. Several small groups within the class could do this on different days.

9. Go to the library and ask for some of the Newbery and Caldecott award books. Study the gold seal placed on the covers: Is the symbolism of the seals creative and appropriate? Read a sampling of the Newbery books and look over several of the Caldecott Medal books. Would you agree that they meet the criteria reviewed in this chapter?

TO THE CLASSROOM TEACHER

1. Ask the art teacher, the physical education teacher, the music teacher, and any others who work with you to identify the creative children in your classroom. Do you agree with them? How many of the criteria listed in this chapter did you use to make your choices? Do you feel you accept and enjoy creative children or are they a nuisance to you?

2. Ask the children to paint a picture of some story they have recently read. At another time ask them to write a story about some recent experience. Do you see any relationship in the creativity in the pictures and in the written stories? In other words, do the creative authors appear to be the creative painters in your opinion? Or are some children highly creative in one skill but not in another? Would you say that creative children often excel in one skill rather than in all skills?

3. On page 523 there are some lists of filmstrips of children's books that may be used in the classroom. Some have accompanying phonodiscs using the voice of a good storyteller. Secure some of these and try them out on children. What are some of the advantages of such media? Disadvantages? How can you use this medium effectively with your reading program?

4. Outline a plan for teaching the history of the United States through the use of children's literature.

5. The best way to use children's literature is through an individualized reading program. If you have not attempted such a program, try to individualize your top group as a starter, allowing the children to select their own materials and keep their own records. Later you can try it on your other reading groups.

6. Select about five books written in very different styles. Read them to your children and follow each with a discussion about style. Have your children rate the books from most favorite to least favorite and note whether they have any preferences for certain styles. See Chapter 12 for a discussion on developing appreciation for style.

7. Ask your students to make lists of their favorite characters in children's literature. Have two of your able students make a composite of the class choices. Does this give you a clue as to the type of books your students prefer? Have some of the students make a chart of the choices for the class to see. Leave space at the bottom of the chart for children to add new characters as they discover them.

8. Make a bulletin board display of the Newbery books and note whether or not it has a noticeable effect on the children's choices in the next few days.

TO THE COLLEGE STUDENT
AND THE CLASSROOM TEACHER

1. There is a great deal of trash sold as children's literature today. Have each member of the class bring a book of recent publication to a group meeting. Using the

criteria for selecting children's literature as defined in this chapter, evaluate the books brought in by the group members.

2. Many creative thinking skills can be developed through the use of children's literature in the classroom. Select some well-known children's book and study it for answers to the following questions:

a. What creative thinking skills does the author develop—challenge in arriving at a creative solution of the plot, appeal to imagination, clever use of words, challenge to the reader's ability to use empathy?

b. What kind of personality characteristics are encouraged or discouraged by the story?

c. Does the author tell a story, moralize, develop a "cautionary" tale, or set a mood, or a combination of any of these? If so, does the work ring true?

d. How can literature develop creative components of the intellect?

3. Read *Island of the Blue Dolphins* by Scott O'Dell, a Newbery Medal book, and discuss all the ways you can think of in which it could be used in the classroom in connection with various areas of the curriculum. Try this with *Slave Dancer* by Paula Fox and *Deenie* by Judy Blume.

4. Set aside a short period of time in class, and ask one student each session to read a child's book or story. Rediscover for yourself the delightful world of children's literature.

5. Discuss the following open-ended situations:

a. How would you make children aware of the style of a book?

b. What could you do to prepare a group of culturally disadvantaged children for a book like *Sounder*?

c. What techniques can a classroom teacher use in general to motivate children to read books?

d. Does a moving picture about a book tend to add to or detract from the book?

e. Why do teachers not teach poetry very often?

6. Discuss and list the criteria you feel appropriate in the selection of outstanding adult books. Compare them with the criteria discussed in this chapter for the selection of children's books. How comparable are your lists?

7. Bring in some books which you loved as a child. How many of them appear on recommended book lists? Can you tell why some do not? Can you identify the reasons for your attachment to the book? Do you feel the criteria listed here are applicable to *all* books? Might not a very creative and worthy book be overlooked because it varied from the usual criteria?

8. Make a display of Caldecott Medal books and give all your co-workers the opportunity to study the pictures. Do you agree or disagree with the author that children are exposed to some superior art work in these books?

9. In the discussion of reading in this chapter, we try to point up the need for experience in order to give books meaning. How does this discussion hold up with books that are flights of the imagination and not based on experience?

SELECTED BIBLIOGRAPHY

Arbuthnot, May Hill, and Zena Sutherland. *Children and Books*. 4th ed. Glenview, Ill.: Scott, Foresman, 1972.

Arbuthnot, May Hill. *The Arbuthnot Anthology of Children's Literature*. Zena Sutherland, ed. Glenview, Ill.: Scott, Foresman, 1976.

Barnet, Sylvan, Morton Berman, and William Burto. *The Study of Literature: A Handbook of Critical Essays and Terms*. Boston: Little, Brown, 1960.

Bernstein, Joanne. "Changing Roles of Females in Books for Young Children," *Reading Teacher* 27 (March 1974): 545–549.

Boutwell, W. D. "How Well Does Johnny Read? Results of the First National Survey of Reading by the National Assessment of Educational Progress," *PTA Magazine* 66 (June 1972): 9–10.

Carner, Charles R. "Case of the Mysterious Awards," *Top of the News* (January 1966).

Chall, J. "Reading Seems To Be Improving," *Instructor* 83 (February 1974): 44.

Children's Books: Awards and Prizes. Children's Book Council. Published annually.

Cianciolo, Patricia. *Literature for Children: Illustrations in Children's Books.* Dubuque, Iowa: Wm. C. Brown, 1970.

Cohen, Dorothy H. "The Effect of Literature on Vocabulary and Reading Achievement," *Elementary English* 45 (February 1968): 209–213.

Cooper, B., and D. M. Smith. "Reactions of Sixth Grade Students to Remembered Favorite Books of Elementary School Teachers," *Elementary English* 49 (May 1972): 1010–1014.

Dalgliesh, Alice, and Annie Duff, comp. *Aids to Choosing Books for Your Children.* New York: Children's Book Council, n. d.

Eakin, Mary K. *Good Books for Children, 1950–1965.* 3rd ed. Chicago: University of Chicago Press, 1966.

Earle, R. A. "Using Literature to Teach Reading," *Reading Improvement* 9 (Fall 1972): 35–38.

Geeslin, D. H., and R. C. Wilson. "Effect of Reading Age on Reading Interests," *Elementary English* 49 (May 1972): 750–756.

Georgiou, Constantine. *Children and Their Literature.* Englewood Cliffs, N.J.: Prentice-Hall, 1969.

Gersoni-Stavn, Diane. *Sexism and Youth.* New York: R. R. Bowker, 1974.

Heinlein, Robert. "Ray Guns and Rocket Ships," in *Readings about Children's Literature,* edited by Evelyn R. Robinson. New York: McKay, 1966.

Hollowell, Lillian. *A Book of Children's Literature.* 3rd ed. New York: Holt, Rinehart and Winston, 1966.

Huss, Helen, comp. and ed. *Evaluating Books for Children and Young People.* Prepared by the Committee of the International Reading Association. Newark, Del.: The Association, 1968.

Izard, Anne. "Behind Closed Doors with the Newbery-Caldecott Committee," *Top of the News* 22 (January 1966): 163.

James, Philip B. *English Book Illustration, 1800–1900.* New York: Penguin, 1947.

Johns, J. L. "What Do Inner City Children Prefer to Read?" *Reading Teacher* 26 (February 1973): 462–467.

Justus, H. "Status Report on Reading, Findings of the National Assessment of Education Progress Series," *American Education* 8 (August 1972): 9–13.

Kingman, Lee, ed. *Newbery and Caldecott Medal Books, 1956–1975.* Boston: Horn Book, 1975.

Kingman, Lee, et al., eds. *Illustrators of Children's Books, 1957–1966.* Boston: Horn Book, 1968.

Klemin, Diana. *The Art of Art for Children's Books.* New York: Potter, 1966.

Lauritzen, C. et al. "Children's Reading Interests Classified by Age Level," *Reading Teacher* 27 (April 1974): 694–700.

Linder, Leslie L. *The Art of Beatrix Potter.* 6th ed. New York: Frederick Warne, 1972.

MacCampbell, James C. "Literature in the Language Arts Program," in *Readings in the Language Arts in the Elementary School,* edited by James C. MacCampbell. Boston: D. C. Heath, 1964.

Miller, Bertha M., et al., eds. *Illustrators of Children's Books, 1744–1945.* Boston: Horn Book, 1947.

Miller, Bertha Mahony, and Elinor Whitney Field. *Newbery Medal Books: 1922–1955.* Boston: Horn Book, 1955.

Miller, Bertha Mahony, and Elinor Whitney Field. *Caldecott Medal Books: 1938–1957.* Boston: Horn Book, 1957.

Miller, Bertha M., et al., eds. *Illustrators of Children's Books, 1946–1956.* Boston: Horn Books, 1958.

Norvell, George W. *The Reading Interests of Young Children.* East Lansing, Mich.: Michigan State University Press, 1974.

Peltola, Bette J. "A Study of Children's Book Choices," *Elementary English* 40 (1963): 690–695, 702.

Pilgrim, Geneva H., and Marianne K. McAllister. "Research on Reading Interests." In *Books, Young People, and Reading Guidance,* 2nd ed. New York: Harper & Row, 1968, pp. 53–68.

Pitz, Henry C. *A Treasury of American Book Illustration.* American Studio Books, 1947.

Pitz, Henry C. *Illustrating Children's Books: History, Technique, Production.* New York: Watson-Guptill, 1964.

Porter, Jane. "National Assessment on Reading," *English Teacher* 50 (January 1973): 107–116.

Saunders, Jacqueline. "Psychological Significance of Children's Literature." In *A Critical Approach to Children's Literature,* edited by Sara Inis Fenwick. Chicago: University of Chicago Press, 1967.

Sayers, Frances Clark. *Summoned by Books: Essays and Speeches.* Ed. by Marjeanne J. Blinn. New York: Viking Press, 1965.

Stanchfield, J. M. "Boys' Reading Interests as Revealed Through Personal Conferences," *Reading Teacher* 16 (September 1962): 41–44.

Stirling, Nora. *Who Wrote the Classics?* New York: John Day, 1965.

Veatch, Jeanette. *How to Teach Reading with Children's Books.* New York: Citation Press, 1968.

Veatch, Jeanette. "Research Studies on Sylvia Ashton-Warner's Key Vocabulary," *Childhood Education* 48 (May 1972): 437–440.

Washburne, Carleton, and Mabel Vogel. *What Children Like to Read: Winnetka Graded Book List.* New York: Rand McNally, 1926.

CHAPTER 4

Children's Literature and Creativity

PUTTING MAGIC INTO ANTS AND GRASSHOPPERS

Mr. Nash was constantly aware of the fact that he must provide situations for his live-wire group of nongraded students in which they could be made to think creatively. With many objectives in mind that he hoped to accomplish with one meaningful activity, he decided to apply the principle of force relationships to his classroom group as a technique for helping them to solve a problem. What resulted was jokingly referred to in the days that followed the project as "the magic grasshopper."

"We decided a few weeks ago," said Mr. Nash one bright October morning, "that we wanted to take part in the assembly program for American Book Week. Some suggestions were made, you recall, and I think we finally decided to present one of our favorite stories in a new and unusual way. Today you were each going to write the name of your favorite story on one of the 3 × 5 cards I gave you. Let's see if we can decide which story we will present and how we will present it."

The cards were collected and Mr. Nash suggested that the children appoint a committee to classify them and then make a list of the stories in order of their preference. No sooner said than done, and the committee, with Peter as chairman, was sent off to the conference room to work.

"Meanwhile," said Mr. Nash, "while our committee is at work, I have something new I would like to show you that I think you will enjoy." He held up a sheet of blank white paper.

"What do you see?" he asked.

"Nothing," the children all said at once.

"Watch closely," said Mr. Nash. "I am going to make some magic. Bill, will you please snap off the lights?"

Now Mr. Nash had pulled down all the classroom shades before school began so the room was immediately plunged into semi-darkness.

"Watch closely," said Mr. Nash. He snapped on the black fluorescent light. He moved the white paper he was holding into the circle of light cast by the fluorescent tube. Immediately the surface of the paper sprang alive with glowing colors in a design which Mr. Nash had painted on the paper with fluorescent paint and chalk.

"Wow!"
"Boy, is that neat!"
"How did you do that?"
"Man, is that keen!"
"Hey, that's magic!"

The children sat with open mouths and popping eyes.

"What makes it work, Mr. Nash?"

So Mr. Nash showed them how the magic light worked. "I know you want to try it," he said, "so I have hung three lights over the large tables in the room. I also have a caddy for each table with some brushes and paint and some chalk and crayons. There are piles of white paper on the shelves. See what you can do. If you paint with the invisible paints under the light, you will see what you have; but when you move it out of the circle of light, it will all disappear and you will have only white paper."

After the children were busily at work, Mr. Nash went to see if he could help Peter's committee. He suggested that they put their findings on a large chart and then join the others in experimenting with the magic light.

The next day the children studied the chart of Peter's committee. Single choices or low-count selections were eliminated from the chart. A discussion cut the list down considerably. Finally, a vote was taken to decide on the remaining three stories of their choice, and the winner was John Ciardi's *John J. Plenty and Fiddler Dan.*

Mr. Nash placed his multilevel group in five smaller groups. "I am going to ask you each to discuss this problem," he said. "How can we use the magic light to best present *John J. Plenty and Fiddler Dan* to the rest of the school at our book week assembly?" (force relationships)

At the end of fifteen minutes, Mr. Nash called the groups together and each chairman reported on the ideas from his group. They were listed on the chalkboard and finally voted upon. Almost unanimously, the class chose the idea that they present a magic scroll movie. As the story was read, a picture (really a blank paper) would roll into view and then the light would snap on and the picture would burst into color before the eyes of the audience.

The enthusiasm of the total group became a highly motivating force in getting them to plan a logical course of action. Mr. Nash made a chart of their ideas:

Plans for Making Our Magic Movie

1. Mr. Nash will read the story to us again.
2. We will form the following committees:
   script committee
   materials committee
   theater committee
   lighting committee
   scroll committee

3. The script committee will make copies of the script.
4. We will all take part.
5. Each person will draw a picture to go with his part. The scroll committee will paste the pictures in order on a roll of shelfpaper.
6. The theater committee will make a large box in which the scroll may be played, and will decorate it.
7. The lighting committee will snap the magic light on and off at the proper times and will put floodlights on the stage beforehand.
8. The materials committee will set up the speaker system and collect materials for our work periods.

The story was read and the committees met to refine their plans.

Inasmuch as Mr. Nash hoped to use dramatics a great deal during the year, he saw a "teachable moment" arise in this situation where the children could learn to write scripts. Consequently, the next day he planned a lesson for this purpose. He asked them to find reading books and grammar books with plays in them. He brought in a few books of children's plays for reference. He asked the children to note how the plays were written. They saw how a cast of characters was listed, how scenery was described, how directions were given, and how the various speakers were indicated. The children also saw how various punctuation marks were used, such as the parentheses around words explaining stage directions, the colon after the speakers' names, etc. Mr. Nash pointed out that all of them needed to know how to write a script even if they were not on the script committee because they would all have an opportunity to write scripts sometime during the year; besides, they all needed to understand how scripts were written so they could read them.

The script committee then went to work while other committees planned their work and then went on to do other things. Mr. Nash met with the script committee to help them.

As soon as the script was completed, it was read to the class. Reading parts were chosen by the children. Scenes were outlined on charts with the pictures for each scene listed under the name of the scene.

Soon each child was drawing his picture to illustrate his own particular part of the script, and the committees were meeting at planned times to carry out their duties.

Because the scroll movie was to be a large one due to the size of the audiences, the theater committee could not decide how to house the scroll so it could be rolled. When they placed their problem before the class, Darlene, whose father ran an appliance store, offered to see if she could get a large refrigerator or television shipping carton to serve the purpose. Darlene's father supplied the box, and the theater to house the scroll movie was made from it.

One day while the children were doing some choral speaking, which Mr. Nash decided to tape, Meg had an idea.

"Mr. Nash," she asked, "why couldn't we tape our parts for *John J. Plenty* and play them like a sound track along with the movie?"

The children were immediately excited over Meg's plan and one idea led to another.

"We could even add sound effects like the wind and the snow blowing outside John J.'s house," said Marge.

"How about putting in music like they do in real movies?" suggested Dick.

"Yes, that's good," Paula added. "Then we could have violin music every time Fiddler Dan comes on the scene."

"We could have a crash of cymbals to open the play," said Peter.

"Wait a minute, wait a minute," said Mr. Nash, holding up his hands in protest. "Wait until I get these ideas down. You're going so fast I can't keep up with you."

A whole new idea came forth with Meg's suggestion—new plans were made and new committees formed. On the day of the taping, signs appeared outside the classroom door which read "PLEASE, do not disturb. Taping session under way."

The children sat in a circle in order of their speaking parts. In the center of the circle were two record players and the chosen records with various musical backgrounds. Other materials were there for sound effects: a pair of cymbals to open the show, a sheet of tin to shake for thunder, a set of blocks to clamp on the table to simulate the sound of marching feet. The sound committee was well versed in fading out one record player and bringing volume up from the other. They were, for instance, playing *Pastoral* as background music for one scene, which gently faded to be replaced by the distant music of a violin (recording by Jascha Heifitz) swelling in as Fiddler Dan entered the scene.

For the occasion, Mr. Nash had borrowed a battery-operated cassette tape recorder so there would be no wires for the children to manipulate or stumble over. As one child spoke, the child next to him held the microphone, then passed it along to the next speaker. The committee in the middle of the circle provided the necessary sound effects.

The taping went well and the children were eager to hear the finished product. They could hardly wait then to put the tape and the scroll movie together. It was a triumph!

After the movie was ready, there were other things to do. The children wrote letters of thanks to people who had helped them. Mr. Nash utilized this need to teach the correct form for business letters, so people such as Darlene's father could be properly thanked.

The principal of the school was so enchanted with the magic movie that he asked the class to present it at a P.T.A. meeting during Book Week. The children felt their parents would like to know how the movie developed and all they had learned from it. So they planned an exhibit for the school foyer which contained their planning charts, copies of the letters they had written, books used, resources, etc. Two committees also gave a live demonstration of the black light.

Mr. Nash felt that he had had a very successful experience in creative problem solving with his children at the same time that he had accomplished many of his language arts objectives for the year.

This story of the magic scroll movie is an example of creative teaching. So is the "Adventure with Halibut Bones," described in Chapter 2. Why are these two verbal observations creative? Because of the importance of the creative movement in the world today and because literature exemplifies the creative products of people, the authors feel that one chapter of this book should be devoted to a discussion of creativity and what it is.

What is creativity? In the past fifteen years many strides have been made in defining it. Before that time creativity was considered to be a trait or characteristic which, like love, could not be defined or measured.

The work of researchers and the growing interest in creativity throughout the world have done much to dispel the mystery surrounding it and have resulted in some definite understandings of it. Creativity, in the space age, is a precious commodity and there is competition throughout the world for the creative minds of men.

Creativity, in this volume, is defined as *the ability to tap past experiences and come up with something new.* This product need not be new to the world, but it must be new to the individual, though highly creative acts also result in something new to the world. The product in some creative thinking is a new or creative process. Creativity can lead to a process and/or a product.

Creativity has often been defined as *the ability to see new relationships between unrelated objects* or to make the strange familiar and the familiar strange.

In order for research to be conducted in the area of creativity, it must be defined in terms of human behavior that can be observed and measured. E. Paul Torrance has such a definition.[1]

... a process of becoming sensitive to problems, deficiencies, gaps in knowledge, missing elements, disharmonies, and so on: identifying the difficulty; searching for solutions, making guesses, or formulating hypotheses about the deficiencies; testing and retesting these hypotheses and possibly modifying and retesting them; and finally communicating the results.

FIGURE 4–1. *Children generate and develop their own ideas in an original puppet show:* Marcie and the Book Worm.

---

1. E. Paul Torrance, *Torrance Tests of Creative Thinking,* Norms: Technical Manual, research ed. (Princeton: Personnel Press, 1966), p. 6.

This definition, says Torrance, "describes a natural human process. Strong human needs are involved at each stage. If we sense some incompleteness or disharmony, tension is aroused. We are uncomfortable and want to relieve the tension. Since habitual ways of behaving are inadequate, we begin trying to avoid the commonplace and obvious (but incorrect) solutions by investigating, diagnosing and manipulating, and making guesses or estimates. Until the guesses or hypotheses have been tested, modified, and retested, we are still uncomfortable. The tension is unrelieved, however, until we tell somebody of our discovery." For our purposes the simpler definition will suffice.

Concepts of Creativity

Some of the current beliefs and concepts relating to creativity differ vastly from those of a decade ago. A review of these concepts will help the reader understand some of the principles underlying the teaching strategies of the teachers mentioned above.

1. All children are born creative.
2. There is a relationship between creativity and intelligence; highly creative people are always highly intelligent, though highly intelligent people are not always creative. But all children can create to some degree.
3. Creativity is a form of giftedness that is not measured by current intelligence tests.
4. All areas of the curriculum may be used to develop creativity.
5. Creativity is a process and a product.
6. Creativity is developed by focusing on those processes of the intellect that involve divergent thinking. This area of the intellect has been greatly neglected in our teaching up to this point.
7. All creative processes cannot always be developed at one time or in one lesson. Lessons must be planned to focus on each process.
8. Creativity cannot be taught; we can only set conditions for it to happen and insure its reappearance through reinforcement.
9. More knowledge, more skills, and more facts than ever before are required for creativity to be developed.
10. The theories of creative development lead us to believe that children must be able to tap all of life's experiences in order to become truly creative; unnecessary rules and actions may force much of their experience into the preconscious or subconscious where it cannot be readily used.
11. Excessive conformity and rigidity are true enemies of creativity.
12. Children go through definite steps in the creative process.
13. Creative teaching and creative learning can be more effective than other types of teaching and learning.
14. Children who have lost much of their creativity may be helped to regain it by special methods of teaching.

A few of these statements bear elaboration, and some can be witnessed in the account of the classrooms above. Because Mr. Nash believes all children are creative, note how he organized and constructed his classroom setting so all children were allowed to contribute. Children in his classroom are comfortable; they feel free to say what they must. They also are willing to take risks, to try out new ideas. Mr. Nash did not dictate what they should do; he set conditions and then he allowed them to discover, manipulate, and explore ideas.

Both Miss Sawyer and Mr. Nash used all areas of the curriculum to develop creativity. They set conditions for creativity to happen. Children put knowledges and skills to work in new relationships. Situations presented to the children were open-ended and required new, rather than old, solutions.

Principles of Creative Teaching

If creativity cannot be taught, what can be done in the schools to promote it? Smith[2] has evolved a set of principles on which he and his colleagues have based their teaching strategies with highly creative results. The illustrations taken from regular classrooms and used in this book are teaching episodes based on these principles. We will describe them in relation to creative teaching experiences in literature. Some of the principles are readily demonstrated by the accounts in the classrooms above. Let's pull those out first:

1. *From creative teaching, some new, different, or unique results.* This new product must be new to the individual creator. The light show and the production of the scroll movie were both products new to the world—at least, the authors had never seen a production like either of them before. In both of these situations, the teachers encouraged the children to pool their ideas and to come up with new associations and inventions. The account of the adventures in literature above point up some other salient facts about creativity: that group production often results in more creative outcomes than individual creativity, although this is not always the case. A creative project such as the Apollo moon explorations could not be accomplished without the creative input of many great minds, yet the artist, poet, author, and musician often come up with highly creative products working by themselves.

2. *Creative teaching stresses divergent thought processes through open-ended problem-solving situations.* Notice, above, how a *definite* specific answer is rarely called for. Known facts and skills were constantly being used in new experiences. All ideas were heard and many were accepted and used. Notice particularly these open-ended incidents in the two situations:

1. The children in Mr. Nash's room were allowed to choose their own book. Notice, too, the clever way Mr. Nash channeled their thinking into exploring new ways to produce a play through the principle of forced relationships.
2. The children suggested ideas for the scenes—and finally related their problem to a medium somewhat new to them—the black fluorescent light.

---

2. James A. Smith, *Setting Conditions for Creative Teaching in the Elementary School* (Boston: Allyn and Bacon, 1966).

3. Note how, in exploring ideas in an open-ended discussion, the idea of using a television box for the movie theater evolved in "The Grasshopper and the Ants."
4. Also note how, through open-ended strategies, Mr. Nash led the children into composing a tape to be presented creatively as a sound track to the scroll movie.

3. *Motivational tensions are a prerequisite to the creative process.* The creative process serves as a tension-relieving agent. It is interesting to observe in both of the above illustrations that the tensions in the classroom that led directly to the creative productions were child instigated. Does this mean that Miss Sawyer and Mr. Nash teach an unplanned curriculum? Although it may appear to the casual observer that this is the case, it is not so. One of the most common misinterpretations of the British Open Classroom concept is that centers are set up and that children "discover" the materials there by chance; learning often appears to be haphazard and by happenstance. The reader must realize that every object selected for a center is chosen for a reason. Much of "discovery" happens because teachers put materials in the way of children, so to speak, to the degree that they must "discover" them or fall over them. Or teachers create situations in which children are almost forced to make discoveries or to think a certain way.

So it is with these teachers. The tension in Miss Sawyer's room came when she was quick enough to seize on the idea of a book suggested by her children as a means to accomplish some of the objectives she held about creativity. Miss Sawyer herself was being creative when she took two unrelated concepts—(1) a book on colors, and (2) a set of objectives to develop creativity in her classroom—and related them, forming a new product, which was, in this case, a strategy for teaching. From the conditions she set in her classroom came the freedom of the children to discuss and explore ideas resulting in the delightful presentation of "Hailstones and Halibut Bones."

Mr. Nash created the same kind of atmosphere for the creation of the Magic Grasshopper movie. All through the development of the project, it must be noted, subproblems of great interest to the children were introduced and solved creatively by the children. Thus, the "tension flow" of the children rises and falls as one problem is solved only to create another, which must also be solved.

Harold Rugg[3] points out that the one great characteristic of people engaged in creating is that they appear to be passionately involved and driven to solve a problem. The motivation is largely intrinsic, although a clever teacher can motivate children to create with a contrived motivational strategy, as we shall see in the case of *The Five Chinese Brothers* below.

Effective creative writing is often open-ended writing. Consequently, many of the principles of creativity developed here are present when a child is engaged in the process of reading a piece of literature. The writing itself stirs his imagination, causes him to conjure up pictures in his mind, forces him to manipulate situations and ideas, arouses his emotions, and forces

---

3. Harold Rugg, *Imagination: An Inquiry into the Sources and Conditions that Stimulate Creativity* (New York: Harper & Row, 1963), pp. 185–186.

him to project and anticipate. We might say that good children's literature develops these behaviors and consequently results in creative reading.

4. *In creative teaching, the outcomes are unpredictable.* To truly teach creatively, the teacher must have trust and faith in the children and must be willing to take risks, to be adventurous, to dare to be different. At the beginning of any really creative experience, it is impossible for the teacher to tell what the result of her lesson or experience may be. It is true that she may be able to predict some activities to a general degree, such as the fact that at the close of her lesson or at the close of a particular class experience, most of the children will write a poem or story or will participate in the production of a play or puppet show. Unlike content areas in the curriculum, however, she cannot predict the *content* of the product. If she can do this, there is a strong chance that the experience is *not* a creative one.

This fact has created a great deal of conflict in the minds of many teachers who have become influenced by the writing of behavioral objectives. On the surface, the writing of behavioral objectives appears to be a sound and sensible concept. It springs from the principle that education is the process that changes human behavior. In order to teach effectively, consequently, the teacher must search for changes in the behavior of each student. To be a good teacher, then, she must be aware of the behavior that needs changing and the type of behavior that she hopes will result after her lesson(s). If the resultant behavior is to be achieved, a system for measuring it must be included in the statement of the objective.

The concept of behavioral objectives has not been fully accepted as logical or reasonable by all educators, especially those concerned with creative teaching. Some criticisms center around such thoughts as: behavior is unpredictable in creative teaching incidents; the concept can apply *only* to cognitive, short-term learnings, which tends to recognize them as more important than affective, long-range learnings; behavior of any one child is not always interpreted alike by all teachers; the result of many lessons cannot truly be measured at the end of the lesson, but must be observed in the many days and months that follow; and writing behavioral objectives does not insure that the teacher will make teaching or learning any more relevant or creative. Other arguments used against the writing of behavioral objectives are: the behavior of the creative child is different from that of other children and these children will be judged by the norms for normals; the trend toward the open classroom means the teacher must have objectives for each individual and writing behavioral objectives for all children is impossible; objectives written for groups, however, do not allow for individual differences in children; many reliable evaluation devices are not usable in measuring the fulfillment of behavioral objectives; creativity is relegated to the background; the lower limit of acceptable performance is stated, thus depriving many children of the joy of developing their full potential; and no attention is given to the *process* of teaching.

While the writing of behavioral objectives is entirely suitable for some areas of curriculum study, this plan contributes little or nothing to the prediction or measurement of creative development in children.

5. *In creative teaching, conditions are set that make possible preconscious thinking.*

Lawrence Kubie[4] states:

> ... the creative person is one who in some manner, which today is still accidental, has retained his capacity to use his preconscious functions more freely than is true of others who may potentially be equally gifted.

Kubie defines preconscious mental processes as those having the highest degree of freedom in allegory and in figurative imagination. The contribution of preconscious processes to creativity depends upon their freedom in gathering, comparing, and reshuffling ideas. The preconscious state lies between the unconscious and the conscious. Kubie says that the essential quality of the creative person lies in his ability to allow preconscious material to readily achieve conscious expression, as against filing it away in the unconscious. He believes that the preconscious system is the essential implement of all creative activity ... "unless preconscious processes can flow freely there can be no creativity."

In terms of the classrooms above, the teachers were extremely careful to be certain that children could feel free to discuss and explore ideas. No child was ridiculed: we can see in the taped conversation that the children themselves had come to respect each other largely because they were respected by their teachers. Both teachers barred no topics for discussion. To a great degree, the children determined their own behavior by the careful plans they made. When there are few inhibitions and children are not always "on guard" not to say things to which the teacher objects, more ideas can be put before a group to be discussed. No child's contribution is considered silly or irrelevant. When a child offers a far-out idea, he is asked to explain in more detail about what he is thinking. Often his explanation throws new light on an inventive idea.

In the creative classrooms such as those planned by Miss Sawyer and Mr. Nash, both verbal and nonverbal communication is promoted and the children, like the teachers, learn to take risks, to be adventurous, to be willing to explore new experiences: this is the only path to creative production.

6. *In creative teaching, students are encouraged to generate and develop their own ideas.* In the brief excerpts taken from the total classroom experience above, we can list many examples of this principle.

- Peter served as chairman of the committee. Other committees were meeting to make plans for the movie. Children were encouraged to propose their own ideas for the entertainment.
- All children in the class were encouraged to choose their favorite piece of children's literature. This was also true in Miss Sawyer's room when it was decided to present a play.
- Mr. Nash encouraged (but did not dictate) the exploration of new ideas in order to present the play effectively. He kept the situation open-ended so the children could continue to explore their own ideas.
- Planning was carefully recorded on charts so ideas could be remembered

---

4. Lawrence S. Kubie, *Neurotic Distortion of the Creative Process* (Lawrence: University of Kansas Press, 1958), pp. 47–48.

and developed from day to day. Planning sessions were held daily so new problems could be dealt with.

- The two boys who constructed and decorated the theater from the discarded TV box used their own creative and original ideas.
- The clever and unique ideas of the group brainstorming sessions (see below) were used in the various scenes, such as the use of the glo paint to make magic, the use of Christmas tree lights for fireflies, the use of the opaque projector to develop color and shadows, the ideas formed by the different groups to show specific colors, etc.
- Mr. Nash prepared the children by teaching new and needed skills (such as script writing, business letters, etc.) so that they knew how to properly and efficiently record their ideas and use their skills in practical situations.
- Costuming the "Hailstones" play showed a great deal of ingenuity and the clever use of old materials.

It is a characteristic of highly creative people that not only are they able to solve difficult problems, but that they are also capable of identifying problems. Evidence of this ability is demonstrated in the classrooms described above.

7. *In creative teaching differences, uniqueness, individuality, and originality are stressed and rewarded.* The individual differences among people are our greatest national asset. From individuals or from groups of individuals come the many ideas that can be termed highly creative because they have changed the world: the invention of the wheel, the electric light, the steam engine, the telephone, the theory of relativity, the fight for civil rights, and on and on. No person ever became great, renowned, or famous by copying some other great person. It is only the people who dare to be different, who are willing to take risks, to be adventurous, who differ from the masses who become highly creative and influential in the life of everyone. Conformity and creativity are opposite concepts. Yet our public schools emphasize conformity in almost everything children do, even to the work exercises they do in books, the books they read, the pictures they draw. In a democratic society, individuals should count. But they won't count for much unless they remain individual. One of the problems of a modern classroom is to help children to determine when they must conform because it is for the good of the group as a whole, and when they may be individual for the group as a whole. In the studies of creative children, we find, interestingly enough, that creative children seem to be neither compulsive conformists nor nonconformists. They seem to know, almost intuitively, when to conform for the good of all and when to remain themselves.

In the classrooms of the teachers described above, the children were having many experiences in offering ideas of their own and in learning to blend those ideas into a plan. They were also learning to conform in order to help the group accomplish its goals. Progress is really nothing more than the result of cooperative problem-solving. A teacher must remember that, although developing self-actualization in children means she affords many opportunities for them to be individual, nonetheless one of the human needs of individuals is social interaction. Social actualization, then, cannot be attained in isolation: a person's work cannot be recognized as different or unique unless it is done in relation to the work of other persons. Consequently, the development of individuality does not mean children work in

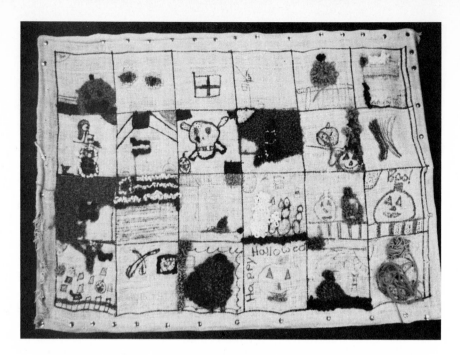

FIGURE 4–2. *The process is as important as the product: Children try their hand at making a hooked rug after reading Margaret Farquhar's* Colonial Life in America. *Each child drew and "hooked" a square for this rug.*

isolation pursuing their own interests; it means that children must learn to project, to empathize, to communicate with others, and yet maintain their own personalities and contributions to the degree that they can understand and respect the personalities and contributions of others.

8. *In creative teaching, the process is as important as the product.* In the process of creating, the children engage in real learnings. Often the process used in creating is also the product, as in the development of a process in the new math, for instance. Scholars have tried to analyze the creative process in recent years, hoping to discover certain steps they could plot and use with children, thus making possible the teaching of creative problem-solving. In these investigations many insights have been gained into the creative process.

There is no one creative process. This is perhaps due to the fact that there are many kinds of creativity and there are probably just as many processes. One book by Marksberry does indicate that in the many attempts to identify a creative process, one pattern of components tends to appear again and again. It would seem that these could best be labeled components of the creative process, and readers must remember that some processes of creating may have many more "steps" than the components recorded below.

Marksberry[5] classifies creativity into three types on the basis of the

5. Mary Lee Marksberry, *Foundation of Creativity* (New York: Harper & Row, 1963), p. 37.

object produced (the product): under the first type, unique communication, she includes creative writing and art experiences (this would include children's literature); under the second type she includes problem-solving, critical thinking, comprehension, application, analysis, and evaluation; under the third type she includes the formation of appropriate hypotheses in light of known facts and the ability to modify such hypotheses when new facts and considerations are found, the ability to make social studies generalizations, word-attack generalizations, mathematical discoveries, and science generalizations.

Marksberry feels there is enough evidence to conclude that the creative process consists of four definite stages: (1) a period of preparation (where high motivations to solve a problem creatively are established); (2) a period of incubation (where the creator is plagued and even tortured by the many facets of the problem and weighs them one against the other. This incubation period may last for a few minutes or for several years); (3) a period of insight, illumination, or inspiration (where all the pieces of the problem seem to fall into new relationship and a solution to the problem comes); and (4) a period of verification, elaboration, perfecting, and evaluation (where the creator checks the solution against the original problem to see if the problem is really solved and if the solution needs some adjustments or alterations. This stage is generally accompanied by feelings of release, self-satisfaction, and pride).

In the conversation taped in Mr. Nash's class above, we can see the children in the incubation period and also their arrival at some insights. In the final production, we can see stage (4) of the process.

9. *In creative teaching certain conditions must be set to permit creativity to develop.* We have stated that creativity cannot be taught. We can only set conditions for it to appear and encourage its reappearance through reinforcement. So important are these conditions to the development of creativity in any of the subject-matter areas that we have devoted a section of Chapter 5 to a description of those conditions necessary for creative development through the teaching of literature.

10. *In creative teaching, teaching is success, rather than failure, oriented.* No child left school on any day in the classrooms described above without experiencing success. Failures in school, if repeated too often, can destroy personality. It is true that failure may lead to creative thinking, but when the teacher uses failure experiences as a basis for creative production, they do not remain failures, for the problems are resolved and the failures are turned into successes.

11. *In creative teaching, provision is made to learn knowledge and skills, in order to apply them to new problem-solving situations.* Observe how Mr. Nash taught the children about script writing for the purpose of using their newfound skill in writing the scenes for the play. He taught them some accounting in arithmetic so they could record their expenses. New punctuation was learned to be applied to the script writing. Recording skills were learned and applied to the making of the soundtrack. Construction skills were learned and applied to the making of scenery. In creative teaching, the teaching process seems almost reversed from the traditional teaching process, for children are taught skills when they can be learned

FIGURE 4–3. *Conditions for creativity can be set by providing a variety of materials through which children can express their ideas of the literature they read.*

for a reason through direct application, not as something to be memorized and stored for future use.

12. *In creative teaching, skills of constructive criticism and evaluation are developed.* Notice how the children, in their conversations with each other, were able to build idea on idea without slighting anyone's contribution. In each classroom, the final evaluation of the work came in the children's group discussions of the scenes as they were planned, and of the final production.

13. *In creative teaching, ideas and objects are manipulated and explored.* Think for a moment of the many ideas the children suggested in either of the illustrations above. In Miss Sawyer's and Mr. Nash's rooms, they not only built idea on idea but had experience in manipulating paint, construction paper, scissors, paste, fluorescent chalk, fluorescent paint, black light, cardboard, cloth, paper bags, plastic bags, feathers, cellophane, shadows, light, string, yarn, thread and needle, tapes, tape recorders, record players, tin, musical recordings, sound recordings, and ditto materials.

Studies of creative people have shown that there is a high correlation between their creativity and the fact that they were allowed to manipulate and explore materials when they were young.

14. *A creative teacher employs democratic processes.* In these classrooms, individuals count. The children take part in planning the work and are responsible for creative output. The teacher guides, suggests, helps, and sets realistic limits.

FIGURE 4–4. *Ideas and objects are manipulated and explored: One frame of* The Five Chinese Brothers, *a transparency show.*

Children have many options from which they make choices. The greatest freedom in a democratic society is the freedom to make choices. To be creative, children need guidance and practice in making choices so they may enjoy or suffer the consequences thereof. In the above classrooms, decisions are made by the group and the children conform to the will of the group. Decision making and judgment passing are not only characteristics of democratic citizens, they are also capabilities of highly creative people.

Characteristics of Creative Teaching Situations

Two of the characteristics of creative teaching situations follow:

1. *There seems to come a time in creative teaching when the teacher withdraws as leader and the children face the unknown.* Our illustration at the beginning of the chapter begins with Mr. Nash and the class about to explore the unknown. The children, at this point, must pose the problem or begin to work on it. Often in a classroom, the teacher motivates the entire group, perhaps for the purpose of writing stories or poems, then she reaches a point where she is no longer in the foreground but becomes a guide and helper while the children begin the actual writing. In Mr. Nash's room we saw this happen when he helped the children outline the scenes for their play, teach them the skills needed for script-writing, and then turn them loose to write the scenes and make other preparations. He was also able to remain in the background while the children held discussions on production.

2. *In creative teaching, self-initiated learning seems to be encouraged.* Because the children in these classrooms were planning together and because each was making selections regarding his own particular job, each was happily busy and occupied. Children, on their own, read to find information to include in their scenes, they worked in their spare time on costumes, scenes, special effects, and they planned and suggested much of their own curriculum.

SPECIAL STRATEGIES TO DEVELOP CREATIVITY

For the past fifteen years, scholars have been experimenting with a variety of strategies to develop creative thinking among children and adults. From this experimentation, some ideas have come that may be of use in the creative teaching of literature.

Brainstorming

Brainstorming is a special technique by which creative ideas can be put quickly before a group in a limited length of time. It is most effective in a group of ten to fifteen, although it can be used effectively with larger groups under some circumstances. In brainstorming, a problem has to be limited in scope: too broad a problem generally leads to no specific solution.

In brainstorming, the following procedures are observed: the moderator poses the problem very specifically and generally sets a time limit for the session. A recorder is appointed to list the ideas as they are spoken. All ideas, no matter how foolish they may sound, are recorded. No judgment is passed on any idea until the end of the session. The moderator may encourage the flow of ideas (creative ideation) by stopping the session and asking the recorder how many ideas have thus far been recorded. He may say, "In the first ten minutes we have come up with fifty ideas. Let's see if we can double it in the next ten minutes." In order to keep similar ideas together on the recorder's list, the "hitchhiking" technique is used. If one person gives an idea that sets off a related idea in another person's mind, the latter snaps his fingers and the moderator calls on him so his hitchhiking idea will come after the one that prompted it.

After the session is closed, a committee meets and leisurely evaluates the ideas resulting from the brainstorming session. Some are immediately discarded as impractical: too expensive, etc. The rest are discussed further. A sample of the results obtained in a brainstorming session may be seen below.

Brainstorming Put to Use: The Five Chinese Brothers

This is an example of the skillful manipulation of unrelated experiences into a new product, new thought, or new experience—thus, a creative situation.

The children had decided to make a puppet show for their part of an assembly program for Book Week. Because the sixth grade was the highest grade in this particular school and all the children viewing the puppet show would be younger, Mr. Adams asked the children in his slower reading group to serve as a committee to choose the story to be dramatized —one that they had enjoyed very much and that held universal appeal. They chose *The Five Chinese Brothers* by Claire Hucket Bishop.

Now, translating *The Five Chinese Brothers* into a puppet show presents many problems different from those of presenting it as a dramatization or in some other art form. Mr. Adams identified these problems as follows, and felt that they were excellent opportunities for brainstorming practice.

1. How will we show the first Chinese brother swallowing the sea in scene 1?
2. How can we show each Chinese brother going home to say goodbye to his mother?
3. How will we show the second Chinese brother's iron neck?
4. How will we show the third Chinese brother's legs "stretching and stretching" to reach the bottom of the sea?
5. How will we show the fourth Chinese brother being burned in the fire?
6. How will we show the fifth Chinese brother being smothered? How will we push him in the oven?

"Before we begin brainstorming Problem 1," said Mr. Adams, "I'd like to remind you of a few of our rules for brainstorming. First, let's get out all ideas, even if they seem silly. Second, remember that no one can speak negatively about an idea—we will put them all down and evaluate all of them later. We will work for five minutes and then we will see what we have. Walter and Sonja will take down the ideas on the chalkboard. Walter will write down the first idea, Sonja the second, and Walter the third, and so on. Any questions? Then I'll read the problem again. Today we are exploring ways we can show how the first Chinese brother can swallow the sea. O.K. Let's go!"

Hands were already up. "Marcia?"

"We could have a square fishbowl on the stage and put scenery around it to make it look like the sea. When the first Chinese brother sucks up the sea, we could siphon off the water."

Walter wrote: 1. Square fishbowl—siphon off water.

"Good," said Mr. Adams. "Carolyn?"

"We could not use scenery at all and let the audience know what was going on by the way the Chinese brother talked," said Carolyn.

Sonja wrote: "2. No scenery." At Mr. Adams's suggestion, she added the words: "Dialogue defines scene."

Johnny added, "We could paint the sea on a curtain and when the Chinese brother slurps, the curtain could be opened and show the bottom of the sea painted on another curtain behind it."

Brian snapped his fingers. "Brian has a hitchhiking idea," said Mr. Adams. "What is it, Brian?"

"It would look more real if we painted the sea on the bottom of the curtain and let the curtain drop when the Chinese brother slurps," said Brian.

Judy was snapping her fingers excitedly.

"Now Judy has a hitchhiking idea—what is yours, Judy?"

"I think it would be better if we didn't use a curtain but a cardboard or something so all the top of the curtain wouldn't have to drop down."

Now Francie was snapping her fingers. "Yes, Francie?"

"That's a good idea, I think. We could paint the backdrop like a Chinese village by the water only instead of water we could paint dead fish and old bottles and things like you'd find under the sea. Then in the front of the stage, we could paint the sea on a cardboard like Judy says and when the Chinese brother slurps, we could drop the cardboard and the bottom of the sea would show."

Walter couldn't resist asking a question. "How would we make the sea go up and down?"

"Someone behind the stage could move the cardboard up and down," volunteered Bett.

"That might get in the way of the actors, but what about nailing the sea painting to a stick with strings on each end of it, and then someone backstage could raise and lower the string?"

"All of this sounds good," said Mr. Adams, "but let's hear from some more people."

"How about painting the sea on a transparency and throwing it on a plain background? Then when the Chinese brother slurps, we can slide the transparency down on the overhead projector and it will look like the sea going down," said Jimmy.

Connie said, "Or we could project a light from the rear and do this scene with shadows. It would be easy to lower the sea if it was only a shadow."

And so the discussion went. At the end of five minutes the children had fifteen possible ways to show the first Chinese brother swallowing the sea. No more ideas were forthcoming. Seeing the class was pleased with the ideas presented, a committee was chosen to evaluate them. The idea agreed on is shown in Figure 4–5.

Then Mr. Adams met with the committee responsible for each scene. Each committee was made acquainted with the technical and staging problems of a puppet show, and each idea was weighed for its practicability, general effect, possibility in terms of materials, expense, time, and skills that might be needed to put the idea into effect. Sometimes one idea led to another. Then each committee reported to the entire class.

The creative ideas resulting from the first of the above problems were as follows:

To show the first Chinese brother swallowing the sea, the backdrop of the scene of the puppet stage was painted from the middle to the top to represent a Chinese fishing village tucked at the base of a mountain range. From the middle down, the backdrop was painted to resemble the bottom of the sea. It was a muddy color spotted with dead fish, old bottles, the hulk of an old boat, shells, and other debris.

In the proscenium arch, the children hung a piece of heavy cardboard with strings on the sides (invisible to the audience) so that the cardboard could be slowly lowered. The cardboard was cut along the top like the choppy little waves of the sea, and the rest of the cardboard was painted to look like waves with tiny white caps.

To give the illusion of the Chinese brother swallowing the sea, the

a   b

c

FIGURE 4–5. *The first Chinese brother swallows the sea* (a). *The sea recedes, exposing the ocean bed* (b). *John and Heather show how it is done with strings* (c).

first Chinese brother appeared with the little boy of the story on a wharf painted on the backdrop. He leaned over and made a great "slurping" noise. The cardboard was gently lowered with each slurp, giving the impression that the sea was lowering as the bottom with its dead fish, shells, and wrecked ship came into view. The little boy jumped down into the sea and ran around back and forth. When it was time for the first Chinese brother to release the sea and the little boy would not come back as he promised, it was simple for the first Chinese brother to make a huge noise as though he were spitting up the sea, the cardboard was then raised until the little boy was covered, giving the illusion that he had drowned. The realism of the scene held children and adults spellbound!

Concerning the second problem, Mr. Adams pointed out to the children that the puppet stage was not very wide and that it would not seem real for the Chinese brothers to walk across the stage solely to give the impression that each was going from the city out to his mother's home in the country.

Brainstorming with the concept of reversals, the children decided they could give the illusion of the brothers walking home if they would paint all their scenery on one big long mural and put it on rollers on each side of the rear of the stage, so the scene could be rolled like a scroll movie. At one end of the mural would be the fishing village, leading to the public square of the village, then on through the village with the thinning out of houses, on to the country and eventually the mother's house would come into view. By making the Chinese brother walk in place and having the scenery slowly go by behind him, the illusion was created that he walked from the village to the country.

As to Problem 3, the iron neck of the second Chinese brother was shown simply by using a small potted meat tin can with its ends cut out and painting it to look as though it had bolts on it—somewhat like a Frankenstein effect. The can was dulled to resemble iron and every time the executioner hit the second Chinese brother with his axe, a child backstage slapped together two iron wrenches to give the sound effect of iron on iron.

To make the third Chinese brother stretch and stretch his legs, long legs were cut from cloth like pajama legs with heavy little lead feet attached to the bottoms. The tops were sewed up under a long kimono-type costume. Up the back of the puppet a long stick was fastened under the kimono-like blouse. When it came time for his legs to stretch and stretch, the feet were held to the stage, just below the level of the cardboard sea used in the first scene, and the child operating the puppet pushed the stick up and out of the puppet stage toward the audience. As he did so, the carefully folded cloth legs slowly unfolded and came down below the kimono, giving the effect of long, growing legs.

On Problem 5, the children simulated a fire by daubing red, yellow, orange, and some blue color with flo-pens on an old large square white handkerchief and cutting it in from the edges with scissors. This they fastened to the wire cage of an electric fan. When the fan was held flat just below the eye level of the audience, the pieces of silk flew up and licked the fourth Chinese brother like fire. To add to the illusion, one child stood backstage and flashed a red floodlight around the stage to give the illusion of flickering flames.

Problem 6 was solved thus: An oven was made from a flat sheet of tin with big high doors that could be opened above and behind the proscenium arch. It was put on a shallow box, the back of which was covered with cotton balls. When the fifth Chinese brother was to be smothered, the great oven doors were opened, some of the "whipped cream" cotton balls spilled out, and he dove in to have the doors close behind him. When he emerged the next morning, he had fluffs of cotton stuck to him.

The results of the brainstorming sessions that Mr. Adams held with his sixth grade gave this production a uniqueness and special quality that raised it far above the commonplace. These sessions provide an excellent example of divergent thinking processes. They also serve to demonstrate certain other principles and strategies that may be used to develop creative thinking.

FIGURE 4–6. *The principle of new uses: David created this puppet from a popcorn pan.*

Creative Ideation

In order to stretch creative thinking, the following criteria can be applied to creative products: new uses, adaptation, modification, magnification, minification, substitution, rearrangement, reversing, and combining. In his course at the University of Buffalo, Dr. Parnes[6] suggests attribute listing, forced relationships, and structure analysis.

New Uses

An uncreative person will use a bobby pin only to hold her hair in place. A creative individual will find that she can use a bobby pin to substitute for a paper clip, to serve as a crochet hook, to use as a spring or an instrument, and to pick a lock. One way to stretch the mind and make it work creatively is to subject objects to uses besides the one for which they were intended. "What are all the uses you can think of for a brick?" you might ask. The first suggestions are generally the practical ones such as: as a door stop, to build a house, as a bookend, etc. Then, as the practical ideas are used up, more unusual and creative ones appear such as: to drown a cat with, to heat and warm a bed with, to pulverize glass with.

6. Sidney J. Parnes, *Instructor's Manual for Semester Courses in Creative Problem Solving,* rev. ed. (Buffalo: Creative Education Foundation, 1963).

In the story of the Chinese brothers, brainstorming was employed to find materials for each solution to the problems posed and a committee finally decided on the materials to be used. Note the *new use* of the following materials: cardboard painted to replace the sea; the scroll movie used horizontally instead of the usual vertical position; the silk handkerchief used to represent flickering flames; cotton used to replace whipped cream.

Adaptation

Adaptation is taking something and changing it, however, slightly, to fit another purpose. It is often a low form of creativity, as when children write new words to a popular song. It can be a high level of creativity, however, as when a whole new principle is adapted to a new use, e.g., adapting skis to a small motorized vehicle to invent the snowmobile.

The principle of adaptation is illustrated in the production of the *Five Chinese Brothers* when the children change the story to fit the puppet show, and add sound effects and music to create a sound track.

Modification

Modification is changing something that exists so it looks different or serves another function. The principle of modification is exemplified in the *Five Chinese Brothers* when the children changed the costume of the third Chinese brother, modifying the legs of his pants by making them extremely long and tucking them up under the jacket so they did not show until he stretched.

Magnification

This is making something larger than it is to serve a new or different purpose. A good example of magnification is when a group of children made a Robin Hood book cover larger than ordinary so they could use it as a backdrop for a play, allowing characters to emerge from it. This is reported in Chapter 5.

Minification

Minification means making things smaller so they can be used in a creative and different way. An example of the use of minification to solve a problem occurs in Mr. Carr's classroom in Chapter 5 when the children were reminded that the stage was too small to store or move large scenery about. Viktor's idea of using a book that opened to reveal two pages, one of which was covered with print and the other with a picture that came to life, made possible the creation of five small scenes, painted on large flat pieces of cardboard, which could be placed on the picture side of each page. These small flats were easy to store: they were simply left stacked, one on top of the other, and the top one was slid off to become the bottom one to change the scene. The illusion of size was kept because the frame of the book page determined the boundaries of the scene.

Substitution

This is shown in many ways in the illustrations presented in this book. In the puppet play, cellophane and light substitute for waves; tin, pebbles, and cymbals substitute for the sounds of a storm; a TV box substitutes for a miniature puppet theater, etc. Asking the question "What materials can I substitute for this one to obtain the same or a better effect?" generally leads to some creative ideation.

Rearrangement

This means exactly what it implies: how can we change the structure, form, or parts within a product to make it more useful, more functional, or more aesthetic? For instance, Miss Sawyer displayed a creative solution to a common problem of suggesting to the children that they think of ways to present unusual effects rather than solely by a play. The result was the rearrangement of scenes so the story could effectively be presented in a colored-light show.

Reversing

Reversing is exemplified in the story of the Chinese brothers when the children made the scenery move instead of the characters to create the effect of walking along the road. Reversing is a process whereby ideas, concepts, or objects are used in reverse to produce a new product.

Having the sea drop when the Chinese brother slurped is another example of the use of the reversal technique. Rather than having the little boy get larger, the sea grew smaller.

Combining

In combining we use the principle of putting two or more ideas together to produce a new idea. Mr. Nash combined music and art media with all the subject-matter areas of the curriculum to provide situations for creative problem-solving. Creative ideation is stimulated when we ask children, "What can we put with this cone of cardboard to create a hat that will look like that worn by Milady of the Middle Ages?"

The Principle of Deferred Judgment

Even at the onset of the creative act, excessive evaluation may be construed by children as disapproval and may check the creative flow. The work of many researchers would propose that evaluation and criticism of ideas be postponed until all ideas are out. This is often called the principle of "deferred judgment."

In the illustrations above, the principle of deferred judgment is almost a necessary component of the projects because the children could not evaluate their work until each project was completed. Like all evaluation, deferred evaluation creates last minute changes and alterations in the product that make it more utilitarian, more functional, and more creative.

Attribute Listing

This is a kind of checklist procedure. The problem solver lists the various attributes of an object or an idea. Then he turns his attention specifically to each of these attributes, thinking of ways to improve or duplicate it. When Mr. Carr was ready to work on the costumes for the *Adventures of Robin Hood* (Chapter 5), he brought in several pictures of medieval life in castles, at the fairs, and on the jousting field. From these pictures the girls made generalizations about court costumes and everyday costumes. The list from the court costumes looked like this:

head covered—peaked hat with silk, or a frame draped with silk
long gown
flowing sleeves
slit sleeves
low waist line
cord around waist
rings
necklaces
open or high neck
low-heeled slippers
soft, colorful materials

When the attributes of medieval court costumes were applied to modern dress, the nearest the girls could come to it was a house coat or a caftan. There being no modern equivalent to the headgear, they set out to invent an appropriate substitute.

Forced-Relationship Technique

In this technique the teacher may place two seemingly unrelated objects before a child and say, "Put these two objects together in such a way as to make something new." In a course one of us was teaching in creative problem solving, he had his students make a list of the topics in their student teaching with which they seemed to have trouble motivating children. Three of the topics were: (1) introducing children's literature, (2) preparing interesting science quizzes, and (3) meaningful multiplication drill.

He then introduced the black light, such as Mr. Nash used in the opening part of this chapter, and the fluorescent chalk as a medium with which they were unfamiliar. After they had learned about the light and the chalk and knew how to use them, he said, "Here is a new medium and here are three problems to solve. I am going to put you into three groups and will assign each group one problem. Using the fluorescent chalk and the black light, find a solution to your problem."

The results were exciting. Mr. Nash, a student in his class at that time, came up with the idea related in the first illustration in this chapter. The other groups became enthusiastic over the suggestions that came out of their sessions.

Answers to problems can sometimes be solved creatively through forced relationships as Mr. Nash has shown us in the account of the Magic Grasshopper.

Blocks to Creativity

Studies of creativity have indicated many blocks exist that minimize creative production in a classroom. Some of them are as follows:

LACK OF KNOWLEDGE. Sometimes problems cannot be solved creatively because the creator does not have the necessary knowledge. Notice how Mr. Nash taught the children to write scripts before he expected them to write a script.

HABIT. We become hidebound and uncreative through habit and often this stands in the way of solving problems in new ways.

ATTITUDINAL BLOCKS. These are "sets" in our minds that close them to imaginative thinking. Among common attitudinal blocks are: lack of a positive outlook, conformity, reliance on authority, and lack of effort towards positive thinking or positive problem-solving.

Other Strategies

There are some other strategies which should be mentioned that seem to enhance creative problem solving. Creative evaluation is one. Another is helping children become more sensitive to problems and teaching them to state their problems specifically. Breaking down a broad problem into more specific ones serves to make the problems more manageable and better adaptable to brainstorming techniques. Allowing a problem to "incubate" over a period of time tends to bring forth more practical and more creative solutions than working on it as soon as it is presented.

A MODEL FOR CREATIVE PRODUCTION

Another marked contribution to the development of creative processes, especially in the elementary school, is the work of Frank Williams[7] at Portland State University. Williams operates on the premise that pupil-teacher interactions dealing particularly with both cognitive and affective behaviors are vitally responsible for releasing creative potential. He has purposely programmed the ongoing curriculum for developing those thinking and feeling abilities that contribute directly to the creative process. These are then measured by a combination of cognitive and affective instruments and provide scores to show each child's progress.

---

7. Frank G. Williams, *Classroom Ideas for Encouraging Thinking and Feeling* (Buffalo: D. O. K. Publishers, 1970).

Williams believes in the training and measuring of teacher competencies in the use of certain strategies that have been found to elicit most effectively those pupil behaviors which contribute to their creativeness. He feels that a measurement of teachers' understanding and performance of these strategies is necessary to discern how well they are causing creativity to take place in the classroom. Williams has developed an interaction model for teaching and learning and new assessment instruments for measuring the effective installation of this model in the classroom. He indicates that although creativity tests allow for divergent thinking, they are actually cognitive, since they are scored for how well a child can think fluently, flexibly, elaboratively, or originally. Williams has also designed guidebooks and workbooks giving specific examples of the employment of the strategies and behavior changes demanded by the use of his model. His tests include those that measure children's feelings, attitudes, and temperament factors of the affective domain. These aspects of personality are included because Williams, like many other scholars today, believes that children cannot become fully functioning, self-realized, creative individuals until all their thinking powers have been aroused and used.

Because his model is comparatively new, an evaluation of its worth at this point is premature. A great deal of success has been reported in the material published by the people who have applied the model and its concepts. The Williams model makes possible the classification of strategies and methods employed by the teacher and thus organizes them into categories for scientific study. The model has the advantage of encouraging the teacher himself to invent or create new strategies, thus teasing his own creative powers.

The Williams model bears significance here because literature is one of the areas designated as subject matter in which plans may be devised to develop creative thinking. In that sense, the Williams model supports the philosophy of this book in stating that the relationship between literature and creativity is cyclic: creative process begets creative products, which in turn beget creative thought, which in turn beget etc., etc.

SUMMARY

Literature is the product of creative people. The teacher in the modern school not only needs to know about literature and the people who write it, she needs also to know about the processes by which it is attained. She needs to understand about creativity and how children may be helped to develop their creative thinking abilities and their creative output, especially their creative writing, which is, in essence, literature.

Research in the area of creativity in the past fifteen years has provided some new concepts for the teacher. Creativity is defined as the ability to see new relationships between unrelated objects. Some misconceptions about creativity have been erased by research, namely, that it is a special talent for a chosen few, that it is highly related to intelligence, that it is developed solely through activities in the fine arts. Creativity is seen currently as a process *and* a product and has its basis in divergent thinking. Creativity, of itself, cannot be taught, though many of its components can.

Conditions can be set to help creativity appear, and blocks to creativity, such as rigid conformity, attitudinal blocks, lack of knowledge and habit, can be removed in helping creativity to develop. Creative teaching can be based on a set of principles derived from this research.

Some special methods for developing creativity have been devised. Among these are the strategies of brainstorming, creative ideation (new uses, adaptation, modification, magnification, minification, substitution, rearrangement, and reversal), deferred judgment, forced relationships, and attribute listing.

Models for teaching creatively are now in practice. Literature can be taught creatively and can also contribute to the creative development of boys and girls in the elementary school.

TO THE COLLEGE STUDENT

1. In the "Adventure with Halibut Bones" at the beginning of Chapter 2, how do you imagine the teacher was able to pull so many creative ideas from the children? How do you feel she organized her classroom so that she could have this production?

2. Select a color as the children did in the "Adventure with Halibut Bones" and write a poem about it. Share these poems with each other and then brainstorm ways to have a production—making your production as creative as possible.

3. In which of your college classes do you have instructors who plan *adventures* for you as against *experiences*? Plot some adventures for the class for which you are using this text. For example: An experience might be to read about some aspect of children's literature and report to the class. An adventure might be to take the same topic and go directly to some classroom to observe or work with children. Note especially the risk-taking involved in adventuring. Could this be a threat to some students? Could we say that risk-taking is a threat to most uncreative people? (Refer to Chapter 4.)

4. Suppose you went into a teaching situation next fall eager to try many new ideas and anxious to put into effect a program modeled to promote the philosophy in this book, only to find a completely old-fashioned, traditional library. Children are scolded continually for making any noise, shelves are beautifully kept but seldom used, the librarian has no concept of the resource center or of helping teachers; the library is *her* domain. Children are seldom found there. What could you do as a new teacher to wisely and subtly begin to change the program to make the library the core for your classroom program?

5. Think of all the ways other than a magic scroll movie to effectively produce *John J. Plenty and Fiddler Dan*.

6. Take each of the special strategies mentioned on p. 129 and show how it was applied to creatively solve a problem in contemporary society, such as: (1) magnification—doubling highways to provide greater safety with one-way traffic on each highway; (2) reversal—throwing light *up* instead of down to create a more pleasant indirect lighting.

7. Recall your own elementary school experiences. Using the principles of creative teaching described in this chapter, do you feel you ever had a creative teacher? If so, share your ideas about her with other people in your class. Why do you remember her as being particularly creative?

8. Make a list of the creative activities on campus in which college students are involved, such as dramatics, musical programs, float parades, May Day exercises, initiations, etc. How are these creative products generally obtained—by a creative or an uncreative approach to problem solving? Why are more college classrooms not operated on a more creative approach, do you suppose?

TO THE CLASSROOM TEACHER

1. Read "Hailstones and Halibut Bones" to your class and have them brainstorm ways they can create a production dramatizing each color. Instead of encouraging the children to build their production around colored light, try suggesting they do it through the use of movement and see what happens.

2. Find a list of characteristics of creative children. Make a chart by listing the characteristics in such a way that you can check each child against the chart. Using the chart, see if you can identify the creative children in your classroom. You will add interest to this project if you will give the *Torrance Tests of Creative Thinking* to the children and correlate your selections with the scores the children receive on the tests.

3. Keeping in mind the principles of creative teaching outlined in this chapter, evaluate your literature program and note the number of groups you meet each day that can honestly be termed creative in terms of teaching children's literature.

4. Observe the books your children cherish. What clues does this observation give you for creative teaching in your classroom?

5. Examine your classroom and note the stimuli you have provided for interesting children in literature. Are you doing enough? How can you do more? How can you get the children to help? Have you provided materials on many reading ability levels?

6. Have each student make a list of the books he remembers from his childhood. Make a composite and note which books were enjoyed most by the members of the class. Check your favorite books against the favorite books of children today. How well has your choice withstood the element of time?

7. Examine your daily program for the past week and notice the amount of time you spent on children's literature. Do you have a well-balanced reading program?

8. Think of all the ways to teach art through the use of children's literature.

9. Make a list of all the current television shows based on children's literature. View some and discuss them in class with the following aspects in mind:

a. Did the presentation catch the flavor of the story?
b. What justifiable changes were made for television presentation?
c. How creative was the producer in transferring the book to the television screen?
d. Do you think television programs of this sort encourage or discourage the children from reading good literature?

10. Check your own teaching with the principles of creative teaching mentioned in this chapter. What percent of your own teaching is creative, would you say? Think through ways you can gradually change your teaching strategies so that the creativity of the children is developed.

TO THE COLLEGE STUDENT
AND THE CLASSROOM TEACHER

1. From the material you have read so far in this book, show how literature can become the core of each subject-matter area of the curriculum.

2. Discuss the following statements:

a. Writing behavioral objectives enhances creative development.
b. A systems approach to teaching is an excellent way to develop creativity.
c. The "process" approach to teaching is closely affiliated with the creative approach.

d. A teacher who is short of supplies could turn this catastrophe into a very creative problem-solving situation.

3. Make a list of the logical methods you might employ to evaluate or measure creative growth.

4. A description of bibliotherapy is given in Chapter 5. Discuss this question: Is bibliotherapy a creative way of using children's literature?

5. After reading this chapter, see if you

can determine an instance at the college or adult level identifying each of the following strategies:

a. An open-ended problem
b. An incubation period
c. Deferred judgment
d. Adaptation
e. Modification
f. Magnification
g. Minification
h. Substitution
i. Reversing
j. Attribute testing

6. Experiment with the brainstorming technique as the children brainstormed problems for *The Five Chinese Brothers,* by brainstorming the following question:

a. How could you design a set to show the inside of a whale in producing a play of *Pinocchio?*

7. Brainstorm ways you can apply the principles listed in this chapter to the course for which you are reading this book, to make the teaching more creative.

SELECTED BIBLIOGRAPHY

Beechold, Henry F. *The Creative Classroom: Teaching Without Textbooks.* New York: Charles Scribner's Sons, 1971.

Bissett, Donald. "Literature in the Classroom," *Elementary English* 50 (May 1973): 729–738.

Cobb, Stanwood. *The Importance of Creativity.* New York: Scarecrow Press, 1968.

Davis, Gary, ed. *Imagination Express.* Buffalo: D. O. K. Publishers, 1974.

Eisner, Elliot. *Think with Me about Creativity: Ten Essays on Creativity.* Dansville, N.Y.: F. A. Owen, 1964.

Evans, William, ed. *The Creative Teacher.* New York: Bantam, 1971.

Getzels, Jacob W., and Philip W. Jackson. *Creativity and Intelligence: Explorations with Gifted Students.* New York: John Wiley & Sons, 1962.

Ghiselin, Brewster, ed. *The Creative Process.* New York: Mentor, 1955.

Gowan, John Curtis, George D. Demos, and E. Paul Torrance, eds. *Creativity: Its Educational Implications.* New York: John Wiley & Sons, 1967.

Guilford, J. P. "Three Faces of Intellect," *American Psychologist* 14 (1959): 469–479.

Guilford, J. P. "Factors That Aid and Hinder Creativity," *Teachers College Record* 63 (February 1962): 380–392.

Guilford, J. P. *Intelligence, Creativity and Their Educational Implications.* San Diego: R. R. Knapp, 1968.

Kneller, George. *The Art and Science of Creativity.* New York: Holt, Rinehart and Winston, 1965.

Kornbluth, Frances S. *Creativity and the Teacher.* Chicago: American Federation of Teachers, 1966.

Marksberry, Mary Lee. *Foundation of Creativity.* New York: Harper & Row, 1963.

Massialas, Byron G., and Jack Zevin. *Creative Encounters in the Classroom: Teaching and Learning Through Discovery.* New York: John Wiley & Sons, 1967.

May, Rollo. *The Courage to Create.* New York: W. W. Norton, 1975.

Michael, William, ed. *Teaching for Creative Endeavors: Bold New Venture.* Bloomington: Indiana University Press, 1968.

Miel, Alice. *Creativity in Teaching: Invitations and Instances.* Belmont, Calif.: Wadsworth, 1961.

Muenzinger, Karl F. *Contemporary Approaches to Creative Thinking.* New York: Atherton Press, 1967.

Rosner, Stanley, and Lawrence E. Abt, eds. *The Creative Experience.* New York: Grossman Publishers, 1970.

Rugg, Harold. *Imagination: An Inquiry into the Sources and Conditions That Stimulate Creativity.* New York: Harper & Row, 1963.

Shumsky, Abraham. *Creative Teaching.* New York: Appleton-Century-Crofts, 1965.

Smith, James A. *Setting Conditions for Creative Teaching in the Elementary School.* Boston: Allyn and Bacon, 1966.

Taylor, Calvin W., ed. *Creativity: Progress and Potential*. New York: McGraw-Hill, 1964.

Taylor, Calvin W., ed. *Widening Horizons in Creativity*. New York: John Wiley & Sons, 1964.

Torrance, E. Paul. *Guiding Creative Talent*. Englewood Cliffs, N.J.: Prentice-Hall, 1962.

Torrance, E. Paul. *Creativity: What Research Says to the Teacher*. Washington, D.C.: National Education Association, 1963.

Torrance, E. Paul. *Rewarding Creative Behavior*. Englewood Cliffs, N.J.: Prentice-Hall, 1965.

Torrance, E. Paul. *Encouraging Creativity in the Classroom*. Dubuque, Iowa: Wm. C. Brown, 1970.

Torrance, E. Paul, and R. E. Myers. *Creative Learning and Teaching*. New York: Dodd, Mead, 1970.

CHAPTER 5

Setting Conditions for the Teaching of Children's Literature

ROBIN HOOD RIDES AGAIN!

The children in Mr. Carr's class ranged in age from nine through twelve. The school building was old, but it contained a small kitchen, an auditorium-gymnasium combination room, and an extra classroom.

Mr. Carr believed in having his children work together as much as possible. Consequently, when a group of older boys came to school one morning full of tales of a film they had seen on television over the weekend, Mr. Carr perked up his ears, hoping he might get some clues for new reading materials and new areas of study. He did. It turned out that the film had been *Ivanhoe*, and the boys were all excited about knights and castles and tournaments.

Mr. Carr found them at noontime role-playing knights at a tournament on the playground. Many times during the day he saw them pretending to pull a knife or ride a horse. Sensing that interest ran high, Mr. Carr checked various subject guides for material on the Middle Ages.

So the children in Glenmont School were introduced the next day to *Sir Gawain and the Green Knight, The Sword and the Grail, One Is One, Sword at Sunset, Hidden Treasure at Glaston, The Adventures of Robin Hood,* and later to *Stories of King Arthur and His Knights, The Prince and the Pauper, Black Fox of Lorne, Adam of the Road, A Door in the Wall, The Sword and the Stone, The High King,* and other tales of the Middle Ages. Interest ran high among all the children, so an entire unit was developed in which the children studied life in the Middle Ages. They made booklets, went on field trips, invited guests to the school (a monk from a nearby monastery came one day to show them some early hand-painted books), gave plays, did reading research, gave reports, made charts, wrote stories and poems, and collected a small museum of materials.

One day Mr. Carr said, "We have learned a lot about the Middle Ages and why that time is important to us now. We have many fine things in our room that I would like to share before we put it all away to begin work on another unit. Do any of you feel as I do, and if you do, what ideas do you have about sharing?"

Immediately the class responded and Mr. Carr was given the idea for a worthwhile culminating activity. The children decided they would plan a large exhibit of the things they had collected and made. They felt they could have certain children talk about these artifacts and creations while dressed in costumes of the Middle Ages. Some children felt this would not be enough, and that the class should give a play to round out the evening set aside for the exhibit.

At a later meeting, the class chose *The Adventures of Robin Hood* as their favorite Middle Ages story. This classical piece of literature provided many creative experiences for the children, as we shall see below. It also helped them to pull together the concepts they had learned in their unit on the Middle Ages. The project called for correlation of all the subject-matter areas that helped the children learn and apply many new skills such as script writing, business letter writing, account keeping, new punctuation, sewing, and making scenery.

The first job at hand was to rewrite the script so they maintained the flavor of the story yet made it adaptable to production on a stage. A class discussion identified the scenes they wished to portray as follows:

Scene	*Setting*
1. Robin Hood Becomes An Outlaw	1. Outside of Robin's Castle
2. Robin Hood Meets Little John	2. Sherwood Forest
3. Robin Hood Meets Friar Tuck	3. Sherwood Forest
4. Robin Hood Meets Maid Marian	4. Sherwood Forest
5. The Marching Song	5. Sherwood Forest
6. Robin Hood Goes to the Tournament	6. Tournament Field
7. Robin Hood Marries Maid Marian	7. The Chapel
8. Robin Hood and the Sheriff of Nottingham	8. The Castle
9. Death of Robin Hood	9. Sherwood Forest

Each child in the class signed up to work on a scene. Mr. Carr made certain that each committee had at least one person who was a fluent writer and a fair speller so that this student could act as secretary to the group.

Before the class could write the scripts, Mr. Carr had a lesson on script writing, as Mr. Nash did in Chapter 4. He brought in some play scripts and some reading books with plays in them. The children searched through the reading books and examined the scripts and how they were written. They noted the manner by which the name of the speaker is set to one side and separated from his words with a colon. They noticed particularly how stage directions were shown, how characters were listed, how scenes were described. They made a chart of "stage talk," which included words such as upstage, downstage, exit, enter, aside, proscenium, flats, backdrop, flys, props, climax, plot, wings, etc. After they had discovered all these things about play writing, they wrote the opening of their play together on a chart with Mr. Carr there to help them.

The initial planning sessions for the play posed some problems for the children at once. They felt a need to tie the isolated scenes together. Here is a part of the conversation from a tape of their second planning session.

Paul: We can't just have a scene end and have everybody sitting there while we change scenery and all that stuff. We ought to have something between acts to keep the acts together.

Bruce: Maybe we could sing some of the songs we learned then, or have music playing.

Patty: We're going to sing one song we wrote in the play. I think too many songs will be tiresome.

Buddy: We ought to do something between the scenes to give the audience an idea about the next scene.

Ruth: Don't forget, we've got to change scenery between the acts.

Paul: Yeah, Mr. Carr, can we have real scenery? You know, paint some?

Mr. Carr: Well, that's up to you. I need to remind you that our stage is very small and there is not room to store or move big scenes. Perhaps we will have to use props or small scenery to *suggest* the scenes.

Gwen: Maybe we could read some from the book between the scenes. You know, we'll be in costumes and maybe we could play some record music while we read.

Ruth: Hey, Gwen, I think that's a neat idea—then we can choose stuff from the book that ties the scenes together.

Viktor: Hey, Mr. Carr—I got a better idea. As long as we can't make big scenery, why don't we make the front of a big book—then when each scene takes place, the book will open a little and the characters will come out on the stage and act the scene?
(The dialogue on the tape is interrupted at this time by the enthusiastic exclamations of the children. After a while Buddy gets the floor.)

Buddy: That's a great idea, Viktor—and listen! Why don't we have one of the little guys who can read O.K. dress as a page boy. He can come out from the book, blow his trumpet, and announce each scene or tell what happens from one scene to the next.
(Again the tape is full of exclamations of delight. Ruth's voice eventually can be heard.)

Ruth: I don't quite understand—how is the book going to open a little?

Viktor: It won't. We'll fake it!

Ruth: Well, I was wondering why we can't have it open wide and there will be a printed page and a page with a picture. The picture will be us and it will come alive when we come out on the stage. We can make small flats for that much space, and in the big scenes other people can come in on the stage from the wings.

An enthusiastic discussion followed, in which many immediate problems were creatively resolved.

The committees set to work writing the scenes the next day. After each scene was written, it was read to the entire class and suggestions were made. When necessary, the script was changed. Arnie was chosen for the page boy so he could work outside of school on the script that would tie the scenes together and plan the announcement for each.

Soon the play was ready. Mr. Carr typed it on ditto paper so all could have a copy. The cast of characters was listed on a chart and some criteria were discussed for each character. Many children wanted one specific role and when they were the only one who wanted it, they were given it. For the coveted parts, tryouts were held. Some children had to play two parts.

Letters were written home for costume materials. A windfall came when one ex-Marine father donated twelve of his old green skivvy shirts. They made wonderful tunics when used with a belt around the middle. The costume box along with feathers and materials from the junk box provided the necessary cache to make the costumes. As a base to their long gowns, the girls wore caftans or housecoats. Cones made of chipboard, rolled to fit the head and embellished with a colored silk handkerchief floating from the peak, made effective headgear.

The book front was constructed of lath covered with rolled construction paper. Buddy, the class artist, drew the cover and solicited the help of all the other children in painting it. (*See* Figure 5–1*a*.) Each scene was planned and painted by the committee that wrote the script for it. (*See* Figures 5–1*b* to 5–1*d*.) Many problems arose each day. Often new ideas were born during such discussions, as in the incident below.

"I think we ought to have a song for Robin Hood to sing as he and his merry men come on to the stage," said Jimmy.

"Right," said Bill.

The children and Mr. Carr were sitting at a planning conference.

"Mr. Carr," Tom turned to him, "could we have time this morning to work on a song?"

"How about our report period at 11:30?" asked Mr. Carr, "I think we can work it in there."

So at 11:30 Mr. Carr asked the children to meet in a circle to make up a poem for a marching song.

To determine the tempo of the lyrics and the music, Mr. Carr asked the boys to march like Robin Hood's band around the room and invited the other children to join in. Soon they were clapping the beat of the marching. As soon as they were again seated in a circle, Mr. Carr asked anyone who had an idea to write it on the chalkboard. Rhythm was clapped for the ideas and soon the following poem took shape.

THE MARCH OF ROBIN HOOD'S MEN

We are the band of Robin Hood
Marching, marching!
Each day we do our deeds of good
Marching, marching!
We take from the rich and give to the poor
We go from forest to field and to moor
We help all we can to save and to store.
Marching, marching!

a

b

c

d

FIGURE 5–1. *The cover of* The Adventures of Robin Hood (a); *in the chapel* (b); *outside the castle* (c); *in Sherwood Forest* (d).

Mr. Carr then asked some of the boys to bring in a set of tuned bells (which the class had used many times previously), and the boys on the production committee explained the problem of creating a song to the group.

Mr. Carr asked anyone who had an idea to try it out on the bells. He explained that, as the children experimented and each became satisfied with his tune, it would be recorded so they could later remember what each sounded like. He encouraged children to work for entire tunes or phrases.

Mr. Carr had placed pieces of colored tape on each bell. As each child came up with an idea that he thought was good, he was asked to make a notation on the chalkboard.

The notations were simply made—pieces of chalk, the same colors as those on the bells, were on the chalk tray, and a child who played a tune went to the chalkboard and repeated the color scheme from the bells to the chalkboard. Past experiences of the children were utilized to give the phrases proper accent and beat. The poem looked like this on the chalkboard.

Red-Red-Red-Red-Red-Red-Red-Blue
Blue-Red Blue-Red
Orange-Orange-Orange-Orange-Orange-Orange-Orange-Violet
Violet-Orange Violet-Orange
Orange-Orange-Orange-Orange-Orange
Yellow-Yellow-Yellow-Yellow-Yellow
Yellow-Yellow-Yellow-Yellow-Yellow
Green-Green-Green-Green-Green
Green-Green-Green-Green-Green
Blue-Blue-Blue-Blue-Blue
Blue-Red Blue-Red

Mr. Carr utilized every situation in which the children were highly motivated to develop new concepts and skills in music. Before the class met the next day he constructed a melody chart. He felt this chart would serve two purposes: (1) it would help the children take a step toward notating their song, showing pitch intervals; and (2) it would lead to a creative scene in the play.

Placing the melody graph (Figure 5–2) before the children, he encouraged them to transpose the color symbols of the song into note names on the scale. The children knew note values so notes were used.

The children could easily sing their melody, using the note names. Mr. Carr suggested that it might be fun to show the audience of their play how easy it is to compose songs by using the note names and showing how this particular song was composed.

In the play immediately after the scene where the marching song was sung, the book opened and a group of boys stuck their heads through the note holes and sang the marching song by singing the notes, each boy his own note. The effect was very pleasurable.

Mr. Carr did not lose sight of the fact that once the children had made the melody chart, he could easily help them to transpose the music to a scale by adding key signature, time measure, and tempo terms. The children here worked directly on music paper. After the task was accomplished, each child received a dittoed copy of the song for himself.

Needless to say, *The Adventures of Robin Hood* was a smashing success. As Mr. Carr watched the play from the audience, he felt his adventure into literature had provided a sound base for teaching many meaningful creative experiences.

Mr. Carr's project with Robin Hood was successful because he had carefully set conditions in his classroom so adventures in literature could

A Melody Graph. The March Of Robin Hood's Men.

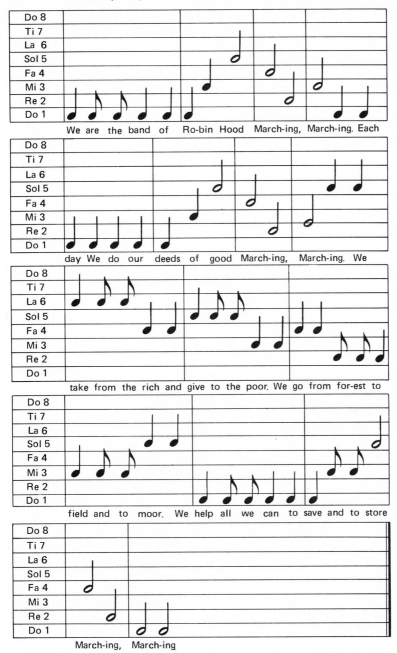

FIGURE 5–2.   *A melody graph: The march of Robin Hood's men.*

take place. These conditions may be classified as physical, social-emotional, intellectual, and psychological conditions.

CONDITIONS FOR THE CLASSROOM

The classroom must, first of all, be stimulating and respectful of literature in that there are bulletin boards, displays, paintings, realia, and other material consistently being changed to provoke the children to read and adventure in literature.

A library center is necessary and, if the situation is an open school, several library centers may be available. The classroom reading center is considered in the next chapter.

Even if there is a classroom library center, the teacher must have access to a school library and a resource center.

Teachers will need moving picture projectors, tape recorders, cassette recorders, filmstrip machines, and overhead projectors. A file of pictures from books and pictures of authors should be easily accessible somewhere. Good recordings of literature and interviews with authors are an enrichment to any literature program.

Teachers will want to survey the community to locate places for field trips. These resources are discussed in Chapter 17.

Above all, in preparing physical conditions for adventures in literature in the classroom, the teacher will need to plan for open working areas, display centers, tool repositories, and good listening conditions for the students. Listening habits need to be taught because listening is a necessary skill for each child to fully appreciate literature.

FIGURE 5–3. *This behavior indicates appreciative listening.*

Listening

As part of the regular language arts program, listening can be taught. There are four kinds of listening skills: attentive, appreciative, marginal, and analytical.[1] These special types of listening will be discussed later.

The following conditions are important to the listening program:

1. Be sure the physical conditions are properly set up. Remove all distractions that you possibly can—both noise and movement. Make sure that all chairs face the right direction so that eyestrain and uncomfortable sitting positions are erased. Place materials to be used in a prominent place and remove materials not to be used. Make sure that each child is comfortable and can see well.
2. Speak in an animated and interesting manner, as though you yourself can hardly wait to tell the children what you have to say.
3. Make sure your speaking speed does not exceed the children's listening speed.
4. Help children make up rules for good listening.
5. Help the children to understand what they have heard, much the same way you would check comprehension in a good reading lesson. Ask children such questions as: "What did Bill tell us about?" (selecting a main idea); "What was the first thing that happened to Bill?"
6. Praise the children often for good listening. When you give directions and they are carried out well, motivation for listening is enhanced when the teacher says, "Good. I am proud that you did such a good job! It shows that we all listened well!"
7. Be a good listener yourself. Teachers so often only half-listen to a child as their eyes roam around the room taking in all the other children at work. Develop the habit of looking directly at the child when he talks and respond specifically to him.
8. Avoid needless repetition, especially in giving directions. It is better to say, "Do all of you understand that?" than "Listen once more and I'll say it all over again." The child who thinks he has it correct (and most of them will) will not listen the second time. This discourages good listening.
9. Avoid needless demands of pupil attention. Instead try using interesting gimmicks and devices to gain immediate attention.
10. Allow the children to talk. Remember that most teachers talk too much!
11. Help children eliminate bad listening habits. Make a list of the poor habits you notice in your children. One teacher's list looked like this.
    a. Children are distracted by playthings on or in their desks.
    b. Children "fake" attention—they are really day-dreaming.
    c. Children interrupt with unrelated thoughts.
    d. Children look out the window or at the clock.
12. Do not place too much emphasis on regurgitative materials. To foster creative listening, seek to develop an attitude of mental alertness in children. Attitude or "set" toward listening is important. Much of the time that children are required to listen is for the purpose of reproducing what they hear. More emphasis should be placed on encouraging them to *think about* what they hear.
13. In the teaching of listening, teachers should be sure that the children realize that there are varying degrees of attention required for different

---

1. James A. Smith, *Adventures in Communication: Language Arts Methods* (Boston: Allyn and Bacon, 1973), pp. 121–135.

kinds of listening. Part of the task of the teacher is to set the mental and physical conditions necessary for listening in each new lesson throughout the school day.

Social-Emotional Conditions

There are certain social-emotional factors the teacher should maintain in the classroom for literature to be taught creatively. They were well exemplified in Mr. Carr's classroom.

- Each child must feel that he is an accepted member of a congenial group. Notice how all the children freely entered into the discussion and activity in Mr. Carr's class.
- He must feel comfortable enough to communicate freely with his teacher and his peers.
- He must feel that he has worthy alternatives from which to choose should the material being read or used in the classroom not appeal to him. Instruction should remain as individualized as possible. Mr. Carr offered the children many options from which to choose.
- There must be an "air of expectancy" about creating and adventuring. Mr. Carr acted as though he expected his children to come up with ideas, so they did.
- Uniqueness and differences in the children will be praised and valued. Many children had ideas and all were accepted.
- Children will be helped to accept the highly creative child.

Intellectual Conditions

In setting intellectual conditions for developing a love and appreciation for literature, there are a few hints a teacher might follow:

Remember that it is not only the plot that makes the story a good one; it is the way it is told. Encourage the children to use the author's words as much as possible. Be sure that the Elephant's Child does not look only for the crocodile, but also for "the great grey greasy Limpopo River all set around by fever trees." Mr. Carr's children spoke in the dialect of the times of Robin Hood.

Children can interpret the author's words only in light of their own experiences. Do not try to force your interpretation of a story on them. Let them dramatize or retell it in their own way. Although their interpretation may not be the same as yours, the retelling does give you an opportunity to correct gross misconceptions.

Enjoyment of the piece of work, not perfection of performance, should be the goal. Should some child's or some group's contribution be exceptionally well received, the class may work on it to "polish it up" for other classes or for parents. This should only happen occasionally, for polished performances take too long to prepare. Children should receive enjoyment from experiences with literature every day.

Continually draw attention to phrases or words in the writing that make it unique or give special delight: All over America children love to chant.

He meant what he said
And he said what he meant
And an elephant's faithful
One hundred percent.

and

Listen, my children, and you shall hear
Of the midnight ride of Paul Revere . . .

Phrases listed from literature are as much a part of life as learning itself. To know them is part of the children's rightful heritage.

Hold discussions that point up the literary aspects of the writing as well as the story aspects.

Plan many exciting adventures that grow out of your literature choices. Notice how the original song grew out of a need in the Robin Hood production.

Be sure that the children have developed listening skills.

Psychological Conditions

In setting conditions for the creative teaching of literature, the teacher must remember the following psychological conditions necessary to develop creativity in literature and to make possible the full enjoyment of literature.

* The child must feel secure in the classroom.
* He must be stimulated by the material read and must often have a part in selecting it.
* He must be considered as an individual as well as a group member, and valued as such.
* He must feel free to love and must feel that he is loved, that he is worthy.
* He must experience success at something every day of his school life and must have a sense of achievement.
* He must be given the opportunity to experience affective learnings as well as cognitive ones.
* The classroom situation must provide children with a permissive atmosphere; a freedom to explore, to test, and to experiment. "Silly" ideas must be accepted as creative ones, *new* solutions to problems must be sought as well as correct solutions; children must have the opportunity to share and learn from each other. Mr. Carr's classroom provided a classic example of this.
* Proper motivation and tensions must be built to agitate creative thinking.
* The teacher must value literature and also creativity, and the children must know this.

Literature has been known to have a decided psychological effect on child growth in specific cases. For this reason the area of bibliotherapy has become much discussed.

Bibliotherapy

Bibliotherapy is a technique that can best be used to help individuals adjust socially, although some teachers have had a great deal of success using this technique with groups of children. The teacher chooses a book for a child to read wherein the main characters have the same social or emotional problems as the reader. The theory is that the child will identify so closely with the main character of the story that he will live successfully through the solution of his problem. A series of books dealing with the same or similar problems eventually help the child to see that his own problem is not insurmountable.

One example of the use of such a book is the case of a fourth-grade teacher who used Eleanor Estes's *The Hundred Dresses* to help a child who was rejected by her peer group. A second-grade teacher used *And to Think That I Saw It on Mulberry Street* by Dr. Seuss for a child who had a vivid imagination that was not accepted at home. This was followed by Louis Slobodkin's *Magic Michael* and other such stories. A third-grade teacher who had an especially troublesome class read them such stories as "Bad Trouble in Miss Alcorn's Class" to give them a more objective look at their behavior.

Some objection has been raised to the deliberate use of this technique. Arbuthnot and Sutherland point out the dangers of bibliotherapy:

> There is also considerable danger in giving a child a book dealing with his particular behavior problem. In the process of growing older, a child may be confronted with pressures and problems too difficult for him to sustain or solve. As a result, he may lapse into temper tantrums or timid withdrawal or aggressiveness. To give such a child, already harassed, a story about a hero who conquers a similar fault may simply make the child more self-conscious or so resentful of the virtuous example in the book that he turns with increased fervor to the uninhibited excitement of television and the comics. A child going through one of these temporary periods of rebellion or withdrawal needs to discover books so absorbing and exciting, so alight with adventure or warmth or satisfying accomplishment, that he is heartened in his own struggle to achieve and encouraged that life is worthwhile in spite of its limitations.[2]

There is much truth in this statement. The fact remains, however, that teachers cannot control the selection of children's books at all times, nor should they, and children *may* read books that deal with their own problem anyway. Inasmuch as it is difficult to determine the effect any book may have on children, the teacher's role is that of guide and counselor: she can help the child interpret books so that they become meaningful and helpful to him and by suggestion can help him in making selections. Many children have been helped through bibliotherapy, but no teacher should ever regard it as a cure for the psychological problems of any child.

Books *can* be of great help in guiding children through emotional experiences difficult for them to understand, such as birth and death. One such book by Judith Viorst, illustrated by Erik Blegvad, deals with the death of a pet, in this case a cat named Barney. It is called *The Tenth Good Thing about Barney* and simply but beautifully presents the cycle of life in a manner that children can understand. Another book which deals effectively with death is Charlotte Zolotow and William P. Du Bois's *My Grandson Lew.*

---

2. May Hill Arbuthnot and Zena Sutherland, *Children and Books*, 4th ed. (Glenview, Ill.: Scott, Foresman, 1972), p. 16.

Children who experience emotions about which they feel guilty find solace in knowing they are not alone with these feelings.

Charlotte Zolotow's book, *When I Have a Little Girl,* is a delightful bit of rebellion against the conventional behavior expected of little girls. Every little girl must have felt the same as the heroine of this book, who seeks independence and freedom, yet is sensible enough to understand that there is a reason for all behavior. When children read this book, they empathize to the degree that it is not uncommon for them to nod their heads as they read, as if they were agreeing with everything they were reading. Knowing that other children have felt as they have gives them a sense of comfort.

General Classroom Conditions Necessary to Build an Appreciation of Literature

A teacher must work at keeping good literature before her class. Some activities employed by successful teachers are listed below:

1. Have a library corner with good books easily available as described above.
2. Keep a bulletin board of good books before the class. Discarded book jackets, posters, and pictures of favorite authors will help make these bulletin boards attractive.
3. Read a poem or story to the class at least once a day.
4. Encourage children to share the good books they have read by providing time during "sharing" periods.
5. Provide time every day for children to choose favorite books and to read silently.
6. Encourage the children to tell and write stories, poems, and books.
7. Take the class to good motion pictures of great pieces of literature or show these films in the classroom.
8. Use film strips, such as those of the Weston Woods, to create an interest in new books.
9. Use creative book reports for children to share each other's literature experiences.
10. Draw or paint pictures of favorite poems, books, or characters.
11. Encourage children to share their home libraries with the class. Ask them to bring three or four books from home and tell the others about them while they show the pictures.
12. Encourage frequent trips to the town library or the school library.
13. Reserve time occasionally for the school librarian to come into the room and show new books from the library or tell a story.
14. Encourage children to take advantage of local children's theater groups or traveling companies who do a notable adaptation of some piece of children's literature.
15. Watch the paper for good commercial television shows that portray some great children's literature.
16. Play some of the better commercial recordings of dramatizations of children's stories, such as *Hansel and Gretel, The Littlest Angel, A Christmas Carol, Peter and the Wolf.*
17. Organize a book club or a literary group that meets once a week in your classroom.
18. Children can make their own book jackets for their favorite books.
19. Make up good book lists for parents and have them dittoed to be sent home. This may be done around Thanksgiving time as a guide for parents in purchasing children's books for Christmas gifts.

20. Watch for radio programs that dramatize children's literature.
21. In art class, have the children make posters of books they like. When made in three dimensions, these posters add interest to book exhibits, library displays, and bulletin board exhibits.
22. Devote a few assemblies each year to programs about books. If each grade would take responsibility for putting on one assembly program during the year to which other classes were invited, the children would be constantly exposed to books on all reading levels and all topics.
23. Celebrate Book Week with assemblies, exhibits, visits from authors, library trips, story hours, displays, and special programs. Be sure all children have a part in preparing for Book Week. (Many ideas for Book Week programs may be found on the following pages.)
24. Hold at least one or two Book Fairs a year where the materials made by the children may be exhibited.
25. Correlate literature with all your classroom work. In social studies, read great books to help children understand the life of any given country. *Heidi* correlates well with a study of Switzerland, *The Secret Garden* with England. Kipling's stories relate well to India, and *The White Stag* is perfect reading when studying the history of countries of central Europe. Many books provide excellent material for dealing with social problems (*see* Chapter 15).
26. In grammar classes, styles of writing may be studied by reading from various authors. Much literature has been set to music, such as *The Lord's Prayer, The Owl and the Pussycat, Little Boy Blue, A Nautical Ballad, Cradle Hymn, The Nutcracker*. Others that are part of the children's rightful heritage are *A Visit From Saint Nicholas*, nursery rhymes, and folk ballads of the West, the mountains, and the plains. Music and literature can be closely correlated by singing some of the great poems set to music or by hearing them sung by great artists on high fidelity recordings. Every aspect of the school curriculum may be correlated with some great children's story or poem.
27. Art work is a close companion to literature. Some correlations in art have already been suggested, and others include the following:
    a. Use cut-out illustrations for children's favorite selections.
    b. Use crayon sketches.
    c. Use block print designs for posters and for covers for Book Week programs.
    d. Have the children fingerpaint pictures of the literature they read.
    e. Spatter paint designs can be used as variety in illustration.
    f. Make silhouette designs of favorite scenes from their readings.
    g. Colored chalk lends variety to illustrations, especially in covering large surfaces such as murals or backdrops for scenes.
    h. Favorite characters can be depicted with soap carvings.
    i. Sand-table scenes of favorite stories may be constructed.
    j. Wood models may also be constructed.
    k. Dolls may be dressed to represent storybook characters (real and paper dolls).
    l. Prints (potato prints, cork prints, and linoleum prints) may be used to make book covers, program covers, and invitations to Book Week programs.
28. Set up a listening post in your classroom or resource center if convenient. Provide earphones so children may enjoy literature from readings and cassette tapes by themselves. Cassettes on visits with authors should be included.
29. Study the techniques of various illustrators of children's books through discussions, bulletin board displays, and recordings.

SUMMARY

In order for literature to be taught effectively and creatively, certain physical, social-emotional, psychological, and intellectual conditions need to be developed in the classroom. Special attention should be focused on helping children develop their listening abilities; listening is a much-needed skill in adventuring with literature.

Literature sometimes serves to help children with specific social-emotional problems, but must be used for this purpose with care and by an understanding teacher.

The most vital element in promoting a literature program is a good school library and a classroom center library, both of which will be discussed in Chapter 16.

TO THE COLLEGE STUDENT

1. Identify instances in your college classes where each type of listening indicated on p. 147 is used. Into which category would you place each of the following:
a. Listening to a lecture to identify the types of listening
b. Watching a television tape that demonstrates the four types of listening
c. Listening to a child make a book report
d. Listening to the librarian read a poem
e. Listening to a teacher explain the use of a card catalogue
f. Watching a Weston Woods film on *Mike Mulligan and the Steam Shovel*
g. Listening to a recording of *The Adventures of Robin Hood*
h. Listening to a child read his own story

2. Select an idea from the list of general suggestions for using literature in Chapter 5, and use it to present a report in your college class or before your faculty. Determine whether this type of presentation is as effective at your age level as a verbal report or a written one.

3. Plot the ideal college classroom for teaching children's literature creatively and with relevancy to you as a college student.

4. Do you feel that bibliotherapy can be used on adults? Would it, for instance, be effective with you? Have you ever read a book that gave you a great deal of comfort? Changed your outlook? Refreshed your viewpoint? Helped eliminate a problem? If you have, list a few and share them in a discussion with each other.

5. Read *The Tenth Good Thing About Barney* together in class and share your reactions. Then discuss this statement: Books of this nature help children understand the unknown by giving them a fresh viewpoint. Find other books that accomplish this goal and share them in class.

TO THE CLASSROOM TEACHER

1. Evaluate your classroom in terms of what you have read in this chapter: Have you set conditions for a creative program in children's literature? What is lacking? One teacher recently said to us, "I couldn't get through the day without reading something beautiful to my children! And how it pays off! The beautiful things they write provide us with so many hours of pleasure that the time I spend in preparation for our literature periods together is amply repaid." How do you feel about this?

2. Keep a list on your desk next week of all the opportunities available in your environment to plan some adventures in literature. Start with your room, then consider the library, the learning resource center, the museums in town, the moving pictures, television shows, and the artifacts

handy in old homes and stores.

3. How might you use each of the following to motivate children to a worthy piece of literature? An umbrella, a balloon, a white rabbit, a top hat, a cane, a silver spoon, a cocked hat, a stuffed monkey, a large egg, a fishpole? Think of more than one way for each item.

4. How could you plan a creative book fair?

TO THE COLLEGE STUDENT AND THE CLASSROOM TEACHER

1. List all the ways that Mr. Carr's lesson developed creativity in the children and followed the principles of creative teaching. (See Chapter 5.)

2. Make a card file of new books that may be used for bibliotherapy. Explore the writings of Judy Blume, a comparatively new author in this field. Such books as *Are You There God? It's Me, Margaret, Then Again, Maybe I Won't,* and *It's Not the End of the World* deal with religion and puberty, growing up and divorce. Read these books and others, and decide whether you would recommend them to children engrossed in these problems.

3. In the open-classroom concept, the room is set up in centers that become places where children can engage in self-learning and can also receive a great deal of individual help from their teachers. Design such a center for literature and reading.

4. Think through the objectives Mr. Carr hoped to accomplish with his project on Robin Hood. Do you think he met these objectives? Do not forget such social objectives as developing responsibility in the children, teaching skills of independent study, and the like.

5. From the story at the beginning of this chapter, do you get a feel for the environment Mr. Carr had set up in his classroom so learning could take place? What were some of the materials included? How do you think the furniture in this classroom was arranged?

SELECTED BIBLIOGRAPHY

Barlow, Mildred. *Human Relations in the Primary Grades*. National Conference of Christians and Jews, n.d.

Beechold, Henry F. *The Creative Classroom: Teaching without Textbooks*. New York: Charles Scribner's Sons, 1971.

Borten, Helen. *Do You Hear What I Hear?* New York: Abelard-Schuman, 1960.

Carlson, Ruth Kearney. *Literature for Children: Enrichment Ideas*. Dubuque, Iowa: Wm. C. Brown, 1970.

Dale, Edgar. "Education for Creativity," *Newsletter* 3 (December 1964).

Edmonds, Edith. "Matching Books to a Child's Need," *Instructor* 82 (October 1972): 160–164.

Evans, William, ed. *The Creative Teacher*. New York: Bantam, 1971.

Fenner, Phyllis, ed. *Something Shared: Children and Books*. New York: Day, 1959.

Getzels, Jacob W., and Philip W. Jackson. *Creativity and Intelligence: Explorations with Gifted Students*. New York: John Wiley & Sons, 1962.

Gordon, W. J. J. "On Being Explicit about Creative Process," *Journal of Creative Behavior* 6 (1972), 295–300.

Gowan, John, and George Demos. *Creativity: Its Educational Implications*. San Diego: R. R. Knapp, 1968.

Homze, Alma. "Interpersonal Relations in Children's Literature, 1920–1960," *Elementary English* 43 (January 1966).

Kircher, Clara J., comp. *Behavior Patterns in Children's Books: A Bibliography*. Washington, D.C.: Catholic University Press, 1966.

Kneller, George. *The Art and Science of Creativity*. New York: Holt, Rinehart and Winston, 1965.

Kohl, Herbert R. *The Open Classroom*. New York: Random House, 1970.

Krumboltz, John, and Helen Krumboltz. *Changing Children's Behavior*. Englewood Cliffs, N.J.: Prentice-Hall, 1972.

Mandel, R. L. "Children's Books: Mirrors of Social Development," *Elementary School Journal* 64 (January 1964): 190–199.

Mars, David. *Organizational Climate for Creativity*. Buffalo: Creative Education Foundation, 1969.

Massialas, B. G., and Jack Zevin. *Creative Encounters in the Classroom: Teaching and Learning Through Discovery*. New York: John Wiley & Sons, 1967.

Newell, G. "At the North End of Pooh: A Study of Bibliotherapy," *Elementary English* 34 (January 1957): 22–25.

Rosner, Stanley, and Lawrence E. Abt, eds. *The Creative Experience*. New York: Grossman, 1970.

Saunders, Jacqueline. "Psychological Significance of Children's Literature," in *A Critical Approach to Children's Literature*. Edited by Sara Innis Fenwick. Chicago: University of Chicago Press, 1967.

Smith, James A. *Setting Conditions for Creative Teaching in the Elementary School*. Boston: Allyn and Bacon, 1966.

Smith, James A. *Adventures in Communication*. Boston: Allyn and Bacon, 1972.

Taylor, Calvin W., ed. *Widening Horizons in Creativity*. New York: John Wiley & Sons, 1964.

Torrance, E. Paul. *Encouraging Creativity in the Classroom*. Dubuque, Iowa: Wm. C. Brown, 1970.

PART II

People Who Create
Children's Literature

CHAPTER 6

Classical Authors:
A Reference for the Teacher

I like books that remain faithful to the very essence of art; namely, those that offer to children an intuitive and direct way of knowledge, a simple beauty capable of being perceived immediately, arousing in their souls a vibration which will endure all their lives. And books that awaken in them not maudlin sentimentality, but sensibility; that enable them to share in great human emotions; that give them respect for universal life—that of animals, of plants; that teach them not to despise everything that is mysterious in creation and in man . . . I like them especially when they distill from all the different kinds of knowledge the most difficult and the most necessary—that of the human heart.[1]

A classic has been referred to in this volume as a book that has universal appeal and has survived the test of time. Classics belong to the past, the present, and the future. Of course, a classic is not born a classic. It earns its place by its enduring popularity due to the enjoyment it gives the reader. Consequently, there are modern books that will be classics of tomorrow. An example is E. B. White's *Charlotte's Web,* published in 1953 and recently made into a motion picture, which gives every indication of becoming a modern-day classic. When judging any book, old or new, apply the criteria for excellence discussed in Chapter 3, rather than revering a book because it is old or because it is a "reputed" classic.

Despite the criteria for universality, no one child or adult can like

---

1. Paul Hazard, *Books, Children and Men* (Boston: Horn Book, 1960), pp. 42–43.

every book that is considered a classic. By the same token, two lists of children's classics by different authorities will by no means contain the same entries. Reading tastes are subjective. Consequently, it is important that no one *impose* a so-called classic upon an unwilling child, lest it have devastating effects on his attitudes towards reading. It is all too easy for an eager teacher or parent to assume that because he has fond memories of a book read in his youth, the same book will be, or ought to be, gobbled up by his children. Often the adult is moved by a nostalgic drive to return to the innocent idyls of his own childhood, and consequently recommends a classic to a child who has no reading taste for that particular selection.

The classics are divided into genres or types, as are all books. We are talking here about books of fiction with stories that are "made up" as children are wont to say. The list of classics discussed in this chapter fall into four genres: (1) fantasy, (2) fairy tales, (3) adventures, and (4) realistic fiction. A child will enjoy one classic because he prefers fantasy and will reject another because he does not like realistic fiction. Young readers often get stuck in reading only one genre: all fantasies, all mysteries, all fairy tales. Children usually grow out of this one-type-of-book period. We find few young readers have developed catholic tastes at an early age.

If a child enjoys a good adventure story, and it is difficult to find one who does not, a book like *Treasure Island* reveals a realm of experience totally different from the humdrum of everyday living. Such a book contributes to the child a world bigger than his own environment. At the same time, while reading of young Jim Hawkins's experiences and the level-headed manner in which he conducts himself, the child is offered a vicarious sense of confidence, finding pleasure in thinking that he too would handle himself in much the same way. Almost all adventures consist of a character about the age of the reader, maybe a bit older, who functions admirably in a hostile world. The child of Western culture is conditioned to be essentially helpless, dependent upon his parents and other adults. Adventures offer the compensation that the reader, if ever offered the opportunity, also has the power to control his situation.

While adventure stories temper the child's outlook upon the world and reinforce his confidence, fantasies help to develop the inner world of the child's imagination. Childhood is the most imaginative period of one's life. Adults often lose sight of the fact that children have yet to form a comprehensive picture of the world; a child's familiarity is at first concerned only with his small world of family, school, and friends. Life is such a novelty that the young child is still not quite aware of what is possible and what is not possible. Fantasy offers an extension of a child's life often combined with humor, and every child loves to laugh. A successful fantasy requires certain realistic elements to save the story from becoming boringly nonsensical. A good example of fantasy is Kenneth Grahame's *The Wind in the Willows,* which depicts animals behaving as idiosyncratically as humans. The beautiful characterizations heighten the quality of genius in this favorite fantasy.

Fairy tales, such as those of Hans Christian Andersen and the Brothers Grimm, present a child with the magic that fascinates children, for the child still half-believes that anything magical is possible. Fairy tales portray a world where evil is punished and goodness eventually triumphs.

The child can empathize with *The Ugly Duckling* and *The Steadfast Tin Soldier.* Children are quick to note hypocrisy in adults, so humorously told in *The Emperor's New Clothes.* Fantasies offer simple plots with themes that fulfill the child's emotional needs.

Realism in literature, exemplified by Mark Twain's *The Adventures of Tom Sawyer* and *The Adventures of Huckleberry Finn* and by Louisa May Alcott's *Little Women,* is a source of satisfying reading because these books show real-life boys and girls as they truly are, not as stereotypes of good, evil, vice, and virtue. Many children are literal and reject literature that does not show life and people realistically. In Twain's books, humor is an important ingredient, which delights the child. In *Little Women,* a child gets a feeling of family solidarity and security, and the story is honestly told with the ups and downs that all families experience.

Since the field of children's literature is relatively young, and it was not until the late eighteenth and nineteenth centuries that authors wrote expressly for children, many of the classics now listed for children were actually written for adults. Since children had no books of their own, they adopted these books. Examples are *Gulliver's Travels* and *Robinson Crusoe.* The reverse is now true. Many children's classics are also listed as adult reading, e.g., *Sounder* by William Armstrong.

The classics are books that create a special world, one so unique that it lives in the mind of the reader forever. It may be the scene one remembers, such as Rat rowing peacefully down the river while extolling the pleasures of boating in *The Wind in the Willows,* or the setting of the clean air and beautiful flowers on the mountains in *Heidi.* It may be the characters who create a special world in one's memory, for instance Tom Sawyer, Pinocchio, or Winnie-the-Pooh.

When children enjoy a book, they often read it over and over. Soon they begin to search for other books by the same author. Their interest in authors may reach the level of the group described in Chapter 12. Because of the strong interest in an author, Mrs. Galvin was able to develop an entire unit around Lois Lenski and her work. From a pedagogical standpoint alone, teachers should be acquainted with the classics and their authors when children become curious about them.

We are aware of the many well-written and informative biographies about authors of children's books. We also know that the type of teacher using this volume will need information quickly with little time for research, so thumbnail sketches of many authors of the classics are given here. It is hoped that their inclusion not only will be a convenience but will whet the appetites of college students and teachers in training so they will want to learn more about the people who have created the masterpieces.

Obviously, not all authors of children's classics can be included in one chapter. Those that are included have created the *milestones.* In some way they have made an especially significant contribution to the development of children's literature.

Lewis Carroll's *Alice in Wonderland,* for instance, represented the early departure in writing from Victorian didacticism and was the first fantasy created solely for the purpose of entertaining children. Mark Twain and Louisa May Alcott are significant because they introduced the entire realm of realistic literature. Robert Louis Stevenson wrote adventure stories that made no attempt to preach, as stories were suppose to do at that time.

FIGURE 6–1. *Jim made a pocket chart* Story of Robinson Crusoe, *by Daniel Defoe, for a book report.*

Each milestone provided a new concept in children's literature: a turnstile to a new path for exploration.

Daniel Defoe (c. 1660–1731)

Daniel Defoe's *The Life and Strange Surprising Adventures of Robinson Crusoe of York, Mariner* is considered the protean adventure story of the English language. Written in 1719, it was originally intended for adults. Like many other children's classics, however, *Robinson Crusoe* was subsequently discovered by children. Until this time, whatever books were available to children tended to be merely instructional or heavily moralistic. Thus, within four months of Robinson Crusoe's first publication, an unauthorized abridged edition was available to children and soon became extremely popular. Interestingly, *Robinson Crusoe* is now regarded as a children's classic, although it is still enjoyed by adults.

Daniel Defoe, who changed his name from Foe at the age of forty-three, was born about 1660, the son of a London butcher and candlemaker. Like many other intelligent men of his time, he entered the church; but, also like many others, he later found church life unsuitable, embarking upon a series of careers. Defoe became a successful merchant and later was an adventurer himself, traveling to Portugal and Spain.[2]

He subsequently turned to newspaper journalism and novel writing, contributing greatly to the novel as a literary form. Defoe was a social reformer vitally concerned with politics and religion. So controversial were

2. Brian Doyle, ed., *The Who's Who of Children's Literature* (New York: Schocken Books, 1969), p. 72.

his pamphlets that he was tried in court and imprisoned. Topics of concern to Defoe included the construction of insane asylums, the building of better roads, and the organization of schools for women.

Upon his release from prison, Defoe wrote his first novel, *Robinson Crusoe,* and later that same year he wrote a sequel, *The Farther Adventures of Robinson Crusoe.* He wrote these imaginative fictional yarns so realistically, presenting them as actual, authentic accounts, that readers believed them to be true. All his romantic novels contain a plethora of minute, convincing details. Defoe based his plot partially on the life story of a Scottish sailor, Alexander Selkirk, who was shipwrecked on a desert island for four years. Selkirk not only told his story to Defoe, but also gave him his papers. *Robinson Crusoe* recounts how a man ingeniously survives on a desolate island, making clothes, raising his food, building his home, and making life comfortable. Crusoe rescues a man from his fellow cannibals, naming him Friday after the day of his discovery. Friday becomes more than the sailor's trusted servant; he becomes a friend. Thus, the term "Man Friday" means someone who is more than a servant, a symbol of loyalty.

Not only did this book become important in the development of the novel, but it also became the pattern for similar romantic adventures of castaways on desert islands, giving us the French term *robinsonnade.* Among the many novels Defoe wrote, his other popular ones are *Moll Flanders* and *A Journal of the Plague Year,* generally read by adults. But neither of these achieved the fame of *Robinson Crusoe,* a book that satisfies children's need for excitement and their hunger to achieve self-reliance.

Jonathan Swift (1667–1745)

Jonathan Swift was one of the world's greatest satirists; his writings, although they contain bitter irony, are full of humor and charm. His most famous book is *Gulliver's Travels,* a tale of adventure and fantasy.

Swift was born on November 30, 1667, in Dublin, Ireland, of English parents. Because his father died before he was born, his mother was poor. Luckily for Swift, the family had well-to-do relatives who paid for his education at Trinity College, Dublin. Later Swift received a degree from Oxford University in England. When he returned to Ireland to a town near Belfast, he became a clergyman in the Church of Ireland, the Irish counterpart of the established Church of England. Swift developed ties with both Ireland and England, and for the rest of his active life, he divided his time traveling back and forth. In 1713, he was appointed Dean of Saint Patrick's Cathedral in Dublin, but it remained a constant disappointment to him that he was never made a bishop of the church, a position he greatly coveted. As years passed, this made the misanthrope more bitter.

Like Defoe, he was a pamphleteer, also writing on social, religious, and political subjects, probably the most prolific writer of his era. In one pamphlet called *A Modest Proposal,* Swift suggested that Irish children should be sold or eaten by their parents, thereby limiting the size of the rapidly growing Irish population (the population explosion was a concern then too). He was making the bitter point that it would be kinder to eat one's children than to raise them ignorant, hungry, and poverty-stricken. Considering Swift's background, his interests, and his personality, it is not

FIGURE 6–2. Children simulate the capture scene of Gulliver's Travels with finger puppets and one large paper bag puppet.

surprising that he finally turned to writing *Gulliver's Travels,* a satire on the human race, pointing out its follies and stupidities. Also satirized is the foolishness of the English court, its government officials and statesmen. It is interesting that Swift did not publish *Gulliver's Travels* immediately after writing it, and when he did, he used an anonymous name: Dr. Lemuel Gulliver. Apparently he worried that the satire was explosive subject matter.

Amusingly, we can note that this satire was so disguised by humor and inventiveness that London society warmly received the book, undoubtedly to Swift's relief. It is said that many of the British statesmen who were lampooned did not even recognize themselves until years later, and so it was that the same period that produced *Robinson Crusoe* brought another unusual book, one also written for adults but eventually taken over by children. This satire, now listed as a classic for children and adults, can be enjoyed on two levels: first, a fantasy of fun for children who are unaware of any double meaning; and second, a spoof on mankind, an entertainment for adults.

First published in 1726, this book has been abridged and adapted for children. Only Parts I and II are considered suitable for children, the other parts involving excessive political discourse. Modern adaptations have been included in many children's anthologies and have been translated into virtually all major languages. The book has attracted the skills of prestigious illustrators such as Charles E. Brock, Fritz Eichenberg, and the most famous, Arthur Rackham.

Why do children still love *Gulliver's Travels*? It tells a wonderful, fascinating story. In Part I Gulliver, writing in the first person singular, tells of his shipwreck, his being the sole survivor, and how he swims ashore to Lilliput where the people are only six inches high. Children love the details of the lives of the comic Lilliputians and all the humorous situations in which Gulliver finds himself. In Part II Gulliver journeys to the land of the giants, Brobdingnag, where his situation is reversed and he, a man, becomes a toy. Swift put together all the ingredients of a good adventure, including exciting action and unforgettable characters, told with rollicking high humor. Unfortunately, Swift spent the last years of his life bitter, unhealthy, and at times insane. He died in Dublin on October 19, 1745, but left a memorable legacy for the children of the world.

Johann David Wyss (1743–1818), *Johann Rudolf Wyss* (1781–1830)

Wyss (pronounced *Vees*) is the surname of a family of a Swiss minister and army chaplain and his sons, who together produced *The Swiss Family Robinson*.

The father was Johann David Wyss, born in 1743 in Berne, Switzerland. The clergyman did not start this story with publication in mind; it was merely a narrative told to his four sons for their enjoyment and moral instruction and was continued each night. The pastor-father was greatly influenced by Defoe's *Robinson Crusoe*, whose story and style he admired. Therefore, this adventure fits into the previously mentioned *robinsonnade* pattern of the sea, a shipwreck, an island, and man versus nature, beasts, savages—man's ability to survive by his own ingenuity. The entire Wyss family enjoyed reading and telling each other variations of the Robinson Crusoe motif, imagining themselves shipwrecked on an isolated desert island and giving an account of what each would do under such circumstances.

The father Johann David decided to write these stories as the family made them up, while his son Johann Emmanuel drew illustrations with watercolors. Years later Johann Rudolf took his father's manuscript of *Swiss Family Robinson*, revised and edited it, and gave it to a Swiss publisher. Johann Rudolf was a professor of philosophy and theology at the Berne Academy.

The basis of the actual story of *The Swiss Family Robinson* was the supposedly true account of a sea captain who found a Swiss minister and his family who had actually been shipwrecked on an island in the South

Pacific. The book was published in two parts, the first in 1812, the second in 1813, under the complete title *The Swiss Family Robinson or Adventures on a Desert Island*. It was first published in German, translated into French in 1814, then into English, and since then into virtually all major languages. When the story was published in French, it was lengthened with permission of the son. (The father, Johann David Wyss, had died in 1818.) There have been three well-known English editions; perhaps the best of these was edited in 1879 by William H. G. Kingston, now beautifully illustrated by Lynd Ward.

The story tells of a Swiss pastor, his wife, and their four young sons, their adventures and discoveries after they were shipwrecked on a tropical island. It is claimed that over three hundred versions have been published in the English-speaking world. Children love the daily accounts of the family's good and bad fortunes, their endeavors to make a civilized life, eventually naming their home New Switzerland. Modern scientists find many errors in the frequent and lengthy but interesting explanations of natural history, geography, flora, fauna, and other scientific discussions.[3] Pastor Robinson takes every opportunity to give scientific lectures to his children, not neglecting religious instruction. However, it is not so moralistic or didactic that modern children find it dull or boring. In fact, it is the sort of book that even today's college students, scientifically knowledgeable, have told us they still enjoy rereading after five times.

Johann Rudolf Wyss also copied Swiss folk songs and legends, and he wrote "My Country Calls," the Swiss National anthem. He died in Berne in 1830, but *Swiss Family Robinson* has been copied and sequels written. Some are rather good; some are inferior and cheap imitations. It is interesting that the great Jules Verne wrote a long sequel that appeared in France, entitled *Second Fatherland*, which was translated into English in the same year (1900). Thus generations of readers, young and old, still thrill to what has often been called the perfect desert island story. Each reader likes to think of the Swiss family as still living in New Switzerland, the same Robinson family of Pastor Wyss who told stories around the fireside to amuse his own children so many years ago.

The Brothers Grimm: Jacob Ludwig Karl Grimm (1785–1863)
Wilhelm Karl Grimm (1786–1859)

The Brothers Grimm can be considered among the first to have taken a scholarly approach toward the sources of folklore.

Born in Hanau, Hesse (Germany), the brothers lived a rather impoverished youth due to the early death of their lawyer father. Nevertheless, they were enabled to attend the University of Marburg through the help of an aunt. Both studied law; Jacob, however, chose to remain at the university as an assistant to one of his professors. At one point he traveled to Paris to become Jerome Bonaparte's personal librarian. For all of their lives, however, the two brothers were virtually inseparable. When Wilhelm married, Jacob moved into his house. They spent most of their lives in universities, living and teaching at the University of Gottingen and later

---

3. *Ibid.*, p. 298.

at the University of Berlin. Early in their university lives, they developed a love of medieval German literature and philosophy.

Jacob Grimm, perhaps one of the first real linguists, developed "Grimm's Law," which illustrates the correlation between certain Germanic consonants and early Indo-European consonants. His *History of the German Language* (1848) contributed greatly to the emergence of comparative linguistics as a science.

The early nineteenth century was a time of great turmoil for the loosely organized German states; nationalism, therefore, became something of an obsession. The Brothers Grimm, through their travels around the German countryside, contributed greatly to this growing sense of national pride. In their attempt to study native dialects, the brothers hoped to capture an all-pervasive *volk* spirit that would transcend mere political boundaries.

As Christina Kamenetsky points out in "The Brothers Grimm: Folktale Style and Romantic Theories":

> With many other German Romantic writers the Brothers Grimm shared a deep concern for the sources of German folkdom. In their nation's cultural heritage they searched for a time when man had still lived in unity with God and nature. When they spoke about the child, they usually thought of it not so much in realistic terms as a potential reading audience, but rather as a symbol of innocence, purity, and naivety, which corresponds to their concept of the "childhood" of the nation . . . as genuine students of Romanticism, they did not analyze and dissect the folktale style, but they absorbed its melody and rhythm, hoping to affect again the heart and soul of the nation.[4]

Therefore, the published folktales of the brothers were the coalescence of the effects of both the Romantic movement in literature and the rise of German nationalism. In looking at the publication dates of the brothers' first two volumes of *Nursery and Household Tales*, one sees the significance of the political events that were occurring. The first volume of tales was published in 1812, that famous winter of Napoleon's retreat from Moscow. The second volume was published in 1815, the year of the Battle of Waterloo. The armies of Napoleon had invaded Kassel. The brothers wrote that "while foreign persons, foreign manners, and a foreign, loudly spoken language" were seen and heard, "poor people staggered along the streets, being led to death," but the brothers stuck to their work tables, to reconstruct the present through the past.[5] The political atmosphere encouraged the two scholars to escape the horrible life by writing about better times and pleasanter events. They hoped that the results of their studies of Old German would ease their depression and also give them hope that the fruition of their labors would contribute to a brighter future for their country. How little did these brothers dream what a milestone they were creating, not only for their country, but for children and adults all around the world! Translations of the tales came almost immediately in Dutch,

---

4. Christina Kamenetsky, "The Brothers Grimm: Folktale Style and Romantic Theories," *Elementary English* 51:3 (March 1974): 381.
5. *The Complete Grimm's Fairy Tales,* revised by James Stern (New York: Pantheon Books, 1974), p. 836.

English, Polish, Russian, Hebrew, Armenian, and many other languages. And so the brothers worked quietly alone from 1812 until 1857, proceeding slowly, but continuing their research.

The major purpose of the Grimms' work was a linguistic research into the origins of German folktales as told orally from generation to generation. The tales were gathered and transcribed as they were told to the brothers by friends, relatives, and simple folks from farms and villages. They also studied medieval German manuscripts, tales from the time of Martin Luther, Charles Perrault, and Hans Christian Andersen. Although Jacob and Wilhelm always caught the natural speech of the oral tradition, as their work progressed they weeded out needless repetitions, added lively conversations, and simplified plots. Consequently, the literary style of the tales improved, although still authentic, not because they were interested in aesthetics of style, but because they were interested in the effect of the tales upon the listeners or readers, and ultimately upon the patriotic spirit of the German nation.

For the above reasons, it is a paradox that the tales were not written for children, although Jacob said he was glad children liked them. Although the scholars' work was primarily scientific, they, chiefly Wilhelm, had the creative spirit of the poet. This is why children and adults are able to read and enjoy such tales as *Snow-White, Rumplestiltskin, Tom Thumb, Hansel and Gretel, Puss in Boots, Cinderella*—about 210 tales in all!

Throughout the years, there have been many translations from the original Grimms' tales in German into English. In 1972 and 1973 there were three notable reprintings and translations. One is *The Complete Grimms' Fairy Tales*, introduction by Padric Colum, folklorist commentary by Joseph Campbell, and illustrated by Josef Scharl, Pantheon Books, 1974. In 1973 Farrar, Straus & Giroux published *The Juniper Tree and Other Tales from Grimm*, translated by Randall Jarrell and Lore Segal, illustrated by Maurice Sendak. The third is *The Classic Fairy Tales*, edited by Iona and Peter Opie, Oxford University Press, New York, 1974.

When *The Complete Grimms' Fairy Tales* was first published by Random House in 1944, the poet W. H. Auden wrote the review in the *New York Times*. He said, "It would be a mistake if this volume were merely bought as a Christmas present for a child," and he went on to say that this volume of Grimms' tales is "among the few indispensable, common-property books upon which Western culture can be founded." Auden classed the Grimms' tales with the Bible, Shakespeare, and Dante, copies that every household should possess, "for the reader who has come to love the unaltering, fundamental verities that these stories possess will never again be able to endure the insipid rubbish of contemporary entertainment."[6]

Hans Christian Andersen (1805–1875)

Hans Christian Andersen is considered the author of the modern fairy tale. Unlike the Brothers Grimm, who collected folktales that had been told orally and then written down, Andersen used his especially creative imagination and invented fairy tales. Although some of his stories are adaptations of

---

6. *The New York Times Book Review* (Fall 1974): 23–24.

FIGURE 6–3. *An original flannel board story that resulted from reading* The Fir Tree *by Hans Christian Andersen.*

old folktales, he put his own stamp of individuality on them when he wrote them.

Andersen was born in 1805 in Odense, Denmark, the son of poor peasants. Although his father was only a shoemaker, he had educated himself by reading. These precious books, which he kept on a shelf over his workbench, he read to his son. Not only did Hans hear the best of Danish literature, but also the Bible, the Arabian Nights, classic dramatic plays, legends, and folktales. His father cut out puppet figures and Hans began to dress these dolls, making a puppet theater and writing dialogue. The boy obviously had talent at a young age, for he began to write poems, stories, and plays. For the rest of his life, he enchanted children when he told fairy tales while cutting out paper puppets for the characters.

Hans's mother was uneducated, ignorant, and very superstitious, but she loved her odd, unusual boy and helped his literary career by taking him into the fields to gather wheat among the peasants. There Hans learned superstitions and legends and folklore from other peasants. The boy had little formal schooling and said of himself that he grew up "pious and superstitious," two traits we find in all his writing. He was a shy, awkward, odd, introverted child, laughed at by other children. He had a habit of half-closing his eyes, which made people think he had poor eyesight, when actually he keenly observed everything, storing sensory and auditory impressions that he kept in his mind. Later, when he was educated and writing, he drew upon these early, invaluable impressions.

His interest in reading and his unusually beautiful soprano voice enabled him to meet the gentry of the countryside, and through them he gained access to books, adding to his education. He was especially attracted to Shakespeare. One can see the appeal the dramatic scenes would have upon the sensitive boy—e.g., the three witches from *Macbeth* and the ghost of Hamlet's father.

At fourteen Hans left home to go to Copenhagen. The awkward, poorly educated boy carried with him glorious dreams of becoming successful as an actor or a dancer or as a singer, a poet, or a playwright. Unfortunately, for long years life was hard; he succeeded in none of the artistic goals he so passionately desired. His first bit of luck came when well-to-do friends sent him to school, and at eighteen he entered a grammar school where he suffered the humiliation of being placed in a class of the youngest boys in the school. He finally completed his formal education with a private tutor paid for by his friends. For the rest of his life, Hans was fortunate in attracting friends among the nobility; he must have had personal magnetism and talent, recognized by the educated and rich, who were consequently willing to help him. Hans profited by his association and friendship with these cultivated people so necessary to his sensitive nature.

At last, in 1833, his luck changed; he started to receive an annual stipend granted to promising writers. This was a custom at that time, namely, that patrons of literature encouraged young writers by giving them money to live on while they wrote. One stipulation was that he travel, and he later wrote in his autobiography that this was more valuable than his formal education. He loved traveling and was always received at the fine homes of the most famous people. Eventually, he traveled to every European country, particularly enjoying Germany and Italy.[7]

At the age of twenty-four, he seriously began his career of writing poems, novels, and plays. They had only minor success; most failed. It was not until he was thirty, when he needed money, that he wrote and published four fairy tales. The book sold well; the tales were popular so he immediately wrote another and another. He kept writing fairy tales for the rest of his life, and these brought him success and fame. Before he was forty, he received the adulation he had sought. Yet, even at the end of his life, he regarded these tales only as "trifles," not judging them as worthy as his novels, plays, and poems.

Probably his most remembered fairy tale is *The Ugly Duckling*. He admitted its theme came from his life and that the idea occurred to him after he had visited a luxurious country manor where he saw the beautiful petted swans floating majestically in the pond. He had just returned to Odense, his home in the rustic village, and he began to think what an ugly duckling he had been and what a transformation his life had taken. He later wrote that many of his simple fairy tales were autobiographical.

The list of his fairy tales most popular with children is too long to enumerate, but some of the most famous are: *The Princess and the Pea, Thumbelina, The Steadfast Tin Soldier, The Fir Tree, The Snow Queen,* and *The Emperor's New Clothes.*

After fame finally came, he enjoyed a happy life although he never married. He died in 1875, having enriched children's literature in his re-writing of old folktales and in his creation of the original "trifles" that came

---

7. *Ibid.*, pp. 23–24.

from his own experience in life. Fairy tales became an accepted form of literature for children, and such tales, particularly Hans Christian Andersen's, are just as appealing to children today as when they followed him, begging him to tell them "one more."

Carlo Collodi (1826–1890)

The creator of the world's most famous puppet, Pinocchio, was Paolo Lorenzini, born in Florence, Italy, on November 24, 1826. When he became a writer, he took the name Collodi, his mother's birthplace, a small village in northern Italy. As a child, he roamed the streets of Florence and, like the author Charles Dickens, he associated with all types of people, many unsavory criminal types who, no doubt, furnished the author with real-life characters for his later stories. In Florence, he entered a seminary to study for the priesthood; however, he discovered he did not care to be a priest, so he left the seminary and began his writing career in 1846.

The author who entitled his famous story *The Adventures of Pinocchio* seems to have had only one interesting adventure and that was as a soldier fighting for the independence of Italy from Austria in 1848, a period of emerging nationalism for Italy. He won a medal for valor. After the war, he returned to Florence and became a political journalist. He founded his own newspaper *Il Lampione* (The Lampoon), which was eventually banned by the government. Undaunted, Collodi started a theatrical journal, which led him into writing plays and novellas; eventually, at the age

FIGURE 6–4. Pinocchio *is born: A puppet show of Carlo Collodi's story constructed by middle-graders.*

of fifty, he translated three of Perrault's fairy tales from French into Italian.[8]

As we have previously pointed out, because there was so little literature available for the young, published stories for children, if they had any merit, were greeted with immediate success. Consequently, Collodi decided to write an original story, one that would appeal to children as amusement, not merely as instruction. At first, Pinocchio appeared in "A Children's Journal," a Roman newspaper edited for children in 1881. Collodi wrote episodes about a wooden puppet, and they were published in installments. The story of the mischievous puppet was an instant success, so in 1882 Collodi published it in book form; almost one hundred years ago this version became a best seller that is said to have immediately sold a million copies. It was translated into foreign languages and is now a classic, a story known and loved by every child today.

The adventures of the rascal-boy-puppet are episodic, each chapter finding Pinocchio in more trouble. But we are repeatedly told he is a good boy at heart; he is like all children, good at heart but easily misled by poor companions. He frequently repents while continuing to do the things all children wish they too could do. Pinocchio meets marvelous, interesting animals, characters, and magical beings whom every literate child today knows—the talking Cricket, the Pigeon, the Snail, Tuny the fish, and the Good Fairy. Children are delighted when Pinocchio's nose grows longer when he tells a lie, and when he is swallowed by Dogfish, a whale. Like all good fairy tales, this one ends well. Pinocchio learns to be a good boy, is reunited with his long-suffering father Gepetto, and is rewarded by turning into a real boy.

So very popular with each generation is *Pinocchio* that the book has been adapted, dramatized, made into a recording, and Walt Disney made a full-length color cartoon in 1940, which became extremely popular.[9] Many feel, however, that Collodi's original version is still the most delightful form for children to enjoy. Unlike many of the classics, this book can be read by children as young as ten; it does not demand the older age, better reading ability, and greater sophistication that many other children's classics do.

Collodi wrote other stories for children, but none was ever so successful as *Pinocchio*. He died October 26, 1890, having created one of the best-loved little rogues in literature. His great innovation in children's books was that he was the first author to personify an inanimate object—a puppet carved of wood. Up until this time, only human boys and girls were thought to be appropriate as the chief characters in a story.

Jules Verne (1828–1905)

The world of literature received a new genre of fiction from Jules Verne, who is called the creator of science fiction, one of the most popular types of books that children enjoy.

Jules Verne was born on February 8, 1828, at Nantes, France. He was the son of a lawyer, and he himself trained for and practiced law for a

---

8. Doyle, *op. cit.*, p. 56.
9. *Ibid.*, p. 57.

short period. But, for a young man who possessed such a vivid imagination and who yearned for wild adventures, a legal career could only be boring. He began to write stories, plays, and comedies in verse. In moving to Paris, he met Alexander Dumas, Sr., who produced a play of Verne's in 1850. To support himself while writing, he became a secretary at the *Théatre Lyrique;* this was particularly necessary since he had married a widow with two children. Later, he became a stockbroker.

His literary success began by his writing on what was then a new sport—ballooning. In 1863 he started writing the prototype of the science fiction novel, *Five Weeks in a Balloon.* This is an amazing adventure of three men who travel in a balloon over Africa. This tale captured the imagination of the French public and was the beginning of an extremely prolific and successful career. Verne began writing stories for a new periodical, stories that were published serially, but were later published in book form as *Voyages Extraordinaires.* For the next forty years, Verne happily continued writing these fantastic science fiction adventures. The irony is that what was science fiction for Verne and the world at that time is now science fact, because many of the things Verne wrote about are now reality. For example, he wrote about such inventions as the airplane, the submarine, the radio, television, the electric clock, the incandescent light bulb, and space travel. Not only have children and adults always loved his novels, but scientists have always studied them with great interest. Before Verne began writing each book, he thoroughly researched, studied, and experimented with his subject.

The list of his novels is too long to include, but following are his most popular ones: *A Journey to the Center of the Earth* (1864); *From the Earth to the Moon* (1865); *The English at the North Pole* (Part I), *The Wilderness of Ice* (Part II) (1866); *Round the Moon* (1870); *Twenty Thousand Leagues under the Sea* (1870); *Around the World in Eighty Days* (1873); *The Mysterious Island* (1875); *The School for Crusoes* (1882); a sequel to Wyss's *Swiss Family Robinson* written in two parts, *Their Island Home* and *The Castaways of the Flag* (1900). Verne spent the last years of his life at Amiens, France, where he died on March 24, 1905.[10]

In spite of all the new inventions and discoveries in science, his books are not outdated. Recent space and sea exploration has stimulated new interest in them. Because of the high interest level in Verne's books, easy-to-read abridgements have been published for young children. The stories are so exciting and full of suspense that even reluctant readers will avidly persevere through the pages of a Jules Verne adventure. Verne's most popular book with older elementary-age children is *Around the World in Eighty Days,* which has also been brought to the stage, filmed, and set to music. Verne called it the "story of perpetual motion." It concerns one of the most lively, exciting races ever put down on paper. Everyone loves a wager and the thrill of seeing whether it is won or lost, but in this story the adventure is how the wager was won. All the elements of adventure are felt and perceived, from travels on elephants, to boats, to planes and locomotives. The setting includes exotic countries and people, ranging from crafty Indians in the East to savage Indians in the United States's wild

---

10. Stanley J. Kunitz and Howard Haycraft, eds., *The Junior Book of Authors* (New York: H. W. Wilson, 1951), p. 290.

West. The characters are unforgettable, comic, and charming: Phileas Fogg, the taciturn English bachelor; his servant, the wily Passepartout; and for romance, the lovely Aonda.

Lewis Carroll (Charles Lutwidge Dodgson; 1832–1898)

Clifton Fadiman has remarked that the Victorians often suffered psychologically from a split personality. He did not mean that this generation was abnormally mentally ill; instead, he was concerned with conflicting patterns in the personality of the Victorian: one tendency was a strong feeling for materialism, witnessed by the rise of the merchant class and the love for the products of industrialization; the second tendency was a strong feeling for piety, propriety, and sentimentality. A perfect example of this Victorian split personality was The Reverend Charles Lutwidge Dodgson, a tutor and lecturer of mathematics at Oxford University and his alter ego, Lewis Carroll, the creator of one of the most whimsical fantasies of literature. Fortunately for the world of children's literature, Lewis Carroll was the dominant part of the two personalities. Lewis Carroll wrote *Alice's Adventures in Wonderland* and *Through the Looking Glass*, often referred to as the *Alice* books, and it is in this personality that the literary world is interested. In the following biography of this famous man, when the author is discussed, he is called Lewis Carroll; and when the Oxford don is discussed, he is called Charles Dodgson.

The Reverend Charles L. Dodgson, the son of a canon of the Anglican Church, was shy, religious, and scholarly. His favorite subject was mathematics. Although ordained as a clergyman, he never had a parish,

FIGURE 6–5. *Papier mâché puppet characters for* Alice in Wonderland *by Lewis Carroll.*

probably because he was nervous in the presence of adults and suffered from a bad stammer. This stammer magically disappeared when he was in the presence of *young* children, in whose company he found great pleasure. When children reached the age of thirteen, which Dodgson called in his diaries "the awkward age of transition," the friendship suddenly ended.

As a young boy, Dodgson started making up stories, usually fairy tales, to entertain his brothers and sisters. He also invented games, made a train, a railway station, and with the aid of a carpenter, he made a troupe of marionettes and a stage. He wrote plays and took all the acting parts in his dramatic productions. This was the beginning of Charles's lifelong interest in the theater, including pantomimes and burlesques, similar to the American vaudeville. Although Canon Dodgson was amused by his young son's theatrical productions, like most proper Victorians, he frowned on his son's interest in commercial theater, which was often gaudy and common. Despite the elder Dodgson's disapproval, young Dodgson was able to reconcile his love of the theater with his conscience. It is reported, however, that although he loved the fun and jokes in a comedy, if a joke was made on a sacred subject, Dodgson would get up from his seat and leave the theater.

Charles's schooling took place at Rugby and Christ Church, Oxford University. All through his academic career, he achieved highest marks and won many prizes. From the time he matriculated at Oxford and then became a resident tutor, he remained at Christ Church for the rest of his life. He was a precise bachelor who kept diaries and journals, wrote poems and stories, sent them to magazines, and wrote mathematical treatises; yet, with all this he would be almost forgotten today if it were not for the *Alice* books. However, he did also have one hobby that might have earned him a footnote in history: he was a pioneer in amateur photography.[11] Many consider him the most outstanding photographer of children in the nineteenth century.

Literary history, a true turning point in children's literature, was made on a sunny July 4th in 1862 when Dodgson took the three young daughters of his friend George Liddell, the Dean of Christ Church at Oxford, on a picnic. While rowing a boat on the river, Dodgson extemporaneously made up a story. One of the girls was eight-year-old Alice, who is immortalized in the fanciful tale he told, which he called *Alice's Adventures Under Ground*. Later in life, Alice Liddell said that Dodgson was a gifted storyteller, had an endless supply of "fantastical tales," often drawing illustrations on a big sheet of paper.[12] Alice and her sisters especially loved the story he told on that happy picnic, and Alice begged him to write it down. Four months later at Christmas, Dodgson presented Alice with the story written by hand and illustrated by the author himself. Not only did the Liddell family enjoy it, but also their literary friends, who urged its publication. Finally, the famous illustrator John Tenniel was suggested for the illustrations. When Tenniel read the manuscript, he readily accepted the commission. *Alice's Adventures in Wonderland* was published in 1866.

---

11. Lewis Carroll, *Alice in Wonderland,* edited by Donald J. Gray (New York: W. W. Norton, 1971), p. 291.
12. *Ibid.,* p. 275.

Later, Dodgson wrote *Through the Looking Glass.* Both books were immediate successes. Fame bothered the shy don. He never changed his manner of living, remaining at Oxford until he died in 1898.

The *Alice* books are dream fantasies. The plots of both books are simple. In *Alice in Wonderland,* Alice goes to sleep and falls down a rabbit hole into a strange land where her adventures become "curiouser and curiouser." She finds herself "always growing larger and smaller and being ordered about by mice and rabbits." Alice meets many strange and wonderful animals and characters whose names are known to every literate adult, such as the White Rabbit, the Cheshire Cat, the Pig Baby, the Mad Hatter, and the Dormouse. At the climax Alice awakens, runs off to get her tea, and thinks what a wonderful dream it has been.

In *Through the Looking Glass and What Alice Found There,* Alice discovers a game of chess and more unique characters, such as the Red Queen, Tweedledum and Tweedledee, and Humpty Dumpty. On the surface, both books seem simple, but in fact they are complicated fabrications that have been studied and analyzed by mathematicians, linguists, psychologists, and students of children's literature. They can be read on many levels: the child enjoys the fun, the nonsense, the puns, and the unforgettable characters. Adults see hidden meanings, originality, caricatures, and ironic wit. Not every child or adult likes the *Alice* books: one either likes them or hates them. There is no middle ground. One reason the *Alice* books are often obscure and meaningless to adults is that in order to appreciate their originality, one must know about the author, how the books originated, and the meaning of the jokes, puns, and parodies that Carroll employed. An adult is helped to understand these complexities if he reads a fully annotated edition.

Carroll produced a masterpiece that was a turning point in the history of children's literature. In studying the text, one sees that its author was ridiculing the moralistic story, which was the prevalent type of literature in the Victorian age. He wrote a delightful fantasy "simply to amuse and entertain." Underneath the story line, Carroll parodies the obedience and prudence and restraints enforced upon Victorian children. If one studies the *Alice* books, examining literature available to Victorian children, one can see it was an innovative, unique creation. *Alice* can also stand on its own merits, for it is a synthesis of fine writing for children. It has stood the test of time because of its genuine emotion and its artistic style. These books are truly classics and have delighted children for over a hundred years. Next to the writings in the Bible and in Shakespeare, the *Alice* books are most often quoted and are universal in appeal.

Louisa May Alcott (1832–1888)

Louisa May Alcott's *Little Women,* published in 1868, is one of the most popular and widely read books in children's literature. Like so many classics, this book has a special place as a landmark in the history of children's literature. It is the prototype of books written for girls and also one of the first novels classified as realistic fiction. Although far removed from the 1970s brand of realistic fiction, nevertheless it is realistic in style. Especially amazing is that it was written in the Victorian Age. Reticence, particularly about one's family, was always practiced. Yet Miss Alcott simply wrote about her own family life from a point of view never before recorded.

One can hardly separate the book *Little Women* from Louisa May Alcott's own life. It was such an interesting life that children who love this book will enjoy knowing about its author. There are many good biographies of both Miss Alcott and her father Bronson Alcott, an unusual man.

Born in Germantown, Pennsylvania, in 1832, Louisa was the daughter of highly individualistic parents. Her father Bronson Alcott was a school teacher, a progressive educator, a writer and a transcendentalist philosopher. His wife Abba May was self-educated, intelligent, kind, an unusually good wife and mother. Both parents were native New Englanders; Abba May's ancestors were Boston Brahmins, the Quincys, Sewells and Mays. Although born in Pennsylvania, Louisa soon moved to the Boston area, where she and her family were to move again about twenty-six times, mostly from Boston to Concord, back and forth. The family moved from Germantown because Bronson was fired; his educational theories were too radical for the Quakers. For one thing, he admitted a black girl to his school. His tragedy was that he was ahead of his time. Bronson's educational philosophy is accepted today.

At Concord, Bronson Alcott knew the famous transcendentalist philosphers. Among them were Ralph Waldo Emerson, who was a lifelong friend and benefactor of the family, and Thoreau, who taught Louisa her lessons in botany while he was living in his cabin at Walden Pond. Nathaniel Hawthorne and his family later moved to Concord, and his daughter Ellen was taught by Louisa.

In 1843 the Alcott parents, their four daughters, along with other transcendentalists, formed the Con-Sociate Society, a utopian commune called "Fruitlands," a ninety-acre farm.[13] The poor Alcott family almost starved because no one worked except the beleaguered Mrs. Alcott with the aid of her two oldest daughters (Louisa was the second). The story of this experiment in communal living is both amusing and sad. The group were vegetarians, wore odd clothing (cotton was forbidden because the Alcotts were abolitionists, and cotton was the product of slave labor), wore long beards when other men were close-shaven, and concentrated on feelings of love rather than the practical affairs of harvesting crops.[14] One by one, the commune members left, and by winter the poor Alcott family had little to eat and almost froze to death. Fortunately, Mrs. Alcott was practical as well as laborious and valiant, for Bronson was a visionary who was never able to provide successfully for his family.

However, Bronson Alcott, aided by his wife, provided an environment richer than money; they gave their children high literary and artistic tastes, intellectual stimulation of some of the most famous men and women of all times, and in spite of poverty, these parents gave their children the love, affection, and security of family life on its highest level.

This is the background of the girl who wrote *Little Women*. A few biographical facts add interest to the life of the author herself.

Early in her life, two separate but significant traits developed in

---

13. Marjorie Worthington, *Miss Alcott of Concord* (Garden City, N.Y.: Doubleday, 1958), p. 22.
14. *Ibid.*, p. 27.

Louisa's personality. One was kindliness, humor, and high spirits, which formed a pleasing personality. The second was a strong determination to earn money to support her family. From her personal diaries, there is never an insinuation that Louisa felt that her father was a failure for not being a good provider. She respected him, and later, when she was financially successful, she provided Bronson with the money for the school that he had desired for so long: a school that was a testing ground for his advanced educational theories. Her adored mother became prematurely old with hard work, and Louisa luckily was able to provide her with luxuries that as a young woman Mrs. Alcott had so nobly sacrificed. Louisa kept writing until she literally wore herself out, to earn money not only for her parents but also for her sisters and their children.

At sixteen Louisa started working to help out family finances by teaching school, a job which she disliked. Her students were apparently fond of her because of her warm personality. She then went to Boston and became a maid, a governess, and a seamstress. It was at this time she began to write for money by contributing lurid romances to second-rate magazines. Her first novel was *Moods,* published in 1864. Although Louisa thought it very good and always favored it above *Little Women,* it was not a success.

When the Civil War started, she went south as a volunteer nurse. Unfortunately, she returned to Boston seriously ill, and the girl who had always been robust and healthy never again was strong. She developed vague nervous disorders which plagued her the rest of her life. But from these nursing experiences came her first literary success, a book called *Hospital Sketches,* which were realistically told accounts of her encounters with the war's wounded men. By this time, she was rather well known in the Boston literary world. The editor of the then prestigious firm Roberts Brothers asked her to write a book for girls. With the publication of *Little Women* in 1868, she became famous and financially secure, but never rich enough, for she had a whole family to support, so she kept on writing in spite of her poor health.

She wrote a sequel to *Little Women* that first appeared in the magazine *St. Nicholas* and was later published together with the first part of *Little Women* in 1869, the two parts forming the book as we now know it. Other books about the March family and their relatives followed: *Little Men, An Old Fashioned Girl, Eight Cousins, Rose in Bloom.*

Miss Alcott never married and only lived until fifty-six, dying the day after her father. This kindly, warm, sympathetic New England lady was an innovator in children's literature. The innovation seems so simple; she wrote about her family in a warm, loving, humorous way, but one must remember that at that time novels about families were didactic, moralistic, artificial, and overly sentimental. Miss Alcott's fame rests on her warm, truthful, quietly told story of a real family, their hopes, failures, frustrations, moods, and tragedies. In spite of the changes in family life today, the book contains universality. It delights girls now as much as it did their grandmothers. In spite of poverty, Louisa enjoyed her sisters, her parents, her family.

In her last years, she was always asked how much of the March family was true, how much was fiction. The gentle Victorian lady always answered that she had cut off the sharp edges of the family's genteel poverty, and the rest went like this: Louisa was Jo, the tomboy heroine; Beth was truly her sister Elizabeth; Marmee, her mother, was Mrs. March; the plays, the costumes, the parties were true; and the romance with Laurie—well, she was always mysterious about that. Her journals indicate he was a Polish pianist, younger than she, whom she met in Europe, or else a composite of all the young attractive boys she knew.

In 1888, Louisa May Alcott died without completing her last novel, which she had intended to call *Success*, but perceptively and ironically she had changed its name to *Work*.

Mark Twain (Samuel Langhorne Clemens; 1835–1910)

Samuel Clemens, using the pen name Mark Twain, is perhaps America's foremost literary humorist. More than a humorist, however, Clemens is significant for his uncanny ability to capture the color of the distinctly American frontier spirit.

Born in 1835 in Florida, Missouri, Samuel Clemens soon moved with his family to Hannibal, Missouri, where he stayed until he was eighteen. Clemens's father was something of a frustrated visionary, always expecting to make a small fortune on some risky business venture. His 1847 death consequently left the family in rather dire straits. Mrs. Clemens proved more practical and energetic than her husband, however, and the family

FIGURE 6–6. *In an open-school situation, all ages enjoyed* The Adventures of Tom Sawyer *by Mark Twain, and all ages tried their hand at dramatizing the fence-painting scene for a classroom production.*

seems to have survived somewhat comfortably in the casual Mississippi River community.[15]

These were idyllic times for young Clemens, providing the substance for many of his most entertaining stories. The childhood adventures rhapsodized in such books as *Tom Sawyer* and *The Adventures of Huckleberry Finn* are largely unexaggerated accounts of his own youth, demonstrating a genuine gusto for life. Most of the characterizations in those books are based upon real people that Clemens grew up with; many consider Tom Sawyer to be modeled after the author himself.

A certain restlessness of spirit characterized Clemens's early manhood. Traveling throughout the country, he was at times a printer, a Mississippi riverboat pilot, prospector, newspaper reporter, and at all times a keen observer and a philosopher. As a reporter in Virginia City, Nevada, however, Clemens began to hear his calling. Originally harboring no particular literary ambitions, he limited himself to the frontier burlesques and lampoons so common to that period. Moving to California, Clemens soon found nationwide recognition with his *Jumping Frog of Calaveras County.* The culture-hungry west latched onto him as its literary hero, and Clemens subsequently found newspapers sponsoring traveling expeditions with his acting as a correspondent. The 1869 publication of *The Innocents Abroad,* the result of a sponsored voyage to the Mediterranean, cemented his reputation.

An indirect result of this voyage was that Clemens met Olivia Langdon and her brother. Smitten with Miss Langdon, he soon married her. Critics have often speculated upon the effect Miss Langdon, coming from a conservative, Victorian, middle-class family, had upon Clemens. She often criticized the topics of Clemens's colorful, flamboyant style. He loved her deeply, often deferring to her, and it is entirely possible that Clemens's career might have taken a totally different shape had it not been for her. The following twenty years demonstrate a departure from his previous broadly satiric style, a departure that resulted in his largest successes with the public.[16]

The Adventures of Tom Sawyer (1876) is the episodic story of young Tom and his friends in a small town on the Mississippi of the 1840s. Simultaneously an adventure story and realistic fiction, *Tom Sawyer* is significant as one of the forerunners of the latter. The book, although relating such exciting scenes as Tom fighting it out with brutal Injun Joe in a cave, also depicts the cares and concerns of a boy growing up. Tom emerges as the protean all-American boy.

The Adventures of Huckleberry Finn (1884) is considered by many to be the "great American novel." Once again, this book is of great value as realistic fiction because of its tolerant portrayal of Huck, son of the town drunk; Huck smokes and swears and does not go to school. At the same time, however, he is "redeemed" by his gentle kind-heartedness and warm simplicity. *Huckleberry Finn* also gently encourages a more accepting attitude toward blacks and attempts to communicate the flagrant injustice of slavery through the memorable runaway slave, Jim.

---

15. Allen Johnson and Dumas Malone, eds., *Dictionary of American Biography,* vol. IV (New York: Charles Scribner's Sons, 1930), p. 192.
16. *Ibid.,* p. 193.

Both books represent the freewheeling frontier spirit of the 1840s. The Mississippi River almost becomes a character itself and is, at the same time, symbolic of nothing less grandiose than life itself, as it bears the characters from one exciting adventure to the next. We read an accurate portrayal of all forms of river life, from the aristocratic Grangerfords to the river low-life of the Duke and the Dauphin.

In later years a series of impractical business ventures necessitated a European lecture tour in order to repay his many debts. The early 1900s brought tragedy to Clemens in the death of his wife and two of his daughters. Greatly saddened, Clemens himself died in 1910 as America's most loved author. William Dean Howells called Clemens "the Lincoln of our literature."

Robert Louis Stevenson (1850–1894)

Robert Louis Stevenson is the author of two of the world's most loved adventure stories, *Treasure Island* and *Kidnapped*. Born in 1850 to a well-known Edinburgh civil engineer, Stevenson was a sickly child with weak lungs. Showing little inclination toward engineering, a profession in which many Stevensons had excelled, Stevenson was steered by his father toward the law. Stevenson himself had felt inclined towards a literary career since childhood; at Edinburgh University he became something of a free-thinker. Stevenson never seriously practiced law; instead he became an essayist who contributed articles to contemporary magazines.[17]

On his first trip to the Continent, which provided the basis for his first novel, *An Inland Voyage*, Stevenson met Fanny Osbourne, an American whom he followed back to San Francisco and married in 1880. It was his stepson Lloyd Osbourne who provided the inspiration for *Treasure Island*. Twelve-year-old Osbourne was passing the time one day by idly drawing a map of a desert island. Stevenson watched with interest and began to make additions of his own, including descriptive geographic names and crosses marking buried treasure. Little Osbourne was delighted and remarked that such an island could inspire a good yarn. By the next morning *Treasure Island's* first chapter was complete. Stevenson wrote quickly, reading a new chapter each day to Osbourne. A friend of the family read the manuscript and urged its immediate publication. Stevenson had originally entitled the work *The Sea Cook*, but it appeared serially in the magazine *Young Folks* as *Treasure Island* between October 1881 and January 1882.[18]

As a serial, the adventure caused little stir; when it appeared in book form in 1885, however, *Treasure Island* became a sensation. Critics hailed it as a refreshing break with the verbose, often boring adventure stories of the time. The story involves the search for the buried treasure of a now-dead pirate. Young Jim Hawkins and his friends, Dr. Smollet and Squire Trelawney, outfit a ship in pursuit of the treasure. Complications include a mutinous crew led by Long John Silver, certainly one of the most remembered characters in children's literature.

Stevenson contributed other works to *Young Folks*, *Kidnapped* being

---

17. Doyle, *op. cit.*, p. 251.
18. *Ibid.*, p. 252.

the most notable. It depicts the adventures of young David Balfour, who has been cheated out of his inheritance by his greedy uncle. Balfour is kidnapped but escapes to the Scottish highlands, where he meets the daring Alan Breck Stewart.

Plagued by poor health throughout his life, Stevenson moved to Samoa in 1890 in search of a more suitable climate. He stayed there until his death in 1894. Stevenson was a favorite with the natives, who called him "Tusitala," teller of tales. It is said that sixty Samoans bore his body to the top of the mount where he is buried.

Even though Stevenson's two adventures, *Kidnapped* and *Treasure Island,* were written almost a hundred years ago, they are not outdated and are extremely popular with today's young readers. Although the original manuscripts written by Stevenson are preferred, there are many shortened, abridged editions available for elementary children too young to read the original. *Treasure Island* remains the classic adventure, mystery, sea story in children's literature.

All Stevenson's stories are written with a clean, descriptive, unexaggerated style. Each story maintains the reader's unflagging interest and enthusiasm, painting clear and vivid word images.

L. Frank Baum (1856–1919)

Few authors have held as many occupations as Lyman Frank Baum. Born in Chittenango, New York, educated in Syracuse, Baum began his career as a New York newspaper reporter, also managed several theaters, and, in addition, acted and wrote several minor plays.[19] Baum left New York and theater work while in his late twenties, devoting himself to raising chickens. His first book, *The Book of Hamburgs* (1886), was an instructional manual on chickens. At the same time, Baum and a friend went into business developing, of all things, a brand of axle grease, Baum's Castorine. Abandoning chickens and axle grease, he and his wife moved to Aberdeen, South Dakota. There he opened a general store, "Baum's Bazaar." Baum apparently missed journalism, because a few years later he sold out and went to work for the *Dakota Pioneer,* becoming editor in 1888. After the *Pioneer* went bankrupt, the Baum family moved to Chicago where Baum sold crockery and did newspaper reporting. He changed occupations once again in 1897, founding an association of store window decorators. He edited the *Chicago Show Window* and published *The Art of Decorating Dry Goods Windows* in 1900.[20]

Baum, however, developed an interest in writing for children, having published *Mother Goose in Prose* in 1897 and *Father Goose—His Book* in 1899. Baum's real literary achievement, however, was *The Wonderful Wizard of Oz,* published in 1900. The premier American fantasy, it is the story of a Kansas girl, Dorothy, and her adventures in the land of Oz. Whimsically told, the book was an overnight success. Many critics have read the story as a political allegory concerning the gold standard and the Populist movement of the day. This approach, however, is not recommended for children, as it

19. *Ibid.,* p. 22.
20. *Ibid.,* p. 23.

FIGURE 6–7.   *An attractive shadow box of* The Wizard of Oz *by L. Frank Baum.*

detracts from the delightful nonsense and can ruin the child's enjoyment.

The Wizard of Oz was almost immediately adapted for the stage, where it was a tremendous success. It was later adapted for the screen; three versions have been made—two silent movies and the 1939 Judy Garland extravaganza. The public wanted more Oz books and, against his will, Baum wrote a series of fourteen more, initiating many new characters. These books are considerably inferior in quality to *The Wizard of Oz*.

Under the name Floyd Akers, he wrote six boys' books, and as Edith Van Dyne he wrote twenty-four books for girls. These works are generally ignored today but were popular at the time of their writing. Baum died in Hollywood in 1919; nevertheless, Oz lived on. Twenty-six more Oz books were written by a total of five different authors, one of them Baum's son. The forty Oz books together are said to have sold over seven million copies.[21]

The Wizard of Oz is a milestone in literature for children. It is the first distinctly American fairy tale, signifying a vast departure from the traditional European genre. The heroine is not a princess but an American farm girl. One of the elements of the typical fairy tale is the quest; in European tales, the characters search for marriage to royalty or wealth and fame. The characters of *The Wizard of Oz* instead seek the good old American values of intelligence, kind-heartedness, and courage. Dorothy desires only to see her Aunt Em and Uncle Harry and to return to the Kansas prairie. *The Wizard of Oz* portrays perhaps the best-known characters in American fantasy; almost every child knows Dorothy, her dog Toto, and her friends

---

21. *Ibid.,* p. 24.

the Lion, the Scarecrow, and the Tin Woodsman. The Judy Garland movie is shown almost every year on television. Fortunately, librarians and teachers report that after seeing it on television, many children ask to read the book.

Kenneth Grahame (1859–1932)

Born in 1859 in Edinburgh, Scotland, Kenneth Grahame was the son of a Scottish barrister. The Grahames were an old family, tracing their ancestry back to Robert the Brave. Grahame lived in Scotland until he was five, when his mother's premature death brought about a move to his grandmother's Berkshire estate. Despite his mother's death, young Grahame enjoyed his childhood. He showed an early appreciation for nature, which was easily fulfilled by the beautiful grounds and lovely countryside. The River Thames flowed through the estate and Grahame seems to have had many fond memories of river idylls. Two years later, however, his grandmother moved Grahame and his sister and two brothers to Cranbourne, a setting much less enjoyable to him. He did well at St. Edward's school, excelling both scholastically and athletically. Grahame's grandmother thwarted his plans of attending Oxford University with her intention of securing him a clerk's position with the Bank of England. He rose steadily in the bank, attaining the position of secretary in 1898, a post he held until poor health forced his resignation in 1907.[22]

During his years with the Bank of England, Grahame began submitting essays and small poems to papers and magazines; the large majority were refused. Gradually, however, some of his works began to be published, eventually gaining approval in W. E. Henley's *National Observer*. In 1895 Grahame published *The Golden Age*, followed in 1898 by *Dream Days*. Both books won widespread critical approval, containing sketches of children at play that appealed to adults much more than to children.

Grahame married late in life in 1899 and the following year Alistaire, Grahame's only child, was born. On Alistaire's fourth birthday, Grahame began what was to become the immortal *The Wind in the Willows* as a bedtime story. Mouse, Alistaire's family nickname, so enjoyed the story that it had to be continued by mail when he went on a seaside holiday three years later.

The Wind in the Willows is one of the most superbly conceived and written fantasies in children's literature. The secret of its appeal is the delightful adventures of Mole, Rat, Badger, Mr. Toad, and a host of other animals whose characters possess the most endearing and charming foibles of humans and animals. *The Wind in the Willows* is considered a children's classic because of its three qualities: the imagination of Grahame, who transports the reader into another world; the exceptional characterization of the animals; and the beauty of its style. The language is perfectly fitted to each scene, dialogue, and mood. Grahame's style is poetic, pastoral, allegorical, and worthy of comparison to any classic in the field of adult literature. Since it was originally written as a bedtime story, *The Wind in the Willows* lends itself to being read aloud by a parent to children at bedtime or by the classroom teacher. The book is full of sensory appeal: the feel of

---

22. *Ibid.*, p. 119.

earth, water, food, woods, and meadows. It is truly one of the greatest masterpieces in the English language.

James Barrie (1860–1937)

Sir James Matthew Barrie is perhaps best known for his timeless play about a boy, Peter Pan, who never wanted to grow up. Barrie was a prolific author, writing many successful novels and plays which continue to be staged and filmed, such as *Quality Street, The Admirable Crichton, The Twelve-Pound Look,* and *Dear Brutus.*

Born in 1860, son of a Scottish weaver, Barrie displayed an unusually strong attachment to his mother, later making her the model for the heroine of his novel, *Margaret Ogilvy,* entitling the book after his mother's maiden name. Mrs. Barrie seems to have been a remarkable woman. Despite the poverty of their home, she was no doubt directly responsible for the subsequent fame and culture of her son. She insisted that young Barrie be well educated. Nevertheless, he was somewhat less than a diligent student at Dumfries Academy, much preferring cricket to his schoolwork. Consequently, Barrie had quite a struggle later at Edinburgh University, eventually receiving a Master of Arts Degree in 1882. He was an avid reader, however, greatly enjoying Robert Louis Stevenson and James Fenimore Cooper. These two authors, though possessing radically conflicting styles, demonstrate a commitment on Barrie's part to reading. Barrie corresponded with Stevenson, and the two grew to be great friends through letter writing. Barrie undoubtedly would have eventually traveled to meet him in Samoa had not Stevenson died in 1894. Stevenson's death inspired Barrie's only serious poem.[23]

In later life Barrie seems to have cultivated the public conception of himself as a shy, retiring Peter Pan figure. In fact, nothing could be further from the truth. Barrie loved to make speeches, although often posing as something of a recluse. He was, in fact, a shrewd businessman who lived quite comfortably.

Curiously, despite his many whimsical stories appealing to children, Barrie did not really like children. He was, however, fond of W. E. Henley's daughter, Margaret, caring for her after the death of her father. Little Margaret served as the model for Wendy in *Peter Pan,* but it is Barrie's mother who seems to have greatly conditioned his writing. It has been noted that the only form of love he portrayed in his works was mother love. Even little Wendy mothers Peter.[24]

As often happens, a children's story, in either poetry or prose, is first conceived by being actually told for the amusement of one or two real children, and after the successful telling and retelling, the story is finally written down. And so it was with *Peter Pan,* which was originally told by Barrie to some young boys in Kensington Gardens. Barrie first created Peter as a baby who appeared in one section of his book *The Little White Bird* (1902). This section was later republished separately in 1906 under the title of *Peter Pan in Kensington Gardens,* excellently illustrated by Arthur Rack-

---

23. Kunitz and Haycraft, *op. cit.,* p. 79.
24. *Ibid.,* p. 80.

ham.[25] Editions of *The Little White Bird* are still published and read by children. Many simplified, shortened adaptations of the story of Peter Pan appear each year, but the original is still the best, the most whimsical, and most fey. Mary Martin played Peter Pan in a charming musical that is occasionally repeated on television.

Peter Pan is loved because of its exciting adventures in Never-Never Land, and it has unforgettable characters: Wendy, Tinker Bell, Tiger Lily, the good Indians, Captain Hook and his pirates, and the crocodile that swallowed a clock which goes tick-tock and is always trying to catch Captain Hook so it can eat him. But most memorable is Peter Pan, the little boy who never grows up or even wants to, a feeling many children experience.

When Barrie died in 1937, he left as a legacy one of the most unforgettable characters in all children's literature.

Howard Pyle (1853–1911)

Howard Pyle is truly the father of American illustrators, and, as a writer, his books have become classics enjoyed equally by juveniles and adults. Pyle's career created another milestone in the history of children's literature, altering its course in America. First, beginning with Pyle, America at last broke her dependence upon English illustrators. After Pyle became well known, he set up his own art school in Wilmington, Delaware, and taught Maxfield Parrish, N. C. Wyeth, Frank Schoonover, and Jessie Wilcox Smith, all of whom became well-known artists and illustrators who were as American in their style of painting as Mark Twain and Louisa May Alcott were in their style of writing.

Second, since Pyle could both write and illustrate his own books, he foreshadowed the present time in which remarkably talented individuals like Maurice Sendak and Ezra Jack Keats write and illustrate their own books, truly producing a perfect fusion of both arts. Today it is not uncommon for one person to practice both arts in producing children's books, but in Pyle's time, authors like Lewis Carroll and Kenneth Grahame wrote the texts and commissioned an artist to illustrate their books. Before Pyle, it was the English illustrator who held prestige in America.

Born in Wilmington, Delaware, in 1853, Pyle came of Quaker parents who were deeply committed to the intellectual climate of their city. Pyle's relationship with his mother was particularly close, and she in turn took great pains to foster in him an ability to appreciate all that was beautiful. Consequently, when Pyle demonstrated an early inclination toward art and writing, it was quickly encouraged. He studied at the Friends School and chose not to go to college, instead studying art in Philadelphia.

Pyle is perhaps best remembered for his *The Merry Adventures of Robin Hood* and his four King Arthur books. Many critics consider Pyle's interpretation of *Robin Hood*, both in its writing and in its artistry, to be his finest work. Almost all critics, however, consider it the paramount version of the Robin Hood adventures. Pyle's Robin Hood success inspired his Arthur books, perhaps his most ambitious feat. This involved total mastery of all the Arthur literature in all its previous forms. After seven years, a testimonial to one man's scholarship, *The Story of King Arthur and His Knights* appeared in 1903. *The Story of the Champions of the Round*

---

25. Doyle, *op. cit.*, 225.

Table (1905), *The Story of Sir Launcelot and His Companions* (1907), and *The Story of the Grail and the Passing of Arthur* (1910) followed.[26]

A. A. Milne (1882–1956)

Alan Alexander Milne, the father of world famous Christopher Robin, the little boy of *Winnie-the-Pooh* and *The House at Pooh Corner,* was born in London in 1882 and educated at Westminster School and Trinity College, Cambridge, where he edited its literary magazine. Graduating in 1903 and armed with a gift of three hundred pounds from his father, Milne returned to London to become a journalist. In his first year he went through his money and the twenty pounds he had made from his writing. Two years later, Milne was faring slightly better, having made three hundred pounds on his own. He was no doubt surprised and pleased when *Punch,* the famous English magazine, offered him an assistant editorship. He remained at that position until the First World War. In early 1915 he enlisted in the Royal Warwickshire Regiment. While in service in 1915, he wrote his first children's book, *Once on a Time,* a story about fairies. It was published in 1917. After his demobilization, Milne was well enough known so that he left *Punch* in order to devote all his time to writing.

At the suggestion of a friend, Milne wrote some children's poems for a new magazine, *Merry-Go-Round,* in 1923.[27] Finding writing for children enjoyable, he wrote more verses, using three-year-old Christopher Robin, his son, as a subject. These verses eventually became *When We Were Very Young,* a collection that met with immediate success upon its publication in 1924.[28]

The word always used to describe Milne's *Winnie-the-Pooh* (1926) and *The House at Pooh Corner* (1928) is "whimsical." Christopher Robin makes his first appearance in prose surrounded by the wonderful characters: Pooh, Piglet, Eeyore, Owl, Tigger, Rabbit, and Kanga; each animal has a distinct, endearing personality. As with Grahame, the stories were based on bedtime stories. They generally involve the light misadventures of the impetuous but purposeful Pooh, the bear with very little brain.

The original Pooh was a stuffed bear that Christopher Robin had owned since early childhood; Winnie was a favorite bear that he liked to watch at the London Zoo.

Milne would, perhaps, have preferred to be remembered for his many adult works. Nevertheless, his contributions to children's literature are eminently memorable in themselves. Milne died in 1956.

SUMMARY

The creative use of the classics in literature can meet some of the objectives of teaching in the elementary school. Books of fiction by the most original, creative authors that have stood the test of time are called classics. They

---

26. *Ibid.,* p. 226.
27. *Ibid.,* p. 200.
28. *Ibid.*

are the heritage of every child. Although a child should be exposed to the classics, he should never be forced to read any book he does not like. Reading tastes are personal, individual, and subjective.

Since classics, like all books, are divided into types or genres, a child is able to find many that he will enjoy. A child can choose among stories of adventure, fantasies, fairy tales, science fiction, and realistic fiction. Professionals who have worked with children and have observed their reading find that the classics reviewed in this chapter, plus many more not included, are still being read and enjoyed. The classics must, however, subject themselves to the criteria of excellence that all books must undergo, namely the pleasure and joy a book gives to a child.

In reviewing the so-called classics, one finds that some were first written for adults but were readily embraced by children because there were few books written especially for children. Writing for children is the most recent branch of literature. When children read the books written for adults, they read them on a different level, not understanding the political, social, or satirical meaning of the authors. Children read these books because they are interesting and tell a good story. Today we find that many books written for children are equally enjoyed by adults. The multilevels in which certain classics are written speak for their originality and depth of meaning.

Any list of classics is controversial. Everybody has his favorite ones and those he ardently dislikes. The rationale for choosing the books in this chapter was that each was a turning point in the history of children's literature. Each author produced a work unique and innovative. Therefore, it is important for those adults who guide children's reading to become familiar with the classics and with the authors who wrote them. Children are curious to know about the person who wrote a book they love and enjoy. One of the best approaches to the creative teaching of literature is the biographical and historical approach. Who wrote the book? What kind of person was he or she? How did he happen to write this book? Anecdotal sketches of authors' lives intrigue children and add to the total enjoyment of the book. Knowledge of the classics and their authors signifies to the child interest and approval. Hopefully each reader of the classics can experience an adventure, an important part of each child's cultural heritage.

TO THE COLLEGE STUDENT

1. Encourage members of the class to select one of the children's classics not discussed in this chapter and have them do research about the author. Include interesting anecdotes and material concerning the author's life that will intrigue the children and make them want to read the book.

2. Start making a file folder of biographical material about famous authors. This will be an invaluable resource. Material can be found in the *New York Times Book Review,* magazines, and newspaper articles. Try to find pictures and visual aids as well as printed ones.

3. Start a reading program for yourself, one in which you reread the classics. Maybe your opinions of these books have changed since you read them as a child. Keep an index card with notes about each book as you read it.

4. Watch for film versions of children's classics at your local theater and on television, and then compare the book with the adaptation.

5. Select one author of children's classics whom you especially like. Collect material about him, but, more important, read everything you can find about this author. In other words, become a specialist on Charles Dickens or Hans Christian Andersen. Every year new books—biographical and critical analyses—appear about famous authors. This can become a useful and interesting reading hobby. Your knowledge of the author will enable you to find creative ways of presenting a writer whom you are genuinely interested in and know about.

This kind of knowledge benefits you as a teacher and your students, who are quick to realize the difference between a surface knowledge and genuine understanding. Your students will react more enthusiastically to your true knowledge of your subject.

6. Write a paper on one of the intriguing literary aspects of a classic. For example, write a paper on the concept of reality in a classic adventure story, comparing this concept with that of a modern realistic novel.

TO THE CLASSROOM TEACHER

1. One way to help children become interested in classics is to use the biographical approach to the author's life. Think of ways you can do this in the classroom. Many ideas are mentioned in Chapters 13 and 14. Try bulletin board displays, library research projects, dioramas, and so forth. Try out projects in which the child can use his own creative ability. Such an assignment might be: "Write an imaginary diary pretending you are Louisa May Alcott during the year she spent at Fruitlands."

2. In planning your next unit, see how many ways you can use a classic piece of literature in correlation with social studies, science, arithmetic, and the creative arts. *Robinson Crusoe* and *The Swiss Family Robinson* are good examples for this experiment.

3. For a period of time, assign your students oral reports on the lives of the authors of the classics. Encourage them to give interesting, vital information about the author, rather than a dull recital of facts and dates. You might give an example of one yourself so they can understand what kind of information is exciting. These reports may encourage the students to want to read these authors' books.

4. Let the children plan a play about an author's life, featuring some of the highlights of the author's career. This is often done with historical figures such as George Washington or Abraham Lincoln, but the lives of authors also contain dramatic excitement, such as Daniel Defoe's imprisonment, Baum's many business adventures, Mark Twain's colorful life, or a scene of Lewis Carroll rowing a boat while telling the story of *Alice in Wonderland* extemporaneously to the three little Liddell girls.

5. After the students have learned about famous authors' lives, develop games for the children to play, using a guessing-game approach, such as written reports about an author's life with a folder on which is printed "Who Am I?" Each child can read his and then ask the class to guess. Or children could draw pictures of events in an author's life and show them to the class, individually or on a bulletin board. The drawings should be labeled "Who Am I?" Or a child could be "it," pretending to be a famous author and go to the front of the room. Then the rest of the class could play "Twenty Questions" which the author-impersonator would have to answer. Questions might be: "Were you a nurse in the Civil War? Are you Louisa May Alcott?" "Were you a college teacher of mathematics before you became a famous writer? Are you Lewis Carroll?"

6. The ideas in the preceding three exercises can be assigned using the books themselves, rather than the authors' lives. For example, the twenty-questions game can be played about a specific book. When children get accustomed to playing these games, the teacher finds that the children start doing more close reading, noting details, rather than skimming books for the enjoyment of plot alone.

TO THE COLLEGE STUDENT
AND THE CLASSROOM TEACHER

Although we hope children receive pleasure from reading, other intrinsic values of good literature can be fostered by the teacher. These values have been discussed throughout this book; some are the development of creativity in a child's oral and written expression, the development of his artistic and esthetic sense, the fulfillment of emotional and intellectual needs, the examination of life's moral code, and so forth. Consequently, because the classics contain the best that literature offers, the teacher can use these books to meet some of the child's developmental needs that have just been mentioned. Therefore, the teacher should design assignments and projects using the classics towards these goals.

1. For development of imagination in using the classics, ask members of the class to rewrite the ending of a classic. Let each child read aloud his own creative effort to the class. Be prepared for some highly imaginative results.

2. Encourage the children to write their own adventure story or fantasy or whatever type each wishes, after he has read some classics.

3. Have the students write or tell about a character in a classic that they could identify with, or a character they liked or disliked, and tell why.

4. Ask each student to write or tell about a specific situation or scene in a classic that was most meaningful or poignant or sad or funny to him.

5. Ask each child to find a passage from a classic and read it to the class. The part he chooses should be one that he decides is beautiful and poetic in language.

6. Ask each child to prepare a report, in either written or oral form, in which he thinks a character is dealt with or treated either fairly or unfairly, and tell why.

7. Ask each child to think about and then report orally why one classic is a good or poor book, stressing the point that the book is good if it is meaningful to him and that the book may be considered poor if he rejects it as meaningless. In this way, literature can serve the most difficult function of the mind, that is, the ability to think critically and analytically.

SELECTED BIBLIOGRAPHY

Arbuthnot, May Hill, and Zena Sutherland. *Children and Books*, 4th ed. Glenview, Ill.: Scott, Foresman, 1972.

Carroll, Lewis. *Alice in Wonderland.* Edited by Donald J. Gray. New York: W. W. Norton, 1971.

Crusoe, Robinson. *My Journals and Sketchbooks.* New York: Harcourt Brace Jovanovich, 1974.

Darton, F. J. Harvey. *Children's Books in England: Five Centuries of Social Life*, 2nd ed. New York: Cambridge University Press, 1958.

DeVries, Leonard. *Little Wide-Awake: An Anthology of Victorian Children's Books and Periodicals.* Selected from the Collection of Anne and Fernand G. Renier. New York: World, 1967.

Doyle, Brian, ed. *The Who's Who of Children's Literature.* New York: Schocken Books, 1969.

Fenner, Phyllis. *The Proof of the Pudding.* New York: John Day, 1957.

Georgiou, Constantine. *Children and Their Literature.* Englewood Cliffs, N.J.: Prentice-Hall, 1969.

Godden, Rumer. *Hans Christian Andersen: A Great Life in Brief.* New York: Alfred A. Knopf, 1955.

Graham, Eleanor. *Kenneth Grahame.* New York: Henry Z. Walck, 1963.

Grahame, Kenneth. *The Wind in the Willows.* Illustrations by Arthur Rackham. Avon, Conn.: Heritage Press, 1971 (reissue of 1940 edition).

Grimm Brothers. *Grimm's Fairy Tales.* Illustrated by Arthur Rackham. New York: Viking Press, 1973.

Grimm Brothers. *The Juniper Tree and Other Tales from Grimm*. Randall Jarrell and Lore Segal, trans. New York: Farrar, Straus, and Giroux, 1973.

Gulliver, L. *Louisa May Alcott A Bibliography*. New York: B. Franklin, 1973.

Hazard, Paul. *Books, Children and Men*. Boston: Horn Book, 1960.

Hoffman, Miriam, and Eva Samuels, comps. *Authors and Illustrators of Children's Books. Writings on Their Lives and Works*. New York: R. R. Bowker, 1972.

Huck, Charlotte S., and Doris Y. Kuhn. *Children's Literature in the Elementary School*, 5th ed. New York: Holt, Rinehart & Winston, 1975.

James, Philip. *Children's Books of Yesterday*. London: The Studio, 1933.

Johnson, Allen, and Dumas Malone, eds. *Dictionary of American Biography*. New York: Charles Scribner's Sons, 1930.

Jordan, Alice M., and Helen Masten. *Children's Classics*. Boston: Horn Book, 1960.

Jordan, Alice M. *From Rollo to Tom Sawyer*. Boston: Horn Book, 1975.

Kaplan, Justin. *Mr. Clemens and Mark Twain: A Biography*. New York: Simon and Schuster, 1966.

Larsen, Svend. *Hans Christian Andersen*. Odense, Denmark: Flensted, 1961.

Lonsdale, Bernard J., and Helen K. Mackintosh. *Children Experience Literature*. New York: Random House, 1972.

Manning, Sanders, and Ruth Manning. *Swan of Denmark: The Story of Hans Christian Andersen*. London: Heinemann, 1949.

Meigs, Cornelia L. *Invincible Louisa*. Boston: Little, Brown, 1933.

Meigs, Cornelia, et al. *A Critical History of Children's Literature*. New York: Macmillan, 1969.

Milne, Christopher. *The Enchanted Places*. New York: E. P. Dutton, 1975.

Moore, Annie E. *Literature Old and New for Children*. Boston: Houghton Mifflin, 1934.

Muir, Percy. *English Children's Books, 1600–1900*. New York: Frederick A. Praeger, 1954.

Opie, Iona, and Peter Opie, eds. *The Classic Fairy Tales*. New York: Oxford University Press, 1974.

Sayers, Frances Clark. *Summoned by Books: Essays and Speeches*. Ed. by Marjeanne Blinn. New York: Viking Press, 1965.

Smith, Lillian. *The Unreluctant Years: A Critical Approach to Children's Literature*. Chicago: American Library Association, 1953.

Spink, R. *Hans Christian Andersen and His World*. New York: Putnam, 1972.

Stern, James, illus. *The Complete Grimm's Fairy Tales*. New York: Pantheon, 1972.

Stirling, Monica. *The Wild Swan: The Life and Times of Hans Christian Andersen*. New York: Harcourt, Brace and World, 1965.

Worthington, Marjorie. *Miss Alcott of Concord*. Garden City, N.Y.: Doubleday, 1958.

CHAPTER 7

New Models, New Faces

Kids are keenly aware of the world around them; it is their misfortune that nobody talks to them intelligently about anything, much less about the important things. They want to find out, on their own terms (without being bored), what life is all about. That's why they sometimes sit and read instead of running and looking.[1]

MAIA WOJCIECHOWSKA

NEW FACES, NEW STYLES

Authors of children's literature today have the advantage of drawing on the themes and popularity of the authors of the past. Creative writers, however, have also developed new styles and themes of their own. The young reader is thus presented with a massive collection of books of seemingly unlimited scope. Children are placed in a position of continually making choices for their reading pleasure. Since the right of making choices is basic to the democratic way of life, children not only learn much from the books they read, they also begin to build reasons for making choices. The child's choices are related not only to topic and interest but to type of writing as well. One task of the teacher of children's literature is to encourage the child to become acquainted with all types of literature: folktales as well as realism, fantasy as well as adventure. An exclusive diet of any one genre presents an unbalanced picture of life to children.

Every type of literature is being written by modern authors. Fantasy has been written by modern authors in such a way as to make it more relevant to children of the late twentieth century. One example is Maurice Sendak's *In the Night Kitchen*. This fantasy tells about young Micky, who one night falls out of his bed and his clothes and into the "night kitchen." Also available to the young child is Barbara Cooney's *Chanticleer and the*

---

1. Miriam Hoffman and Eva Samuels, *Authors and Illustrators of Children's Books: Writings on Their Lives and Works* (New York: R. R. Bowker, 1972), p. 418.

Fox, a modern adaptation of Chaucer's *Canterbury Tales,* which retains fantasy from the past. Children's literature, like adult literature, has kept pace with the culture of which it is an integral part, while preserving the good from yesteryear.

In the modern elementary school, books may be used in a variety of ways, as discussed in other chapters of this volume. If children are to adventure meaningfully with books, they will soon want to know something about the authors of their favorite stories. To help the busy teacher, this chapter presents biographies of modern authors, all of whom have contributed to the reservoir of books accessible to children today. Some, such as Lois Lenski and E. B. White, began publishing decades ago; others, such as Judy Blume and S. E. Hinton, are relatively new.

Different genres are represented in the works of these modern authors, who also employ different styles of writing the same *type* of literature. These authors offer contrasts in concept, approach, and technique. They are representative of many notable modern writers, each representing a trend in children's literature. For instance, one emphasis in education today is the reinforcing of a child's positive self-concept; another is the attempt to present various life styles by showing children who are different —physically, emotionally, intellectually, in nature, culture, race, and ethnic grouping. Modern authors have been influenced by such trends, and their writings reflect them.

These modern authors show a progression in the new realism. Beverly Cleary's *Fifteen* precedes Elaine Konigsburg's *George.* Dr. Seuss anticipates Maurice Sendak. Lois Lenski writes realistically about poor sharecroppers in the South; S. E. Hinton writes realistically about rival gangs in the city. There are differences in the degree of realism presented. The younger authors deal with recent problems in our society, or problems that society is now willing to discuss. Many of the newer authors also realize that as life becomes more complicated, its problems are sometimes unsolvable; therefore, happy endings do not always resolve the conflict of the story. Many resolutions of the characters' problems are open-ended, for life is like that. This stark realism is particularly true in literature for older children. Realistic fiction is becoming increasingly popular, and more and more children ask for books that tell about life as it really is.

All of the authors discussed in this chapter feel deeply about their characters and their hardships; all are compassionate writers, and most balance the tension created in their stories with a great amount of humor. They were chosen to be represented here because of their popularity with children and because their works have been used as a basis for many of the adventures in this book. A modern author is considered as one who is still alive or who died recently.

Lois Lenski (1893–1974)

Lois Lenski was one of the greatest contributors to children's literature and one of the most prolific author–illustrators of our times. She was the interpreter of regional America. Her many books demonstrate a warm empathy for all the children of our country, and through these books children have gained insight into many cultures that they could not personally encounter.

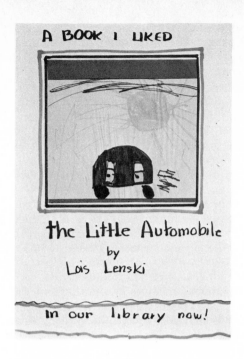

FIGURE 7–1. A first-grader's concept of The Little Auto *by Lois Lenski.*

She was a versatile writer who produced books of many genres and for different age groups; yet she never sacrificed quality for quantity.

Born in Springfield, Ohio, the fourth of five children, Miss Lenski was the daughter of a Lutheran minister. When she was six, the family moved to a small town, Anna, Ohio; a favorite family joke was that the Lenski family increased the population of the town from two hundred to two hundred and seven. Miss Lenski enjoyed a happy childhood, and it was then that she developed her everlasting love of the countryside. Her father moved the family to Columbus in 1911 when he became a professor at Capitol University. Later he became dean of the Theological Seminary. That same year Miss Lenski entered Ohio State University College of Education, anticipating a teaching career. Upon graduation, however, she followed the advice of an art teacher and went to New York City to study at the Art Students League. She subsequently decided that art was her main interest. In 1920 she went to London to study at the Westminster School of Art. It was in England that she did her first illustrations for a book.

Miss Lenski married Arthur Covey, the well-known muralist, in 1921 and the couple moved to an old colonial farmhouse in Harwinton, Connecticut. It was in New England that she was first inspired to write historical fiction and her famous regional books. Because of Miss Lenski's poor health, the family spent many winters in the South, so again she was exposed to another part of the country. When Mr. Covey died in 1960, she and her son Steven moved to Florida. Writing books and working in her garden were her greatest pleasures.

Although Miss Lenski was best known for her regional stories, she began her career by writing historical fiction for older children. These novels were well written and authentic in detail, which is also characteristic of her later regional stories. She showed her perception of and empathy for all human beings, their personal relations, their adjustments. Lois Lenski wrote of all people, past and present: Yankees, Southerners, Indians—no matter what their culture or ethnic group. She declared:

> My travels have taken me to all parts of the country—the mountains of North Carolina, the oil fields of Oklahoma, and the corn fields of Iowa. I have tried to describe how people live in these different places. Actual people, seen and known in different regions, become my main characters. Each time I draw a character, I hold in my memory the image of the real person I saw who inspired it.[2]

Lois Lenski's regional stories are written for two age groups: the Round-about America Series is aimed towards third and fourth graders, and her Regional Series is directed towards slightly older children. The books are written realistically; her portrayal of her characters is always honest. Characters speak in dialect and use the idiomatic language of their culture. True to life, she includes drunken fathers, impoverished parents, and the harsh realities that children and adults face. Despite her adherence to realism, none of her stories is oppressively harsh or sordid. There are family love and security and joy combined with poverty, despair, and sadness. Her books exude warmth, demonstrating that all cultures have become a part of America.

In addition to her famous regional stories, Miss Lenski wrote excellent picture books for pre-school children. The Davy books convey the excitement and enthusiasm of the young child who immediately recognizes and identifies with Davy's tasks. Mr. Small, who is tiny so that children see themselves in him, is the subject of Miss Lenski's series for children between five and seven. This series answers many of the questions children ask about the outside world by depicting Mr. Small in such situations and occupations as operating a fire engine (*The Little Fire Engine*), sailing (*The Little Sail Boat*), and being a policeman (*Policeman Small*). Miss Lenski's four books on the seasons of the year answer children's curiosity about their environment. All these books are miniature in size and are thus cherished all the more. Miss Lenski's picture books once again demonstrate her knowledge of children of all ages.

Miss Lenski illustrated all her own books; her style was unique and showed an understanding of the appropriateness of illustrations to text. For example, her books for very young children demonstrated simple, almost childlike drawings, suitable to the child's visual perception. Her illustrations for older children were more detailed and more realistic.

Lois Lenski's contribution to children's literature is monumental. Her love for all children of America shines throughout her books. Her versatility is emphasized in the account of the unit taught by Mrs. Galvin with her books as a basis, as related in Chapter 12.

---

2. Lee Bennett Hopkins, *Books Are by People: Interviews with 104 Authors and Illustrators of Books for Children* (New York: Citation Press, 1969), pp. 133–134.

FIGURE 7–2. A child's diorama of Stuart Little *by E. B. White.*

E. B. White (1899–)

E. B. White has written only three books for children, but these three—
Stuart Little, Charlotte's Web, and *The Trumpet of the Swan*—are so exceptional that Mr. White is considered by many to be the foremost modern
writer of children's fantasy books.

Elwyn Brooks White, son of a piano manufacturer, was born in
Mount Vernon, New York, where he says he "lived the pleasant life of a boy
in the leafy suburbs." Mr. White traveled about the country for several
years after his graduation from Cornell University in 1921. During this
period his two most notable jobs were as a reporter for the *Seattle Times*
and as a mess-boy on an Alaska-bound ship.

Eventually White returned to Manhattan, where he became a production assistant in an advertising agency. His frequent contributions to
the then-fledgling *New Yorker* magazine were enthusiastically accepted by
editor Harold Ross. In 1928 Ross persuaded White to join the staff of *The
New Yorker;* thus began an illustrious career.[3] It is interesting to note that
two other *New Yorker* contributors, William Steig and Robert Kraus, have
also written children's books.

For years Mr. White wrote the celebrated "Talk of the Town" column
of *The New Yorker,* also contributing many satires, essays, and serious
poetry. He has written eighteen books of prose and poetry, including *Is Sex*

---

3. Stanley J. Kunitz and Howard Haycraft, comps., *Twentieth Century Authors*
(New York: H. W. Wilson, 1941), p. 1508.

Necessary?, a hilarious essay co-authored with James Thurber. Thurber, a close friend, said of Mr. White that he is:

> ...a poet who loves to live half-hidden from the eye... He understands begonias and children, canaries and goldfish, dachshunds and Scottish terriers, men and motives... He plays a fair ping-pong, a good piano, and a terrible poker... He is a good man with ax, rifle, and canoe, and sails a thirty-foot boat expertly.[4]

In 1929 Mr. White married Katherine Angell, *The New Yorker's* literary editor. They have one son and three grandchildren. In 1938 the Whites moved to a farm in Brooklin, Maine, which Mr. White still farms. Many of his barnyard animals have provided the inspiration for the lovable characters of his books. White ruefully speaks of farming as the only profession in which the object is to nurture and care for animals, only to slaughter them later, a theme of his *Charlotte's Web*.[5]

Of *Stuart Little*, published in 1945, Mr. White says, "The character Stuart Little appeared to me in a dream one night when I was traveling by rail. A writer is always grateful for small favors and I recall that I jotted down fragments of the tale the next morning."[6] Stuart is a mouse born to normal human parents, who never grows higher than two inches. Mr. and Mrs. Little accept their child's handicap and, at times, it even has its advantages. In one episode Stuart bravely descends into a drain pipe in search of his mother's wedding ring. The book is episodic in nature and the sequences could be read in any order. The details of Stuart's birth to a human family somewhat disturbed some of the more straight-laced parents of 1945. Nevertheless, children adore the resourceful little mouse and his adventures.

Charlotte's Web, published in 1952, is perhaps Mr. White's most famous book. Wilbur, a pig, realizes that he will be killed when he gets fat. Fern, the farmer's daughter, also realizes that Wilbur will die and tries to save him. From spending long periods of time with Wilbur and the other barnyard animals, she finds that she can understand what the animals say to each other. Charlotte, a loquacious spider, Templeton, a greedy rat, and all the other animals plot together to save Wilbur's life. He lives but Charlotte dies, leaving many eggs to take her place. *Charlotte's Web* is an exciting book; children are greatly moved by the many hilarious scenes and by Charlotte's tragic death. Garth Williams's illustrations are to *Charlotte's Web* what E. H. Shepard's are to *The Wind in the Willows*.

The Trumpet of the Swan, published in 1970, beautifully blends realistic elements with fantasy. It is the story of a mute swan who learns to play a trumpet in order to sing to his love. Edward Frascino's illustrations are brilliantly interpretive. *The Trumpet of the Swan* was a leading contender for the children's category of the 1971 National Book Award.

John F. Kennedy awarded E. B. White the Presidential Medal of Freedom in 1963. He has also received a Gold Medal for Essays and Criticism from the National Institute of Arts and Letters, and honorary

---

4. *Ibid.*

5. Hoffman and Samuels, *op. cit.*, p. 410.

6. Muriel Fuller, ed., *More Junior Authors* (New York: H. W. Wilson, 1963), p. 225.

degrees from seven colleges.[7] In 1970 he received the Laura Ingalls Wilder Medal for a lasting contribution to children's literature. E. B. White's contribution is three imaginative fantasies that promise to be classics.

Ruth Krauss (1901–)

Ruth Krauss's special talent is her remarkable understanding of young children. She writes with the exuberant spirit of a surrogate child, a high compliment for a children's author.

Born in Baltimore, Miss Krauss never finished high school but went on to study art and music at the Peabody Conservatory, graduated from the Parsons School of Fine and Applied Arts, and has taken extensive anthropology courses at Columbia University. In 1941 she married Crockett Johnson, author-illustrator of many fine children's books and creator of the Barnaby books. The Johnsons live in Rowayton, Connecticut, on the northern edge of Long Island Sound.[8]

Miss Krauss is particularly aware of the young child's fascination with language, a skill which the child has not yet mastered. Her nonsense syllables and light-hearted style reflect the child's striving to express his feelings. This treatment is evident in *A Hole Is to Dig: A First Book of First Definitions;* it is a charming compilation of definitions from a child's point of view—"mud is to jump in and yell doodleedoodleedoo." *How to Make an Earthquake* delights children with its mock-serious advice. Upon its publication in 1954, many librarians catalogued it with all the other how-to books![9] Two of her other books, *A Very Special House* and *I Write It,* have also enthralled readers.

All Miss Krauss's books appeal to the imagination. Today, when realistic fiction is the reigning force in children's literature, it is refreshing, and indeed necessary, that books which are imaginatively written still exist.

Dr. Seuss (Theodore Seuss Geisel; 1904–)

Theodore Seuss Geisel, better known as Dr. Seuss, is probably the most popular author and illustrator for children in America. Nine times out of ten, when asked what her child is reading, a mother will only be able to remember Dr. Seuss's name. *The Cat in the Hat* and *The Cat in the Hat Comes Back* are the ninth and fourteenth best sellers in children's literature, with total sales of 1,588,972 and 1,148,669 copies, respectively.[10]

Geisel was born in Springfield, Massachusetts, where his father was an official with the parks department. At Dartmouth College he edited the school humor magazine; he was known for his offbeat cartoons featuring bizarre animals. Hoping to become a literature professor, Geisel did graduate work at Oxford University. He never finished, however; instead, he met and married fellow American student Helen Palmer.[11]

---

7. Hoffman and Samuels, *op. cit.*, p. 411.
8. Fuller, *op. cit.*, p. 120.
9. Hopkins, *op. cit.*, p. 123.
10. *Ibid.*, p. 257.
11. Fuller, *op. cit.*, p. 182.

Mr. Geisel sold a cartoon in 1927 to the *Saturday Evening Post*, signing it "Dr. Seuss." His motivation in using his middle name was to reserve "Geisel" for the Great American Novel he intended to write later. He now says,

> ...I already wrote my Great American Novel, unpublished and deservedly so. This was over forty years ago and I can't even remember what it was about. First I wrote it in two volumes. Then I trimmed it to one volume, then I cut it to a long short story, then a paragraph. Finally I sold it as a two-line caption for a cartoon.

One of his cartoons made reference to a then-popular insecticide: "Quick, Henry, the Flit." Soon Geisel was working in the advertising department for its manufacturer, Standard Oil of New Jersey.[12]

Geisel's first book was the now-famous *And to Think That I Saw It on Mulberry Street* (1936). However, it was rejected twenty-seven times before finally being accepted by an old Dartmouth friend at Vanguard Press.[13] Since that time, he has published over two dozen delightful and zany books, among them *The 500 Hats of Bartholomew Cubbins, Horton Hatches the Egg, Green Eggs and Ham,* and more and more.

The underlying attraction of the Dr. Seuss books is, as Selma Lanes notes, their ability to raise young readers to dizzy heights of vicarious anxiety.[14] In the world of *The Cat in the Hat* and company, this anxiety does not take the form of monsters, hobgoblins, and ferocious beasts. Worse, it takes the form of all the things the child fears in his everyday life— breaking lamps, staining clothes, destroying furniture, and, worst of all, the parental punishment he knows will be forthcoming. The Seuss illustrations picture every household item perched on the brink of destruction. No object is content merely to rest sedately on another; rather, whirlwind lines and the fact that these objects hover precariously above their appropriate place contribute to the total feeling of chaos. Any child reading these books rejoices that all these horrible things are happening in a book to someone else.

The Cat in the Hat launched Random House's Beginner Books division, with Geisel as one of the editors. Always using only a few one-syllable words, often as few as fifty, the Beginner Books have enabled many pre-schoolers to read, thus giving encouragement in what seems a monumental accomplishment.

Most important of all, children love Dr. Seuss and his books. Mail from adoring children offers such praise as: "Dr. Seuss, you have an imagination with a long tail"; and from a nine-year-old, "This is the funniest book I've read in nine years."[15] Dr. Seuss has given rise to new creatures, such as the Tufted Mazurka from the Isle of Yerka, the obsk which eats corn on the cobsk, and the seersucker. Alma mater Dartmouth came the closest to summing up Dr. Seuss when it awarded him an honorary doctorate

---

12. *Ibid.*

13. Hoffman and Samuels, *op. cit.,* p. 170

14. Selma Lanes, *Down the Rabbit Hole: Adventures and Misadventures in the Realm of Children's Literature* (New York: Atheneum, 1971), p. 83.

15. Hoffman and Samuels, *op. cit.,* p. 166.

in 1955 (making him an "official" doctor). Dartmouth said that Dr. Seuss already possessed a D.D.C.—Doctor of Delighted Children.[16]

Some of his recent books include such titles as *Did I Ever Tell You How Lucky You Are?*, *Great Day for Up*, *Shape of Me and Other Stuff*, *There's a Wocket In My Pocket*, and *Oh, The Thinks You Can Think*.

Eleanor Estes (1906–)

Eleanor Rosenfeld Estes combines a rare understanding and love of children with superb literary craftsmanship to produce books of high literary quality, loved and appreciated by all who read them.

Born and raised in West Haven, Connecticut, Mrs. Estes remembers the town as a pleasant village, rather than the New Haven suburb it has become. It is located on Long Island Sound, and she has vivid memories of forest streams, fishing, and clamming in the ocean.[17]

Mrs. Estes cites her mother as having influenced her writing. Mrs. Rosenfeld quoted Tennyson, Shakespeare, and Heine profusely and would often tell old folktales to her four children. In addition, she would draw, paint, and compose light verse.[18]

Upon graduation from high school in 1923, Mrs. Estes became a children's librarian at the New Haven Free Public Library. Only five years later, she found herself in charge of the children's room. As a result of her outstanding work, Eleanor was awarded the Caroline M. Hewins Scholarship for Children's Librarians in 1931, and she went to New York to study at the Pratt Institute Library School. The following year she married fellow student Rice Estes, who is now head of the Pratt Library and Secretary of the Institute.[19]

Mrs. Estes is probably most noted for her Moffat stories: *The Moffats*, *The Middle Moffat*, and *Rufus M.* Like E. B. White's *Stuart Little*, these stories are episodic; each chapter is a distinct unit. The Moffats are a rollicking family and they make reading fun.

Perhaps the most moving children's book ever written on the effects of prejudice and isolation, *The Hundred Dresses* is the story of young Wanda Petronski. Poor and different from her classmates, she is the object of scorn and derision because she wears the same dress to school each day. Yet Wanda insists that she has a hundred dresses at home, often describing them. When she wins a medal for her pictures of a hundred dresses in an art exhibition, the children realize their cruelty. It is too late; Wanda and her father have moved away.

Mrs. Estes also wrote *Miranda the Great*, published in 1967. Miranda is a cat in ancient Rome. When barbarians sack the city, Miranda rescues other cats, including a lioness from the Colosseum. Miranda is a resourceful feline and the book makes interesting reading. Children learn a great deal about Rome in reading about Miranda.

---

16. May Hill Arbuthnot and Zena Sutherland, *Children and Books*, 4th ed (Glenview, Ill.: Scott, Foresman, 1972), p. 482.

17. Stanley J. Kunitz and Howard Haycraft, eds., *The Junior Book of Authors* (New York: H. W. Wilson, 1951), p. 114.

18. *Ibid.*

19. *Ibid.*

FIGURE 7–3. *Papier mâché figures from* Ginger Pye *by Eleanor Estes.*

All of Mrs. Estes's books are beautifully illustrated. *The Moffats* is the first book artist-sculptor Louis Slobodkin ever illustrated. His crisp pen and ink sketches also highlight *The Middle Moffat, Rufus M.,* and *The Hundred Dresses.* Edward Ardizzone's sketches for *Miranda the Great* are equally delightful.

A book by Eleanor Estes is certain to be distinctive and popular, especially with girls.

Charlotte Zolotow (1915–)

Charlotte Zolotow is one of today's authors who has become increasingly concerned with writing realistic fiction. As an author of more than fifty books for children and as the senior editor of the Junior Books Department of Harper and Row, she has been a leader in the revolution in children's books; she is vitally concerned about writing and publishing books that honestly mirror today's society.

Zolotow was born in Norfolk, Virginia, and attended the University of Wisconsin for three years. She is married to Maurice Zolotow, a writer. They are the parents of one girl and one boy and live at Hastings-on-Hudson, New York.

The following quotation tells of Mrs. Zolotow's criteria for a good children's book. The interesting thing to note is that her criteria are reflected in her own writings, which have helped to set high standards in children's literature. She has written, "The idea for a child's book—to make it publishable—must come to a definite sense of form and scheme. I prefer a sensory type of book, in which the sounds of the words communicate the meanings of the words, or a king of children's lyrical poetry in prose. I like words that sound like what I want to say to children so that something in the lift of the line will engage them."[20] In the last sentence she is describing her own style of writing.

The following are the very best of her many books: *When I Have a Little Girl, When I Have a Son, The Quarreling Book, The Hating Book, The Storm Book, A Father Like That, My Friend John, New Friend, William's Doll* (illustrated by William Pené du Bois), *My Grandson Lew* (also beautifully illustrated by du Bois), and *When the Wind Stops*.

William's Doll and *My Grandson Lew* have come to grips with the new realism. The first is discussed in Chapter 9 on Modern Illustrators. *William's Doll* discusses sexism or the rigid rules that society places upon young children. Mrs. Zolotow rightfully points out that it is appropriate and normal for a young boy to have a doll so that he can learn to take care of a baby, and that playing with a doll does not make him a sissy but prepares him for when he will become a father.

In *My Grandson Lew*, published in 1974, Zolotow discusses the death of a beloved grandfather. In the story a young boy Lew wakes up in the night and tells his mother than he misses his grandfather, who died when he was two. Now he is six, but he still misses him. The boy waited for the grandfather to come back, since he was never told that his grandfather had died. It is true that children are often not told when family and friends die because many parents think that children should be shielded from death. And so in *My Grandson Lew*, the boy and his mother share their own wonderful memories of Grandpa. The book poignantly concludes with Lew saying, "I miss him." His mother says, "So do I . . . but now we will remember him together and neither of us will be so lonely as we would be if we had to remember him alone."

This book is a masterpiece of simple, understated prose and will undoubtedly become a classic, one that will be treasured for years to come. As Mrs. Zolotow has said, "We have to tell young people the truth. I don't see how this position can be altered."[21]

Recent books by Mrs. Zolotow that deal with the problems children confront are *May I Visit* and *It's Not Fair*, both published in 1976.

Beverly Cleary (1916–   )

Yamhill, Oregon, was too small to have its own library. Beverly Cleary remembers eagerly waiting each week for the crate of books that the state library sent to her mother, who acted as the town librarian. The "library" was located in a lodge hall over the town bank, and Beverly Bunn (her maiden name) would read every children's book in the crate. Joseph Jacobs's *English Fairy Tales* became such a favorite that she insisted on taking it, rather than her teddy bear, to bed each night! She soon decided that she would become an author when she grew up.

---

20. Anne Commire, *Something about the Author*, vol. I (Detroit: Gale Research, 1971), p. 228.
21. "Charlotte Zolotow," *Publishers Weekly*, June 10, 1974: 68.

Mrs. Cleary graduated from the University of California at Berkeley and also received a degree from the School of Librarianship at the University of Washington. With her interest in writing children's books, it seemed natural that she become a children's librarian. She married Clarence T. Cleary in 1940, and it was he who encouraged her to finally sit down and write a book.[22]

The book was *Henry Huggins*. Written in much the same spirit as Robert McCloskey's *Lentil* and *Homer Price*, it nonetheless seems more modern. Henry is a typical American boy who gets into such situations as flooding the neighborhood and his mother's mason jars with ever-increasing numbers of guppies. *Henry Huggins* was so successful that Mrs. Cleary wrote a series of very funny books with Henry as the chief character.

Mrs. Cleary has written several very good books for teenage girls, particularly *The Luckiest Girl* and *Sister of the Bride*. They effectively capture the feelings of adolescent girls in a way with which all readers immediately identify.

Beverly Cleary writes her books about the people who read them. She says of her childhood reading: "It seemed to me that all the children in books lived in foreign lands or were very rich or very poor or had adventures that could never happen to anyone I knew. I wanted to read about boys and girls who lived in the same kind of neighborhood I lived in and went to a school like the one I attended." She has also written a humorous book, *Ramona the Pest;* a fantasy, *The Mouse and the Motorcycle;* and *Mitch and Amy,* a book about twins and their problems. In 1975 she published *Ramona, the Brave*. Mrs. Cleary's books strive for normalcy more than realism. As a result, they are almost universally read and loved.

Margaret Wise Brown (1910–1952)

The books of Margaret Wise Brown are known for their extraordinary sensitivity to young children. She was one of the early experimenters in modern children's literature: her *Noisy Book,* which began a seven-title series, made children guess the origin of particular sounds before turning the page, increasing their involvement and demanding "honest sensory responses." The *Little Fur Family* pioneered a new promotional packaging device in children's books; bound in rabbit fur, the book was sold in an attractive little box with a hole in it displaying the fur. A hundred thousand fur-bound copies later, however, it was discovered that rabbit fur is particularly prone to moths, and a cloth edition soon replaced it.

Altogether Miss Brown wrote over a hundred books for children, with total sales of over fifteen million. Vitally interested in the total impact of a book, she was an excellent collaborator with illustrators, bringing out the best in them. *The Little Island,* published under her often-used pseudonym of Golden MacDonald, won the 1947 Caldecott Medal for illustrator Leonard Weisgard. Jean Charlot, largely popularized by Miss Brown, was a 1944 Caldecott runner-up for *A Child's Goodnight Book,* as was Tibor Gergely in 1954 for her *Wheel on the Chimney*. The Dead Bird (1958) is probably one of her most popular books and one of the first to deal with death.

---

22. Hoffman and Samuels, *op. cit.*, pp. 70–72.

Miss Brown was born in Brooklyn, New York, to a well-to-do rope manufacturer. Her parents were from Kirkwood, Missouri, where Mr. Brown's father had been state governor and a United States senator. When she was four, the family moved to Whitestone Landing on Long Island.[23] Miss Brown enjoyed an idyllic childhood there, amassing some "thirty-six rabbits, two squirrels (one bit me and dropped dead), a collie dog, two Peruvian guinea pigs, a Belgian hare, seven fish, and a wild robin who came back every spring."[24]

Miss Brown studied two years abroad in a Swiss school and at Dana Hall in Wellesley, Massachusetts. She graduated from Hollins College in 1932, where she demonstrated a strong interest in experimental writing. Nevertheless, a short-story course at Columbia disappointed her because she "couldn't think up any plots." It was Miss Brown's experience with the Bureau for Educational Experiment, now known as the Bank Street School, that provoked her interest in writing for children. Under the tutelage of the brilliant Lucy Sprague Mitchell, Miss Brown rapidly became adept at her lyrically poetic approach towards writing.[25]

By 1937 Miss Brown was the editor of the W. R. Scott Company, a new publishing firm interested in publishing books for the "neglected" nursery-age child. As editor, her proudest accomplishment was persuading the famed Gertrude Stein to write a children's book (which later proved rather controversial).[26] Miss Brown died tragically in France in 1952 while recovering from a routine appendectomy.[27]

Helen E. Buckley (1918–   )

This author of picture books has several distinctions that set her apart from other authors included in this chapter. Dr. Buckley is a professor in the English Department at the State University College at Oswego, New York. Through her teaching she has influenced hundreds of students who have become teachers and writers. Due to the popularity of her courses, many students enroll in her classes for the joy of learning about literature for children. Dr. Buckley also has the talent of putting theory into practice, for she has written twelve picture books whose worth both critics and children recognize.

Dr. Buckley was born and educated in Syracuse, New York, receiving both a Bachelor of Arts and a Master of Arts at Syracuse University. In 1962 she received a doctorate in early childhood education at Columbia University. She began her teaching career as a public school elementary teacher in Syracuse for eight years. In 1949 she went to Oswego, where she began her career at the college, first as a first-grade teacher at the campus school. She then taught seminars in early childhood education, supervised student teachers, and was the coordinator of early childhood education programs. Since 1961 she has been teaching children's literature and

---

23. *Ibid.,* p. 20.
24. Kunitz and Haycraft, *Junior Book of Authors,* p. 55.
25. *Ibid.,* p. 20.
26. *Ibid.,* p. 21.
27. *Ibid.,* p. 25.

seminars in writing for children. She married Francis E. Simkewicz, a newspaperman; they have one daughter, Niesha.

Dr. Buckley claims that her books do not spring from actual situations that happened to children she has known, except for one: *The Little Pig in the Cupboard.* The inspiration for her books is her understanding of children and her sensitivity to all the facets of a child's life—his emotional, intellectual, and psychological makeup. Her books reflect the fact that she not only likes and understands children, but also that she never "talks down" to them as if they were underdeveloped adults. She meets children on exactly the right level, and her books reflect this rare quality.

Grandfather and I, written in 1959, was her first book, a Junior Literary Guild selection; this was followed by *Grandmother and I* in 1961, and *My Sister and I* in 1963. All three were illustrated by Paul Galdone, whose work perfectly complements the text. These books contain the concept of the security of family relationships. *Grandfather and I,* a favorite of children, warmly describes the special love and warmth a grandparent gives to a child. The little boy in the story says, "Grandfather and I are going for a walk. It will be a slow walk because Grandfather and I never hurry. We walk along and walk along and stop and look . . . just as long as we like." The emotional tone of the book is quiet, tranquil, contented, and loving.

Dr. Buckley has written four books about a little girl named Josie: *Where Did Josie Go?, Some Cheese for Charles, Josie and the Snow,* and *Josie's Buttercup.* All were illustrated by Evaline Ness. Josie is a happy child who has a little dog named Buttercup, a "cozy dozy" cat, and a mouse named Charles, who naturally loves cheese. The repetition and the rhythm of the words make these books a delightful experience for children. These are not controlled vocabulary books. However, older children often claim they learned to read these books after having listened to them once or twice. *Where Did Josie Go?* was chosen for the International Library at Geneva, Switzerland, and reviews have compared it to Mother Goose nursery rhymes.

The five books Helen Buckley has written more recently are aimed toward older children: *The Little Boy and the Birthdays,* also a Literary Guild selection, *Too Many Crackers* (illustrated by Tony Chen), *The Little Pig in the Cupboard, The Wonderful Little Boy,* and *Michael Is Brave.* All are excellent examples of the best in picture books; all are sensitive and whimsical. Their popularity is shown by the fact that children enjoy reading them over and over, and they are often hard to find on the public or elementary school library shelves.

Helen Buckley is modest about her talents as a writer and always encourages her students to send their manuscripts to publishers, as she once did to Lothrop, Lee & Shepard, who have published all her books. She maintains, "There are many good unpublished stories in people's heads or written on paper but tucked away. Even though you are unknown, send in your story." Children are fortunate that the professor followed her own advice of "Write and send."

Russell Hoban (1925–)

Russell Hoban was born in Lansdale, Pennsylvania, and after high school went to the Philadelphia Museum School of Industrial Art. In 1944 he married Lillian Aberman, and she has illustrated most of his books. They are the parents of four children, and Hoban admits that the inspiration for most of his stories comes from "ordinary domestic problems, so I have to pay close attention to what is going on in the house, looking for whatever humor may be in the situation and the resolution of it, and the resolution of it has to be one that really works."[28]

Hoban is one of the authors who has until recently been connected with many different phases of advertising. He started out in 1945 as an artist and illustrator for an advertising agency. Since then he has been a story board artist and character designer, television art director, and a freelance illustrator for advertising agencies and magazines including *Time, Life, Fortune,* and *Saturday Evening Post.* In 1956 he began concentrating on writing children's books.

All books by the husband-and-wife team have been consistently outstanding. Hoban's best-known books are the stories about Frances, a young female badger, and her problems and victories within her family. By using animals as characters, Hoban's messages are less didactic. He writes of animals that act like human beings, and his stories are told so that a child can see himself and his family and hopefully understand the interactions and relationships within family life.

The Frances books, charmingly illustrated, include *Bedtime for Frances* (1960), *A Baby Sister for Frances* (1964), *Best Friends for Frances* (1969), *A Bargain for Frances* (1970). These books show familiar family situations, sibling rivalry, stalling at bedtime, and fussy food habits—all humorously told.

One of the most delightful of all picture books is Hoban's *The Little Brute Family* (1972), a story about a family of ugly features, habits, and manners. As they go through life snarling, kicking, and acting rude, they are unhappy. But one day something happens: "a wonderful little lost feeling" comes to Baby Brute; he takes the feeling home and he changes. He remembers to say "Please" and "Thank you." As a result, the whole family changes, acts politely, and finally they change their name from Brute to Nice. This is a charming allegory with which children and parents can identify.

Hoban admits that most of his ideas for the Frances stories have come from observing his own family life. He has stated that ever since he has been writing, "There has always been a child less than three feet high around, and this is the point of view I've generally written from."[29]

Hoban has written one novel for children; it is a touchingly poignant fantasy, *The Mouse and His Child* (1967). In addition to personifying animals, Hoban writes of toys, so this is a story of a wind-up toy father and son who are broken, discarded, but repaired by a tramp. Then the pair set out on a quest to find a home, love, and security.

Maia Wojciechowska (1927–   )

Maia Wojciechowska (pronounced *Voi-che-hov-skah*) was born in Warsaw, Poland, where her father was the chief-of-staff of the Polish Air Force. After

---

28. Commire, *op. cit.,* p. 114.
29. *Ibid.*

the German invasion in 1939, the father remained in Poland while the family fled to France. Later they moved on to Spain, Portugal, and England before coming to America in 1942 and settling in Los Angeles. Miss Wojciechowska has been leading an interesting life ever since she fled from Poland. She is now a renowned author of juvenile realistic fiction.

A versatile woman of many talents and varied interests, Miss Wojciechowska has been a detective, a bullfighter, a professional tennis player, a masseuse, a ghost writer, a foreign language translator for Radio Free Europe, an assistant editor, a literary agent, and a publicity manager. She has recently written an autobiography, *Till the Break of Day: Memoirs: 1939–1942,* and if she had written nothing else, she would be singled out as an interesting person and author.

An interesting comment she has made about her education in France, where she was dismissed from seventeen schools in one year, reveals the beginnings of strong feelings about children, education, and perhaps explains why she writes about juveniles with problems. She said, "There has never been a love affair between me and education, especially since the time when at eleven I was asked by a teacher what I was doing. Thinking, I said. Stop it! said my teacher".[30] Life, however, has been exciting for Miss Wojciechowska in spite of her traumatic school experiences.

In 1950 she married Seldon Rodman, a writer; they are the parents of one daughter Oriana. Divorced seven years later, and remarried, Miss Wojciechowska and her daughter now live in Jamaica.

In 1965 Maia won the Newbery Medal for *Shadow of a Bull,* which tells the inner conflict of a young Spanish boy who is afraid to be a bullfighter, although he feels the duty to follow the skill of his father who had been the greatest bullfighter in Spain. Even though the setting is Spain, the theme is universal; and children identify with the boy's turmoil and with the final resolution of the plot, when at age eleven, Manuelo admits he is afraid to fight the bull. He quits, thereby exhibiting the kind of courage to confront an unreal expectation.

Maia's second notable book is *Tuned Out,* written in 1968 and generally recommended for teenagers. Due to the subject, a boy's problems with drugs, younger children of eleven and twelve find the book absorbing. The story is realistically told by an adolescent boy whose older brother returns from college addicted to drugs. The subject is presented in an honest, straightforward style, telling how the brother becomes addicted. The agony of both boys and their parents is painful, but, unfortunately, it is a subject that should be told. Miss Wojciechowska achieves the appropriate tone.

Don't Play Dead Before You Have To was published in 1970 and is another fine example of the best of today's realistic fiction. The book explores the problems young people face—divorce, self-alienation, the generation gap (which Miss W. labels a "chasm"), and identity crises. This sounds like dreary, oppressive reading, but Miss Wojciechowska has interspersed a great amount of humor into the story that lightens the seriousness of the crises and problems the characters face. This book is appealing to young and old, and in reading it, an adult can perhaps learn how to bridge the chasm between the generations.

---

30. *Ibid.,* p. 228.

Maia Wojciechowska has added new dimensions to realistic fiction, dimensions that today's youth want to read about. A woman of deep convictions, she has said, "I am pretty much concerned about this generation of kids, not because so much attention is being paid them but because they are so little understood and so lacking in understanding."[31] Her two latest books, *How God Got Christian into Trouble* and *The Crazy Old Lady and Me*, show her concern for the problems of children everywhere.

Louise Fitzhugh (1928–1975)

Louise Fitzhugh is the author-illustrator of *Harriet the Spy*, realistic fiction aimed at the ten to twelve age group. This important author was born in Memphis, Tennessee, the daughter of Louise Perkins Fitzhugh and Millsops Fitzhugh, an attorney. She attended the Hutchison School and Southwestern College in Memphis and then Florida Southern College in Lakeland, Florida. She went north to New York City and enrolled at New York University in the School of Education; she was a literature major but stopped six months short of earning a degree. Her interest in art caused her to switch to the Art Students League and enroll later at Cooper Union. She did well, and in 1963 she received enthusiastic critical reviews for a one-person show of her paintings at a New York gallery.

Miss Fitzhugh wrote from the time she was a child. Her first published book was *Suzuki Beane* (1961), written in collaboration with Sandra Scoppetone. It was her second book, *Harriet the Spy*, which made Louise Fitzhugh a success and set a new trend in realism for young people. This novel, which she illustrated as well as wrote, was selected by the *New York Times Book Review* as one of the year's best books for juveniles and won the 1967 Sequoyah Children's Book Award of Oklahoma. In 1968 *Family Circle Magazine* chose it as one of the "most loved children's books."[32] Her third book, *The Long Secret*, is a sequel to *Harriet the Spy*. Her fourth book, *Bang, Bang You're Dead* was again written in collaboration with Sandra Scoppetone. All books have been illustrated by Miss Fitzhugh. One can hardly imagine Harriet the Spy looking anything except the way Miss Fitzhugh drew her.

Miss Fitzhugh lived in Washington, D.C., and then in New York City, the setting of *Harriet the Spy*. She continued to write and illustrate and paint until her death in 1975. Her hobbies were tennis and playing the flute.

It now seems amazing that *Harriet the Spy*, published in 1964, stirred such a controversy at the time; however, many adults felt that it was a harmful book for juveniles to read. They objected to Harriet, an eleven-year-old, who went about spying on her parents, friends, teachers, and neighbors and recording her witty but honest comments. Critics claimed that children would be encouraged to spy, as if many normal children had never thought of pretending to spy. The Child Study Association removed *Harriet* from its list of recommended books. But children loved the book

---

31. *Ibid.*
32. Doris de Montreville and Donna Hill, *Third Book of Junior Authors* (New York: H. W. Wilson, 1972), p. 86.

and its sequel. When one reads the more graphically realistic books that have been published since, *Harriet* seems tame. The book is written with a great amount of humor, and Harriet is a unique child in one way, yet typical of all children in another. The book is a delight, and children are still enjoying it. Fitzhugh's recent book, *Nobody's Family Is Going to Change* (1974), discusses contemporary issues: children's rights, women's liberation, and sibling rivalry.

Maurice Sendak (1928–   )

Most critics agree that Maurice Sendak is the prevailing genius of children's literature and that three of his books have already become classics. This prestigious author-illustrator is equally well known and admired in Europe. Sendak's biographical background helps to explain his work, for he is a philosophical, intense, serious, and dedicated man whose personality prevades his work.

Maurice Sendak was born in 1928 in Brooklyn, New York, the child of Jewish immigrants who came to the United States from Poland before World War I. His father was a dressmaker and did well until the Depression, but Maurice says they still did well enough to be termed middle-class. The climate of his home was intellectual; books were treasured, and the creative interests of the three Sendak children were encouraged. The elder Sendak was a storyteller who told fantasies to his children; now it is the son who writes fantasies for other children.

Mr. Sendak has given many interviews that enlighten his public about himself as an artist and author. Sendak considers himself a creator

FIGURE 7–4. Children prepare a puppet show of one of their favorite stories: Where the Wild Things Are *by Maurice Sendak.*

of books. He does not believe in writing just for children. He says there is no such thing as a children's book; he claims that children just happen to like his books. Actually, he seems to write books for himself, to express a strong creative urge combined with a recall of the feelings, fears, and fantasies he had when he was a child. Sendak does not view children as his inferiors, but rather as his peers. Consequently, he scorns the idea that anyone sits down and writes *for* children a book suitable for ages four through eight. The fact that college students and all adults enjoy Mr. Sendak's books substantiates his claim that there is an arbitrary division between children's and adults' books. He has often said that adults enjoy *Alice in Wonderland* as much as children, so why can't adults enjoy picture books or any kind of books for children? Furthermore, he argues, quite rightly, that it takes as much creative effort to write children's books as adult books.

Sendak's strong feelings about the importance of books go back to his childhood, about which he says, "I felt that books were holy objects to be caressed, rapturously sniffed, devotedly provided for. I gave my life to them. I still do. I continue to do what I did as a child: dream of books, make books, and collect books."[33]

As a child, the youngest in his family, Sendak was close to his brother Jack. When Jack began writing and illustrating books, so did his admiring younger brother. When Jack went off to war in World War II, Maurice was in high school. He worked afternoons and evenings for All-American Comics, filling in backgrounds and working on lines for comic strips such as "Mutt and Jeff." When Jack returned from the army, both brothers, who had always been passionately interested in toys, started to make their own and tried to sell them to F. A. O. Schwarz, the New York toy store. The firm was not interested, but Maurice was offered a job working on display windows. At the time, he was studying at the Art Students League but, like many creative geniuses, his talent was within himself, and he now feels that he taught himself more than he learned from formal instruction. In many interviews Sendak has said that about this time he started studying the classical illustrators, particularly those of the nineteenth century in England. He admired Randolph Caldecott, Sir John Tenniel, Arthur Rackham, and William Blake.

For Sendak success came in the 1950s. In 1952 he had the opportunity to illustrate *A Hole Is to Dig* by Ruth Krauss, whom he admires as an author. His illustrations for the book were so delightful that Sendak became well known to publishers. He did seven books after that with Miss Krauss, from whom he said he learned the art of collaboration. Ever since, as he became an author-illustrator, his text and graphic designs have been a supreme example of the perfect harmony between the two arts. In the 1950s he also illustrated the *Little Bear* books by Else Minarik. He has illustrated for many top-grade authors, but it is Sendak's own books as an author-illustrator that give him the distinction he holds in children's literature.

In 1964 Sendak won the Caldecott Medal for *Where the Wild Things Are* and was runner-up for the Caldecott Medal for five other works. He has

33. Saul Braun, "Sendak Raises the Shades on Childhood," *New York Times Magazine*, June 7, 1970: 40.

been on the *New York Times* list of best-illustrated children's books fifteen times. So far, he has written and/or illustrated seventy books. In 1966 Sendak received the Hans Christian Andersen Award, the first American to win this international honor for excellence in the illustration of children's books.

Fame and devotion to his work have weighed heavily upon Sendak; to him the creation of his books is a mission. He suffered personal tragedies when his parents and his dog Jennie, a Sealyham terrier, all died within a short period of time. His dog is immortalized as Jennie the nurse in *Higglety Pigglety Pop!* The book is dedicated to her. Sendak suffered a heart attack, but has fortunately recovered his health and is now well and working on several books. A bachelor, he lives and works in a Manhattan duplex and has recently bought a farm in New England. Both homes are filled with books, records, and toys he keeps from his childhood. He has a huge collection of Mickey Mouse toys which he says he looks at when he is depressed. He writes and illustrates while listening to music that sets the mood for his work.

Some critics do not like his illustrations of children, which are not romanticized or realistic-looking. Some critics have called his children ugly, European, and un-American. Sendak says they are a curious "admixture of Brooklyn remembered and *shtetl* (Jewish small town) life in Poland fantasized, never actually experienced but passed on to me as persuasive reality by my immigrant parents."[34]

All of Sendak's books are popular, but his five most admired are *Where the Wild Things Are, Higglety Pigglety Pop: Or There Must Be More to Life,* the *Nutshell Library,* and *In the Night Kitchen.* Each has sold several hundred thousand copies; librarians claim they never have enough copies of his books to lend.

In Sendak's books children have learned the word "No," which children in real life have been saying for a long time. Sendak's characters show the frustration, aggression, fear, and delights that children experience. In *Pierre: A Cautionary Tale,* one of the miniature volumes in the *Nutshell Library,* Pierre keeps saying, "I don't care. I don't care." Children love Sendak's injection of chaos and his inclusion of hostility, which children do feel. Naturally Sendak's books have aroused controversy among parents and educators. Many feel that children should not be exposed to boys and girls who are "naughty." But, as has previously been stated, the final critics are the children who love Sendak's books.

This unique man has no one style of illustrating his books. Sendak says that one style is boring; when an artist has only one style, he is actually doing the same book over and over. Having a flexible style allows him "to walk in and out of all kinds of books." Flexibility Sendak has, from *Higglety Pigglety Pop!,* which has the finely engraved Victorian English style of pen and ink sketches to the most modern cartoon strip, pop culture style of *In the Night Kitchen.*

One of Sendak's latest works is the illustrations for *The Juniper Tree and Other Tales from Grimm* (1973). First, the selection of the stories from the complete 210 tales of the original Grimm Brothers collection is notable.

---

34. *Ibid.,* p. 42.

Lore Segal and Sendak jointly chose 27, and their choices are very good. Four tales were translated by the late poet Randall Jarrell; the remaining 23 are the work of the novelist Lore Segal, who writes prose and poetry and teaches writing at Princeton and Columbia Universities. She has written children's books, including *Tell Me A Mitzi* and *All the Way Home*. Together Segal and Sendak have produced a masterpiece. In appearance, *The Juniper Tree* resembles a book published in nineteenth-century Germany. The two boxed volumes are small in size; they are published by Farrar, Straus & Giroux. Sendak's pen and ink drawings measure only 3½ by 4½ inches, but as if by magic these drawings seem much larger. Many art critics feel that these drawings are among Sendak's best. They have been compared to Durer's "Little Passion of Christ." Also seen are the influences of the classical illustrators John Tenniel and Edward Lear. The bearded peasants look the way one pictures the rural folks who actually told these stories to the Brothers Grimm. But, last of all and most important, they have the genius and creativity of Sendak himself. Each tale has one illustration, once seen not easily forgotten. Wistful peasants, sometimes serious and often mocking, cats, crows, dogs, skeletons, princesses, and devils appear against interesting compositions of leaves and foliage. To understand exactly what was needed for his drawings, Sendak spent years studying German, traveling to the mountains and forests where the originals were told. It is such perfectionism that has earned Sendak his prestigious reputation.

Mr. Sendak thinks of himself first as an author, then as an illustrator. In fact, he doesn't think of the pictures at all until the book is written. He finds it more difficult and interesting to write, admitting he suffers greatly. "A book being printed is a major topic in itself; it is a very difficult thing to see through. What was once very dreamlike and transparent and what you thought was a magic moment has now become a real thing in a printing press . . . and it looks lousy, and it has to be done all over again."[35]

These are the words of a perfectionist who conjures up many moments of magic—an original creator who writes wonderful fantasies that are wry, witty, and fun. His latest work is *Some Swell Pup: Or Are you Sure You Want a Dog?* and his illustrations for Randall Jarrell's *Fly by Night* (1976) and George MacDonald's *The Golden Key* (1967).

Elaine L. Konigsburg (1930–)

In 1967, Atheneum Press published two books by a young, unknown author, Elaine L. Konigsburg. The first book, unusually titled *Jennifer, Hecate, Macbeth, William McKinley, and Me, Elizabeth,* is a warm, subtly humorous story of an interracial friendship. That same year Mrs. Konigsburg published *From the Mixed-Up Files of Mrs. Basil E. Frankweiler*, the detailed account of a brother and sister who leave home and move into the Metropolitan Museum of Art in New York City. The story is so impeccably crafted that the plot seems plausible.

With the publication of these two books, Elaine Konigsburg accomplished an unusual feat in children's literature. She won two awards: *From*

---

35. Hoffman and Samuels, *op. cit.*, p. 375.

the Mixed-Up Files of Mrs. Basil E. Frankweiler was awarded the Newbery Medal, and *Jennifer, Hecate, Macbeth, William McKinley and Me, Elizabeth* was voted a Newbery Honor Book.

In 1970 Mrs. Konigsburg published (*George*), a realistic yet humorous story of a boy with a split personality, a schizophrenic. The subject does not sound funny, but the author's tender story of this intelligent, lovable boy strongly urges a more enlightened approach towards mental illness and toward understanding that a child can be different yet lovable. Because of Mrs. Konigsburg's amusing style, what could be an unpleasant subject becomes enjoyable reading.

Elaine Konigsburg never set out to become an author. Raised in the mill town of Farrell, Pennsylvania, she was an excellent student, majored in chemistry at the Carnegie Institute of Technology in Pittsburgh, and continued her studies at the University of Pittsburgh. In interviews she jokingly claims that she was a chemist until a few minor explosions in a laboratory caused her to turn to teaching. Actually, the end of her chemistry career was brought about when she and her husband David, who has a doctorate in psychology, moved to Jacksonville, Florida. The couple began rearing their children, and it seemed that Elaine would eventually settle into being a suburban mother. However, when the family moved to New Jersey and her youngest child entered school, she suddenly had more time. She took lessons at the Art Students League and soon began winning art prizes. Mrs. Konigsburg began to write, testing her work on her children when they came home for lunch. Then she began to write and publish.

In addition to the three books discussed above, Mrs. Konigsburg wrote a novel *About the B'nai Bagels* in 1969 and *Altogether, One at a Time* in 1971, a collection of four well-written short stories. In 1974 she published *The Dragon in the Ghetto Caper*, a humorous assortment of cops, crime, dragons, and amateur detectives.

Elaine Konigsburg is one of the new exponents of the ever-growing trend towards greater realism in juvenile fiction, although she also writes fantasies such as *A Proud Taste for Scarlet and Miniver* (1973), a fantasy about Eleanor of Aquitane. She writes for both sexes and for all ages. Her latest book is *Father's Arcane Daughter*, published in 1976.

Joan Lexau

Joan Lexau is blessed with the ability to write consistently excellent books upon a diversity of topics. Highly prolific, she has written more than thirty books since *Olaf Reads*, her first book, was published in 1961.

Miss Lexau was born in St. Paul, lived her first five years in Washington, D.C., and then returned to St. Paul. Her parents divorced when she was quite young, and her mother struggled to make ends meet for young Joan and her brother Henry:

> When I was a small child, I went to the little store for bread one day and heard the store manager telling a customer about a courageous woman who lived nearby and was bringing up two kids on very little money. I went home and told my mother about this marvelous creature and then wondered why she didn't have anything to say about it. It wasn't

until years later that I recalled the scene and realized that she was the woman.[36]

Although she disliked high school, Miss Lexau stayed because "No one told me I could drop out."[37] She has since studied philosophy at St. Paul's College of St. Thomas. In the years between school and writing, Miss Lexau was at times a department store saleswoman, library clerk, bookkeeper, a kitchen girl in a Montana resort, and a reporter for several magazines and journals. In 1957 Miss Lexau began doing production and liaison work on children's books for Harper and Row. Coming into contact with so many books, she herself finally decided to write.[38]

Olaf Reads is a highly entertaining story about a boy just learning to read who takes the "pull" sign of a fire alarm too literally.

Many of Miss Lexau's books concern minority children. *Benjie,* published in 1964, is about a small black child in search of his grandmother's lost earring. During his hunt, he loses a lot of his shyness. The 1971 *Benjie on His Own* shows Benjie lost in the city and overwhelmed. His grandmother is ill and he must find help. *Me Day,* written in 1971, is about a boy whose parents are divorced. *Striped Ice Cream,* published in 1968, is about a girl from a poor family who eagerly anticipates her birthday.

Miss Lexau currently lives in a converted church parsonage where she continues to write her wonderful books that delight children of all ages.

S. E. Hinton (1948–   )

S. E. Hinton is a masculine-sounding name, and intentionally so. Author Susan Hinton feared that no one would believe her books about gangs and drugs if it were obvious that a girl had written them. Nevertheless, her two books, *The Outsiders* and *That Was Then, This Is Now,* are read by hundreds of thousands of high school and junior high school students.

The Outsiders, published in 1967, is the story of the conflict of two high school cultures: the Socs (middle-class) and the Greasers (people from the "other side of the tracks"). We empathize with the situation of Ponyboy, a sensitive and reluctant Greaser, and we are made to feel the hopelessness of his situation. Man's inhumanity is displayed in a new context. Miss Hinton was only sixteen when she wrote *The Outsiders.*

That Was Then, This Is Now, published in 1971, provides deep insight into the drug world. Byron is faced with the decision of whether or not to turn in his best friend Mark for dealing in drugs. He remembers the horrible effect drugs had upon another friend. Byron turns in Mark but undergoes tremendous guilt feelings. This book is written in a matter-of-fact style. It does not moralize over the evils of drugs but instead demonstrates some of the pitfalls.

Susan Hinton is neither Soc nor Greaser nor addict. Rather, she is a girl from Tulsa, Oklahoma, recently graduated from Tulsa University, who objects to the dearth of books about topics of concern to teenagers:

36. Hopkins, *op. cit.,* pp. 144–145.
37. *Ibid.,* p. 145.
38. Commire, *op. cit.,* p. 144.

Have you ever looked at the books on the Young Adult Shelf? They are written by aging writers who either try to remember their own youth—which was at least fifteen years ago—or they try to write about today's teens without knowing them.[39]

After all, who is better qualified to write about teenagers than a teenager? Obviously, her books involve controversial subjects, and many mistakenly feel that Miss Hinton is condoning gang fights and drug use or else is guilty of sensationalism. She received many critical letters in response to an August 7, 1967, article in the *New York Times Magazine*:

"I have three teenage children, and they just don't know any people like those in your book."

"I feel that Miss Hinton is a cliché grabber, not a free thinker . . . America has more responsibility to the people of the world than to think teenagers are to be looked up to or catered to."[40]

Miss Hinton replies that the same parents that object to the gang fights in *The Outsiders* think nothing of their children's watching several hours of TV violence.[41]

Of course, this controversy took place in 1967; few people object to Miss Hinton's *That Was Then, This Is Now* in 1976. Her recent book *Rumble Fish* is a story of a tough fourteen-year-old boy whose drive to be like his older brother, "The Motorcycle Boy," leads to some problems that seem very real among today's life styles.

SUMMARY

Children today are fortunate to have a great variety of literature available to satisfy their needs and desires. The books written in the past have been preserved and are still being enjoyed. Modern books display a seemingly endless assortment, for within their beguiling covers are modern adaptations of every type of literature—myths, folklore, fairy tales, and fantasies, in addition to a new type of realistic fiction.

Although there has always been some realism in children's literature, it is continuously moving towards a new peak. Realism today echoes the child's world. Many current books candidly discuss subjects that were once forbidden and considered shocking. These books are extremely popular with children, who are more sophisticated and more knowledgeable than children were twenty-five years ago. The subjects mirror our culture: violence, war, drugs, divorce, alcoholism, inhumanity, self-alienation, and racial, ethnic, and sexual discrimination. The writers of children's literature have responded to these crises of our society, attempting to help the child find a better self-concept and to serve as a guide to the solution or explanation of these problems.

---

39. Zena Sutherland, "The Teen-Ager Speaks," *Saturday Review,* January 27, 1968: 34.
40. *Ibid.*
41. *Ibid.*

Honest realism is written for very young children in picture books as well as for older children, who reach maturity at a younger age than formerly and are eager to read about life as it really is. Although there are many examples of realistic books with high literary merit, some are merely sensational, written by authors who wish to capitalize on the latest movement. A judicious teacher follows her own criteria for good and bad literature, judging realistic fiction by the same standards used for other types of books. She can guide her students and can offer a balanced literature program in the classroom as well as to children individually.

Knowledge of the lives of the authors of children's books can provide both the teacher and the children with deeper understandings of the circumstances which prompted the writing of the books, and a deeper appreciation of the motives, philosophy, and circumstances that help to develop the author's special world.

TO THE COLLEGE STUDENT

1. Make a study of books published in the last year. Divide them into types, such as fantasy, realistic fiction, biography, and so forth. Divide the books into age groups: picture books for young children, books for intermediate age groups, and books for early adolescents. When the study is completed, note the variety of subject matter, genres, and literary value.

2. Develop a philosophy or set your own criteria of what good realistic fiction should be for each age group.

3. Think about and discuss what themes have relevancy to today's youth. Try to find books on these themes.

4. Compare how realism for young children and juveniles has changed between 1930 and the present. Find one or two examples from each period, and note the similarities and dissimilarities in theme, style, mood, tone, and humor.

5. Keep a file card system of books listed together which have the same theme, such as divorce, drugs, violence, alienation, ethnic and racial problems, and so forth. This list will be very useful when your teaching career starts.

6. As you read modern literature, keep a list of books that you decide will lend themselves to reading aloud to a classroom during story hour. Some books are better for a child to read by himself; others are appropriate for group enjoyment.

7. As you read modern literature, keep a list of books with themes and episodes of everyday problems that will be useful to you for role-playing or for classroom dramatic productions. The purpose for these books is not for school plays but for on-the-spot situations, as when jealousy or arguments arise between two children or two groups, as illustrated by Maurice Sendak in Janice Udry's *Let's Be Enemies.*

TO THE CLASSROOM TEACHER

1. Think of ways you can use modern realistic fiction so that your students see the connection between literature and life. Children hear the word "life" but often have only a vague concept of what this mysterious word means. Try to find ways that the adventures and experiences in books have a real connection with those that children have every day.

2. Using the criteria for selecting good books discussed in Chapter 3, make a list of twenty to fifty books of recent publication dates, and ditto this list to send home to parents for suggested reading for their chil-

dren. Most parents want to buy or help their children find books that a teacher recommends.

3. Work with your school librarian to help select new books. Most librarians are very happy to have teacher recommendations.

4. Invite the school librarian or one from the public library to come into the classroom and show some new books and give short book reviews.

5. Participate in district and county book selection committees.

6. If possible, set aside some time each week or each month to review new books within your classroom. One of the easiest sources for keeping up with new books is the Sunday *New York Times Book Review* section, available at all public libraries. Clip out and save the page of book reviews from newspapers and magazines and try to find these books or order them at the library.

7. Build a unit around the works of one author mentioned in this chapter.

8. Using some of the strategies mentioned in Chapters 13 and 14, have the children present reports on the authors of their favorite books rather than on the books themselves (e.g., puppet shows, dramatizations, peep shows).

TO THE COLLEGE STUDENT AND THE CLASSROOM TEACHER

1. Discuss and evaluate books containing controversial issues. Are these books good literature, or are they capitalizing on such sensational topics as drug addiction, divorce, sex, the generation gap?

2. In analyzing books of realistic fiction, discuss whether style, mood, humor (or lack of it) add or detract from the literary merit of the book and the subject it discusses. Compare and contrast such differences in the styles of Eleanor Estes, Lois Lenski, Elaine Konigsburg, Louise Fitzhugh, Maia Wojciechowska, and Judy Blume.

3. Compare realistic fiction in literature for children with the presentations of television and cinema. Do all three have their own merits as well as lack of distinction? Watch for the showings of films or television dramatic productions based on books you use in the classroom.

4. Compare and contrast some classic fantasies, such as *Alice's Adventures in Wonderland* or *The Wizard of Oz* or *Peter Pan*, with modern fantasies, such as E. B. White's *Stuart Little* or *Charlotte's Web*, and Eleanor Cameron's *The Court of the Stone Children*.

5. Compare and contrast the classic picture books with modern ones. Try to find ones on the same subject or of the same genre. Compare a traditional edition of *The Three Little Pigs* with William Pené DuBois's *Three Little Pigs*. Try to find as many books from the nineteenth century and compare them with books of recent publication, keeping in mind that you might want to present both the old and the new treatment of the same subject.

6. Borrow *Publishers Weekly* (R. R. Bowker) from your library to keep up on new children's books published by modern authors.

SELECTED BIBLIOGRAPHY

Arbuthnot, May Hill, and Zena Sutherland. *Children and Books*, 4th ed. Glenview, Ill.: Scott, Foresman, 1972.

Commire, Anne, ed. *Something about the Author: Facts and Pictures about Contemporary Authors and Illustrators of Books for Young People*, vols. 1–7. Detroit: Gale Research, 1971–1975.

de Montreville, Doris, and Donna Hill, eds. *Third Book of Junior Authors.* New York: H. W. Wilson, 1972.

Fuller, Muriel, ed. *More Junior Authors.* New York: H. W. Wilson, 1963.

Hoffman, Miriam, and Eva Samuels, comps. *Authors and Illustrators of Children's Books.* New York: R. R. Bowker, 1972.

Hopkins, Lee Bennett. *Books Are by People: Interviews with 104 Authors and Illustrators of Books for Young Children.* New York: Citation Press, 1969.

Huck, Charlotte S., and Doris Young Kuhn. *Children's Literature in the Elementary School,* 3rd ed. New York: Holt, Rinehart and Winston, 1976.

Hurlimann, Bettina. *Picture Book World.* Edited and translated by Brian Alderson. Cleveland: World, 1969.

Kingman, Lee, ed. *Newbery and Caldecott Medal Books, 1956–1965.* Boston: Horn Book, 1965.

Kunitz, Stanley J., and Howard Haycraft, eds. *The Junior Book of Authors,* 2nd ed. New York: H. W. Wilson, 1951.

Lanes, Selma G. *Down the Rabbit Hole: Adventures and Misadventures in the Realm of Children's Literature.* New York: Atheneum, 1971.

Larrick, Nancy. *A Teacher's Guide to Children's Books.* Columbus: Charles E. Merrill, 1960.

Lenski, Lois. *Adventure in Understanding: Talks to Parents, Teachers and Librarians by Lois Lenski, 1944–1966.* Tallahassee: 1968.

Lonsdale, Bernard J., and Helen K. Mackintosh. *Children Experience Literature.* New York: Random House, 1972.

Robinson, Evelyn Rose. *Readings about Children's Literature.* New York: David McKay, 1966.

Smith, James Steel. *A Critical Approach to Children's Literature.* New York: McGraw-Hill, 1967.

Townsend, John Rowe. *A Sense of Story: Essays on Contemporary Writers for Children.* Philadelphia: J. B. Lippincott, 1971.

CHAPTER 8

Classical Illustrators:
A Resource for the Teacher

Alice was beginning to get very tired of sitting by her sister on the bank and of having nothing to do; once or twice she had peeped into the book her sister was reading, but it had no pictures or conversations in it, "and what is the use of a book," thought Alice "without pictures or conversations?"[1]

Lewis Carroll knew the importance of illustrations in a children's book. Back in 1865, in the first sentence of the first paragraph of his famous *Alice's Adventures in Wonderland,* he wrote the quotation which opens this chapter.

It was his century that produced those artists we now refer to as the classical illustrators, beginning with the famous trio Walter Crane, Randolph Caldecott, and Kate Greenaway. The advent of literature for children, which was in itself a milestone, created another milestone: the development of appropriate art work to enhance the children's stories and poems. Criteria have developed over the years for judging this art work; these criteria are presented on page 95.

Much of the flavor and style of a book are enhanced by its illustrations. Many illustrations, after a passage of time, are updated or copied by a modern artist, which is a tribute to the timeliness of the original illustrations. The updated art may also give the story more appeal to a new generation. However, many books are still most appealing with their original illustrations.

---

1. Lewis Carroll, *Alice in Wonderland,* edited by Donald J. Gray (New York: W. W. Norton, 1971), p. 7.

Just as they want to know who wrote the stories they read, children will also want to know who painted the pictures or made the drawings in their favorite books. Excellence in artistic ability does not go wasted on children. A good artist's work is ageless. Children find delight in beautiful pictures regardless of the year they were painted or drawn, just as all art is appreciated because of its beauty, not its origin in time.

One of the classics still loved by modern children contains Beatrix Potter's charming sketches of *Peter Rabbit*. It demonstrates that children are still finding pleasure and delight in a book written and illustrated at a time when the world was far different than it is today. The child cares little when these drawings were produced. He only knows his enjoyment.

A teacher who wishes to be able to answer children's questions about the books and pictures that they experience will learn that modern illustrators have been greatly influenced by the classical illustrators. Knowing about these artists supports the teacher in her ultimate goal of teaching literature through using a variety of approaches. A lack of understanding of the styles of classical illustrators would be tantamount to a history teacher's knowing nothing of ancient history while attempting to teach students modern history. Sensible pedagogy suggests that a teacher know the past and the present and the links connecting them so that she may be a more creative teacher. In coming to a complete understanding of any area of the fine arts, an appreciation of the work of artists in ages past is important in order to judge the work of artists today.

Let children discover, see, and enjoy the beauty preserved in the

FIGURE 8–1. *Primary children draw their versions of* Jack and the Beanstalk.

book illustrations from the past so that they can learn to understand the elusive, mysterious quality of beauty today and in the future. The love of beauty, once nourished in a child, is rarely lost.

Literature written especially for children is a new kind of literature. However, children from primitive times who looked at the drawings on the walls of caves, at Japanese scrolls, or Renaissance parchments have always had some form of art to see. If the production and publication of children's books developed slowly, the illustration of books developed even more slowly. Before the invention of movable type by Johann Gutenburg about 1450, books were written and illustrated and printed by hand. They were expensive, and only the clergy and the nobility could own them.

It was not until the seventeenth century that a book called *Orbis Pictus* (World in Pictures) made history. It was the first illustrated book for children in the Western world. Written in Latin in 1637, translated into English in 1658, this book with pictures was written by John Amos Comenius (1592–1670), who was a bishop in the Moravian church in Hungary. Comenius is called the father of the picture book because he believed children could learn more by seeing illustrations printed in their books. After Comenius wrote his book, he traveled to Nuremburg, Germany, to have his illustrations engraved on plates. The illustrations were woodcuts, and it is reported that the illustration, printing, and publishing of the book took three years to complete. The book contains 150 chapters covering many subjects. Each page had a text explaining the nature of the world to children, and each page had an appropriate woodcut illustration. What a delight *Orbis Pictus* must have been to the children fortunate enough to have seen it! To our modern tastes the pictures seem crude and elementary, but this book marked the beginning of the idea of the fusion of text with the art of illustration.

Since writing stories for the entertainment of children was slow in acceptance, so was the idea of illustrating a book for the child's pleasure, rather than as a visual aid for moralistic instruction. The first illustrators of children's books were anonymous, as were the authors, since working on children's books was not considered a respectable occupation.

The only books available to the masses of poor people were gaudy *chapbooks*, so named because they were sold by peddlers called chapmen. These chapbooks were sold for a few pennies and were written on a variety of subjects: humorous, religious, legendary, historical, biographical, supernatural, and so forth. The stories were not original but were rewritten legends, folktales, and action-filled adventures. Not many were great works of literature and they were designed for adults, but children read them because they were the only literature available.

In the 1860s, publishers in London began to sell what we now classify as children's picture books illustrated in color. One publisher and artist, Edmund Evans, was responsible for launching the careers of three great illustrators: Crane, Caldecott, and Greenaway. Evans was an innovator in color printing. It is said that he hated the chapbooks and their low-quality illustrations. He believed that books could be produced for the nursery child that would be artistic in color and design and could sell for a small price. He became the first printer of paperbacks in color, for the books he produced had soft-bound covers. Evans was essentially a color printer, but he also owned machinery for wood engraving. He operated a large shop with many machines for printing both types of art work of the highest quality. He printed what were called "yellowbacks," soft-bound books and magazines. Between jobs his machines were idle, which in business is obviously not a desirable financial state. In order to fill up these idle times, he conceived the idea of publishing toy books, small-size children's books printed in color. Not only was Evans a good businessman with a fine artistic taste, he was apparently a good artist himself. The first artist Evans found to illustrate his books was Walter Crane, then came Kate Greenaway, then Randolph Caldecott, all of whom were innovators in the art of illustrating children's books.

Walter Crane (1845–1915)

Crane was the first illustrator whom Edmund Evans, the printer of children's toy books, hired to produce picture books for children that were beautiful in color and design. Crane's success gave him great pleasure and gave children picture books of great artistic value. His genius for design and color have made his illustrations classic masterpieces that are studied and admired by modern illustrators.

Crane's life was interesting. He possessed an inventive mind and was deeply involved in the artistic and social influences of his age. Perhaps this is one reason why his work still has validity today.

Crane was born in Liverpool, England, the son of a well-known portrait painter. Growing up in an artistic environment, the young boy began to draw. As early as fourteen, the youth drew color illustrations for Tennyson's *Lady of Shalott* that were so good that when W. J. Linton, the famous London wood-engraver, saw them, he accepted Crane as an apprentice for three years, from 1859 to 1861. Consequently, not only did Crane learn to draw on the block and all about wood engraving from a master, he was also able to absorb many different facets of the exciting world of London. For example, he liked to go to the office of *Punch Magazine* and look at the cartoons of famous artists, and in the evenings he studied at an art school. At this time he met J. R. Wise, a writer, who became his intellectual mentor. Wise, a lover of both history and nature, took the boy to the countryside on traditional English walking tours, introducing him to the natural beauties of the forest. Through Wise, Crane was also introduced to the writings of Ralph Waldo Emerson, whose *Conduct of Life* was intellectually stimulating.

At seventeen, Crane's illustrations for the verses of Wise's ballad, *The New Forest, Its History and Scenery*, were published and highly praised. In the following year, 1863, Crane illustrated his first children's book, *The True, Pathetic History of Poor Match*, a story about a dog. At this time he began to design railway bookstall novels, the gaudy, commercial yellowbacks popular with the public. This led to his meeting the printer Edmund Evans who, upon seeing Crane's work, invited him to illustrate the first series of children's toy picture books. The titles of these books show that nineteenth-century children for the first time had a selection similar to that of the modern child. The list includes: *The Farmyard ABC, The Railroad Alphabet, The House That Jack Built, The History of Cock Robin, Sing a Song of Sixpence, This Little Pig, One, Two, Buckle My Shoe, Cinderella,*

Little Red Riding-Hood, Jack and the Beanstalk, Beauty and the Beast, and *The Sleeping Beauty.*

The second set of toy books, begun in 1873, shows that Crane had become more experienced in drawing for children, since he used more colors and designed the pages in a more spacious manner. Crane's first set were a bit too elaborate and sophisticated for children. However, as Crane matured, he experimented with theories of design, color, and format. He can be considered a forerunner of the modern illustrators in that he thought illustrating for children was an art worthy of serious effort, drawing each picture painstakingly so that there was a harmony between text and art. In fact, he himself even drew parts of the text in bold red and black letters. And, as many modern artists do, he drew charming title pages and end papers. He loved to decorate the borders of his illustrations, a practice which many modern artists still keep.

Crane's work shows the effects of three influences: his love of Japanese art (a Navy friend brought him prints from the Orient), his visits to Italy where he learned to admire Botticelli and the early Florentines, and his friendship with William Morris and his school of craftsmen. Crane developed a sophisticated art style of bold, black outlines drawn with a forceful heavy stroke, highly detailed designs which, when combined with primitive colors, made fanciful and often humorous illustrations.

After Crane finished his commission for Evans, he illustrated seventeen books for Mrs. Molesworth, a popular writer for children. Crane also illustrated two plays of Shakespeare, and *The Happy Prince* by Oscar Wilde. Many critics feel that Crane's most illustrious work was the pen and ink sketches of Grimms' *Household Stories,* translated by his sister Lucy.

Crane was a teacher of art and had frequent exhibitions as he became well known. He and his family traveled extensively, going to America where he exhibited in Boston, Philadelphia (where he met Howard Pyle), Chicago, and St. Louis. In Boston Crane was asked to illustrate Nathaniel Hawthorne's *Wonder Book for Girls and Boys.*

Anyone interested in Crane's life will enjoy his autobiography, *An Artist's Reminiscences.* The history of illustrators of children's books is enriched by Walter Crane's lifelong artistic striving, which impelled his imagination to make new syntheses in children's books.

Randolph Caldecott (1846–1886)

The second illustrator of this famous triumvirate was Randolph Caldecott, whose work was so distinguished and admired that in 1938 the medal given annually in America to the artist who designs the most distinguished picture book for children was named for him.

Caldecott was born in Cheshire, England, the son of an accountant who wanted him to be a banker instead of an artist. At the age of fifteen, Caldecott started working in a bank in Shropshire. The youth cared little for banking and spent his free time drawing on old bank receipts and traveling around the country, enjoying the pursuits a young country squire followed in those days. He went fishing and hunting, went to country fairs and developed a love for the vigor of the English rural life; these impressions stamped themselves on his personality and artistic work for the rest of his life. Finally in 1870, Caldecott gave up banking and went to London to establish himself as an artist, for he had already made friendships with prominent artists. His illustrations soon appeared in *Punch* and in the American magazine *Harper's Monthly*. His first success was his illustrations for Washington Irving's *Old Christmas* and *Bracebridge Hall*. Finally, like Crane, he was asked to illustrate children's books in color by the printer Edmund Evans. In 1878 Caldecott's first famous picture book was published, *The House That Jack Built*, which, incidentally, is still being published today exactly as Caldecott drew it. He also successfully illustrated William Cowper's poem *John Gilpin*. Caldecott's reputation as an outstanding illustrator was established, and he went on to produce sixteen picture books. The familiar stories he illustrated were *Sing a Song for Sixpence, Hey-Diddle-Diddle, A Frog He Would A-Wooing Go, Ride a Cock Horse to Banbury Cross*, and *Three Jovial Huntsmen*.

Caldecott apparently did not have to find his style, for it seemed formed in the beginning of his career, and his illustrations are not uneven in quality. All his illustrations are whimsical, original, humorous, and robust in action, thereby giving him the reputation of the classic illustrator for children. In looking at illustrators from the late nineteenth century to the present, it is obvious that Caldecott's work has been studied, admired, and copied. He never used an unnecessary stroke or line, for each line gives life, animation, and action. If his successor, Kate Greenaway, was a master of painting children in gardens while playing and having tea parties, Caldecott was a master of drawing animals and people who lived the robust English country life. It is virtually impossible to estimate the pleasure children have received from Caldecott's art, and his reputation lives on with the medal awarded to picture books whose merit is judged worthy of bearing his name.

Few people realize that Caldecott (who never was physically strong) and his wife went to St. Augustine, Florida, where he hoped the warm climate would restore his health. However, his health did not improve and he died in 1886 at the age of forty.[2]

Kate Greenaway (1846–1901)

The third of the three best illustrators of children's books in the nineteenth century was Kate Greenaway, whose books can hold their own with the best books published today. In fact, many modern artists are copying the Greenaway style. Miss Greenaway was born in London, the daughter of a well-known artist and engraver whose work was often published in *Punch*. Although most of her early childhood was spent in London, she often visited the country on a farm at Rolleston in Nottinghamshire. These quiet scenes of English country life and the children and the gardens made an everlasting impression on her. Born with artistic ability, her environment nurtured her talent. She began to draw, sketch, and paint at an early age although she was not given formal art lessons until she was twelve. At art school her talent was recognized, and she won many prizes and awards. When she was twenty, she first exhibited her work, one watercolor and "six little drawings on wood."

2. Brian Doyle, ed. *The Who's Who of Children's Literature* (New York: Schocken, 1969), p. 320.

She began her career as a greeting card artist by designing valentines, Christmas and birthday cards. The printer Edmund Evans saw her work and was impressed by its charm and originality. In 1879 Evans printed her first book, *Under the Window*, a picture book with verses that Miss Greenaway composed and illustrated. On each page is an illustration of children running, playing, sitting, skipping—all looking happy in a beautiful sunlit world. *Under the Window* was an innovation in children's picture books and an immediate success, making Kate Greenaway famous in America as well as Europe. The book sold about 70,000 copies and is still available, printed by Evans's firm. "K. G.," as she was known to her close friends, continued illustrating and writing children's books the rest of her life. The public loved her work, particularly her calendars or *Almanacks*, which were published every year except one for the next fourteen years. Her most famous illustrated books were *The Language of Flowers, Marigold Garden, A Apple Pie, A Child's Garden of Verses, A Birthday Book for Children,* and *Mother Goose.*

Miss Greenaway's style of illustrating is characterized by simplicity, freshness, humor, and purity. In looking at the children in her illustrations, one is fascinated by the way they are costumed. When her books were first published, the Kate Greenaway look in children's clothes was copied and, at one time, she thought of manufacturing children's clothes as a business venture. The girls' clothing is distinctive, including frills, high waists, ribbons, and mobcaps. Many have speculated on the source of her inspiration for the children's costumes. The distinctive Greenaway look is due to three sources: (1) she undoubtedly remembered from her Rolleston days the quaint clothes worn by the country children; (2) her mother at one time had a children's clothing store where she sold fancy clothing, lace, and accessories, which made Miss Greenaway unusually aware of clothes for children; and (3) she studied pictures of children's clothing from previous generations. Then she added the extra ingredient of her imagination, thereby creating a style of her own, belonging to no specific period. The picturesque look of these children appeals to children now, as it did almost one hundred years ago. It gives one a sense of security and contentment to gaze at Miss Greenaway's children as they sing, dance, run, play games, march together, and have tea parties in charming English gardens. Kate Greenaway saw beauty in everything in the world; she often said she saw little that was ugly.

Her private life, in spite of her success, remained quiet. She lived modestly and devoted herself to her work, her family, and her garden of flowers. One of her most often quoted lines expresses the philosophy behind her work: "Children like something that excites their imagination—a very real thing mixed up with a great unreality like Bluebeard." She deserves her place in the art of illustrating children's books, for she was truly a pioneer.

In 1955, the Kate Greenaway Medal was established in Great Britain. It is awarded annually to the artist who has produced the most distinguished illustration of children's books during the year. It is equivalent to the Caldecott Medal in America.[3]

---

3. Edward Ernest, *The Kate Greenaway Treasury* (Cleveland: World, 1967), pp. 24–43.

John Tenniel (1820–1914)

Born in London in 1820, John Tenniel was interested in drawing at an early age. He studied art at the Royal Academy School, but he learned more from taking his sketching pad to the British Museum than from art lessons. At sixteen he exhibited one painting at a small art gallery, and a year later he showed an oil painting at the prestigious Royal Academy in London. He continued exhibiting his oil paintings while he started illustrating books— three in all, one of which, *Aesop's Fables*, was for children. Like most illustrators of that time, he worked on wood blocks.[4]

In 1850 he started his lifelong career, that of a cartoonist for *Punch*. He continued this work for the next fifty years. As *Punch* was a magazine with a wide circulation, much like our modern *New Yorker* magazine, his cartoons made his name well known. The subject matter of his cartoons was topical, both social and political. Although Tenniel's name was familiar to the British public as a cartoonist for *Punch,* the world today would not know his name or his work had he not been the illustrator of Lewis Carroll's *Alice* books. Although other artists have illustrated Carroll's fantasy, for many readers Tenniel's illustrations remain the most perfect. His interpretations of the characters and their settings are unique and different. Once one has seen Tenniel's drawings of Alice, the rabbit, Humpty Dumpty, the Cheshire cat, one can never forget them.

When Lewis Carroll's friends urged him to publish *Alice's Adventures in Wonderland*, Tenniel's name was suggested. After Tenniel read the manuscript, it is said that he readily accepted the commission. An interesting sidelight of the book's illustration is that at first Carroll thought he himself would draw the illustrations, but when he discovered they had to be done as wood engravings, he knew he did not know that process.[5] There are differing accounts of the relationship between these two men during the time when the book was illustrated and published. Some report their collaboration was difficult and that they quarreled over Tenniel's sketches because Carroll rejected many. However, Carroll says nothing of this in his diaries, only noting the dates when he received Tenniel's sketches. The first book appeared in 1865, but both Tenniel and Carroll disliked the poor printing so they recalled the entire published collection, now a collector's item. In December 1866, Macmillan issued the second edition, of which both men approved, and its success was immediately apparent by the book's sales, which constantly increased. *Through the Looking Glass and What Alice Found There*, also illustrated by Tenniel, was published in 1872.

A subject intriguing those who study Tenniel's illustrations is who was the model for Alice. She did not resemble the Alice Liddell to whom the story was originally told, for the real Alice had her hair cut straight across her forehead in bangs. Tenniel's Alice has long, straggly hair brushed back from her forehead, probably a product of Tenniel's imagination, because he hated using live models.[6] At any rate, Tenniel's Alice, once seen, is easily remembered; one recalls her serious, prim face, her plain dress and pina-

---

4. Doyle, *op. cit.*, p. 353.
5. Carroll, *op. cit.*, p. 277.
6. *Ibid.*

fore, her striped stockings, as one remembers the unique way Tenniel drew all the characters. Like the *Alice* books themselves, one finds himself either repelled by or attracted to Tenniel's illustrations, but that he remains one of the classic illustrators of children's books is indisputable.

Arthur Rackham (1867–1939)

Arthur Rackham's name must be added to the list of classic illustrators contributed by Great Britain to the world of children's books. Rackham created a world of fantasy through his illustrations. His painstaking work, laboriously sketched, included visions of fairies, witches, goblins, gnomes, and maidens. He was born in southeast London, the eldest son of a middle-class family of twelve children. His parents believed in hard work and frugality and inculcated these qualities in their son, who spent his money cautiously and was able to become affluent later in life. He had some formal art training in London and Paris. His career started with his contribution of his drawings to magazines. He soon received commissions for illustrating books. When he illustrated Lamb's *Tales from Shakespeare* in 1899, he became well known.

The following list attests to the fact that he is often called the classic illustrator of the classic authors. He illustrated these well-known books: *Grimms' Fairy Tales* (1900), Swift's *Gulliver's Travels* (1900), Irving's *Rip Van Winkle* (1905), Barrie's *Peter Pan in Kensington Gardens* (1906), Lewis Carroll's *Alice's Adventures in Wonderland* (1907), Shakespeare's *A Midsummer-Night's Dream* (1908), *Aesop's Fables* (1912), Dickens's *A Christmas Carol* (1915), Malory's *King Arthur and His Knights of the Round Table* (1917), Hawthorne's *A Wonder Book* (1922), and Andersen's *Fairy Tales* (1932). And his last is the one many adults remember him for —*The Wind in the Willows,* published in 1940 after his death.

Rackham's philosophy was that the author and the illustrator should form a union of equals in producing the book. He said the artist was the author's "partner, not servant." His art work shows the strong force of his own personality, individual taste, and emotion to a much greater degree than that of any illustrator before him. He was highly independent; no author could tell Rackham which line, passage, or episode of the text should be illustrated. Rackham himself decided, and the results are often unconventional, untraditional, and surprising. For example, instead of taking an important event in a text and illustrating it, he would choose lines or sentences from the text, ones that the reader, without seeing illustrations, would overlook, and ones that many artists would consider could not be illustrated. If one watches for this, his genius of making written words into art magic is fascinating.

Nothing about this man's appearance, that of a bespectacled, balding, long-nosed man, suggested that he himself lived in the imaginative world of visual fantasy. He had an intellectual, subjective view of art, and many of his magical effects are due to his mixing together of objects spiritual and materialistic. Although much of his work is described as airborne— fairies, ghosts, and humans—he also gave inordinate attention to the minute details of earthly objects such as fabrics, rugs, crockery, pillows.

He thought his greatest work was the illustrations for *Grimms' Fairy*

Tales. He enjoyed working on them so much that he reworked his illustrations many times, always finding pleasure. Many critics thought him bold and daring when he illustrated *Alice in Wonderland,* because by that time (1907), the world was used to Tenniel's illustrations, which were thought perfect. But many critics joyfully received these new illustrations, and one wrote that his Alice made Tenniel's Alice look like a wooden puppet.

In his choice of colors, he used a subdued pallette of somber browns and greys. Whereas Kate Greenaway's pictures were set in the sunny weather of summer, Rackham's pictures were set in cold weather. Yet they are not depressing; their setting adds to the sense of enchantment, magic, and fantasy so prevalent in his work. On inspecting his work, one realizes why this illustrator of the Edwardian period in England enjoys enduring popularity that places him in the group of classic illustrators.[7]

Beatrix Potter (1866–1943)

Born in Victorian London, Beatrix Potter was the daughter of well-to-do parents. Her childhood was sterile and devoid of warmth, for her parents were oppressively cold. Miss Potter found some solace, however, in her watercolor set and a few wild pets she would smuggle into her nursery.

Each spring the family took its holiday in either Scotland or the Lake Country. It was on these vacations that Miss Potter developed her vast appreciation for the English countryside. Unlike Kate Greenaway, her author-illustrator counterpart who drew children and gardens, Miss Potter was fascinated by the woodland creatures she observed. Numbered among the animals in her nursery were rabbits, mice, bats, snails, and even a hedgehog. These animals became the substitute for the love that her parents denied her.

Emerging into womanhood, Miss Potter devoted more and more of her time to her drawings and watercolors. She began to study and draw animals in their woodland habitat. Her introduction to writing came in the form of a letter written to young Noel Moore, the son of Miss Potter's former governess. Little Moore was ill and the letter contained a story intended to cheer him up. For the duration of his illness, she continued to send him little stories. Moore loved them so much that Miss Potter began to think of publishing them. She sent one of the stories, her now immortal *The Tale of Peter Rabbit,* to six publishers; it was rejected each time. Miss Potter's family was horrified that she would commit such an unaristocratic act as to write a book and then solicit its publication. She proved indomitable, however, paying for the publication of five hundred copies herself. The copies sold so well that in 1901 the well-known Frederick Warne and Company agreed to publish *Peter Rabbit.* The following year they published Miss Potter's *The Tailor of Gloucester;* altogether she wrote and illustrated fourteen toy books for children.

Through her association with the Warne family, Miss Potter felt familial warmth for the first time in her life. She met the Warne's son,

7. Bertha E. Mahony, Louise P. Latimer, and Beulah Folmsbee, eds., *Illustrators of Children's Books: 1744–1945* (Boston: Horn Book, 1947), p. 168.

Norman, and the pair, approaching middle age, fell in love. A severe and tragic blow was dealt Miss Potter, however, when in 1905 Warne suddenly became ill and died.

Miss Potter saved herself by taking another one of her bold steps. She bought Hill Top Farm in the tiny Lake Country village of Sawrey. She devoted her time and energy to remodeling her cottage, tending the garden, keeping animals, and, above all, writing and drawing. In 1913 she married William Hellis, a solicitor. Miss Potter then followed the daily pursuits of an English country woman. In these years only *The Tale of Johnny Town-Mouse*, published in 1918, was comparable to her earlier work.

Beatrix Potter remains today the classical author-illustrator of the nursery, and *The Tale of Peter Rabbit* is still published by F. Warne and Company, a miniature-sized book which even now sells over forty thousand copies annually in America alone. It is the simple little story of a young rabbit, dressed in a blue jacket and tiny shoes, who ignores his mother's advice and almost meets tragedy in Mr. MacGregor's garden. Beatrix Potter's work enjoyed a renewed interest in the mid-1970s.

The small size of Beatrix Potter's books alone appeals to the young child. Pictures and text blend to form a perfect and inseparable harmony. The endearingly quaint illustrations are not maudlin, nor is there cloying oversentimentality. The soft pastel hues create a "bathed in sunlight" effect. All the pictures are irrepressibly happy. They are perhaps the first to give animals human attributes and affectations.

Miss Potter is especially remarkable at imparting a simple humor to her animal characters. For example, *The Tale of Mrs. Tittlemouse* portrays Mrs. Tittlemouse as a fastidious housekeeper. She is plagued, however, by a ceaseless parade of animals walking through her abode. One picture shows her anxiously watching a beetle, who she is sure has six dirty feet, pass through her home. Mr. Jackson, a fat toad who lives in a ditch, pays a visit; the subtle pictures of the pompous toad contentedly sitting in front of the hearth as ditch water drips down his coattails are amusing. Of course, poor Mrs. Tittlemouse almost has a breakdown.

Truly Beatrix Potter's tales are written and illustrated with a classic blending of verbal and visual beauty.

Ernest H. Shepard (1879–1976)

Although born in the late nineteenth century, enough time has passed so that literary critics consider Shepard among the preeminent classic illustrators. His fame rests on his sketches for A. A. Milne's *Winnie-the-Pooh* books and Kenneth Grahame's *The Wind in the Willows*. Arthur Rackham also illustrated the latter book, but most people prefer Shepard's pictures, and most copies found on the shelves today contain Shepard's illustrations.

Ernest Shepard was born in London, the son of an architect. He attended St. Paul's. Like most artists, he started drawing as a young boy, especially excelling at painting portraits. He soon settled into a career as a cartoonist for *Punch*, and this association continued for a half-century.

His drawings for Milne's Christopher Robin books, *When We Were Very Young* (1924), *Winnie-the-Pooh* (1926), *Now We Are Six* (1927), and *The House at Pooh Corner* (1928), are unequalled. Some critics feel that Shepard's illustrations of these texts contributed to their success and popularity. Most of these illustrations are done in black and white, but later color plates were added, and are found in the compiled edition of the *Pooh* stories. In these books one finds a perfect blending of text and illustration.

In looking at Shepard's sketches, one first notes their simplicity; they are not intricate, detailed drawings, but literally sketchy. However, it is a deceiving simplicity, for not a stroke is wasted; there are no unnecessary lines, and the illustrations suggest rather than reveal. At first, the pictures look flat and static, for there is no obvious robust action as in Caldecott, but when one looks again, there is movement and action. For example, in one drawing where Pooh is going up in the air beside a tree while holding onto a balloon, to investigate whether the bees have honey, there is the distinct feeling of movement. How Shepard accomplishes this action and three-dimensional depth is the secret of his genius. His illustrations are usually small in size, rarely covering a whole page. The sketches also suggest emotion on the faces of the animals. Pooh looks hungry; Eeyore looks gloomy; Piglet looks confused; Owl tries to look wise. The reader smiles and delightfully chuckles.

Shepard perfectly illustrated Grahame's text *The Wind in the Willows*. For example, in one scene Rat and Mole go to Toad's house. The text says that Toad is "resting in a wicker garden chair, with a preoccupied expression on his face, and a large map spread out on his knees." Beneath this short paragraph is a masterpiece. There sits Toad, dressed like an English country squire. His facial expression, his physical attitude, and emotional expression are delightfully humorous and suggest Toad's personality.

Although Shepard has illustrated many books for authors other than the two mentioned, he remains famous and loved by children for these. His latest work (and probably his third most famous illustration) is his 1962 edition of Hans Christian Andersen's fairy tales.

Shepard's daughter is the Mary Shepard who illustrated the *Mary Poppins* books.[8]

Howard Pyle (1853–1911)

Howard Pyle was one of America's most prestigious illustrators, authors, and teachers. As such, he started the stream of American illustrator-authors who continue today to produce a style that we can proudly call American.

This talented American was born in Wilmington, Delaware, the son of intellectual parents. From his mother he inherited his artistic and literary talents; she gave him the best in literature and the best of the English illustrators, particularly John Leech and John Tenniel. Like most artists, he started to draw as a young child and was encouraged by his mother, who gave him private art lessons for three years. Later he had a few lessons at the Art League in New York, but he was largely self-taught.

Although Pyle was well known to contemporaries for his illustrations in *Harper's Weekly Magazine* and in books written by other authors, he is

---

8. Doyle, *op. cit.*, pp. 348–349.

best known as a classical author-illustrator, the first American to combine these two talents. He wrote and illustrated *The Merry Adventures of Robin Hood* (1883), *Pepper and Salt* (1886), *The Wonder Clock* (1888), and four volumes of *The Story of King Arthur and His Knights* (1903–1910).

As a teacher, he helped develop the talents of artists such as Maxfield Parrish, Jessie Willcox Smith, N. C. Wyeth, and Frank Schoonover. These people in turn influenced other illustrators, and Americans began to see their books illustrated by native sons rather than British illustrators. The men Pyle accepted in his school, both at Drexel Institute and later at his home in Wilmington, were selected carefully, and most went on to do great illustrations.

Pyle's art style is characterized by a good sense of draftsmanship and balanced composition that give his drawings vigor and life. He was versatile; he used oils and watercolors, but his pen and ink sketches were his masterpieces. His most famous illustrations were those for *Robin Hood* and *King Arthur;* the sketches were painstakingly drawn, medieval in flavor, and often compared to the work of Durer. For the first time, an American attracted the attention of English illustrators. His work is today enjoyed by all children who see his illustrations.[9]

N. C. Wyeth (1882–1945)

Newell Converse Wyeth founded one of America's most creative families. N. C. Wyeth is the grandfather of Jamie Wyeth and the father of Andrew Wyeth, one of America's best-known painters. For American children growing up from 1910 to the present, N. C. Wyeth is the best-known illustrator of the classics found on bookshelves of libraries and homes. He illustrated twenty juvenile classics, sometimes called the Scribner classics, as they were published by Charles Scribner's Sons, each containing nine color pictures.

N. C. Wyeth was born in Needham, Massachusetts, attended a mechanic art high school, a two-year college, and an art school in Boston. He studied art under Howard Pyle, whose biography we have just given. In 1908 Wyeth settled in Chadds Ford, Pennsylvania, where he continued painting until he died in 1945. While he was busily engaged in his own career, he nurtured his family clan that includes seven respected artists.

His art style reflects a mastery of composition and draftsmanship, and he had the talent to instill visual excitement in the adventure story. Many mistakenly think he had only one style of painting, but upon close inspection, his work reveals that he suited his painting style to the emotion or tone of the episode he wished to represent. Although he was a robust man with a great zest for life, some of his illustrations portray delicate movement, others show danger and terror, while others are dreamlike and airy. In 1916, Wyeth began experimenting with the techniques of the French Impressionists, and this accounts for his variety of style.[10]

One of us carefully examined his illustrations for Jules Verne's

---

9. Dumas Malone, ed., *Dictionary of American Biography*, vol. 15 (New York: Charles Scribner's Sons, 1935), pp. 287, 288, 289.

10. *Who Was Who in America*, vol. 2 (Chicago: A. N. Marquis, 1950), p. 596.

Michael Strogoff: A Courier of the Czar, printed by Scribners in 1927. This book not only was exciting to look at but gave the viewer a sense of magic because the nine illustrations were all so different. Each had its own individual style, suited to the subject. The variety includes illustrations that are romanticized, vibrant, robust, sentimental. Some are traditional and stylized; some are impressionistic and suggestive. In *David Balfour* by Robert Louis Stevenson, printed in 1933, one illustration had the look of an old master of the classic Flemish School. As the author was standing by the shelves of the public library looking at these books, studying them, analyzing their artistic merit, a boy about twelve grabbed one and exclaimed, "Hey, look at the neat pictures!" In a short time, Wyeth has become a classic illustrator, and he still passes the final criterion: he appeals to youth today. This speaks for Wyeth's universality.

SUMMARY

As the writing and publishing of books written especially for children developed slowly, so did the art of illustrating children's books. It is important that a teacher understand this slowly evolving process, which gained impetus in the nineteenth century in Great Britain. When the teacher attains an understanding of the innovations of artists in the past, she can more easily evaluate the styles and trends of modern artists. In studying the lives and art of the great illustrators of the past, we are reminded that the richness of their color and design still have validity that speaks to children today. This is a part of children's cultural heritage.

One goal of those educating children is the transmission of culture from one generation to the next. One aspect of culture is art; another is literature. Teaching children the best in visual art goes hand in hand with teaching the best in the printed word. Great art increases the power of perception in the eye of the beholder so that he may experience new delights. There are things seen that increase the power of words, and sometimes there are elusive things seen that cannot always be said in words. Today we believe that illustrations in children's books play an important role in their lives. Not only do children's first experiences with books prepare them to read and enjoy literature, but the graphic art also expands their knowledge of their limited world. If each child is exposed at an early age to the best in art, he may very well develop aesthetic taste and a love of beauty.

TO THE COLLEGE STUDENT

1. Begin to develop a card file on classic illustrators. Watch for material in professional magazines and newspapers.

2. Go to a library and find illustrations of the artists discussed in this chapter. Study them and note their individual styles.

3. Decide which artist or artists you like and critically analyze the illustrator's style. Can you determine why children have found the artist's work so appealing?

4. Read some biographies of the well-known classic illustrators.

5. Think of ways you could use a knowledge of an artist's life in a creative way in the classroom.

6. Look at some modern illustrators, such as Maurice Sendak or Tomi Ungerer or Barbara Cooney, and see if you can detect influences from the illustrations of classic artists.

7. Go to the library and look at one story that has been illustrated by many artists; for example, begin with Tenniel's *Alice* books, and then find other illustrators who have drawn the *Alice* books. Compare them.

8. Find different editions of *Mother Goose:* Kate Greenaway's, Arthur Rackham's, and Brian Wildsmith's modern one. Contrast them.

TO THE CLASSROOM TEACHER

1. Conduct a survey to find out how much your students are affected by the pictures or art work in picture books. Find out whether the members of the class select a specific book because of its title, subject, or appearance, or because of the illustrations. Use the results of the survey to talk to the pupils about the importance of illustrations. Note to what degree a book's illustrations affect the child's enjoyment of the book.

2. Arrange a display of picture books; use the display in such a way that the children become more aware of differences in art style. For example, print a sign saying: *"Which Pictures Would You Choose for This Book?"*

3. Ask the children to illustrate their own picture book. Some will be able to make up their own; others will need ideas from the teacher, such as the teacher reading a simple story and asking the children to draw pictures for it.

4. Arrange a bulletin board of reproductions of illustrations from the classics using Crane, Caldecott, Greenaway, Tenniel, Rackham, Potter—as many as you can find. Encourage the children to discuss what they like about them or what is good about them or why they prefer some over others.

5. Obtain from the library one book that has been illustrated by several artists, such as both Tenniel's and Rackham's illustrations for the *Alice* books or *The Wind in the Willows.* Note the children's reactions. Ask the children to compare and contrast the illustrations.

6. In planning the curriculum, think of ways you can help the children become aware of the importance of book illustrations, always keeping in mind their reactions to the art work in the books they select and enjoy.

TO THE COLLEGE STUDENT
AND THE CLASSROOM TEACHER

1. Choose a classical illustrator such as Kate Greenaway or Caldecott, any artist who portrays another generation's culture —its homes, clothes, and games—and show the pictures to some children. Ask them to tell you what they notice that is different from modern-day life. An especially good example is Miss Greenaway's illustrations in *Under the Window:* children are seen having tea parties, rolling hoops, playing a game of shuttlecocks. Or show her *Book of Games,* in which children are shown spinning tops. Also ask the children to note similarities to their own lives. Aspects of social studies are thus discussed, in addition to encouraging the class to observe well.

2. Collect some of the famous paintings of all times, such as *The Vigil* by Pettie, and compare them to the illustrations by Howard Pyle in *The Adventures of Robin Hood.* Note how each:

a. Catches the flavor of the period about which the painter is painting.
b. Follows the principles of good art work.

c. Captures a feeling and a style different from other paintings and illustrations.
d. Makes use of a particular medium in a worthy manner.

Other comparisons may be *The Race Track* by Albert Ryder with Howard Pyle's illustrations for *The Legend of Sleepy Hollow; In the Ozarks* by Thomas Benton with Laura Ingalls Wilder's illustrations for *Little House on the Prairie.* Try this activity with children to see if they appear to benefit by it.

3. Compare the illustrations in children's books with caricatures, with comics, with oil paintings, with watercolor, with lithograph, and with sketches. Can you find children's books where all these techniques and media have been applied?

4. Many famous paintings might well be illustrations for children's books. Leaf through some books of great paintings and note which ones make you feel that they were painted especially for a child's book that you like.

5. Write and illustrate a children's story of your own.

6. Collect names of classical illustrators not mentioned in this chapter. Assign different people in your group to do some research on these and to report on their work. Be sure to show samples of each artist's work.

7. A film that teachers and children will enjoy is *The Story of a Book*. It shows the creation and publication of *Pagoo* by Holling.

SELECTED BIBLIOGRAPHY

Arbuthnot, May Hill. *Children and Books,* 4th ed. Glenview, Ill.: Scott, Foresman, 1972.

Ashton, John, ed. *Chap-Books of the Eighteenth Century.* New York: Benjamin Blom, 1965. Reprint of 1882 ed.

Caldecott, Randolph. *The House That Jack Built.* New York: Warne, 1878.

Caldecott, Randolph. *John Gilpin.* New York: Warne, 1878.

Caldecott, Randolph. *Sing a Song for Sixpence.* New York: Warne, 1880.

Caldecott, Randolph. *The Three Jovial Huntsmen.* New York: Warne, 1880.

Caldecott, Randolph. *A Frog He Would A-Wooing Go.* New York: Warne, 1883.

Caldecott, Randolph. "The Great Panjandrum Himself." From *Picture Book No. 4.* New York: Warne, 1885.

Crane, Walter. *The Baby's Opera.* A book of old rhymes with new dresses. Engraved and printed in colors by Edmund Evans. New York: Warne, 1900.

Davis, Mary Gould. *Randolph Caldecott, 1846–1886: An Appreciation.* Philadelphia: J. B. Lippincott, 1946.

Doyle, Brian, ed. *The Who's Who of Children's Literature.* New York: Schocken Books, 1969.

Ernest, Edward, ed. *The Kate Greenaway Treasury.* Cleveland: World, 1967.

Freeman, Larry G., and Ruth Freeman. *The Child and His Picture Book.* Watkins Glen, N.Y.: Century House, 1967.

Hoffman, Miriam, and Eva Samuels. *Authors and Illustrators of Children's Books: Writings on Their Lives and Works.* New York: R. R. Bowker, 1972.

Hudson, Derek. *Arthur Rackham: His Life and Work.* New York: Charles Scribner's Sons, 1967.

James, Philip B. *English Book Illustrations, 1800–1900.* New York: Penguin, 1947.

Klemin, Diana. *The Art of Art for Children's Books.* New York: Clarkson-Potter, 1966.

Lane, Margaret. *The Tale of Beatrix Potter: A Biography,* 2nd ed. New York: Warner, 1968.

Linder, Enid, and Leslie Linder. *The Art of Beatrix Potter.* New York: Warne, 1973.

Mahony, Bertha E., Louise P. Latimer, and Beulah Folmsbee, eds. *Illustrators of Children's Books: 1744–1945.* Boston: Horn Book, 1947.

Miller, Bertha E., *et. al.,* eds. *Illustrators of Children's Books, 1946–1956.* Boston: Horn Book, 1958.

Muir, Percy. *English Children's Books, 1600–1900*. London: Botsford, 1954.

Moore, Anne Carroll, ed. *The Art of Beatrix Potter*, rev. ed. New York: Warne, 1967.

Pitz, Henry C. *Illustrating Children's Books*. New York: Watson Guptill, 1963.

Pitz, Henry C. *Howard Pyle: Writer, Illustrator, Founder of the Brandywine School*. New York: Clarkson and Potter, 1975.

Potter, Beatrix. *The Art of Beatrix Potter*. New York: Warne, 1964.

Rackham, Arthur. *Arthur Rackham Fairy Book*. Philadelphia: J. B. Lippincott, 1950.

Sloane, William. *Children's Books in England and America in the Seventeenth Century*. New York: King's Crown, 1955.

Yolen, Jane H. *Writing Books for Children*. Boston: Writer, 1973.

CHAPTER 9

Modern Illustrators: Smorgasbords of Visual Delights

> *Children's books . . . hold a peculiar position. They are attractive to designers of an imaginative tendency, for in a sober and matter of fact age they afford perhaps the only outlet for unrestricted flights of fancy open to the modern illustrator, who likes to revolt against the "despotism of facts."*
>
> WALTER CRANE[1]

One of the newest illustrators of children's books is Tony Chen. A visit with him reveals that not only does he paint beautifully to illustrate children's books, but his life philosophy, his concepts of his world, and his theories of art are reflected in his pictures.

A Visit with Tony Chen

"I consider myself an illustrator," said Tony Chen as he sat in a comfortable chair talking to Mrs. Park and sipping a glass of punch. "I do not pretend to call my work anything other than illustrating—illustrating a book. One can call it fine art or anything else, but I simply call it illustrating."

Mr. Chen went on to point out that regardless of the art medium he is using, he tries his best to get the most he can from it. It does not occur to him that he must direct his work to any particular age level: he simply does his very best with all media. When he is illustrating a children's book, however, he is even more aware that he must give his best, for it is part of his philosophy that the young, impressionable child should be exposed to the best art forms of every culture.

---

1. Quoted in Lillian Smith, *The Unreluctant Years: A Critical Approach to Children's Literature* (Chicago: American Library Association, 1953), p. 118.

FIGURE 9–1. *Tony Chen's* Hello, Small Sparrow *inspired the children in Mr. Perry's room to make this exhibit of their own Haiku writings.*

"The experience of fine art is one of the greatest things in my life," exclaimed Mr. Chen, "and even the memory of great works I've seen gives me a feeling of exhilaration. For the first time in history, the works of all cultures, from the dawn of mankind to the present time, are available in museums and books. These have become our human heritage, personally and collectively. These are the heritage and birthright of our children. With just a little opening up of our eyes, the concepts and skills of even the most exotic culture can be assimilated and become factors of artistic and cultural enjoyment, a source of inspiration, a point of departure for artistic growth. Our own work as artists should compete with the best of each period: the Tang and Sung Dynasties of China, the Egyptians, the Greeks, the Renaissance, pre-Columbian, primitive, the folk art of America —right through to contemporary art. The amalgamation of all civilizations is available now for our children and they deserve the best from us. It is the force of the amalgamation of these cultures, their vitality, that is the driving power of the things I try to express in my art."

"When you are called to illustrate a book," said Mrs. Park, "do you ever feel restricted by the text?"

"I wouldn't accept a book that would do that," said Mr. Chen. "A job must excite me before I will accept it. If I can read a text and become excited, then I immediately conceive all the pictures in my mind as they shall be in the book. In this situation, the book provides me with a great deal of leeway and freedom. It really unchains the talents of the artist to interpret, to use his imagination. The thing that starts the brush working is the visualization of the story in my mind. I create a visual world to accompany the text. Whatever the writer does not put into the text, that is the area which gives the artist complete freedom to conceptualize."

"Your work reflects a strong feeling and love for animals," Mrs. Park observed. "Your illustrations show an empathy for animals, both the familiar and the exotic ones."

At this point Mr. Chen became very animated. Leaning forward in his chair, he exclaimed that not only does he love animals and nature, but he is extremely concerned about many species of wildlife that are becoming extinct because of man's hunting and lack of general concern. Ecology is a subject about which Mr. Chen feels very strongly, and he conveys his sympathy and empathy for the world of nature in his books. He reached over to the table, picked up and opened a copy of his book *Run, Zebra, Run,* the one book he has both written and illustrated.

This book is a statement about ecology. The cover is a colored painting of zebras: a mass of dazzling black and white stripes swirling in circular movement and contrasted against a background of luxuriant, breathtaking flowers in tropical color.

Mr. Chen turned to the page from which he took the title of the book and read. "Listen," he said,

> *Run, wild zebra, run!*
> *Run, free zebra, run!*
> *Here comes the hunter with his gun*
> *His customer wants your skin—*
> *To decorate his living room wall.*

In explaining how he illustrated this particular book, Mr. Chen said, "As an artist, I am concerned with the feeling of mass, curves, light, shadow, and texture, but all must be unified. In this book, I strove for an orchestration of movement."

Mrs. Park remarked that the illustrations in this book are powerful and show great graphic impact.

"Yes," said Mr. Chen with great animation. "Power, visual power. To be effective, a painting must have power of expression. But balanced against power must be tenderness. You know, I think these qualities that I try to put into my art are the same qualities we should impart to children. We want children to develop power *and* tenderness. By tenderness, I do not mean weakness or sloppiness or lack of discipline."

Both Mrs. Park and Mr. Chen agreed that the main purpose of a book should not be didactic, but when a concept like ecology is the theme of a book that also contains good art, it is a good thing. We began to talk about how art, literature, and music can be combined or interrelated and be passed on to young children. Mr. Chen had definite ideas on this.

"Yes, I think parents and teachers should set the standards for the taste of a child. Give the child a positive approach to art, to life itself! Give him the best in music, literature, language—for instance, the sheer beauty and magic of the English language in the great tradition of Elizabethan prose and Victorian poetry. Expose the child to these things, and he shall, in beauty, find a new horizon, a new dimension to his life—an appreciation and an inner joy that will remain with him throughout all his years."

One feels the dynamic presence of Mr. Chen's personality and can sense the power and delicacy that show so often in his art work.

Mrs. Park asked him about the format and layout of his books. He said he could not speak for other illustrators, but he designs the typography, the layout—almost everything having to do with the visual aspects of his books. He prefers paper with a white background and black printing because he believes that is easier for children to read. He is very interested in the location of the printing of the words on each page, so that his art work can blend with the text. For example, one illustration has a rhinoceros on double pages. The animal has a big curving horn. The text, consisting of four lines, is printed within the curve of the horn. His format obviously promotes the unity of the text and illustrations.

The conversation drifted back to the subject of the use of picture books within the school curriculum. Mr. Chen agreed that his book *Honschi* not only stands on its own merit as a work of art, but that much can be learned from it about Oriental places. The landscapes in the book tell the children a great deal about a foreign land. The houses the people live in are depicted, and the fact that there is snow in the Far East is shown. And the theme of the book has a universal concept that all children understand: the concept of fear.

Honschi is a story of the adventures and emotions (particularly fear) of a Japanese chickadee after she leaves the nest. Mr. Chen uses the flowers in the book to symbolize Honschi's emotions. The illustrations are painted in bright, bold colors: the anemones symbolize diversity and distress; the iris symbolizes friendship.

Mrs. Park was interested in the fact that some of the green leaves showed imperfections, as though the leaves were suffering from a disease. Mr. Chen laughed, "Yes, my leaves show imperfection, true of nature. Besides, it's boring to see illustrations of perfect green leaves!" He added parenthetically that drawing trees fascinates him. He is always searching for new ways to draw trees. He thinks of concepts of trees. "Modern painters do conceptualization rather than representation. An artist creates his own world and tells things that are not readily evident."

In further discussion about *Honschi*, Tony Chen said that Honschi as a little chickadee is constantly singing, so he tried to suggest music in paint and color.

Mr. Chen is also aware of the psychological nature of life and this shows in his books. For example, *Honschi* deals with tangible dangers: the young and fearful bird is afraid of fear itself. A fascinating "psychological" painting appears on the book ends. Mr. Chen draws Honschi pursued by Japanese wind socks made in the form of fish. The huge, fierce, and colorful paper fish represent Honschi's fears, but the fears are ill founded because the fish are only paper and have no teeth, so they could not possibly harm Honschi.

From listening to Tony Chen, one soon gets the impression that art, to him, is a joyful creation, that he makes his illustrations come alive for his readers by doing them with love, care, devotion—and with his own creative skills. His final words were, "A single book illustration is as important a statement about life as a painting or a piece of sculpture."

Tony Chen (1929–   )—*Some More About Him*

Tony Chen is an extremely talented artist and sculptor who has recently become an illustrator of children's books. He has been a free-lance illustrator, and until 1970 he was Assistant Art Director of *Newsweek*. He left this position in order to devote more time to book illustrations. In his studio he continues painting and has had five one-man shows and won numerous awards. Mr. Chen enters children's book illustrations with an impressive background of professionalism and art work of the highest quality.

Born and raised in Kingston, Jamaica, West Indies, Mr. Chen began drawing at the age of six. An uncle bought him a set of watercolors and painted a head for young Chen to copy. Chen quickly drew a better one and decided that he would become an artist. He attended a Chinese school where he learned calligraphy, the art of rendering Chinese characters. Following the Chinese custom, Mr. Chen was given a notebook in which to repeatedly draw flowers, birds, and bees. Today, he draws these subjects of nature exquisitely and can quickly make a whole series of one subject. Living in Jamaica, Mr. Chen grew up in a lush environment abundant with the beauty of exotic flowers and animals. Summers in his grandmother's homestead in the hills fostered his affections for a pet donkey and numerous goats, cats, and rabbits. His closeness with animals is easily seen in his art work today.

After graduating from high school, Chen realized that he must go to New York City in order to establish an art career. There he attended the Art Career School and Pratt Institute, where he graduated with honors and won a cash prize from the Society of Illustrators.

In 1955 Mr. Chen began an apprenticeship at an advertising agency. He is an example of one of the many fine children's illustrators whose careers began in commercial art. He quickly mastered such skills as layout design and developed a thorough knowledge of photography and printing. Chen's current work in children's books reflects this professionalism both in the mechanics of graphic art and in the skill of painting.

Chen's first children's book assignment was Helen E. Buckley's sensitively written *Too Many Crackers* in 1966. The pictures are perfectly suited to the mood of anxiety felt by a little boy whose parents have left him with an aunt while they have gone on a vacation. The muted blue and mauve illustrations create a dreamlike atmosphere which tones down the mounting anxiety and lonesomeness that the little boy feels as the days go by.

In 1971 Mr. Chen illustrated Hannah Lyons Johnson's *Hello, Small Sparrow,* a picture book of haiku poetry. The art work is impeccable in its choice of color and design. Chen is actually describing how we relate to the earth and how balance and rhythm with nature are necessary. Chen claims, "Haiku is really wildlife poetry—poems about ecology."

Mr. Chen wrote and illustrated *Run, Zebra, Run,* also published in 1972. Again each illustration is a work of art; each picture is a notable painting.

Mr. Chen lives with his wife and two sons on Long Island, New York, in a beautiful old home. He now teaches art at Nassau Community College. The interview at the opening of this chapter gives many insights into Mr. Chen's philosophy of life and children.

Tony Chen continues keeping busy with many projects that revolve about his varied interests and talents. Five of his paintings have been exhibited at the National Gallery of Fine Arts in Washington, D.C.; the Delaware Museum in Wilmington, Delaware; the Virginia Museum of Fine Arts in Richmond; and the Wadsworth Atheneum in Hartford, Conn. Since this interview took place, he has completed six books: *Follow a Fisher* (T. Y. Crowell), *About Birds* (Golden Book Press), a UNICEF Cookbook *Many Hands Cooking* (T. Y. Crowell), *About Owls* (Scholastic Press) and *Once We Went on A Picnic* (T. Y. Crowell). Tony Chen is an author and a prolific artist—a Renaissance man. As such, he is an important contributor on the list of illustrators of children's books.

THE MODERN ILLUSTRATORS

Modern illustrators of children's books are interested in "conceptualization rather than representation. An artist creates his own world. An artist tells things that are not readily evident," as Tony Chen stated in his interview. Today's illustrators for children's books are concerned with creating a visual, aesthetic experience for the child, rather than just decorating the pages. Naturally the illustrations must help tell the story, complementing the text, and they must be accurate in such matters that if the text says, "Johnny has three red balloons," the illustration must show three red balloons. But today's illustrator is interested in more than accuracy and realistic drawings. The truly creative illustrator hopes to stimulate the child's mind so that the child can envision beyond the text, sending him into creative "flights of fancy" that Walter Crane spoke of in the quotation that begins this chapter. In early childhood education we hear of the term "reading enrichment"; perhaps the term is applicable to the rewards a child receives in "reading" the pictures. The goal of the dedicated illustrator is to extend the text, not merely to duplicate it. Illustrations are often suggestive rather than portraitlike.

In this golden age of picture books, not all illustrations are good art; some are cheap, marshmallowy, and trite. However, since illustrating for children is now big business, artists with talent and imagination will be the ones to survive.

Furthermore, the illustration of children's book is not only an art, but also a trade and a craft. An illustrator must know his trade in order to see his work accurately reproduced. In addition to fine arts painting, which most modern illustrators study, the illustrator must master highly technical skills of photography, the limitations of color separation, called overlay, typography, format, and other techniques too complicated to explain to the nonprofessional. The process an illustrator goes through from the blank page to the galleys to the final book production is an intricate one.

In an age in which our society is deploring the loss of craftsmanship and trying to promote renewed interest and pride in one's craft, it behooves those interested in guiding children to become aware that book illustration is a craft worthy of respect. Although the artist is aided by machines, he is a craftsman who works with his hands, his imagination, and his talent. With the aid of technology he is free to practice his skill by constantly experimenting, by following his flights of fancy using a variety of styles, media, and techniques as he works alone in his studio. Although there are many illustrators who do their own writing, the illustrator who does not write his own text but illustrates for authors is free to interpret the text as he wishes. The author does not tell or advise the illustrator. One authoress of many picture books for children said she never once met the illustrator for her books until after the books were published.

The most common procedure is that a writer sends his text to a publisher. If the text is accepted, the children's book editor selects the illustrator, who then submits his sketches exactly as he wishes. As one editor has said, "No one is looking over the shoulder of the author telling him how to write, so the author should not tell the artist how and what to paint."

More illustrators are now writing their own texts. Few started with this intention; it happened for either aesthetic or economic reasons. Sometimes an illustrator, such as Maurice Sendak, Leo Lionni, or Ezra Jack Keats, is genuinely talented in writing as well as in drawing, or else the illustrator is both talented and independent, possessing a desire to tell his own story. The artist then fares better financially since he does not have to share his royalty rights. If he does not write his own original story, he can rewrite and adapt old fairy tales or nursery rhymes now in the public domain. He can produce ABC books and counting books. Many of the illustrators in this chapter are also authors. They are included here rather than in Chapter 7 on modern authors because their art work is especially innovative, creative, and representative of a particular style.

Variety of Styles in Picture Books

Picture books contain two styles of illustrations. One style is the traditional, representational, true-to-life style. Some critics believe that children's first books, nursery tales, counting books, and those often called nonliterary books, should be representational. The authors of this book disagree, for young children do not have rigid standards of or opinions on traditional versus modern art. Children know what they like and will reject a book with pictures they dislike. How else can one explain the popularity of Brian Wildsmith's *1, 2, 3's, ABC, Circus,* and his other books for young children?

The second style, such as that of Wildsmith, is nonrepresentational. The artist is more free to use symbols, unusual designs, shapes, sizes, forms, colors, textures, and often a combination of media. It is frequently more difficult for an adult to understand and accept such art than it is for a child. Nonrepresentational artists do not use blobs of paint that are splashed helter-skelter on a page so that objects are unidentifiable. Rather, the artist, using color, *suggests* design, texture, and media in order to produce an emotional, imaginative picture.

A look at the most recently published books shows that more artists are turning to the nonrepresentational style of illustrating. However, some illustrators are content to stay with one style; examples are Dr. Seuss, H. A. Ray, and Wanda Gag. Certain illustrators achieve a variety of styles and choose the most suitable one for the text they are illustrating; examples are Maurice Sendak and Marcia Brown, both of whom are very versatile. Some illustrators change, like Ezra Jack Keats, who said that he found his style when he wrote and illustrated *The Snowy Day.* Compare any of his books after *The Snowy Day* with *The Ballad of John Henry.* Once he found his style, he stayed with it, and the popularity he enjoys shows that children love his constant experimentation.

FIGURE 9–2. *Alvin Tresselt and Roger Duvoisin's* White Snow, Bright Snow *motivated this bulletin board.*

Keats uses collage extremely successfully. Like many nonrepresentational illustrators, he uses non-art materials, such as scraps of fabric and wallpaper in *The Snowy Day*. In *Amy's Hat* he used dried leaves, fabrics, valentines, and cut-up paper flowers for that delightfully amusing hat.

Evaline Ness said in her acceptance speech for winning the Caldecott Medal for *Sam, Bangs, and Moonshine* in 1967:

I steal anything that will help me resolve a piece of art: sunlight falling across a half-finished drawing, a dirty fingerprint, knots in wood, accidents like spilled ink, broken pens, ripped paper. Even the muddy waters I rinse my brushes in can be the answer to a color problem.[2]

It seems that colors and shapes in nonrepresentational art are more exaggerated, exuberant, forceful, and unorthodox. Brian Wildsmith paints in a dazzling, unique style, using bright bold colors. His illustrations have marbleized effects, geometric shapes and patterns. An excellent example of Wildsmith's style is *Puzzles* (1970), which is stimulating to the imagination and a joy to the beholder.

The modern illustrator often combines different media: pen and ink, crayons, watercolors, acrylics, gouache, linoleum block printing, wood cuts, stone lithography, and, as one illustrator has said, "even spitting."

2. Selma G. Lanes, *Down the Rabbit Hole: Adventures and Misadventures in Children's Literature* (New York: Atheneum, 1971), p. 52.

New Trends in Children's Illustrations

Since the subject matter of children's books has changed and enlarged the scope of topics, modern illustrators have kept abreast in the emotion and tone of their art work. The newest trend is realism; topics such as death, poverty, sickness, physical and emotional handicaps, alienation, racial differences, and discrimination are discussed. As a consequence, illustrators portray subjects never before thought worthy of illustrating. For example, Ezra Jack Keats illustrates his stories with black and white children, and he places them in the setting of a big city where, in reality, they do live and play together. His illustrations show garbage cans, clothes hanging on the rooftops, graffiti on the fences, run-down tenements—the way many children live and the things they see in real life. The illustrations make Keats's book relevant to the child who lives in a big city and extends the knowledge of the child who lives in a suburb or in a rural area.

Some illustrators, like Leo Politi, show the activities of small children of minority groups. *Pedro, the Angel of Olvera Street* (1946) and *Juanita* (1948) are about Mexican-Americans of Los Angeles. *Moy Moy* (1960) is about a young Chinese-American girl. Politi has also written a book with illustrations of Italy in *Little Leo* (1951), the story of a young boy who travels to Italy and teaches the children of the village how to play being Indians.

Photographs, both black and white and with colors, are increasingly used as illustrations in an imaginative and impressive manner. The photographs are not merely pictures of people, places, and objects. Photography is used to stimulate imagination so that children can see in actual photographs the beauty, joy, and humor of people, places, and objects. Outstanding examples are *The Red Balloon* by Albert Lamorisse (1956), and *Black Is Beautiful* (1969), written by Ann McGovern, photographs by Hope Wurmfeld.

In keeping with the subject of realism, many illustrations portray visual reality. Consequently, we no longer see children always dressed up or clean or being good or living in tidy upper-class suburban communities. Children can see other children as they often are—dirty, naughty, poor, and physically and emotionally handicapped. Books now contain illustrations of people who come in colors other than white, and who speak different languages and observe different cultural customs. Unlike some early books designed for children's reading, Daddy is not necessarily dressed in a business suit wearing a shirt and tie. Fathers are often shown cooking and taking care of babies. Mother is not apron-clad, baking cookies, and looking perennially cheerful in the kitchen. Brothers, sisters, mothers, and fathers fight, quarrel, run away, and sometimes they die. Mother, Father, Dick, Jane, and Spot have vanished. But with all the choices avaliable, a child does not have to feed on this alone. He can still find comfort in looking at books published today that are filled with beauty, drawn with pictures of things the way they're "supposed to be."

Children today can still have books with illustrations of classical authors. A popular children's book club continues offering *Marigold Garden,* written and illustrated by Kate Greenaway; *The Pied Piper of Hamelin,* written by Robert Browning and illustrated by Miss Greenaway;

The Pooh Story Book, written by A. A. Milne and illustrated by E. H. Shepard; and all the tales written by Beatrix Potter.

Thus children now can select books with illustrations that vary from traditional to impressionistic, executed by illustrators from one hundred years ago or from one year ago. Children do not care about the age of a book nor how recent was its publication.

It is the depth, range, and diversity of illustrations that impresses us as we evaluate today's picture books. As Henry C. Pitz, the illustrator and author of *Illustrating Children's Books* (1963), said, "When we look at American illustrations I think one of the first reactions is to note their diversity. They speak in so many voices. One finds individual voices having their say. Nowhere in any of the European countries can one find anything comparable to that. Even when we say things badly, we usually say them with a certain amount of vigor and conviction. There is no wonder, of course, when we consider the artists who are making the pictures for these books and the people who preside over the manufacture of them." As Pitz continues his discussion on the diversity of the artists, he notes, as we all do, the wealth of racial, ethnic, and cultural backgrounds of American-born illustrators: Wanda Gag, William Pené du Bois, Robert McCloskey, Maurice Sendak, Lynd Ward, Leonard Weisgard, Leo Politi, and Lois Lenski. And consider too that some of our finest illustrators were not born here but migrated to America and added their diversity and richness of national and cultural heritage to modern American illustrating: Feodor Rojanovsky, Kurt Wiese, Ludwig Bemelmans, Roger Duvoisin, Ingri and Edgar Parin d'Aulaire, Tony Chen, and Tomi Ungerer, to name only a few. When, in the future, a new generation examines our children's books, perhaps our legacy will not be the written word, but rather the talent, diversity, creativity, and imagination of the graphic images.

THE VALUES OF ILLUSTRATIONS TO CHILDREN

Although children like to study the details of illustrations, many children have no idea how the pictures got into the book. Yet there are many values to be gained if both teachers and children learn a bit about the fascinating work and skill of illustrators. A child studies a picture intently; his face shows emotion—sadness, frustration, anger, happiness, and laughter. If a child is old enough to note the name of an illustrator whose work has meaning for him, he will often ask for books with "pictures" by the same artist. He will ask, "Who drew the pictures?", "Does he have any children?", "Where does she live?" A child's curiosity can be aroused and satisfied if the teacher can relate anecdotes about the life of the illustrator or how he paints or what inspires him. If a teacher or parent interests a child in illustrations, there are many adventuresome lessons to be learned, and new experiences await the child.

From studying illustrations, a child begins to grow in developing appreciation of art and is helped in his expression of it. Children love to draw, paint, and work with art supplies, no matter how simple or sophisticated. How often teachers have heard a child complain, "I don't know how to draw a camel." Or "Mary's animals look better than mine." It is at this point that a teacher can discuss how artists draw the same object in different ways. There is no one right way. Illustrations in picture books show how literally hundreds of artists draw, how each has his own unique style. It is worthwhile for teachers to learn more about illustrators and how they work.

The Weston Woods's film on Ezra Jack Keats is especially good. Keats shows how he searches for and experiments with techniques, such as his collage and his marbleized backgrounds, like the dark sky in *A Letter to Amy.*

When the teacher takes the time to know about the lives and illustrations of artists who appeal to children, she can use picture books in all areas of the curriculum: art, science, social studies, reading, music, and math. Finally, in learning about illustrations and how illustrators have experimented with techniques, children learn to think more creatively. We are not trying to make children become book illustrators or asking the teacher to learn complicated processes of the production of illustrations. But when the teacher and child note the individuality of an illustrator, both can discover new ways of thinking about and seeing people and the world.

Gathered together in the following biographical sketches is information about unusual aspects of some well-known modern illustrators' lives. Perhaps a child's interest will be sparked by learning that Wanda Gag was orphaned at age fourteen and struggled to bring up her brothers and sisters, keeping them together as a family; that Tomi Ungerer was a member of the African Camel Corps; that John Steptoe wrote and illustrated his first book at age seventeen.

Because of lack of space, it is obvious that many eminent illustrators cannot be included in this chapter. Every year about three thousand new books for juveniles appear on the market. Almost all contain some type of illustration. Many illustrators are worthy of comment.

The criteria for selecting the illustrators who appear here are as follows: (1) They are well-known names to many teachers who can use information on them in teaching units in their classrooms, for projects described in this book; (2) they represent a cross-section of *types* of illustrations—each has a different style, technique, and medium; and (3) they have contributed significant innovations to modern illustration.

Wanda Gag (1893–1946)

Wanda Gag died thirty years ago, yet today the books she wrote and illustrated are regarded as classics. She demonstrated how perfectly text and illustrations can be combined into a perfect harmony. She was one of those true geniuses who created a special world for children. Her first book, *Millions of Cats,* published in 1928, is a landmark in the development of the American picture book. Wanda Gag's influence among author-illustrators is still felt today; more important, her books remain extremely popular with children, because they seem modern to children who are unaware that they were written years ago. This great appeal and popularity will undoubtedly be maintained for years to come, testifying to the universality of her talent.

It is ironic that Wanda Gag's *Millions of Cats* marked the beginnings of the high quality of the *American* picture book because her background was very European. Due to this old-world influence in her early life, she brought to the field of children's literature interest in and knowledge of European folklore.

Born in 1893, Miss Gag was the daughter of parents born in Bohemia who had immigrated to New Ulm, Minnesota. Both parents were extremely artistic. She grew up in an environment that fostered her innate sense of creativity.

Mr. Gag painted houses and churches on weekdays, but on weekends he painted pictures. All the seven children started to draw as soon as they were able to hold a pencil. Every evening the family gathered around the kitchen table to draw and paint throughout the evening. Miss Gag said, "It never occurred to me that life might go on without these things, and when I discovered that to many people drawing was not as important as eating and sleeping, I was puzzled and disillusioned."[3]

The family life of the Gags was very happy until, when Wanda was fourteen, she and her brother and sisters were orphaned. Against the advice of family friends, Miss Gag insisted that all seven children finish high school and, more important, stay together. Those were very hard times for the children, but their success was due to the determination and courage of Wanda, who modestly claimed that all the children worked together to contribute to their support.

Later Miss Gag left Minnesota, where she had studied art, because she felt she had to go to New York City. She attended the Art Students League. Before she became a children's book author-illustrator, she had achieved success as a commercial artist and as a "fine arts" artist who did drawings, paintings, wood cuts, lithographs, and etchings. She had a successful exhibition at a New York gallery. Her eventual financial success enabled her to buy a farm in rural New Jersey, which she appropriately named "All Creation." The younger Gags joined her, and they created art, farmed, and lived together until they moved on to lives of their own.

Miss Gag claimed that the stories for *Millions of Cats, The Funny Thing, Snippy and Snappy* were among those she had written down and illustrated after having told them over and over to children who begged to hear them again and again. Because she had told them so many times after their original invention, she said they became more and more compact. This is one of the hallmarks of her style as an author—the tightness of her stories in which not an extra word could be added nor could one word be deleted.

Millions of Cats is a cumulative tale told and illustrated by a master craftsman. Children respond with delight to the story of an old man and woman who look for a cat to love. The gnomelike old man goes to search for one cat to take home, but because of his indecisiveness, he takes home "hundreds of cats, thousands of cats, millions and billions of cats." Children love the repetitive refrain of these words. The black and white etchings are charmingly drawn. They are vital, simply executed, and form a natural blending of text and illustration. The pictures tell the story to a child who cannot read, and when a child hears the story orally, he under-

---

3. Stanley J. Kunitz and Howard Haycroft (eds.), *The Junior Book of Authors,* 2nd ed. (New York: H. W. Wilson, 1951), p. 135.

stands it well and appreciates it. When a child sees the pictures, he can also "read" the story.

Another book of Miss Gag's that shows the generative force she gave to children's literature was an alphabet book, *ABC Bunny,* published in 1933. This book is considered a classic model of the large assortment of alphabet books that constantly appear on the market. Each letter of the alphabet places the bunny in a new situation. The facial expressions of the bunny and all the animals he meets are unusually descriptive. The rhythmic text and the offbeat rhymes mesmerize children. The illustrations are dark woodcuts with large scarlet capital letters resembling a child's wooden ABC blocks.

In using her European heritage of traditional folklore, Wanda Gag rewrote and illustrated tales originally told by the Grimm Brothers. In *Tales From Grimm, More Tales from Grimm,* and *Snow White and the Seven Dwarfs,* she gave these old and beloved tales her personal touch, using her skill as a masterful storyteller, combined with heavy black lines, sophisticated and yet childlike, drawn with humor and charm, including exactly the right amount of details that children love. In *Gone Is Gone,* published in 1935, Miss Gag retells the folk tale of a man who wanted to do all the housework. The illustrations done in dramatic black and white give the story an authenticity of a writer who seemed to feel the magic of the funny *märchen.*

In placing Wanda Gag in historical perspective and evaluating the contribution she has made to American children, Lynd Ward, the illustrator, said that at the time Wanda Gag started producing her masterpieces, "It was still a little heretical for an artist whose reputation was grounded in what the critics call 'the fine arts' to work seriously and without pretentious apology in the field of illustrations for children. The children of America, of course, are immeasurably richer because of what Wanda Gag brought them within the covers of her books."[4]

Ludwig Bemelmans (1898–1962)

Born in the Austrian Tyrols, Bemelmans came to America because he almost fatally wounded the headwaiter at the hotel where he was working. Luckily, the hotel was owned by Bemelmans's rich uncle; the local police gave him the choice of reform school or leaving the country. In 1914, he was on a boat, armed with sufficient ammunition and guns to fight off all the Indians that he thought roamed the American countryside.

Instead of fighting Indians, Bemelmans found himself waiting on table in New York City. Despite the fact that he was an inept waiter, Bemelmans eventually became part owner of a restaurant. His first thought of writing was the result of encouragement by a book editor friend. Bemelmans published *Hansi* in 1934, the story of a boy's skiing holiday.[5]

Bemelmans is most remembered for his *Madeline* series. The

---

4. Lynd Ward, "Wanda Gag, Fellow Artist," *Horn Book Magazine* 23 (May–June 1947): 195.

5. Miriam Hoffman and Eva Samuels, *Authors and Illustrators of Children's Books* (New York: R. R. Bowker, 1972), p. 7.

youngest of twelve girls in a Paris convent school, Madeline is also the most independent. She gets into all sorts of mischief and children love her. There are five Madeline books: *Madeline* (1939), *Madeline's Rescue* (1953), *Madeline and the Bad Hat* (1956), *Madeline and the Gypsies* (1959), and *Madeline in London* (1961). *Madeline's Rescue* won the 1954 Caldecott Award, and *Madeline* was a Caldecott runner-up.

All of Bemelmans's illustrations demonstrate a rejection of formalized art in illustrating. Rather, the pictures are as lighthearted as the stories. The splashy watercolors often overlap their outlines, giving each character vibrant energy. He is an expert at communicating artistically the gaiety and humor of his texts.

The *Madeline* books are among America's best-loved picture books, and Ludwig Bemelmans is one of the great children's authors and illustrators.

Roger Duvoisin (1904–)

Roger Duvoisin is one of the most prolific illustrators in children's literature. He has illustrated well over 125 books, using a variety of techniques. Whether he combines his talents and works as an author and illustrator, or whether he illustrates for his wife Louise Fatio or for writer Alvin Tresselt, the results are delightful.

Duvoisin has led an interesting life. Born in Geneva, Switzerland, his early interest was music and he studied at the Geneva Conservatory of Music. He soon developed an interest in murals and stage scenery, however, and subsequently worked as a designer. Duvoisin also managed a ceramics plant that had been founded by Voltaire. He met Miss Fatio in Paris; they married and traveled to Depression America. They now live in rural New Jersey.

Duvoisin uses colors very effectively in a symbolic sense. The object painted quickly calls to mind its real-life counterpart; yet, at the same time, its reality has been embellished. Despite this representational treatment, which largely ignores the details of the subject, Duvoisin unerringly captures its essence with grace and delicacy. His sense of arrangement is excellent. Mr. Duvoisin won the 1948 Caldecott Medal for *White Snow, Bright Snow*, written by Alvin Tresselt. Some of his popular books are *Hide and Seek Fog* (1965); *What Is Right for Tulip* (1969); *The Beaver Pond* (about ecology); *Veronica; The Hippopotamus and Petunia; The Goose;* and *The Crocodile in the Tree*.

William Steig (1907–)

William Steig's *New Yorker* cartoons are famous. His adult books, especially *Small Fry and The Lonely Ones*, have been enthusiastically received. And recently Mr. Steig has turned his attention to the field of children's literature with excellent results. His third book *Sylvester and the Magic Pebble* won the 1970 Caldecott Medal.

A Manhattan native, Mr. Steig comes from a highly creative family. Both his parents were artists. All three of his brothers are artists; one is also a writer, one a musician and writer, and the third a poet. Furthermore, Steig's daughter Lucy is an artist, and his son Jeremy is too! Jeremy is also an up-and-coming jazz flautist who has released several albums. Lucy and Jeremy, both married, live in the same Greenwich, Connecticut, neighborhood as their father, and all see each other often. Mr. Steig is a withdrawn person who enjoys solitude; nevertheless, he is a devoted family man.

Sylvester is the story of a young donkey who finds a red pebble that has the ability to grant wishes. Suddenly frightened, however, Sylvester turns himself into a rock, and the pebble, which needs to be held while wishing, falls by the wayside. It looks as if Sylvester is doomed to lead the life of a rock until his despondent parents picnic on top of him one day, reuniting him with his pebble. He bursts back into donkeyhood as plates of food clatter off his back. Parenthetically, many librarians became quite incensed when Sylvester won the Caldecott: Steig had drawn policemen as pigs! They bemoaned the irreverence for authority.

All of Steig's illustrations bear the mark of a seasoned cartoonist. They are boldly assertive and have a larger-than-life quality about them. The pictures are mock-humorous, depicting animals with precise human affectations in dress and in mannerism. Steig makes effective use of bright primary colors.

Other books by Mr. Steig are *Roland the Minstrel Pig; CDB!; An Eye for Elephants; Dominic; Amos and Boris; Farmer Palmer's Wagon Ride;* and *Abel's Island.* His last four books are on the American Library Association's Notable list.

Leo Politi (1908–)

Leo Politi's picture books, beyond being entertaining stories, are important for preserving the charm and flavor of his native California. He portrays the Sicilian fishermen of Monterey, the Chinese-Americans of Los Angeles' Chinatown, and the Mexican-Americans of his beloved Olvera Street in Los Angeles. Unlike those of John Steptoe, Tom Feelings, and others, Politi's stories are directed more towards children outside these cultures, and thus the stories take on an interestingly informative dimension. They tell how children of minority cultures live and think. The books, however, have universal themes and stories that all children can readily understand.

Born in Fresno, California, Mr. Politi went with his family to Italy when he was seven. There he was raised in Brani, his mother's childhood home, and at fifteen he won a scholarship to the University of Art and Decorations in Monza. Returning to America shortly after his graduation, Politi settled on Olvera Street, the heart of Los Angeles' Mexican section. It is the oldest street in the city, and its rich sense of heritage provides the setting for many of Mr. Politi's stories. *Pedro, the Angel of Olvera Street, Juanita,* and *Piccolo's Prank* take place here. These books emphasize the flavor of Mexican culture and, at the same time, encourage its more easy-going, less materialistic values.

Particularly effective is Mr. Politi's *Song of the Swallows,* winner of the 1950 Caldecott Medal. It is a lovely story of the friendship between a young boy and an old man who together eagerly await the coming of the

FIGURE 9–3. *Poster made by a child for Leo Politi's* The Butterflies Come.

swallows to Capistrano each year. Their stoic patience and the cycles of the seasons are beautifully conveyed. Other books are *Little Leo, Moy Moy,* and *Emmet.*

Mr. Politi's illustrations in all his books are perfectly suited to his subject matter. Bright splashes of color and stylized detail create a delightful aura of gaiety and simplicity. His wonderful illustrations totally immerse children in a relievingly peaceful world too often foreign to their realm of experience.

Virginia Lee Burton (1909–1968)

Intensely creative, Miss Burton brought life to all of her artistic pursuits. She was born in Newton Center, Massachusetts, and her father was the Dean of the Massachusetts Institute of Technology. The family moved to California where, as a junior in high school, Miss Burton won a scholarship to the California School of Fine Arts. She excelled in both art and dance. She returned to Boston within the year, however, becoming a sketcher for the drama editor of the *Boston Transcript.* While taking art lessons at the Boston Museum School, Miss Burton met George Demetrios, a teacher and sculptor-artist. They married only a few months after meeting and settled on Cape Ann, Massachusetts. There, Miss Burton established the Folly Cove Designers, a group interested in textile design.

In 1937 Miss Burton published *Choo Choo,* the hilarious story of a mischievous train engine. Her famous *Mike Mulligan and His Steam*

Shovel appeared in 1939. In the story Mary Anne, the steam shovel, is becoming outdated; the newer diesel shovels are awarded all the jobs. Still chipper, however, she and Mike bet that in one day she can outdig one hundred men working for a week. Of course, Mary Anne and Mike win, and the book ends with a charming surprise. Miss Burton's *Calico the Wonder Horse or The Saga of Stewey Stinker* caused a small controversy when it was published: a librarian strongly objected to a character in a children's books having a name like Stinker. *The Little House* won the 1943 Caldecott Medal. It is the simple and poignant story of a house built in the country. As time goes by, a village envelops it and eventually a huge, sprawling city has swallowed up the once pastoral house. Now fallen into disrepair and dwarfed by dingy skyscrapers, it is rediscovered by descendants of the original family. The little house is moved to the country where once again it is nestled in the idyllic setting in which it so appropriately belongs.

The Little House is a vital book that has valuable sociological significance to children. The reader witnesses the progression of a city's development in all its awesome complexity. What was once a blissful, rural setting ultimately becomes chaotic confusion ensnarled by an elevated train, traffic jams, and innumerable throngs of people. The barest trace of human expression is evident in the little house's "face," and it conveys a sense of despair. Children easily identify with the house, as they too often feel dwarfed by adults, and they delight in the house's reaction.

FIGURE 9–4. *A montage drawing by two primary children of* The Little House *by Virginia Lee Burton.*

Virginia Lee Burton's best stories characteristically involve inanimate objects. Her artistic style readily displays her experience with dance. Swirling whirlwind lines whisk through each picture, constantly creating an energetic sense of motion. Text and illustrations are always in perfect harmony; often the text is arranged in such a configuration as to complement the action of the accompanying illustration. Miss Burton's watercolors are always bright and appropriate. Virginia Lee Burton is one of the great contributors to the picture book in its emergence as an art form.

Leo Lionni (1910–   )

Few approach Leo Lionni's talent in coordinating words and pictures. He is superb in his ability to synthesize a highly imaginative story and art of unrivaled excellence into a single cohesive unit. Yet, at the same time, both the words and the pictures are so vivid that either could effectively tell the story alone.

Remarkably, Dr. Lionni never studied art; he is self-taught. Born in Amsterdam in 1910, he is quick to point out that he lived within two blocks of two of Europe's most important museums. Lionni lived in Amsterdam until he was twelve, then moved about between Holland and Belgium until he entered the University of Genoa, Italy, where he received his doctorate in economics. Dr. Lionni came to America in 1939 to act as art director for a Philadelphia advertising agency. He has also been art director of *Fortune Magazine*, design director for the Olivetti Corporation, head of the Graphics Department of Parsons School of Design, and editor of *Print*.

Dr. Lionni takes pride in his lack of identifiable style, preferring instead the flexibility of adapting art to his story, solely on the basis of that story. He experiments with combining a variety of media, particularly painting and collage. If he feels he cannot do illustrations that will perfectly unite with a story in question, he will abandon the story. Perhaps it in this philosophy that accounts for the numerous awards Dr. Lionni has received for works such as *Little Blue and Little Yellow* (1959), *Inch by Inch* (1960), *Swimmy* (1963), *Frederick* (1967), *Alexander and the Wind-Up Mouse* (1968), *The Greentail Mouse* (1972), and *Pezzeltino* (1976). Many of his stories are sophisticated enough to be thought of as allegories; Swimmey, for example, is a lone black fish among a school of red fish, suggesting racial overtones to many.

Lionni is one of the best craftsmen in illustrations and when he draws animals and nature, a child can see new dimensions of graphic art.

Dr. Lionni lives in Lavasna, Italy.

Evaline Ness (1911–   )

Evaline Ness is one of the best-known illustrators still producing new books that delight children and adults. Born in Union City, Ohio, she attended Ball State Teachers College and has done further work at the

Art Institute of Chicago, the Corcoran Gallery Art School in Washington, D.C., the Art Students League of New York, and the Academia de Belles Artes, Rome. Before becoming a children's book illustrator, Miss Ness drew dress advertisements for New York's famous Saks Fifth Avenue. Later she worked for such mazagines as *Ladies' Home Journal, Good Housekeeping, Seventeen,* and curiously, *Sports Illustrated.*

Like many illustrators, Miss Ness began to write books in addition to illustrating them. Her fifth book *Sam, Bangs, and Moonshine* won the 1967 Caldecott Medal. Sam is a little girl who tells stories which her widowed father calls "moonshine." One day Sam tells a story that leads her pet cat, Bangs, and her friend Thomas into a dangerous storm. Of course, Sam learns her lesson and resolves to tell only "good moonshine." Young children easily perceive Sam as a lonely little girl who tells her stories to compensate for the fact that her mother has died. They sympathize with Sam's problems that are related with such compassion. The pictures help a great deal to tell the story. They are done with a variety of techniques, such as painting, sketching, and realia. On one page, she uses a wad of string. Miss Ness experiments until she obtains the effect she desires.

Miss Ness makes highly effective use of color woodcuts. Each picture requires a separate pictorial unit for each color. The blocks are then inked and pressed by hand. Her colors are deep and impenetrable. The resulting impression is a very layered and dimensional effect, showing texture and utilizing the richer colors as a background.

Other books are *The Girl and the Goatherd, Yeck Eck,* and *Old Mother Hubbard and Her Dog,* which she both wrote and illustrated. Her illustrations for Helen Buckley's Josie books were considered avant-garde when they were first published. Her latest book, *A Paper Palace To Cut Out and Color,* is a new type of adventure into color for children (1976).

Robert McCloskey (1914–)

Even though Robert McCloskey has not written since his 1963 *Burt Dow: Deep-Water Man,* he is a perennial children's favorite. He is also a favorite of the critics, the only man to be awarded two Caldecott medals and two runners-up.

Mr. McCloskey was born and raised in Hamilton, Ohio. He thinks of his life as having had three phases. At an early age McCloskey began to play the piano, harmonica, drums, and oboe. This first phase ended rather abruptly when he became infatuated with inventing mechanical gizmos. McCloskey might have continued blowing fuses had he not begun drawing for his high school paper. He subsequently won an art scholarship to the Vesper George School in Boston and later studied at the National Academy of Design.

Children are fascinated to know just how much of himself McCloskey puts into his books. *Lentil, Homer Price,* and *Centerburg Tales* all loosely chronicle his Ohio childhood. The picture of *Lentil* bathing and playing his harmonica in an old-fashioned bathtub is McCloskey in his own childhood upstairs bathroom. The crazy inventions of *Homer Price,* if not actually invented by McCloskey as a youth, very well might have

FIGURE 9–5. *A diorama illustrating the creative principle of substitution: Robert McCloskey's* Homer Price and The Donut Machine. *The donuts are Cheerios. The stools are pencils and Coke bottle tops.*

been. While writing *Make Way for Ducklings,* it was so important to Mc-Closkey that the mallards be realistic that he bought four mallards at an open-air market (only to find that two were impostor puddle ducks). The four ducks quacked around his Greenwich Village apartment until his neighbors could not take any more. McCloskey even consulted a Cornell University ornithologist about his problem.

Not only does Mr. McCloskey write about himself, he writes about his family. Sal of *Blueberries for Sal* is his daughter, who has since grown up and married. The family, pets, and younger daughter Jane appear in *One Morning in Maine.* All the McCloskeys and their Maine home are found in the beautifully written *Time of Wonder.*

Many of McCloskey's illustrations may seem old-fashioned to children and adults now. The Maine stories, those involving the whole McCloskey family, lend a peaceful, serene sense of tranquility that ultimately conveys a satisfied sense of well-being. The illustrations of Mc-Closkey's more autobiographical boyhood stories are superlative in their ability to communicate the comic exuberance of the texts. He does exceptionally well at artistically re-creating each scene that he describes in writing. The pictures are highly colorful, but always appropriate, and stylized with just enough detail to heighten the imagination.

Mr. McCloskey is presently involved with puppetry and works in his Maine home creating new types of puppets. Perhaps this is a fusion of his inventive phase and his artistic phase.

Paul Galdone (1914–   )

One of the most sought after illustrators today, Paul Galdone has twice been a Caldecott Medal runner-up, for *Anatole* (1956) and *Anatole and the Cat* (1957). Today he has over one hundred books in print.

Born in Hungary, Galdone came to America at fourteen. He can still remember the embarrassment of reading Shakespeare's *A Midsummer Night's Dream* aloud in his American high school class; not only did the class find Mr. Galdone's accent highly amusing, but he himself could make neither head nor tail of Shakespeare's language. The Galdone family moved to New York City where young Galdone worked by day as a busboy, electrician's helper, and fur dyer. At night he studied at the Art Students League and the New York School for Industrial Design. Eventually Mr. Galdone worked in Doubleday and Company's art department. There, and later as a free-lancer, he built a busy career as a book jacket designer. It was not long before he realized the advantages and challenges to be found in illustrating children's books.

Mr. Galdone is a painter as well as an illustrator and studied under such notables as George Grosz, Louis Bouché, and Guy Pené du Bois.

Using color sparingly, Galdone relies instead on pen and ink shading with a thin wash. The pen and ink creates an informal feeling; nevertheless, his work is much more painstaking than is initially apparent. Every object is meticulously proportioned and all his shading lines are thoughtfully placed. His style is easily adaptable to humor, as in Mary Lynn Solot's *100 Hamburgers*. Other recent Galdone notables are *The Monkey and the Crocodile, Little Tuppen, Three Aesop Fox Fables, The Three Bears, The Three Little Pigs, Henny Penny,* and *Honeybee's Party,* which was written by his daughter.

Paul Galdone's pictures are of consistently high quality. One of the more prolific illustrators, his name is a household word among teachers, librarians, and parents.

William Pené du Bois (1916–   )

William Pené du Bois is a giant in the field of children's literature. His books have delighted readers since he published his *Giant Otto* (1935) at the age of nineteen.

Born in 1916, the son of famous painter and critic Guy Pené du Bois, young du Bois lived in Nutley, New Jersey, until age eight. He was then sent to the Lycée Hoche, a boarding school in Versailles, France. He credits the school as one of the major influences on his life, a mathematics teacher in particular. He says this about that teacher:

> Every morning he would stack our homework papers in a neat pile in the middle of his desk and then proceed to look at them one by one, not as correct or incorrect, but as neat and sloppy examples of orderly procedure. He would hold them up as if he were studying etchings, look at the name of the student and express his sentiment of the work. He would either say, "Ah, c'est beau!" and stack it in a pile to his right, or make a sad, dejected grimace and tear it in four

FIGURE 9–6. *A bulletin board for* Lazy Tommy Pumpkinhead *by William Pené du Bois. The quilt is real and was made by children.*

equal parts which he stacked to his left. I remember doing a magnificent page of arithmetic, my favorite subject, in which I neglected to rule one short line under a subtraction of two one-digit figures. "What have we here?" he said. "An artist? Monsieur du Bois is drawing free hand."[6]

As a result, Mr. du Bois is meticulous to this day; before he starts work, he painstakingly arranges his brushes and pens until they are all in their proper places. He will not use an ordinary glass to rinse his brushes, rather, an antique ceramic fulfills that function. Mr. du Bois paints exactly one picture a day, no more, no less—the picture must be perfect, however. Most recently, Mr. du Bois has illustrated Charlotte Zolotow's *William's Doll.* Mr. du Bois's meticulousness manifests itself in his illustrations. When he draws with sharp, efficient pen and ink lines, the illustrations seem drawn by a draftsman. He changes his style to suit his words; recently, in *My Grandson Lew,* written by Charlotte Zolotow in 1974, he uses misty shadings with no broad-stroke outlines because this type of illustration is better suited to the mood of the text. There are touches of whimsicality and warmth in every illustration.

All of du Bois's stories are highly imaginative. The Otto books are about a giant dog; *Lion* is about an animal factory in the sky; *Lazy Tommy Pumpkinhead* is about a boy so spoiled by his automated house that he is

6. Stanley J. Kunitz and Howard Haycraft, eds., *The Junior Book of Authors* (New York: H. W. Wilson, 1957), p. 103.

totally dependent upon it; and *The Twenty-One Balloons* won the 1947 Newbery Medal. Du Bois pays exquisite attention to detail in both his stories and his illustrations. Children are truly fortunate to have his books. In 1976 he illustrated *The Runaway Flying Horse* by Paul Bonzon, and *It's Not Fair* by Charlotte Zolotow.

Ezra Jack Keats (1916–)

Ezra Jack Keats began drawing as a young child in a Brooklyn tenement. He found quick encouragement from his mother; an early opus, drawn all over the kitchen table, was so admired that she covered it with a special tablecloth and proudly uncovered it for guests. Young Keats, of course, had expected quite a scolding. This encouragement was not shared by Keats's father, however. A waiter in a Greenwich Village cafe, Mr. Keats viewed firsthand the life of the struggling artists. But he often brought home tubes of paint, explaining that a destitute artist had traded them for a bowl of soup. When Mr. Keats died, shortly before his son's high school graduation, his wallet revealed newspaper clippings of every award Keats had won.

After graduation Keats could not even afford to accept his scholarship to the Art Students League. Often he had to paint with house paint. Instead of going to school he went to work painting the comic strip hero, Captain Marvel. After World War II, Keats devoted himself to illustrating. Several magazine covers, including *Reader's Digest* and *Collier's,* caught the attention of publishers, and Keats has since been in demand. He still lives in New York City and is much attached to it.

The Snowy Day, the first book Mr. Keats wrote and illustrated, is of primary importance in children's literature. Peter wakes up one morning to find that it has snowed overnight. The snowball he brings inside melts, to his dismay. It snows again the next night, and Peter knows he'll play again tomorrow. It is significant that Peter is illustrated as being black, yet the text never alludes to color. *The Snowy Day* heralded the beginning of a more easy-going approach towards ethnicity. In fact, it is a non-approach because race is irrelevant to the story. *The Snowy Day* won the 1963 Caldecott Medal.

Mr. Keats is noted for his effective use of collage. Using all sorts of scrap papers and cloth, some sent to him by admiring children, each particular scrap suggests a specific object. Keats achieves his translucent backgrounds by dipping his paper into a pan in which he has swirled several related oil colors. The result is an ethereal, marbled effect. A feeling of depth contributes towards a sense of dimensionalism.

All of Ezra Jack Keats's books portray children with real feelings in real situations. The characterizations are superb, both textually and artistically. Most of his books, including *Apt. 3, Peter's Chair, Goggles,* and *Pet Show!,* take place in urban run-down neighborhoods, yet the stories are warm and friendly. The texts are sparingly written, but in combination with the illustrations, there is a feeling of many emotions. Mr. Keats shows the city as it really is—its stark reality, its garbage cans, the writing on the sidewalks, the laundry on the rooftops. Yet all is clothed in a magic that wraps the city into a world that in itself is both ugly and beautiful.

Other popular books written and illustrated by Keats include *Whistle for Willie, Hi, Cat!, Dreams,* and *Louie.*

Leonard Weisgard (1916–)

As a young boy Weisgard loved to paint. He excelled so in art courses in high school that he decided to make art his lifelong career. He studied at Pratt Institute in New York City, first became a commercial artist, then turned to illustrating children's books, winning one Caldecott medal and placement on the Caldecott honor list. Later he wrote and illustrated his own books.

Weisgard's reputation as an illustrator was established when he won acclaim for illustrating twenty-two of Margaret Wise Brown's little books. Two examples of his best work are seen in *The Little Island* by Golden MacDonald (a pen name of Margaret Wise Brown), which won him the Caldecott Medal in 1947, and *The Little Lost Lamb* (1946), also written by Golden MacDonald. He illustrated *The Golden Egg Book* (1958) for Margaret Wise Brown, and this book designed for Easter is one of his most charming, as it suggests Easter as well as spring. It still remains popular and delights children.

Other authors with whom this prolific illustrator has collaborated are Sesyle Joslin in her delightful stories about Baby Elephant, Phyllis McGinley's *A Wreath of Christmas Legends* (1967), and Charlotte Zolotow's *Wake Up and Goodnight* (1971). Some of his finest art work is the biblical *And It Came to Pass* (1971), a book of Bible verses and carols arranged by Jean Slaughter.

He also illustrated *Alice's Adventures in Wonderland* in color, different from the original black and white sketches by Sir John Tenniel. Weisgard was placed on the Honor List as a Caldecott runner-up for his illustrations for *Rain Drop Splash* by Alvin Tresselt (1946).

Leonard Weisgard wrote and illustrated *My Peaceable Paints,* about the colonial period in America, and *Down Huckleberry Hill,* a cumulative tale full of action, fun, and sound. The illustrations for both are representative of his humor, imagination, and fine sense of rhythm. *Silly Willy Nilly,* an animal story of a baby elephant who runs away, is a delightful tale that he wrote and illustrated.

Weisgard can be classed as a fine-arts painter who uses brilliant colors as well as soft ones for shade, and a mistlike quality when appropriate. His illustrations contain details of flowers and birds, and he especially excels in drawing animals.

Leonard Weisgard has made a significant contribution to the beauty of children's books. Many, many children know him as a friend because of his prolific attainments in writing and illustrating.

Marcia Brown (1918–)

The only woman to receive the Caldecott Medal twice, Marcia Brown is truly a dynamic force in the field of children's literature. In addition to *Cinderella or The Little Glass Slipper* and *Once a Mouse,* her two winners, Miss Brown has had two runners-up for the honor.

Miss Brown was born in Rochester, New York. Her father was a minister, and his calling led the Browns to several towns in the state. She studied at the State University of New York at Albany and won a scholarship to the Woodstock School of Painting, where she studied under the well-known Judson Smith. Upon graduation, however, she found herself teaching high school English and drama until the possibility of book illustrating finally lured her to New York City. Lee Bennett Hopkins reports that Miss Brown went to Scribner's with her first book, *The Little Carousel*, only to find the children's book editor busy. Determined, she marched around the corner to Viking, where she found herself confronted with an elevator operators' strike. Not quite determined enough to climb infinite stairs, Miss Brown returned to Scribner's, waited, and has been with them ever since.

Once a Mouse is a simple Indian tale about a hermit who, out of pity, turns a defenseless mouse into a series of progressively more important animals. Finally a tiger, the ex-mouse is ungrateful and finds himself abruptly transformed back to the mouse he once was. Miss Brown did the illustrations in simple woodcuts that precisely fit the nature of the parable.

Miss Brown's illustrations are minutely descriptive. She seems to strive for the total effect. As in a photo negative, Miss Brown pays so much attention to each background that the more simply drawn object stands out. Still, her pictures demand much more concentration than is often the case with other illustrators. Her *Felice* (1958), for example, contains one picture with more than forty cats, but no more than ten or so are immediately apparent. Children who know this book spend much time looking for and counting the cats.

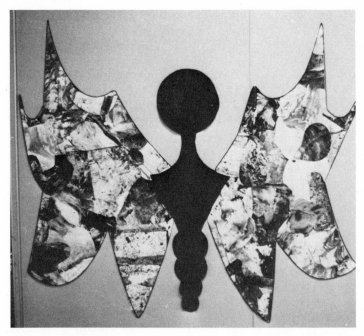

FIGURE 9–7. *A bulletin board created by older elementary children to promote Marcia Brown's* All Butterflies.

Children love Marcia Brown's books and it is evident that she loves children. Her *All Butterflies, An ABC* (1974), with words in pairs and illustrated with elegant woodcuts, clearly indicates that she understands how children learn.

Brian Wildsmith (1930–   )

Brian Wildsmith greatly enlarges the soul of illustration at the expense of text. In fact, the text is often so reduced that the art work can hardly be called illustrations, for the pictures become both the text and the illustrations: a picture book in the truest sense of the word.

The text of *Brian Wildsmith's Circus* (1970) consists of one simple sentence; the first page (the book is unpaged) reads, "The circus comes to town . . . ," and the last page concludes " . . . the circus goes on to the next town." Every page between the phrases depicts scenes of circus life. As in all Wildsmith's books, the kaleidoscopic colors are arranged in an assertively prismatic sense. His full-page, full-color illustrations create a wonderfully different world. Each picture is so suggestive that the images inspire the child to provide his own text. The illustrations are unique and each one would make an excellent poster for a child's room. In fact, Wildsmith does make imaginative and artistic posters for children, which are sold commercially.

Mr. Wildsmith is a native of Yorkshire, England. He and his family live alternately in Gerona, Spain and Dunwich, London. His *Brian Wildsmith's ABC* (1961) won the 1962 Kate Greenaway Medal. Other recent Wildsmith books include *The Twelve Days of Christmas* and *Brian Wildsmith's Puzzles*.

Tomi Ungerer (1931–   )

Tomi Ungerer's picture books are consistently delightful because of their imaginative plots, offbeat characters, and satirical and ironic illustrations.

His life has been as offbeat as his books. Born in the Alsace district of France, where Ungerer's father was a painter, historian, inventor, and a builder of astronomical clocks, Ungerer viewed the horrors of World War II firsthand. After the war he traveled extensively, hitchhiking and skipping borders. He met his Waterloo in Africa, however, when illness cut short his tour with the Camel Corps. Still ailing, he came to New York in 1956. Since then Mr. Ungerer, in addition to being a highly successful author and illustrator, has been a cartoonist, designer, and advertising artist.

Ungerer's stories characteristically involve a bizarre animal as the protagonist in a somewhat outlandish situation. *Crictor*, for example, is a boa constrictor who has been mailed to a French school teacher. In the small village Crictor acts as a jump rope for the girls; Boy Scouts practice their knots on him; and eventually he even ties up a burglar. *Orlando, the Brave Vulture* saves a prospector by flying to "Prattleborough, Vermont" to contact his family. *Monsieur Racine and the Beast* is a delightfully droll animal story. His recent book, *A Storybook*, is a compilation of stories by

FIGURE 9–8. *A stocking puppet show of* Crictor *by Tomi Ungerer.*

Wanda Gag, Hans Christian Andersen, the Grimms, and others; it has earned him the title of the Charles Addams of children's illustrators.

Tom Feelings (1933–)

As one of the few black illustrators involved in children's literature, Tom Feelings takes a purposeful approach toward his work. As with John Steptoe, Mr. Feelings was made aware at an early age that books were written for whites only. Certainly no story was about blacks, nor did plots depict blacks living in real-life situations. This dearth of literature for blacks only served to reinforce the notion of second-class citizenship so dominant in America.

Born and raised in New York's Bedford-Stuyvesant section of Brooklyn, Feelings attended the School of Visual Arts. His first major employment was to write and illustrate an informational comic strip for a Harlem newspaper. After graduating from art school, no one would buy Feelings's art work because his subjects were the black people of Bedford-Stuyvesant:

> Most magazines and book publishers just weren't interested. "Don't you draw white people?" they asked. "Your scope seems limited; why don't you be practical and include more white people? You shouldn't place so much emphasis on race. It just shows that you are different."[7]

7. Lee Bennett Hopkins, *Books Are by People* (New York: Citation Press, 1969), p. 70.

Feelings's autobiographical *Black Pilgrimage* is simply and movingly written. While describing the specific trials of one man, it is simultaneously accessible and relevant to all blacks. Yet it is almost as important that white children read this book; it will be an introduction to a culture that they know little about.

The sketches of *Black Pilgrimage* successfully capture the flavor of Bedford-Stuyvesant. The careless poses, the forlorn hopelessness, and the drab buildings confront the reader. These sketches effectively contrast with the vivid colors of the pastels that Feelings drew while in Ghana, Africa. These pictures are rich and luxurious, expressive of an inner warmth and tranquility. Feelings's sketches have beauty, strength, and power reminiscent of those of Leonardo da Vinci.

Other books by Tom Feelings include the 1972 Caldecott runner-up, *Moja Means One: The Swahili Counting Book, Zamani Goes to Market,* the 1969 Newbery Medal runner-up, and *Jambo Means Hello: The Swahili Alphabet Book*—all of which were written by his wife Muriel Feelings. He also illustrated *To Be a Slave* by Julius Lester.

Uri Shulevitz (1935–   )

One of the bright, more recent figures in children's literature, Uri Shulevitz won the 1969 Caldecott Medal for his colorful illustrations in Arthur Ransome's *The Fool of the World and the Flying Ship.* In addition to illustrating other people's books, Mr. Shulevitz has written and illustrated outstanding picture books of his own, *The Moon in My Room, One Monday Morning, Rain Rain Rivers,* and *Dawn.*

Forced to flee Warsaw, Poland, during Hitler's invasion, the Shulevitz family was among the homeless refugees that flooded through Europe. When he was eighteen, the family moved to Tel Aviv, Israel. There, in addition to attending the Teachers Institute, Mr. Shulevitz was at various times an apprentice to a rubber stamp maker, a house painter, a carpenter, and the Tel Aviv city dog license issuer. Now an American citizen, he lives and works in New York's Greenwich Village. Mr. Shulevitz is an ardent student of *tai-ch-chuan,* a Chinese physical discipline similar to shadow boxing.

One Monday Morning is a novel story about a meek little boy who tells us that the King and Queen and various other royalty came to his run-down apartment one day. He's never home, so the ever-increasing retinue must come back the next day until, finally, the little boy is home. It is then that we see that the boy has never left his room and has fantasized the whole affair—he has been playing with a deck of cards and the face cards and joker have sparked his imagination.

Mr. Shulevitz's illustrations always capture the flavor of the scene; they evoke feelings beyond those that create the reaction, "What a pretty picture!" His pictures are invariably beguiling and low-keyed. Mr. Shulevitz possesses a remarkable ability to present great detail without becoming tedious or without stealing the show from the mood of the story. Whether he draws his illustrations in pen and ink, or whether he adds a wash or uses full color, his pictures are always delightfully appropriate. Recently

(1976) he has illustrated a new book of Robert Louis Stevenson's *The Touchstone*.

John Steptoe (1951–   )

John Steptoe is a young black from Brooklyn's Bedford-Stuyvesant district of New York. Noting that almost no picture books were written for black children by blacks, he wrote and illustrated *Stevie* at the age of seventeen. Using idiomatic language that black and white city children use, Steptoe wrote a book that communicates immediately to all children and portrays a universal situation with which all children can identify. Young Robert resents little Stevie, a boy whom his mother cares for every day. Yet when Stevie and his family move away, Robert finds himself reminiscing over such events as finding dead rats together and cooking mickies and marshmallows in the park. Since *Stevie,* Steptoe has written a book a year: *Uptown, Train Ride,* and *Birthday.*

In 1974, Steptoe illustrated *She Come Bringing Me That Little Baby Girl* written by Eloise Greenfield. Also in 1974 he wrote and illustrated *My Special Best Words.* His art is often described as poetic and lyrical in quality.

He studied art at Manhattan's High School of Art and Design but left early, finding it overly commercial. His illustrations are anything but commercial, however. Intensely impressionistic, the colors are deep rich oils, the total effect soft and muted. The pictures are excellent art.

John Steptoe is extremely talented, and books like his are long overdue. They help children of all ethnic groups to understand the life of a special ethnic group in America.

SUMMARY

A child's first introduction to reading and literature is through his experience with picture books. A picture book is defined as a harmonious blend of text and illustrations. The adult reads the story; the child "reads" the pictures. If the combination of the two media—writing and illustration—is well done, a child's first experience with books is enjoyable and will facilitate the child's ability to read by himself.

As a child grows older and can read better, he still enjoys pictures. As texts become longer and more complicated, the illustrations tend to be fewer in number. These books are referred to as illustrated books. Today the illustrations in both types of books are so imaginative that young children continue to enjoy books with illustrations as they grow older and their perception of beauty is sharpened.

In this generation a child can enjoy books illustrated by classical artists whose works are still available, as well as books illustrated by modern artists, many of whom have been influenced by their predecessors in the field of graphic art. Some of the modern artists continue to re-create settings and people of ages past, while others explore new media, styles, and techniques. Consequently, the Space Age child is presented with a wealth of visual choices in the books he selects to read. Today's child is sophisticated in his response to visual stimuli because of the influences of comics, cartoons, films, and television. Children naturally and instinctively love art in all its forms.

And so we have reached the golden age of books produced especially for children. Through innovations in photography, printing, and lithography, it is possible to produce outstanding books judged by literary and artistic criteria. As the number of books increases, exciting new artists have appeared in the last thirty years. Many have come from foreign countries, many from the field of commercial art and advertising, but no matter by what route they have traveled, they have brought devotion and change to the art of illustration.

Realism is a new trend that has developed in the literature of recent years, and the illustrations have developed accordingly. Children now see the harsh facts of life in a world which is not always beautiful and perfect. Thus, the graphic arts have helped literature become more relevant to the child and his experience. Art has helped literature expand the joys of the child's world.

It is important for a teacher to know the criteria of good illustration, and it is helpful for her to know biographical facts and vignettes of the lives of illustrators. For children are curious to know about the life of an artist, how he works, who he is, and so forth. This adds another dimension to children's interest in books. Knowing a little about an artist's life helps the teacher realize that each artist has a different approach, philosophy, and style, but that all share a dedication to their work. Mediocrity can always be found in illustrations, as in any field of human activity, but the majority of the artists working in children's books are excellent.

The classroom teacher can effectively use the illustrations in children's books as a part of the school curriculum. When children become aware of illustrations, they develop an appreciation of the differences in man's perceptions of the world. Children can see different cultures, different races, different value systems. Consequently, illustrations can be correlated with other subjects in the curriculum such as science and social studies. The artist enlarges the viewer's perception of the beauty and the reality of the world. As such, he deserves attention, study, and careful consideration.

TO THE COLLEGE STUDENT

1. Examine books from recent years that have won the Caldecott Medal (see page 93). Try to find books with differences in style and compare them.

2. Read three or four acceptance speeches of the Caldecott Medal. Some suggestions are Robert McCloskey, Ludwig Bemelmans, Ezra Jack Keats, and Maurice Sendak. Compare the philosophies expounded.

3. Find several well-known picture books and analyze the illustrations. Suggestions are *Childhood is a Time of In-* *nocence* by Joan Walsh Anglund, *Once a Mouse* by Marcia Brown, *About Owls*, illustrated by Tony Chen, *Swimmy* by Leo Lionni, *In the Night Kitchen* by Maurice Sendak. Note the similarities and differences in illustrations.

4. Compare and contrast the illustrations of some of the well-known classical illustrators of the nineteenth century, such as Randolph Caldecott, Kate Greenaway, and Beatrix Potter, with those of some well-known modern illustrators, such as Dr. Seuss, Evaline Ness, and Leo Lionni.

Discuss your observations with your class.

5. Compare and contrast illustrations of one subject, such as houses, animals, nature, people, means of transportation (cars, trains, horses, carriages) by finding picture books with illustrations that portray these objects in different styles.

6. Find one illustrator who uses a variety of styles and see how differently he treats the text of each book he illustrates. Such an artist is Paul Galdone. Compare his style of illustrating Helen E. Buckley's *Grandfather and I* with the illustrations in *100 Hamburgers*. Note the

appropriateness of his style to varying subjects in these books.

7. Find one illustrator such as Dr. Seuss and note how his style of illustration is much the same in each book. Does his style always suit the text? Which do you prefer, an illustrator with different styles or one whose style is readily recognizable? Which do you think children prefer? Or does it make no difference as long as the illustrations suit the story?

8. Try to write and illustrate your own children's book.

TO THE CLASSROOM TEACHER

1. Collect pictures of and anecdotes about modern illustrators. Think of the times in your curriculum when you can best use this reference material. A bulletin board display of illustrators is one way. Another way is telling anecdotes about an illustrator's life before you read a book during story hour. Robert McCloskey has written many amusing accounts of his experience with ducks in his preparation for writing *Make Way for Ducklings*. *Horn Book Magazine* contains many articles about modern illustrators.

2. Ask your classroom students to find books with illustrations that they especially enjoy. Encourage them to discuss *why* they like the illustrations.

3. Encourage your students to make a picture book with their own illustrations. Children should be made aware that no one artist's style is more correct than any other. This is demonstrated in the different styles of professional illustrators.

4. Provide your class with pictures from magazines and newspapers. Think of different ways you can stimulate their imagination to use these pictures in creative ways; for example, let them make a collage or illustrate their own picture book by using the cut-out pictures.

5. Plan an activity in which the class can draw a mural of scenes from picture books. Divide the class into groups and let each group take turns painting a scene from the book.

6. Encourage members of the class to act out the scenes illustrated in a picture book. Two good choices would be *Let's Be Enemies* by Janice May Udry, illustrated by Maurice Sendak, or *The Brute Family* by Lillian and Russel Hoban. Children need not necessarily follow the action portrayed in the illustrations; instead, they can role-play how they feel the scene can be illustrated, by using body actions, facial expressions, or pantomiming.

7. If possible, arrange to invite an illustrator to visit your school so that he can tell how he illustrates his books.

8. Write to Weston Woods (see address in Appendix C) and obtain their list of films of illustrators; arrange to show one or more to your class. There are many excellent films by such illustrators as Maurice Sendak, Barbara Cooney, Ezra Jack Keats, and Robert McCloskey.

9. Plan an exhibit of children's book illustrators for a school program or a school fair.

TO THE COLLEGE STUDENT
AND THE CLASSROOM TEACHER

1. When you next visit the children's library or bookstore, become more aware,

by browsing through many books, of a book's format, illustrations, use of colors, and the wide variety of styles of illustrators.

2. Bring to class some picture books with illustrations of didactic writing. Compare these with modern picture books. Note the subtle ways modern illustrators can teach children lessons.

3. Bring to class picture books that are examples of illustrations meeting high as well as low artistic standards. Does the class agree which are good and which are poor? Show the same books to a classroom of children. Can children see the difference between the ones that are universally considered good illustrations and those considered trite and cheap?

4. Collect and share books that contain illustrations of people from different countries and environments, from different racial groups, and from different occupations. Think of the ways these illustrations can be used in many areas of the curriculum, such as social studies, science, music, and art.

SELECTED BIBLIOGRAPHY

Arbuthnot, May Hill, and Zena Sutherland. *Children and Books.* 4th ed. Glenview, Ill.: Scott, Foresman, 1972.

Bland, David. *A History Book of Illustrators: The Illuminated Manuscript and the Printed Book,* rev. ed. Berkeley: University of California Press, 1969.

Cianciolo, Patricia. *Illustrations in Children's Books.* Dubuque, Iowa: Wm. C. Brown, 1970.

Commire, Anne. *Something about the Author: Facts and Pictures about Contemporary Authors and Illustrators of Books for Young People,* vol. 7. Detroit: Gale Research, 1975.

de Montreville, Doris, and Donna Hill, eds. *Third Book of Junior Authors.* New York: H. W. Wilson, 1972.

Feldman, Edmund Burke. *Becoming Human Through Art: Aesthetic Experience in the School.* Englewood Cliffs, N.J.: Prentice-Hall, 1970.

Fuller, Muriel, ed. *More Junior Authors.* New York: H. W. Wilson, 1963.

Hoffman, Miriam, and Eva Samuels, eds. *Authors and Illustrators of Children's Books: Interviews with 104 Authors and Illustrators of Books for Young Children.* New York: R. R. Bowker, 1972.

Hopkins, Lee Bennett. *Books Are by People.* New York: Citation Press, 1969.

Huck, Charlotte S., and Doris Young Kuhn. *Children's Literature in the Elementary School,* 3rd ed. New York: Holt, Rinehart and Winston, 1976.

Hurlimann, Bettina. *Picture Book World.* Edited and translated by Brian Alderson. Cleveland: World, 1969.

Klemin, Diana. *The Art of Art for Children's Books.* New York: Clarkson-Potter, 1966.

Klemin, Diana. *The Illustrated Book: Its Art and Craft.* New York: Clarkson-Potter, 1970.

Kunitz, Stanley J., and Howard Haycraft, eds. *The Junior Book of Authors,* 2nd ed. New York: H. W. Wilson, 1951.

Lanes, Selma G. *Down the Rabbit Hole: Adventures and Misadventures in the Realm of Children's Literature.* New York: Atheneum, 1971.

Lindstrom, Miriam. *Children's Art: A Study of Normal Development in Children's Modes of Visualization.* Berkeley: University of California Press, 1957.

Lonsdale, Bernard J., and Helen K. Mackintosh. *Children Experience Literature.* New York: Random House, 1973.

Mahony, Bertha E., Louise P. Latimer, and Beaulah Folmsbee, comps. *Illustrators of Children's Books, 1744–1945.* Boston: Horn Book, 1947.

Pitz, Henry C. *Illustrating Children's Books: History, Technique, Production.* New York: Watson-Guptill, 1963.

CHAPTER 10

A Blume with a View

The golden age of new candor did not really dawn until the past two years and its real heralds were Maurice Sendak and Judy Blume.[1]

DIANE I. ZIMMERMAN

A MODERN AUTHOR: MEET JUDY BLUME

We have seen in previous chapters the conditions under which the writers of the classics have been inspired to write. What inspires the modern author? What motivates him so he feels he must write upon themes that are relevant to the life of today's children?

Clues to the conditions and inspirations of modern writers can hopefully be found in this chapter, which contains a biography of Judy Blume and a taped conversation with her. Her books are very popular today; once a child has read one of her books, he returns and asks for "another book by Judy Blume." The sincere candor and honesty of these books is currently having an astonishing impact on literature written for today's youth. She has written two picture books and eleven novels for juveniles.

Judy Blume's most popular books are *Are You There God? It's Me, Margaret; Then Again, Maybe I Won't; Iggie's House; It's Not the End of the World;* and *Deenie.* In *Margaret,* Mrs. Blume explores the problems of Margaret, a sixth-grade girl who expresses her concern over religion, bras, boys, menstruation, and her relationship with her peers. In *Then Again, Maybe I Won't,* Mrs. Blume examines the problems of Tony, a seventh grader, whose father suddenly becomes rich, enabling the family to move from Jersey City to an affluent Long Island community. The book explores Tony's emotional and physical problems as well as the change

---

1. Diane I. Zimmerman, "Goodbye to Never-Never Land," *New York News,* April 29, 1973: 16.

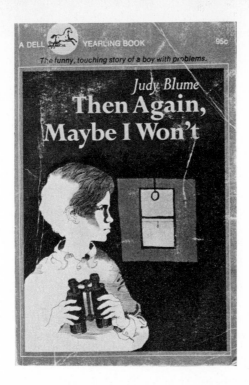

FIGURE 10–1. Judy Blume's books do not generally contain pictures other than the cover. Many of them are now available in paperback. (Illustration by Charles Gehm)

that money makes in Tony's life and family. In *Iggie's House*, Mrs. Blume writes about a black family that moves to an all-white community. *It's Not the End of the World* discusses the effect of divorce on a family. The subjects of Judy Blume's books are handled with humor and insight. Although some parents have been shocked by what they consider an overly frank treatment of "things children shouldn't know about," many parents enthusiastically read the books themselves. Children accept them wholeheartedly.

Judy Blume and her family live in suburban New Jersey. She is the wife of John M. Blume, a lawyer, and the mother of a daughter and a son. Mrs. Blume graduated from New York University, where she majored in early childhood education. Mrs. Blume wrote the following account of herself:

I had a typical middle-class suburban upbringing—but somewhere along the way, I started to think for myself, probably because of my father, a dentist, who was a bit of a philosopher and shared his ideas with us.

I always wanted to get married and have children, but deep inside was the wish of becoming a great actress or artist or something very exciting. But it wasn't until my children were both off to school that the urge came back. I knew I had to do something for myself—something that belonged to me as a person, apart from having a family. I was lucky. I have the best of both worlds now, and my husband and children share my excitement.

When I write books for children, I become a child—whether it's a boy or girl doesn't matter. I love my work, and I love to hear from children who read my books. I shall continue writing for children forever.[2]

Dorothy Park, one of the authors of this book, went to Judy Blume's home and taped the following conversation. In this conversation, Mrs. Blume spoke with the same candor with which she writes.

An Interview with Judy Blume

Park: Do you consider your books as realistic fiction?

Blume: I consider most of them to be realistic fiction, but I don't think that I am as conscious of that as you might be.

Park: How does it happen that you write this way? Is it a psychology that you have, as the kids say today, to tell it as it is, or do you just record the story you have to tell in a realistic manner?

Blume: All I want to do is tell a good story, and give the kids a character they can identify with, and a lot of feeling.

Park: Would you like to tell me how you go about writing a book? Do your books have basis in actual facts, people you know, real situations, or are they products of your imagination?

Blume: Let's take it slowly from the beginning. Shall we talk about the novels, first—like *Are You There God?* and *Then Again?* Okay, now ask me little questions.

Park: Are the characters people you have known; do you draw them from your imagination, or half and half?

Blume: I think it's both, it's definitely both—a lot of it is me. I seem to have something called total recall. I can remember everything from third grade on and every feeling I ever had and all kinds of little incidents, so that *I* go into all my characters, I guess, and then things that I see, people that I see, and there are a lot of real things and made-up things, a combination, I guess. Does that make sense?

Park: Yes, it does. Your books are so realistic that when I read them to my students in classes, they are amazed.

Blume: About my characters—it's funny, because I'll keep a little notebook when I'm writing a book, and I'll write down names of characters I know I am going to use in the book. I really don't know anything about them. A lot of children write and ask about the grandmother in *Then Again.* . . . When I tell them the truth, it sounds terrible because, I mean, it was just a family and I really didn't know them; yet when I wrote their names down, I had too many people in this family and so I did this terrible thing to Grandma because I did not want her to talk; and because she didn't talk, she grew into a character she never would have become had she been a regular member of the family that had dialogue. People are crushed that I did this to her, but I didn't know her when I did it, and it was only after I started writing, I decided this is the way it would be.

---

2. Anne Commire, *Something about the Author,* vol. 2 (Detroit: Gale Research, 1971).

Park: You're talking about her laryngectomy?

Blume: Right, I'm talking about that. It was after I did that to her that she became real to me, like now, in a new book I am doing, there are two girls named Wendy and Caroline, and I really didn't know very much about them in the beginning except their names. Now they are growing into people and I know them, and I have to go back to the beginning of the book (I'm forty pages into it), and I have to say, "Now, Wendy wouldn't say that, but Caroline would."

Park: So you feel that your characters are products of your imagination and your creativity, but some of them are based on families and situations you knew?

Blume: There are little parts of them that are, I am sure, but basically I think they are made up.

Park: Do your children give you many ideas? I don't mean they say, "Mother, write a book about me," but are you aware of their characters? Do they enter into your books?

Blume: More so now, because they have reached an age of the characters in my books, and I'm very aware of them, but when I started to write, when I wrote *Are You There God?*, it was from my imagination.

Park: In literature we speak of an author's concept, the idea behind a book. Do you say to yourself (using as an example *Are You There, God?*) I'm going to show how a twelve-year-old feels under such and such conditions; or does the book just happen?

Blume: Again, every book is different, but we'll talk about the novels for the older children (the twelve-year-old's books). I would say as far as the concept, I think what I do is that I walk around for a long time, maybe six months, thinking about the next book I'm going to do, usually at the same time I'm writing a book, and by the time I'm halfway through with one book and knowing pretty much where it's going to go in my mind, the next book is beginning to work. *Margaret* was the first book I did that I felt was really me. Before that I just wanted to be published. I wrote *Iggie's House,* not in my style really, because I had no style then. That is something that comes. In *Margaret,* I really let loose, and I can't remember anything except enjoying it tremendously, and, I think, wanting to show what it was like to be a certain twelve-year-old girl. You know people will say to me, "Not every twelve-year-old girl is like Margaret," and I say, "Okay, but this is what Margaret is like, and there *are* twelve-year-old girls like Margaret."

Park: I think it is very typical of girls of this age.

Blume: Yes, it seems to be from all the letters I receive because all the girls who write think they are Margaret. They say they know that I don't know them, but I wrote this book all about them and they really are Margaret. They do identify with my characters; Margaret certainly is the child that I was at twelve. I would say that I'm a part of Margaret more than any of my other characters.

Park: After you wrote *Margaret,* did you decide to yourself that you would write a book explaining how a boy feels?

Blume: I can tell you I have a great memory for how I did the next book because at that time I really wasn't sure that anyone would publish *Margaret,* and while I sent it to the editor at Bradbury Press, who had worked with me on *Iggie's House,* because I think he's very talented and I like him and we work well together, I didn't know at that time whether or not they would publish it and because I was so anxious, I sat down and started to write *Then Again, Maybe I Won't* in longhand. My husband said to me, "I'll bet by the time you hear from that publisher, you'll have finished this other book," and I think I probably was halfway through it.

Park: That is interesting, because you got into the mind of a twelve-year-old girl in *Margaret* and when I read *Then Again, Maybe I Won't* last week to my class, a boy said that was exactly the way he felt when he was that age too, and we thought how fine it was that one person could do this with a girl and a boy.

Blume: I don't know how that happened but I'm glad I did it then, because now that I've been around more I hear others say that women should never write about men; they cannot possibly know what it's like to be a man, and a man should never write about a woman because he doesn't know what it's like to be a woman; and blacks shouldn't write about whites, and whites shouldn't write about blacks. I think part of it is if you can put yourself in the other person's shoes and say, "Oh, I know just what he would feel like." I mean I never knew Tony; he was totally fictitious.

Park: That's why you are a good writer. I don't hold to the theory that you have to be black to write from a black person's viewpoint, or that you have to be a pigmy to write from a pigmy's viewpoint. I think that if you have empathy, you can put yourself. . . .

Blume: I'm not sure; I'm very confused on this issue. It seems to me that I really do write basically what I know about. I always set my books in the suburbs or New York City because those are the two places that I lived, and I think when I know something that the scene is much better.

Park: I can't see you putting a book in Asia, that would be out of it, but you do seem to get into the mind of a person. The setting is something else.

Blume: Well, I enjoy doing that, I guess. It's like a game of pretend, you know; when I was a child I always played games of pretend. I was perfectly happy playing alone, and I always talked to myself and I was all different kinds of people. I even at one point gave imaginary piano lessons. I kept a whole notebook full of children's names that I taught; I graded them and gave them report cards and everything. So maybe I finally found an outlet, you know?

Park: This is interesting. Were you an only child?

Blume: No, and I liked having lots of friends, and I liked traveling with a crowd and being very popular, and all the things I wrote about in *Margaret,* and here was another part of me that I never would have told my friends. I was younger when I did this. I can remember doing it with a set of paper dolls. I didn't play with paper dolls the way little girls are supposed to. I made up regular stories, and then my dolls were in accidents and they were in the hospital. All kinds of things happened and I liked it.

Park: I had forgotten in reading stories like *Margaret* how you go back to your own childhood, to the clubs, the secrets—ours was shaving legs.

Blume: Ah, shaving legs came later. Great . . .

Park: Yes, that was later. I think it was seventh or eighth grade. It brought back the feeling that it was very true to that age group.

Blume: You're right. Our friends are really very important. At least, we think our friends are more important than our family. Certainly, we would rather be with our friends.

Park: That's the time when you are breaking away from your family and getting in with your peer group, which is preparing you for life.

Blume: This is the time when you have to hate your parents and see how dumb they are, and "yuk," as Winnie says.

Park: Your dialogue is realistic and very true to life and sounds the way the youngsters speak in the age group you are really writing about. Is this a hard thing for writers to accomplish successfully?

Blume: I can talk about dialogue, because that is one thing I know about. Now when I write a book, I rewrite it many, many times— many. I start the first draft; it is really torture. I know the book because it goes by my mind in a second and yet having to put all those words down on paper can be very difficult. I always think of the first draft as torture. After that, it is pleasure, and dialogue is the only thing I can do spontaneously. It comes right out sitting at the typewriter from the first time, and it never has to be rewritten. Dialogue just comes spontaneously.

Park: That is probably why it comes out so well.

Blume: I don't know. I can tell you about one scene and where the dialogue came from. That's in *It's Not the End of the World*. There is a scene where the mother takes the fourteen-year-old son and Karen, the lead character, who is twelve, and Amy, the little sister who is six, to Howard Johnson's, and the mother and the son have a fight, and the son walks out. Now years ago I was sitting in Howard Johnson's with my children and they were very small, and there was a mother and son in a booth behind us. They had a terrible fight over the fact that he ordered fried shrimp. She said, "You know you don't like fried shrimp." "These are breaded," he said. "You'll have to eat them anyway," she said. "Lay off," he told his mother. I took a little card out of my wallet, and I wrote it all down, the whole thing about the fried shrimp. I don't know how many years later I wrote the book, but I always remembered that little card, and I used it word for word. Otherwise I just don't know where dialogue comes from.

Park: You told me you received many letters from your young readers, and you delight in reading them. Would you tell me some of the things they write?

Blume: Oh, their letters are wonderful. Sure, do you want me to show you some? Do you want me to try and tell you?

Park: Try to tell me first. You said that they always say, "I'm Margaret." What about the boys?

Blume: Well, ninety percent of the letters, I would say right now, are from girls and they're about *Margaret*. But *Margaret* is the only book right at this minute that's really around everywhere in paperback. And you could see the letters increase from the time the paperback came out until I'm getting, I don't know, sometimes twenty to twenty-five letters a week. Every now and then I get a letter from a boy, but . . .

Park: What do the boys say? The same things?

Blume: Boys say different things. Boys are funnier, at least I think they're funnier, and they want to know what do I look like? How old am I? How much do I make? Girls' letters are very touching, and they're writing just to me. They would die if anyone else saw it. That kind of thing.

Park: Probably hero worship.

Blume: They're very sweet. I can give you examples, you know.

Park: Yes, I would like to see them very much. Do you write answers? Do you have time to write any answers?

Blume: Up until two weeks ago I personally hand-wrote an answer to every child that wrote to me, and I loved doing it; but a few weeks ago I spent all day Saturday and all day Sunday answering about forty letters, and at the end of that weekend, it had become a chore and that was no good for the children. I don't want to dread getting their letters; I want to look forward to it and truly enjoy it. So what I've done now is that instead of a printed sheet, which a lot of publishing companies will put out for you, I've written a dated newsletter. I plan to do four a year. I've started this spring. It's a handwritten letter two pages long, explaining to my letter writers why I can't write a personal letter and telling them all about me, my family, and my work. It's being Xeroxed. On the back there's enough room for me to write a couple lines to each child who writes to me, and I send them a list of the books with this newsletter in my handwriting. I hope that they'll accept it and be happier with that than with a printed sheet.

Park: That's a very good solution—instead of a Rolling Stone Fan Club, we can have a Judy Blume Club!

Blume: Well, it just makes me feel badly because I feel deeply toward any child who sits down and writes to me not just because of a school project. I know the difference when I get the letters, and they usually tell me if it's a school project. But most of the kids who write to me sit down and write spontaneously because they enjoyed what I wrote. I think that they deserve a personal answer, and I feel badly about it when I can't send one. This week I received a booklet that I showed you from the child near Chicago who made a project for school about me and my books. I got a personal letter from her mother and her teacher thanking me for taking the time to write this personal letter to her, and they said how much it meant to her and how much it meant to them. I was just crushed because since then I've been sending out Xeroxed letters.

Park: I think you've arrived at a very good solution. Now to return to the books themselves. This is something we haven't talked about so far. Even though the subject matter in *Iggie's House, Are You There God?* and *Then Again, Maybe I Won't* is very serious, there's a great deal of humor that pops out. Are you aware of it? Do people comment about the humor?

Blume: Children like them because they're funny, and I think that's very important. I like to make people laugh because first of all, the books have to be good entertainment. You can't say, "Something funny happened; everybody laughed." The funny things are the most touching and sometimes the most embarrassing. I rarely know when I'm writing something that it is funny. Sometimes I don't even think it's funny until my editor will look at it and just burst out laughing. I say, "Well, what is funny there?" and he'll show me. I don't even realize that it's there, that it's funny. But I know that the books have lots of humor, and I certainly want them to stay that way. I think one of the things that depressed me about writing *It's Not the End of the World* was that it wasn't a funny subject. I mean, divorce to this child, and to any child probably, just broke her heart. It tore me apart writing the book, every day suffering with this kid and crying. I cry when I write; I laugh and cry at my own words. Once they're on the page, it's like they're not mine anymore. You know, I'm very emotional over my characters, and I cry. And I not only cried when I wrote that book, but I cried when I read the galleys, and I cried when I read the book. And I love to laugh. Nothing delights me more than sitting at the typewriter and laughing. You know, it's such fun, but that doesn't happen every day.

Park: Today I was reviewing *Iggie's House,* and I laughed so.

Blume: It's not my favorite book. You just won't be able to get me to talk about it because it's much more forced than the others. It's a book that everybody has to write when they're starting out maybe. I was really feeling my way; I had no idea that I could write a long book. I wrote that book chapter by chapter, week by week, while I was taking a writing course, and each week I would hand in another chapter. It was forced writing because I had deliberately set out to write a book about blacks and whites. It was very big then. And I wanted to be published badly. You know, I'm trying to be honest about it. I would hate to call it a rip-off book because I certainly wasn't at the point where I could have done a quickie book. I did feel for it and thought it was important because the town that I lived in was very much like the town that I wrote about. But I just don't feel that it's me.

Park: But again I felt this terrific empathy that you have for your characters and for people in situations—this poor young girl, first of all, she's so sad that her friend had moved away, and then she likes the black family who moves in . . .

Blume: Well, she wants to like them.

Park: And then she feels so terrible about how they're treated, and then her mother and father—it did ring true.

Blume: I worked very hard; I had an editor who sat with me and talked for hours and hours and sent me home so enthusiastic that I totally rewrote the book. It was really melodramatic and dumb in the beginning, and after talking to him (which we now do on every book), I went home so enthusiastic that I just couldn't wait. Of course, it did grow and it did get better and the new scenes that I wrote changed the value of the book, so it is better. But I feel that if I did it today, it would be a better book still. I'm glad that it was my first novel because I took a terrible beating from *School Library Journal.* I'm glad that that happened to me in the beginning rather than in a situation where I might write a book like *Margaret* first and have it wildly popular and then write *Iggie's House* and be stepped on. Many reviewers were kind to *Iggie's House. Library Journal* gave it not just a bad review, but a terrifying review, which I'll be happy to show you, saying that it wouldn't do middle-class children any favor; it was featherweight sociology. This, you know, really kicked me, and I took it very hard. Probably *Iggie's House* never would have sold any copies at all because of that review, except for the fact that the other books have made children go back and say to the librarian, "I would like to read *Iggie's House.*" Now they're writing to me and telling me that they like it.

Park: Do you think you'll ever take that subject and write about it again—the racial integration problem?

Blume: I just don't know. Not right now.

Park: Well, you've got other books in progress.

Blume: I feel for it and I'm interested to see what's happening, but I don't think so. I rather think that once one has done a subject, it's time to go on to something else, even though one is really writing about people and not subjects in novels.

Park: All of your books, I've noticed, contain the concept of personality adjustment, the early adolescent, his environment in school, family, among his peers, and each character's attempt to establish good meaningful relationships. Your characters are interesting and believable and realistic.

Blume: I have strong feelings about a book for children, and it is that a child's life is divided in two: school life and home life. I vowed that I wouldn't try to get them away from school and home because they spend most of their time there. School is very important to them, and I've discovered from their letters that what they really want is that interaction that takes place among them in school. They love to recognize situations that they face in school—school, home, family, friends; that is their life.

Park: Another thing I noticed, all the characters you write about are very typical and very normal; they're not abnormal, they're not psychopathic, they're not neurotic, even though Tony . . .

Blume: Tony definitely wasn't a neurotic child.

Park: They're all very normal. I can see that would be a big reason why so many people could identify, because they're typical problems that adolescents have, even though each one is individualistic and each character is believable and real. Do you see what I mean, they are not . . .

Blume: Even when you have a wonderful and supportive family, no matter how great your family is, no matter how well adjusted you are at twelve and thirteen or before or after, you still are going to have some problems. Nobody can grow up without facing some problems. It can be a small thing, but it's very important to the child.

Park: You want to know what my reaction was when I was reading *Then Again, Maybe I Won't*, when the family moved to their Long Island home, Rosemont?

Blume: Yes, that's really Roslyn. But I changed it. I had a good friend that moved to Roslyn.

Park: In my mind, I pictured it Manhasset, because I know Manhasset. So I thought, he isn't going to play basketball, he isn't going to have any friends, and he isn't going to adjust—and I was pleased that he *did* fit in, and it was very natural. You know, he didn't jump into the situation, and it wasn't the same as it was back in Jersey City. But he went to church and met some people there, and he had that little girl who wrote him notes and then the family next door . . . it was all natural and believable. He was a normal kid, but he did find an adjustment, and he had problems. Let's talk about that. I was interested in this because it is a typical situation that's happening all over America. We talked about this with my students the other day after we read the book. I said, "Have any of you ever known a family who had a sudden rise in fortunes? What happened to them? Was it like this book? Is this book the way it really is?" They could really identify; they all knew not only one, but two or three or four.

Blume: And yet, something that I wanted to make very sure of coming through in the book was that he didn't want to go back to the way it was in Jersey City. He liked it in Rosemont.

Park: You felt at the end of the book that this boy Tony was going to make it.

Blume: Well, I was very fond of him. You know, I was really attached to him and, again, I knew that I was going to write a book about money. That was all that I knew when I started. And, of course, it may be hard for an adult to believe that it could happen just this way; that might have been a little bit strained, having the father get the money that way. I remember that one reviewer called it a Horatio Alger kind of story, and yet children believed it. I believed it while I was doing it.

Park: I believed it. It does happen. I've known people that this happened to.

Blume: Yes, it can happen. I had to find a way for it to happen, and that was the only thing that was a little bit difficult. How was this going to happen? I felt that it couldn't just happen slowly; it had to be a big change.

Park: Well, it's like the fairy godmother . . .

Blume: Right! Of course! And also I think an awful lot of kids that live the way Tony lived in Jersey City are very curious to know what it would be like to have money and be "rich," even though Tony's family was not "rich rich." They were rich by comparison, and I think kids are very interested in that. I can see that even where we live. We have all different socioeconomic groups going to school together. Some children come home with mine, look around and say, "Oh, you must be rich," and it's simply because we have more than they have. It's very embarrassing to my children to have to say, "Oh, no, we're not rich. We're just ordinary."

Park: Because everything is relative. This *is* a problem for children. Another thing I like about the book is the way it dealt with phoniness. Did anybody ever compare that with *Catcher in the Rye?*

Blume: Well, I, of course, loved *Catcher in the Rye* and the first few times I read it, I didn't know what kind of book it was. I just knew that it was a book to sneak out of my parents' bookcase and hide upstairs because it had some bad words in it. That's what we were interested in then. That's what I vowed to do for kids who read my books; to satisfy the things that they really are interested in, to satisfy their interests so that they don't have to go looking for certain things in other books. It wasn't until I was in high school, probably, that I knew *Catcher in the Rye* was not just a book where you could find these certain words, but that it had a wonderful story and a great character. I loved it, and I went on to read everything of Salinger. I can remember when I read *Franny and Zooey.* I just loved everything that he wrote.

Park: I was talking about the phoniness that Tony felt when he moved to Long Island, and how he had to deal with that. What I liked about it was that the father remained the same.

Blume: I seem to be nicer with fathers in my books. I found this out recently. For instance, in the book that I've just finished, the girl has a real problem with her mother; although her mother is a perfectly decent human being, she is pushing her daughter to gratify her own needs. The father is very definitely the one in the family that the girl counts on and is close with. And I wonder now, am I writing from the way I felt, because I was definitely closer to my father and admired him more?

Park: I liked the way the father acted in *Then Again, Maybe I Won't,* and I thought that was very realistic. He was just, proud, and generous and he was pleased. There wasn't any "keeping up with the Joneses"; he wasn't like the mother.

Blume: My father, I think, was very much that way. It pleased him to be able to do things for us.

Park: And it wouldn't have rung true if both the mother and father had been that way. There's a balance in the characters in that book. The mother and the brother, what do the kids say, cop out, sold out. The grandmother, of course, has the wisdom of age, and she knows what's going on, and typical of an older person, she recedes into her room and stays there. And the poor father doesn't know what to do, so he buys a color television set for the grandmother. He's confused about it all. There was a nice balance of inner reactions. Maybe you didn't plan it that way?

Blume: No, no, talking about it makes me say to myself, "My goodness, how did I do all that?" Because you really don't know exactly what you're doing; I don't until I see it as a finished product, or sometimes until I read a review. Then I say, "Oh, is that what I meant? I knew there must be something." Usually I can ask my editor, and he'll tell me what I'm saying.

Park: I've been meaning to reread *Catcher in the Rye*. But what I was thinking about was how Holden Caulfield resents people being phony, and yet he is so phony himself. But anyway, meeting you, you look so ladylike and are ladylike and act so ladylike . . .

Blume: Oh, no. Oh, I'm not. Now you're telling me the wrong thing. That's not true.

Park: You are not the kind of author who would say "puke."

Blume: Yes, oh yes. You ask my children. We use every four-letter word in this house regularly, and that's the truth. The children, too. As long as they understand what's socially acceptable outside of the house so that they don't get expelled from school.

Park: But you're not vulgar.

Blume: I can be. In the book that I'm doing now, which I'll show you, there is a paragraph on the opening page where I have a description of a boy in fifth grade picking his nose.

Park: I wouldn't consider that vulgar. That's what kids do. And yet, on the other hand, many teenagers who read your books have never read books where these things have been discussed or told or presented before. The college students have never read books like this, and they're all fascinated by it because realistic fiction is a new thing for young people. It's been in existence for adults, but it hasn't been for young people.

Blume: It still isn't completely realistic. I think that it's going to be, but now I think that most people are still not writing really realistic fiction for children the way children really are. I don't think I've done it quite yet, but I keep hoping that I will. I think in *Deenie* I get to it a little bit more. We have held back because a year or so ago it was a question of "Will anybody publish it?" and then money being what it is, "Will anybody buy it?" Or are the librarians going to say, "Oh, no, that's disgusting; we're not going to have that," even if it's the way kids really are.

Park: Have you ever had any reaction or any letters from irate parents or librarians?

Blume: Never. I've had only the nicest letters, the dearest, sweetest letters and that includes many, many from librarians who have encouraged me to go on when I really have had it at certain points. But there have been many librarians who have *told* me of their troubles—they're the ones that are left holding the bag, you know. I only hope that they won't get scared and stop because of any one parent. You know, many parents say, "This is great. I'm glad my children are reading this." But they may not come to school and tell the librarian this. But there's *one* parent, and there's always one who's against it—that one will make trouble. Most of the reactions have been with *Then Again, Maybe I Won't.* I can think of two examples. One was a boy's father. The librarian handed the sixth-grade boy the book and said, "I think you'll like this." She thought that it would be a good book for him. Now most parents don't pick up the books their kids are reading, they really don't, but if the child comes to the parent with a question because it's there and it's spontaneous, it is a perfect opportunity for that parent and child to sit down and discuss it. But when this boy went to his father about wet dreams and his father picked up the book, he slammed it shut and said, "This is a dirty book." He went to the school and threatened to have the librarian fired and all kinds of things, instead of just sitting down and discussing it with the boy. The perfect opportunity was lost. . . . Why do parents do this? I think it's because they're afraid, because they can't handle it, so they don't know what to do. Most of the other incidents, I think, have been with girls who have read *Then Again* and come with the question of wet dreams. The thing that really makes me mad and makes my editor mad (and my editor is a young man) is the fact that *Margaret* is being accepted more readily because *Margaret* is a girl, and because most librarians and teachers are women right now, and they'll accept *Margaret*. The perfect example is a mother who came up to see me. (This is unbelievable, but absolutely true.) She was a supposedly intelligent, well-educated woman and told me how much her twelve-year-old son loved reading *Then Again, Maybe I Won't.* I said, "Oh, I'm so glad," and she said, "But I cut out two pages." I thought this was a joke and I said, "Well, what do you mean, you cut them out?" She said, "I took a scissors and I cut them out." I know it's unbelievable but it's true. I just looked at her. We were face to face at a party and I said, "Oh, I don't believe you." She said, "Yes, I cut them out with the scissors." I said, "What did your son think?" She said, "He came to me and said, *'Look!'*" and she said, "When they're printing these books, it happens all the time. Just keep on reading the story." Then I started to get angry and I asked her "Why?" She said, "Because I don't think he's ready to know about wet dreams; it could upset him." I said, "If you had a daughter, a twelve-year-old daughter, would you let her read *Are You There God? It's Me, Margaret,* which talks about menstruation?" She replied, "Well, of course. Menstruation is normal." So what happens to a boy? As my editor said about *Then Again, Maybe I Won't,* sex rears its ugly head. That's just too much for some people to accept. It's a shame because even in New Jersey, where we're very conservative and we have no sex education at all in our school system, they do show a movie in fifth grade about menstruation, and they hand out little books. But for boys— nothing! They are completely ignored. There's no puberty for them. That's it. I certainly think that if boys learned about girls and girls learned about boys, this mystery, this giggling, this nonsense that takes place would all be natural, the way it should be.

Park: That's right, that's true, because we have sex education in seventh grade now in New York state, and girls and boys go to the class together. I know they discuss menstruation, but I bet they don't discuss wet dreams. And why should you discuss one thing and not discuss the other thing?

Blume: I believe this very strongly. You know, I don't sit down to write a sex book or a book about sex. But I do feel if it comes along and it belongs, it should be there because children are very interested; their bodies are their biggest interest, and they are entitled to find satisfaction in their literature, and not just literary satisfaction, but total satisfaction.

Park: You said that you didn't think that your books were as realistic, that you had a sense of holding back; you may think you're holding back and that they aren't as realistic as you might get to be, but they are still very realistic.

Blume: I know that. I shudder sometimes when a teacher or librarian tells me that she's reading these books out loud because I really feel that they're personal books. They're personal experiences, just between me and that child who's reading them. An awful lot of people tell me that they read *Margaret* out loud, and lots of mothers tell me that they read it out loud with their daughters. I suppose that's all right. The best way for me is that I love to get a good book and go off alone and read it, and I don't want anybody to discuss it with me, and I don't like to discuss a book really after I've read it. I've enjoyed it, I've loved it, that's it. I just want to keep it inside me. I think we over–book report our kids, you know, trying to get them interested in books. I can't say I'm all in favor of the constant book reporting that has to be done. A book is to enjoy and love and think about. I know this from my own daughter. She'll love a book, but she'll say, "I don't want to talk about it." It doesn't mean she didn't understand it. It's just something nice that she keeps inside.

Park: Has she read your books? She must have.

Blume: Oh, my goodness. Oh, of course. Randy is a super junior editor. She was only eight when I wrote *Margaret,* and she has reread it every year. By now she knows it by heart, and it's made many friends for her because when we moved over the summer, she was the new girl in sixth grade and she said, "I have lots of friends because of your books, Mom."

Park: And what about your boy?

Blume: Oh, Larry has not read everything that I've written. He read *Then Again, Maybe I Won't.* He liked that best of all my books. He read it this year; he's in fourth grade. Now that's young, except that we're very open and he knows all about puberty and sex. He read it to enjoy the story, and he liked it. And he's read the books for younger children.

Park: I would think they would both get a kick out of *Freckle Juice*.

Blume: *Freckle Juice,* you see, they both now consider to be a baby book.

Park: But when they were younger—weren't they about that age when you were writing it?

Blume: Yes, I wrote *Freckle Juice* because—that is, I came up with the title *Freckle Juice* and then had to write a book about it simply because I liked the title!

Park: That's a very charming book.

Blume: Randy used to play in the bathtub, and she had lots of freckles. She used to make mush out of soap and things and call it freckle juice; but I personally get more satisfaction out of writing the novels for the older children, the twelve-year-old character . . . . That's my favorite thing; I really get involved with it.

Park: So far, from what you've written, do you have a favorite book? Or is your favorite book your last one?

Blume: Always! My favorite book is always the book that I'm working on or that I've just finished or that's about to come out. I guess that *Margaret* will always have a special place; I don't know whether it's because so much of me is in it, or because it was my first, or because that's what most of the children write to me about. So I think that it will always be special.

Park: Do you think it's possible that there is too much realistic fiction for children and teenagers now, that it's wrong to give them only realistic fiction? We discussed this in class.

Blume: I don't think there's enough realistic fiction. I don't know where you get that, because in the ten to thirteen age group which I write for, there really is not enough.

Park: *Saturday Review* had an article, I think in October, 1972, saying that realistic fiction is flooding the market for children and juveniles in children's literature, whereas the trend for adults is going toward fantasies. Witness the popularity of *Jonathan Livingston Seagull*. Everybody's noticing that there's more and more realistic fiction, particularly in picture books, such as *The Tenth Good Thing About Barney* by Judith Viorst.

Blume: Well, I think that's great.

Park: The college students are excited because they say, "Well, we still have to have a place for fairy tales, and we still have to have *Winnie the Pooh.*" You see, this becomes a conflict in our students of children's literature who are going to be teachers or librarians.

Blume: I think that you have to offer children everything, and let them read what they want to read. Now I can't write fantasy and I can't write adventure; I mean, I write what I can write and what I feel must be done. I think one writes what one likes to read. I like to read a realistic adult novel with a strong woman character. I like that, and I think that I write what I like to read. I have a child in sixth grade who only wants to read realistic fiction. Realistic fiction doesn't mean hard knocks and terrible problems and shattering existence. It just means that she wants to read about kids whom she recognizes as being real people in real situations. It doesn't mean drugs and sex and abortion necessarily. *Tales of a Fourth Grade Nothing* is exaggerated realistic fiction but strictly for humor. I wrote that book to entertain, and that's it. It's supposed to make kids laugh wildly, and they tell me that they do.

Park: If a child is experiencing the situations in life that he encounters in realistic fiction, is reading about it going to help him?

Blume: That's up to the child. Strictly up to the child.

Park: Which is what I always say—one has to know the child.

Blume: They know what they like to read. They absolutely know it. Randy can tell me what kind of book she wants to read, and she'll pick up a book and read two pages and say, "I don't want to read this book," so I just don't see how it can hurt. I get angry, again, at the rip-off books, you know, that are done just one, two, three, to cash in on some subject, rather than having the books be about people, because fiction (I keep getting back to this)—fiction is people and feeling. I think *feeling* is the key word. If you can make kids feel for your characters, love them or hate them, or sympathize with them, but recognize them and see themselves and see other people and say, "Maybe this is what it's like to be that way. Maybe this is what it's like when you're big and developed and in the sixth grade and everybody's looking at you and making fun of you." That kind of thing.

Park: That book brought me back to childhood and I thought, how good if I could have read a book like that when that was happening to me. I would have understood myself better.

Blume: I hope so. The book that I've just finished, *Deenie,* is about a child who is beautiful. Her mother wants to exploit her beauty and then suddenly they find out that she has scoliosis, which is a curvature of the spine, and she has to wear a brace from her neck to her hips for the next four years. This idea came from a mother who was telling me about her daughter. I had never heard of it before. Now that I've studied it and researched it and I've been to hospitals, I find that it's very common. This is not what one would call a physically handicapped child, and she does not think of herself as handicapped at all, and yet other people think of her as handicapped.

The interview between Mrs. Park and Mrs. Blume was interrupted when guests began to arrive. Since Mrs. Park had visited with Mrs. Blume for three hours, she felt she had taken enough of her time.

The above interview has been edited. It is printed here with the approval of Judy Blume.

Since the time of this interview, *Deenie* has been published and is in paperback. Although *Deenie* did not receive from critics the highest accolades of *Are You There God? It's Me, Margaret,* and *Then Again, Maybe I Won't,* the book is popular with juveniles, and they are the ones for whom the book was written.

In 1974, Mrs. Blume published another book, entitled *Blubber.* In 1975 her new book *Forever,* a story of first love, was released.

Books by Judy Blume

1. *The One in the Middle Is the Green Kangaroo*
   A picture book about Freddy Dissel, the middle child in the family. For grades K–3 (Chicago: Reilly and Lee, 1969).

2. *Iggie's House*
   A novel about Winnie Barringer, trying to prove what a great neighbor she is to the Garber kids. But the black Garbers aren't looking for a neighbor. They're looking for a friend. For Grades 4–6 (Scarsdale, N.Y.: Bradbury Press, 1970).

3. *Are You There God? It's Me, Margaret*
   A novel about Margaret, a sixth grader who talks everything over with God, including menstruation, bras, boys, and school. For grades 5–7 (Scarsdale, N.Y.: Bradbury Press, 1970; paperback edition—Dell Yearling, 1972).

4. *Then Again, Maybe I Won't*
   A novel about Tony Miglione, in seventh grade. He's just moved from Jersey City to a suburban Long Island town. He's interested in basketball and the beautiful sixteen-year-old girl next door . . . and the changes money makes in his life. For grades 6–8 (Scarsdale, N.Y.: Bradbury Press, 1971; paperback edition—Dell Yearling, 1973).

5. *Freckle Juice*
   A story in chapters with pictures. It's about Andrew, who's in second

grade and needs freckles to hide the dirt that his mother is always looking for. And about Sharon, the crafty girl who tells him how to get them. For grades 2–4 (New York: Four Winds Press, 1971; paperback edition—Reader's Digest, 1973).

6. *Tales of a Fourth Grade Nothing*
Episodes about nine-year-old Peter, Fudge, his three-year-old brother, and Peter's pet turtle Dribble. For those who like to laugh. For grades 3–6 (New York: E. P. Dutton, 1972; paperback edition—E. P. Dutton, 1973).

7. *It's Not the End of the World*
A novel about Karen and her family and divorce. She's in sixth grade and wants more than anything to make her parents love each other again. For grades 5–7 (Scarsdale, N.Y.: Bradbury Press, 1972; paperback edition—Bantam Pathfinder Books, 1973).

8. *Otherwise Known as Sheila the Great*
About Sheila Tubman, a ten-year-old know-it-all. She's a character from *Tales of a Fourth Grade Nothing*. Funny episodes about Sheila's summer. For grades 3–6 (New York: E. P. Dutton, 1972).

9. *Deenie*
A novel about a seventh-grade girl who is very beautiful. Her mother wants her to be a model, but the doctors discover she has scoliosis, a curvature of the spine. She has to wear a brace from her neck to her hips. How her family and friends treat her and how she thinks of herself are all part of the story. For grades 6–8 (Scarsdale, N.Y.: Bradbury Press, 1973).

10. *Growing Up and Liking It*
A booklet that gives the basic facts of menstruation in story form. (Milltown, N.J.: Consumer Education Dept., Personal Products Co., free).

11. *Blubber*
A novel about a fat fifth-grade girl whose classmates nickname her "Blubber." Judy Blume is usually sympathetic with her chief character, but in this novel Mrs. Blume's message is that nobody should *allow* herself to be victimized. The book shows Blubber's helplessness: "Let's everybody walk all over her . . . she really looks for it." The book deals with the unrelenting cruelty of children against one or two victims. The sad truth is that children unfortunately have to learn at an early age to stand up for themselves. The author's concern about cruelty and injustice is accentuated when Blubber later joins the inhumane group as they select a new victim for ridicule. (Scarsdale, N.Y.: Bradbury Press, 1974.)

12. *Forever*
A story about first love at a summer camp where eighteen-year-old Kath faces the dilemma of how a girl can be in love with one person and yet be attracted to another. (Scarsdale, N.Y.: Bradbury Press, 1975).

SUMMARY

This chapter demonstrates how a person creates. Judy Blume's overwhelming success with critics, parents, and children testifies to her masterful ability to write a story that is truly meaningful. This ability springs from an interaction of several vital qualities: empathy, imagination, sensitivity, a sense of humor, a total recall of childhood, and a sense of discrimination for what is appropriate.

It is evident that any creative process is by no stretch of the imagination a science. What one does is both observable and describable; how one modulates the forces that provoke this action is not. A description of the creative act of writing is, in the final analysis, elusive and mystical.

Writing is essentially a problem-solving process. At times everything clicks, and at times writing is torture. The successful author transcends this tedium. This special breed can create a world so vivid that readers feel compelled to become involved. It is apparent that Judy Blume's magic results from her intuitive as well as intellectual and emotional resources. Her writing reflects a deep personal involvement. Furthermore, she has few preconceived notions that restrict her. In writing each book, Mrs. Blume embarks on a bold new adventure.

TO THE COLLEGE STUDENT

1. What aspects of juvenile realistic fiction also apply to adult realistic fiction?

2. After you read Judy Blume's books, decide whether the subjects of the books are truly relevant in a meaningful sense, or are they isolated for the sake of dramatic effect?

3. Do these books have meaning for a child who has not undergone any of the crises discussed? Should a child be asked to confront a problem that he might not ever have to face?

4. Does realistic fiction rob children of their innocence by imposing adulthood on them too early? Can we expect children to cope with problems that are often too difficult for adults?

5. By exposing children to the problems of life at an earlier age, do we help children learn to cope with adulthood?

6. Assign some members of the class to select passages from current realistic fiction, both good and poor. Have each member read a selection from his choice, but do not tell the title or author of the book. Ask the class members to assign one of the following ratings: Excellent, Good, Fair, or Poor. After reading all the passages, tell the title and author of the passages read.

7. Hold a Judy Blume (or some other author) Day where you plan activities and exhibits around her work.

TO THE CLASSROOM TEACHER

1. You may be able to bring an author to your school for an interview such as this. Consult the addresses listed on page 497. Plan what you will ask him/her.

2. Read Margaret Wise Brown's *The Dead Bird*, Judith Viorst's *The Tenth Good Thing about Barney*, and Charlotte Zolotow and William Pené du Bois's *My Grandson Lew*. Compare the manner in which these authors treat the subject of death.

3. Read the Book Review section of the *New York Times*. Watch for books identified as realistic fiction. Clip the reviews and add them to your files. Try to find them in your library and read the ones that interest you.

4. Read a passage from a book of realistic fiction to your class. Perhaps the children will want to role-play a problem presented in the book. Discuss possible

solutions to the problem. Or let the children write their own ending of the problem.

5. In the periods you set aside for creative writing, encourage the children to write realistic stories about problems they perceive to be relevant.

TO THE COLLEGE STUDENT
AND THE CLASSROOM TEACHER

1. Discuss the problems of whether or not a teacher should impose her interests in realistic fiction on children. For example, one teacher may be interested in the subject of racial or ethnic discrimination; another teacher in alcoholism of parents; another in teenage drug addiction; another in divorce. Is it possible for a teacher to overemphasize any of these social problems?

2. Discuss the matter of relevance in children's reading programs. How much time should be spent on relevance as seen in realistic fiction as balanced against the time spent on fantasy, folklore, poetry, and other genres? What is a balanced program of various types of literature for elementary children?

3. Discuss whether or not the reading of realistic fiction tends to do the following:
   a. hide worthwhile values
   b. find the solution to children's problems
   c. develop empathy

4. What about possible negative effects of reading realistic fiction? Are these books too depressing? Do children who have these problems always care to read about them? Do they want to escape the problems? Does it depend on the individual child? Could these books be used in bibliotherapy?

5. In this interview, Mrs. Blume states that she feels children should choose their own reading. Do you see this statement as being contradictory to the philosophy of this book? Is it not possible for children to miss some very exciting adventures with books if they are not frequently introduced to new ideas?

6. If you like to read interviews with authors, get the following books from your library:
   a. Lee Bennett Hopkins. *Books Are by People: Interviews with 104 Authors and Illustrators of Books for Young Children.* New York: Citation Press, 1969.
   b. Justin Winette and Emma Fisher. *The Pied Piper.* New York: Paddington Press, 1975.

CHAPTER 11

Adventuring with Poetry

THE MAGIC TALKING BOOK OF WORD MUSIC

Do you remember Sara from Chapter 1 who named our book for us? "Poems are really word music," Sara said. "You just can't *read* them. They sing back at you!"

Sara's comment started a project going in her class: the magic talking book of word music. It didn't start out to be magic, or talking either, for that matter, but everyone was interested and got excited and one idea led to another until there it was: a book that was magic, that talked and held singing words!

Miss Baxter had suggested that each child find a poem he liked best from the many modern poems that the class had read together or that each child had read separately. Each day at conference time a few children read their selections. Many of the children wrote poems and planned to read them. As it turned out, the *Magic Talking Book of Word Music* was made in two parts: Part I was called *Poems We Like Written by Others,* and Part II was called *Poems We Like Written by Us.*

The *Word Music* part came after the discussion in which Sara called the poems word music. The book they made was big—and on the decorated cover was the name WORD MUSIC. On the last page of the book, after the very last poem, was another pretty page on which was written the rest of Sara's quote: "This is word music. It sings right back at you!"

The *magic* part of the book came from an idea Miss Baxter had. One day she gave everyone a sheet of white construction paper and showed them some "magic" chalk and crayons such as those used by Mr. Nash in Chapter 4.

The children went wild over the magic chalk; they couldn't wait to get to work. They made beautiful pictures to illustrate their chosen poems, and they wanted to use the magic light some more, so they decided to illustrate their own poems the same way. That's when it was determined to add Part II to the magic book.

The *talking* part came one day when Bob said, "You know, Miss Baxter, I really have to *hear* poems to appreciate them. Now, take that poem you just read to us, for instance. I started to read it the other day and quit about halfway through. Now today you read it to us and it sounds great!"

"Bob," said Miss Baxter, "I have always felt the same way. My mother used to read poems to her children when I was little. I love to read poems now, and when I do, I actually hear my mother reading them."

"When we show our Magic Word Music Book, why don't we have each person read his poem?" suggested Tammy.

The class agreed it was a good idea and for many days they practiced reading their poems. One day during conference time, Miss Baxter made a suggestion.

"I've been thinking," she said, "how nice it would be for us to present our magic word music book to the library after we are finished with it so other boys and girls could go there and enjoy it. But then I got thinking of what Bob said about how nice it would be to have each person read his own poem, and the question came to my mind, 'Why not make a tape recording of each person reading his poem?' Then other people could play the tape while they looked at the pages."

The class cheered. Everyone wanted to do it.

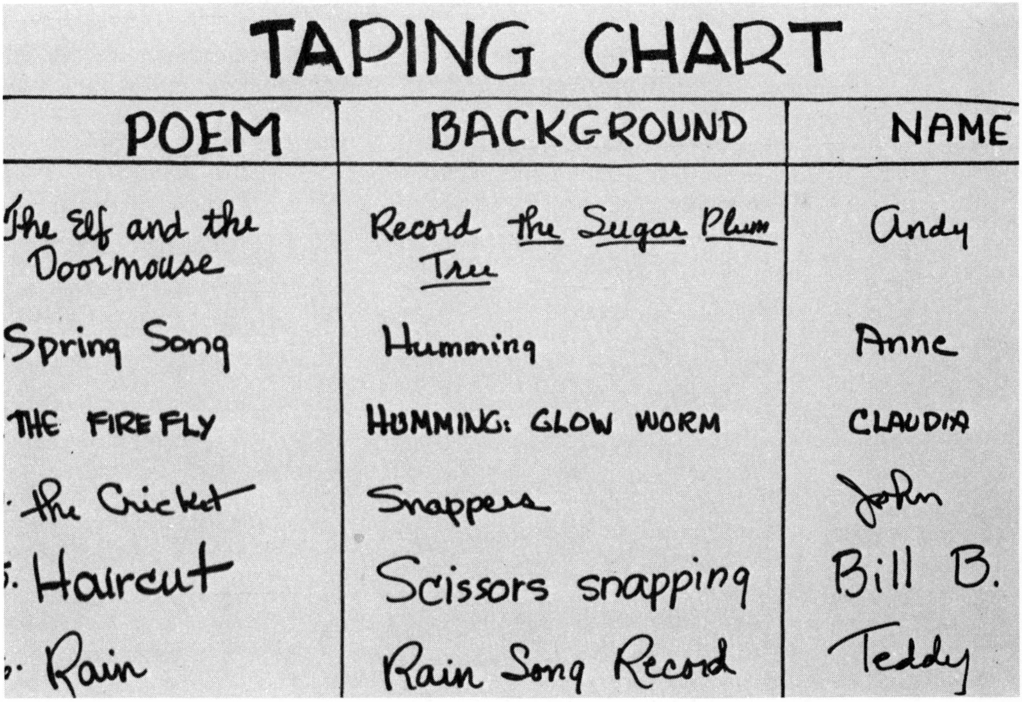

TAPING CHART

POEM	BACKGROUND	NAME
The Elf and the Doormouse	Record the Sugar Plum Tree	Andy
Spring Song	Humming	Anne
THE FIRE FLY	HUMMING: GLOW WORM	CLAUDIA
the Cricket	Snappers	John
Haircut	Scissors snapping	Bill B.
Rain	Rain Song Record	Teddy

FIGURE 11–1. *Planning chart for* The Magic Talking Book of Word Music.

"I also wondered," said Miss Baxter after the excitement had died down, "if perhaps we couldn't find a piece of music to play softly in the background while we read our poem. It would set the mood for what we are going to read."

The class liked that idea, too. Charlie, who played a guitar, offered to make up some of his own music.

The other children listened to recordings to find music suitable for their poem, or played with the recorder, the piano, or the autoharp in pairs so one might read while the other played.

A chart was designed and hung before the room on which each child put his name in the sequence he wanted to be. Across from his name was the music he would have as background to his reading. Miss Baxter encouraged the children to explore all kinds of noises that might be appropriate. Cindy asked the class to hum "Glowworm" while she read her poem about a firefly. John brought a snapper to school and his buddy played a rhythm on it while John read his poem, "The Cricket." Anne had written a poem about thunder so she taught Marie to play drum rhythms for a background to her poem.

As soon as the chart was complete, a taping day was set up and each child read his poem with the appropriate background along with it.

Miss Baxter began the tape by saying, "This is a Magic Talking Book: *Word Music* by Miss Baxter's group." Then Claudia began with her favorite poem, "The Elf and the Dormouse" by Oliver Herford. In the background she chose recorded music of the "Dance of the Sugar Plum Fairy." Bill was next. He read "Haircut" by William Packard while the boys snipped scissors in a rhythm in the background. Then it was Anne's turn, and she read "Spring Song" by Rod McKuen while the children softly hummed "It Might As Well Be Spring." The children continued until Part I was finished.

On another day they taped Part II. Claudia began with her poem "Rain." In the background the record player played the "Rain Song" from *The Fantastiks.*

RAIN

The sky is crying
Tiny tears
Upon my roof
My mother hears
Their plinking noise,
And says to me
"Put on your rubbers!"
I know that she
Can't stand the rain.
It makes her sad
Like teardrops should.
But me? I'm glad;
I love to run and shout and play
And let rain wash my tears away.

Arthur was next. He had some of his friends hum "Down by the Station" while he read his poem, "The Moon Goon."

There once was a man in the moon
Who was a happy old goon
His hair was red, red
His feet were of lead
And his nose was shaped like a spoon.

Sara had brought a set of bells to school. Marcia played "Twinkle, Twinkle, Little Star" on the bells while Sara read her poem, "Little Star."

Little star, O little star,
Who do you
Think you are?
Are you a sun that shines at night?
Or are you a jewel that twinkles bright?
Could you be a raindrop set aglow?
Or a piece of ice or frozen snow?
Or are you a wish that I once made
That floated off while I kneeled and prayed?
Little star, O little star
Who do you
Think you are?

After each child had read his poem on the tape, the entire project was put together. As the pages of the book were turned, they burst into color while the music and the voices spoke the poetry of the children.

POETRY AND CHILDREN

Children are natural poets. The opening story of this chapter shows they are sensitive to rhythm and are eager to experience. They have a fresh way of looking at things and respond to their experiences with all their senses. They see words as things to investigate and manipulate for their own purposes. They hum tunes before they speak, they tap rhythms on their crib slats before they walk, they learn nursery rhymes and short poems before they understand their meaning.

Miriam Blanton Huber says this about the child's experience with poetry in school:

> It is unfortunate if the school cannot continue poetry as a simple, natural experience of childhood. But the enchantment will be destroyed if chores and requirements and obligations become a part of the program. All that is really needed is to let children hear poetry read casually and pleasantly but well. At first they may not talk much about a poem, but they will listen. Before long they will ask to hear certain poems again, then again and again. Then they begin saying certain lines with the reader and perhaps even repeating whole poems for themselves. This happens, though, only in an atmosphere free from compulsion. It cannot be forced or hurried.[1]

---

1. Miriam Blanton Huber, *Story and Verse for Children*, 3rd ed. (New York: Macmillan, 1965), p. 17.

Huber has hit the nail on the head. Few schools do much with poetry. It seems that teachers are afraid of it, perhaps because of the unpleasant memories they have of poetry in school in their own childhood years. Typical of "schoolness," educators have not been content simply to incorporate poetry into the curriculum for its enjoyment; something had to be done to it in order to justify its being there. Consequently, it has been bisected, dissected, analyzed, memorized, and mutilated into dull, tedious exercises until children have rebelled with an attitude that shouts, "Forget it!"

Poetry is read, chanted, and enjoyed in nursery schools and kindergartens. From there on, it is a losing battle. We find it being used less and less as the child progresses through school. Girls tend to take to it in the middle grades, but most boys regard it as "sissy" and will not read it. Inasmuch as most teachers use it very little, it is no wonder that many children grow into adults who do not really enjoy it and cannot use it as a means of sharing human experience or expressing creative thoughts.

Building appreciation in poetry is a delicate thing. Even though samples are given in this book of conversations teachers can develop with children in order to build an appreciation of the poet's work rather than to conduct a comprehensive examination on the poem itself, it must be remembered that the reading of a poem calls for many considerations. Its effectiveness depends on the motivation of the children, the timeliness of the situation, the appropriateness of the poem, the type of children who are to hear it, their backgrounds, and the ability of the teacher.

Children who can scan a poem and decide how it should be read by its pattern on the page are usually above-average readers. Consequently, many average and all slow readers can only labor through the poem, confused by the fact that it does not "read" like other selections in the book. Once they experience lack of satisfaction from trying to decode a poem, they sense failure and, like all children, shy away from reading poems to avoid such experiences.

Some handicapped children also cannot read poetry effectively: the blind, the partially sighted, some physically handicapped, and the retarded. Unfortunately, the deaf child cannot hear it, and if he is ever to enjoy it, it will be through the use of his eyes. Poetry read aloud each day could be enjoyed by all the class, with the exception of the deaf, and those who were capable of reading poetry well by themselves would pursue it further for additional enjoyment.

A review of many anthologies would lead teachers to believe that a child must be exposed to poetry before he can write his own. It has been our experience that the opposite is true. When children have become excited about writing their own poems, *then* they have wanted to read and share the poems of others.

This experience does not begin with the use of full-blown poems, however. It begins with recognizing and utilizing the components of poetry that children already have built-in and ready-made when they come to school: rhythm, simile, metaphor, analogy, and sometimes rhyme. It also includes the use of a sensitivity to "experiencing" and the unique use of an oral vocabulary.

Generally the teacher uses the poems the child knows when he comes to school and recites them over and over, which children enjoy. She adds regularly to these verses and jingles and thus the child's concept of *rhyming* verse is developed.

But this is not enough—all along the way she must be developing the poetry inherent within each child, recognizing it in its crude and undeveloped form. She does this by employing the beautiful phrases of oral expression the child uses in his everyday speech.

A weakness in books on children's literature and various anthologies is their lack of support for the concept that poetry is "a beautiful expression set on paper with a definite rhythm and/or style." Few of the older books available on this subject contain any free or blank verse for children. Consequently, children often look upon poetry as something written for them but only by adults; they think there is a definite style and form for writing poetry and that any style or form they may use themselves doesn't really count.

Children say many beautiful and poetic things during the course of the day. The authors have been able to help children capture the essence of their own poetic intuition by using these expressions daily on reading charts or in poems. They made a conscious effort to develop this ability. It seemed a natural thing to do: to take something already there and develop it to the point where it could be expressed in a variety of ways rather than always exposing children to rhyming, jingling words which said to them, "This is really poetry," and led them to think theirs must also rhyme or jingle to be worthy of acceptance.

The first formal experience most children have with poetry is through the nursery rhymes or Mother Goose. Actually, many Mother Goose rhymes are highly structured and often contrived pieces of writing for all their apparent simplicity. Children experience great difficulty in trying to write like these highly structured poets.

Following are some examples of children's sayings which the authors have collected and used in their classrooms by listening carefully to the children and jotting down their original expressions. Always before a saying was used as part of classroom instruction, we received permission from the child who said it.

"The seeds are riding tiny parachutes to the ground." (Michael, age 4, after he blew a milkweed.)

"Loneliness is being all by yourself even when there are people around." (Marion, age 12, who is a very lonely child.)

"A raindrop is a bead of glass." (Patricia, studying a rain-drenched rose.)

"Your eyes are like two spoonfuls of the sky." (Lloyd, age 6, to his blue-eyed teacher.)

"The snowflakes are poking each other on their way down." (Missy, age 6, watching a gentle snowstorm.)

"He made that old bat smack like a rifle shot." (Shawn, age 12, after hearing Jim hit the ball for a home run.)

"Man, did that ball go—just like a li'l ole rocket headin' for the moon!" (Jim, telling about his home run.)

Material like this is flying around every classroom and playground and is there to be used to develop poetic ability. All the teacher need do is listen.

Children who are encouraged to come up with poetic ideas begin at an early age to write these ideas as free or blank verse. If they cannot write, they dictate their thoughts to the teacher.

SNOW
You pack it
You throw it
You cut it
Snow
You are great fun!

ALICE
Grade 1

GRANDMA'S KNITTING
Grandma is sitting
Doing her knitting
Kitty has the yarn
I hope she'll do no harm.

SCOTT
Grade 1

FOAM
Little rain drops,
I saw you yesterday,
Running down the trumbling
Summer waves.

SHIRLEY WIGGAND
Grade 4

They continue writing through the middle grades.

PURPLE
Purple is fruity,
Grapes are purple,
It's the color of lady's fingernails,
Also Granny's old fashion grape jam,
And bruises on a leg.

Purple is the binding of a book,
Also the eyes of a Teddy Bear,
Purple is yarn to make a picture,
And a flower called a Pansy,
Purple is a colored basket,
With designs on it.

JANE
Grade 5

GIRLS
Kissable, pretty
Hopping, skipping, playing
Mean, dumb, nice, teasing
Girls.

TONY LIGOCI
Grade 6

BOYS

Handsome, cute
Kissing, looking, watching
I love some boys,
Wonderful.

> Casolee Forgets
> *Grade 6*

WHAT AMERICA MEANS TO ME

America is a free country
You say anything you please!
You worship as you please.
You speak what you think is right.
In America you do anything you like.
Some people think you can break laws like: killing,
*   shooting, breaking windows, stealing, robbing.*
These are easy rules to follow,
But everything else you can do.
You can go to school and get an education instead of
*   someone saying, "Get out, this is just for rich*
*   people." Or if you're walking on the sidewalk no*
*   one stops and tells you to walk in the street.*
Nobody really knows what the Statue of Liberty means,
*   I think it means this:*
This is the land of the free. The land of Good Will—
Where all people are treated equal.
For no man is different, the rich or the poor.
God bless America the land of the free.
Where all men are treated equal and fair.

> Peter
> *Grade 6*

GOLD

Standing high on a hill
Looking down upon all
Stands a tall and handsome tree
Letting fall her golden leaves.
They lie at her feet
Making a golden path
For all to see.

> Phyllis D.
> *Grade 6*

INTERLUDE

A cold, dark night—
The moon above
A sigh—
A de—ep breath—
Ah ———love?
No. ———Skunk!

> Jim
> *Grade 6*

Carried throughout the school years, the poetry children write for themselves is interwoven with the poetry written *for* them, so that they become steeped in it. They can think poetically and write about any subject at almost any time if the spirit moves them, as the following poems indicate. Particularly interesting is the use of subtle humor in some of these poems.

PUSSY WILLOW

Pussy, Willow! Pussy Willow!
Pretty! Pretty! Pretty!
Kitty! Kitty! Kitty!
Come out, come out
And play with me—
No! I have more fun
Playing on the willow tree!

SAYRA
Grade 1

FUN POEMS

Once there was a shoe
Who said "I always walk with you."

PAM
Grade 2

I once saw some llamas
That were in pyjamas.

CATHY
Grade 3

THE FUNNY CLOWN

A clown jumps from place to place
With a funny painted face.
He gets himself in a fix
When he does his funny tricks.

MICHAEL
Grade 4

THE GHOST

The ghost is creeping
  Up the old broken steps
Of the old dark house
  Wakening all the ghosts
With a yell—and—
  Oops! He fell!

EILEEN
Grade 4

SLEET STORM

White fingers waving to the freeze—
Heavy trees on bended knees
Road of glass, sky so gray
Such a gloomy, lovely day!

MARION
Grade 6

FIGURE 11–2. *Michael's illustration for his own poem, "The Funny Clown."*

I NEVER KNEW

I came and I cried,
I laughed and was happy,
I saw a man die and saw a man born.
I learned and retained knowledge,
I saw beauty and horror,
I heard beautiful music and sang.
I danced and was joyous,
I respected and hated,
I worshipped and believed.
I was ecstatic and depressed,
I was glad and I was lonely,
I loved and was loved.
I lived and I died—and Oh, God! what I'd
Give to do it over again!

SUSAN
Grade 7

It has been our experience that children conscientiously attempt to think "like a poet" when they realize that we value their own ability to put words and phrases together. Charlie came running to his teacher on a dark, gloomy day and said, "Hey, Mr. Smith, how's this for an idea for a poem: The world is grumpy today?" Ellen added, "What about: The world is scowling at us?" When they begin to think this way, we realize they are sensitized to their roles as poets. They are certainly acquainted with the skill the poet must have with words.

In his book on creative teaching of the language arts, Smith[2] gives an illustration of the use of children's built-in, intuitive thinking in designing poetry. This illustration also demonstrates the meaning of timeliness and the need for sensitivity to the teachable moment in the developing of poetry appreciation.

Lloyd, a first grader, came to school on a foggy day and said, "If the church steeple didn't hold the fog up like a tent pole, it would all fall down and smother us."

Mr. Smith printed Lloyd's phrase at the top of a sheet of chart paper. When the class had assembled, Mr. Smith said, "I'd like to talk about the fog you have all enjoyed on your way to school this morning. Lloyd already had a way of telling me about it. Let's read it."

After the chart was read, Mr. Smith asked, "Can each of you think of a different way to tell me about the fog and how it makes *you* feel?"

Here are some of the things the children said:

"The fog has drawn white curtains over our school windows and we cannot see out."

"The fog is wet on my face like my dog's tongue."

"The fog is like frost on my glasses and I cannot see."

"The fog is like a white night."

"Can we think of some words that might describe the fog?" asked Mr. Smith. "You may want to use them later in your own poems and stories." The list that followed included these words:

mysterious	gentle
creepy	misty
sly	opaque
soft	

Mr. Smith did not let the experience die at this point. "I know of a famous poet who wrote about the fog," he said. "I think I can remember how he told about it. There is only one word I will have to explain to you and then I think you will understand this poem."

Mr. Smith proceeded to explain to his inland group the meaning of the word "harbor" and then recited Carl Sandburg's poem, "Fog."

Imagine his delight when, upon finishing the poem, Lloyd, the innovator, commented, "Gee, that's pretty good too!"

Later the children wrote about the fog.

This account is a combination of experiences in which the whole concept of poetry was explored and enjoyed by the children for the ultimate purpose of writing their own thoughts about the fog. From experiences such as this, teachers develop children's intuitive ability to express themselves poetically.

Somewhere along the line, children discover rhyming—that is, they take it from the intuitive role it plays in their lives and put it in a conscious role—making direct efforts to utilize it in their writing. The awareness of rhyming so it can be verbalized is likely to come at almost any age level.

2. James A. Smith, *Creative Teaching of the Language Arts in the Elementary School,* 2nd ed. (Boston: Allyn and Bacon, 1973), pp. 144–146.

For a time, one of us was affiliated with a nursery school at a large university. In studying the three- and four-year-olds, he found that they chanted nursery rhymes they had learned at home and in nursery school, but that they also chanted phrases *with rhythm and/or rhyme* of their own. One three-year-old spilled some pungent-smelling glue down the front of his smock. He curled his nose and said, " 'Ott (for Scott) 'ou's (for you) a Stinky-Poo."

Then he stopped and listened to himself. He said the phrase over and doubled up with laughter. He turned to his teacher and said, " 'isten: 'Ott ou a Stinky-Poo!" and was again convulsed with laughter. He had discovered he could rhyme. For days he went around saying his rhyme over and over and a few days after his discovery he said, " 'Ott ou—Stinky-Poo like Jack and Jill faw down a hill"—and the wise teacher concluded he had discovered the fact that both rhymed, so she sat with him and explored the sounds of other nursery rhymes. At the discovery of each set of rhyming endings, he squealed with delight.

The poetic words and phrases of children can be used in teaching. Note how Miss Baxter used the children's poems for reading charts at the beginning of this chapter.

Poems about children are not necessarily children's poems any more than poems about adults are only for adults. This realization has helped teachers by providing a broader selection of poems for children and helping them to be more discriminative about the poems they bring to the classroom for general use. Caution must be exercised in selecting poems for individuals, however. Some children may select poems to read and

FIGURE 11–3. *Five-year-olds re-create stories and poems about Indians with enthusiasm.*

enjoy that the teacher might not include on her list of poems to be used with the entire class. If children are capable of reading certain poems, they will decide whether or not the poem is enjoyable to them. Much permissiveness in reading should be allowed children on the individual level.

Recommended anthologies and modern books of poetry are listed in Chapter 17 under *Resources for the Teacher*.

Criteria for Selecting Poetry

In choosing poems to read to children, the teacher should be sure that the criteria discussed in the following paragraphs are considered.

1. THE CHILDREN MUST ENJOY THE POETRY.   It is impossible, of course, for a teacher to tell whether the children will enjoy a poem before she reads it to them. But she probably will know at once if they will *not* enjoy it. There are certain factors that will help a teacher to be sure the poems she chooses will be enjoyed. She should consider the tastes of the children and will not choose something she knows they already dislike; and she must know something about the background of each child, his home life, and his interests. The jingle or rhythm of Mother Goose rhymes can sell them to children so that the children chant them and love them even though they do not understand the words. This does not, however, extend to other poetry. A child soon reaches a phase where he wants to know what the poem is about. Poems outside the realm of his experience mean little to him and are so packed with unfamiliar words that he is soon confused, frustrated, bored, and then rebellious. However, some older children will enjoy the powerful sounds of the poem even when they do not clearly understand its meaning.

A teacher in a ghetto school would have little cause to read Longfellow's "The Village Blacksmith" to her class. Such a poem *might* be read but it would require a great deal of preparation; first, perhaps a discussion of the village blacksmith, who he was, what he did, what tools he used, where he worked, how he worked, and why his shop was such an attraction to the villagers. A film would help to develop the necessary concepts for understanding the poem. At least pictures could be collected to help the children visualize the colorful village blacksmith. Some of the words of the poem might need explaining, for what ghetto child of this age would understand the meaning of bellows, sledge, sexton, forge, threshing-floor, and anvil? On the other hand, "The Village Blacksmith" would be a natural for a teacher who had just taken her class on a trip to Sturbridge Village or for one living in a community where there was a village blacksmith. She must make sure above all else that the subject matter of the poem she chooses is relevant to the children.

Aspects other than subject content must be considered in selecting poems for children, e.g., emotional content. Poems should not be selected for children if they would upset them unduly. For instance, children who are very insecure will probably not enjoy poems that frighten them.

Sometimes, however, children who have had a dramatic frightening experience, such as a flood or fire, may find great comfort in reading poems and stories about other children who have survived floods.

Poems selected to read to children must be based on a direct or vicarious experience in order to be understood. This does not mean that children cannot read about experiences they have not had: it means that a backlog of experiences must be built up within children so that they may make transferals of feelings and understanding to unknown experiences and thereby live them vicariously.

Although all men experience the same emotions and the same inward drives, the emotional tone of a poem and the imagery it paints are understood in varying degrees by different people. "Park Pigeons" by Melville Cane is a poem all ghetto children can understand because they have experienced it. "Haircut" by William Packard is a poem that can be universally understood because all children get haircuts.

The grade and age level of the children for whom the poem is to be read must be considered. Many middle-grade children will be insulted if they are asked to read "baby" books or poems unless the teacher is skillful enough to introduce them cleverly. This is unfortunate because many easy books of poetry have interesting stories and can be read by slow readers. Use of a guide for books children prefer at different age levels may help the teacher to decide the best topics for a variety of grade levels.

Timeliness and motivation are other factors to be considered in choosing poems children will enjoy. *Timeliness* means introducing the right poem at the right time so that children literally get the total essence and flavor of the poem with little preparation or motivation. Timeliness and motivation are demonstrated in the above illustration of Lloyd and the discussion he aroused on fog, which ended in the reading of Carl Sandburg's "Fog."

One way a teacher can always be sure of successful attempts to read poetry that children will enjoy is to start with poems that are universal, that is, that appeal to all children everywhere, and to all ages, even adults.

2. THE POEM MUST BE SINCERE AND HONEST. This means that the poem is real; it is not a phony. Much of the trash on the market today is not real —it is a composite of those elements about books that appeal to children but make no real contribution to literature. Its sole purpose is to make money from the children and their unsuspecting parents.

Highly artificial or contrived poems do not generally appeal to children. A sincere poem presents a clear image or series of images in a logical manner. The main intent of the author is to tell a story, paint an image, provide enjoyment, create music. He aims to reach children and employs all the resources at hand to do so. He is a student of children and has retained many of their qualities.

3. IT WILL BE UNIQUE. Something about the poem will set it aside from all other poems in its category. This is where the true creativity of the author comes through, because to be creative his work must be unique, individual, or new. Uniqueness may come through the style, in the narrative, in the form, in the description, or in a combination of all these.

4. The Poem Appeals to the Feelings As Well As to the Intellect. A good poem holds a strong sensory element—the reader responds to it with a chuckle, a guffaw, a smile, a tear, a frown—something must happen inside the child. Lack of sensitivity to emotional passages may well mean that the children have been deprived of many sensory experiences, and the school should consider providing these experiences as part of the curriculum.

5. Narrative Poems in Particular Possess Those Qualities Necessary for a Good Story. The qualities are an adequate theme, a lively plot, memorable characters, and a distinctive style. Because poems differ from prose, they are subject to additional criteria.

6. Poems Capture the Music and Rhythm of the Language. The rhythm of the piece should come through so clearly that each child taps a rhythm, nods a head, moves a toe, sways his body, or shows in some way that the poem makes him *feel* its music.

7. The Writing Must Be Rich in Vigorous Description, Using Clear, Precise, Imagery-Filled Words. These words must create pictures in the mind, feelings in the heart, chuckles in the throat, and ideas in the head.
    One quality of good writing is that it gives new importance to the common everyday experiences of life.

8. The Poems Must Be Heard. The poems should be read aloud to children. Poems are for hearing. Only persons who possess some skill in reading should read poems to children or else the rhythm, rhyme, and music may be lost. In some instances the meaning will be lost with the music. The teacher should read many poems to children and should practice reading poetry aloud for them. Just as a good storyteller adds invaluable richness to a good story, so can a good reading add to the richness of a poem. Reading poetry well is even more important than reading prose well, for a poor reading can destroy a child's feeling toward a poem forever.
    Arbuthnot has said, "Children who have had the good fortune to hear a poem that gives them shivers up their backbones or a swift upsurging flood of elation or a sense of quietness and peace are discovering the joy of good poetry."

Poetry: A Heritage

Poetry is the rightful heritage of every child. How rich the world is in verse and song! How truly necessary it is to read the record of man's feelings and life through the rhythm of his life styles in order to maintain a sense of balance and a spirit of joy within the heart!
    Poetry is a natural expression of man's rhythm: the rhythm of breathing, of the heartbeat, of sex, of running, walking, dancing, or skipping. It is as natural as sunshine for children to make "word music" and to love the poems of others.
    The expression of man's natural rhythm through speech goes back to the early ballads, legends, and folktales told by the wandering minstrels. Many of them were in verse.
    Way back in 1715, a young man by the name of Isaac Watts wrote

a book of poetry for children called *Divine and Moral Songs for Children.* Watts used his songs to moralize to children, but among the songs in his little book were some lovely hymns, many of which are still found today in church hymnals.

In 1789 a great poet by the name of William Blake published a book of poems for and about children called *Songs of Innocence.* This book remains a classic. In 1794 Blake followed it with a second, *Songs of Experience.* Poets today feel that Blake's books marked the beginning of the Romantic Movement in English poetry. The appeal of Blake's works for children was in the melody of the verse.

In 1804 Ann and Jane Taylor published another book of "moralizing" songs: *Original Poems for Infant Minds, by Several Young Persons.* These poems, however, are gay and fun loving and tell a great deal of life in rural England. Many of their works were miniature sermons, tedious and overly long, with rather poor verse. Of all the poems written by the Taylors, "Twinkle, Twinkle, Little Star" has always been the favorite.

In 1807, William Roscoe, a lawyer and member of Parliament, wrote "Butterfly's Ball" for his young son. It was light, gay, and pleasing to the ears. There was no moralizing in it; it was fun and became very popular at the time.

Among the writers about fairies and wee folk is one William Allingham (1824–1889), noted for his famous poem, "The Fairies." All his poems are printed in a volume called *Robin Redbreast.*

Another writer of fairy tales in verse is Rose Fyleman (1887–). Her works have been published in four volumes: *Fairies and Chimneys, The Fairy Flute, The Fairy Queen, Fairies and Friends.* Rose Fyleman combined her fairy folk with the habits and activities of real people, thus making them more believable.

Kate Greenaway (1846–1901), another author of children's works, was an illustrator and poet. The winsome, dainty pictures that decorated her books are treasured even today. Many students of children's literature feel that her illustrations give charm to her verses and that without them, her verses are not strong. The quaintness of the pictures appears to be an almost perfect complement to the light, lyrical flavor of the rhymes. One of her most successful works was a tiny book of illustrated Mother Goose rhymes, which is today a collector's item. Her works also include *Under the Window* (1879), *Birthday Book,* and *Marigold Garden.*

Kate Greenaway's works are well remembered by adults, who associate them with their youth. Her work was simple, direct, and delightful. Time has coated it with nostalgia, however, and her works are less popular among today's children.[3]

Most poets after Greenaway's time wrote of the child's world. Probably no child in America has not heard of or read Robert Louis Stevenson's *A Child's Garden of Verses.* Born in 1850, Robert Louis Stevenson grew up to be the outstanding children's poet of his time. His poems were about children and for children, as were his stories. They are as popular today as they were at the time of their publication.

---

3. Selma G. Lanes, "Greenaway Went Thataway" in *Down the Rabbit Hole: Adventures and Misadventures in the Realm of Children's Literature* (New York: Atheneum, 1971).

Another milestone in the field of children's literature is *Under the Tree,* a book of poems by Elizabeth Madox Roberts (1886–1941). Her books and poems are unique in that she has been able to artfully capture a child's point of view, and uses as her content the simple topics that delight children, in a language which enchants them. Her poems are about children as they really are and the pleasant people who live with children, all highly reminiscent of Miss Roberts's childhood.

Winifred Welles (1893–1939) wrote *Skipping along Alone,* a book of poems with a delightful blend of realism and fantasy. The lovely poems in this book can be read now mostly in anthologies.

Rachel Field (1894–1942) is an author well known to both adults and children. Her novel *All This and Heaven Too* was made into a successful motion picture. In 1930 she won the Newbery Medal for a historical novel for children called *Hitty.* She has written plays, fiction, and three books of poems: *The Pointed People, A Little Book of Days,* and *Taxis and Toadstools.* Her poems are mostly realistic; they deal with things as they are. Yet Rachel Field captures the child's sense of wonder and his love of nature. Some of her poems are fantasy and deal with fairies but, for the most part, she writes about such things as the floral shop, taxis, city rain, and mushrooms.

Other writers who have contributed to the heritage of children in the early years of this century are: Dorothy Aldis (1897–   ), who wrote four books in verse that have now been published in one volume, *All Together;* Harry Behn (1898–   ), who wrote three little books of verse, *The Little Hill, Windy Morning,* and *The Wizard in the Well,* which contain some nonsense verse but are largely about the child's imaginative and play world; Mary Austin, who writes of children in the southwest United States in *The Children Sing in the Far West;* and Carl Sandburg, who wrote for children in *Rootabaga Stories* and *Rootabaga Pigeons.* A selection from his poems of those that seem most suitable for children has been published in a volume called *Early Moon.*

There are other writers who have left a rich heritage to children. This is the group often classified as lyricists. They include William Shakespeare, William Blake, and Christina Rossetti. Three who have written beautifully about nature are Sara Teasdale, Elizabeth Coatsworth, and Hilda Conkling.

Modern poets continue to contribute to the joy of poetic communication in all forms. A delightfully humorous collection of poems, *Cat and Mouse: A Book of Rhymes* by Rodney Peppe (Holt, Rinehart and Winston, 1974), is highly reminiscent of the happy jingles of Edward Lear. Shel Silverstein's *Where the Sidewalk Ends: Poems and Drawings* (Harper and Row, 1974) is a delightful collection of poems for children with vivid imaginations. Stephen Dunning's *Reflections on a Gift of Watermelon Pickle and Other Modern Verse* (Lothrop, Lee and Shepard, 1967) has already become a classic.

Humor

Humor in children's poetry deserves special recognition. Starting with Mother Goose rhymes, children's poetry has contained nonsense rhymes and droll humor throughout its history.

In 1846 Edward Lear published *The Book of Nonsense*. This was probably the first book since Mother Goose that used poetry to excite laughter. His second book, *Nonsense Songs and Stories* (1871), contained the ever-loved narrative poem, "The Owl and the Pussycat."

Next to make an impact on the children's world was Lewis Carroll. In 1865 he produced *Alice's Adventures in Wonderland,* which was not only a highly imaginative story but was spiced with delightful poems, including "Jabberwocky." This was followed by *Through the Looking Glass* and it, too, contained delightful nonsense verse.

Laura E. Richards, the daughter of Julia Ward Howe, enriched the world of poetry for children with her jingles and stories, which first appeared in the *St. Nicholas Magazine.* She wrote many books, all of which were popular with children. When she was an old lady, many requests were made for her now-famous jingles and verses, and in 1932, May Lamberton Becker was largely responsible for the publication of a book of Laura E. Richards's verses called *Tirra Lirra: Rhymes Old and New.* All in all, in her lifetime Laura E. Richards published some sixty books for children. Her lyrical poems and nonsense verses remain some of the best in the world.

In 1903, Leslie Brooke published *Johnny Crow's Garden,* which was followed a few years later by *Johnny Crow's Party,* both highly amusing books. All of these books of nonsense verse, limericks, and rhymes have made great contributions to the development of more serious poetry for children.

Other writers of humor were also writing for children during these times. Humor differs from nonsense verse in that humorous verse deals with amusing things that happen to real people or to animals that have human characteristics.

Among them was A. A. Milne (1882–1956), whose *When We Were Very Young* and *Now We Are Six* became popular as soon as they were published. Of course, his *Winnie-the-Pooh* is a classic, and although Milne wrote a great deal of literature for adults, he is best known for his writing for children.

Eleanor Farjeon is an English writer who contributed a great deal to developing humor in children's poetry. She had the knack of making fun out of characters from history. Most famous of her history verse books are: *Mighty Men from Achilles to Caesar* and *Mighty Men from Beowulf to William the Conqueror.* She is also known for two other volumes, *Nursery Rhymes of London Town* and *More Nursery Rhymes of London Town.*

Vachel Lindsay (1879–1931) is famous for his writing for older children and adults, but he has also written many excellent children's fun poems, such as "The Potatoes' Dance" and "The Mysterious Cat." Lindsay's poems have a definite rhythm, which children feel and act out the minute they hear them.

James Whitcomb Riley's (1849–1916) wonderful narrative poems, "Little Orphant Annie," "The Raggedy Man," "The Schoolhouse by the Road," and others, are homespun and appealing to adults as well as to children. His poems are not happily funny—he does more to tickle the funny bone in a moment of nostalgia than to seek for outright guffaws and belly laughs.

David McCord (1897–   ) is well known for his nonsense poems and for his serious work as well. William Jay Smith (1918–   ) wrote *Laughing Time,* a book full of delightfully humorous verses that appeals to all ages. Ogden Nash (1902–1971) has written mostly for adults, but his writing is peppered with nonsense poems that can be used successfully with children.

Another poet whose works remain popular with children and who deals with nostalgic fantasies is Eugene Field. "The Duel" is one of his funniest poems. More nostalgic than humorous are "Wynken, Blynken and Nod" and "The Hush-a-bye Lady from Rock-a-bye Street." A tragic poem written by Field that is still popular is "Little Boy Blue."

Walter de la Mare (1873–1956) contributed a rich legacy to the entire field of literature. He wrote prose and poetry for adults and for children. All of his poems for young people are now collected in *Rhymes and Verses: Collected Poems for Children.* Many of de la Mare's poems provoke creative thinking in that they are open-ended and the child can provide his own endings. Walter de la Mare has written on all subjects and for all ages.

Presenting Poetry to Children

Any group of children who has a teacher who reads or recites some poetry to them each day is lucky indeed. A teacher who loves poetry will find many opportunities during the day when she can appropriately read a gem or two that the children can ponder.

But poetry horizons need to be expanded like all other horizons. And teachers who do not have children who respond to poetry will need to devise many ways to motivate them. The following ideas used by some teachers have been successful.

All the ideas suggested in the preceding pages are applicable to setting conditions for the creative teaching of poetry. Because poetry is a unique form of written expression, however, some additional suggestions are entered here.

- Use choral speaking for the teaching of many poems.
- Write a poem on the chalkboard and divide the class into groups. Encourage each group to think of a different pattern to present the poem through choral speaking.
- Print a rhyming poem on a large sheet of paper. Cut the poem into rhyming strips and pass out the strips. Allow the children who have the strips to go to the front of the room and reassemble the poem by rhyming it. Then allow them to do the poem in choral speaking.
- Create special moods by reading such poems as the following to the children. In these lists, *I* indicates intermediate grade level; *P* indicates primary grade level; and *A* is for any grade.

> "The Song of Hiawatha" by Henry W. Longfellow (with drum beats)   (*A*)
> "The Bells" by Edgar Allan Poe (with bells)   (*I*)
> "Gerald McBoing-Boing" (with "boings" and other sounds suggested by the story)   (*P*)
> "The Monotony Song" by Theodore Roethke (with clapping patterns)   (*A*)

"An Easy Decision" by Kenneth Patchen (with a whistling tune)
   (*I*)
"The Song of the Jollicles" by T. S. Eliot (with a phonograph record
   in the background softly playing "Buffalo Girl, Won't You Come
   Out Tonight") (*A*)

Special moods may also be created simply by reading certain poetry
that is beautifully written. Discuss with children the mood created by such
poems as these:

"Flight" by Steve Allen (*I*)
"The Coming Star" by Juan Ramon (*A*)
"The Prayer of a Butterfly" by Carmen Bernos de Gasztold (*A*)
"Loneliness" by Haskin (*A*)
"Youth" by Langston Hughes (*I*)
"Within a Word" by Karla Kuskin (*A*)

• Read action poems and then have the children create sounds or actions
  to go with them:

"Washing Day" by Lillian F. Taylor (*P*)
"Ding, Ding" by Eve Merriam (*A*)
"The Rainwalkers" by Denise Levertov (*A*)
"Mix a Pancake" by Christina Rossetti (*P*)
"The Mitten Song" by Marie Louise Allen (*P*)
"Paddling" by Gertrude Monroe Higgs (*A*)
"Stop-Go" by Dorothy Baruch (*P*)
"Action Rhyme" by G. H. Adams (*P*)
"Duke-o'-York," nursery rhyme (*P*)
"The Wind" by James Stephens (*I*)
"The Bells" by Edgar Allan Poe (*I*)
"The Cuckoo-Clock Shop" by Rachel Field (*A*)

• Collect "noisy" poems and weave the noises into the poem. Some good
  ones are:

"Taxis" by Rachel Field (*A*)
"Chicago" by Carl Sandburg (*I*)
"The Duel" by Eugene Field (*A*)
"Frolic" by G. W. Russell (*P*)
"Motor Cars" by Rowena Bastin Bennett (*P*)
"Johnny's Farm" by H. M. Adams (*P*)
"Shoes and Stockings" by A. A. Milne (*P*)
"The Barnyard" by Maude Burnham (*P*)
"Sneezing" by Marie Louise Allen (*A*)
"Riding the A" by May Swensen (*A*)

• Collect "hopping" poems and hop to them:

"The Frog" by Hilaire Belloc (*P*)
"Ladybird, Ladybird" by Vachel Lindsay (*P*)
"This Is the Way the Ladies Ride," nursery rhyme (*P*)
"Grasshopper Green" by Walter de la Mare (*A*)
"A Cat Came Fiddling," Mother Goose (*P*)
"Trains" by James Tippet (*P*)
"A Hop, Skip and a Jump," old rhyme (*P*)
"The Road to Town" by H. M. Sarson (*A*)
"Ding, Ding" by Ann Merriam (*P*)

FIGURE 11–4. A primary-grade montage of Robert Louis Stevenson's The Swing.

- Look for poems with movement and action. Do the action suggested by the poem, as in:

  "The Swing" by Robert Louis Stevenson (*P*)
  "Polly, Put the Kettle On," nursery rhyme (*P*)
  "A Swing Song" by William Allingham (*A*)
  "The Swing" by Mary I. Osborn (*A*)
  "Lullaby" by Christina Rossetti (*P*)

- Collect "quiet" poems and read them to soft music:

  "The Little House" by Christopher Morley (*P*)
  "Hiding" by Dorothy Aldis (*P*)
  "Hush-a-bye Baby," nursery rhyme (*P*)
  "The Rock-a-bye Lady from Hush-a-bye Street" by Eugene Field (*P*)
  "Antique Shop" by Carl Carmer (*A*)
  "Park Pigeons" by Melville Cane (*A*)
  "Stars" by Carl Sandburg (*I*)
  "Soft Steps" by Georgette Agnew (*A*)
  "Sweet and Low" by Alfred Tennyson (*P*)
  "Spring Song" by Rod McKuen (*I*)
  "Stopping by Woods on a Snowy Evening" by Robert Frost (*A*)
  "Fog" by Carl Sandburg (*A*)

- Collect "swaying" poems and sway to their rhythm:

  "Who Has Seen the Wind" by Christina Rossetti (*P*)
  "Daffodils" by William Wordsworth (*A*)
  "Wynken, Blynken and Nod" by Eugene Field (*A*)
  "Sweet and Low" by Alfred Tennyson (*P*)

"Slumber Song" by Louis V. Ledoux   (P)
"Why the Gray Cat Sings" by Arthur Guiterman   (A)
"In My Garden," anonymous   (A)

- Collect "walking" poems and walk to them:

    "The Little Turtle" by Vachel Lindsay   (A)
    "Twinkle, Twinkle Little Star," by Ann and Jane Taylor   (P)
    "The Rock-a-Bye Lady from Hush-a-bye Street" by Eugene
        Field   (P)
    "Goblin Feet" by J. R. R. Tolkien   (I)
    "Marching Song" by Robert Louis Stevenson   (P)
    "The Rainwalkers" by Denise Levertov   (A)
    "Feet" by Irene Thompson   (A)
    "The Jungo Ring," anonymous   (A)
    "Velvet Shoes" by Elinor Wylie   (A)

- Encourage the children to find as many poems as they can on one topic, such as *the City,* and discuss the many interpretations and feelings people can have of the same place. For instance, a comparison among David Budbell's "New York in the Spring," Quandra Prettyman's "Still Life: Lady with Birds," and John Updike's "Scenic" can show children dramatically that much of beauty *is* in the eye of the beholder!
- Mr. Thompson and his middle school students studied poetry through its emotional content. They first identified and listed the basic emotions of man: hate, love, fear, rage, anger, pride, happiness, courage, depression, etc., and discussed how important emotions are in determining actions. The children, in their discussions, concluded that anger and pride have been responsible for causing most wars; that love made men marry and have children; that fear often caused them to steal or commit crimes. One boy said during a discussion, "It seems that people tell about their emotions best through poems." That started a really heated discussion, which led to the suggestion that the children collect poems and classify them according to the emotions they portrayed.

    Several exciting bulletin boards grew out of this project and the children began to write fluently about their own feelings. Mr. Thompson secured some films which the children viewed, such as *The Toymaker,* and they identified the feelings these films evoked. Music was also explored as an outlet for emotions.

    Under the heading of *Love* on the bulletin board, the children put such poems as "Nikki-Roosa" by Nikki Giovanni, "Poem" by Langston Hughes, "Emily Jane" by Laura Richards, and "Love Is a Special Way of Feeling" by Joan Walsh Anglund.

    Under the heading of *Hate,* they found no poems. This created some interesting discussions, but none of the poems brought into the class were ever placed under this category.

    For *Fear,* among others, they put "Table" by Merrill Stone and "House Fear" by Robert Frost.

    For *Compassion,* they collected: "The Ballad of the Light-Eyed Little Girl" by Gwendolyn Brooks, "To a Poor Old Woman" by William Carlos Williams, "Poem to Be Read at 3 A.M." by Donald Justice, and "Muttering Over the Crib of a Deaf Child" by James Wright.

    At the end of the unit, the children decided to choose their favorite poem from each classification. Some of their favorites were: "If I Must Die" by Claude McKay (pride), "Yet Do I Marvel" by Countee Cullen (hope), "Coal for Mike" by Bertolt Brecht (compassion), "Modifications" by Ron Koertge (empathy), "I Woke Up This Morning" by Karla Kuskin (joy), "The Lamb" by Rachel Field (tenderness), "Loneliness" by Robert Frost (loneliness), "The Blind Man" by Rachel Field (courage), and "In This City" by Alan Brownjohn (loneliness).

Needless to say, Mr. Thompson's unit not only introduced the children to poets and their poems, but led them to a much deeper understanding of themselves and of each other.

- Find a mood picture and place it on the bulletin board. Under it place a placard saying "What poems tell how these people feel?" or "What poems describe the feeling of this picture?" Help children find appropriate poems by providing books of collections of children's poems.
- Some poems lend themselves especially well to dramatization, such as:

  "The Pied Piper of Hamelin" by Robert Browning   (I)
  "A Tragic Story" by Albert Von Chamisso   (A)
  "Casey at the Bat" by Ernest Laurence Taylor   (I)
  "Concord Hymn" by Ralph Waldo Emerson   (I)
  "The Armful" by Robert Frost   (A)
  "The Elf and the Dormouse" by Oliver Herford   (P)
  "Mr. Nobody" by Eugene Field   (I)
  "My Shadow" by Robert Louis Stevenson   (P)
  "A Tragic Story" by William Thackeray   (I)

- There are poems especially suited to puppet shows, such as:

  "The Pied Piper of Hamelin" by Robert Browning   (I)
  "The Duel" by Eugene Field   (A)
  "Robin Hood and Little John," old ballad   (I)
  "The Leak in the Dike" by Phoebe Cary   (I)
  "Thanksgiving Day" by Eleanor Farjeon   (A)
  "A Visit from St. Nicholas" by Clement Moore   (A)
  "The Owl and the Pussycat" by Edward Lear   (A)
  "In Praise of Johnny Appleseed" by Vachel Lindsay   (I)
  "Three Little Kittens" by Eliza Lee Follen   (P)

- Some poems lend themselves especially well to pantomime:

  "In School Days" by John Greenleaf Whittier   (I)
  "The Village Blacksmith" by Henry W. Longfellow   (I)
  "The Blind Men and the Elephant" by John Godfrey Saxe   (A)
  "Abou Ben Adhem" by Leigh Hunt   (I)
  "Evening at the Farm" by John Townsend Trowbridge   (I)
  "Robin Hood and Little John," old ballad   (I)
  "I Woke Up This Morning" by Karla Kuskin   (A)
  "Hubert and the Glue" by Karla Kuskin   (A)

- Poems especially suited for shadow plays are these:

  "The Elf and the Dormouse" by Oliver Herford   (P)
  "The Courtship of Miles Standish" by Henry W. Longfellow   (I)
  "A Visit from St. Nicholas" by Clement Moore   (A)
  "The Owl and the Pussycat" by Edward Lear   (A)
  "The Leak in the Dike" by Phoebe Cary   (I)
  "The Song of Hiawatha" by Henry W. Longfellow   (I)

- Some poems are especially suited to group action, such as:

  "The Merry-Go-Round" by Dorothy Baruch   (P)
  "Fog" by Carl Sandburg   (A)

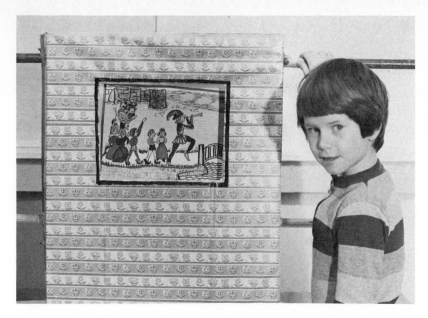

FIGURE 11–5. *A scroll movie of a favorite poem, Robert Browning's "The Pied Piper of Hamelin."*

    "Riding in an Airplane" by Dorothy Baruch   (*P*)
    "Tugs" by James S. Tippett   (*P*)
    "Riding in a Motor Boat" by Dorothy Baruch   (*P*)
    "The Little Jumping Girls" by Kate Greenaway   (*P*)

- Fingerplays provide a good way to introduce poems.
- Collect unusual pictures and put them on the bulletin board. Encourage children to find poems that *describe* the pictures.
- Find many pictures for *one* poem and make a bulletin board display of them. An example of a good poem to use for this activity is Joyce Kilmer's "Trees".

- Collect poems "to make things to." If the children are making boats, such poems as these can be read:

    "Sea Fever" by John Masefield   (*I*)
    "I Saw Three Ships," folk song   (*A*)
    "A Good Play" by Robert Louis Stevenson   (*P*)
    "A Nautical Ballad" by Charles Edward Carryl   (*I*)
    "Old Ships" by David Norton   (*I*)
    "A Number of Numbers" by Eve Merriam   (*A*)
    "Counting" by Karla Kuskin   (*P*)

- Occasionally children can read a classic together and write an alternate ending or imagine the story with a different ending, such as:

    "A Visit from St. Nicholas" by Clement Moore
    "Little Boy Blue" by Eugene Field
    "Casey at the Bat" by Ernest Laurence Taylor
    "The Gingham Dog and the Calico Cat" by Eugene Field
    "The Sugar Plum Tree" by Eugene Field

- Scrapbook collections of poetry can be encouraged. Collect poems under various headings and enter them in the class scrapbook. Examples:

HOLIDAY POEMS

"Birthdays" by Marchette Chute   (P)
"At the Seaside" by Robert Louis Stevenson   (P)
"Thanksgiving Day" by Lydia Maria Child   (A)
"Christmas Bells" by Henry W. Longfellow   (A)
"Conversation about Christmas . . . After Dinner, . . . The Useful Presents" by Dylan Thomas   (A)
"Halloween Song" by Marjorie Barrows   (A)
"What? No More Witches in New York?" by Rachel Field   (A)
"The Rose on My Cake" by Karla Kuskin   (A)

FUN POEMS

"Mr. Nobody" by Robert Louis Stevenson   (I)
"The Owl and the Pussycat" by Edward Lear   (A)
"The Plaint of the Camel" by Charles Edward Carryl   (I)
"A Nautical Ballad" by Charles Edward Carryl   (I)
"Eletelephony" by Laura E. Richards   (A)
"Father William" by Lewis Carroll   (A)
"The Purple Cow" by Gelett Burgess   (A)
"Dinky" by Theodore Roethke   (A)
"Mrs. Gilfillan" by James Reeves   (A)
"Praise to the End" by Theodore Roethke   (I)
"But Outer Space" by Robert Frost   (A)
"Ollie's Polly" by Eve Merriam   (A)
"Anne's Fan" by Eve Merriam   (A)
"Tee Vee" by Eve Merriam   (I)

TASTE POEMS

"Pop Corn Song" by Nancy Byrd Turner   (A)
"The King of Hearts," nursery rhyme   (P)
"Animal Crackers" by Christopher Morley   (P)
"The Ice Cream Man" by Rachel Field   (P)
"The Sugar Plum Tree" by Eugene Field   (A)

ANIMAL POEMS

"The Rabbit" by Edith King   (P)
"Wooly Lambkins" by Christina Rossetti   (P)
"The Little Turtle" by Vachel Lindsay   (A)
"Mouse" by Hilda Conkling   (P)
"Choosing a Kitten," author unknown   (P)
"My Dog" by Marchette Chute   (P)
"The Tyger" by William Blake   (I)
"Ma Cavity: The Mystery Cat" by T. S. Eliot   (I)
"The Elephant or the Force of Habit" by A. E. Housman   (I)
"The Lion" by Herbert Asquith   (I)
"Creatures in the Zoo" by Babette Deutsch   (A)
"Deer" by Harry Behn   (A)
"Ungainly Things" by Robert Wallace   (A)
"Inside the Zoo" by Eve Merriam   (A)

POEMS OF ADVENTURE

"To China" by Leroy Jackson   (I)
"A Boy's Song" by James Hogg   (I)

"The Wonderful World" by William Brighty Rands   (*A*)
"It Is Not Far" by Sara Teasdale   (*P*)
"A Vagabond Song" by Carmen Bliss   (*A*)
"Go Fly a Saucer" by David McCord   (*A*)
"Wynken, Blynken and Nod" by Eugene Field   (*A*)

- Make collections of poems chosen for particular people. Examples:

POEMS FOR MOTHER

"Mother" by Theresa Helburn   (*A*)
"Cradle Hymn" by Martin Luther   (*P*)
"The Courtin' " by James Russell Lowell   (*I*)
"The Vinegar Man," author unknown   (*I*)
"The Rock-a-Bye Lady from Hush-a-bye Street" by Eugene
   Field   (*A*)
"When Mother Reads Aloud" by Theresa Helburn   (*I*)
"Her Words" by Anna Hempstead Branch   (*I*)
"Sale" by Josephine Miles   (*A*)
"Florist Shop" by Rachel Field   (*A*)
"Houses" by Rachel Field   (*A*)

POEMS FOR FATHER

"The Deacon's Masterpiece" by Oliver Wendell Holmes   (*I*)
"Sea Fever" by John Masefield   (*I*)
"In Flanders Fields" by John McCrae   (*I*)
"I Hear America Singing" by Walt Whitman   (*I*)
"Chicago" by Carl Sandburg   (*I*)

FIGURE 11–6. *Cover of a collection of poems by primary-grade children.*

"Father's Story" by Elizabeth Madox Roberts   (*P*)
"The Thinker" by Berton Braley   (*I*)
"Father" by Frances Frost   (*A*)
"Automobile Mechanics" by Dorothy Baruch   (*P*)
"Daddy Fell into the Pond" by Alfred Noyes   (*P*)
"The Man of the House" by David Wagoner   (*A*)
"Those Winter Sundays" by Robert Hyde   (*A*)
"The Unknown Citizen" by W. H. Auden   (*I*)
"Old Man Cutter" by Rachel Field   (*A*)

POEMS FOR BABY

"The Baby" by George MacDonald   (*P*)
"Infant Song" by William Blake   (*A*)
"A Baby's Feet" by Algernon Charles Swinburne   (*P*)
"Little" by Dorothy Aldis   (*P*)
"Slippery" by Carl Sandburg   (*A*)
"Cradle Song" by Sarojini Naider   (*A*)
"Slumber Song" by Louis V. Ledoux   (*P*)
"Cradle Hymn" by Martin Luther   (*P*)

POEMS FOR SISTER

"Skating" by H. Asquith   (*I*)
"Sisters" by Eleanor Farjeon   (*I*)
"Little Orphan Annie" by James Whitcomb Riley   (*I*)
"In School Days" by James Whitcomb Riley   (*I*)
"Our Silly Little Sister" by Dorothy Aldis   (*P*)

FIGURE 11–7.   *A middle-grade collection of poems for father.*

"Marjorie's Almanac" by Thomas Bailey Aldrich   *(I)*
"The Playhouse Key" by Rachel Field   *(A)*
"The Lost Doll" by Charles Kingsley   *(P)*
"The Centaur" by Mary Swenson   *(I)*
"The Picnic" by John Logan   *(I)*

POEMS FOR BROTHER

"The Rum Tum Tugger" by T. S. Eliot   *(I)*
"A Feller I Know" by Mary Austin   *(I)*
"Big Brother" by Elizabeth Madox Roberts   *(I)*
"The Quarrel" by Eleanor Farjeon   *(I)*
"The Fishing Pole" by Carolyn Davies   *(I)*
"A Good Play" by Robert Louis Stevenson   *(P)*
"A Boy's Song" by James Hogg   *(A)*
"My Dog" by Marchette Chute   *(A)*
"Mr. Nobody" by Robert Louis Stevenson   *(A)*
"Little Brother's Secret" by Katherine Mansfield   *(P)*
"Hiding" by Dorothy Aldis   *(P)*
"Fred's Bed" by Eve Merriam   *(A)*
"Mother to Son" by Langston Hughes   *(I)*
"The Brothers" by John Logan   *(I)*
"The Aura" by James Dickey   *(I)*
"The Pitcher" by Robert Francis   *(I)*
"Ties" by Dabney Stuart   *(I)*
"Haircut" by William Packard   *(A)*

FIGURE 11–8.   Primary collection: Poems for sister.

FIGURE 11–9. *A child's drawing for the cover of* Poems for Brother.

- Combine the reading of poems with humming or singing music softly, such as:

   "The Landing of the Pilgrims" with "The Doxology"
   Excerpts from "Snowbound" with "Jingle Bells"
   Reading of the Christmas story with "Silent Night"
   The Twenty-Third Psalm with "The Battle Hymn of the Republic"
   "The Daffodils" with "April in Portugal"

- Read poetry while children fingerpaint or paint pictures.
- Have children show especially well-worded passages in paint or finger-paint. Example: paint "The Humble Bee" by Ralph Waldo Emerson.
- Mrs. Green and her middle school students studied the history of the United States through poetry. After the children had discussed poetry and had learned to identify various kinds of poetry and the many forms that could be used in writing it, they tried writing some of their own. A poetry collection of other people's poetry was started. First they collected poems that told about historical events, such as:

   "The Midnight Ride of Paul Revere" by Henry W. Longfellow
   "The Concord Hymn" by Ralph Waldo Emerson
   "In Flanders Fields" by John McCrae
   "Memorial Wreath" by Dudley Randall
   "Indian Children" by Annette Wynne
   "Columbus" by Joaquin Miller
   "The Wilderness Tamed" by Elizabeth Coatsworth
   "Wild West" by Robert Boylan
   "In Praise of Johnny Appleseed" by Vachel Lindsay

"The Prairie Schooner" by Edwin Ford Ryser
"Barbara Fritchie" by John Greenleaf Whittier
"The Falling Star" by Sara Teasdale

These were arranged in chronological order. The children felt that most of the historical poems they found dealt with war periods and did not fully represent all of American history. So, they set out to find what they labeled as "events" poems. These included such poems as:

"Dust Bowl" by Robert A. Davis
"Wild West" by Robert Boylan
"The Excellent Machine" by John Lehman
"Brooklyn Bridge" by Vladimir Mayakovsky

Another category used to expand their poem collection was "descriptive" poems about America and life therein, and these included:

"Chicago" by Carl Sandburg
"America for Me" by Henry Van Dyke
"America the Beautiful" by Katherine Lee Bates
"Scenic" by John Updike
"Miracles" by Walt Whitman
"Dragon Fly" by Harry Behn
"The Dream" by Harry Behn
"Star Swirl" by Robinson Jeffers
"The Diver" by Robert Hayden
"Night Sound" by Eve Merriam

Other categories included "people" ("Runagate, Runagate" by Robert Hayden, "When Mahalia Sings" by Quandra Prettyman, "The Flower Man" by Rachel Field); "special events" ("Outer Space" by Robert Frost, "Casey at the Bat," etc.). The unit afforded an interesting, new approach to studying history and a lasting appreciation and love of poetry.

• Collect poetry describing life and feelings in all places in America. Use these in correlation with social studies. Suggestions:

"Cross" by Langston Hughes   (I)
"Those Winter Sundays" by Robert Hayden   (A)
"A Moment Please" by Samuel Allen   (A)
"Southern Mansions" by Arna Boutemps   (I)
"The Negro Speaks of Rivers" by Langston Hughes   (I)
"Lincoln Monument: Washington, D.C." by Langston Hughes   (I)
"Brooklyn Bridge" by Vladimir Mayakovsky   (I)
"Corner" by Ralph Pomeroy
"Highway: Michigan" by Theodore Roethke   (I)
"Schenectady" by Eve Merriam   (I)
(See James Daugherty's book, Walt Whitman's America.)

Poems listed in this chapter may be found in the books listed in the second section of the bibliography at the end of the chapter.

Poetry, like all literature, must be a source of enjoyment to children in order to be appreciated. The study of the structure of poetry has little place in the elementary school except as it relates to helping children structure their own poems.

In selecting poems for children, certain criteria can be kept in mind. A poem should do one or more of these things:

FIGURE 11–10.   *Children share their poems with their principal.*

. . . it should catch moments of beauty; it should penetrate the honest feelings of the author and the reader; it should picture interesting people; it should release hearty laughter or it should tell appealing stories.[4]

Teachers should be very skeptical of poems that attempt to teach lessons, contain remote adult ideas, or drip with sentimental doggerel.

Poetry can be *lived* by children and *loved* by children.

SUMMARY

Poetry is part of a child. The poems written by the artists of word manipulation are the rightful heritage of every child in the world. Conditions may be set in the elementary school so that the natural role of the poet may be released in the child and he can develop his own creativity through the rhythmic use of words.

Poetry begins when the child's speech begins. It develops in his instinctive use of metaphor, perception, analogy, simile, rhythm, and

---

4. Leland B. Jacobs, "Children's Experiences in Literature," in *Children and the Language Arts,* edited by Virgil E. Herrick and Leland B. Jacobs (Englewood Cliffs, N.J.: Prentice-Hall, 1955), p. 195.

rhyming sense. Children who create and eventually write poetry quickly learn to appreciate and enjoy the poetry of others.

In selecting poetry to read to the children, the teacher can be guided by certain criteria: (1) the children must *enjoy* the poem: this means the teacher must know the children, their backgrounds, their interests, and their tastes; the poem must be relevant, the emotional content must be considered, the poem should be based on direct or vicarious experiences of the children; the grade and age level, timeliness, and motivation are all important; (2) the poem must be sincere and honest; (3) the poem must have uniqueness; (4) it must appeal to feelings as well as to intellect; (5) narrative poems must possess the qualities of a good story; (6) the poem must capture the rhythm and music of the language; (7) the writing must be rich in vigorous description, using clear, precise, imagery-filled words; and (8) poems must be heard to be appreciated.

The history of poetry has left children with a valuable heritage. Creative teachers will find a multitude of ways to use and enjoy poetry daily in connection with their regular classroom activities. This chapter suggests some activities as possible starters.

TO THE COLLEGE STUDENT

1. Read some of the books of poetry for children listed in the bibliography at the end of this chapter. Read the works of some of the modern young poets, such as Rod McKuen, or listen to them reading their poetry on records. Do you think children will respond to this type of poetry? Try some on children and note their reactions.

2. In your college class, assign a group of students to present some modern adult poetry to the class in a manner which captures the mood similar to the idea used by the children in the magic talking book. For instance, one student who plays a guitar may provide some musical background while others read the poem, etc. Do you feel that this type of activity enhances or detracts from the poetry?

3. Fit the criteria for selecting poetry to your own tastes—must poetry fit these criteria for you to enjoy it?

4. In the account of the magic talking book of word music told at the beginning of this chapter, the children worked in an environment where an "air of expectancy" prevailed; in other words, they took for granted the fact that they would write poems. Discuss these statements:

a. By her attitude a teacher can set conditions for children to write poetry naturally; i.e., her attitude is more important than any other condition in the classroom.
b. "Adventuring" in a classroom has more emotional impact than experiencing.
c. Poetry can be taught effectively when teachers like Miss Baxter capitalize on the "teachable moments" that arise in their classrooms. How must a teacher prepare herself for a "teachable moment"?
d. Children cannot and should not write free or blank verse when they are young.
e. There has been a revival in the interest in poetry in the past five years.

TO THE CLASSROOM TEACHER

1. If you are interested in the child's ability to use words beautifully, present a child with many sensory experiences and ask him or her to find words to describe them. To encourage this, put items in a bag so children can feel but not see the items.

Color can be made more vivid by projecting a film such as *Fiddle Dee Dee* on a wall or by putting swatches of cellophane on an overhead projector.

2. Constant exposure to good writing in literature generally fosters good writing in children. Would you guess that the children who wrote in this chapter were in a classroom where literature was used frequently? How do you think you can go about building appreciation and taste in poetry?

3. Find some records of modern poets and play them for the class. Then choose an appropriate strategy for presenting the poem before the group in an effective manner. Rod McKuen, a modern poet, has several interesting records of himself reading his poems. He uses a guitar a great deal to help set the mood for his poems.

TO THE COLLEGE STUDENT
AND THE CLASSROOM TEACHER

1. In the magic talking book of word music described at the beginning of this chapter, Miss Baxter blended the role of the child as a poet with his role as a listener. This was accomplished in a very creative manner. Discuss ways Miss Baxter might continue to guide the children to play each role after the completion of the magic talking book.

2. This is a book which promotes the theory of creative teaching, but which also provides the reader with many verbal observations so he can see how the theory can be carried out. Discuss this statement: Using visual observations so heavily in the book destroys the reader's ability to think for himself how to put the theories into creative classroom practice.

3. Some poets have said that the way to develop appreciation for poetry among children, as well as the ability to write poetry, is to concentrate on the development of the child's natural ability to use metaphor, simile, rhythm, perception, analogy, and rhyme. How do you feel about this? How would you design lessons on each of these skills?

4. If you have never tried writing poetry, do so. Try writing some for the children with whom you work. Read it to children and note their reactions.

5. A valuable asset to any teacher is a file on children's poetry. Explore children's poems by having each member of your class bring poems to class and read a few each day. Ask each to be responsible for a thumbnail sketch about the author. If the class members take notes on 3×5 cards, they will have a substantial file by the end of the semester.

6. Children are capable of developing quality in their poetry, as you can see by the poems in this chapter. How will you, as a teacher, help children develop quality in their poems?

SELECTED BIBLIOGRAPHY

Books about Poetry

Alexander, Arthur. *The Poet's Eye: An Introduction to Poetry for Young People.* Englewood Cliffs, N. J.: Prentice-Hall, 1967.

Arbuthnot, May Hill, and Shelton L. Root, Jr. *Time for Poetry,* 3rd ed. Glenview, Ill.: Scott, Foresman, 1968.

Arnstein, Flora. *Adventure into Poetry.* Palo Alto, Calif.: Stanford University Press, 1951.

Arnstein, Flora. *Poetry in the Elementary Classroom.* New York: Appleton-Century-Crofts, 1962.

Barnes, Walter. *The Children's Poets.* Chicago: World Book, 1924.

Behn, Harry. *Chrysalis: Concerning Chil-*

dren and Poetry. New York: Harcourt, Brace and World, 1968.

Benet, Laura. *Famous Poets for Young People*. New York: Dodd, Mead, 1964.

Benet, Rosemary, and Stephen Vincent Benet. *A Book of Americans*, rev. ed. New York: Holt, Rinehart and Winston, 1952.

Boyd, Gertrude A. *Teaching Poetry in the Elementary School*. Columbus: Charles E. Merrill, 1973.

Brewton, John E., and Sara W. Brewton. *Index to Children's Poetry*. New York: H. W. Wilson, 1942, with supplements to date.

Cox, Harvey. *Feast of Fools: A Theological Essay on Festivity and Fantasy*. Cambridge: Harvard University Press, 1969.

Dawson, Mildred, and Mary Alberta Choate. *How to Help a Child Appreciate Poetry*. Belmont, Calif.: Fearon Publishers, 1970.

de Regniers, Beatrice Schenk, et al. *Poems Children Will Sit Still For: A Selection for the Primary Grades*. New York: Citation Press, 1969.

Deutsch, Babette. *Poetry in Our Time*. New York: Holt, Rinehart and Winston, 1952.

Dunning, Stephen; Edward Leuders; and Hugh Smith. *Some Haystacks Don't Even Have any Needle And Other Complete Modern Poems*. New York: Lothrop, Lee and Shepard, 1969.

Haviland, Virginia, and William Jay Smith, comps. *Children and Poetry: An Annotated Bibliography*. Washington, D.C.: Library of Congress, 1969.

Hopkins, Lee Bennett. *Pass the Poetry, Please!* New York: Citation Press, 1972.

Huber, Miriam Blanton. *Story and Verse for Children*. 3rd ed. New York: Macmillan, 1965.

Hughes, Ted. *Poetry Is*. New York: Doubleday, 1970.

Koch, Kenneth. *Rose, Where Did You Get That Red? Teaching Great Poetry to Children*. New York: Random House, 1973.

Koch, Kenneth. *Wishes, Lies, and Dreams: Teaching Children to Write Poetry*. New York: Vantage Press, 1973.

Larrick, Nancy. *Somebody Turned on a Tap in These Kids: Poetry and Young People Today*. New York: Dell, 1972.

Livingston, Myra Cohn. *When You Are Alone It Keeps You Capone: An Approach to Creative with Children*. New York: Atheneum, 1973.

Painter, Helen W. *Poetry and Children*. International Reading Association, 1970.

Perrine, Laurence. *Sound and Sense: An Introduction to Poetry*, 4th ed. New York: Harcourt, Brace and World, 1973.

Sell, Violet, et al., eds. *Subject Index to Poetry for Children and Young People*. Chicago: American Library Association, 1957.

Terry, Ann. *Children's Poetry Preferences: A National Survey of Upper Elementary Grades*. Urbana, Ill.: National Council of Teachers of English, 1974.

Witucke, Virginia. *Literature for Children: Poetry in the Elementary School*. Dubuque, Iowa: Wm. C. Brown, 1970.

Books with Poetry for Children

Adams, Adrienne. *Poetry of Earth*. New York: Scribner's, 1972.

Adoff, Arnold, ed. *I Am the Darker Brother: An Anthology of Modern Poems by Black Americans*. New York: Macmillan, 1968.

Adoff, Arnold. *Tornado Poems*. New York: Thomas Y. Crowell, 1976.

Adoff, Arnold, ed. *My Black Me*. New York: C. P. Dutton, 1974.

Agree, Rose, ed. *How To Eat a Poem and Other Morsels: A Collection of Food Poems for Children*. New York: Macmillan, 1969.

Aldis, Dorothy. *All Together: A Child's Treasury of Verse*. New York: G. P. Putnam's Sons, 1952.

Aldis, Dorothy. *The Secret Place and Other Poems*. New York: Scholastic Book Services, 1962.

Benet, William Rose, ed. *Poems for Youth: An American Anthology*. New York: E. P. Dutton, 1923.

Bissett, Donald J., comp. *Poems and Verses to Begin On*. San Francisco: Chandler, 1967.

Blake, William. *Songs of Innocence*. New York: Peter Pauper, 1938.

Brewton, Sara, and John Brewton. *Birthday Candles Burning Bright*. New York: Macmillan, 1960.

Ciardi, John. *The Monster Den or Look What Happened at My House—And to It*. Philadelphia: J. B. Lippincott, 1966.

Coatsworth, Elizabeth. *The Sparrow Bush*. New York: Norton, 1966.

Cole, William, ed. *Humorous Poetry for Children*. Cleveland: World, 1955.

Cole, William, ed. *Poems of Magic and Spells*. Cleveland: World, 1960.

Cole, William, ed. *Pick Me Up: A Book of Short, Short Poems*. New York: Macmillan, 1972.

DeVries, Leonard, ed. *Flowers of Delight: An Agreeable Garland of Prose and Poetry, 1765–1830*. New York: Pantheon, 1966.

Dunning, Stephen, et al., eds. *Some Haystacks Don't Even Have Any Needle, And Other Complete Modern Poems*. New York: Lothrop, Lee, & Shepard, 1969.

Dwyer, Jane Ellen, ed. *I See a Poem*. Racine, Wis.: Whitman, 1968.

Ferris, Helen, comp. *Favorite Poems Old and New*. New York: Doubleday, 1957.

Fleming, Alice. *Hosannah the Home Run! Poems about Sports*. Boston: Little, Brown, 1972.

Fujikawa, Gyo, comp. *A Child's Book of Poems*. New York: Grosset and Dunlap, 1969.

Gregory, Horace, and Marya Zaturenska, eds, *The Crystal Cabinet: An Invitation to Poetry*. New York: Holt, Rinehart, and Winston, 1962.

Hazen, Barbara. *A Haunting We Will Go: Ghostly Stories and Poems*. New York: Albert Whitman, 1976.

Hazen, Barbara Shook. *World, World, What Can I Do?* Reading, Mass.: Addison-Wesley, 1976.

Hopkins, Lee Bennett. *Pass the Poetry, Please!* New York: Citation Press, 1972.

Jacobs, Leland B., ed. *Poetry for Summer*. Champaign, Ill.: Garrard Press, 1970.

Jacobs, Leland B., ed. *Poetry for Space Enthusiasts*. Champaign, Ill.: Garrard Press, 1971.

Johnson, Hannah Lyons. *Hello, Small Sparrow*. New York: Lothrop, Lee and Shepard, 1971.

Kherdian, David, and Nonny Hoagrogian. *Poems Here and Now*. New York: William C. Morrow, 1976.

Kuskin, Karla. *The Rose on My Cake*. New York: Harper & Row, 1964.

Larrick, Nancy, ed. *Poetry for Holidays*. Champaign, Ill.: Garrard Press, 1966.

Larrick, Nancy, ed. *On City Streets: An Anthology of Poetry*. New York: M. Evans, 1968.

Larrick, Nancy, comp. *I Heard a Scream in the Street: Poetry by Young People in the City*. New York: M. Evans, 1970.

Lewis, Richard. *Miracles: Poems by Children of the English-Speaking World*. New York: Simon & Schuster, 1966.

McCord, David. *Far and Few: Rhymes of the Never Was and Always Is*. Boston: Little, Brown, 1952.

McDonald, Gerald D., comp. *A Way of Knowing: A Collection of Poems for Boys*. New York: Thomas Y. Crowell, 1959.

McGinley, Phyllis. *Wonderful Time*. Philadelphia: J. B. Lippincott, 1966.

Mary-Rousselière, Guy, photographer. *Beyond the High Hills: A Book of Eskimo Poems*. New York: World, 1969.

Merriam, Eve. *Rainbow Writing*. New York: Atheneum, 1976.

Noyes, Alfred. *Daddy Fell into the Pond, and Other Poems for Children*. New York: Sheed and Ward, 1952.

O'Neill, Mary. *Hailstones and Halibut Bones*. New York: Doubleday, 1961.

Prelutsky, Jack. *Nightmares: Poems to Trouble Your Sleep*. New York: William C. Morrow, 1976.

Rasmussen, Carrie. *Let's Say Poetry Together and Have Fun*. Minneapolis: Burgess, 1962.

Reed, Gwendolyn, ed. *Songs the Sandman Sings*. New York: Atheneum, 1969.

Ross, David, ed. *Illustrated Treasury of Poetry for Children*. New York: Grosset and Dunlap, 1970.

Sandburg, Carl. *Sandburg Treasury: Prose and Poetry for Young People*. Edited by Paula Sandburg. New York: Harcourt Brace & Jovanovich, 1970.

Shakespeare, William. *Seeds of Time.* Compiled by Bernice Grohskopf. New York: Atheneum, 1963.

Thurman, Judith. *Flashlight and Other Poems.* New York: Atheneum, 1976.

Wallace, Daisy, ed. *Monster Poems.* New York: Holiday House, 1976.

Whitman, Walt. *I Hear America Singing.* New York: Delacorte Press, 1974.

Withers, Carl. *A Rocket in My Pocket: Rhymes and Chants of Young Americans.* New York: Harcourt, Brace and World, 1948.

FURTHER READINGS

Adams, Bess Porter. *About Books and Children.* New York: Henry Holt, 1953.

Arnstein, Flora J. *Children Write Poetry: A Creative Approach.* New York: Dover, 1967. Original title: *Adventure into Poetry.*

Benet, Laura. *Famous Poets for Young People.* New York: Dodd, Mead, 1964.

Brewton, John E., and Sara W. Brewton. *Index to Children's Poetry.* New York: H. W. Wilson, 1942, with supplements to date.

Bodger, Jean. *How the Heather Looks.* New York: Viking, 1964.

Cole, William, ed. *The Birds and the Beasts Were There.* Cleveland: World, 1963.

Isaacs, J. *The Background of Modern Poetry.* New York: E. P. Dutton, 1952.

Lennon, Florence Becker. *Victoria Through the Looking Glass.* New York: Simon and Schuster, 1945. Reprinted by Dover Press (1972) as *The Life of Lewis Carroll.*

Parker, Elinor, comp. *100 Story Poems.* New York: Thomas Y. Crowell, 1951.

Parker, Elinor, comp. *100 More Story Poems.* New York: Thomas Y. Crowell, 1960.

PART III

Adventures with Literature

CHAPTER 12

Developing Appreciation for Children's Literature

There's an Author In the House!

Mrs. Galvin watched her group of eight-year-olds carefully when they visited the main library in their school building for the first time. "What kinds of books do they read?" she thought. "What types of books are they interested in?"

Both Mrs. Galvin and the librarian became aware that several children asked for books by Lois Lenski. In investigating this situation later in a discussion, Mrs. Galvin learned from the children that they had read all of Lois Lenski's picture books in grades one and two, and many of her true stories of children living in other places.

Part of Mrs. Galvin's curriculum for the year was to stress contrasting cultures (both current and historical) to the children in this small city of Bloomdale where she was teaching. These children had studied community helpers and their urban community in the primary grades and had read the Mr. Small books by Lois Lenski as part of their interest in studying the family. They had also read Lenski's books: *The Little Auto, The Little Airplane, The Little Fire Engine, The Little Farm, The Little Sail Boat, The Little Train, We Live in the City,* and others, in studying transportation systems within their city.

With interest in Lois Lenski so high, Mrs. Galvin suddenly had an idea: she went to the library and reviewed all the books written by Lois Lenski and found so many that would help in presenting her work on contrasting cultures that she decided to build her unit for the next few weeks around the general interest of the children in Lois Lenski.

First, Mrs. Galvin wrote to Miss Lenski's publishers for any material they could send her—or any bookjackets. Scott Foresman sent her a beautiful chart with a picture of Lois Lenski and a picture of the covers of many of her books. Companies sent her other material. Mrs. Galvin used various resources to find out what she could about Lois Lenski. She withdrew from the library as many of the early reading books by Lenski as she could find. One morning before school she made a beautiful bulletin board of some of the material she had received. A large attractive sign on the top of the bulletin board asked, "Here is a friend of ours. Do you recognize her?"

Below the question was the large picture of the friendly, motherly face of Lois Lenski. Around her photograph were illustrations from many of her books clipped from book jackets. Below the bulletin board, on a bookshelf Mrs. Galvin had made by stacking bricks and planks to create a series of planes, were all the books these children had read by Lois Lenski.

The bulletin board created the type of reaction Mrs. Galvin had hoped it would, for some children recognized the picture. The display of Lenski's early books had a psychological effect on this group of children, because many of them asked if they might check a particular book out and take it home to read. Of course, Mrs. Galvin was delighted that this happened but was somewhat surprised as well. Always before, she had had to be very careful not to suggest too many "easy" books to her students because they tended to say, "They are baby books." Displaying them to the whole class in this manner seemed to legitimize the appearance of the books in the classroom and the children poured over them as if they were meeting a long-absent friend. Several children suggested they read some of the books together again.

Mrs. Galvin agreed to this idea and a plan was devised whereby a *Lois Lenski Hour* was held each day for the next week of school. Five or six children chose a Lois Lenski book they wanted to read during that time and announced it through a creative advertisement put on the Lenski bulletin board. These "ads" told the name of the book to be read, the reader, the place in the room where the listeners should assemble, and the times the book would be read during the Lois Lenski Hour. In order to keep some sort of balance, each group was limited to ten children and they signed up on the "ad" for their own choices. This afforded the children the opportunity to plan their own program for an hour each day. Five or six children were reading the Lenski stories during the same hour, and repeating the readings three times within the hour so all the children could move from group to group and hear each story. For those who did not want to spend the entire hour listening, the bookshelf below the Lenski bulletin board was kept supplied with new books by Lois Lenski, and the children were invited to spend the time reading books of their own selection.

Among the books chosen for reading were the following:

Animals for Me
Let's Play House
Cowboy Small
The Little Airplane
The Little Auto
Little Farm
Little Train
Papa Small
We Live in the City

Big Little Davy
Davy Goes Places
Davy and His Dog
Davy's Day
A Dog Came to School
Surprise for Davy
Papa Pequeno
The Little Fire Engine
The Little Sail Boat
Policeman Small
I Like Winter
Now It's Fall
On a Summer Day
Spring Is Here
Lois Lenski's Christmas Stories

In a discussion of Lois Lenski's books soon after, Mrs. Galvin asked the children, "If we could get Lois Lenski to come to visit us, what would you like to ask her?"

"Does she have children?" asked Marcia.

"How old are they?" Bill added.

"Where does she live?"

"How did she begin to write?"

"Does she always draw all her own pictures?" asked Benny.

"I'd like to know if she draws her pictures first or writes the stories first," said Gerry.

"How many books has she written?"

"Does she write books for adults too?"

FIGURE 12–1. *A shadow play of* Corn-Farm Boy *by Lois Lenski*

"Would she come to visit us?"

"How is a book printed?"

Mrs. Galvin made a list of these and other questions asked by the children.

Now, among the materials Mrs. Galvin had received free of charge was a record made by Henry Z. Walck, Inc. of an informal talk by Lois Lenski. On this record she tells how she makes a picture book.[1] "The making of a picture book is always sheer pleasure to me," Miss Lenski begins. In the message that follows, she tells how the children themselves help her to write her books through their suggestions and criticisms.

Mrs. Galvin felt that this record would have great value to the children at this time so she said, "I don't know if Lois Lenski can ever come to our school, but we can do the next best thing to talking to her. We know what she looks like by her picture on the bulletin board, and we can hear what she sounds like by listening to a record she made that I have here. On the record, I believe, Miss Lenski will answer many of the questions you have just asked me."

The children were very anxious to hear the record. A part of this recording is devoted to singing some of the songs in Miss Lenski's song books. The children enjoyed this recording a great deal and asked that it be left in a place easily available to them for replaying.

Mrs. Galvin discovered that most of the children did not know that Lois Lenski had written music. A committee was sent to the library to find any books by her that might contain songs. On the record the children heard the *Songs of Mr. Small, At Our House, I Went for a Walk,* and *When I Grow Up.* They quickly learned to sing these and sang along with the record.

Mrs. Galvin saw an excellent opportunity to integrate her music, literature, social studies, and art in the weeks that followed. The committee that went to the library found several Lenski books containing songs and brought copies of *Songs of Mr. Small* and *We Are Thy Children* (music by Clyde R. Bulla), which provided much interesting material for the children.

After the children had listened to the record, they discussed the answers to several of the questions they had asked.

Mrs. Galvin spent some time on the following day making a presentation with the overhead projector and pictures she had found about the life and work of Lois Lenski. At this time she informed the children that one of the areas of study set for the third-grade curriculum was that of finding out how people in other parts of the United States lived differently from people in Bloomdale. She also informed them that people in Bloomdale did not live now as they had lived years ago and that they would study together the differences between life in other places and life in Bloomdale, and between life in former years with life now.

"I think," said Mrs. Galvin, "that our friend, Lois Lenski, can be of great help to us. She has written more books about people in other places than anyone I know, and she has also written many books of people living long ago. I would like to suggest that we plan a trip to the library

---

1. "A Message from Lois Lenski: The Making of a Picture Book" (New York: Henry Z. Walck) P 3M–9418.

soon, and that we have a Lois Lenski Treasure Hunt on that day to see what materials we can come up with. Let's plan the trip this afternoon so we will know exactly what we are looking for. Meanwhile, will you be thinking of all the places you have been *or* have read about where people live differently than we do here. Plan to tell us about these places tomorrow."

Part of the next afternoon was spent with children telling about life in different places. Several had spent their summer at the seashore and indicated that life there was quite different from life in the.city. Albert had lived in a small country town before he moved to Bloomdale and life there had been very different. Billy had spent the summer with his cousin on a dairy farm in upstate New York and that life, he felt, was very different from city life. Jill had moved into town after living in the suburbs for several years, and she told about living there. Madeline had spent the summer in Paris with her father and mother. Peter had been to Disney World. Tricia had been on a dude ranch for a week.

All of these shared experiences led the children into a discussion with the following questions (planned by Mrs. Galvin) as a base:

Why is life different in these places?
Is it different because the people want it so, or is it different because people *must* live in this fashion for other reasons?
Where can we find out about the life styles of many groups of people?
How can we find out why these people live as they do (or did)?

Some worthy concepts and understandings grew out of the discussions held of other life styles the children had experienced.

On the following day Mrs. Galvin encouraged them to ask their mothers and fathers and grandmothers and grandfathers where they lived and what life was like in that place when they were eight years old. They then shared these experiences. As a result of their discussion, they came up with some very basic concepts which Mrs. Galvin recorded to use as a base for further studies. The first list of conclusions the children made were as follows:

- There are many different ways of living.
- People sometimes live as they do because of the geography of the land.
- People sometimes live as they do because of their history. Repeated acts of living create customs and tradition.
- People sometimes live as they do because of wealth or poverty.
- People sometimes live as they do because of politics and government.
- People sometimes live as they do because of climate.
- People sometimes live as they do because it is their choice or their dream.
- People sometimes live as they do because of the way they earn a living.
- People sometimes live as they do because of education.
- All styles of living have a history, and styles of living in one place change from generation to generation.

Mrs. Galvin suggested that the children divide an outline map of the United States into natural land areas. These were set apart on the map with colored chalk. Then she suggested they form committees of three or four people to study the life style of the people in these areas, both currently and historically. She planned with the children the Lois Lenski Treasure Hunt. One day they went to the library. Each child looked for Lenski books that would tell him about life in his selected region of study, both currently and historically. When they returned to their classroom, they charted their findings.

HOW OTHER PEOPLE LIVE
Books by Lois Lenski

Place	Today	Long Ago	Name of Book
Swamp Area—			
New Orleans	X		*Bayou Suzette*
New England		X	*Bound Girl of Cobble Hill*
		X	*Phoebe Fairchild, Her Book*
The Plains	X		*Corn-Farm Boy*
		X	*Prairie School*
Mountain People	X		*Blue Ridge Billy*
Country Life		X	*We Live in the Country*
	X		*Blueberry Corners*
City Life	X		*We Live in the City*
	X		*Project Boy*
Middle Atlantic		X	*Indian Captive*
States		X	*A Little Girl of Nineteen Hundred*
Water and Waterfront	X		*Ocean-Born Mary*
Ranch Life		X	*Texas Tomboy*
Indians		X	*Indian Captive*
	X		*Little Sioux Girl*
The South: Florida		X	*Strawberry Girl*
The South	X		*We Live in the Southwest*
	X		*Cotton in My Sack*
	X		*Judy's Journey*
		X	*Mama Hattie's Girl*
		X	*Peanuts for Billy Ben*

Some children became so interested in the life of Lois Lenski that they did some research about her. One group reported to the remainder of the class on the awards she had won for her writing and drawing. Because *Strawberry Girl* had won a Newbery Award, the class asked Mrs. Galvin if she would read the book to them. This was done chapter by chapter.

The committee for each region of the United States to be studied met after the material had been classified and decided how they should read the material. Three committees decided they would read their books together, with each person on the committee reading to the others for part of each period. Another committee decided that each member of the committee would read each book. Inasmuch as there were three books and three members on the committee, the books were simply rotated among the members until all the children had read them. Other groups of children chose the good readers in the group to read the entire book or books to them at various intervals. Sessions were held to determine how the stories in the books would then be presented to the remainder of the class. Many heated discussions were held until each committee came up with a unique way to give their material.

The children reporting on life in the swamp presented a talking roll movie of *Bayou Suzette*.

The group presenting life in New England wrote a play and presented it for *Bound Girl of Cobble Hill*.

Indian Captive was presented by reading passages of the book between tableaus posed inside a large picture frame made from an old screen.

Another committee reproduced the country store at Blueberry Corners to show early American rural life, and held an exhibit of early American toys and tools.

After the Lenski book lists were exhausted, children held a treasure hunt for books by other authors that would help them in their study of other times and other places, and these books also provided the incentive for some highly creative planning and working.

Some of the books by other authors that seemed to fit well into the regional studies were:

> *Riding the Pony Express* by Clyde Bulla
> *Thanksgiving Story* by Alice Dalgliesh
> *The Time of the Wolves* by Verne T. David
> *Tom Whipple* by Walter Edmonds
> *One Long Picnic* by Neta Lohnes Frazier
> *This Dear Bought Land* by Jean Latham
> *Calico Captive* by Elizabeth George Speare
> *His Indian Brother* by Hazel Wilson
> *Little House Series* by Laura Ingalls Wilder
> *Wilderness Journey* by William Steele
> *The Far Frontier* by William Steele
> *Bonanza Girl* by Patricia Beatty
> *How Many Miles to Sundown* by Patricia Beatty
> *Soup* by Robert Newton Peck
> *Maple Harvest* by Elizabeth Gemming
> *Amish People* by Carolyn Meyer
> *Skinny* by Robert Burch
> *The Story of George Washington* by Bernice Carlson Wells
> *Three Ships Came Sailing In* by Miriam Evangeline Mason
> *Fourth of July Story* by Alice Dalgliesh
> *Ice Cream Next Summer* by Elaine R. Govern
> *If You Lived in Colonial Times* by Ann McGovern

The unit was culminated in a Lois Lenski festival to which other classes were invited. At the festival, all the work of the children was on exhibit, an exhaustive display of Lois Lenski's books was set up, mobiles of book characters decorated the ceilings, bulletin boards telling of the work of the children were on view, and the children dressed as characters from the books they had read. The program consisted of selections from their favorite reports among those given to the class and were announced

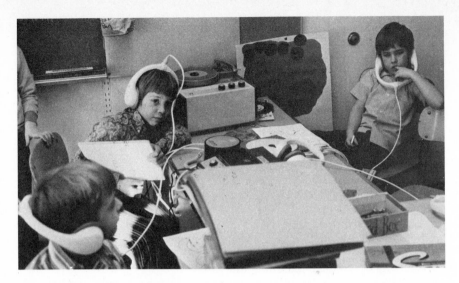

FIGURE 12–2. *Using modern technology to learn more about Lois Lenski.*

by a guest first grader, dressed to look like a little man who represented Papa Small. Many of the children had made dioramas and box scenes of their favorite Lenski stories and these, too, were on display.

One day in class Mrs. Galvin helped the children tape the songs they had learned that were developed around Lois Lenski's stories. These recorded songs were set up in a listening center, a small room adjoining the classroom, and small groups of children could go into this room and listen to the tapes. Also available in the listening center was a record player where children might listen to the record by Lois Lenski, "The Making of a Picture Book."

The final act of the program was a fashion show where all the children had the opportunity to tell about their own costume, the character who wore it, and the book in which the particular character was to be found.

Mrs. Galvin felt that the children learned a great deal about writing from their unit on Lois Lenski. Consequently, she made lists, as the unit progressed, of topics of interest to the children about life styles of various peoples. One day she placed the topics on the chalkboard with the intent of stimulating the children to write their own literature. Many stories and poems resulted, such as, "A Boy at Valley Forge," "An Attack on Fort Stanwix," and "Four Girls and a Conestoga Wagon."

Mrs. Galvin felt that building her unit around the works of one writer had paid off well. Because of the diversity of stories written by Lois Lenski, she was never at a loss for something of a child's interest or reading ability. Mrs. Galvin's own evaluation of her unit contained one very interesting statement, "I feel," she said, "that the children developed a real 'feel' for people in other places and for people who lived at other times. Before this, when I have used social studies books for resource material, the children have learned many isolated facts from which they developed concepts and arrived at conclusions. Often these concepts were misconceptions. This time, they seemed to have a total picture about a time or a place from which they were able to pull out specific facts. Learning about a time in history or a place in the country through identification with a character, often their own age, was a very unifying experience. I never had to pressure them to read...they literally consumed Miss Lenski's books. She has become a friend and teacher to them."

Mrs. Galvin's experience with her children helped them to develop a love of books and a taste and appreciation for a specific author's work. In this instance, taste and appreciation are almost inevitable by-products of a rich teaching experience. But appreciation and taste may be developed through direct, conscientious planning by the teacher, as we shall see in the following discussion.

APPRECIATION AND TASTE IN CHILDREN

Holding a book fair is one of the surest ways known to help children develop an *interest* in books, especially if the fair is like the one described on page 465 and each child has been individually involved. With real involvement comes relevance.

How does a teacher go further than this and build in children *a love and appreciation of good books*? For this is a deeper thing than interest. It is the power that holds children to books for the rest of their lives.

Many teachers are rightfully concerned about the cheap, tawdry, yet impressive, writing to which children are exposed daily, and they wonder how they can help children see and understand the differences between writing such as this and writing that is beautiful. They wonder how they can build "appreciation" in literature—how they can help a child see that real literature calls for a certain beauty and style of writing.

What Is Appreciation?

In stating the philosophy of this book, a discussion was presented on the meaning of appreciation and taste. In this discussion the following concepts were presented as the type of activity that builds appreciation and taste in children.

Appreciation and Taste Can Be Developed

Experiencing Contrasts

A logical way to develop a background for building an appreciation for books and a specific personal taste in children, then, is to deliberately expose them to many kinds of books and all sorts of writing. In doing this it may be necessary for the teacher to minimize her own tastes to be objective in her selection of material for the children. As mentioned above, appreciation and taste develop as a result of studying contrasts.

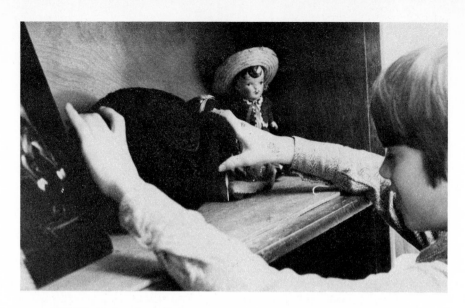

FIGURE 12–3. Appreciation for literature manifests itself in many be-haviors: Kevin makes a collection of realia to illustrate his favorite stories.

A child cannot really know what hot is until he has experienced cold. He does not really understand sadness until he has been very happy. He cannot know true lightness until he has experienced weight. All these concepts are relative and are not understood except in relation to something else. A child cannot understand the qualities of *good* literature until he has also experienced *poor* literature.

Often a child brings a book to school for the teacher to read. It may be an inexpensive book picked up at the dime store by his mother. He asks the teacher to read it. Certainly this request is a compliment to the teacher! Read it she should, even though it is no great piece of literature. When a child has something that is precious to him and he wants to share it, he should be commended—he is empathizing his enjoyment. Through subtle discussion the teacher may help the children to see that the piece is shallow, or she may simply express enjoyment over the story, appreciation over the sharing of it, and do little if anything more with it. The important thing is that the child felt that his contribution has been accepted and appreciated.

An understanding of good writing will not come full-blown. It will evolve gradually as the teacher and the children, through discussion and experience, find those qualities which elevate some writing above the commonplace.

Little by little, through discussion and other selected activities such as those described below, children can be helped to understand reasons for their choices in books. From contrasts of his own experiences, each child becomes his own critic of literature and can verbalize his reasons for his general choices in books (appreciation) and his own particular choices (tastes).

Adventures and Experiences

We take the stand that both appreciation for good literature and taste in literature are developed through the types of experiences children have with it or with the "adventures" planned for them by the teacher. Such adventures have been illustrated many times in this volume. Certainly, with experiences such as those described in each chapter, children can really develop a warm, affectionate feeling for characters and stories. It must be remembered that appreciations are built as a result of knowledge and *emotional feeling*. Emotions play a great part in determining one's appreciation of a book.

Empathy

Empathy, the ability to project one's own consciousness into another being, is necessary in order to experience literature, and the ability to project oneself into any situation is dependent on one's own related experiences and feelings. It is not enough that children hear good literature in the classroom—they must *experience* it or have adventures with it. This means that though sometimes the reading of a poem or story will suffice in itself, in most instances conditions must be set so that the children can experience or live the material being read. It is this additional attention paid to the "good" stories and poems that makes children realize they are

FIGURE 12–4. *The props are ready; now for the costumes for* Little House on the Prairie *by Laura Ingalls Wilder.*

special. By living and feeling the story with the characters, and by learning to express their own feelings in carefully chosen words, they come to see the skill of the author—and to appreciate the quality of the work. Through classroom experiences with literature, they build their own values and standards, and learn to evaluate the writing of others.

Appreciation for literature may be a by-product of the teacher's direct attempts to develop empathy in children. Many strategies have been used recently to develop understandings of various subcultures and ethnic groups. Among them is role-playing, which calls for a child to play a role in a free dramatic situation. By playing roles in any dramatization, a child is called upon to project. Dramatizations with role-playing are used by many teachers for solving school social problems. For instance, an argument arises on the playground that almost results in a fight. The teacher, who did not witness the circumstances leading to the fight, asks the children involved to dramatize the situation from the top down. If the situation is a highly emotional one, she may ask a group of witnesses to play the scene as they saw it. This dramatization provides the class with a common base for discussion and leads to questions which often, when explored, get to the root of the problem. The ability to empathize is necessary in order for children to grow in their capacity to make moral judgments.

Another effective technique requiring empathy is that of role reversal. In Mr. Dickson's class one child accused another of stealing his sneakers from his locker. Mr. Dickson was concerned over the fact that one child was accusing another publicly with no evidence. He asked the boys involved to play the scene. Then he asked them to reverse roles and play the scene. Immediately, Ron, the accuser, said, "I shouldn't have blamed Dick in front of everybody until I was sure he had my sneakers. I'm sorry, Dick."

Other techniques that help to develop empathy are: the open-ended story (where children must listen carefully to a problem story and provide the solution), films, filmstrips, and records (which present open-ended stories), and problem pictures (wherein children must identify and solve problems presented through the use of pictures).

Creative dramatics where children become involved in a relaxed, informal presentation of a story they have heard (without the pressure of memorizing parts) can be very effective in developing empathy and appreciation.

The effective reading of literature requires that the child place himself in the various roles of the characters. Helping children to project, to see the other fellow's viewpoint, enhances their enjoyment of literature and enables them to appreciate the power of words.

Evaluative Discussions

In developing appreciation and taste, discussions of stories and poems after a reading will differ from the usual type of discussion so the thrust of the dialogue will be toward helping children identify those aspects of *the writing* which make it superior or beautiful. Refer to page 8 to note the type of questions that might be asked to help the children become sensitive to and appreciative of style.

Relevance

Relevance is a factor to consider in developing appreciation for literature. Creative teachings helps to make learning relevant. One job of the teacher in working with children's literature is to help the children select material relevant to them. Another job is to provide adventures in the classroom that will involve children completely and thus bring many types of literature into relevance.

Little motivation was needed, for instance, to encourage the children in Mr. Carr's class to read *The Book of Three, Taran Wanderer, The Black Cauldron, The Castle of Llyr*, and *The High King* by Lloyd Alexander after their work with *The Knights of the Round Table* and *The Adventures of Robin Hood*.

Sensory Experiences

Appreciation is an emotional as well as an intellectual reaction to a given stimulus. Appreciation in any of the creative arts calls for a reaction from any or all of the senses. Deliberate attempts to provide sensory experiences for children enhance their likelihood of appreciating creative products. Many illustrations of classroom situations are presented in this book where sensory experiences have been deliberately planned for the children.

Sensory experiences can be integrated successfully with any of the subject matter areas of the elementary school. Miss Culkin, a primary teacher, taught a science unit on tastes. The children learned about taste buds and the effect of the sense of smell and sight on taste. Blindfolded children could not always tell what foods they were eating. Children with clothespin clamps on their noses found that they could not always taste the food they were eating. Some children were nauseated on being presented with meat that was green or apples that had been colored brown. After their explorations with food, Miss Culkin had them put into words their feelings about some of these experiences. This helped them appreciate the difficulties of finding the most effective words for the situation.

Sharon wrote: "Eating horseradish was like a needle explosion in my nose." Pete wrote:

> *I discovered something new,*
> *A way to put your food to waste*
> *Is—put a clothespin on your nose*
> *And you will find it has no taste.*

Mr. Marks, a middle school teacher, conducted a science unit on sounds. The children learned about the function of the ear and how sound is carried. They experimented with materials that would carry sound. They ran a 2"×4" board through a hole in a large cardboard, which created two cubicles on one side of the classroom. One child made a noise by hitting the end of the 2 × 4 with a spike. At the other end, a child put his ear close to the 2×4 and listened for a vibration. When a vibration was felt or a noise was heard, it was recorded. The 2×4 was replaced with yarn, rope, a metal bar, a necktie, a piece of carpeting, a copper wire, an aluminum wire, a plank, a hollow pipe, a strip of cardboard, and a pane of glass. Mr. Marks also helped children find words to express their feelings about sounds.

Many of the experiences children normally have in school can be carried into the realm of verbal expression: Halloween parties, Valentine parties, and Christmas parties provide excellent opportunity to develop the sense of taste and smell in the food prepared; sight, in the decorations, costumes, centerpieces, etc.; sound, in the programs presented; and touch, in the multitude of materials used.

Perception Development

Perception is a part of learning.[2] The way a child sees things is the way he learns about and understands them. Aesthetic perception deals with seeing the beauty in line, color, texture, realism, rhythm, contour, posture, etc. Aesthetic perception in children's literature means seeing the beauty of the characters, the rhythm of the words, the joy of the rhyme, the trueness of the description, the subtlety of the humor, the sentiment in the portrayals, the style of the author, the emotional appeal of the phrases, the tone quality of the piece, and other characteristics of the work as a whole.

All humans see things differently because perception is more than observing. It is interpreting what one observes. And when one interprets, he can do so only in terms of his own feelings and experiences. Because the background of experiences and emotional reaction of any two people is never exactly the same, they cannot interpret the same. Consequently, no two people perceive the same, even though they are observing the same object. Understanding this, the teacher will not expect all children to react the same to any piece of literature.

Conditions can be set, however, for making direct attempts to develop perception in children so they become more careful in their observations and consequently more discreet in their interpretations.

Because art is a visual medium, much can be done through art to develop perception. Lessons can be built around any topic, and art can be integrated in a manner similar to the following.

Take a lesson about transportation. Airplanes and airports are familiar to all children and they accept the wonder of flight without even considering how it is possible. In talking about flight, the teacher can introduce talk about birds, and in so doing, she can talk about the beauty that others have perceived in birds. To do this successfully, there is a very real need for the teacher to have adequate reference material in her classroom. This might take the form of large mounted prints or large-size or well-illustrated art books in color. The teacher might show pages from John James Audubon's *Birds of America* or examples of early Chinese brush drawings in which the birds were drawn with a minimum of beautifully controlled strokes. There are the prints of the magnificent carvings of falcons that appear so often in ancient Egyptian art, and there

---

2. Some of the material in this section was borrowed from John G. Ritson and James A. Smith, *Creative Teaching of Art in the Elementary School* (Boston: Allyn and Bacon, 1974).

are paintings such as *The Singing Birds in a Tree,* a tomb painting from the twelfth dynasty that is very close to the perception of children. Art appreciation used in this fashion is not an added nicety but an integral part of the learning process that has as much to do with what the child becomes as with how much he knows. In order to help the children appreciate the subtle skills of both perception and control of the media that are an intrinsic part of the Chinese print, the teacher herself must be able to appreciate it to the fullest. The process of imparting this appreciation to the student is best done by asking the right kind of questions:

"What kind of brush did the Chinese use and how did they hold it?"

"We have all kinds of art materials; what kind did the Chinese use, or the Egyptians?"

"Does their art look like that because of their materials, or did they choose their materials to match the way they saw things?"

"How can we choose materials for special purposes?"

"In all the examples shown, the artists were interested in birds for very different reasons. Can you see what the interest of each one was?"

"When you draw a bird, what is it that interests you?"

The questions are all aimed at making the child examine the art work in some way that relates to himself. This may be in the way that he sees things, or feels about things, or it may have to do with the problems that he has faced in trying to deal with the same subject or area of experience. Much of the art work in children's books can be used in this manner.

In applying these principles to literature, questions such as those described on page 9 can be used to develop perception of aesthetic writing.

"I just love *Caddie Woodlawn,*" says Marcia.

"I do, too," the teacher replies. "What was your favorite part of the book?"

"The part where Caddie warned the Indians that the white men were going to attack them," Marcia replies.

"That *was* good," says the teacher. "I made up some words to describe Caddie at that moment. I wonder if your words would be the same as mine?"

"Let's see," says Marcia thoughtfully, "she was courageous—boy, did she have courage!"

"I agree," says the teacher. "That was one of my words, too."

Jimmy also has read the book. "She had guts!" he blurts out.

"That's another word for it, isn't it?" said the teacher. "What were some of her other characteristics, would you say?"

"Well, she was loyal. She wasn't about to let her friends break up her friendship with the Indians."

"Yes, I would say she was loyal. I also put down honest. Would you say Caddie was honest?"

"Oh, yes," said Sally, who had also read the book. "I'd also say that Caddie was aggressive—you know, she pushed herself—she made herself do things that the other kids didn't."

"I think she was reliable," said Marcia.

After more discussion, the teacher said, "We have said that Caddie Woodlawn was a girl who was courageous, loyal, "gutsy," honest, aggressive, and reliable. Tell me, do you boys know of any boy character in any book who has these characteristics?" After some thought, Darin said he felt Johnny Tremain had these characteristics. The children then became interested in finding passages in the books showing how the author had made the reader aware of these characteristics.

Darin chose a passage to show how Johnny Tremain had the courage to face his crippled hand for the first time. The children flipped through the books on their desks to find passages for other purposes: those that described the settings of the story, showed the hero's or heroine's relationship to other people, showed changes in character, made them laugh, made them sad, and those where the author created unusual and beautiful images.

All of this sharpens perception of style. Perception is really the ability to be aware: *awareness*. When discussions such as those mentioned above are not held, children do not become aware of those elements that make a piece of literature appealing to them.

Because each author approaches his writing with his own unique style, these experiences need to be continuous. The teacher's job is to maintain a continual sense of awareness.

To be fully aware means constant challenge and change, flexibility and fluency. All this demands the output of physical, emotional, and intellectual energy. It is easier *not* to be aware.

Perception is often heightened by shock. Our awareness of the automobile undergoes extreme changes after an accident. Gone is the feeling of shining strength and worth. The vulnerability of thin steel is revealed. The same changes in perception can be managed by providing mildly shocking experiences. Look up at things that you normally look down on, and the reverse. Look at things while standing on your head or lying on your side. Enforce selection by viewing things through a hole punched in a card or through the view finder of a camera. Look at things through a magnifying glass or the wrong end of a telescope. Look at things through pieces of colored acetate. Look at the parts separately from the whole.

Record the sounds of things and play them without visual context, play them louder than normal. Locate things solely by the sense of smell. Color meat green with food coloring and discover how one area of perception fools another—in this case, taste. Play the game of filling paper sacks with objects that simulate the feel of other things: wet grapes feel like eyeballs, a water-filled plastic bag feels like liver, etc. These activities help to make the point that true understanding and awareness come from an integration of all the senses.

PERCEPTION AND EXPERIENCE. We all undergo experiences but only the perceptive individual is able to fully understand them and store the vital information for future use.

Literature springs from the desire to express past and present experiences. The creative nature of the process and product will depend upon the degree to which the individual has made the experience his own.

It is inevitable that perception will be modified by the individual's uniqueness and individuality. There is the story about the honeymoon couple, the engineer, the golfer, and the artist staying at a small guest house by a picturesque waterfall. The honeymooners went away talking about the

FIGURE 12–5. *Children's perceptions differ: Umbrellas drawn by first graders after reading* Rain *by Robert Louis Stevenson.*

romantic sound of falling water and the dampness of the grass. The engineer was intrigued by the possibilities of hydroelectric generation. The golfer felt his time had been wasted, the local golf course lacked any challenge. The artist went away with images of refracted light, the intricacies of the pattern of falling water, the subtle change in night smells as one approached the moist air around the falls, and the feel of the moisture on his face. He had climbed to all sorts of viewpoints seeking new visual compositions.

Perception, it seems, is very much a part of experience. If we want our children to develop fully, then we have to help them find both worthwhile experiences and the means to perceive their meanings. Experiences can be as significant for the child in the wheelchair as for the healthy, active child. It is not so much the magnitude of the experience, but the quality that becomes important.

Development of Metaphor, Simile, and Analogy

Simile and metaphor are examples of the creative act in action: making new relationships between unrelated things.

Simile is an expressed comparison of two different things or ideas, especially as a figure of speech for rhetorical effect. In *Secret of the Andes* by Ann Nolan Clark, the author uses simile richly.[3]

---

3. Ann Nolan Clark, *The Secret of the Andes* (New York: Macmillan, 1952).

Miss Cane used this book to help her ten- and eleven-year-olds work directly with similes. After they had discussed a simile, the children held a simile hunt in the book and copied some beautiful expressions on 3 × 5 cards which they then posted on a chart before the class.

On pages 14 to 15 of *Secret of the Andes* (which the teacher had read to the class), Maxine found the following similes:

"The boys' thoughts were whirling like the foaming rapids on the far side of the valley."

"It was Inca music as old as the rocks of the canyon walls, as mysterious as the mountains."

"He bore the proud look of the giant condor circling a cliff nest on a mountain crest."

"He had the grace of a puma waiting to spring upon its prey."

"The minstrel was wild and free as sound can be wild and free."

John thought one paragraph of the book was particularly rich in simile so he copied the entire paragraph to be placed on the chart.

> The minstrel played softly at first on his Panpipes, and the grazing llamas stopped to listen. Then, as the music continued, they folded their feet beneath them and rested. They began humming. No music is more beautiful than llamas humming. It sounds like wind over water. It sounds like water rippling over moss-covered stones. It is wind-and-water music. It made a moving background for the sweet crying of the minstrel's pipes. Cusi stopped braiding the grass strands to listen. Chuto stopped twisting tortoru reeds and long grass to listen. Suncca crouched by his young master and forgot to whine and forgot to be afraid in the beauty of the music. The minstrel began to sing, softly at first, then louder and louder to the music of the Panpipes and the llama-humming.[4]

Metaphor is an implied comparison between two different things: a figure of speech in which a word or phrase that ordinarily means one thing is used in place of another thing in order to suggest a likeness between the two. In *Secret of the Andes,* Miss Clark uses metaphor beautifully. Miss Cane's children found several examples of it:

> *the foaming rapids tossing their crystal spray (p. 63)*
> *the sunlight did not reach the crevice trail (p. 78)*
> *the steps were blotted in purple shadow (p. 78)*
> *fire smoke curled upward in a blue line (p. 81)*
> *the valley that lay hiding just beneath the line of eternal snow (p. 85)*
> *to soothe his aching disappointment (p. 87)*

Miss Cane did not use the terms "metaphor" and "simile" with her students. They had discussed certain pieces of writing and she and the children had found favorite passage in books they liked. They discussed how the words were put together to make them sound lyrical or to paint beautiful images. They discussed the importance of words in writing and the need of using the best word in the best place. They discussed "describing" words and noted that some authors used describing words a great deal in their writing. Another technique they used was to compare one

---

4. *Ibid.*, p. 25.

thing with another. Miss Cane urged them to create some comparisons themselves. Thus they discovered simile. Some of the similes they invented follow:

> *The sky is like a tie-dyed scarf.*
> *The wind is shouting today like a grouchy father.*
> *The Christmas tree shines like broken glass.*

Miss Cane pointed out the fact that another technique often used by these authors is to put together words not usually used together to create beautiful "mind pictures." The children tried to do this. Some of their metaphor appears below:

> *the fluttering lights on the Christmas tree*
> *tinsel stars*
> *teardrop rain*
> *monster clouds and thunder*

Of course, teachers will not teach metaphor, simile, or analogy as such, but one way to develop students' appreciation for good writing is to work with these concepts in their discussions about authors and their writing, helping children to see and understand why the writing is unique.

To develop the ability of the child to use simile, metaphor, and analogy is to use the principle of developing new relationships and to help the child find new ways to express his own emotions.

Miss Barclay has planned a series of activities that she hopes will result in an ability to see relationships.[5] "I am going to show you a collection of photographs that I have cut out of magazines. See if you can find things in these that will make them match a second picture."

The first efforts result in *people* being matched with *people*. "Very good, now let us see how many other things you can find that match them."

Jim chooses an elephant and a fireman with a hose. "Jim, that's clever, why don't you take a magazine and see what you can find."

Analogy can be developed on a more concrete level using art media. Provide paint and paper but no brushes. The child is forced to look at other materials which have similar characteristics as brushes: things that will hold the paint long enough to allow it to be applied to the paper. Some of the possibilities are pieces of cardboard, sponges, tissues, popsicle sticks, Q-tips. Once this has been understood, substitutions can be made for both paper and paint. Paintings can be made without any commercial materials. Children can be encouraged to discover the possibilities of coffee, tea, ketchup, mustard, food coloring. These can be applied to such things as paper towels, paper sacks, cloth, wood, stones, or the sidewalk. The important thing is the discovery of common relationships.

The ability to deal freely with relationships means that we do not have to resolve every problem as a thing separate from all others. The analogy is a means of speeding the learning process.

This type of learning takes place naturally at an early age during play. It is reasonable to suggest that if children lose the ability to deal with analogy freely, it is because learning has become divorced from play.

Consider some of the following intellectual and psychological

---

5. Ritson and Smith, *op. cit.*

factors involved in play and how necessary they are to learning and making analogies.

Challenge	Perception	Discrimination
Discovery	Improvisation	Exploitation
Excitement	Abstraction	Imagination
Reward	Curiosity	Fantasy
Patience	Analysis	Flexibility

The ability to deal with analogy can only be developed if these other factors are being satisfactorily developed at the same time. The child's own stories, his writing and his art work are, in many ways, a symptom of his emotional, intellectual, and psychological health.

Sue's paintings include, time after time, a house, a tree, and a swing set between a ribbon of blue sky and another of green grass. This repetition of stereotypes is not so much an art problem as a symptom of something else.

Miss Jackson perceives the problem and structures some art experiences that can excite Sue's interest and make it difficult for her to rely on the old stereotypes.

"Look what funny shapes these pieces of scrap construction paper make; these two together look like a huge head with a wide open mouth."

Sue cannot see the connection until the jaw is made to move. "What kind of head is it?" she asks.

"We could tell that better if it had a body and legs. See if you can find some other pieces to fit."

Sue's problem is so deep that she does not feel that she can modify the pieces that she chooses. "Can I cut out some pieces?" Miss Jackson senses that cut pieces will result in rigid stereotyped thinking.

"Why don't you try tearing them, maybe you will find some fun shapes that way."

Sue finally realizes that she can achieve her ends without the necessity of conscious intellectual thinking. Her intuitive powers come into play and she begins to perceive relationships between shapes and the developing image. The exercise has involved her in many of the factors on our list.

The power to use analogy is strengthened by the ability to use metaphors. The metaphors can be used to help the strange become familiar and the familiar strange.

Miss Jackson looks at Sue's monster with his gaping jaws and says, "With jaws like that he would be great for cracking nuts. What should we call him?" She is using direct analogy.

"Wouldn't it be fun if he could tell us about himself? He looks like a storyteller from another time." She is trying to help Sue perceive fantasy analogies. With any luck the total artistic and verbal experience will produce a play situation in which Sue will feel free enough to move into new areas of understanding and learning.

Writing Literature

Perhaps the most effective way to develop "taste" and appreciation for literature is through providing a program in creative writing designed to encourage children to continually struggle with the conversion of ideas into words so they may communicate their moods, feelings, ideas, and emotions to other people. When a child has worked hard at putting words together to tell of a sad situation, he comes to recognize the skill of an author who does effectively what the child himself has been trying to do.

Activities Built Specifically Around Books

Activities built around books do more than acquaint children with books: they help develop values. When children see adults busily and seriously engaged in presenting a book fair, they conclude that anything that requires so much planning, time, and energy must be a worthy and important project.

When teachers allow children to devote time to adventures in literature as we have seen throughout this book, children come to realize that something happens to them which feels good and right, and they come to treasure these experiences.

We have already said that appreciation and taste can be developed through the study of various authors, such as the unit on Lois Lenski described above. Children come to know and appreciate the people who write their books through activities of this nature and often develop a taste for writing simply because they identify closely with the life style of a certain writer.

SUMMARY

Developing interest, appreciation, and taste in children's literature is an elusive act at best and is often confused with the imposition of the teacher's tastes and values on the children. Appreciation, taste, and interest are personal qualities and may differ greatly from individual to individual.

A properly conducted book fair is one activity which helps to develop interest in books. Children appreciate those activities on which they see adults placing values and which become relevant to them.

Appreciation comes from feelings within the child developed over a long period of time through meaningful encounters with many types of literature.

Taste develops after an appreciation of all books in general and is a result of a combination of factors: strong interests within a child, appeal of writing style of an author, sensitivity to psychological makeup of the child, and that which supplies escape for a child.

Appreciation and taste are not developed in children by telling them what they should like or by continually selecting for them books considered excellent by adults. They can be developed in children by: (1) the use of contrasts in the selection of teaching materials; (2) providing adventures with many types of books in the classroom; (3) developing the quality of empathy in children; (4) holding evaluative discussions of literature with children; (5) making material relevant to children; (6) developing the child's sensory experiences; (7) the development of perception; (8) the development of metaphor, simile, and analogy; (9) fostering creative writing among the children; and (10) activities designed specifically around books.

Focus on the development of these traits rather than simply on children's books can be maintained throughout the day in the total school curriculum, thereby making literature a dynamic part of life.

TO THE COLLEGE STUDENT

1. Could world history and state or national history be taught through the use of adult literature? Working in groups, select an era or a place and see if you could promote a course in college that would be taught through the use of the literature of the particular era or place. (Example: *The History of New York State Through Literature.*)

2. How many of the techniques listed here for the development of taste and appreciation of literature in children also apply to adult literature, college level?

3. The ability to draw analogies and to create metaphor and simile are indications of a creative mind. See what you can do with adaptation by writing television commercials or fractured fairy tales around some current theme of political or social interest similar to the children's work mentioned on page 342.

4. Visit a playground, a cafeteria, a movie theater, a ball diamond, a circus, or any place where groups of children are assembled. Listen carefully to their dialogue. Record some of the things they say that show their own ability to use analogy, simile, metaphor, and rhyme. Discuss how you might use these sayings in the classroom.

5. Make a list of other concepts you feel children must develop in order for them to fully develop appreciation and taste in literature, such as: vocabulary, sensitivity, a sense of humor, etc.

TO THE CLASSROOM TEACHER

1. You may be able to bring an author to your school. See the addresses on page 493.

2. Plan some lessons that will develop empathy and perception through the use of dramatics in your classroom.

3. Contact with good literature and awareness of style in literature should make children better able to write their own literature. Encourage the children to write short stories, books, plays, or poems about social studies or science topics. Keep them in a folder after the children have read them. Note as the months pass whether or not you become aware of an emergence of style in each child as he is in contact with good writing and as he writes more fluently on his own.

4. Order some of the filmstrips and phonodiscs (listed in Appendix D) from your A-V department and use them with your children. How many ways can you think of to use them creatively? Be sure to define your objectives for using each filmstrip.

5. The next time a problem arises in your classroom involving a group of children, allow them to role-play the problem and then to discuss possible solutions. Note whether or not *seeing* the problem as well as hearing it helped the children perceive the problem better and *empathize* more fully with the characters.

TO THE COLLEGE STUDENT
AND THE CLASSROOM TEACHER

1. Brainstorm as many ways as possible to develop perception through the use of science teaching. How could you make some of these transferrals to art and literature?

2. Seek out authors such as Lois Lenski and make lists of their books so you can consider how to use them in teaching units as Mrs. Galvin did in this chapter.

3. Search through the supermarket book-shelves and those in the dime stores and try to find some children's books you feel are excellent. Compare them to books you have read in connection with this book. Also seek out some you feel are terrible. If possible, purchase them and bring them to class. Note the reactions of others in your group. Can you determine the criteria of taste in the group? Did some people like the book you brought as a poor sample? Why?

4. Note the use of simile and metaphor in the poems by the children in Chapter 1 and those scattered throughout the book. All of these children did not have training to use simile and metaphor. To some children it is almost an intuitive act to use them. Study the poem on p. 288 and the one on p. 295. In one classroom the teacher had been working like Miss Cane to develop picturesque speech. In the other classroom the teacher worked with each individual, always praising but never suggesting. Can you tell by the poem whether or not metaphor and simile had been promoted among *all* children?

SELECTED BIBLIOGRAPHY

Carlson, Ruth Kearney. *Literature for Children: Enrichment Ideas.* Dubuque, Iowa: Wm. C. Brown, 1970.

DeLisi, Rita. "An Experiment in Visual Education." In *Programs of Promise: Art in the Schools,* edited by Al Hurwitz. New York: Harcourt Brace Jovanovich, 1972.

Eisner, Elliot. *Think with Me about Creativity: Ten Essays on Creativity.* Dansville, N.Y.: F. A. Owen, 1964.

Fearing, Kelly; Clyde Martin and Evelyn Beard. *Our Expanding Vision.* Austin: W. S. Benson, 1960. This is a series of which there are several titles.

Fisher, Margery. *Intent upon Reading.* New York: Watts, 1962.

Goodfriend, Ronnie Stephanie. *Power in Perception for the Young Child: A Comprehensive Program for the Development of Pre-Reading Visual Perceptual Skills.* New York: Teachers College Press, 1972.

Hochberg, Julian. *Perception.* Englewood Cliffs, N. J.: Prentice-Hall, 1964.

Holstein, B. I. "Use of Metaphor to Induce Innovative Thinking in Fourth Grade Children." *Education* 93 (1972): 56–60.

Hopkins, Lee B. *Books Are by People: Interviews with 104 Authors and Illustrators of Books for Young Children.* New York: Citation Press, 1969.

Khatena, J. "Use of Analogy in the Production of Original Verbal Images." *Journal of Creative Behavior* 6 (1972): 209–213.

Kircher, Clara S., comp. *Behavior Patterns in Children's Books.* Washington, D.C.: Catholic University of America, 1966.

Larrick, Nancy, ed. *Somebody Turned a Tap on in These Kids: Poetry and Young People Today.* New York: Delacorte, 1971.

Lewis, Richard. *Journeys: Prose by Children of the English-Speaking World.* New York: Simon and Schuster, 1969.

Massialas, Byron G., and Jack Zevin. *Creative Encounters in the Classroom: Teaching and Learning Through Discovery.* New York: John Wiley & Sons, 1967.

Mearns, Hughes. *Creative Power: The Education of Youth in the Creative Arts.* New York: Dover, 1958.

Michael, William, ed. *Teaching for Creative Endeavor: Bold New Venture.* Bloomington: Indiana University Press, 1968.

Petty, Walter T., and Mary Bowen. *Slithery Snakes and Other Aids to Children's Writing*. New York: Appleton-Century-Crofts, 1967.

Pratt-Butler, Grace K. *Let Them Write Creatively*. Columbus: Charles E. Merrill, 1973.

Smith, James A. *Adventures in Communication Language Arts Methods*. Boston: Allyn and Bacon, 1972.

Smith, James A. *Creative Teaching of the Language Arts in the Elementary School*, 2nd ed. Boston: Allyn and Bacon, 1973.

Smith, Ralph. "The Three Modes of Perception." *Instructor* (April 1969): 57–64.

Torrance, E. Paul. *Education and the Creative Potential*. Minneapolis: University of Minnesota Press, 1963.

Torrance, E. Paul. *Encouraging Creativity in the Classroom*. Dubuque, Iowa: Wm. C. Brown, 1970.

Van Witsen, Betty. *Perceptual Training Activities Handbook*. New York: Teachers College Press, 1967.

CHAPTER 13

Strategies for Adventuring in Children's Literature

A Museum Is For Living

Jerry was giving a book review. "Well," he said, "all I can say is that this is a real *cool* book."

The book in question was E. L. Konigsburg's Newbery Medal winner, *From the Mixed-Up Files of Mrs. Basil E. Frankweiler.*

"It's about a girl named Claudia, and her brother Jamie. They run away from home and go to New York and hide out in the Metropolitan Museum of Art."

"The Metropolitan Museum!" exclaimed Betsy. "Why in the world did they ever hide out in a place like that?"

"Well, Claudia was a big know-it-all, the way most sisters are, and she had read all about the Metropolitan Museum so they hid there."

"What did they do?" asked Bob.

"Well, they got all mixed up in a mystery over some statue. It was a statue they thought was made by Michelangelo, but no one could be sure."

"I saw the television show about Michelangelo," interrupted Sadie. "Boy, was he something!"

Miss Spencer, teacher in this nongraded situation, felt that the conversation at this point had given her many leads into some "teachable moments." Also, it was part of her plan that the children would visit the city museum in the near future so she thought she could capitalize on Jerry's report.

"Did any of the rest of you see the television program about Michelangelo?" she asked.

Seven of the children in the group had. "I'm going to write your names on this card and put it on the bulletin board so we can come back to this topic later after Jerry has finished his report. Perhaps you can each tell us something about Michelangelo. Now, Jerry, suppose you continue with your report."

Jerry gave an idea of the plot, told how well the book was written and that he especially enjoyed the easy way the author wrote so that he, Jerry, laughed a lot. He showed some of the illustrations from the book and recommended it to everyone. Immediately there were "takers" from the other children.

Miss Spencer had been sensitizing children to the resources available in the community where the children could go to seek information for their many units of study. Here was an excellent opportunity to explore another resource: the museum. Inasmuch as her school was located in a fairly large city with an excellent museum, Miss Spencer had planned that the children might take a trip to that museum. Some of her students had been in to New York and had already visited many famous museums there.

Miss Spencer also felt that this was an excellent opportunity for her to draw attention to other books about museums and about Michelangelo, such as Betty Cavanna's *The Mystery in the Museum*, Elizabeth Ripley's *Michelangelo*, Helen Acker's *Michelangelo Buonarroti, 1475–1564: Five Sons of Italy*, and Anne Merriman Peck's *Wings of an Eagle: The Story of Michelangelo*.

When the book reports were over, Miss Spencer said, "I'd like to go back awhile to Jerry's book report. We have been talking about resources we can use to look up information, and the museum is a wonderful place for that. Let's let Jerry begin a list for us of all the things we could find out about in a museum. Then, those of you who have been to museums can add your ideas."

A lively discussion followed from which an initial list resulted.

Help We Can Get at a Museum

We can see: paintings   filmstrips
             artifacts   sculpting
             models   inventions
             original items costumes
             mock-ups   weapons
             films   animals

We can read about: history
                    authors
                    models
                    countries
                    houses
                    cultures
                    arts and crafts

Sometimes we can see demonstrations of:
             weaving
             making flax
             furniture making
             pottery making
             dancing
             arts and crafts
             printing

Some museums have live models where you can:
        use telephones
        operate cars
        operate exhibits
        print
        dance
        make things
        take things out to your classroom and/or home

Naturally, the interest aroused in the discussion of the museums the children had seen, and the chart listing the resources, led to further discussion as to how a museum might be of help to the class in their current studies. Eventually a trip to the city museum was planned. Each child took with him a notebook of things he wanted to find out. In addition to this, various committees were going to split into small groups after a general tour to look up or view material on the topics of great interest to them in their classroom work, namely: Life in the Middle Ages, Life in Ancient Egypt, African Culture, Steam Engines and Their Uses, Michelangelo, Leonardo da Vinci, Modern Art, and Weathervanes.

The trip to the museum was a great success. By this time half the class had read *From the Mixed-Up Files of Mrs. Basil E. Frankweiler* and had come to understand and appreciate the plight of Claudia and Jamie. Some children were already writing museum stories of their own.

A bus trip to a living museum was planned later in the year when the group became interested in a study of New York state. The children arranged a trip to the Farmers' Museum in Cooperstown, New York, where they participated in making flax, milking cows, casting pots, and folk dancing. They saw early tools made, patchwork quilts being sewed, books being bound, sheep being sheared. While they were in Cooperstown, they also visited the Baseball Hall of Fame, a different type of museum.

These children developed a healthy respect and a high regard for museums, thanks to the mixed-up files of Mrs. Basil E. Frankweiler. Every child in the class eventually read the story.

Toward the end of the year, the entire school entered into a school fair, a project where each class presented to every other class something about its favorite study of the year. Inasmuch as Miss Spencer's group had enjoyed their museum trips so much and had discovered so many exciting books during their studies, they chose as their theme: *A Museum of Books.* Various children and groups of children made dioramas of scenes from their favorite books, one group presented a puppet show, bright paintings appeared all over the walls, and several short dramatizations were given. The main feature of the evening, however, was an exhibit of favorite books of the children arranged in true museum style, with the books the children had come to love arranged chronologically to best show how history could be learned through the reading of books. The first book in the exhibit, placed on a special dais, was a copy of *The History of Little Goody Two-Shoes,* written by Oliver Goldsmith and published by John Newbery, often considered the first novel ever written for children. It was an original edition copy passed along by one of the parents' fathers to his son. The last books in the exhibit were an array of the Newbery Medal books for the last five years.

Around the doors of the classroom, paper had been hung on which the children had painted the entrance to the Metropolitan Museum. A sign told the patrons that they were entering the Metropolitan Museum of Art, only it was worded this way: "Claudia and Jamie Kincaid invite you to the Metropolitan Museum of Art." The sign was painted on a violin case.

The main feature of the evening was a *slide-film* showing of *From the Mixed-Up Files of Mrs. Basil E. Frankweiler*. For this production, the children had carefully edited the story, selecting what they considered to be the main scenes. These they spoke into a tape, with a narrator and musical background tying the spoken scenes together. Conversation was used as directly as possible from the book to maintain the flavor of E. L. Konigsburg's delightful writing. After the story was on tape, the children selected various scenes and each drew a picture to go with his scene. The pictures were drawn on overhead projector transparencies with bright flo pens and showed a great deal of ingenuity. Synchronized with the sound track, they made a beautiful presentation.

With all the activity going on in the room, the children erased forever the old concept of the museum as a dull, boring place and showed instead that their concept was that *a museum is for living!*

STRATEGIES FOR ADVENTURING WITH CHILDREN'S LITERATURE

On the following pages are many strategies and techniques that teachers have employed in the creative use and creative teaching of literature. Each is presented in context, showing how some teacher was able to create a remarkable experience: an adventure. Often the ideas came from the children.

These adventures are not described with the intent that they should be copied. To copy is to violate creative thought. They are given as idea-spurring suggestions to teachers, hoping that each will fire some strand of her own imagination that will cause her to adapt, enlarge, remodel, and adjust the ideas so that she comes up with a creative product of her own.

Dramatizations

Dramatics provide an excellent strategy for children to adventure with literature. There are many forms of dramatics that can be effectively employed to develop imagination, to encourage interpretation, to develop listening and speaking skills, and to introduce new words into a child's spoken vocabulary.

Most obvious of all the ways to live literature is through dramatization, which helps the children get the feel of the characters and sense the mood of the story. Many stories and poems lend themselves well to dramatization.

From the beginning of life every human enjoys "play-acting" and imitating life around him. By mimicking life in early years, a child learns to behave like his parents and his peers. This joy of imitation is often

FIGURE 13–1. *A second-grade class engaged in dramatic play.*

squelched in children at an early age and seeks its legitimate outlet in role-playing throughout life. Children play roles in their games, in their play, and in mocking their peers. Later, when this is frowned upon, they continue to imitate in their games, in school plays, and in behaving like people they admire. High school and college students give vent to this creative drive by appearing in plays and joining dramatic clubs where they can pretend they are someone else. Often such roles provide therapy by permitting them to become someone they would like to be. Our choice of a profession or a vocation is often determined by our ability to identify with a role we see others playing that appeals to us.

We play dramatic roles every minute of every day—and the roles change considerably from hour to hour, minute to minute. A female college freshman may play the role of a campus coed from 8:00 A.M. to 9:00 A.M. She changes her costume, her behavior, and even her mode of speaking at 9:00 A.M. when she assumes the role of the student teacher. At 4:00 P.M., with school over, she returns to campus again to play the role of the student—doing her homework for the following day. At 7:00 she plays the role of the leader as she acts as chairman of a sorority committee making plans for Spring Weekend. At 8:00 her young man comes to call and she plays the role of a sweetheart. Over the weekend she acts differently when going to church than when going to a basketball game. She behaves differently as Student Council president than she does as big sister when she returns to visit her family. "All the world's a stage!"

Many terms are used to identify the use of dramatics in a child's life. A definition of each of these terms is valuable.

FREE PLAY.   Free play is a simple type of dramatic play. Children play out life situations such as a scene in the home on wash day or a ride on the school bus or whatever interests them, and they do it with no script and very simple props. Often, after reading a story to young children, the teacher will find them acting out the story of their own accord, making up dialogue and assigning parts as they go along: "You be the mother, Mary, and Billy, you be the father," and "You're coming home from work; I'm going to be the baby," and the play proceeds, one child bouncing dialogue off another. Free play is very creative because it is almost completely open-ended. Little preparation is needed for using it.

The introduction of realia such as a pair of red wings, or a basket and a red hood, may be all that is necessary for the children to launch into a dramatization of *The Little Rabbit Who Wanted Red Wings* or *Little Red Riding Hood*. Free play is spontaneous and almost totally unstructured.

PANTOMIME.   Pantomime is literally the basis for all characterization. It can become an art form of mimicry. Little children are experts at it. Any parent has only to converse with and observe his own child to see himself reflected in the child. Children copy gestures, sayings, ways of walking, wearing apparel, etc. A teacher may play a hopping record one minute and they are bunnies, and the transition is immediate when she plays galloping music and they become horses.

Pantomime serves many purposes in the elementary grades. Children can be helped to observe and listen by asking them to watch someone and then be that person. They can pantomime entire scenes and the remainder of the class can identify the situation. To improve the quality of mimicry, the teacher will want to hold a discussion after each incident. The following questions are good leads.

"How did you know Karen was Father Bear? What did she do that bears always do?"

"Who played the old lady in the scene? How did you know she was an old lady? Do old ladies always walk slowly?"

"How did Freddie make us know that the little rabbit wanted red wings?"

Pantomime can be correlated with children's literature all through the elementary school. In the middle grades it can be developed as an art form. Older children will greatly enjoy studying films of the great pantomimists such as Red Skelton and Marcel Marceau. One film, *A Fable* by Marcel Marceau, has become a classic.

DRAMATIC PLAY.   This term is also used in referring to the spontaneous play of children, generally in an adult-prepared environment. Many theories have been advanced regarding its meanings and functions. Some educators believe this to be a recapitulation of the experience of the race. Some interpret children's dramatic play as a rehearsal for the future role of the individual. Therapists and psychologists see it as a channel for growth in individual and social areas. Others see it as a means of emotional outlet— or a means by which the child works out his problems. All agree that playing out a situation is the most natural way a child learns to live in the world around him, and that permitting a child to play freely in a setting of security and acceptance is a sound way to enable him to deal satisfactorily and healthfully with the problems he faces in life. It aids in his emotional development and his social adjustment. It is essential to normal growth. Through dramatic play the child develops an empathy for others in his world.

A good kindergarten and primary-grade program makes provision for dramatic play as a technique by which children learn. Proper conditions are set for its development by providing dolls, pounding games, homemaking corners, large dollhouses, small dollhouses, a costume box, water and soap, replicas of life tools such as ironing boards, toy trucks, simple musical instruments, etc., and an out-of-doors play area. A part of the school day in all primary grades should be set aside for free dramatic play.

Hartley, Frank, and Goldenson[1] state that dramatic play serves many functions. Through this activity the child is given the opportunity to (1) imitate adults; (2) play out real-life roles in an intense way; (3) reflect relationships and experiences; (4) express pressing needs; (5) release unacceptable impulses; (6) reverse roles usually taken; (7) mirror growth; and (8) work out problems and experiences with solutions.

In many schools dramatic play is not provided for in the curriculum above kindergarten or first grade. A common belief that as children mature this "baby stuff" should be put away is, indeed, unfortunate. Dramatic play goes on in life and should be a part of the entire school program. A group of boys will play cops and robbers, Robin Hood, or King of the Castle just as ardently at the age of eleven as they played milkman at the age of four.

Dramatic play may be legitimately sustained throughout the elementary school program by role-playing the great characters of history or of children's literature, by developing creative thinking, and by the spontaneous dramatization of children's literature.

From the above description of dramatic play, we can conclude that it is one of the most natural ways of creative expression a young child has. In fact, dramatic play is proof positive that all children are born creative, because no one "teaches" a child how to dramatically play these roles— from the age of two or three, he just does it. Dramatic play is a spontaneous, natural way for children to develop their creative powers.

ROLE-PLAYING.   This term has two general meanings. First, it means acting out by the child of the sex role he or she will play in life. Studies of children's play indicate that even at the nursery school age, there are sex differences in the play of three- and four-year-olds, as children identify with adults in their society. Girls tend to play at being mothers; they cook food, play with dolls, clean the house, have tea parties, and dress up. Boys play roles of father, boat captain, baseball star, garageman. This role identification helps the child to play his or her role in society. If it is used excessively, i.e., if boys are not allowed to cook, play with dolls, etc., and girls

---

1. Ruth E. Hartley, Lawrence C. Frank, and Robert M. Goldenson, *Understanding Children's Play* (New York: Columbia University Press, 1952), pp. 27–28.

FIGURE 13–2. Role-playing: The First Thanksgiving.

are not allowed to be boat captains, less understanding of the opposite sex role is developed and some of the ability to empathize is lost. Allowing children to engage in divergent roles in their play helps to develop their creativity. Creative children are more open to life experiences and can draw on more experiences from which to create. With the changing roles of the sexes in current society, the roles children play are also changing. Second, role-playing means playing out specifically assigned roles in a dramatic scene or in a sociodrama.

DRAMATICS OR DRAMATIZATION. When dramatic play becomes structured and teacher-controlled, it becomes dramatization. In dramatization, the teacher may deliberately use scenes from life or literature to conscientiously develop some objectives she has in mind. Dramatics may be instigated by the reading of a story and may consequently be more structured than free play in that the teacher has given the children an idea for a story and they are following the general plot pattern.

Care should be taken in the selection of stories to be dramatized in the primary grades. Some stories are too structured and children have difficulty in sustaining the story line. On the other hand, stories such as *The Three Billy Goats Gruff* can be dramatized with joy because the plot is simple and much repetition takes place.

In dramatizing stories in the primary grades, the teacher will want to discuss the incidents with the children as they happened in sequence. Then a cast is chosen and the children proceed. A big box of simple props should always be on hand. Often more than one cast will want to play the story. Then a discussion such as that mentioned above should be held.

Such dramatizations contribute substantially to a child's growth in oral expression, in characterization, in ability to empathize, and in speech development. From creative dramatics children come to understand plot, characterization, and how to portray and understand feelings.

Dramatics can also mean the acting out of a play from a written script. This can be an excellent tool for the development of creativity, especially when the script is an original one written by the children. Dramatics may take many forms: puppet shows, shadow plays, pantomime, radio and television plays, choral speaking, book reports, etc. Dramatizations are generally planned to present before an audience. They may be impromptu and read off the cuff, or they may be a highly polished performance with scenery and costumes.

FREE DRAMATIZATION. Actual historical scenes, pieces of literature, events in other countries, or stories of other times and places which children love can be dramatized to help children feel the event, the time, or the place more fully. Often the entire class can take part in such "free" dramatizations with no audience, because the emphasis is on the participation and involvement of each child with the intent to develop empathy and creativity. One middle school group dramatized a Mexican Christmas, a piñata party, and a Mexican fiesta. Every child chose a role and played it to create the situation. Another group dramatized a medieval fair. Other events that lend themselves to total dramatization are: a medieval tournament, a visit to a Spanish marketplace, the election of a president, a day in Plymouth, a trip to New York, an evening around a campfire, the meeting of an Indian council, a visit to a carnival, a day at the horse races, etc. Many children's books lend themselves to total group dramatization of this nature: the Boston Tea Party in *Johnny Tremain,* the opening of *Pandora's Box* (each child who comes forth must represent some evil), the Munchkin scenes and the Wizard's scene in *The Wizard of Oz,* the scene at the French Court in *Ben and Me.*

DRAMATICS GAMES. Some games are planned around dramatizations and are excellent for use with some literature, particularly biography. *Who Am I?* is one such game. One child sits before the group and tells about himself. Once in a while he stops to act out certain parts of his life. The rest of the class guesses what character from literature he represents.

In Mr. Jones's class, one boy acted as Ben Franklin from *Ben and Me,* and told about his boyhood. He pantomimed his experimentation with the kite and his invention of the Franklin stove. This particular dramatization was so well done that Mr. Jones used it as a means of introducing *Ben and Me* to the class.

Another technique for developing individual dramatic interpretation is the *You Are There* game. Children dramatize a historical event and the rest of the class tells what it is. The Boston Tea Party, the assassination of Lincoln, the launching of a spaceship, and innumerable other events lend themselves well to this sort of treatment.

Historical fiction can be dramatized in social studies to make history more realistic and to develop creativity. Many scenes from children's novels lend themselves well to such dramatic interpretation: the landing of the Pilgrims, the signing of the Declaration of Independence, a meeting of the United Nations Security Council, the inauguration of the president, the daily life of a cowboy, a day in a colonial school, and many others.

A popular radio program of a few years back called "Minute Dramas" is appropriate for creative interpretation. An opening scene of a book is described, and the children make up and dramatize an ending with no preparation; they do it as they go along. Example: "You are at the airport waiting for a plane, and suddenly a strange man rushes up to you, clasps your hand, calls you by name, and says, 'I haven't seen you for years. It's just luck that I should see you now! I am in deep trouble and I need your help!'" Often, after the dramatization has been given, the author's ending to the story is read.

Contrived dramatizations introduce many new words into the child's oral speech. Place five unrelated objects in a bag, such as a thumbtack, a water pistol, a hair curler, a stick of gum, and a measuring cup. The class is divided into groups of five. Each group takes a bag and must construct a story using all the five objects, which they then dramatize for the rest of the class. Children enjoy making up the bags for each other.

A variation of this is to put in a bag five objects relating to a story the children have read and loved, and to ask them to guess the story, then, using the objects, to dramatize a scene from it. For example, in a bag place a parka, a picture of a wolf, a piece of fur, a plastic snowflake, and a Newbery medal taken from an old book jacket. The story is obviously *Julie of the Wolves,* the 1973 Newbery Award winner.

Most children enjoy playing fractured dramas. Instead of dramatizing stories exactly as they are written, children are encouraged to change the endings and "ham" them. Thus, in "Casey at the Bat," Casey does not strike out. Comic relief is encouraged, and children have a way to expend the wisecracks they so enjoy at this age, in a legitimate and acceptable manner.

Children are jolted into breaking away from traditional patterns of thinking in inventing new endings. The imaginative aspects of their thinking are brought into play. Creative ideation through the use of modification, minification, elaboration, substitution, and techniques mentioned in Chapter 4 is encouraged.

It is important to recognize that taking such liberties with established pieces of literature should not destroy the literature itself. It can add meaning and beauty to the writing if the children are able to catch the author's style or understand his skill through the story contrasts they invent.

Mrs. McCarthy showed us how she could use dramatics, literature, and music to develop many skills and understandings that eventually led to some creative writing by her children.

On the first day of her work with the children, she gave each child a slip of paper on which she had written a direction. Each child acted out this direction and the class guessed what it was. Some of the slips of paper read as follows:

be an Indian stalking a deer
pretend you are a cowboy setting up camp
act like the nurse to a wounded soldier

be Dr. Marcus Welby
imitate a woman shopping at the bargain basement
pretend you are a cow chewing her cud

No evaluation was given at the end of the dramatizations because Mrs. McCarthy wanted the children to be completely comfortable with themselves.

The next day she asked them to play by groups a character suggested by a piece of music. She prepared a Sousa march for one group who decided to be soldiers; the "Dance of the Sugar Plum Fairies" was played for another group who became elves and fairies. "Night on Bald Mountain" produced a witch, etc.

On each succeeding day they were to imitate a favorite character from literature or from their acquaintance. For those who could not think of a character, Mrs. McCarthy had prepared names on slips of paper in a box on her desk, and the children could choose one of these slips if they liked. The next day there were excellent interpretations of Sherlock Holmes, Davy Crockett, Daniel Boone, Amelia Earhart, Charles Lindbergh, Frankenstein, Florence Nightingale, Heidi, and others. Again musical selections were played and matched with the character.

On the following day Mrs. McCarthy began to work on the skills of dramatization by having the children choose slips of paper calling for unique interpretations and special actions to portray character. She prepared slips from which the children chose; she asked them to observe such a situation or such a character at home or on the streets, and then to dramatize it the next day. Some of these slips read as follows:

be an old man
be a shy boy
imitate a cat catching a mouse
imitate a cat lapping up milk
cry like a little baby
sit down like an old lady
run like a four-year-old
walk like a Marine

Following the dramatizations the children were encouraged to evaluate each interpretation.

After a few periods of this work, Mrs. McCarthy held a discussion with the children and asked them how many expected to go to town with their parents over the weekend. Several planned to do so. She asked them to watch people on the street and a particular person or scene that appealed to them, and to be prepared to dramatize it on Monday morning in pantomime so the rest of the class might guess what each saw. We were present in Mrs. McCarthy's room on that Monday morning and spent a delightful half-hour watching the children act out their skits. Five girls dramatized a mother taking a group picture at a Sunday family picnic. One was a little child who wouldn't stand still. Of course, the inevitable happened when he turned his head just as the mother clicked the shutter.

Four boys showed how their powers of observation were sharpened when they presented their scene. They stood in various slouching positions, leaning against the doorway, hands in pockets, bored expressions, listless actions. One tossed a coin, another twirled a watch, one scratched the ground with his toe. Suddenly they all became electrified. All eyes turned in one direction, bodies tensed, hats were shoved back on foreheads, eyes popped. All eyes and heads turned to the left and slowly swept to the right. Each boy stopped at least once in this process and let his eyes fall from eye level to the floor and up again. When all eyes and heads were finally as far to the right as possible, the boys all joined in one unanimous "wolf" whistle. They had observed a group of sailors loitering on a street corner when a pretty girl passed by.

Other dramatizations were equally imaginative and challenging. One girl imitated a Boy Scout helping an old lady across the street, and one group imitated a Sunday school teacher trying to quiet her brood.

We visited Mrs. McCarthy's room many times after that. She added voices to the dramatizations as her next step, and then music, and the creative dramatizations these children were producing were superior in every way. Many of the children were writing their own plays and musicals.

One day when we visited, a lively discussion was in progress. The children had been assigned as homework to watch Marcel Marceau, the French pantomimist, on television. They were delighted with what they had seen, and many times during the discussion a child would leap to his feet and imitate the great artist with no inhibitions at all. Mrs. McCarthy had led this group from a shy, inhibited, self-conscious one to where they could use their own bodies, uninhibited and free, to communicate creatively.

Open-ended stories provide excellent situations for creative dramatizations. The teacher reads the beginning of a story and the children are divided in groups—each group dramatizes a possible ending. Often the children are encouraged to use music to accompany their dramatizations.

These children gave many of their book reports in dramatic form. Props and scenes made for the reports were saved. At the close of the year, Mrs. McCarthy's class held a gala *Literature Drama Festival* out-of-doors in the evening. A stage was erected on the sports field with floodlights directed on it, and the scenes from the book reports were played for entertainment. Booths held literature exhibits for the parents to admire, and the children, acting as hosts and hostesses, were dressed in costumes they had made representing their favorite characters from literature.

Puppets

There are many types of puppets and many ways they can be used to develop meaningful adventures in literature, as well as meeting other objectives in the curriculum of the classroom: (1) to develop good speaking habits, (2) to foster an oral vocabulary, (3) to develop ideas in a sequence, (4) to promote creative thinking, and (5) to encourage creative writing.

Fist puppets can be made quickly. So can balloon puppets. The

FIGURE 13–3. *David and John prepare a marionette show of* The Painted Pig.

children can crouch behind a table and hold the fist or balloon puppets in view and dramatize dialogue simply and directly.

Needing some puppets in a hurry when the children asked if they might have a puppet show—"now, right away," Mr. Crane got the idea of blowing up balloons for puppet heads and drawing faces on them with flo-pens. The children cut a slit in a square of cloth through which they put the stem of the balloon so they could hold it and at the same time conceal their hands.

This turned out to be a very successful idea. Not only was the puppet show a hit, but the children became intrigued with making story characters out of balloons. Exploring the properties of balloons, they concluded that characters might blow up or disappear (bursting the balloon), or melt away (letting the air out of the balloon). This discovery set their imaginations running and soon they produced a play wherein characters blew up or melted away before their eyes.

In the spring when the annual book fair, sponsored by the entire school, was held, Mr. Crane's class volunteered to make signs for the booths from balloons. Large balloons were tied together. Faces were drawn on them with flo-pens and cloth, paper, and yarn were added to indicate the character each portrayed. The animal characters were particularly exciting.

Paper bag puppets can be made quickly and used for dramatizing stories and poems, just as Mr. Crane used the balloon puppets. Stick puppets are a little more complicated but very easy for the children to make.

FIGURE 13–4. *Paper-bag puppets made by children in an open classroom.*

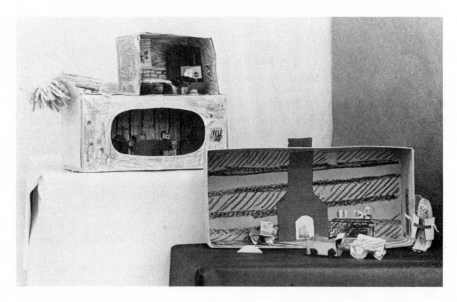

FIGURE 13–5. *Stage settings made in boxes for a variety of finger puppet shows.*

A tissue box or small shoebox makes a small theater for two children to present shows to each other or to small groups. (*See* Figure 13–5.) The tips of the fingers can have faces put on them with colored chalk, colored (washable) markers, colored pencils, or paint, or they can be made up to represent puppets.

Finger puppets can also be made with the fingers being used for legs, thus providing many opportunities for desk-top dramatizations.

Papier mâché puppets provide excellent opportunities for all sorts of dramatizations. Children may be given boxes of junk or bags of materials that might be useful in making puppets, and encouraged to make the puppet, using a variety of these materials.

Teaching children to make puppets will help them to perfect skills. The creative puppet will be the one the child invents to make a character to help him to solve a life problem with which he closely identifies.

A puppet play may be used as a projective technique to present a current classroom problem. Puppets are sometimes more appropriate for telling stories than for an actual dramatization. They are a superb device for tapping a child's creativity. Not only do they provide an opportunity for purposeful vocabulary development, but they also afford one of the best opportunities possible for developing voice control, the power of projection, and clear speech.

Children who use puppets a great deal to interpret literature soon become skilled in using them creatively.

Marionette shows and puppet shows of various kinds delight children of all ages and provide an excellent opportunity to play out beloved stories and to acquire the language of the authors.

An account of a creative adventure is presented below, showing how forcing new relationships results in creative products:

FIGURE 13–6. *Kindergarten children created a story using these stick puppets.*

Mr. Hunter's fifth grade decided to dramatize Robert Browning's "The Pied Piper of Hamelin" with marionettes. Certain production problems were discussed, and many unique ideas were offered to solve them. One problem was how to give the illusion of the Pied Piper walking down a long street with the rats following him and then, later, the same street with children following him. One child suggested that the Pied Piper go through the motions of walking while the scenery went by. The children put a sheet of shelf paper on the floor and painted houses, lamp posts, fences, trees, bushes, and shops on it. Then, using the roll-movie technique, they rolled the scene up on two dowels which they inserted through holes in the back of the puppet stage. Two boys rolled the street scene from one dowel to another while the Pied Piper walked in place. The effect delighted the children.

The same technique was later used to dramatize *The Little Engine That Could* for a second grade. The engine stayed in one place on the stage while the scenery went by. In this way, the engine was able to go up one side of the mountain and down the other.

Puppet shows sustain the quality of make-believe that permeates much of children's literature and are, therefore, very well suited to dramatizing children's stories and poems.

Felt-o-grams and Flannel Boards

Felt-o-grams and flannel boards are especially effective for stories that are developed by adding a character or two as the story progresses (such as *The Gingerbread Boy*) or for stories where there are not many scene changes but a building up of one or two scenes (such as *The Duchess Bakes a Cake*).

Stories with several scenes can be effectively depicted by tacking several layers of flannel along the top of a board and drawing a simple scene on the flannel with crayon. The pieces of flannel can then be flipped as the scenes unfold and the characters added in their logical sequence.

Many creative effects can be developed with the flannel board if children are cautioned to keep alert to find all materials that might adhere to the flannel. Colored pipe cleaners can be bent quickly into many shapes and they will stick readily to felt or flannel. Blotters will also stick to felt and flannel, and many figures and objects can easily be cut from them. Decorative materials, such as glitter or Christmas snow, also adhere to flannel and can create interesting illusions.

In telling "The Night Before Christmas," Mr. Torsey sprinkled Christmas snow over the last scene as he said, "Happy Christmas to all and to all a good night!" Mrs. Cohen used silver glitter on her flannel board to create the illusion "Sailed on a river of crystal light, into a sea of dew," from "Wynken, Blynken and Nod."

Telling stories by use of a flannel board is an excellent way for children to share words they know and to add new ones to their vocabularies. Commercial cutouts can be used for flannel board stories. Pictures from any old worn-out books provide a wealth of material if they are cut out and a small piece of flannel is pasted on the back so they will stick to the board. A new dimension in creativeness is developed, however, when children design and paint their own figures and symbols for use on the flannel board.

Flannel boards serve many purposes besides the telling of stories. Because children must *tell* about the materials they are putting on the flannel board, vocabulary may be developed in all subject areas.

LITERATURE. Miss Carmen asked her fourth-grade children to give a third dimension to their flannel board stories by making the figures and objects from construction paper and designing them so they moved or opened. In presenting the "gingerbread boy," the children found that by bending one leg of the figures, they could give them the appearance of running. They made the barn door open; the oven door opened so the little gingerbread man could be shut in; the mowers' pitchforks were separate from the mowers so they could throw them down; and a big gingerbread boy folded his arms and legs, and finally his head disappeared.

As part of a Christmas program, Mr. Fuller's fifth grade presented *The Small One* by Charles Tazewell in the following manner: The children read the story and listed the eight major scenes on the chalkboard. They then signed up for the scene on which they preferred to work. Working in committees, they first made large flannel boards of the same size by taping outing flannel over cardboard cut from towel cartons. Then each group made characters, scenes, and props to tell about its part of the story. The night of the program, the curtain opened to reveal the eight blank flannel boards resting on easels across the stage. Christmas music was playing softly in the background. A spotlight picked up a narrator standing on the side of the stage. The narrator began to tell the story and the spotlight moved to the first flannel board. Two children came forward from the back of the stage and proceeded to build their scene as the narrator told the story. Then the spotlight shifted to the second scene and down the line until, at the end of the story, the footlights were brought up, revealing a mural of the entire story across the stage. The children, grouped behind the pictures, sang a Christmas carol to end their portion of the program.

ORIGINAL FLANNEL BOARD STORIES. After the teacher has utilized the flannel board effectively with the children, creativity is evidenced in using it as a motivator for their own creative work. The ultimate goal is to have children create their own stories and use their own ideas to present them.

Making Films

Film-making is less expensive today that it was, and children can have many worthwhile experiences making a real movie and showing it to other children. Actually, making a moving picture is not much different from making a play—only much more permanent! An 8mm camera can be used with black and white or colored film. Taking movies is so simple with modern built-in viewfinders that children can be taught quickly how to do it.

Mrs. Briggs's fourth grade enjoyed reading "Hansel and Gretel" so much that they decided they would make a moving picture film of it. Mrs.

Briggs borrowed a camera for the shooting of the film. The children had raised some money for classroom activities and they used it to purchase the film.

First they adapted the story to a movie version. Then, as they had no indoor lighting equipment, they obtained some large sheets of cardboard from a box manufacturer, and on this they painted a cottage scene to set up outdoors. For the woods scene, they used the woods behind the school. They also painted, on heavy cardboard, a gingerbread house to set up in the woods.

Costumes were simple and for the most part were made from crepe paper. Props were gathered from around the school or brought from home.

A book on making movies was obtained from the library. The children learned movie-making vocabulary and talked in terms of "going out on location" or "building the set."

The cast of main characters was chosen through a discussion where criteria was established for each part; then children tried out for the parts. Voting was done in terms of the established criteria and performance.

While only a few children were chosen for the main parts, all of them took part some way. Some made titles, some painted scenes, some cared for costumes. There were scene designers, directors, camera men, editors, and a make-up crew. All the children took part in one dance, "Brother, Come and Dance with Me," which they called their "production number."

The scenes were shot in true Hollywood fashion—not in sequence

FIGURE 13–7. *Children enjoy making animated cartoons as much as they do making movies. It takes three drawings for Marcus to take one step down Mulberry Street in animation. With each step, the background mural is moved a trifle to the left.*

but whenever they were ready—providing, of course, that the weather was suitable.

After the film was developed, returned, edited, and shown, the children decided to put the songs, music, and script on a tape to go with the moving picture. Keeping track of the expenses provided some excellent arithmetic experiences.

The children showed the film at a P.T.A. meeting, where Mrs. Briggs explained the learning values that came from the work. They called this showing their "World Premiere" and advertised it as such.

These children lived this story with every fiber of their beings. Such an experience made them appreciate good stories and gave them the opportunity for many social and academic experiences.

Bulletin Boards

Bulletin boards can be exciting condition-setters for adventures with literature. They may be constructed for a variety of objectives; in the realm of children's literature some of these are:

1. Motivation to interest children in new books or poems.
2. To have the children share their writing and reading with their classmates.
3. To summarize an experience in literature.
4. To impart information.
5. To provide individual instruction or individual work for the children.
6. To share beautiful passages, phrases, or words.
7. To encourage creative writing on the part of the children.
8. To advertise or announce new books and events about books.
9. To display first editions, unusual books, or illustrations in books.

Let us see how some teachers used the bulletin board to fulfill each of these objectives.

Miss Lowe used book jackets to motivate the children to read new books in the room. She put a sign above the colorful jackets which read, "Have You Read These New Books?"

On another occasion she used riddles. She pasted on cards pictures from the book jackets and then beside them printed "Who was it that became lost in the haunted house?" or "What book in this room tells about a family that lived through a terrible hurricane?"

Miss Lowe also kept a record of the children's favorite authors. When one of these authors published a new book, she put a picture of him on the bulletin board and surrounded it with titles of his works or a book jacket, captioning the bulletin board with "A new book by Dr. Suess!"

Book catalogues were also clipped apart and used to make summary cards of books. Miss Lowe first of all used these on a bulletin board, and then in a file to guide children in selecting books that were of interest to them.

Miss Gilbert used her bulletin board to post the children's own writings. She often built the bulletin board around a theme such as, "It is snowing, and our authors have written about the snow," or "Poems for Children *by* Children."

FIGURE 13–8.   A bulletin board designed by a library committee.

Often she asked the children to choose lines of poetry or selections of prose and print them on a 5 x 8 card. Each child then painted or drew a picture to go with his selection. This material provided a great deal of interest over a long period of time.

Miss Gilbert also used some of her own favorite selections illustrated by a picture or a painting. Once she had the children fingerpaint for her, with the purpose of selecting a line of poetry to go with each painting. The next day the children found poetry of their own to match the paintings.

Bulletin boards provide motivation for editing any sort of personal writing or painting so that it will be in proper form to share with other people.

Miss Nelson used her bulletin board a great deal as a summary of experiences with literature. After her fourth grade had read Kippling's "How the Camel Got His Hump," the children built a scene of the story from cut construction paper.

Miss Nelson brought in an armful of old magazines one day. After she read them the poem, "America the Beautiful," the children went through the magazines and found pictures to illustrate the poem. These were then mounted on the bulletin board around a printed copy of the poem. On another occasion, the children drew their own pictures.

Miss Nelson used the bulletin board a great deal to integrate social studies with literature. Bulletin boards built around such topics as "Stories about Mexico," "Children in Other Lands," "Children in Trouble," Books About Living Together" helped Miss Nelson direct the children's attention to the literature dealing with the topic being studied.

When the fourth grade was studying Indians, Miss Nelson introduced the unit by reading *Songs of the Chippewa* while she played soft drum music on the record player. From this reading came a dramatization followed by questions about Indian life. This led to a bulletin board built around the questions and pictures of Indians depicting the answers.

Mr. Lowery used bulletin boards a great deal to impart information. Beside the more common uses of the bulletin board (such as posting announcements of school functions, radio and television programs worth seeing, and the like), he used it for current events, community activities and problems, and outstanding current world problems.

Often Mr. Lowery used his bulletin board to impart news about a certain author in whom the children were interested. Generally he found a picture of the author and selected interesting facts about his life to dramatize by printing and illustrating them on cards. He always made a bulletin board on the Newbery and Caldecott award-winning books.

Mr. Lowery found the bulletin board was of great value in summarizing stories. Often he wrote a summary of a book and encouraged the children to fill out the bulletin board by providing space for their book summaries on it.

When Mr. Lowery was teaching a unit, he often used the bulletin board as a reference center. Under the title "Resources for Our Unit," he would pin envelopes to the bulletin board with titles printed on them such as these: "Legends of Mexico," "Stories Written in Mexico," "Mexican Authors," "Picture Books of Mexico," "Books for Research on Mexico."

FIGURE 13–9. *Mr. Lowery's bulletin board.*

Inside the envelopes were cards on which were printed the author, title, publishing company, and publishing date of many books under each category. A sign at the bottom of the bulletin board ("Can You Add to These Packets?") encouraged the children to make a record of the books they found.

Mrs. Gaines used a bulletin board in her room to meet individual differences and as a means of providing individual instruction.

One day the children decided to make a marionnette show of *Alice in Wonderland.* The day after the show was planned, a simple set of directions for stringing a marionnette appeared on the bulletin board and below this the necessary materials for doing so. This gave the children a worthwhile independent activity to pursue when their other work was finished and freed Mrs. Gaines to work with those children who needed her most.

On another occasion, Mrs. Gaines placed step-by-step directions for binding a book on the bulletin board; she also used the board to instruct the children in the basic process of cutting a block print; and at one time she showed them how to take a book out of the library by use of the call numbers.

Mrs. Gaines used one bulletin board next to the chalkboard to meet individual differences in children's reading ability and interests. Each child was given an envelope on which to print his name. Each envelope was pinned on this bulletin board under the sign, "Here Are Some Special Books You Will Enjoy." Mrs. Gaines then made simple cards of books best suited to each child's ability and interest and dropped them into the child's envelope. All the children were encouraged to go to these envelopes when they had any free time during the day. The envelopes were also explored previous to each trip to the school library so that the children could look for definite books while they were there.

Sometimes Mrs. Gaines suggested special activities in the children's envelopes. Billy, who was a slow reader, was not only directed to read a certain book whose vocabulary was compatible with his reading level; he was also encouraged to make a picture of it for the bulletin board. And Maxine, who was reading on a grade level three years in advance of her own grade, was encouraged to read a more adult book and to write an illustrated summary of it for the bulletin board.

Many suggestions have already been given as to how to use bulletin boards to share beautiful passages, phrases, or words and as a motivation for encouraging creative writing. The teacher can readily see that bulletin boards can be made exciting by displaying original illustrations borrowed from publishing houses or by displaying first editions of great children's classics.

Mrs. Eggert selected some great paintings and tied art and literature together in various ways. One day she mounted a lovely reproduction of Winslow's "Blue Boy" on the bulletin board. Below the bulletin board she opened a book to Eugene Field's "Little Boy Blue." Then she printed beneath the picture, "An artist expressed his idea of a blue boy this way. A poet expressed his idea about Little Boy Blue this way. How would you do it?"

One day she displayed a picture from a magazine showing an icy abstraction done in shades of blue. Above it she lettered, "This picture made me think of these poems. What does it make you think of?" Around the picture she mounted such poems as Robert Frost's "Stopping by Woods on a Snowy Evening," excerpts from Lowell's "The First Snowfall," Shakespeare's "When Icicles Hang by the Wall," James Stephens's "White Fields," and Sara Teasdale's "February Twilight." Books of poems below the bulletin board on a table encouraged the children to look for other poems.

Often Mrs. Eggert found a beautiful picture from a magazine or a calendar which she saved for the bulletin board, using this caption, "List the poem this reminds you of." A cardboard of empty lines with a flo-pen attached encouraged the children to write titles under the picture.

Bulletin boards can be very creative and helpful in setting conditions for the enjoyment of literature. To be creative they must be ingenious, fresh, and interesting so as to provide an outlet for creative expression much as a painting or a clay modeling will. Here are a few suggestions that should be considered in making bulletin boards that place no restrictions on the creator.

The overall effect of the completed bulletin board should be as good in design and as pleasing to the eye as a painting. Too much material can make bulletin boards confusing and cluttered.

Any lettering should be as much a part of the total design as the other material on the bulletin board. It should not be tacked on as an afterthought.

Bulletin boards are more attractive if material is grouped according to related ideas rather than simply spread out in any manner. Rest spaces for the eye help the purpose of the bulletin board to become more apparent.

Every bulletin board should be centered around an idea or purpose, and that idea or purpose should be outstanding enough both to be immediately recognizable and to be conveyed across the room. The main idea should attract the children so that they are drawn to the bulletin board to read or see the subtopics. Importance can be obtained for the outstanding idea by having it larger in size, brighter in color, or more prominently placed than any other idea on the bulletin board.

Many commercial companies distribute beautiful material that is excellent for bulletin board use and is supplied free of charge to the teacher. These materials tie in with the children's literature appearing in basal reading books but are used as advertising and available to all. A Scott, Foresman poster is made up of all the characters of classic stories of children's literature with the question over them "Who Are Your Storybook Friends?" Under each character is the key word that ties in with the reading program such as *giant, fairy, bear,* etc. Children enjoy identifying these characters. The posters can be cut up after they have served their initial purpose and used for other purposes. Miss Jarvis used the colorful pictures as covers of booklets by pasting them on construction paper. The children then filed their stories appropriately in each booklet after they were typed on a primary typewriter by a student aid from the high school child care program. Bill's craze for giant stories filled the giant book very quickly. Miss Jarvis kept this material on a special shelf in the reading center, under a bulletin board that said, "Stories for children by children."

These class-made books were read by the children more than any others in the classroom.

Another poster published by the same company is divided into nine sections and in each is a drawing presenting a scene from a good piece of literature accompanied by a selection from the text. The poster reads, *Can You Solve This Mystery?* In one corner of the poster is a list of authors and a list of titles to help the students. The idea is to match the correct title, quote, picture, and author.

Miss Barnes made a contest of this poster by announcing to the children that she was going to place a puzzle poster on the bulletin board on the following day, and ditto sheets below the bulletin board on which each child could attempt to match the pictures and prose selections with the authors and titles. The ones who were able to do this correctly were to have the honor of selecting quotations from other pieces of literature the class had shared, drawing a picture to accompany the illustrations and plotting a bulletin board of their own.

Teachers can often develop the habit of studying advertising materials of this nature and putting them to creative use.

Scott, Foresman and Company also offers a 17″ × 22″ poster of folk-tale heroes suitable for use in designing an exciting bulletin board.[2]

Teachers who feel that children spend too much time watching television or reading comic books may well use these activities for clues to the preferences of subject matter for these children. They may then expose children to books having similar content or to those with characteristics similar to the comic book. These include the use of pictures, short easy dialogue, humor, adventure, etc. Mrs. Johnson went so far as to set up a bulletin board of "Comic Book Stories" and on the table beneath put out books such as the following for her mixed-age group:

Horton Hatches the Egg, Dr. Seuss
Did I Ever Tell You How Lucky You Are? Dr. Seuss
Curious George, H. A. Rey
Uncle Ben's Whale, Walter D. Edmonds
King Grisley-Beard, Maurice Sendak
Mr. Popper's Penguins, Richard and Florence Atwater
The Day the Circus Came to Town, Glen Rounds
Georgie, Robert Bright
Frog on His Own, Mercer Meyer (a wordless book)
The Horse Who Lived Upstairs, Phyllis McGinley
Little Toot on the Mississippi, Hardie Gramatky
Honk the Moose, Phil Strong
What's the Matter with Wakefield?, June Lewis Shore
Andy and the Lion, James Daugherty
Andy Says Bonjour, Pat Diska and Chris Jenkyns
Alphonse, That Bearded One, Natalie Savage Carlson
A Bear Named Paddington, Michael Bond
The Biggest Bear, Lynd Ward
The Five Chinese Brothers, Claire Hucket Bishop
Lentil, Robert McCloskey
Slappy Hooper, the Wonderful Sign Painter, Bontemps and Conroy

---

2. Scott, Foresman and Company, 1900 East Lake Avenue, Glenview, Illinois.

Another bulletin board was covered with book jackets, with this caption overhead, "Adventures That Beat the Comics." On the table beneath the bulletin board were the following books:

The High King, Lloyd Alexander
Blind Colt, Glen Rounds
Lord Rex, David McKee
Calico, the Wonder Horse, Virginia Lee Burton
Three Jovial Huntsmen, Susan Jeffers
A Pony Called Lightning, Miriam E. Mason
Clarence and the Burglar, Patricia Lauber
Buffalo Bill, Ingri and Edgar Parin d'Aulaire
Have Spacesuit, Will Travel, Robert A. Heinlein
Custer's Last Stand, Quentin Reynolds
Chicken Soup with Rice, Maurice Sendak
The Matchlock Gun, Walter E. Edmonds
Pugwash in the Pacific, John Ryan
Strange Island, Marian Boyd Havighurst
Why Cowboys Sing in Texas, Legrand
King Basil's Birthday, Miriam Young
Duffy and the Devil, Harve and Margot Zemach
Deenie, Judy Blume
Flash Flood at Hollow Creek, Marjorie Paradis
Nobody's Family Is Going to Change, Louise Fitzhugh
Jasmine, Roger Duvoisin
Everyone Knows What a Dragon Looks Like, Jay Williams

Book Reports

There are many ways of giving book reports so that they are creative and challenging to children. Too often books are read for the primary purpose of making a report on Book Report Day, which makes the literature secondary. Book reports assigned in this manner often make a child hate a book. If he has liked the book, he will *want* to tell others about it! The inventive teacher will find many ways to encourage the child to tell about his book.

Miss Wagner organized her class into a Book Club that met from one to two o'clock every Friday. Each Friday morning the members of the class were divided into five groups. Then the children took their weekly trip to the library, where, in addition to other books, each child chose one book he wanted to read for fun and brought it back to the classroom.

During Book Club time the groups met around five tables, and for the first five minutes everyone looked at the books each child chose for fun reading. Then each group selected one book and a child to read it to them. The five groups sat at different places in the room where a story was read to them. After half an hour they discussed whether they wanted to report on their book to the rest of the class. If they did, they decided on interesting ways in which they might present the book and selected one. During the following week they had time to prepare their report.

The last fifteen minutes of each Book Club meeting was spent in the presentation of one group's report. Thelma's group read *The Five Chinese Brothers,* and with Miss Wagner's help they gave the following presentation:

The six girls on the committee made flowers for their hair from colored facial tissues. They made their eyes look oriental with an eyebrow pencil. Then each made a picture of one of the Chinese brothers, accenting his unique feature—such as the legs that stretched or the neck that could not be cut off. These pictures were made on wrapping paper so they rolled up easily. Each girl brought an oriental Hallowe'en costume from home or a kimono or house coat.

At the beginning of the presentation, the children played the record "The March of the Siamese Children." Then Thelma tiptoed into the room and stood before the group. The five other girls minced in behind her, holding their rolled-up pictures, and stood in a row behind Thelma. Thelma bowed deeply to Miss Wagner. "Honorable Teacher," she said. Then she bowed to the class, "And Honorable Classmates," she added, "I would tell you a story about five Chinese brothers. Now each brother had something very strange about him. One had a neck that could not be cut off." At this line, Becky tiptoed to the front of the improvised stage and let her picture unroll. Each character was introduced in this way.

After this, Thelma invited the class to read the book to find out what happened to them, and the six Chinese sisters minced out of the room while Miss Wagner turned off the record player.

Bill and Sid gave their book report by using a flannel board. It worked out very well for *Robinson Crusoe*, because new characters and objects could be added to develop the scene as they went along.

A group of five boys gave scenes from *Treasure Island* by using a sheet with a light behind it to make a shadow graph. Scenery was made by simply tearing or cutting shapes from wrapping paper and pinning them to the sheet so that the shadow made a setting. Another group chose different scenes from their story and pasted them in sequence on shelf paper, thus making a roll movie.

Projects such as these not only arouse children's creative thinking, but serve the additional objective of making literature live.

Box Theaters

Box theaters provide another form of dramatization that can be adapted to many different uses in presenting children's literature. Box theaters are actually dioramas with some sort of movement added. Sometimes the movement comes simply from slits in the bottom of the box through which stick figures make their appearance on the stage. Larger box theaters can be used with hand puppets.

One group of children, who were studying magnets, used a box with a thin cardboard bottom and made their characters move about the stage through the use of magnets. This was done by making cardboard figures and inserting a paper clip in the base that held each figure upright. The powerful magnet, when touched to the cardboard floor, attracted the paper clip. By moving the magnet about on the underside of the floor, the figures in the box theater moved about also. To stop them in a particular place, the magnet was simply pulled away from the cardboard floor. One group of children used this technique very effectively in dramatizing *Hans*

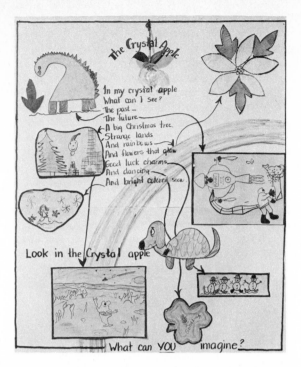

FIGURE 13–10. Creative work motivated by The Crystal Apple *by Beverly Brodsky McDermott.*

Brinker and the Silver Skates, where the magnet was especially effective in making the skaters glide.

Box theaters can be adapted to finger puppets or simple marionettes, or to using commercial figures effectively. They are particularly effective if the teacher wants to depict a scene or a story without too much preparation. In presenting the poem "Wynken, Blynken and Nod," Miss Carey used a box theater and made the wooden shoe sail about the sky simply by making a cardboard shoe and fastening it on a thin dowel with a tack. The dowel was left protruding from the back of the box; a slit was cut there so that Miss Carey could grasp the dowel, and, by moving it in the slit, could give the illusion of a wooden shoe sailing the skies. She also used this simple idea to present "The Duel." The gingham dog and the calico cat could really fight when she moved the dowels protruding from the back of the box theater. With this simple device, trains and cars can move, ships can rock, Jack can climb the beanstalk, and Humpty Dumpty can fall.

Box theaters are effective for giving book reports, for use at school exhibits, and for sharing books read at home.

The Book Fair

A book fair makes possible the use of the strategies suggested in this chapter. Many purposeful objectives can be accomplished through a book fair. An account of an excellent one is given in Chapter 16.

SUMMARY

Many strategies may be used by the teacher to develop an appreciation and understanding of literature in children and to develop their creative ability. Among these are the use of dramatizations, puppets and marionettes, Felt-o-grams and flannel boards, film production, bulletin boards, book reports, box theaters, and book fairs. These strategies can be the basis of a program in literature that helps the teacher meet many of her objectives creatively in the subject-matter areas of the curriculum.

TO THE COLLEGE STUDENT

1. Select some of the types of dramatizations suggested in this chapter and demonstrate each before your college class, making an application to children's or adult literature.

2. Divide the class into groups and allow each group to identify a strategy with which it would like to work. Choose a children's story or book liked by each member of the group and plan a presentation that captures both the theme and the style of the author. Using the chosen strategy, present your book to an audience of children if possible. Note their reactions to your presentation. If feasible, work out some type of evaluation with the children.

3. In Appendix D is a list of filmstrips that have been made of children's books. Some have records that accompany the filmstrips and use the voice of a good storyteller. Get some of these from your learning resource center. Is this technique of telling children stories as effective as having the teacher read them to the class? What are some of the advantages and disadvantages of such a medium? Can you think of creative ways to use these filmstrips and records with children?

4. After your class has had the opportunity to demonstrate strategies as suggested in 2 above, read one children's book of high standards together and then test your creativity by seeing the variety of ways you can present the idea of the book using *one* medium. Divide the class into groups as before and have each group try to capture the theme and style of the author through the construction of an unusual bulletin board. Display them to each other.

TO THE CLASSROOM TEACHER

1. Take any piece of literature with which you are now working and plan a project around it, using one or more of the strategies suggested in this chapter. Use the ideas of the children to make it as creative as you can.

2. Which of the strategies mentioned in this chapter can you apply to adventuring in poetry?

3. Which of the strategies mentioned in this chapter are especially adaptable to individual learning?

4. Devise a plan whereby your students work in groups, each group with a different strategy.

TO THE COLLEGE STUDENT
AND THE CLASSROOM TEACHER

1. Demonstrate the concept of creative dramatics to each other. Divide the class into groups and have each group work out a plan for presenting a creative dramatization; i.e., one that puts them in a situation where they must come up with the solu-

tion to a problem by forcing relationships among unrelated things.

Example: Collect a variety of hats and distribute them to the group (a Boy Scout hat, a cap, a scuba diver's helmet, a top hat, a bonnet, a cook's hat, etc.). Each person is to assume the characteristics of the person who would wear such a hat. The dramatization comes in when the group is challenged to present a play showing how all these characters might come together in a rational situation.

After each group has presented its play, discuss how each technique or situation might be applied to a situation with children's literature.

2. Take the "minute drama" suggested on p. 358 and choose some members of the class to act out an ending. How can this technique be applied to adventuring in literature?

3. Brainstorm all the ways you can think of, other than those mentioned in this chapter, to use bulletin boards for building an interest in children's literature.

4. Notice the many ways children have found to present *The Five Chinese Brothers* in this book. Brainstorm other ways to present this well-loved story.

SELECTED BIBLIOGRAPHY

Anderson, Paul. *Flannelboard Stories for Primary Grades.* Minneapolis: T. S. Dennison, 1962.

Atlea, Mary. *Turning Children on Through Creative Writing.* Buffalo: D. O. K. Publishers, 1974.

Batchelder, Marjorie. *The Puppet Theater Handbook.* New York: Harper & Row, 1956.

Batchelder, Marjorie H., and Virginia Comer. *Puppets and Plays: A Creative Approach.* New York: Harper & Row, 1947.

Burger, Isabel B. *Creative Play Acting: Learning Through Drama,* 2nd ed. New York: Ronald Press, 1966.

Burrows, Alvina T.; June D. Ferebee; Doris C. Jackson; and Dorothy O. Saunders. *They All Want to Write: Written English in the Elementary Schools,* 3rd ed. Englewood Cliffs, N.J.: Prentice-Hall, 1964.

Carlson, Bernice Wells. *Let's Pretend It Happened to You.* New York: Abingdon, 1973.

Carlson, Ruth Kearney. *Literature for Children: Enrichment Ideas.* Dubuque, Iowa: Wm. C. Brown, 1970.

Chambers, Dewey W. *Story Telling and Creative Drama.* Dubuque, Iowa: Wm. C. Brown, 1970.

Coody, Betty. *Using Literature with Young Children.* Dubuque, Iowa: Wm. C. Brown, 1973.

Crosscup, Richard. *Children and Dramatics.* New York: Charles Scribner's Sons, 1966.

Cullinan, B. C. "Teaching Literature to Children, 1966–1972." *English Teacher* (November 1972).

Cullum, Albert. *Push Back the Desks.* New York: Citation Press, 1968.

Cullum, Albert. *Shake Hands with Shakespeare. Eight Plays for Elementary Schools.* New York: Citation Press, 1968.

Cullum, Albert. *Greek Tears and Roman Laughter: Ten Tragedies and Five Comedies for Schools.* New York: Citation Press, 1970.

Cullum, Albert. *Aesop in the Afternoon.* New York: Citation Press, 1971.

Decker, Isabelle M. *100 Novel Ways with Book Reports.* New York: Citation Press, 1969.

Engler, Larry, and Carol Fijan. *Making Puppets Come Alive. Methods of Learning and Teaching Hand Puppetry.* New York: Taplinger, 1973.

Fitzgerald, Burdette S. *World Tales for Creative Dramatics and Storytelling.* Englewood Cliffs, N.J.: Prentice-Hall, 1962.

Jacobs, Leland B., ed. *Using Literature with Young Children.* New York: Teachers College Press, 1965.

McCaslin, Nellie. *Creative Dramatics in the Classroom,* 2nd ed. New York: David McKay, 1974.

Newkircher, Mary Beatrice. *Classroom Activities for Literature and Reading.* Buffalo: D. O. K. Publishers, 1973.

Phillips, Ward H., and John O'Lague. *Successful Bulletin Boards*. Dansville, N.Y.: F. W. Owen, 1966.

Platts, Mary E., Sr.; Rose Marguerite; and Esther Shumaker. *Spice: Suggested Activities to Motivate the Teaching of the Language Arts*. Benton Harbor, Mich.: Educational Service, 1960.

Shaftel, Fannie, and George Shaftel. *Role-Playing for Social Values: Decision Making in the Social Studies*. Englewood Cliffs, N.J.: Prentice-Hall, 1967.

Siks, Gertrude. *Creative Dramatics: An Art for Children*. New York: Harper & Row, 1958.

Siks, Gertrude. *Children's Literature for Dramatizations: An Anthology*. New York: Harper & Row, 1964.

Stewig, John Warren. *Spontaneous Drama: A Language Art*. Columbus: Charles E. Merrill, 1973.

Tiedt, Iris M., ed. *Drama in Your Classroom*. Champaign, Ill.: National Council of Teachers of English, 1974.

Whitehead, Robert. *Children's Literature: Strategies of Teaching*. Englewood Cliffs, N.J.: Prentice-Hall, 1968.

Williams, Helen V. *Puppets Go to School*. Philadelphia: Winston, 1955.

Woods, Margaret. *Creative Dramatics*. Washington, D.C.: American Association of Elementary, Kindergarten, Nursery Education, 1967.

Woods, Margaret. *Creative Experiences for the Young Child*. Buffalo: D. O. K. Publishers, 1974.

Woods, Margaret, and Beryl Trithart. *Guidelines to Creative Dramatics*. Buffalo: D. O. K. Publishers, 1970.

CHAPTER 14

More Adventures in Books

Once Upon A Time

"Once upon a time," says the teacher, and all faces turn in her direction. Books fall to desks, pencils are put away, easels are deserted, and little by little a pool of children forms at her feet.

This is the power of words. Children are easily motivated to hear a story, that is, unless the teacher flubs it.

For storytelling is an art. It is not enough for the teacher to simply recount the events of a story she has read. To be a storyteller worthy of the attention of the children, she must become skilled at it. She "flubs" it when the following behavior is observed: children play with other things in their hands, their eyes leave the face of the teacher frequently, they begin to whisper or to touch each other, horseplay develops among them, they appear listless or inattentive, or they wander away from the storytelling group.

Telling stories and reading them are two different processes. Some stories need to be read to be effective, but many stories are more effective when told.

When the teacher *tells* a story, something different happens from when she *reads* it. When read, the book is the focus of attention for both teacher and children; but when a story is told, the focus of attention is the teacher's face. Her voice inflections, her expression, her degree of animation, and her own enthusiasm play the major part in putting the story across. The art of storytelling has almost become lost. It is due for a revival. Children gain something unique and special from this kind of experience with literature.

Adventures through Telling Stories

In telling stories the teacher need not memorize them; this often makes for a stilted and wooden performance. She needs to know the story well, with the logical sequence of events carefully organized in her mind. Even more important than this, she should repeat the words, lines, or phrases that give the story its personality and charm—and repeat them in exactly the right places.

Because folktales have always been passed along from mouth to mouth, they lend themselves particularly well to telling. Such stories as "Henny Penny," "The Man Who Kept House," "The Gingerbread Boy," "East of the Sun and West of the Moon," and "The Princess of the Glass Hill" are especially suitable for telling. Legends and fairy tales fall into the same category.

Perhaps the main criterion for choosing a story to tell or to read is: Does it appeal to those emotions that are true and desirable in childhood: humor, compassion, a love for adventure, a desire for courage, joyfulness, a sense of congeniality and good fellowship, happiness, love, a sense of comfort, and a fresh imagination?

Proper physical conditions should be considered in storytelling. All distractions should be removed. Children should probably sit facing the quietest wall in the classroom. The teacher should stand if children are seated—at any rate she must be easily seen. Her own voice must be sure and clear. Her face must show the animation and expression necessary to project the story as well as the mode or feeling of the words. She must see herself as the author, telling the story directly to the audience for whom it was written.

Storytelling becomes highly personal in that it is person-to-person, with no barriers or distractions. It is communication in its most elementary and most beautiful form. The great literature of the past was all passed along this way before man could read and write. All children should experience the joy of hearing their teachers tell stories, since this is the way young children will communicate at home before *they* can read and write. Storytelling is an art children should be encouraged to keep through their lives, and teachers can set conditions for this art to develop in their classrooms.

If the teacher has been accustomed to reading stories, she will find a whole new experience in the telling of stories. She may gain the needed confidence to begin by remembering that she has been a storyteller practically all her life: when she tells the children about the flat tire on her car, she is telling a story. Because this was a natural occurrence in which she was completely involved, she tells the story well. She can think of the things she does to put across such "stories" and apply them to the stories of others when she reads them.

She must enjoy the story herself. The animation of face in expression and sparkle helps the children to know that she has a "good one to tell today!"

Every art has its own special tools for expression. In storytelling it is a pleasing voice and an appreciation of and ability to use words. Often this skill can be greatly enhanced by learning phrases from the story itself as mentioned above. Sometimes this skill can be developed by using the style of the author in the voice as the story is told. If the author uses jingling sentences, tell the story with jingling sentences. If he uses short, clipped sentences, as in Hope Newell's *The Little Old Woman Who Used*

Her Head, the flavor of the story will be greatly retained if it is told in short, clipped sentences.

It is a good idea to check on the effectiveness of style as well as the pleasantness of voice by turning on the tape recorder occasionally while a story is being told and listening to it later on. Nothing spoils a story more than the use of run-on sentences, the overuse of the word "and" to connect sentences, and the lack of proper inflection in the voice. Criteria to look for in listening to one's voice are: (1) Is it well modulated—not pitched too high or too thin and yet not too low so that it mumbles? (2) Does it project well, that is, are all parts of the sentences heard, or are parts regularly lost so that listeners must strain to hear? (3) Does the voice seem flexible, that is, does it have an easy flow and rhythm with a variety of intonations? Can the teacher go from one tone (when the papa bear speaks) to another tone easily (when the baby bear speaks)? (4) Is there good breath control so that the voice is not monotonous or the sentences or ideas broken up unrealistically? (5) Is the vocabulary within the range of the listeners? Too many words outside the realm of the listeners' experience can cause children to lose the logic and trend of the story and thus lose interest.

Simple breathing exercises, some attention to sentence structure, and practice in speaking vowels and words on the out-thrust of the breath will add clarity and strength to the voice and will enhance the speaker's ability to project.

Dramatic effect is important in telling a story. With little children these effects can be exaggerated with voice and facial expression. As children become older, however, they often ridicule exaggeration. The voice carries the drama of the story more than facial expression.

PREPARING A STORY. To prepare herself to tell stories, a teacher may think of a story as it is told in a picture book fashion although she will, of course, have no pictures to show. A teacher must SEE a story to bring it to life. She will plan it as a series of events, picture by picture, so each child, through the magic of words, eventually has a picture painted in his own imagination. She will allow a sufficient number of words for description so the characters become clear, the places are established, and the events are logical, each contributing to a climax. She will allot enough time in the narration so characters and events are formed clearly in the images of the children.

Then she will read the story over and attempt to capture the style as suggested above, by memorizing short, colorful, tongue-tickling lines or by adopting the style of the author. To memorize the entire story is impossible and unnecessary, but to memorize simple phrases is possible and often enjoyable.

Timing is important in telling a story. Many stories require a slow, even, easy tempo. Others should be told quickly, almost in a staccato tongue. Still others start off leisurely and then, as the action grows, become more and more hurried in tempo. The type of story should help the teacher in determining its tempo and the teacher should check to be sure variances in tempo genuinely add to the zest of the storytelling.

Timing from the standpoint of *when* a teacher tells a story is also an important factor to consider. A humorous story goes over better when the class is in a happy mood. It would be poor judgment on the teacher's part to tell or read a hilarious story after some child had come crying to school to tell that his grandmother had died. The teacher must be the judge of timing. Often a story can reshape the atmosphere of a classroom and relieve strain or tension. In one classroom where one of the authors recently visited, there had been a small school fire. The entire school had been emptied with a fire drill. When the children returned to the classroom, there were many drawn faces and signs of anxiety among the children.

Miss Martin, the teacher, relieved some of the anxiety by encouraging the children to talk about the fire. She encouraged them to explore their feelings about it. She herself admitted to being scared. She congratulated the children on their ability to conduct themselves so well under the circumstances. She told them they had displayed courage. And she said, "I know a wonderful story about a girl who displayed courage, and I would like to tell it to you." By the time she had finished the story, the fire was a thing of the past and the tension in the room had been relieved.

The best stories for telling are those with a single idea or plot, a short introduction, a logical, clear development, and an obvious climax followed quickly by an ending. Stories having universal appeal are told most successfully, especially if they are told in simple language.

Master storytellers can now be heard on recordings. Teachers can learn a great deal about the art of storytelling by listening to records made by Ruth Tooze, Gudrun Thorne-Thomsen, Ruth Sawyer, and Marie Shedlock. Children will greatly enjoy these records because of the masterful way the storyteller tells the story, but teachers will learn a great deal about storytelling if they will listen to the records with the above criteria in mind. See Chapter 17 for lists of other storytelling records.

VARIATIONS OF READING AND TELLING STORIES. Since literature often creates a mood, teachers should be conscious of the mood or "tone" of stories and should set conditions for the full enjoyment of these stories.

Some, such as ghost or mystery stories, are effectively told with the lights out in the classroom and the shades drawn. One candle burning on a table in the center or at the front of the room often lends additional mystery to the situation.

Some stories are told more effectively against a background of soft music. This is especially true of poetry, which lends itself to mood very well. Interesting combinations of voice and music can be developed, both when the teacher reads to the children and when they read to each other.

Sound effects sometimes enhance the feeling of a poem or story. A music box makes an excellent background for reading Dorothy Baruch's "The Merry-Go-Round." The teacher can work with a child who might add sound effects as she reads a mystery story—a creaking door, a loud bang, the sound of footsteps, a dripping faucet. Some commercial recordings are excellent for providing "sound" introductions to stories or sound effects during the story.

The children's positions also can be used to develop a mood for a story. Some stories are best felt when children put their heads down on their desks and close their eyes; others lend themselves to reading or telling while children are stretched out on the floor ready for a mid-morning nap. Some stories are best told when the children are grouped at the feet of the teachers, others when they are seated at their desks.

The weather may help decide the mood of a story. Foggy days help set the mood for certain poems, just as rainy days, snowy days, and sunny days do for others.

In all instances, the teacher should take advantage of every possible opportunity to set the appropriate physical conditions for presenting literature to children. Often the initial association a child has with a story or poem determines at once whether he enjoys it and whether it will bear repeating. Every attempt should be made to re-create the author's mood when he wrote the selection. If a similar mood is experienced by the child, the message is communicated. Children come to understand the importance of using the right word in the right place. They get to the heart of the selection so that it becomes an emotional, as well as an intellectual, experience for them.

Adventuring through Reading Stories

Both telling and reading stories have a place in presenting good literature to children. Some stories, poems, and plays are written in such a way that to tell them would be to spoil them. This is especially true of books where the script rhymes or where especially beautiful words are used to set a specific tone for the story. Dr. Seuss's rhyming books need to be read (unless the teacher can memorize the script). Robert McCloskey's *Time of Wonder* is a book that needs to be read because of the way this particular author uses the soft sounds of "s" and "c" to give the impression of the softness of fog and rain, and the way he uses other sounds to develop an audio atmosphere for his story.

Other books should be read because of the close relationship between the story and the pictures. Many primary books are written in such a way that the pictures help tell the story. McCloskey's *Blueberries for Sal* and *Make Way for Ducklings* are good examples of such books. When books of this nature are read, it is essential that the teacher set proper physical conditions so that all children can easily see the pictures.

Adventuring through the Use of Artifacts and Realia

Certain stories provide teachers with clues for motivating children. Often artifacts can be collected or created and used strategically to excite children about a story or a book, or to clarify passages and concepts within the selection.

Mr. Evans put a pole in a bucket of sand. On the top of the pole he placed a pirate flag. As the children entered the room, they were very curious as to why the flag was there. At school opening, Mr. Evans introduced *Treasure Island*.

Mrs. Carl bought a tiny plastic doll in the dime store and put it in a jar of Jello one evening. When the Jello had set she capped the jar with the doll suspended in it. On the outside of the jar she put a sticker which said "Sugarplum." Then she took it to school and put it in a conspicuous place on her desk. The children were whipped into a frenzy of curiosity

FIGURE 14–1. *Children's drawings of their favorite stories give clues to the types of stories they like.*

by the doll in the Jello. Mrs. Carl later introduced the book *Sugarplum* by Johanna Johnson. *Sugarplum* is a story about a careless little girl who is always losing her tiny, tiny doll. Once it fell behind the dresser and even went inside the vacuum cleaner, but someone is always finding it. The story reaches a climax when "Sugarplum," the doll, falls inside a jar of homemade jelly. No one sees her, and Mother hurriedly places the tops on the jars and puts them down cellar. Sugarplum is all alone down there. She can see out through the glass but no one comes until a long time later, when Susie's mother brings her up so Susie, who is sick, can have some jelly. When Susie's mother discovers Sugarplum in the jelly, she goes upstairs with her still in the jar and tells Susie she can have "Sugarplum" jelly. A happy reunion—and Susie is always careful with her now. Of course, the book became a favorite in Mrs. Carl's room.

Artifacts brought home from trips can often serve as a way to introduce a story. Dolls are especially valuable for this use. Sometimes action can take place along with the telling of a story. Miss Mace had a cute little crow puppet she had picked up at the dime store. Using a measuring cup partly filled with water and some marbles, she told the Aesop's fable of "The Crow and the Pitcher" by having the crow puppet try to drink from a low water level. She then added marbles one by one to raise the level of the water so he could drink. This proved to be an excellent introduction to the telling of fables. Miss Mace noticed the children telling themselves the story later in the day while they manipulated the crow puppet and the marbles.

A pile of old caps on a plastic wig holder can excite interest in Slobodkina's *Caps for Sale;* a stuffed animal or play toy can be used to introduce many stories, such as Daugherty's *Andy and the Lion.* A little wooden doll is a natural for a Margery Williams Bianco's *Little Wooden Doll,* and a box of fluffy candy marshmallow chickens spread out on a table will suffice to get children interested in d'Aulaire's *Don't Count Your Chicks.*

Realia can be used most effectively for arousing an interest in specific pieces of literature.

One of our student teachers had a father who enjoyed wood carving and making models. One of his most beautiful products was a miniature Conestoga wagon, complete in every detail. Debbie used this model in motivating the children to reading Western poetry.

She placed the model before the class under a box so they could not see it when they came into the room. Debbie planned to launch into a unit on the westward movement so she was using this activity to set the stage for the studies of the West.

While the children were working on an arithmetic work sheet, she slipped into the teacher's office adjoining the classroom and put on a cowboy hat, a holster, and a half-face mask. Sticking her head around the corner, she said, "O.K., you fifth graders, this is a stick-up for your imagination!" Of course, the children reacted with delight and surprise. Before they could comment, she pulled off the mask and said, "Boys and girls, I really want you to use your imagination today—and we'll begin by showing you what I have here under this box. My father used his imagination in making this."

She took the cover off the model of the covered wagon. The children gathered around while they all talked about it and carefully examined each part and how it was made. Debbie skillfully led the conversation from the model to the real thing, and every item in the covered wagon was discussed. The children were interested in learning why each thing was selected to make the journey across the plains. Many told what they had learned from moving pictures they had seen.

Finally, Debbie had them all sit on the floor around her, and she told them she wanted them to *imagine* they were going west in the wagon. First, she said, they would need a family, so she introduced a chart on which she had lettered the names of the family in the poem. Then she read "Western Wagons" by Rosemary and Stephen Vincent Benet.

The children reacted to the poem in an exciting manner. They discussed the content of the poem and the style of the writers. They picked out selections that gave them the feeling of rolling wagons by the manner in which the words were put together.

When they had talked themselves out, Debbie said, "There is one thing about this covered wagon you do not know. It has a secret compartment." She showed them a concealed section under the floor in the rear of the wagon. "Now, in this secret place the family kept its treasures— jewelry, money, or precious keepsakes. In that secret compartment right now I see some slips of paper. I wonder what they are."

Each child was allowed to draw a small folded piece of paper from the secret compartment. On each was an assignment the children were to do. Some were to work in groups and some alone. Most of the assign-

FIGURE 14–2. *Realia can motivate children to read stories. This arrange-*
ment before the classroom aroused curiosity in many children to read
A Teacup Full of Roses *by Sharon Bell Mathais.*

ments were of the type that encouraged children to write a story, poem, or idea about a specific topic taken from the poem and draw a picture to go with it. Later the poems and stories were shared with the pictures by placing them on a bulletin board.

Debbie had written the following as her objectives for the afternoon. Through the effective use of a model, she had accomplished her goals.

As a result of this lesson the children will: (1) Be acquainted with the poem "Western Wagons" by Rosemary and Stephen Vincent Benet; (2) have an opportunity to follow directions; (3) have an opportunity to do some creative thinking in terms of drawing or creative writing; (4) have an experience in oral expression in reading their stories or showing their pictures to each other; and (5) understand how a series of photographs can be put together to form a short story.

Adventuring with Sound Stories

Sound stories can be used as good listening devices and for developing a good oral vocabulary. Many commercial stories lend themselves to becoming good sound stories, such as *Gerald McBoing-Boing, The Tiger Hunt,* and *The Sound Book* (Margaret Wise Brown).

Often the teacher can set up a beginning situation to create a sound story, and the children can take it from there. Putting such stories on tape contributes to their enjoyment, because children hear the total effect better in the play-back than they do while making up the story.

A sound story must be one that can have sounds added to it in much the same way a "round robin" story has words added to it. Think of noisy situations to get your clue: a visit to a factory, the circus, the carnival, a state or county fair, a living room with TV set, radio, hi-fi, and people talking, or a busy store. Start a plot by having a main character enter this situation, and add to the plot by adding sounds as the plot develops. Then the children in the room add the noises until the whole story reaches a climax.

Reading charts in the lower grades can also provide some interesting material for creative oral work. If the teacher keeps an eye on the charts that children construct, she will often find one that lends itself well to choral speaking. Or she will find many charts that are suitable for making a "sound" story.

Miss Kennedy's first grade had visited a farm. From this experience she had built her first reading experience chart. This was how it went:

THE FARM

We went to the farm
We saw cows
We saw ducks
We saw pigs
We saw horses
We had fun.

On the day after the children had written the chart, Miss Kennedy said, "Boys and girls, after we read about our trip to the farm today, I would like to make a new story from it." Some of the children read the story, and then Miss Kennedy showed the children a card bearing the word "heard."

"This is a new word," she said. "It says heard. If we can learn this one new word, we can write a whole new story." The children then found the word in various places around the room where Miss Kennedy had concealed it. Miss Kennedy had also put the sentences of the story on strips of tag board so the children could reconstruct the story in the pocket chart.

After the story was reconstructed, Miss Kennedy said, "Now, let's see if we can change our story by changing one word." She then put the word "heard" over the word "saw" on each line of the chart where it appeared. The children read the story. Miss Kennedy then said, "Now let's make our sound story. What did we hear the cows say?" The children answered "Moo-moo." Miss Kennedy completed the story this way:

THE FARM

We went to the farm.
We heard cows.
They said, "Moo-Moo."
We heard ducks.
They said, "Quack-Quack."
We heard pigs.
They said, "Oink-Oink."
We heard horses.
They said, "Neigh-Neigh."
We had fun.

The chart was then made into a sound story.

Sound stories may also be used in upper grades. At the end of this text, there is a sound story written by one of the authors for an intermediate-grade group. "The Day of the Bubble," was read to a group of children, and they were then asked to write letters to the author and to react to the story, identify the ages to which it would have greatest appeal, and to then illustrate the part of the story they enjoyed.

Following are some of the letters received from the children:

Brewerton Elementary
Brewerton, New York 13029
November 7, 1974

Dear Mr. Smith,

I really enjoyed your story, "The Day of the Bubble." It was really funny. I liked the part when the bubble picked up old Miss Annie Jones. I also liked the part when the bubble picked up the milk cart. I think kids of all ages will like your story.
I was really happy to meet you because I'm going to be a writer when I grow up, so I was really excited when I met you.
Come and visit us again soon.
Good luck with your story.

Sincerely yours,
Gina Ortola

Brewerton Elementary
Brewerton, N.Y. 13029
November 7, 1974

Dear Mr. Smith,

I really enjoyed your story. I especially liked the part about the sticky mess. That was my favorite.
When you take your story to the publishers, they'll flip it's so good! People will buy it by the thousands!
Your story will probably be liked best by the kids from 3rd to 6th grades. They'll love it!
I'm sending a picture to go with your story. I hope you like it.
You are the first writer I have ever met. I'm glad you visited us. I hope you will come again. Thank you for letting us read, "The Day of The Bubble."

Your Friend,
Karen Vrooman

After receiving such encouraging letters from the children, Mr. Smith again visited the Brewerton Elementary School and made "The Day of the Bubble" into a sound story, using the children's ideas. Some of the pictures drawn by the children also appear at the end of this book. We felt that the teacher might want to use the story and the pictures with her class, and it would be easier to use them if they were placed at the end of the book.

FIGURE 14–3. A picture drawn by two middle graders for the sound story, The Day of the Bubble.

Using Finger Plays

In the primary grades particularly, finger plays provide an excellent opportunity for children to use words orally. Certain work with finger plays can be very creative, especially when the teachers and children write their own.

A sample finger play is included here to illustrate how teachers and children may communicate when they repeat the poems and perform the action of finger plays.

Five little snowmen happy and gay	All fingers up.
The first one said, "What a beautiful day!"	Thumb rigid while others slouch.
The second one said, "We'll never have tears."	First finger rigid while others slouch.
The third one said, "We'll stay here for years."	Third finger up.
The fourth one said "What will happen in May?"	Fourth finger up.
The fifth one said, "We will all melt away!"	Fifth finger up. Then all curl slowly into a fist.

Children can be asked to search for stories that can be made into finger plays. One such story is "Ten Little Indians."

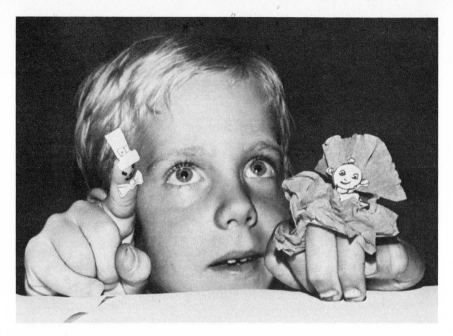

FIGURE 14–4. Two types of finger puppets: One walks and one talks.

Murals

Literature can be expressed very well in mural painting. Tempera paint, cut-out construction paper, and colored chalk lend themselves well to the creation of brightly colored murals for the classroom, the school corridors, or the school library.

Murals can grow out of the telling of one story or poem, or they may be a composite of many of the works of literature the children have read.

Mural-making may be the motivation for art work also. Mr. Harrison taped a long piece of mural paper over the chalkboard along the side of his classroom one day. Then he said to the children, "In the center of this paper I am going to draw a crossroads with this colored chalk. This is where four roads meet. It is Banbury Cross. Remember how all the people came to Banbury Cross to see the fine lady ride on the fine horse? Now each of you will take a section of the paper, and we will chalk in all the people, the animals, the houses, the trees—everything, but with everyone running to Banbury Cross. Let's see how many different ideas we can get and how well you can connect your work with your neighbor's." The result was delightful.

Later Mr. Harrison had his children do a similar mural on "The Pied Piper of Hamelin" with all the children headed for one end of the mural where one student had drawn a river.

Another teacher in Mr. Harrison's school used his idea to make a Christmas mural with all the people and animals heading to the manger.

Murals may be developed like this to convey impressions, or they can be carefully planned in order to express more lasting ideas. Variations of mural-making may be obtained when children make them three-

FIGURE 14–5. The Shape of Me and Other Stuff *by Dr. Seuss led this second grade to an exploration of shapes.*

dimensional. Pieces of discarded cloth can be pasted on for clothing; green burlap can represent grass; yarn can be glued on for wires; corrugated cardboard, flannel, and novelty papers can represent house fronts; cereal can represent bricks or pavement blocks, and so on.

Murals can be used for scenery in puppet shows. Large murals painted on big sheets of cardboard cut from mattress boxes or obtained from box companies make excellent backgrounds for the enactment of plays at assembly programs, especially when the cardboards are taped together with wide masking tape and can be folded like an accordion as the play progresses.

Games

Certain games, such as charades, lend themselves to developing an interest in literature. Children can act out the titles of books while the rest of the class tries to guess what each is. Games such as "Who Am I?" or "What Am I?" also lend themselves to descriptive word usage.

Often the games that children play regularly in gym periods can be adapted to a game dramatization. Bombardment is an excellent game to play along with the reading of *The Adventures of Robin Hood* or "The Charge of the Light Brigade."

One game many children like is "telephone conversation," in which they tell about a book over a toy telephone and the class must guess the book.

Of course, in the primary grades imitative rhythms can be readily applied to the stories the children read. They hop like Peter Rabbit, strut like Paul Bunyan, chug like the Little Engine, and generally pantomime the characters they love.

A physical education teacher will have many suggestions as to how games may be adapted to literature in such a way that children "live" it.

Contacts with Authors

Nothing is more thrilling for a child than to become acquainted with an author through his writings and then to correspond with that author or, what is even more exciting, to see him. Teachers can develop a great love for literature and for reading by writing to live poets and authors or by influencing a local organization to bring one to visit the children during Book Week or any appropriate time. Writers of children's books love children—and are most gracious with them. Acquaintance with these fine people is a constructive and inspiring experience for children.

Consideration for authors is essential, however. If they are to get on with the task of writing good books, they will have little time to answer thousands of letters from children. Consequently, the children's correspondence should be limited to their reactions to the books they read, with possibly some pictures representing their interpretation of the book. Children should be told of the busy lives of authors so they will not expect answers to all their letters. Adults should limit their correspondence to authors to business purposes.

Dioramas

Dioramas serve the purpose of providing children with a three-dimensional picture of the images created in their minds by the stories and poems they read. Similar to a shadow box in construction, the diorama provides an opportunity for the creative use of materials in group or individual projects. They can be made from cardboard cartons or can be constructed as a real art form with heavy cardboard and wood.

Dioramas are especially effective at book fairs and exhibits. A series of them can show scenes from several stories or poems or several scenes from the same story. Sometimes dioramas can be made in various forms to add uniqueness to an exhibit.

Each child in Mr. Rogers's sixth grade made a small diorama. The children worked in groups and built three or four scenes for each of several stories. They then framed their dioramas by cutting poster board in the shape of an open book. A hole the same size as the diorama was cut in the open book so that the resulting effect was a three-dimensional picture on one page of the open book. On the page facing the diorama was the name of the book, the author, and the passage that best described the diorama.

Later in the year, Mr. Rogers's group tried to depict various moods with the creative use of materials in dioramas. One group of children made the locked-up room in *Great Expectations*. They created the illusion of the old, dusty wedding table by spraying a table set with miniature dishes with Christmas snow. Across the front of the box they used string to suggest cobwebs. Old strips from plastic bags cut with ragged edges hung from the ceiling like cobwebs and dust.

Another group depicted *McElligot's Pool* by painting the inside of their box to resemble water and suspending the fish and undersea animals on strings from the top of the diorama to give the illusion of swimming. Across the front they pasted pale blue cellophane to complete the impression of an underwater scene.

Teachers can set conditions for the creative interpretation of children's literature through dioramas by discussing the stories and poems that the children read and by emphasizing the mood or feeling of the poem as much as the story. The teacher can help children see the relationships between available materials and the mood or scene they are trying to depict. Patty's teacher suggested clothespins for bedsteads in the scene from *Peter Pan.* She also suggested that facial tissues be used to make miniature pillows. Once Patty caught on to this type of thinking, she suggested making a three-dimensional fireplace with crumpled cellophane behind it. Patty then cut a hole in the box so light came through the cellophane, giving the appearance of a lighted fireplace. It was also Patty's idea to poke holes in the box outside the window so that the light would represent stars. After Patty added Tinkerbell on a string before the fireplace, she hung a real little bell behind the fireplace which could be tinkled by pulling on a string. Thus Patty added color and sound to her diorama. From discussions of the use of materials, teachers can help children find creative ways of making dioramas both realistic and attractive.

FIGURE 14–6. Diorama and finger puppet show, setting for Rosalie and the Nutshell Kids *by Maurice Sendak.*

Displays and Exhibits

Displays and exhibits can help children develop a love of books. Many schools have Book Fairs during Book Week when all the grades display the creations they have made that relate to good children's books. Often, assembly programs are given to stimulate an interest in stories and poems. Exhibits of commercial books, original sketches for various books, and bulletin boards of the authors and their lives can add a great deal of interest to such an exhibit. To make the exhibit even more meaningful and "live," films may be scheduled at various times. Many schools invite an author to be present to tell stories or to sketch for the children.

Commercial publishing houses will supply catalogues for such exhibits. Children should have the opportunity to handle books and help select those to be purchased for the school library. Good children's magazines and periodicals should constitute a portion of book exhibits.

Often the neighborhood library advertises a children's book exhibit. School personnel should take advantage of these exhibits by taking children on excursions to see them.

The value of displays and exhibits is enhanced when children have a part in setting them up. This involves careful planning, however. Haphazard exhibits are often so confusing that they become ineffective. Material should be grouped topically, by authors or by reading level. When tables are used, they should be elevated at the back in some way so that all books are readily exposed to view and some are not hidden behind others. Books that are to be handled should be on tables low enough for the children to see them easily. Often a theme for the exhibit (such as "A Book Is Like a Ship" or "Adventures Through Books") makes it possible to organize the exhibit more logically and interestingly.

Although a large exhibit once a year is a worthy activity for any school, smaller exhibits and displays should be used constantly. The school library should always have displays of new books and bulletin boards which excite an interest in reading. A showcase near the main entrance of the school building can provide notice of the new books in the library as well as develop an interest in a special gem recently acquired. Such a showcase or bulletin board can also keep children informed of the worthwhile television shows built around children's literature. It can draw attention to fine films in town based on great writing. The showcase can be used to announce unusual events, such as the Book Fair, special noon-hour film showings, and current neighborhood library displays. Such announcements and displays create even more interest among children when they have had a part in creating them.

Peg Board Displays

Peg board is invaluable in the modern classroom. With the variety of hooks, metal pockets, and bars manufactured for the peg board, the teacher is able to display three-dimensional objects very effectively as part of her bulletin board display. The books themselves can be placed in the pockets; through the use of the adjustable wires, they can be displayed open to selected passages. Pegs help to hold pictures in place. Bars make

FIGURE 14–7. Gail Rock's Thanksgiving Treasure *inspired this display.*

it possible to construct simple shelves where clay modeling or other three-dimensional objects may be displayed. Peg board is very adaptable to many uses and purposes, especially in the promotion of children's literature.

Filmstrips and Recordings

Numerous commercial materials are available today that present literature from many interesting viewpoints and can be of great assistance to the classroom teacher in developing a sensitivity to literature. Many of these materials are designed for high school pupils, others for elementary school pupils.

A teacher who feels she needs some background in modern literature herself can derive a great deal of pleasure from spending an evening with some of the materials designed for the upper grades or high school. These materials will not only supply knowledge and enrichment for her own background, but will suggest many techniques for using literature in her own classroom.

Warren Schloot Company publishes material of this nature. A recent set of two color filmstrips, a recording, and teacher's guide is called *Poetry: Commitment and Alienation.* The pictures and accompanying records explore a poet's attitude toward God and how his feeling about God and the world affects his writing. Some poets have achieved forms of commitment not dependent on God. These commitments show in the poets' work. Poets examined in this set include: Auden, Yeats, Cummings, Ginsberg, Donne, Spender, and others.

Another set of filmstrips and recordings is called *Chinese Poetry* and is usable, in part at least, in the elementary grades. It, too, comes with a teacher's guide.

An excellent background record and filmstrip set is *American Writers: Themes and Images*. One set of films deals with Walt Whitman's works, another with Thoreau. Some sets deal with the development of one poem and capture the essence of the author's work with beautiful photography such as the one on Marcel Proust.

Social issues are also discussed through the writings of famous men in some of these filmstrips. One impressive one deals with man's place in society and comes to grips with such questions as: Is he free? What is man?, etc. It is called *Free Will and Utopias* and discusses how Freud, Skinner, Plato, Orwell, and others face such questions. Listening to and viewing this set will give the teacher some viewpoints for discussion in her elementary social studies lessons.

Other companies publish the record-filmstrip combinations and deal with children's literature directly. In Chapter 17, "Resources for the Classroom Teacher," a list of such companies is given, as well as a selected list of records and filmstrips suitable for teaching literature in the elementary school.

Kits are currently available that include colored crayons and pens which may be used to draw directly on film that is made to pass through a filmstrip machine. Each frame is marked to indicate the confines of each picture. Children can plan a sequence of pictures in the same manner as they play a scroll movie and roll them through the filmstrip machine. A sound track may be added by making a tape similar to the account given on page 112 of the making of the sound track for *John J. Plenty and Fiddler Dan*. Such an activity is an excellent exercise in sequence development and can result in some very unusual and creative programs in literature.

Choral Speaking

Both poems and many prose selections lend themselves well to choral-speaking exercises. Choral speaking can enrich the enjoyment of literature by giving the teacher a method of using the words of the author in beautiful and varied ways. It can often be used with many of the activities for promoting children's literature that have already been mentioned in this chapter. Choral speaking provides an excellent background for shadow plays, puppet shows, and pantomime. Probably no other device is as effective in enriching a child's oral vocabulary.

A few years ago choral speaking fell into disrepute because of the way it was used. The purpose of using choral speaking becomes negated when teachers begin to rely on books that give selections to be spoken and the parts are all assigned to various rows, groups, and individuals. When tense and strict drill develops, which is supposed to result in a highly polished choral masterpiece, little value to the children results. When used properly, choral speaking can be a very creative way to set conditions for good vocabulary development.

Choral speaking becomes creative when the children identify closely with a passage, decide to use it for choral-speaking purposes, and then proceed to work out an effective pattern by which to recite it. Even more creative is the group that makes up its own passages and poems to be set to choral-speaking rhythms.

Choral speaking is especially effective because *all* children become involved. *All* children need to say words in order to acquire them, so they may be used later in their creative writing, reading, and spelling. The shy child who rarely volunteers in a class discussion can enter into a choral-speaking exercise with all the poise and security of the confident child. All children learn new words, because the words are spoken in meaningful context. Choral speaking must be conducted in a relaxed, happy atmosphere where the product becomes secondary to the process. The learning comes in the doing and not in the end result. Often the children will be so pleased with a passage they have created that they will want to perform for someone else. In this case, time should be spent in "polishing it up." Most choral speaking should be carried on for the joy of using words in rhythmical patterns, much the way singing is.

Many teachers begin choral speaking by using material the children already know. Then they branch out by introducing unfamiliar material. Next they help the children write their own material.

Here are some ways teachers have begun choral work:

1. Select a poem with precise rhythm, allow the children to tap the rhythm, and then say the poem to the rhythm.
2. Choose poems that *must* be walked or dramatized to be effective, such as "The Merry-Go-Round" by Dorothy Baruch. Part of the class chants the poem while a group in the front of the room become the horses, working out various ways of going up and down like a merry-go-round.
3. Nursery rhymes are always good for establishing the idea of using words to rhythms. They can be used on any age level. The teacher will want to branch out soon, however, or children will consider the material tiresome or babyish.

Mr. Howard used a technique that the children enjoyed very much. Each Friday morning the children chose membership in a specific group and appointed a chairman. As part of their library trip on that morning, the chairman was to find a poem that each group could work into a choral presentation. On Friday afternoon the groups met and worked out their choral patterns. After half an hour, the groups presented their work to each other. Often the whole group decided to tape some of the presentations. After a while the class had a whole tape of interesting poems to listen to.

Another way to provoke creative thinking with choral speaking is to give the children a poem suitable for many adaptations, allowing them to explore various ways of presenting it. Here again is an opportunity for several groups to be working at one time and then share ideas after each has worked out its pattern for presentation.

Booklets

All kinds of booklets can be made as a result of experiences in children's literature. These range from simple booklets containing book reports and illustrations to very highly developed scrapbooks of collections of all kinds.

Bookbinding can be taught to children so that they can make their own scrapbooks or booklets. Attractive covers dealing with themes built around their favorite characters will enhance the value of these booklets. Booklets and scrapbooks can contain many interesting materials relating to children's literature:

Clippings about children's books
Written book reports
Children's illustrations of favorite books
Autographs of authors
Catalogues and brochures collected at exhibits and book fairs
Children's original poems and stories
Records of books children have read
Book lists for children
Book jacket collections
Magazine or newspaper articles about children's authors or children's books
Copies of programs from book fairs, assemblies, and exhibits
Dittoed material given to children by the teacher, such as Caldecott and Newbery Medal winners, books listed under certain topics, and reference materials
Copies of favorite selections from literature
Clippings of TV shows, moving pictures, and recordings made around children's literature
Copies of letters written to various places for materials (catalogues, book lists, and such)

What little girl
  with a bright red hood
Went for a walk
  in the dark, shady wood?

a

What little girl
  with a bright red hood
Went for a walk
  in the dark, shady wood?

b

FIGURE 14–8a, b. Children enjoy pop-up and novelty books and like to make those with surprises on their pages.

Radio and Television Programs

Many children have the opportunity of putting on a live television or radio performance. But too often the "showy" aspects of a school program are exploited in such presentations. Children's literature could be used much more than it is for these programs. This would not only help educate parent viewers as to good literature for children but would motivate child viewers to watch better television shows. Simple or elaborate props can be used for such programs. It is important for the teacher to remember that it is the beauty of the words that makes good literature, so the author's words should be used as much as possible. Many of the suggestions in this chapter are well suited to television programming: choral speaking, puppet shows, shadow plays, dramatizations, reading with music, dance interpretations, pantomimes, book reports, displays and exhibits, dioramas, interviews with authors, flannel boards, pictorial maps, and impersonations.

It is well to remember that although most of this material should grow out of regular classroom work, the class is justified in striving for a polished performance when it is to be presented before the public.

Many children in Miss Thompson's room had become extremely interested in a television show dealing with E.S.P. Their before-school discussions overheard by Miss Thompson helped her to choose two books to share with them: Madeleine L'Engle's *A Wrinkle in Time* and *A Wind in the Door*. The books were a smashing success.

Roll Movies

Roll movies can be an excellent way to introduce stories and poems, to develop the sequence of a story, or to utilize the author's language to translate words into visual imagery.

Miss Fry's class made a roll movie of trees as a result of reading *A Tree Is Nice*. Almost all stories lend themselves to roll movies, which provide a fine opportunity for children to express themselves creatively in a group project.

Shadow Boxes

A large shallow box can be made into a shadow box that will serve as a focal point for arousing interest in good literature in the classroom. The front of the box can be cut out, leaving a frame. It is then painted and hung on the wall. Because of its depth, three-dimensional objects may be displayed in a variety of ways to obtain many interesting effects. A feeling of greater depth may be obtained by painting heavy cardboards to represent various aspects of a scene and placing them one behind the other. Sometimes lights (the Christmas tree variety) can be added to gain more realistic effects.

Miss Arnold's fourth grade made an interesting shadow box of "A Visit from St. Nicholas." They poked holes in the back of the shadow box to allow light to come through to represent stars. The back of the box

FIGURE 14–9. *Children put finishing touches on a scroll movie of* Island of the Blue Dolphins *by Scott O'Dell.*

was then painted a deep blue. Near the bottom, about one-half inch from the back of the box, they set cardboard mountains covered with snow. In front of this they set a cardboard row of fir trees covered with snow. Along the very front of the box they made flat cardboard houses, with windows cut out and covered with tissue paper. Using a string of Christmas tree lights, they set some blue lights before the trees and mountains, and some colored lights behind the windows of the cardboard houses. To top off their scene, they cut out a cardboard Santa and reindeer and suspended them on threads between the top of the box and the houses, giving the illusion of a Santa flying before a star-studded sky.

Shadow boxes can provoke a great deal of interest in poems and stories, and they can provide rich creative activity when the children themselves make them. Often they can serve as a place to put an exciting or colorful object—a lovely arrangement of driftwood and flowers, a place to suspend two or three lighted Japanese lanterns, a coveted shrine to exhibit an artistic madonna, or a center where objects to be seen and not touched are displayed.

Peep Shows

As a variation from the diorama, Mr. John's children became interested in peep shows. This activity not only gave the children an opportunity to make a scene about their favorite book, but also gave them a chance to experiment with color.

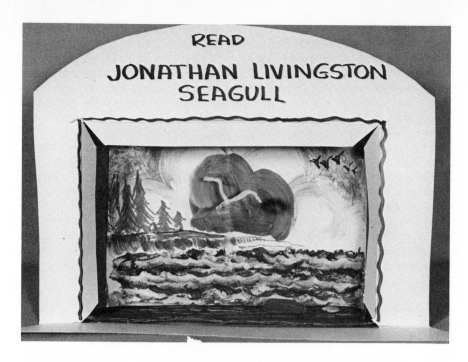

FIGURE 14–10. *A child's diorama of* Jonathan Livingston Seagull *by Richard Bach.*

To make peep shows, a small round hole is cut in the small end of a shoe box through which the children can peek with one eye. To give the illusion of depth, a background sky or wall is painted at the other end of the box on the inside. Then, with pieces of cardboard, the scene is built much like a stage setting is built to show depth. Maryann, for instance, wanted to show a scene from *Heidi.* On the back of her box she made a sky into which she daubed a few white clouds with a sponge. She then cut a mountain range from cardboard and painted snow on the peaks. This she glued in the box about an inch in front of the sky. About an inch in front of the mountain range, she painted a row of smaller mountains. She then made some hills on which she painted the Grandfather's hut. Before this she glued in a strip of green, rolling foothills. Then, on the flat surface of the box she made a little cardboard church to give the illusion of the village square. Two little figures, the old Grandfather and Heidi, were going into the church. The illusion was one of great depth as the children pressed their eyes against the peephole, for they saw the village square with the foothills rising behind it and the tall mountains rising behind the foothills, all in three dimensions. To heighten the illusion, before the top of the shoe box was put over the scene, several long rectangular flaps were cut in it and left fastened on one side so they could be pried up with a fingernail. Over the three openings in her box, Maryann glued a piece of blue cellophane near the back of the box, red cellophane in the middle, and yellow over the slit near the peephole. By opening the slits, the illusion of sunlight on the square was obtained. Blue light over the mountains gave the illusion of dark foreboding or evening. The red in the middle gave the illusion of sunset.

Maryann was a highly creative child. After showing delight over the various effects she was able to get by opening combinations of flaps in her peep show, she attacked the back of her shoe box and cut some flaps in it near the bottom of the box. Over the holes she pasted more colored cellophane. At the top of the box she punched some tiny holes with the point of her scissors. Now when the children looked through the peephole, they could see stars in the sky over the mountains—actually the outside light shining through the little holes Maryann had punched. All her flaps in the back were cut below the mountain line so that when she opened the blue one, the illusion in the box was of evening. Then she opened a red flap and the light flooded the box from behind the mountains, looking for all the world like an early morning sunrise. Opening the yellow flap gave the illusion of daybreak in the Alps. Maryann had made an exciting discovery that resulted in stimulating all the children to experiment with lighting effects in their peep shows.

Field Trips

One teacher took her class to Elmira, New York, to visit Mark Twain's grave. An account of the trip and the impressions it made is best told by one of the compositions written by a boy in the classroom:

MARK TWAIN

In Elmira there are a lot of interesting things about Mark Twain.

The first place which I visited was Mark Twain's studio. To get there you drove or walked up a dirt road. After going about a mile you come to a big parking lot. To get to the studio from there you have to climb an old trail up the hill. Just before you get to the studio you have to go up some rickety stairs. The studio is eight-sided. Inside, there is a fireplace, a desk and two chairs. The studio was locked when I was there. The view from the place where the studio is is just what a writer would want.

The studio looks down upon Elmira which is in a valley. There are mountains in a distance. Through Elmira flows the Chemung River, and from the studio the river is real pretty with all its bridges.

There is one thing in Elmira that is in no other town, that is Mark Twain's grave. Mark Twain's grave is in Woodlawn. There is a big monument at the head of his grave. Right beside his grave is his wife's and graves of some of the others of the family.

Shadow Plays

Shadow plays provide another excellent way to introduce words into the child's oral vocabulary. Here are some ways shadow plays may be used.

Hang a sheet before the room. Place a bright light behind it. Children can make simple scenery by using cardboard to create shadows or simply by cutting newspaper and pinning it to the sheet to make shadows. Turn out the light to change the scenery. Be sure the children perform close to the sheet so that they will make clear-cut shadows.

Take a large carton such as a paper towel carton, and cut a hole in it to represent a stage. Tape a piece of sheeting or unbleached muslin over the hole. Put a bright light behind the carton. Using the towel carton stage, encourage children to cut out cardboard figures and tape them to long wires. Wire coat hangers, when pulled straight, are excellent for this purpose. These figures can then be pressed against the muslin to create shadows without the operator's shadow showing. The operator must sit or stand behind the light that creates the shadow.

Figures can also be cut from cardboard with a tab on the bottom so that they may be operated from beneath the carton simply by putting a slit in the back of the carton and pushing the figures up onto the screen, then moving them about by manipulating the tab.

A simple way to make scenery for this type of shadow box is to paint the scene with thick tempera paint or black flo-pen onto a heavy-grade Saran wrap. The scene can then be pressed firmly against the muslin and it will stick. When the light is turned on, the paint or flo-pen ink casts a shadow, making a fixed scene against which the movable figures can act. This technique provides an easy way to change the scenery quickly.

FIGURE 14–11. *Three middle schoolers constructed this shadow theater and the hand (put together with paper fasteners). Each finger was jointed to a stick so the boys could then make each figure move to demonstrate finger plays.*

Another way to make an effective shadow play is to hang a sheet before the class but far enough from the wall of the room so that rear view projection may be provided by the overhead projector. Place the overhead projector along the wall so it casts a square of light large enough to fill the sheet. Effective shadow scenery can be made by cutting small objects such as trees, houses, porches, pillars, etc., from chipboard or cardboard and simply laying them on the lighted surface of the overhead projector. (See the opening story of Chapter 2.) The shadows can be brought sharply into focus to create the illusion of the intended scene. Characters play the scene standing near the sheet, casting sharp shadows so the illusion continues. Exciting effects may be obtained by adding colored cellophane to change the lighting or by adding moving color to create psychedelic effects. The best part of the whole thing is that the scenery can be changed simply by turning out the overhead light, removing the cardboard, and setting up the next scene.

One group of middle school students who were very fond of the illustrations in *A Story, A Story* by Gail E. Haley were able to capture the color and excitement of the book illustrations by using colored cellophane in cutting scenic backgrounds and cardboard figures to make shadows to represent the main characters. The story was narrated on a tape recorder with an appropriate musical background and shown at a school assembly program.

Lap Stories

"Lap stories" are fun for all age levels. Instead of telling a story some day, the teacher sits down in the middle of a group where all can see and holds a simple piece of wall board on her lap. With a few props, she tells or retells a story by acting it out on her lap board. The one way a lap story differs from any other storytelling is that the teacher gets the children involved in telling it. Here is a description of how Miss Issacs, a first grade teacher, used a lap story.

Miss Issacs was retelling the story of the "The Three Billy Goats Gruff." She used the following props:

blue construction paper
green construction paper
brown construction paper
a small jewelry box that had contained a bracelet
four balls of soft clay

This is how the story developed:

"Today I thought it would be fun to let you help me tell one of our favorite stories a new way. We haven't heard "The Three Billy Goats Gruff" in a long time, so I thought we might enjoy that one again. Billy, Marjery, and Peter, you take the ball of clay and each make me a billy goat. Peter has the small ball of clay, so his will be the little billy goat. Marjery has the middle-sized ball of clay, so hers will be the middle-sized billy goat. And Billy's will be the big billy goat. Henry, you take this ball of clay and make me a funny old troll.

"Now, while these people are making our characters for us, will the rest of you look at my lap and we'll make the scene. What will we need in our scene?"

"The river," said Mickey.

"All right," said Miss Issacs. "You tear this piece of blue paper so it will go across this board to make a river. Now, what else will we need?"

"A green field," said Joe.

"Well, then, you tear this piece of green paper to make a nice green field on this side of the river. Now what kind of a field is on the other side of the river?"

"One where the grass is nearly gone," said Susan.

"Susan, you put this brownish-colored paper on the other side of the river to show the worn-out field. Now, there is something else we need."

"The bridge!"

"Yes, and I wondered if this little box might not make a good bridge."

The children agreed it would as the teacher put the box in place.

"So, our scene is ready," said Miss Issacs. "How are we coming with the goats and the troll? Oh, those are fine; I guess now we are ready for our story. Let's put the troll under the bridge, Henry. Peter, Marjery, and Bill, you put the three billy goats in the old worn-out field, and I guess we're ready. Once there were three billy goats . . ."

And Miss Issacs began the story, allowing the children to tell as much as possible while she manipulated the figures on her lap.

Miss Issacs's ultimate goal was, of course, to encourage the children to tell lap stories of their own and prepare the props for them.

Lap stories can vary from the simple to the complex. Nursery

FIGURE 14–12.   Preparing a tabletop story for a primary-grade presentation.

school and kindergarten teachers can begin with the simplest forms—a candle in a candle holder and a doll or cardboard image of Jack, for "Jack Be Nimble." Almost all the nursery rhymes lend themselves to lap stories; then there are "The Gingerbread Boy," "The Three Little Pigs," "The Three Bears," "The Three Little Kittens," and "Henny Penny."

In the third and fourth grades, children enjoy doing "Hansel and Gretel," "Snow White and the Seven Dwarfs," "Peter and the Wolf," "Jack and the Beanstalk," and "Rapunzel."

Older children can do more elaborate lap stories, working in committees with each child doing a different scene. Some stories appropriate for lap stories on this level are:

> *Robinson Crusoe*
> *The King's Stilts*
> *Homer Price*
> Paul Bunyan stories
> Scenes from *Robin Hood*
> Scenes from *Treasure Island*
> Scenes from *Little Women*
> *The Golden Goose*
> *The Wind in the Willows*
> *The Tar Baby*
> *The Pied Piper of Hamelin*

Lap stories also provide an excellent device for giving book reviews.

Pictorial Maps

Picture maps serve many purposes in helping to develop a love for literature.

Mr. Jones's sixth grade made a large outline map of the United States. In each state they located the authors about whom they studied as a class during the year.

Miss Young's fifth grade made individual maps of each state and of other countries and drew in pictures that best symbolized the places in the stories they read as a class.

The children in Mr. Barrett's third grade made a small book of every book they read by folding a piece of construction paper and printing the title and author on the front page and their own names on the inside page. These were then pasted on a large outline map over the state about which the story was written.

Mrs. Martin's fourth grade made a large map of the United States and pasted around it pictures of stories and poems written by their favorite authors. A ribbon from the picture to the correct place on the map showed where that author lived.

More elaborate maps made by some children had flaps that opened. On each flap was a clue about a great piece of literature, such as "A story was written here about a famous rabbit." On lifting the flap one read "The Tar Baby" by Joel Chandler Harris. Another clue read, "Spare your country's flag!" and under the flap was printed "Barbara Fritchie" by John Greenleaf Whittier.

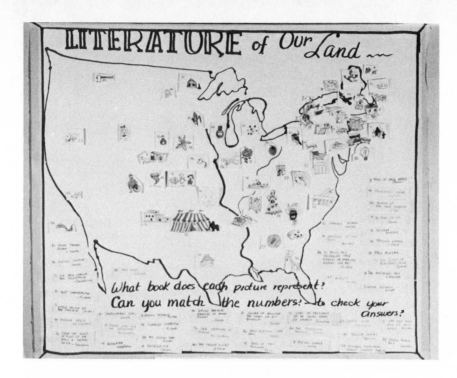

FIGURE 14–13. A pictorial map of children's favorite stories.

Pictorial maps tend to help develop concepts of time and place in children as they relate to authors and their creations.

Creating Ballads

Another way that music and literature can be correlated is to help the children put their favorite stories into ballads. They can pretend they are singing the story just as the old minstrels did long ago. In free or rhyming verse, the story can be retold. Atmosphere can often be added if someone in the room strums a guitar or the teacher plays a recording of guitar or string music. Often one child begins the story and points to another to continue. Children who cannot make rhymes are not pressured to do so; they just tell their portions of the story in their own ways. The musical background will help to determine the tempo and rhythm with which they tell it. Original ballads may also be written.

Mobiles

Mobiles are especially fascinating when units on literature are being taught. Miss French's second grade was reading Dr. Seuss. The children and the teacher read all the Dr. Seuss books they could find. They also read and collected material about Dr. Seuss as an author.

FIGURE 14–14. *Children found many ways to decorate eggs to make their own egg tree after reading* The Egg Tree *by Katherine Milhous.*

Their five favorite Dr. Seuss stories were listed on charts. Each child signed his name under the story he liked best of the five. Then the children met by groups and planned what they would like to put on a Dr. Seuss-mobile. Each group worked out its mobile, which was suspended from the ceiling, in its own way. One group used a tree branch, which they painted white. From it, suspended by threads, were Horton, Maizie, the two hunters, an egg, a circus tent, and a ship. Another group crossed sticks and balanced many grotesque and unique animals to represent *If I Ran the Zoo.*

In the center of the room hung a mobile with a picture of Dr. Seuss surrounded by tiny books on which were printed the names of every book he had written.

Mobiles lend themselves to an excellent representation of poetry and well-written prose. The movement of the floating mobile symbolizes the flow of characters and words through the child's mind. An imaginative teacher can find many ways to match the free, fluent action of a mobile with the free-flowing words of a good poem or story.

Clay Modeling

Children enjoy using plasticine or clay to model their favorite characters or scenes. Clay modeling helps the child capture the feeling of the character he is depicting. Sometimes this can be done by a facial expression, a stance, a posture, or a gesture.

In Miss Arnold's third grade, the children modeled the characters

FIGURE 14–15. Beth's interpretation of Rapunzel, *done in clay.*

from *Treasure Island*. Long John Silver was especially well portrayed with his peg leg. Each pirate had a personality of his own. The modeled figures were used to make a series of box scenes of the story. Over each box the children placed the words chosen from the text that best described the scene.

On another occasion, the children in Miss Arnold's class modeled their favorite characters chosen from all the literature they had read. The models were displayed before a backing made of a folded piece of cardboard on which the children had printed the words best describing their character. Sometimes these words were written in phrases taken directly from the original text; others were made up by the children.

Rosanne made a model of Pinocchio with a long, long nose. Behind it, in her own words, she printed:

He was naughty
He was bad,
Always in trouble
It really was sad.

Sassy and insolent
Always on the go
Silly and sweet:
Adorable Pinocchio.

Bill modeled Homer Price and made a cardboard counter to go before him. On the counter he had piles of Cheerio cereal to represent miniature doughnuts. On the cardboard behind his model, Bill printed:

> *Homer Price was a real boy. He was full of fun.*
> *He was always in trouble. The biggest trouble he ever*
> *had was the day he could not stop the doughnut machine.*
> *This is my favorite story about Homer Price.*

Kenny, who read every Paul Bunyan story ever printed, modeled a huge lumberyard, and on the card behind him printed directly from the text his favorite description of Paul.

> *Paul Bunyan was of tremendous size and*
> *strength, the strongest man that ever swung an ax. Now*
> *a lumberjack always measures things by ax handles*
> *instead of by feet or yards—a thing will be so many ax*
> *handles long or so many ax handles high—and the*
> *various estimates as to Paul's size are given in this way.*
> *Accordingly, the estimate which seems most nearly correct*
> *is that Paul was so big that ninety-seven ax handles*
> *would just barely measure him from hip to hip. This*
> *estimate is a little misleading, however, as no one is sure*
> *whether the ordinary ax handle is meant, or one of Paul's,*
> *which was seven—or perhaps it was seventy—times as*
> *long as the ordinary one. At any rate, it can easily be*
> *seen that he was no little fellow.*
> *He had curly black hair which his loving wife used*
> *to comb for him every morning with a great crosscut*
> *saw, after first parting it nicely with a broadax, and a big*
> *black beard that was as long as it was wide and as wide*
> *as it was long. He was rather proud of this beard, and*
> *took great care of it. Several times every day he would*
> *pull up a young pine tree by the roots and use its stiff*
> *branches in combing and brushing it smooth.*

Clay models can be used for making tabletop or sand-table scenes of favorite stories. Children become more aware of qualities of their favorite characters in literature when they try to translate them into visible forms.

Dance Interpretations

Many poems and stories lend themselves well to dance interpretation.

After the children in the second grade had read "The Elf and the Dormouse," Miss Bradford asked them if they would like to dance the story. A large umbrella was used as the toadstool; it was set in the middle of the room. Some of the children then made up "elf" steps. Others made up "mouse" steps. The children selected two interpretations they liked best, and then Miss Bradford composed music to go with their steps. After one group had danced the story, another group gave their interpretation.

In Miss Harmon's fourth grade the children made up a dance for "A Visit from St. Nicholas." There were many step patterns to be planned— the prancing reindeer steps, the heavy, plodding "Ho-ho-ho" steps of Santa Claus, the airy steps of the sugarplums "dancing through their heads," the fast steps of the "wind and the leaves before the hurricane fly." Miss

FIGURE 14–16. A dance interpretation of Eleanor Estes's The Hundred Dresses.

Harmon used a Fred Waring recording as a background for this dance. At another time her children dramatized "The Elves and the Shoemaker," and she composed music for the dance.

A group of fifth-grade girls and boys created a dance for their Book Week assembly program from "Snow White and the Seven Dwarfs."

Whenever possible, children should have the opportunity to see literature translated into dance interpretations, for example, a corps de ballet dancing the *Nutcracker Suite, The Red Shoes, Peter and the Wolf, Hansel and Gretel, Cinderella, Robin Hood, The Steadfast Tin Soldier,* and other famous stories.

Impersonations

One effective way of creating interest in an author's ability to describe characters is to encourage the children to impersonate characters from the books they have read together while the rest of the class guesses who the character is. These impersonations can be done in many ways. Children can dress in costume and tell about themselves; they may act out a character silently; or they may use the "I Was There" technique, where they sit before the class and pretend they were eyewitnesses to a particular scene of the story in which the character they are depicting took an active part. Some primary teachers have encouraged this sort of activity by using a large cardboard box as a television set on which children tell about themselves.

Impersonations help the children to focus attention on those bits of description in the author's writing which make his characters different and notorious.

Miss Empy used impersonations as the theme of a tea she gave for her fifth-grade mothers. She held a fashion show of children's famous storybook characters, using the boys and girls in her room as the models.

SUMMARY

Telling and reading stories is an art. Certain strategies enhance the telling of a story and stimulate children to a variety of adventures in literature. Among these are: the use of realia and artifacts, the use of finger plays, murals, games, dioramas, displays and exhibits, peg board displays, filmstrips and recordings, choral speaking, booklets, radio and television shows, roll movies, shadow boxes, peep shows, field trips, the use of holidays, shadow plays, lap stories, pictorial maps, writing ballads, making mobiles, clay modeling, dance interpretations, and doing impersonations.

TO THE COLLEGE STUDENT

1. If you have never read or told a story to a child or to a group of children, prepare yourself to do so by studying the first pages of this chapter and putting your knowledge into effect.

2. Listen to some of the recordings suggested in Appendix E for clues to good storytelling.

3. Tape your own voice in reading a children's book or poem, listen to the feedback, and evaluate your own ability to read effectively.

4. Set yourself a creative project to be completed under time pressure. Tape a long, wide piece of mural paper on the wall. Somewhere near the center have someone in the class draw lines to represent the center of the town of Banbury Cross. Now, with paint or colored chalk, have everyone take a place along the mural paper and for a period of fifteen minutes, everyone draws everything he can think of going to Banbury Cross. Each person will need to confer with his neighbor to blend in backgrounds and to give the mural continuity. Of course, the person who stands at the center of town will sketch in the "fine lady on a fine horse."

5. Have your audiovisual department send for the filmstrips and recordings mentioned on pp. 489 and 512 and preview them. They are not all suitable for children, but you will enjoy them.

TO THE CLASSROOM TEACHER

1. Adapt some of the strategies described in this chapter to your own classroom.

2. Think of all the ways you can to give creative book reports.

3. Start a literary club with your class. See p. 373 for suggestions for operation.

4. Encourage the children to play "literature charades." Each child acts out the name *or* the characteristics of a favorite person in a book while the rest guess who it is.

5. Try some of the Weston Woods films with your children and note their reactions.

6. Encourage the children to collect pictures of moving picture ads of films made from children's books and use them on a bulletin board.

TO THE COLLEGE STUDENT
AND THE CLASSROOM TEACHER

1. Why is the situation in which Miss Kennedy made a sound story from a reading chart a good idea? Can you see that this strategy fits in well with the reading incidents described on page 387.

2. What stories are suggested to you by the following bits of realia: a paint brush, an apple, a pile of caps, a doughnut, an axe, a glass slipper, a golden egg? Would you say that an understanding of symbolism enhances appreciation of literature? Discuss ways you might use each to develop motivation for the story it represents.

3. In Debbie's lesson described on page 385, do you feel she accomplished her objectives? What might follow a lesson such as this? What other pieces of literature are appropriate at this time?

4. Try making up a finger play exercise and then do it in a choral poem, spoken in parts.

5. Plan and put on tape an exciting, creative, motivating television shown on children's literature.

SELECTED BIBLIOGRAPHY

Andrews, Gladys. *Creative Rhythmic Movement for Children.* Englewood Cliffs, N.J.: Prentice-Hall, 1954.

Cathon, Laura, et al. *Stories to Tell to Children: A Selected List.* 8th ed. Pittsburgh: University of Pennsylvania Press, 1974.

Chambers, Dewey. *Literature for Children: Storytelling and Creative Drama.* Dubuque, Iowa: Wm. C. Brown, 1970.

Colum, Padraic. *Story Telling New and Old.* New York: Macmillan, 1968.

Colwell, Eileen. *A Storyteller's Choice: A Selection of Stories, with Notes on How to Tell Them.* New York: Henry Z. Walck, 1964.

Coody, Betty. *Using Literature with Young Children.* Dubuque, Iowa: Wm. C. Brown, 1973.

Cundiff, Ruby, and Webb Cundiff. *Storytelling for You.* Yellow Springs, Ohio: Antioch Press, 1957.

Gillespie, John, and Diana Lembo. *Junior Plots: A Book Talk Manual for Teachers and Librarians.* New York: R. R. Bowker, 1967.

Grayson, Marion. *Let's Do Fingerplays.* Washington, D.C.: David McKay, 1962.

Luckhardt, Mildred Correll. *Storytelling at Its Best.* New York: Abingdon Press, 1974.

Petty, Walter, and Mary Bowen. *Slithery Snakes and Other Aids to Children's Writing.* New York: Meredith, 1967.

Ross, Eulalie Steinmetz, ed. *The Lost Half Hour: A Collection of Stories with a Chapter on How to Tell a Story.* New York: Harcourt, Brace and World, 1963.

Ross, Ramon Royal. *The Storytellers Bag.* Columbus: Charles E. Merrill, 1972.

Sawyer, Ruth. *The Way of the Storyteller,* rev. ed. New York: Viking, 1962.

Shedlock, Marie. *Art of the Story-teller.* New York: Dover, 1962.

Tiedt, Sidney W., and Iris M. Tiedt. *The Elementary Teacher's Complete Ideas Handbook.* Englewood Cliffs, N.J.: Prentice-Hall, 1965, Chapter 4.

Tooze, Ruth. *Storytelling.* Englewood Cliffs, N.J.: Prentice-Hall, 1959.

Viquers, Ruth Hill. *Storytelling and the Teacher.* Washington, D.C.: American Association of Elementary-Kindergarten-Nursery Education, 1967.

Wagner, Joseph A. *Children's Literature Through Storytelling.* Dubuque, Iowa: Wm. C. Brown, 1970.

Whitehead, Robert. *Children's Literature: Strategies of Teaching.* Englewood Cliffs, N.J.: Prentice-Hall, 1968.

CHAPTER 15

Using Children's Literature in the Curriculum

The Emperor And The Opera

Miss Black, a classroom teacher, and Mrs. Burns, the music teacher, collaborated on the following project, which proved to be an exciting experience in creating and interpreting.

Some of the objectives copied from Miss Black's notebook read as follows:

As a result of this project, the children will:

Understand the concept of the opera and how it differs from musical plays and dramatizations. This will be evaluated by the children's ability to recognize operatic music when played on records and to produce a small opera of their own with appropriate music style.

Translate a favorite piece of literature into musical expression as evidenced by a final production.

Create operatic music to be used in dramatizing a favorite story.

Learn how to stage a production of this nature, and learn the skills required. These will be: painting scenery, making costumes, creating props, listening to music, writing scripts, speaking and singing effectively, making prints for posters and programs and doing research. Evaluation will lie in the final production.

One of the children brought the book *The Emperor's New Clothes* from the library and gave a report on it to the class. The children selected it as one of the stories to read together. So Miss Black read it one day. The enthusiasm and interest of the children led them to select it as a proper vehicle for fulfilling the objectives of their project.

Following the reading of the story, Miss Black and Mrs. Burns held a discussion. They encouraged the children to list the characters in the story. Next to each character the children then listed characteristics describing his personality. After the weavers, for instance, the children suggested crafty, busy, fussy, energetic, sly, and tricky. After the character of the king, they listed regal, royal, majestic, proud, bossy, stupid, and dressy. After the character of the little boy, they listed innocent, honest, and simple. They described the prime minister as being dishonest, crafty, sly, smug, mean, disloyal, and foxy.

After every actor had been so described, the children were encouraged to go to the piano and to create a theme for each person, trying to invent a musical pattern that would show the character of each.

The weavers needed busy music so certain notes were played to indicate the weavers (see Figure 15–1).

These words were added:

Busy, busy, busy are the weavers of the thread
Hurry, hurry, hurry or the king will chop your head.

The theme created for the king (stately, royal, proud music) is also shown in Figure 15–1.

Words created to accompany his theme were:

Make way
Make way
The king has come today!
He wears
Royal red
And a crown upon his head!

For the innocent, honest, simple little boy, the third theme was invented, and these words were added:

I am just a farmer boy
I only tell you what I see
I never never tell a lie
I'm just as honest as can be.

In addition to writing themes for the main characters, music was created for some of the unusual events, such as the parade in the streets and the final showdown scene.

The story was rewritten as a play by one committee so it could be staged in three scenes: the king's reception room, the weaver's room, and on the street before the palace. Simple costumes were made (mostly from crepe paper). Good lighting effects were worked out and the "opera" was presented.

As each character was introduced in Act I, the theme was played and the character sang his words. From that time on, the theme for each character was played every time that character appeared—sometimes as a background to his spoken words. Parts of the narration were also sung. The teachers and children worked hard at the end of the opera to create a song where all the themes were blended.

They included vocal solos, ensembles, recitative (vocal declamation), as well as orchestral accompaniments from records. They listened to an opera, discovering it was sung throughout. The music teacher told

FIGURE 15–1. "The Weaver's Tune," "The King's Theme," and "The Little Boy's Theme."

them there were exceptions, and that comic opera usually had spoken dialogue.

A children's story, in this illustration, provided the basis for teaching many components of a planned curriculum and helped teachers accomplish some worthy objectives.

Incidentally, the king appeared in his underclothing and pink tights.

LITERATURE IN THE CURRICULUM

One of the assumptions on which the philosophy of this book is based is that literature can be the core of teaching most subjects in the elementary school curriculum. In the illustration above, we have seen how this statement is verified in a music-teaching situation. "The Ballad of Robin Hood" demonstrates another teaching situation in music where literature is used.

The remainder of this chapter presents illustrations of the use of literature in various subject-matter fields as a tool and as an object for developing concepts, attitudes, values, skills, and appreciations.

Literature and Music

Almost all the great poems and ballads have, at one time or another, been set to music. We have already seen how important a part music can play in translating literature into action for children. In this volume children have chosen to use music in their puppet shows, dramatizations, and shadow plays. They have used music to create a mood while they read their poetry, or the poetry of others. We have seen that children can put their own poems and stories to music. They have referred to poetry as "word music." They have created dances to music, and they have created an opera.

How else can literature be used effectively to promote the goals of the music program in the elementary school? It has always been used for such purposes in the past. Unfortunately, it has rarely been used conscientiously to develop a knowledge or appreciation of music and rarely has it been subjected to close scrutiny for the purpose of using music and literature harmoniously to develop creativity in students.

Musical stories built from good pieces of literature have long presented music to children in an interesting form. Examples of such classics are Humperdinck's *Hansel and Gretel* and recordings of Grieg's *Peer Gynt Suite*.

Children's stories have been set to music and made into films— often with excellent results—such as *Alice in Wonderland, Mary Poppins, Dr. Doolittle*, and *The Wizard of Oz*.

The making of cartoons from children's films has become an unsurpassed art, especially as promoted by the late Walt Disney. Music from these productions has run the gamut from poor to mediocre to excellent, but has made a definite contribution to the American way of life.

Perhaps music can be most appreciated by children when they make it work for them, helping them to write and express the mood for their own stories.

Music may be put to many other uses to enhance literature, and literature may be widely employed to enhance music. Too much has been printed about teaching music for music's sake entirely—the same might be said about literature for literature's sake, drama for drama's sake, and dance for dance's sake. Each is an art in itself, but each is a tool to be used to enhance or to serve the other. Children will best make the creative arts a real part of their lives when they can appreciate each as an art and use each as a tool.

Literature and the Language Arts

The accounts of *John J. Plenty and Fiddler Dan* and *There's an Author in the House* are illustrations of the manner by which some teachers met several goals for teaching the language arts through the use of literature. Language arts is that area of the curriculum that deals with communication skills, and how better to learn about communication skills than through those great writers of the ages who excelled in the art of communication?

A review of the natural development of language helps the teacher realize the many ways literature can be used to provide adventures in communication for children.

The Sequence of Language Development

Language develops in a logical sequence. First a child must *experience*. Most of his experiencing in the early years of his life is through *listening* and through the other senses—smell, taste, touch, and sight. After a year or so of listening, the infant selects from the sounds he hears in his environment those which have meaning for him and attempts to reproduce them. *Speech* is born—or *oral* expression. After a period of time when he develops physically to the stage where his tongue, teeth, jaws, and voice apparatus make refined speech possible, he communicates fluently on the oral level. Parallel to this development is the ability to conceptualize and symbolize; soon he can recognize in symbols (print) those words he is able to verbalize (reading). Repeated sight of the visual image of letters and words makes possible the ability to *write. Spelling, handwriting forms, capitalization, punctuation,* and *word usage* are refinements of the handwriting act. The school develops these skills in children because they are arbitrary standard forms adopted by the culture to serve as social courtesies, making handwriting and reading more effective among peoples.

The progression of the development of language skills is shown simply on the chart in Figure 15–2.[1]

As a child progresses from the top to the bottom of this chart, a high level of intelligence is called into play. The slow-learning or retarded child learns best through the use of those skills developed at the top of the

---

1. James A. Smith, *Adventures in Communication: Language Arts Methods* (Boston: Allyn and Bacon, 1972), p. 45.

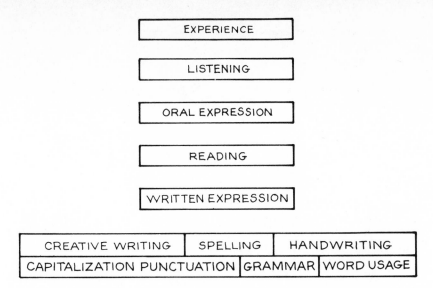

FIGURE 15–2. *The normal sequence of language development.*

chart. His ability to conceptualize and to use symbols is weak. Consequently, he may never read or spell well. Most of his instruction, to be effective, must appeal to his senses and will take place at the listening–oral expression level. Bright children, on the other hand, are capable of using symbols and of dealing readily with concepts and symbols and can be taught to read, write, spell, and use language forms effectively.

Language Arts

In many of the classrooms described in this volume, the children engaged in various kinds of communicative activities, all of which grew out of a project dealing with children's literature. Among other things, they learned to write a script, to use new punctuation forms, to outline and plan on charts, to develop a "stage" vocabulary to expand their regular vocabularies and their reading abilities, to write business letters, to keep accounts, to make programs, and to write invitations.

On the creative side, they wrote poems which they put to music, they developed creative oral expression in planning and making a tape or in speaking on the stage, they wrote scenes for their plays and puppet shows, and many children were motivated to write personal stories and poems during their free time.

Literature and Listening

Once he is established in school, the first concentrated listening the child experiences is listening to stories. In a sense, listening is half the act of communicating. In order for a child to enjoy literature, he must be able to listen.

FIGURE 15–3. *A language arts center: Contracts for individualized learning, games, instructional materials, and story starters.*

FIGURE 15–4. *Fourth graders edit their creative writing for a school yearbook.*

There are many ways to listen. Some children come from home backgrounds where listening is not encouraged or where children have been forced to live with so much noise that they have learned not to hear. The school cannot, therefore, take listening skills for granted. Children have to be taught to listen in a variety of ways for a variety of purposes.

In Chapter 5, under a discussion of the physical conditions that must be set for teaching literature creatively, the various types of listening were discussed and suggestions were made as to how literature could be used to develop certain listening skills. Each type of listening has been illustrated in the accounts given of classroom and school projects in each chapter of this book.

Attentive Listening: Suggestions

1. Read stories that draw attention to the value of listening to sounds, words, letters, or sentences. Examples: "The Sound that Turned Around" (*The Listening Book* by Dan Safier, pp. 13–19); "The Sound that was Lost and Found" (*The Listening Book,* pp. 62–67); "The Changeable Clock" (ibid., pp. 71–85); *Ounce, Dice, Trice* by Alastair Reid; *The Listening Walk* by Paul Showers; *Word Bending with Aunt Sarah* by Al Westcott.

2. Read stories to the children where the plot is constructed around a breakdown in communication due to faulty listening. Discussions of these stories help bring out the need for careful listening. Some such stories are:

"The Hot Weather Mix-up" (*Jack and Jill,* July 1957)
"The Story of Slow Joe" by Dan Safier
"The Tar Baby" by Joel Chandler Harris
"Keeping Still in the Woods" by Charles G. D. Roberts
"Henny Penny," fairy tale
"Lazy Jack," English folktale
"Rumpelstiltskin," Grimms' fairy tale
Bambi by Felix Salten
"The Midnight Ride of Paul Revere" by Henry W. Longfellow
"The Forty Thieves" by Andrew Lang (from *The Arabian Nights*)
"You Can't Please Everybody," Aesop's fable
"Ask Mr. Bean" by Marjorie Flack
The Funny Noise by Romny Gay
"The Emperor's New Clothes" by Hans Christian Andersen
Alice's Adventures in Wonderland by Lewis Carroll
Gerald McBoing-Boing, anonymous
"The Nightingale" by Hans Christian Andersen
The Tale of Peter Rabbit by Beatrix Potter

3. A good "audience-type" situation can be provided for listening by inviting a consultant to read or speak to the children and by preparing them for specific things to listen to. Some people to ask might include: a parent who has an unusual occupation or hobby, the librarian, the school physician, a forest ranger, a town person who has just returned from a trip, the school nurse, the principal, the custodian, a state trooper, a fireman, a policeman, a visitor from a foreign country, etc.

4. Have the children clap for various reasons when they are being read to. For instance: Clap at every word that rhymes with *hat*. (Use Dr. Seuss's books, *The Cat in the Hat* and *The Cat in the Hat Comes Back*.)

5. Many good holiday games can be designed to teach listening skills. One good technique used by Miss Watts to develop attentive listening was the distribution of gifts at Christmas time. Each child brought a wrapped quarter gift. Miss Watts read "A Visit from St. Nicholas" and every child held a gift, but passed it on every time the word "and" was read. At the end of the reading of the poem, the child opened the gift he held in his hand.

6. Young children enjoy the rollicking sounds of Mother Goose rhymes. They can be encouraged to say these rhymes and add rhyming sounds of their own, such as "Hickory, dickory, stockory, mockory" and "Muffet, tuffet, puffet, stuffet," etc. If the teacher records these invented sound words as she hears some children saying them, they can later be read to the class, who will add more sounds.

7. Give the class three titles and ask which one best fits the story or poem to be read to them.

8. Begin a rhyme and let the children make up a new ending.

Appreciative Listening

1. *Reading stories and poems:* Some stories lend themselves to listening exercises. Noises are repeated that children can reproduce. Every time the teacher comes to a certain word, the children are told to make the sound that goes with it. For example, the word "dog" evokes a "grr," the word "telephone" evokes a "ding-a-ling." Some very good stories for this and other kinds of listening activity are: *Gerald McBoing-Boing*, anonymous; *The Listening Book* by Dan Safier; Walter de la Mare's poem "Someone"; "I Know an Old Lady Who Swallowed a Fly" by Burl Ives; "On a Steamer" by Dorothy Baruch; "Riding in a Motor Boat" by Dorothy Baruch; "Tugs" by James S. Tippett; "Riding in an Airplane" by Dorothy Baruch; "Evening at the Farm" by John Townsend Trowbridge; "Strawberry Jam" by May Justus; "The Highwayman" by Alfred Noyes; "In School Days" by John Greenleaf Whittier; "White Snow, Bright Snow" by Alvin Tresselt; *Millions of Cats* by Wanda Gag; *A Kiss Is Round* by Blossom Budney; *On Beyond Zebra, Horton Hatches the Egg,* and *Thidwick the Moose* by Dr. Seuss; *Which Witch Is Which* by Robert Lawson; "The Little Red Hen"; "The Three Billy Goats Gruff"; "Little Galoshes" by Kathryn Jackson and Byron Jackson; *The Little Fat Policeman* by Margaret Wise Brown and Edith Thacher Hard; *Robbins Climbs the Mountain* by Alvin Tresselt; *Growl Bear* by Margot Austin; *Wait Till the Moon Is Full* by Margaret Wise Brown; *Ten Little Fingers: A Book of Finger Plays* by Priscilla Pointer; *Time of Wonder* by Robert McCloskey.

2. Play some beautiful records and have the children paint, draw, or fingerpaint while the music is playing. Suggestions: *Nutcracker Suite*

by Tschaikowsky; "Slavonic Dances" by Dvorak; *Peer Gynt Suite* by Grieg; *William Tell Overture* by Rossini; *Sleeping Beauty* by Tschaikowsky; "A Summer Place"; "Tara's Theme"; "Rhapsody in Blue" by Gershwin; and "Blue Star." A variation is to play the music, listen carefully, and then have the children draw, paint, or write what it means to them.

3. Choral speaking provides endless opportunities for careful listening so that children may work out patterns of their own. Much of choral speaking should be with the children's own creative work and with familiar selections.

4. Often a poem such as "The Sugar Plum Tree" by Eugene Field can be read. Then the teacher asks the children to draw a picture showing everything they can remember about the poem.

Other poems adaptable to this sort of activity are: "Wynken, Blynken and Nod" by Eugene Field, "My Shadow" by Robert Louis Stevenson, "Song for a Little House" by Christopher Morley, "I Like Housekeeping" by Dorothy Brown Thompson, "Stopping by Woods on a Snowy Evening" by Robert Frost, "White Fields" by James Stephens, "Written in March" by William Wordsworth, "Halloween" by Harry Behn, "Thanksgiving Day" by Lydia Maria Child, "A Visit from St. Nicholas" by Clement Clark Moore, "Block City" by Robert Louis Stevenson, "Roller Skates" by John Farras, "The Kite" by Harry Behn, "The Fishing Pole" by Mary Carolyn Davies, "A Sledding Song" by Norman C. Schlichter, "Caterpillar" by Christina Rossetti, "The Little Turtle" by Vachel Lindsay, "My Dog" by Marchette Chute, "Holding Hands" by Lenore M. Link, "Stop-Go" by Dorothy Baruch, "Song for a Blue Roadster" by Rachel Field, and "The Locomotive" by Emily Dickinson.

Analytical Listening

1. Ask children to listen on the way to school to special sounds, which they will reproduce (when possible) in the classroom. Categorize the sounds on charts under such headings as:

Buildings noises (ditch diggers, hammers, saws, pounding, buzz saws)
Play noises (shouting, balls bouncing, skipping rope, playing hopscotch, running hotrods)
Beautiful noises (birds chirping, bees buzzing, wind sighing, ice cream man ringing, church bells ringing, children laughing)
Other categories might be: unpleasant sounds, funny sounds, happy noises, school noises, unusual noises, common noises, machine noises, circus noises.

After a list has been made, ask the children to hunt for books on their next trip to the library which could be read to go with these sounds, such as: (a) *The Little House* by Virginia Lee Burton; (b) *The Moffats* by Eleanor Estes; (c) *Spring Is a New Beginning* by Joan Walsh Anglund; (d) *The Noisy Book* by Margaret Wise Brown.

2. Have the children tell stories or read into a tape recorder and listen to their own presentation in the playback.

3. Use the records *Sounds Around Us* by Scott, Foresman and Company for developing listening skills, and *Listening Activities* by RCA Victor Record Library for Elementary Schools (Volumes I–II).

Other records suitable for this use in the primary grades are: *Come to the Fair*, Young Peoples Records; *Muffin in the City*, YPR; *A Walk in the Forest*, YPR; *Little Cowboy*, YPR; *Listen and Do Series*, Vols. 1–4, American Book Company; *Rainy Day*, YPR; *Let's Play Zoo*, YPR; *Little Indian Drum*, YPR; *Hot Cross Buns*, Children's Record Guild; *Songs, Games and Fun* (Dorothy Olson), RCA; *The Merry Toy Shop*, CRG; *Little Engine that Could*, RCA; *Muffin in the Country*, YPR; *Train Sounds*, RCA; *Children's Concert Series*, CRG; *Fun with Instruments* (Little Nipper Junior Series), RCA; *Let's Dance*, CRG; *Train to the Zoo*, CRG; *Peter, It's Pancakes*, CRG; *Who Wants a Ride?* CRG; *Let's Play* (Children's Musical Action Stories by Kay Ortman. Set I—Farm Lands, Set II—Adventures in the Forest), Kay Ortman's Productions; *Sounds We Hear* (Illa Polendorf), Grosset & Dunlap.

For the intermediate grades: *The Shearing Piano* (George Shearing), Capitol; *Peter and the Wolf*, Columbia LP; *Hansel and Gretel* (Basil Rathbone), Columbia; *Caught in the Act* (Victor Borge), Columbia; *Rusty in Orchestraville*, Capitol; *Big News Series*, Columbia; *Alice in Wonderland* (Jane Powell), Columbia.

Marginal Listening

1. Dramatize action poems that require careful listening. Examples: "The Piggyback Merry-Go-Round" (*The Listening Book*, pp. 57–59); "Bell Horses," nursery rhyme; "A Cat Came Fiddling," Mother Goose; "Feet" by Irene Thompson; "Trains" by James S. Tippett; "Soft Steps" by Georgette Agrew; "Pop! Goes the Weasel," nursery rhyme; "Peas Porridge Hot," nursery rhyme; "To Market," nursery rhyme; "Ride a Cock Horse," nursery rhyme; "The Horsemen" by Walter de la Mare; "A Stick for a Horse" by Sybil Fountain; "Mrs. Hen" by M. A. Campbell; "The Elf and the Dormouse" by Oliver Herford; "Three Little Mice," Mother Goose; "Conversation" by Anne Robinson; "Mix a Pancake" by Christina Rossetti; "I Had a Little Pony," Mother Goose.

2. For intermediate grades: "Casey at the Bat" by Ernest Lawrence Thayer; "Stopping by Woods on a Snowy Evening" by Robert Frost; "Fog" by Carl Sandburg; "A Visit from St. Nicholas" by Clement Clark Moore; "The Duel" by Eugene Field; "The Landing of the Pilgrim Fathers" by Felicia Dorothea Hemans; "Barbara Fritchie" by John Greenleaf Whittier; "The Flag Goes By" by Henry Holcomb Bennett; "The Pied Piper of Hamelin" by Robert Browning; and "The Leak in the Dike" by Phoebe Cary.

3. Listen to records which can be dramatized or interpreted that require special listening skills. Examples: *Peter and the Wolf*, Prokofiev; *I Went for a Walk in the Forest*, Young Peoples Records.

Literature and Oral Expression

Experiences of children are quickly translated into verbal symbols. A good program in oral expression will help children find words to express their experiences effectively and will help them use new words in new contexts. Not only is it necessary for children to use words orally to understand their meaning, but they must also use them orally to understand their *use*. Children will read with comprehension those words which they speak and they will not write words they do not speak.

A glance back over the pages of this book reveals many ways that literature has been used in the teaching of creative oral expression. In Chapter 4, Peter's class worked on oral expression in making a tape for its puppet show. The boys in Mr. Carr's room received plenty of practice in speaking aloud when they put on their Robin Hood play. So did the children who made the tape to go along with the puppet show of *The Five Chinese Brothers*.

Other adventures with oral expression we have described are: the use of games from biographical characters such as *Who Am I?* and *You Are There* (Chapter 14), and the use of puppet shows, which provided excellent experiences in speech for the children in the classes who gave them.

The Felt-O-gram and flannel board experiences mentioned in Chapter 13 of "The Gingerbread Boy," "A Visit From St. Nicholas," and "The Small One" were good listening and oral expression experiences.

The presentation of the many kinds of book reports of *The Five Chinese Brothers*, *Robinson Crusoe*, and *Treasure Island* are examples of creative experiences in oral expression.

Suggestions previously made about employing literature to develop oral expression include: the use of sound stories, making sound stories from reading charts, the use of rhymes and verses for finger plays, using choral speaking, making booklets to be read aloud, developing radio and television shows, making roll movies, using lap stories, creating ballads, making and explaining mobiles, and telling stories to each other.

Literature and Reading

The importance of reading in a successful program in children's literature was explored in Chapter 3. A great deal of emphasis is currently being placed on the individualized teaching approaches to reading. Many new organizational plans have been designed to make possible the concept of individual reading instruction in the classroom. All of these new plans base the reading program on a planned program in children's literature that calls for a wealth of good books for children in each classroom and/or an active, functioning library.

Because reading ability is closely related to intelligence and other factors such as emotional and social adjustment, the reading level and ability of the children will vary greatly. Any personalized approach to reading is beneficial to children. A total personalized or individualized reading program, where each child develops at his own rate of speed and in accord with his own interests, *is* possible. In such a program none of the stages in reading development is skipped, nor is the methodology for teaching reading greatly altered. The difference is largely in the organization of the classroom program.

In organizing a class for individualized reading instruction, the commonly accepted pattern of grouping children according to reading ability or in relation to reading problems is unnecessary. Each child selects his own reading materials, and the teacher so organizes the day that she may spend time hearing each child read, discussing his reading problems with him, and providing individual or group instruction where it is needed.

Because the program is one of self-selection, the individual interests and purposes of the children can be realized and abilities developed as rapidly or slowly as the child's inherent growth pattern permits.

Individualized instruction in reading does not mean that children never meet in groups. They often do because some reading is best taught in groups. Also, in developing an individualized reading program, teachers discover that small groups of children have similar problems or need help in similar skills, so they group these children together.

The individualized reading program recognizes the simple fact that no grouping eliminates individual differences. Almost no two children read at the same level or read the same material at the same time. The teaching of reading as individually as possible gives each child the opportunity for reading without interference, competition, or distraction from other members of a group who may be reading faster or slower than he. In addition to his right to proceed at his own rate, he learns many skills in the self-selection of materials.

Creative teachers have had the success that might well be expected from such a reading program. The number of books children read under the guidance of these teachers has skyrocketed. Interest in reading and associated skills has developed to unexpected proportions, and the skills of reading seem to have developed as much.

The core of all new organizational plans in reading is the school library. The selection and use of books in that library becomes one of the most important tasks of the classroom teacher. The teacher is committed to know a great deal about children's literature under this plan so she can wisely select books of certain ability levels and specific interest levels for individual children. She must become especially sensitive to the wealth of "easy books" which now flood the market and can be used for slow or beginning readers, such as the I Can Read series published by Harper & Row and Beginners' Books published by Random House. Lately, the reading program of many classrooms has been enriched by the introduction of these "easy beginning books" written especially for beginning readers. These books often do what the beginning readers do not. They tell a sensible, exciting story in a simple, direct way that rewards the children by making the reading of the story worthwhile.

Along with the easy beginning books has come much criticism as to their literary value. Literary value or not, they are far superior to the beginning stories in many basic text series. A visit to any classroom where these "easy books" are being used will show how eagerly they are accepted by children. Words are repeated over and over in such a way as to help the child develop a broad sight vocabulary. Various root words, beginning word sounds, word endings, prefixes, and suffixes are so simply introduced and so repeated that children often begin to use phonetic and word analysis skills to figure out the new words for themselves, thereby enabling the teacher to launch into a sound word-attack program at the time the child is most ready for it.

Many bright children have taught themselves to read with the "easy books," and many other children have delighted in their ability to read these books after one or two readings by the teacher.

"Easy books" have made their way into the reading programs of most children, at least out of school, where parents have seen these books as one means to satisfy the hunger of the highly motivated beginning reader. The books can be put to profitable use within the school program if they are carefully integrated into the total reading program.

Literature, then, is the base of a modern reading program. Literature is the reason why children are taught to read in the first place: they learn to read to be able to enjoy their rightful heritage as it has been recorded by the authors and poets of the past and present. But literature is also used to *teach* reading in the new reading programs. The literary value of good books eliminates the apathy that generally overtakes a child who learns to read primers quickly and then grows bored with them just as quickly because of the sterile and tiresome stories which do not challenge his thinking.

Examples of children using their skill of reading for enjoyment were shown in Chapter 2 when the children in Miss Sawyer's room read *Hailstones and Halibut Bones*, and in Chapter 5 when Mr. Carr's children read *Robin Hood*. But in the recording of *The Grasshopper and the Ants* in Chapter 4, Mr. Nash was teaching reading by being certain that the ability level of the passage from the story matched the ability level of the child who was reading it. In the story of *Dandelions and Snowflakes* in Chapter 3, the teacher was using the children's own literature to help develop rhyming sounds, among other things.

In Chapter 13 we saw how Mrs. Gaines used directions for making puppets as a device for teaching children to follow directions. Children

FIGURE 15–5. *Middle-grade children celebrate Thanksgiving at school by preparing a real Thanksgiving feast like the one described in Wilhelmina Harper's* The Harvest Feast: Stories of Thanksgiving Yesterday and Today.

were applying learned skills when they presented the various book reports in Chapter 13. Mr. Nash used a roll movie of a piece of literature to help children develop the concept of sequence of ideas.

Reading can be taught within the context of good books, and good books can be read as a result of the child's reading ability. This inseparable combination is the factor which makes possible the development of an entire school curriculum through the use of literature.

Literature and Grammar Forms

The teaching of grammar forms: punctuation, capitalization, word usage, and form usage, helps children to better read and appreciate the printed page if the lessons for accomplishing this are not dull and boring. They can be creative. Often children can search through their favorite books to note how the usage they are studying is applied in the writing they enjoy. They may also note how the forms they study help to develop effective communication between the author and the reader.

Poetry Forms: Primary Grades

Below is an excerpt from *The Creative Teaching of the Language Arts*[2] describing the creative ways in which some teachers have taught poetry forms.

Most children write their first poems in story form; it is a natural sequence to the instruction they have received in writing stories. In the primary grades, poems generally begin to appear on an individual basis as some children, aware of the concepts of rhyming, make attempts to rhyme their stories. Often these first poems are dictated to the teacher.

The teacher can establish written forms for poetry writing as soon as her children are able to read. Learning poetry forms is a visual skill. Children should see the complete form of a poem as it will appear on a sheet of paper, before they begin to write it. This calls for a sensitivity to the art form or shape of the poem as well as to the wording of it.

There are many acceptable forms for poetry writing. The child must become familiar with numerous such forms and then be encouraged to choose his own. He must also be informed of the different types of poetry such as free verse, blank verse, and rhyming verse so that he may choose a form that suits his purposes. Often a simple piece of written prose is beautiful enough to be written as free verse. The teacher can be alert to the signals of her children's readiness to write poetry and can capitalize on their signals by using them to introduce poetry forms. A rich background of experiences with poetry will make her instructional task meaningful.

Suggestions for Helping Children to Write Poetry Forms: Primary Grades

Put simple poems on reading charts as soon as the children are able to read them. Often simple nursery rhymes the children know may be

---

2. James A. Smith, *Creative Teaching of the Language Arts in the Elementary School,* 2nd ed. (Boston: Allyn and Bacon, 1973), pp. 316–317.

used this way. Draw attention to the fact that the beginning lines are capitalized and that a period ends each idea, but that the beginning lines are not always directly under each other as in an experience chart.

As soon as a child creates a poem, use it to make a reading chart. Explain that one way people can tell whether the material they are about to read is a poem or a story is by the shape of it on the page. Read the poem that was submitted and print it on a reading chart, using a form different from the straight margins usually used in a reading chart. Note the contrast in form. Accent the shape of the indentations of the beginning lines of poetry by drawing a jagged margin with a brightly colored felt pen.

Miss Fleming, a second-grade teacher, printed simple poems her children liked and poems they had written on colored construction paper. She cut out the poems, accenting the pattern of the first lines of the poem by following jagged margins. When mounted on regular tag board, the shape of the poem was easily seen from any place in the classroom and provided an easy reference for the children.

Poems with iambic pentameter may be printed on pieces of cardboard in two-line sections and distributed to the children. They then read the poem and assemble it in a pocket chart at the front of the room, thus drawing attention to the alternate indentation of the lines of this type of poetry and providing the teacher with a method of checking the children's ability to match rhyming lines.

Poetry Forms: Intermediate Grades

Many of the suggestions given for the development of the visual and art form of poetry in the primary grades may be adapted to the instructional program of the intermediate grades. In fact, it will be necessary to develop form consciousness through steps similar to those taken by Miss Fleming if intermediate-grade children have not developed sensitivity to poetry forms.

However, the stress for writing poetry should be on the content of the poem and not the form. Much of the instruction for developing poetry forms will be done on an individual basis as the teacher helps each child edit his draft work for final display or publication in the classroom. (See Chapter 11 for suggestions on teaching poetry.)

Other Grammar Forms

Many library skills can be taught as part of the program in grammar. Many of these skills help children in reading and social studies, especially skills dealing with the use of reference materials.

Other grammar forms can be taught directly through the use of such work as *Grammar Can Be Fun,* an appealing book by Munro Leaf. Books that are written and illustrated well enough to be classified as literature can often be used to enhance the classroom program in teaching grammar. One recent book for primary children by Beth Maestro, *Where Is My Friend?* (illustrated by Guilio Maestro) is a concept book about

Harriet, an elephant who searches for her friend in pages intended to familiarize children with the use and meaning of prepositions. A book by Emily Hanlon, *How a Horse Grew Hoarse on the Site Where He Sighted a Bare Bear* (illustrated by Lorna Tomei) is a tale about homonyms. A crew of animals and a little girl tell a story in words that sound the same but have different spellings and meanings. Books of this nature add style and richness to the classroom teacher's grammar program.

Literature and Art

Throughout the ages, music, dance, literature, drama, and art have provided man with a creative means of communication and a positive outlet for his feelings. The chants and rhythms of the ancient tribes, the sign languages of the American Indian, the ballads of the minstrels, the wagon plays of the medieval church—all were creative forms of teaching long before the average man became literate.

Since literacy has spread among the masses of people, knowledge and skill have developed and have been recorded in the areas of music, dance, drama, literature, and art, and each of these areas of primitive communication has risen to the status of an art in itself. As an art, each has been relegated to a place of honor in the elementary school curriculum where the science and skill of each are taught as part of the general education of all citizens.

FIGURE 15–6. *Art and literature are closely related communicative media. Children made this batik curtain for their puppet play of Tony Chen's* Honschi.

Recent studies and writings in the area of creativity indicate that the creative development of each child would be greatly enhanced if in addition to the teaching of the knowledge and skill necessary for literacy in each of these areas, they were restored in the school curriculum to a place comparable to their place in the history of mankind: that of providing each child with a creative means of communication and a creative outlet for his emotional reactions to his environment.

Art work is a close companion to literature. Correlations in art have already been suggested in bulletin board displays; creative book reports, drawing and painting pictures of stories, books and poems; making posters and book week exhibits and displays.

The principles of art were used extensively in the *Adventure with Halibut Bones* described in Chapter 2 when the children had the opportunity to explore color through lighting effects. Direct experiences of this nature can be planned to help teach certain aspects of art.

For instance, Miss Myers had "color" days. On the Green Day everything in the classroom centered around the color green. Each child wore something green to school. The children covered their desks with green paper. They made green cards, they used green flo-pens to make their charts, they listed green foods (such as spinach, beet greens, swiss chard, celery, peas, mint, etc.), they made green candy (jelly mints), and the stories and poems for the day were about green things, such as Gunilla B. Norris's book of *Green and Something Else, The Visitor* by Rachel Field, and *Green Moth* by Winifred Wells. By the end of each "color day," the children knew the chosen color well.

As authors use illustrations to enhance their stories and poems, so should the teacher feel free to use her own artistic ability to enhance the stories and poems for the children.

Miss Nichols gave the conventional Easter egg tree a creative twist in her primary classroom. About a week before Easter she placed a branch with many twigs on it in a pot of sand. The children sprayed the branch with white paint. They then added decorated eggs to the tree (using real eggs that had been blown out or the shell-shaped eggs that contain pantyhose), but each egg was decorated in keeping with the theme from a book read by each child. Eggs were added each day. On Friday afternoon an hour was set aside when each child showed his egg and briefly told about its meaning in relation to the book he had read.

Later, when enough eggshell pantyhose containers had been collected, the children were encouraged to make some little "secret" object that symbolized the story they read and put it inside the egg. Other children enjoyed peeking inside the shells to see what each story was about.

Literature and Social Sciences

The great problem of the world today is man's inability to live with his fellowman in peace and harmony. The technological revolution has catapulted man into the Space Age more quickly than he is able to cope with the problems that technology has forced upon him.

One thing is certain: nuclear warfare will mean the genocide of the human race. Consequently, man *must* learn to live with his fellowman. Never before in history has there been a mandate so strong or so compulsive.

The problems created by our advances in science cannot be solved as they were in the past. History provides only a portion of the answers, because we are facing problems today which never existed before. New solutions are needed to meet them. In every aspect of human culture, these problems exist—in politics, education, economics, sociology, psychology, industry, medicine, science.

The solution lies in the creative minds of men. But creativity has become a precious commodity, and throughout the world there is competition for the minds that possess it. Since the area of the social studies is that part of the curriculum which attempts to teach children the problems of man and his relation to other men (the skills of living together, the methods of identifying, refining, and solving problems, the skills of research, scientific investigation, and a scientific attitude toward life problems), the elementary school must play a vital part in developing the creativity of each child and in helping children find creative ways of living together. Through the social studies program, children learn most directly how to take their places as participating, contributing citizens in a democratic society.

The block of subject matter designated as the social sciences (or the social studies) in the elementary school curriculum exists for the purpose of helping children to learn to play the role of citizens in a world society. The challenge of the schools today is how best to teach that role. It calls for careful scrutiny on the part of administrators and teachers as to how they can best help young people to understand world problems and how to play an active part in the solution of them.

Learning to live together does not just happen with the act of growing up. We have come to realize more and more that training is needed to develop in people those qualities and skills essential to successful life in a democratic society. Children must *practice* the act of sharing ideas without acting emotionally; they must *practice* critical and creative thinking; they must *learn* to listen to other people's viewpoints; they must *learn* to use democratic processes and group dynamics; they must *develop* empathy and understanding of people different from themselves.

Our schools were founded to perpetuate our political ideology. The primary reason for the establishment of the American public school was to take care of all those needs in the functioning of a democratic society which could not be left to chance. One of the first needs was literacy; today one need is learning to live together in peace and harmony. We are committed to developing these skills in children so that each child may function as an individual in a democratic country. In a democracy, individuals count; their rights and freedoms are respected. Creativity functions best in a free society of free thinkers. Our social studies program should be the core for developing the creative thinkers of our republic.

What Are the Social Sciences?

Because the terms "social studies" and "social sciences" have become clouded with a variety of meanings in their development, the following terms will be used in this chapter.

The *social sciences* are those bodies of knowledge which man has accumulated from his studies of economics, sociology, political science, history, geography, civics, and anthropology.

The *social studies* are the facts selected from this reservoir of truths to be used for instructional purposes and the methods employed to teach those truths that develop worthy human relationships. The term *citizenship education* has often been substituted for social studies, especially when it is thought of in terms of social living and the fostering of effective human relationships.

Social living is the translation of the social studies into action in the classroom. Social living is concerned with the practice of necessary skills and the utilization of knowledge for effective patterns of living together. Social living is concerned with the building of sound, creative human relationships.

The teaching of social studies in the Space Age must incorporate the concept of social living. Children must learn diverse and complicated skills of living together and developing sound human relationships. Relationships may well be defined as the fourth R in the school curriculum. Conditions may be set in the classroom to provide children with opportunities to develop creative and aesthetic living.

The skills of living together are not learned from a textbook. Textbook teaching never has fulfilled the destiny of the social studies program. It was never meant to. In the future it will be even less effective. It has already been demonstrated in recent years that knowledge is accumulating so fast that many textbooks are outdated before they leave the press. In today's social studies program the textbook plays a different role than it has in the past.

Teaching the social studies is concerned with teaching children techniques, attitudes, values, understandings, concepts, and skills, as well as factual matter. School becomes a place where children come to learn *how* to learn. The modern concepts of social studies teaching are directed as much at the development or change of behavior in individuals as at the accumulation of factual knowledge. The school attempts to help each child develop techniques for solving these problems on his own age level. The content of the social studies curriculum, as it has developed through the social functions approach, is concerned with the problems people have faced in all civilizations—those of food, clothing, shelter, pleasure, science, health, safety, transportation, communication, education, government, and organization. Children face these problems of their culture at an early age, and the school can utilize them as the core of the subject matter it teaches. Each area is one that has been accentuated by the process of grouping for better social living, and each is one that must, therefore, be resolved by a group rather than an individual. The school must encourage groups to solve problems through the sound techniques of a scientific method. Many professional groups have organized definite objectives for education in social living.

All school systems define their objectives for teaching social studies in their curriculum guides, designed for teachers to use in their work with children. From major objectives, specific objectives are written for the social studies program. The objective of most social studies programs is stated as follows:

OUR OBJECTIVE: To build certain characteristics, traits, values, knowledges, skills, abilities, understandings, concepts, appreciations, and attitudes in each child in order to develop an effective citizen for a democratic society.[3]

FRAMEWORK FOR A SOCIAL STUDIES PROGRAM

Building Attitudes through Children's Literature

In Chapter 3 the basic needs of children were reviewed. Many of these needs were "feeling" needs.

A child's attitudes toward life are developed not by what he *knows* but by what he *feels*. Although knowledge can temper his attitudes, how he has been treated and the feelings he experiences as a result of his treatment form his attitudes towards people, experiences, and places.

Humans behave as they do because of their basic needs and the degree to which these needs are fulfilled. Lack of fulfillment of basic needs can cause man to fly into a passion, to summon up deep courage, to become obsessed with anger, to call up reserves of colossal strength, to tap wells of love and tenderness, to empathize to the point of heartbreak.

Children's literature serves the unique purpose of giving children a total perspective. In real life a child may react to an immediate situation with an unleashing of his emotions when his basic needs go unmet. In literature he reacts emotionally to what he reads but then reads on to observe the results of his reactions farther along at any given place in the story. This long-range view of situations can do a great deal to help the child modify his attitudes and leave them more open to change.

Emotional reactions to unmet needs have been recorded by each generation of every culture in one way or another. Environments may differ but the emotional structure of people is basically the same throughout the world even though it has been conditioned to a variance of responses in different places. These records of great emotional experiences are the elements that make possible a common understanding among all people. Such records recount the passions, courage, love, hates, frailties, strengths, heartaches. When these are told in a manner so sensitive that the reader finds his or her own emotions called into play and a bond of understanding bridging the span of two different lives—the character's and his or her own—literature is born.

Understanding, then, comes as a result of shared emotions more than as a result of shared facts. This is why the use of children's literature in the classroom can become a great strategy for the teaching of social studies: it builds understanding through emotion, between a child here and a child somewhere else, between a child now and one long ago.

Children come to love Homer Price because they see a little of themselves in him, and they understand that he is a headstrong, clumsy boy who always puts himself in compromising positions. They can under-

---

3. James A. Smith, *Creative Teaching of the Social Studies in the Elementary School* (Boston: Allyn and Bacon, 1967), pp. 27–28.

stand the arrogance in *Pippi Longstocking* because, although she does things they would not dare to do, they are nonetheless things they have all *wanted* to do. They sympathize with Green in *Green and Something Else* because each can recognize the fear that brings out cowardice and the love that creates courage.

They develop a respect for the ancient Inca through the boy Cusi in *The Secret of the Andes* and *Annie and the Old One* because of the quiet dignity of these characters, cloaked in mystery, yet alive and believable.

Often their own needs for change, for expressing arrogance, for showing courage, and for achievement and respect are met vicariously through the reading of these stories.

Developing Skills through Children's Literature

Skills to be developed in a social studies program are: skills of problem solving, self- and group evaluation, critical thinking, creative thinking, map and chart skills, and the skills needed in communication as those discussed in the first part of this chapter.

Suggestions have been made throughout this book as to how literature may be used to develop these skills. Certainly all stories place children in problem-solving situations. Some stories create a higher tension for problem solving than others—mystery stories, for instance. Questions posed by children at the onset of a unit as a problem they would like to pursue can often be answered by reading excellent children's literature.

For instance, in Mr. Arnes's classroom, the children were engaged in a study of the role of the black in America at the time of the war between the states. In answer to the problem, "Was injustice shown the blacks in the South at that time?" Mr. Arnes did not have the class read a text and assume some single author's viewpoint on this important problem. Instead he wanted the children to accumulate a variety of evidence and opinion and then draw their own conclusions. Consequently, he assigned parts of good literature for them to read and report on to the class. To his outstanding sixth-grade readers, he assigned *Uncle Tom's Cabin*, Margaret Mitchell's *Gone with the Wind*, Harper Lee's *To Kill a Mockingbird*, parts of McKinlay Kantor's *Andersonville*, and David Harbison's *Reaching for Freedom*.

To his average readers he assigned such books as *Sounder* by William Armstrong, *Abraham Lincoln* by Genevieve Foster, Philip Spencer's *Three Against Slavery*, Eva Knox Evans's *Araminta*, *Melindy's Medal* by Georgene Faulkner and John Becker, Mabel Leigh Hunt's *Ladycake Farm*, Paula Fox's *Slave Dancer*, and Ann Petry's *Harriet Tubman: Conductor on the Underground Railway*.

What Mr. Arnes was really after was a total picture of the role of the black person in the Southern culture of early America. Since injustice creates emotional reactions, he wanted the children to experience different viewpoints and to share them.

The fact that this adventure was successful was evidenced later when the class role-played a session in Congress with the students taking sides on the issue of the abolition of slavery. Heated, emotional discussions with the children expressing many viewpoints soon led them to see why, in the 1860s, people had become heated and emotional over the same issue.

Reading is a problem-solving adventure, since a plot presents a problem and the story line is developed in solving the problem.

Skills of evaluation are developed when children pursue such activities as those mentioned in Chapter 12 when they learn to develop appreciation and tastes in literature. Evaluation is also used in writing book reviews.

Good stories require critical thinking. Some require creative thinking. Suggestions for the development of these skills and for map and chart skills have been previously presented. These skills are not developed solely in the teaching of social studies; they are also developed through the creative teaching of children's literature. Literature can be used to develop each skill, which can then be used to extend the enjoyment of literature.

Building Values through Children's Literature

Values are the established ideals of life: objects, customs, ways of acting, etc., that the members of a given society regard as desirable. Some values change from generation to generation, but most values change very, very slowly. Rebels in each generation often attempt to change values or impose new values on a culture. The system of "the establishment" is strong, and often rebellious values of the new generation are tempered to fit into the old. On the other hand, new knowledge creates new insights among nations and many values are changed rather quickly almost by common or majority consent.

A society must have a set of values in order to survive. Values provide the code of ethics by which people are able to live together. It is the job of the elementary school staff to examine the values that are important in order for people to live comfortably together and to identify those they feel must be included as targets for instruction in the social studies program. The values recognized as important now must be spelled out in detail and strategies must be plotted so the values are transmitted to the children of the school.

What moral and spiritual values, for instance, are still important to the culture in which we live? Do we still value the old family structure? Marriage? If these structures are on their way out, as some people would have us believe, then the units on family and the concepts of marriage as developed in our social studies programs must be changed.

Children's literature plays a large part in determining the values to be perpetuated in the social studies program in that modern literature provides a way to examine values, and children are as greatly influenced by their heroes in print as they are by real-life heroes. In the literature of the world are found the values of the past and the evolution of the new values of today. Many of the values society still maintains are the subjects of children's books. In reading these books children can see the worth of the value system.

Equality of opportunity is a value we prize dearly at this time in history. It has been the root of riots, burnings, protest marches, assassinations, and rebellion. The right for equality of opportunity is brought home to children with strength and beauty in William Armstrong's *Sounder*.

Part of the task of the elementary school personnel after values have been identified is to select and present books to children which exploit the need and benefits of holding such values. Intuitively, children will take unto themselves those values which seem to make life better. Books that dwell on values (and all of them do to a degree) may also be used beneficially in working with bibliotherapy.

Each year books are published that deal effectively with emotions and values. Some recent examples are: Dorothy Hamilton's *Winter Girl,* which deals with the problem of jealousy between two sisters; Ilse-Margaret Vogel's *My Twin Sister Erika,* a collection of five stories that explore love and rivalry between twin sisters; Joan Hanson's *I'm Going to Run Away,* which deals with the value of juvenile independence; *The Yo-Yo Kid* by Rose Blue, a book for intermediate-grade children that explores violence from the viewpoints of the victim and the perpetrator; Ann Nolan Clark's new book, *Finn Sisu,* that relates the value of courage to a story about immigrants who came to settle Minnesota; Elizabeth Levy's *Lizzie Lies A Lot,* which confronts lying directly; and *What Every Kid Should Know* by Jonah Kalb and David Viscott.

Building Knowledge through Children's Literature

How is the knowledge of the world best transmitted? American teachers have been bombarded with learning theories, modules, kits, organizational plans, methodology, and strategies to encourage the learning of facts and concepts we feel children should know.

Children's literature can develop knowledge in two observable ways: First, it can impart knowledge directly because facts are couched in actions and descriptions of real-life situations that help children learn in a total, natural, relevant setting, rather than in isolated or fragmented bits of irrelevance.

By now, we should realize that usable knowledge is seldom imparted to children through the use of stodgy textbook lessons of learn and recite. What good does it do to know that cheese and other dairy products are produced in Holland if a child has no idea why, and no understanding of the place of cheese in the lives of people? Who cares about the War Between the States and its heroic battles if one does not understand its effect on the lives of the people then and now—the problems it posed, and the lessons learned from it? Few textbooks ever caught the feel of that war as did Margaret Mitchell's classic, *Gone with the Wind,* a book only mildly accepted by literary critics at the time of its publication.

Secondly, children's literature makes real many facts already known and brings them alive largely through enrichment. In this book we have already seen how literature can enrich the social studies. In the account of the unit on Lois Lenski, we have an excellent example of the manner by which literature can bring alive the historical and geographical facts of the country. The reading of stories written about history and places can make history and geography have meaning and relevance for children.

The log cabin Lincoln lived in. Robert G.

a

Abraham Lincoln at the theater and the man sneaking up to kill him.

b

FIGURE 15–7a, b. Lori imparts knowledge to her classmates through a report for which she has drawn scenes. The book is Genevieve Foster's Abraham Lincoln.

A challenge is presented to teachers and administrators in developing courses built around the literature of the world, for every country has its literature both current and for every period of time. Studying social studies in this way would utilize the common understandings among children as it does among men and women: the ability to empathize through native emotions and drives.

Pictorial maps of authors or localities for favorite stories help the teacher to develop geographical concepts. Children can follow the route of *Johnny Appleseed* on a map, plot the adventures of *Tom Sawyer,* or draw out the campaign of *The Matchlock Gun.* From activities of this nature comes an understanding of the purpose and use of maps.

Many of the creative teachers described in this volume have already demonstrated to us how literature may be used effectively in social studies.

In studying faraway places, for instance, the folklore of other countries may be shared through the use of a puppet show, such as that of *The Five Chinese Brothers* recounted in Chapter 4. In Chapter 14, a folk tale of Africa, *A Story, A Story,* was used effectively as part of the study of that continent. In Chapter 13 we saw how bulletin boards could be effective tools for encouraging children to read when the teachers used them for such topics as "Stories About Mexico," "Children of Other Lands," "Legends of Mexico," "Mexican Topics," "Picture Books of Mexico," and "Books of Research on Mexico."

Another way to share the folklore of other countries is to encourage children to give creative book reports, as Miss Wagner's children presented *The Five Chinese Brothers* in Chapter 13. Life on a deserted island was also demonstrated in the unusual book report of *Robinson Crusoe* described in that chapter.

A box theater was used in the same chapter to tell the story of *Hans Brinker or The Silver Skates.* Filmstrips, films, and recordings help children to learn about countries by picturing the environment in which the main character functions.

Other techniques mentioned previously that provide children an opportunity to adventure with a far-off place are: using artifacts from specific places; making murals similar to the one made by Mr. Harrison's class in Chapter 14; making shadow boxes; making peep shows; and presenting shadow plays.

Other examples show how literature helps children to develop concepts about places nearby through the use of stories and pictures. Few children could read McCloskey's *Make Way for Ducklings* without capturing much of the special atmosphere that is Boston. In Chapter 13 Miss Spencer built an entire unit around the local museum to help the children find resources essential to the study of social studies by using *The Mixed-Up Files of Mrs. Basil E. Frankweiler* as a springboard.

Some of the illustrations in this book show how teachers have used books to teach about other times. The adventure that tells how one teacher built an entire unit around the books of Lois Lenski is a classic for demonstrating this strategy. The play by Mr. Carr's class described in Chapter 5 is another illustration of how children could share the behavior and feelings of people living long ago when they dressed, acted, and "felt" like Robin Hood's men in Sherwood Forest. Dramatization techniques are scattered throughout the book; suggestions are made that children dramatize books like *Ben and Me* and that they do free dramatization of historical scenes, of a medieval fair, or of the Boston Tea Party. Ideas for using bulletin boards are presented; one teacher developed an interest in Indians by creating a bulletin board on *Songs of the Chippewa*.

The possibilities are endless. Every technique suggested in this book can be used with social studies content, with involvement being the keynote.

Literature makes possible the identification of children with the problems of here and now, and often it can lead to the creation of literature by the children themselves.

Choral speaking has been mentioned in Chapter 14 as an excellent technique to develop the sense of rhyme and rhythm in children. Much creative work can result from fusing historical facts with the literature read. For instance, reports for social studies may be written in such a way that they read as a cross between prose and poetry and can develop a definite rhyme. With a little practice, children can write such reports, which may be put on ditto paper, distributed to the class, and then chanted onto a cassette tape. A very creative teacher friend of ours, over a period of a few years, had her whole social studies curriculum on cassette tapes in a multitude of types of choral poems. Here is a section from one of her tapes:

> *Across the river by the water there*
> *Stood Paul Revere—waiting, waiting*
> *For a light to appear in the old North Church,*
> *Waiting, waiting.*
> *One if by land and two if by sea.*
> *And the night passed by—*
> *Waiting, waiting!*
> *Suddenly a light in the old North Church*
> *A light, a light—by land they come!*
> *Alert the farmers—tell the world*
> *The British are coming!*
> *Prepare, prepare!*
> *Be off—spread the word*
> *No more waiting, waiting!*

See Appendix J for a list of excellent books that may be used to impart knowledge. These books classify as good literature as well as being factually honest in content.

Information Books

Information books constitute a category that was not discussed in detail in Chapter 2. Many books that can be used in the social studies program fall into this category. Information books are not textbooks. They are written to do what the title implies: impart information. Although many adventure, biographical, and realistic stories impart information, their primary purpose is to weave a story using a definite style, such as the books used to teach the unit on Lois Lenski.

Information books, on the other hand, are designed to impart information without necessarily telling a story. They narrate true incidents, but the narrative is secondary. They readily classify as literature, since their prose has style and the illustrations are superb. In the area of science and social studies, hundreds of these books exist and many have become classics. Examples of such books are: Jeanne Bendick's *The First Book of Airplanes* (and other Firsts), Alice Dalgliesh's *America Begins: The Story of the Finding of the New World* and *The Fourth of July Story*, Genevieve Foster's *Birthdays of Freedom* (and others), Holling C. Holling's *Paddle to the Sea,* Munro Leaf's *Geography Can Be Fun,* Ann Petry's *Harriet Tubman: Conductor on the Underground Railway,* Herman and Nina Schneider's *Let's Look under the City,* Glenn Blough's *Tree on the Road to Turntown,* Clara Ingram Judson's *George Washington: Leader to the People*, and countless others. Appendix K gives a selected list of such books.

Modern authors continue to write exciting information books. A very recent one is Edna Barth's *Hearts, Cupids and Red Roses,* which presents all the folklore and facts about Valentine's Day. It is beautifully illustrated by Ursula Arndt.

Robert C. Cohen has written *The Color of Man,* a timely book with illustrations by Ken Heyman. Deloris Harrison's *We Shall Live In Peace: The Teachings of Martin Luther King, Jr.* is a valuable information book for teachers as well as children.

Maud and Miska Petersham's *Story of the Presidents of the United States of America* falls into the category of information books, as does

FIGURE 15–8. *Books such as Laura Bannon's* Manneba's Birthday, Harry Behn's The Two Uncles of Pablo, *Clyde Bulla's* Benita, Helen Rand Parrish's At the Palace Gates, *and others helped these children glean the knowledge for their activities on Mexico.*

Herbert Zim and James R. Skelly's *Metric Measure* and Zim's *Medicine*. Zim is unparalleled in his books for children in the physical sciences.

The Orchid Family by Lynne Martin is a visual treat. Howard E. Smith and Lorraine Norris have illustrated *Newsmakers: The Press and the President* with news photos that give the book much appeal to upper middle-grade children and juveniles. David Macaulay's *City* is excellent fare for studying a specific life style.

Current information books touch on every topic. *Fun with Seashells* by Claude Nassiet gives the seashell collector suggestions for making designs on household articles or sea sculpture and is illustrated with photographs. Grosset and Dunlap has issued a *Nancy Drew Cookbook* of about 150 recipes. Joseph Davis's *And Then There Were None* is a text with photographs by Nina Leen on the plight of over 100 species threatened with extinction. Many do-it-yourself books continue to be printed, such as Alice A. George's *Creative Toymaking*. For the explorer there are books like Jean George's *Snow Tracks*.

Information books cover all topics: time, language, sex, art, music, foreign lands, crafts, life styles, animals, hobbies, cooking, and the sciences. Name it and there is a good book for it.

Developing Abilities through Children's Literature

The abilities we have been discussing include creative ability, the ability to show self-control, to work in groups, to communicate with others, to think

FIGURE 15–9. Creative writing is posted outside The Writing Shop, where children go to write in solitude.

critically and creatively, to make judgments and decisions, to apply knowledge and learnings, to share other viewpoints, and to organize.

From the many illustrations and verbal observations of classroom situations in this volume, we can see that literature can play a forceful role in developing these social studies goals. Each of the abilities mentioned above is an outcome of the type of literature program advocated by the authors of this book.

The releasing of creative ability is described in every chapter in the many projects carried out by the children. The ability to show self-control is demonstrated when the children hold a discussion and each child is allowed to express his viewpoint; critical and creative thinking is practiced in brainstorming sessions; a discussion where children make judgments and decisions is described; knowledge and learnings are applied in the play presentations, the scroll movies, and the film making, to name a few, and the abilities to plan, organize, and evaluate are also well illustrated.

Developing Appreciations through Children's Literature

Inasmuch as Chapter 6 was devoted to the development of appreciation for literature through creative teaching, one illustration here will suffice to show how the use of literature can help children appreciate the finer things of life.

Reference has previously been made to Mr. Carr's production of *The Story of Robin Hood*. Following is a description of one way Mr. Carr helped children develop an appreciation for style in writing.

After the Robin Hood play was given, Mr. Carr brought passages from other pieces of literature into the classroom and read them. Because the children were sensitive to style, they selected passages they particularly liked and put them on a chart of favorites. One line the entire class felt was most descriptive was this one:

> *The apricot and peach trees stood crucified against*
> *the wall in the sun.*[4]

The use of literature in the teaching of the social studies would practically demand a continual alertness to developing a multitude of appreciations in boys and girls.

Developing Characteristics and Traits through Children's Literature

Part of the job of understanding other people is understanding oneself better. When a child or an adult can understand the reason behind the behavior of others, he is more accepting of it. Consequently, when he understands his own motives, he is more accepting of himself.

Children often set up real and fictitious heroes and heroines. They

---

4. Mary Stewart, *The Crystal Cave* (Greenwich, Conn.: Fawcett, 1970).

identify, especially in the middle grades, with characters in literature and mimic them. It is important at this time in their growth that they have plenty of material around about heroes and heroines worthy of imitation.

Beautiful stories such as *The Hundred Dresses* by Eleanor Estes, *And Now Miguel* by Joseph Krumgold, and *Up a Road Slowly* by Irene Hunt deal directly with the drives, needs, and emotions of the heroes and heroines and help children understand how to cope with them. Such books help the child to understand himself.

Earlier we dealt with the topic of character development through the use of children's books. We mentioned such books as *Up a Road Slowly* by Irene Hunt, *And Now Miguel* by Joseph Krumgold, *Johnny Tremain* by Esther Forbes, *Magic Michael* by Louis Slobodkin, *Two Is a Team* by Lorraine and Jerrold Beim, *Grandmother and I* and *Grandfather and I* by Helen Buckley, and *They Were Strong and Good* by Robert Lawson as examples of books that tell of character growth in some fashion on many age levels.

The development of character has not been neglected in modern writing. Many modern authors have written about old-time heroes—May McNeer's book, *The Story of George Washington,* illustrated by Lynd Ward, is one such example. But they have also invented new heroes who overcome obstacles because of their strength of character. Jean Merrill's *The Toothpaste Millionaire* is a humorous story of a strong character, Rufus Mayflower. Ann Waldron's recent book, *The House on Pendleton Block,* deals well with the trait of determination. Sarah Orne Jewett's story, *White Heron,* illustrated by Barbara Cooney, is a beautifully sensitive piece about the development of character in Sylvy, the heroine. Helen Buckley's little book *Michael Is Brave* deals directly with bravery in a way that can be understood by an early-age primary child. *The Boy Who Sailed Around the World Alone* by Robin Lee Graham and Derck Gill is a story of Robin, whose love for adventure combined with his grit and determination bring him many exciting adventures. It is an excellent "character" story for children aged ten and up.

Ann Irwin deals directly with the grit required to lose weight in *One Bite at a Time,* a story of Neva Allen, a fat girl, and how she solves her problem. The character needed to change a hopeless way of life emerges in Rose Blue's realistic story of *Nikki,* whose brother is a drug addict; her father has deserted her mother; she is failing in the sixth grade. But Nikki has friends; her strong will is brought into play by their help, and she finds a new life.

A striking, memorable story of warm friendship and the conflicts that develop strength of character can be found in Eleanor Estes's recent book, *The Coat-Hanger Christmas Tree. Sky Lab: Pioneer Space Station* by William Suirer and William G. Holder (illustrated by photographs) subtly points up the qualities needed by men participating in NASA's spectacular Skylab operation.

A great deal of nonfiction is published these days that exploits the strong character of certain public figures. Though not exactly a good piece of literature, *Brian's Song* is one such example that has had tremendous appeal to middle-grade boys and girls, especially after seeing the film on television. Figure 15–10 shows the sensitive reaction of one girl in a fifth

FIGURE 15–10. A football helmet and two tears: Sensitive symbolism for a report of Brian's Song by a twelve-year-old.

grade who sums up the entire story by drawing a football helmet and two solitary tears.

Sharon Bell Mathis has written a lovely biography, *Ray Charles,* for ages six to nine. Actually a weaving together of fiction and reality, Barbara Cohen's *Thank You, Jackie Robinson* is an excellent story exploiting character development. Doris Faber has written *Harry Truman,* which is a straightforward account of a man of great character, for children aged eight and up.

Other recent works that deal with character development and that have great appeal to the young are *Muhammad Ali* by Kenneth Rudeen; *The Story of Stevie Wonder* by James Haskins; *Courage to Adventure,* a collection of stories about boys and girls growing up in America, compiled by the Child Study Association; *Scott Joplin and the Ragtime Years* by Mark Evans; and *When William Rose, Stephen Vincent Benet and I Were Young* by Laura Burst.

In the discussion of realistic tales, it was mentioned that children receive a great deal of benefit from reading these tales. Often the problems of the main character are those of the child reader, and he receives comfort, confidence, and self-concept by coming to realize that all problems can be solved, and that he too may be able to work out his problems in time. It was pointed out that realistic tales later help a child understand other peoples and places by showing him the likenesses in the world. They help him to stretch his imagination, to face reality, and to cope with social problems on his own level of thinking. They also help him to identify problems in himself and to develop his sense of empathy.

Piltz and Sund[5] state:

> A page from the history of the advancement of mankind is a page from the history of science. The influence of science in modern life is so powerful that it stimulates and colors all phases of human development. Science has moved out of the laboratory into the living room of man; it has become a discipline integral to his survival in the present and his progress in the future.

Perhaps Piltz and Sund have provided the reason why science has invaded the world of children's literature and vice versa: it is simply too much a part of life to leave out. Many excellent books have been written for children with science as the core of the plot.

Some of these books are fiction and deal with science as fantasy. Madeleine L'Engle's *A Wrinkle in Time* and *A Wind in the Door* are good examples of such books. Robert Heinlein's *Have Space Suit—Will Travel* also falls into this category. *Follow the Whales* by Carl Biemiller and his previous book, *The Hydronauts,* are examples of such books written for upper middle graders.

Others are information books, but they are written and illustrated so beautifully that they can be classified as literature. A few samples of recent books falling into this category are: *Snow* by Thelma Bell, *A Tree Is a Plant* by Clyde Bulla, *The Sea Around Us* by Rachel Carson, *Worlds to Come* by Damon Knight. Jo Polseno, in his recent first book, *Secrets of Redding Glen: The Natural History of a Wooded Valley,* presents wildlife and the change of seasons in a delicate, absorbing manner. Millicent E. Selsam's *Questions and Answers about Horses* is a must for children interested in horses. Hy Ruchlis's *How a Rock Came to Be in a Fence on a Road Near a Town* is a beautiful, informative science picture book. Millicent Selsam and Joyce Hunt's *A First Look at Birds* has clear text, beautiful line drawings, puzzles, and a game to help children observe the differences among groups of birds. Herbert Zim, long known for his science books for children, continues to publish, with such recent books as *Commercial Fishing* (with Lucretia Krantz) and a revised edition of *The Universe.* A different kind of science information book is Robert Welber's illustrated book *Song of the Seasons,* which is a child-sized view of the seasons as reflected in one small backyard. It is written for ages two to six.

Delicate watercolor paintings enhance the text of *Down to the Beach* by May Garelich, a book for ages five to eight that gives much information about life near the ocean. Aileen Fisher's *My Cat Has Eyes of Sapphire Blue* is a beautiful book on cats for ages four to eight. Connie Ewbank's *Insect Zoo* for ages nine to twelve shows youngsters how to house, feed, and observe the habits of many different insects. William C. Grimm and M. Jean Craig have written a fascinating book, *The Wondrous World of Seedless Plants,* which tells about mushrooms, moss, and green fern. Madeline Angell's book, *120 Questions and Answers About the Birds,* tells the young reader everything he ever wanted to know about birds. The

---

5. Albert Piltz and Robert Sund, *Creative Teaching of Science in the Elementary School,* 2nd ed. (Boston: Allyn and Bacon, 1974), p. 1.

drawings in this book are delicate and beautiful. Sigmund Lavine's book, *Indian Corn and Other Gifts,* is not only informative about the history of our crops, but also entertaining. The list of such information books is endless.

The use of science in literature is not new. Jules Verne's *Twenty Thousand Leagues Under the Sea,* a science fiction story, and his other books have long attracted children even though they were written mostly for adults. Many stories dealing with themes of nature and science have become classics through the ages.

The above-mentioned nonfiction books dealing with science report science as fact and do so in a beautiful, effective way with text and pictures. They do not, however, always tell a story or have well-delineated characters. They do pave the way to knowledge and exploration for children and are far superior to the average textbook in showing how children can learn facts in a creative manner. They do, in fact, promote creativity by being so creative themselves.

A third category of science writing is the picture book group, which can hardly be classified as science, but as "getting-ready-for-science" books. These generally extol the beauties and wonder of nature in a charming and interesting manner with exquisite pictures, and do much to help children sharpen their observation powers and make them sensitive to the beauty and usefulness of the world around them. Jeanne Bendick's beautiful little book, *All Around You,* falls into this category.

The objectives for teaching science in the elementary school are many. Most are derived from a main objective: *to develop in children the scientific attitude and knowledge of the scientific method.* Sub-objectives include these: developing a sense of curiosity in the child, arousing a sense of inquiry and discovery, sharpening the child's observation powers, helping him to form realistic concepts, helping the child to identify problems, and teaching him a technique for finding answers to his problems. The technique for answering his problems will be the scientific method: he will learn to state a problem, to make a hypothesis, to gather material about it, to experiment to prove his hypothesis, to synthesize his thinking, to draw conclusions, and to verbalize his results.

The gathering of information in the above process is the stage at which science books are of great value, whether or not they are written in literature form. Excellent books can do much to meet many of the sub-objectives listed above. Whether these books do perform this function lies in the quality of the writing and of the illustrations. In selecting books for the child's reading program, the teacher will, of course, consider accuracy of content. Other factors to be considered are: clarity of presentation; the style of the author (which needs to appeal to the age level for which the book was written); thoroughness of treatment of the subject, so that the book does not develop misconceptions or confusion in the mind of the child; presentation of the material, which should be largely from the child's point of view; the ability to discriminate between books that can be taken as scientific fact and those that are science fiction; the ability to use either or both in their proper place in the curriculum; the organization of the book so that concepts and facts are presented on the child's level of understanding and he is led from the known into the unknown.

One criterion for selection of all information books, especially science books, is to check the copyright date to determine whether the book includes the latest information. Modern technology and research often render these books outdated rather quickly.

SUMMARY

In order to produce literature, children must master the skills of symbolic communication. Since all teaching relies on communication in one form or another, literature can well become the base for teaching these skills as well as the end product.

Language develops in a natural sequence from experiencing to listening to speaking to reading to writing, and then to the refinements of writing, such as spelling, punctuation, handwriting forms, and word usage.

Literature has been used throughout this book to demonstrate how each of these skills can be taught with the thought that exposure to literature all along the way is the foremost factor in leading children to develop an appreciation for literature.

The current trend in the elementary school is individualized reading, which demands a great number of appealing books for children to read. In some schools children are already exposed to the fine writing of excellent children's authors throughout the entire reading program.

Literature is not only a means of communication; it is also an art in itself, a close companion to art and music. In the elementary school each may be used to enhance the other. This marriage of two of the arts is nowhere better exemplified than in the books of children's literature currently available, with their exciting and beautiful art illustrations. Children accept this marriage as natural and important to their understanding of the books they read. This natural, important combination should be used more frequently in developing appreciations of all the fine arts with children.

Both literature and social studies are basically concerned with man's relationships to man, and the manner by which one develops the attitudes, appreciations, knowledges, skills, characteristics, and values necessary to live together in a democratic manner. Consequently, children's literature can stand alone in meeting objectives set for the social studies, or it may be used as a tool to accomplish these objectives by providing social studies enrichment.

The beautiful, effective writing used in children's storybooks has been adapted to other writing for children. This is especially true in the area of the physical sciences. Authors of children's books in this discipline have raised the material presented to a highly creative level through the use of beautiful sketches and photographs, and excellent, accurate script.

A challenge to school personnel is to determine how much of social studies content and experience can be achieved through the use of children's literature.

TO THE COLLEGE STUDENT

1. Do you feel Miss Black and Mrs. Burns met the objectives they set for themselves in the project of *The Emperor's New Clothes*?

2. Using children's literature as your base, try to plan a curriculum unit designed to teach any special aspect of the language arts or the social studies.

3. Plan a curriculum unit whose aim is to teach literature appreciation for itself.

4. Survey the Newbery and Caldecott award-winning lists (see pages 88 and 93) for books that have a language arts base. Is it safe to say that they *all* have a social science base when we use the definition of social science given in this chapter?

5. Make a list of some of the values held important on your college campus today and then note whether or not the ten best sellers of adult fiction truly reflect these values. Would you say that some literature violates standard values for shock value in order to boost sales?

6. Take any one currently popular book of fiction and analyze it for literary value. Does it make a deliberate attempt to:

appeal to people's emotions—to arouse them?

impart knowledge?

exploit or change value systems?

develop sensory experiences?

develop or change a commonly held attitude?

develop or exploit the value of certain traits or characteristics?

be deliberately controversial or shocking?

develop a particular style?

accent effective communication as well as correct communication?

use simile and metaphor effectively?

paint word pictures?

TO THE CLASSROOM TEACHER

1. Make a survey of the times you base lessons on children's literature or use a piece of children's literature in your teaching. Are you using it enough?

2. Take a unit you generally teach in the social studies during the year and plan a new approach basing it on all the children's books you can find related to that unit.

3. Plan to teach a course in your state's history through the use of historical fiction.

4. Refer to Appendixes I and J and ask yourself how you could use the excellent lists given there to teach social studies in the next few months.

5. Repeat Activity 4 by using Appendix J and a science unit you plan to teach soon.

6. Problems for discussion:

a. Fiction is not accurate enough to use as a base for social studies.

b. Affective behaviors cannot be measured accurately enough for the teacher to know whether or not she has accomplished objectives dealing with them.

c. Outcomes in curriculum areas, and particularly in children's literature, can only be determined when objectives are written in behavioral terms.

d. All literature is creative.

e. Subject matter is best taught in classes devoted to each topic. (Use the *Encyclopedia of Educational Research* to do some reading of the research in this area.)

TO THE COLLEGE STUDENT
AND THE CLASSROOM TEACHER

1. In Chapter 12, Mrs. Galvin built her social studies program around the writings of Lois Lenski. What other ways can literature be used to teach social studies?

2. In what ways could you use literature to teach physical education? Home economics? Music?

3. Which of the strategies described

in Chapters 13 and 14 could be adapted to the teaching of literature through the language arts? The social sciences? The physical sciences?

4. In Appendix E, there is a list of individual recordings of various children's classics. Try some of them. What advantages are there in listening to records, rather than watching films of children's stories?

5. Using the "verbal observations" at the beginning of each chapter, find instances where literature was used to develop language skills, social skills, art skills, and physical skills.

SELECTED BIBLIOGRAPHY

Adler, Irving. "On Writing Science Books for Children." *Horn Book Magazine* 61 (October 1965): 524–529.

Applegate, Mauree. *Easy in English*. New York: Harper & Row, 1963.

Baker, Augusta, comp. *Books about Negro Life for Children*, 3rd ed. New York: New York Public Library, 1968.

Bamman, Henry J.; Mildred A. Dawson and Robert J. Whitehead. *Oral Interpretation of Children's Literature*. Dubuque, Iowa: Wm. C. Brown, 1964.

Blough, Glenn, and Julius Schwartz. *Science in the Elementary School and How to Teach It*, 3rd ed. New York: Holt, Rinehart and Winston, 1964.

Broderick, Dorothy. *Image of the Black in Children's Fiction*. New York: R. R. Bowker, 1973.

Carlson, Ruth Kearney. *Literature for Children: Enrichment Ideas*. Dubuque, Iowa: Wm. C. Brown, 1970.

Carlson, Ruth Kearney. *Emerging Humanity: Multi-Ethnic Literature for Children and Adolescents*. Dubuque, Iowa: Wm. C. Brown, 1972.

Charles, Sydney Robinson. *Handbook of Music and Music Literature in Sets and Series*. New York: Free Press, 1972.

Cianciolo, Patricia. "Role of Children's Books in the Open Classroom." *Elementary English* 50 (November 1973): 409–416.

Cole, Natalie. *Children's Art from Deep Down Inside*. New York: John Day, 1966.

Crosby, Muriel, ed. *Reading Ladders for Human Relations*, 4th ed. Washington, D.C.: American Council on Education, 1963.

Deason, Hilary J. *The AAAS Science Booklist for Children*, 3rd ed. Washington, D.C.: American Association for the Advancement of Science, 1972.

Deason, Hilary J., ed. *A Guide to Science Reading*, rev. ed. New York: Signet, 1964.

D. O. K. Publishing Company. *Motivating Readers*. Buffalo: D. O. K. Publishing, 1967.

Edwards, Beverly Sigler. "The Therapeutic Value of Reading." *Elementary English* 49 (February 1972): 213–218.

Gillespie, John Thomas. *Paperback Books for Young People: An Annotated Guide to Publishers and Distributors*. Chicago: American Library Association, 1972.

Greene, Harry A., and Walter T. Petty. *Developing Language Skills in the Elementary Schools*, 4th ed. Boston: Allyn and Bacon, 1971.

Griffin, Louise, comp. *Multi-Ethnic Books for Young Children*. Washington, D.C.: National Association for the Education of Young Children, updated annually.

Guilfoile, Elizabeth. *Books for Beginning Readers*. Champaign, Ill.: National Council of Teachers of English, 1962.

Haman, Albert C., and Mary K. Eakin. *Library Materials for Elementary Science*. Cedar Falls: State College of Iowa, 1964.

Heinlein, Robert. "Ray Guns and Rocket Ships." In *Readings about Children's Literature*, edited by Evelyn R. Robinson. New York: David McKay, 1966.

Hickok, Dorothy, and James A. Smith. *Creative Teaching of Music in the Elementary School*. Boston: Allyn and Bacon, 1974.

Huck, Charlotte S., and Doris Young Kuhn. *Children's Literature in the Elementary School*, 2nd ed. New York: Holt, Rinehart and Winston, 1968.

Huus, Helen. *Children's Books to Enrich the Social Studies*, rev. ed. Washington, D.C.: National Council for the Social Studies, 1966.

Keating, Charlotte Matthews. *Building Bridges of Understanding*. Tucson: Palo Verde, 1967.

Kenworthy, Leonard S., ed. *Studying the World: Selected Resources*, rev. ed. New York: Bureau of Publications, Teachers College, Columbia University, 1965.

Kinnel, Eric. "Can Children's Books Change Children's Values?" *Educational Leadership* 28 (November 1970): 209–214.

Koblitz, Minnie W. *The Negro in Schoolroom Literature*. New York: Center for Urban Education, 1967.

McWhirter, Mary Esther, ed. *Books for Friendship*, 3rd ed. Philadelphia: American Friends Service Committee, 1968.

Martin, Bill, Jr. *Language and Literature*. Washington, D.C.: American Association of Elementary, Kindergarten, Nursery Education, 1967.

Metzner, Seymour. *American History in Juvenile Books*. New York: H. W. Wilson, 1966.

Michaelis, John. *Social Studies for Children in a Democracy, Recent Trends and Developments*, 5th ed. Englewood Cliffs, N.J.: Prentice-Hall, 1972.

Montebello, Mary. *Literature for Children: Children's Literature in the Curriculum*. Dubuque, Iowa: Wm. C. Brown, 1970.

National Council for Social Studies and Children's Book Council. "Notable Children's Trade Books in the Field of Social Studies." *Social Education* 37 (December 1973): 784–792.

Pilgrim, Geneva H., and Mariana McAllister. *Books, Young People and Reading Guidance*, 2nd ed. New York: Harper Brothers, 1968.

Piltz, Albert, and Robert Sund. *Creative Teaching of Science in the Elementary School*. Boston: Allyn and Bacon, 1968.

Platts, Mary E., Sr. Rose Marguerite, and Esther Shumaker. *Spice: Suggested Activities to Motivate the Teaching of the Language Arts*. Benton Harbor, Mich.: Educational Service, 1960.

Plotz, Helen, comp. *Imagination's Other Place: Poems of Science and Mathematics*. New York: Thomas Y. Crowell, 1955.

Porter, Dorothy, comp. *A Working Bibliography of the Negro in the United States*. Waltham, Mass.: University Microfilms, 1969.

Reid, Virginia. *Reading Ladders for Human Relations*, 5th ed. Washington, D.C.: American Council on Education, 1972.

Ritson, John E., and James A. Smith. *Creative Teaching of Art in the Elementary School*. Boston: Allyn and Bacon, 1975.

Schwartz, Julius. *Growing Up with Science Books*. New York: R. R. Bowker, 1966.

Smith, James A. *Creative Teaching of Social Studies in the Elementary School*. Boston: Allyn and Bacon, 1967.

Smith, James A. *Adventures in Communication*. Boston: Allyn and Bacon, 1972.

Smith, James A. *Creative Teaching of the Language Arts in the Elementary School*, 2nd ed. Boston: Allyn and Bacon, 1973.

Smith, James A. *Creative Teaching of Reading and Literature in the Elementary School*, 2nd ed. Boston: Allyn and Bacon, 1974.

Sutherland, Zena. *History in Children's Books*. Philadelphia: McKinley, 1967.

Thomas, R. Murray, and Sherwin G. Swartout. *Integrated Teaching Materials: How to Choose, Create, and Use Them*, rev. ed. New York: David McKay, 1963.

Tooze, Ruth. *Your Children Want to Read*. Englewood Cliffs, N.J.: Prentice-Hall, 1957.

Tooze, Ruth, and Beatrice Perham Krone. *Literature and Music as Resources for Social Studies*. Englewood Cliffs, N.J.: Prentice-Hall, 1955.

Watts, Lois B.; Delia Goetz; and Caroline Stanley. *Books Related to the Social Studies in Elementary and Secondary Schools*. Washington, D. C.: U. S. Office of Education, Bureau of Research, 1969.

Westcott, Alvin M., and Smith, James A. *Creative Teaching of Mathematics in the Elementary School*. Boston: Allyn and Bacon, 1967.

Wolfe, Ann G. *About 100 Books: A Gateway to Better Intergroup Understanding*, 5th ed. New York: American Jewish Committee, Institute of Human Relations, 1965.

CHAPTER 16

The School Library and the Book Fair

THE STORY HOUR BOMBED LAST WEEK

One of the authors was at one time the principal of a four-room elementary school. Because he and his teachers worked with limited resources, he made arrangements for a bookmobile to visit the school each week so students and teachers could enjoy a constant flow of new books into the school. The coming of the bookmobile was always a joyous event for the children. Friday morning became the most coveted time of the week because of the books on wheels and the personable bookmobile lady who came with them.

On alternate weeks he arranged for buses to take the children in to the central school library where they could borrow books, but could also exchange textbooks and reference books and enjoy experiences that were not possible with the bookmobile, like story hours and book fairs.

After two such trips had been taken in the fall, he asked his teachers to write an evaluation of the trip, their experiences in the library, and the planned story hour. One of the author's primary teachers slipped this note on his desk the morning after the trip.

> *Dear Jim,*
>
> *My evaluation of our library trip follows:*
> >   *The ride was great!*
> >   *The bus a blast!*
> >   *The kids were happy!*
> >   *The time slipped past!*
> *And, then—*
> *She met us for an hour*
> *Her jaw was set, her face was sour.*
> *She scowled at us, she gave us rules*

She thinks that little kids are fools!
She lined us up, sat me beside 'er
Clipped out her words like a type-e-writer.
She talked and talked and then she read
With face still stern and voice still dead
The book was funny—she didn't show it
And what is worse, the kids don't know it!
I'm sorry, Jim,
For even though I know you tried
The story hour bombed and died!

MAXINE

Modern libraries are built for modern librarians, and times have changed. We hope Maxine could not write the same evaluation today.

THREE CHEERS FOR MISS LESTER

If Maxine worked in a school where they had a Miss Lester, as one of the authors later did, she would have written me a different evaluation. First of all, Miss Lester knew libraries, she knew children, and she knew books, an essential combination for all children's librarians today.

Miss Lester made certain that the school library was the hub of all

FIGURE 16–1. Miss Lester knows children. A cozy corner in the library with a single child and a good book can be the inspiration for flights of the imagination.

school activities. At one of the first faculty meetings of the year she asked Mr. Martin, the principal, if she might work with the teachers on setting up some plans for the effective use of the school library. All the teachers had ideas that were put into effect as soon as changes could be made in the current organizational plan. By the middle of the year, the library *was* the hub of school activity and was used every minute of every day.

Like many communities, Glendale had a modest budget for library services, so the first big project to make people aware of the need for books in the school program was the presentation of a school book fair. After the fair, Miss Lester held a book drive to add volumes to the library shelves. A committee of children and teachers met and formulated a booklet telling of the need for more books in the school program. Lists were made of the types of books needed and the criteria for good books. A plea was made for donations of books that children had outgrown that might be gathering dust on the shelves at home. A brief explanation was made that some books might not be suitable for a school library and if they were not, they would be returned to the donor or passed along to someone who could use them.

The art teacher met with this committee and helped them design an attractive booklet with simple, appealing sketches. One child made a block print design for the cover, and every person in town received a booklet. Over five hundred books were added to the library this way.

In Glendale the school library is in the center of the school, next to the learning resource center. There are some small conference rooms off the main room which serve multiple purposes. A committee may schedule a room to view a film in one of them. Several of the teachers schedule films and filmstrips for their slow learners who learn more by listening and seeing than they do by reading. These children come to the conference rooms with a list of questions for which they seek answers in the film or filmstrip.

Other groups sometimes use these rooms for listening purposes. Records and tapes are available for music and literature appreciation and for information for children's research. Often when Miss Lester hears that a committee in some classroom is going to make a report on some reading research they have done, she makes plans with the teacher of that group to tape it, and if the tape is satisfactory, she adds it to the collection of tapes. She then catalogues it and makes it available to the next group to study that particular topic. Miss Lester has added to her collection some excellent tapes on ecology, the Vietnam War, drugs, the functions of the government, civil rights, the lives of famous people, and other topics. Many of the tapes made by children are in creative forms, such as interviews, radio and television broadcasts, dialogue, choral speaking, dramatization, and chants.

In the library, near the learning resource center and therefore available to both areas, are record players where children may plug in individually or in small groups to a trunk line of recordings, tapes, or films. This makes it possible for small groups to listen to material without disturbing other children.

The library is open at all times for all children with the exception of one hour each day. Miss Lester sets aside the period from 1 to 2 P.M. for what she calls "Library Time." Outside the library door a large calendar-type chart is attractively displayed. On it is a blank from 1 to 2 P.M. each day. Any class of children may sign up for this time of day for private use of the library. It is during this time that groups of children visit the library for a variety of purposes. One day they may come to learn about library usage. Miss Lester may, at this time, teach them how to locate resources through the use of the card catalogue. She gives them information necessary for developing the skills of locating material and then provides the opportunity for them to practice their learnings by having a treasure hunt. On a set of cards, Miss Lester lists a variety of materials: a book of fiction, a biography, a book of maps, a set of encyclopedias, a tape, a record, a poster, a certain picture, a specific magazine. On the given signal, the children are off to see how quickly they can find the item listed on their card and bring it back to Miss Lester's desk. On another day Miss Lester may be found sitting on a rug with the children around her, a fire in the library fireplace, reading a story. On still another day, the children may all be doing research on a variety of topics for social studies. Often Miss Lester visits one of the clusters (which are the arrangements for children working in this open-classroom situation) and works with the children on some specific library problem, perhaps to prepare them to come to the library for some special purpose as a group. Miss Lester's schedule is outside the library door near the calendar chart, and children are sent by their teachers to sign up for a time when they want her to visit a classroom. Before she makes the trip, Miss Lester finds the teacher in charge of that particular cluster and discusses with her the purpose for her visit, so she can go prepared to help the children with their problems.

Miss Lester offers many services to the children and teachers. She finds out which units of work are being studied in each cluster and pulls together material on that topic and sends it to the classroom or to the cluster bookshelf so it is handy for the children. She keeps the teachers and children informed of all new books by publishing lists of books when they arrive and keeping these lists available on attractive bulletin boards in the library. She often visits classrooms to see what children are interested in, to discover which books they like, and to seek help in ordering new books and materials.

The library is open to all chilldren at all times except for the hour each day when any group who wishes may take it over for a specific purpose. Children are free to leave their classrooms in any cluster and use the library, provided they are not in the process of receiving formal instruction in any group. A specific section of the library is attractive and pleasant with easy chairs, carpeting, and plants placed in such a way as to give a homelike atmosphere. In this reading corner at any time of the day, children are found reading for pleasure.

It is the custom in Glendale that the last period of the day be devoted to children's special interests and this is done through a series of mini-courses. These are taught by the teachers and high school students from the homemaking and child care courses seeking experiences with young children. Many of the students, both boys and girls, from the Future Teachers of America Club in the high school also come to help out. They are trained by the teachers and work with them until they are able and eager to take over a course for themselves. Student teachers from a neighboring teachers' college also work in the Glendale Elementary School and are an asset in running the mini-courses and in helping Miss Lester. She has scheduled some of these students to help her each day. They often take over the care of the library when she is visiting a classroom.

Miss Lester and her helpers offer a series of mini-courses each semester. The titles are such as these: *Famous Authors and the Books They Write; How to Write a Book; The Newbery Award Books; Folktales of Our Community; Mysteries of Our State; The History of Our Community Through Literature; Illustrators of Children's Books; Robert McCloskey and His Books,* and the like.

The library at Glendale is always attractive and friendly. Children help in keeping the many bulletin boards in the library and along the hall walls outside. Miss Lester keeps her eyes open to see if any group is making anything dealing with children's literature which can be displayed in the library. A show case and a display table just inside the entrance always have something attractive in them that is changed every three days: an old manuscript, some dioramas or peep shows, an exhibit made by some class, some dolls of foreign lands, a collection of old toys, a first edition or two. Always somewhere near the display are the book jackets of the books that prompted it.

At any holiday time, appropriate decorations appear in the library and are planned by a committee of children who work with Miss Lester, generally a child chosen from each room. One Christmas these children made a collection of each of their favorite Christmas books for an exhibit in the showcase, and then each child selected one book and made a representative mobile for it. These brightly colored creations dangled from the ceilings all around the library.

FIGURE 16–2. Miss Lester knows how to motivate: A "blast-off" bulletin board of "books we read."

Miss Lester works hard at keeping the library usable, attractive, and simple. The check-out system is easy—even the kindergarten children can check out their own books. A card in an envelope inside the front cover of each book is removed and the child writes his name on it (kindergarten and first-grade children who cannot write hand it to a helper who does it). The card is then left in an attractive box on the library desk. On the desk is another box full of long pink slips. On these slips the day's date has been stamped before school opens. A child slips one into the envelope on his book and off he goes. The librarian has a record of the book and where it is; the child knows the date on which he withdrew it. Children are instructed and practice this procedure on their first trip to the library. They are also told that books may be kept one week—but can be renewed any number of times.

In Glendale the library is the heart of the operation of the school, especially when it functions closely with the learning resource center. The modern elementary school has a type of curriculum much different from the old school, and many new kinds of organizational plans to make possible the operation of the new curriculum. The open-classroom type of school built in clusters of cubicles with the library as a center, such as the one described above, is but one example of the change in purpose and physical plant of one modern school. In order to meet the needs of new educational programs, the library must serve new purposes.

Children are taught to read so they can read and enjoy the materials printed for them. It is absurd but true that some schools today still do not have well-equipped libraries: most of the money budgeted for books

FIGURE 16–3. Miss Lester knows libraries. Here classrooms are placed around a large learning resource center and a small library room.

FIGURE 16–4. *Miss Lester knows how to teach children library skills by working with the teacher.*

goes for the purchase of textbooks. In other words, the children are learning a skill with no place to apply it. *It is an essential aspect of any reading program that the school furnish a library full of excellent children's books.*

Miss Lester allowed me to read a bulletin prepared by the faculty of her school which stated very well the purposes of the school library, especially as they relate to reading. After each statement, the staff, working under her guidance, had made a statement of the type of behavior which would indicate that the objective was being met. An excerpt from the bulletin follows:

OBJECTIVE 1: The pupils' growth in reading ability and in reading interest is a joint responsibility of the teachers, the librarian, and the parents.

Behavior to Accomplish Objective 1: The Individualized Reading Program, which begins in the kindergarten and continues through each successive grade level, stimulates and motivates the development of good reading habits. The program is dependent on and makes extensive use of a rich and varied library collection of books geared to all ability levels of reading and to a multitude of interests.

Teachers and librarians will work together helping each child select books of his interest and in his ability range.

Parents will be informed of the school program. They will be advised on the types of books to purchase for children, and they will be informed of the individualized technique of teaching reading. They will be helped to understand how they can help their children at home. Various lists of books will be provided by the school library: (1) to help parents who wish to buy appropriate books for their children, (2) to keep parents up to date on new books, (3) to recommend holiday books, and (4) to suggest books for vacation and summer reading.

OBJECTIVE 2: The library will be a warm and friendly place with help in library usage and reading guidance available for each boy and girl.

Behavior to Accomplish Objective 2: Children will serve on committees to help run the library and to keep it decorated through the use of bulletin boards, special occasions, holidays, etc. The library and a librarian will be available to children at all times. Each child will be received in a friendly way in the library. There will be a minimum of rules. Library courtesy will be stressed. A time of day will be set aside for meeting group needs. The teachers will send notes to the librarian suggesting special help for the children. Check-out systems will be simple.

A wealth of materials will be available in an attractive and stimulating environment, and boys and girls will be invited physically and verbally to satisfy their many reading interests. Through a reading program geared to individual needs, all students are encouraged to continue their reading interests when formal teaching ceases.

OBJECTIVE 3: The librarian works with all teachers responsible for the developmental, corrective, and individualized reading programs in the school.

Behavior to Accomplish Objective 3: The librarian will consult teachers in the ordering of books. A communication system (visits, notes, etc.) will be worked out between each teacher and the librarian (and her helpers) so that they may know and understand the particular interests and needs of pupils coming to the library. The librarian will be available for scheduled classroom visits. The library will be available at times for the exclusive use of one group.

OBJECTIVE 4: The librarian contributes to the accelerated learning program by cooperating with the teachers in providing challenging reading experiences for the maximum development of gifted students.

Behavior to Accomplish Objective 4: The librarian will keep lists of more advanced books. Gifted children will serve some time helping in the library, so they have a more intimate acquaintance with the available materials. The librarian will keep the gifted children in mind when ordering books, magazines, and materials.

OBJECTIVE 5: The librarian contributes to the total reading program of the school by working closely with the teachers on special cases other than the gifted.

Behavior to Accomplish Objective 5: Teachers will communicate to the librarian the names of children needing special help in the selection and use of books. The librarian will have access to and make use of read-

FIGURE 16–5. *Miss Lester knows how to meet her objectives: An effective display of middle school books.*

ing scores, intelligence quotients, and other pertinent information about the characteristics of individual students. Conference time will be available for the teacher and the librarian to discuss individual cases.

OBJECTIVE 6: A variety of meaningful learning experiences grow out of and are centered around the use of the school library. These experiences have many values, the basic one of which is to build a love and appreciation of good writing and good literature.

Behavior to Accomplish Objective 6: The library will be the hub of the school. Reading guidance is implicit in almost every contact the child has with the librarian whether it be in the classroom, the corridor, or the library. The initiative and creative ability of the libarian will shape much of the activity of these experiences. She will help the classroom teacher in developing dramatizations, scroll movies, videotapes, tape recordings, puppet shows, school fairs, films and filmstrips, traveling theaters, peep shows, dioramas, book units, and studies of authors and illustrators. She will keep the school personnel informed of television shows, radio, commercial film programs, local theater, new books, and all cultural programs that enhance the appreciation of books. She will provide displays, book programs, story hours, mini-courses, and other strategies that will enrich the reading program.

The account of the Glendale school library above tells how these objectives were translated into behavior by the staff of the school. These objectives, of course, deal largely with the reading program. There were

FIGURE 16–6. *Miss Lester knows how to correlate. A library bulletin board results from a reading of* Pilgrim Courage *by E. Brooks Smith and Robert Meredith.*

others of equal importance. All were clustered as subheadings to the two main goals of the elementary school library which were stated as follows: (1) To help children become effective lifetime users of books and libraries through the development of certain basic library skills, and (2) To instill in children a love for books and reading.

Miss Lester, of course, had made a list of the specific objectives she hoped to accomplish dealing with library skills and an outline of these skills she felt were necessary in order to meet the larger objectives.

Objectives of Library Teaching

1. To encourage an attitude of inquiry
2. To teach specific skills in library usage (listed below)
3. To develop habits of independent study and investigation
4. To develop skill in using library resources and tools
5. To stimulate and guide reading for information and recreation
6. To foster the continuing use of and need for books and libraries in order to live richly as an adult

Approach

1. Through group instruction initially in classrooms and/or in library, then through individual instruction
2. Planned program of systematic group and/or individual instruction
3. Close cooperation between classroom teacher and librarian so techniques and skills are taught at logical and teachable times
4. Instruction coming out of real needs of the children

Content: Kindergarten (listed in sequence)

1. Discussing handling of books
2. For children who do not know—caring for books
   a. Turning pages efficiently
   b. Shelving properly
   c. Use of bookmarks
   d. Clean hands in using books

e. Wrapping or placing in book bag to take home (snow, rain, etc.)
f. Keeping book off floors, away from intense heat, etc.
g. Calling attention to tears, etc., that can be mended
3. Visiting the school library
a. Procedure for checking out and returning books
b. Material available in library
c. Location of kindergarten books, other books
d. Learning titles of books

Content: Primary Grades (1–3) (listed in sequence)

1. Knowing school library: picture books, reference material, pictures, etc.
2. Visiting the public library—comparison of books and locations
3. Managing library center in classroom
4. Use of table of contents in finding material
5. Referring to books by author's name and title
6. Alphabetizing short lists of words, then spelling words, then authors' names
7. Opening, examining, and preparing new books for check out
8. Discussing and agreeing on logical library behavior
9. Demonstrations and practice on:
a. Use of the dictionary
b. Use of the encyclopedia
c. Use of an index
d. Other suitable reference materials

Content: Intermediate Grades (4–5, 6) (listed in sequence)

1. Logical library behavior—from class discussions
a. The need and value of quiet
b. Different uses of the library at different times
c. Knowing how to choose books and check them out
d. Knowing how to choose books for individual reading
e. Understanding the role of the librarian and the helpers: assuming this role in checking out books for others
2. Learning how all libraries operate
a. Learning how books are arranged
b. Knowing what numbers on books indicate
(1) what the subject matter of the book is
(2) where the book should be shelved
c. Knowing what the card catalog is
3. Using the physical parts of a book
a. Title, table of contents, chapter headings, index as aids in finding material
b. Taking into account the copyright date on the reverse side of title page
4. Finding materials in books to answer questions
a. Using an abridged dictionary for definitions
b. Using a children's encyclopedia (after demonstrations by teacher or librarian)
c. Using a telephone directory
d. Librarian demonstrating use of *World Almanac*
e. Librarian demonstrating use of card catalogue
5. Making reading records and simple bibliographies
a. Learning to state sources
b. Grouping books according to special topics

c. Keeping records of books read that include name of author, title, and a short comment
6. Reviewing information regarding classification of books and the arrangement of the library
7. Learning how to find books on the shelves from the call number on the catalog card
8. Becoming familiar with the main classes of the Dewey Decimal system and microfilm systems
9. Using the vertical file for pamphlets and pictures
10. Increasing skill in using reference material
   a. Acquiring ability to use a railroad timetable
   b. Using the encyclopedia independently—using key words
   c. Understanding and using cross-references
   d. Using an abridged dictionary more easily and for more purposes
   e. Beginning to use the unabridged dictionary
   f. Using general reference tools that are arranged alphabetically, such as *Children's Catalog, Junior Book of Authors*
   g. Determining that informational books need to be used through the index
   h. Acquiring the ability to make simple bibliographies and reading lists
   i. Librarian demonstrating more difficult uses of the unabridged dictionary, the encyclopedia, the atlas, cookbooks, and other books of directions
   j. Exploring book collections and libraries for books to meet interest
   k. Opening and studying each new book—to determine what user should know about the physical parts of a book in order to use it most effectively
   l. Using more complicated indexes in books
   m. Following cross-references and supplementary references in card catalogue, encyclopedia, and other reference tools
   n. Using a second encyclopedia to compare or increase information
   o. Using an atlas
   p. Learning to use the gazetteer and biographical sections of the unabridged dictionary
   q. Learning to use Webster's *Biographical Dictionary*
11. Introduction to the total role of the librarian with each child serving an internship that will include:
   a. Checking books in and out of the library
   b. Placing books on shelves
   c. Preparing new books for circulation
   d. Preparing cards for the card catalogue
   e. Reading to younger children in the library and in their classrooms
   f. Helping in story time and/or mini-courses
   g. Arranging bulletin boards and exhibits
   h. Proper filing of library material
   i. Helping in the preparation of magazines and papers for circulation
   j. Dittoing and distributing library materials to teachers
   k. Helping individual children choose reading material

The Classroom Library

If the physical construction of the school building is such that it is impossible or awkward for the children to have access to the school library, plans should be made to set up a library center in each room. Many schools that are constructed so a central library is easily accessible to all personnel maintain library centers in each classroom or cubicle in addition, because they feel that children are apt to use books more readily if they have them at their fingertips. There are many advantages to having library centers in place of or in addition to a main library.

Inasmuch as the major objective in having a library is to persuade children to read books, any step taken to bring children and books together is legitimate. Because the success of an individualized reading program is dependent on a wealth of books of various interests and a wide range of reading levels, the major disadvantage of a library center is that the available number of books is greatly reduced for each child.

Most of the activities mentioned above as beneficial for a school library can be carried out in a library center on a smaller scale. One necessary precaution that a teacher must take is that the books in the center be rotated regularly. Often, a trip to the main library by the entire class, planned once a week, may make possible a complete turnover of books for the library center if each child is responsible for replacing a few books of his own interests by new ones of his own interest and reading level. The teacher can take the responsibility of exchanging other books, such as those she may need in the development of new units of work, new reference material, and books she may need for her own work with the children.

Library centers can often be well supplemented by book drives in which children are asked to bring books from home. Although much of the material brought in may not be suitable for putting on the library shelves, it may serve for other uses. So-called "junk" material can be greatly reduced if some criterion is established, or if a few guidelines are given in the material that goes home to the parents.

Excessive rules and regulations void the objective of bringing children and books together; they should be kept to a minimum and planned to meet individual differences. A slow-reading child needs longer to finish a book than a child who reads fast. He may need the entire week to read a book at home, and he should have it. Instead of insisting that a book be returned in one week, it is more realistic to point up this problem to children and come up with a list of proposals such as: "It is suggested that each book be returned in one week. If you have not finished your book in that time, please change the date on your own check-out card." This makes allowance for many variations in children's reading ability as well as the size of books, and certainly removes the pressure from the child. If children really operate the library center, as is suggested in this section, they will have the responsibility of seeing that cards are kept up to date, and this may be a reminder that books are due. Aides may help them, thus relieving the classroom teacher of manual duties.

Many of the skills of using a large library, such as using files, locating books on shelves, and others, cannot be learned in the library center, so trips to the school library and/or town public library will be necessary for fulfilling objectives dealing with these skills. Others can be practiced in the classroom, such as checking out books, using a card catalogue, and filing cards. Lists should be made of all the skills the teacher hopes to develop and should be placed in two categories: those that can be met in the objectives for visiting the main library, and those to be met through the objectives of the library center.

The head librarian will need to have more of her time scheduled to visit classrooms in situations where children cannot visit the school library at any time. She can help the children in each classroom and the teacher in many ways and can also keep in touch with the total library picture of the school.

Other Library Resources

In rural areas teachers do not always have the help of a librarian and the resources of a central library. In such schools the bookmobile plays an exciting and important part in the life of the school. In schools where bookmobiles are not available, plans should be made to bus children in to a main school or public library at least once a week. Teachers will need to work closely with the librarian of the bookmobile, the public library, or the central library if these trips are to accomplish their purposes. Teachers will also need to plan carefully with the children for each of these trips or for each visit from the bookmobile if the objectives of library education are to be met.

In spite of the fact that a good library is one that has innumerable books, the success of the library program can best be measured by the emptiness of the library shelves because the children love the books so much that they have checked them out.

Selecting Books for the School Library

There are many aids available for selecting books for the school library. Most popular among these is the *Elementary School Library Collection: A Guide to Books and Other Media,* an up-to-date resource for all children's literature. Other useful aids are *The Horn Book Magazine,* which is published six times a year and reviews new books for children, and *The School Library Journal.*

Each year the *New York Times,* the *Christian Science Monitor,* and the *Chicago Tribune* run an entire book section of children's books of the year. These editions contain advertisements of all the new children's books by the various publishing houses, well-written reviews of the books by experts, and other general information of interest to the teacher.

Chapter 17 deals with resources and gives many references for help to the teacher and the librarian.

THE BOOK FAIR

A book fair can be a very creative enterprise and can do much to: (1) acquaint children with books, (2) arouse children's interest in new books, (3) provide information regarding resources and sources, and (4) bring the entire school together in a worthy emotional experience. Book fairs

FIGURE 16–7. *Characters from rug tubing were made to designate booths at the book fair.*

can be sponsored by a classroom group, a librarian and her workers, by the entire school, or by a group of townspeople, and can result in a worthwhile adventure for the entire community.

Setting Objectives

Careful plans must be made for a book fair in order to accomplish the objectives for holding it. First in the planning will be a statement of objectives: just what, exactly, are the purposes of having the book fair? Sample objectives are suggested above, but there can be a score of others, some of which will be unique to each place in which the fair is held, such as, "As a result of this experience, the children will become better acquainted with local folklore," and "As a result of this experience, children and adults in our community will come to meet and know some children's authors."

Once the objectives are set, certain tasks must be resolved immediately in order to get the wheels moving. These tasks may be met in a highly creative manner and may result in many valid and exciting learning adventures.

Preplanning for the Fair

Certain matters that will need immediate attention include the following:

- A date should be selected and publicized several months ahead of time, so all people may zero in on the fair and be prepared to fulfill their assignments in plenty of time.

• Although it is not mandatory, a fair often hangs together better if it has a theme. Such themes as "Books Are Friends" or "The Story of Man in Books" or "Adventures in Reading" can be broad enough to plan many sub-themes. Themes such as "Books Take Us Far Away," "Folklore of Our Country," "Books That Win Awards," "The Golden West in Fact and Fiction" are more limited and explain the general focus of the fair. Once set, the theme should be exploited so the goals of the fair are demonstrated from the minute the patron comes in contact with his first poster up to the time he leaves the building in which the fair is housed. Sometimes, too broad a theme can result in such a hodgepodge of books that the viewer is more confused than guided.

• The place where the fair will be held should be decided as soon as possible. Brainstorm all the possible experiences you want people to have at the fair and then plan for all these activities. This may mean that many rooms will be needed: one for the exhibits, one or two for entertainment, a few for listening stations (see below), one or two for film showing, etc. Pay attention to the anticipated flow of traffic at the fair and plot your activities with care. For instance, do not plan to have listening rooms next to the noisiest exhibit of the fair.

• Explore commercial exhibits that you want at the fair and contact the companies at once to see what they can do for you regarding book exhibits, filmstrips, films, pictures, recordings, cassette tapes, viewers, demonstrators, etc. (See Appendix J for addresses for this purpose.)

• Decide on the length of time that you will run your fair. With so many demanding activities, modern families need to plan adequate time to attend such an important function. It is wise to run the fair for two or three days, all day if possible, with special attractions in the evening. This plan allows teachers to bring their classes to the fair during the day and to take advantage of its offerings at a leisurely pace better suited to the concentration of children.

• Publicize the fair well. Here are some suggestions for getting the news around and for making the fair a success:

• *Get as many people involved in the fair as possible.* Each class in the school can take responsibility for one aspect of the fair. Many outside groups can be asked to help and contribute: the P.T.A., the local library staff, service organizations in town, local bookstores, etc. Plan so each organization and each class can be represented on the Book Fair Planning Committee, and each committee member can be responsible for informing his class or his organization of the needed jobs and the progress of the fair. Children can distribute flyers, give out lists, and act as ushers or hosts and hostesses at the fair itself.

• *Plan many creative events to advertise the fair.* In one school a poster contest was held among the children of the middle school. The posters were all later used for advertising purposes in the local stores. In this same school, one class provided an exhibit in keeping with the theme by making a series of dioramas that were displayed in the public library and downtown store windows. The dioramas were rotated by a committee of children who went to perform this task after school each Monday and Friday.

• Another group provided a wandering minstrel show utilizing the theme of the fair. They went from room to room in the school buildings, presenting their program on various days.

• Still another group made enormous paper dolls (built on the large cardboard rolls that form the core of rolled carpeting) to be used for each sub-theme of the fair. As these dolls were completed, they were placed in strategic places around the school and created a never-ending interest in the coming fair.

Other worthwhile activities may become a part of the regular school curriculum. In Glendale, the students of the art classes designed bookends that were exhibited and sold at the fair. The industrial arts teacher helped the elementary classes design bookmarks that were very decorative but also advertised the fair. These were printed by the hundreds and distributed to all parents and patrons, so that almost every person in town had an individual reminder of the fair.

One art teacher in Glendale helped children make mobiles of their favorite authors and books, and all the rooms in the district sparkled with these attractive, floating designs.

Programs were planned and printed by the industrial arts department ahead of time, so everyone could plan his activities at the fair and see for himself the many attractions being offered.

A committee of teachers and students visited the local newspaper office and told of their project and received a great deal of help and publicity in the local paper. One of the fathers who published a small newspaper, gave the children advertising space in three different issues so they could tell about the fair.

Publicity stories were sent to other school newspapers.

Many new activities were introduced to classes. For instance, in Glendale on Friday afternoon each child could select from a series two mini-courses he wanted to pursue for the last hour and a half of the day. Two new courses were introduced by the school librarian: (1) *Story Telling Time* and (2) *Book Review Time.* In these courses the children told the stories and gave the reviews. All the stories told and all the books reviewed were to be exhibited at the fair. In the primary grades, these mini-courses were simplified and held in the classroom in group meetings. Girls and boys from the high school Child Care program came into the classroom to read stories and show books to groups of children who wanted to listen. Sometimes they showed films or filmstrips in an adjoining room. In the middle grades, these courses were scheduled in various rooms and were guided by the classroom teachers.

You will want to *spend time with the principals of all the schools in the district planning a schedule of visitations* for all classes to the book fair at certain times of the day. In some communities, this will mean the scheduling of buses also.

Send material to your local radio stations to advertise the fair. If possible, have children write dialogue with appropriate musical background to make up the spot announcements over the air. Many television stations reserve time during the day for local news and may welcome a short puppet show or dramatization or on-the-spot preparation scenes of the fair. A local newscaster is always happy to come to the school and take pictures for the regular evening news if the pictures are newsworthy.

Form a telephone committee for word-of-mouth promotion.

Make your advertising and promotion material symbolic of the theme of the fair, so that patrons come to associate a symbol or a saying with the function.

Providing Experiences to Meet Objectives

After objectives are carefully stated so everyone knows why the fair is being held, plans must be made to provide experiences for meeting these objectives. These experiences will make or break the fair. Many well-meaning groups have failed in planning their book fairs by putting books on tables, out of the reach of children and well protected by a battery of slogans printed on cards such as: DO *NOT* TOUCH THESE *BOOKS!* If one objective of the fair is to encourage children to read books, it is certain to be voided by the above activity. Books could be covered with plastic and placed where children can easily reach them. Special experiences will be planned to meet the unique objectives such as the two mentioned above; for example, children may become better acquainted with folklore through a variety of experiences.

A good storyteller can be scheduled to tell local folklore at specific times in a room set aside for this purpose.

One section of the fair, an entire booth perhaps, can be set aside to exhibit books on local folklore. Sketches or paintings of folklore by local artists can be displayed, maps indicating the places of various literary events may be shown, writing by schoolchildren can be bound and displayed, bulletin board exhibits can be planned.

A part of the evening program can be devoted to local folklore, with ballads sung by the schoolchildren and dramatizations or puppet plays given by children or local theatrical groups.

"Hand-out" materials should be available so patrons may take home with them carefully organized references giving not only the information about each available book, but the age levels for which the book is suitable, the type of book it is (biography, fiction, poetry, etc.), the price of the book, whether it is on the shelves of the school or public library, and other welcome information for the family.

Unusual exhibits of dioramas, light shows, shadow boxes, peep shows, and dances or pantomimes can be planned and scheduled as part of the main entertainment or as a sort of independent "side-show" where small groups may come and be entertained throughout the evening while they rest. These are the activities mentioned above that can be planned by various classes.

Listening stations in the form of carrels, small rooms, or screened-off places can be set up where patrons may continually stop by to listen to cassette tapes or recorders that not only tell local folk stories but "plug" literature by explaining its value to the people at the fair.

In developing the second objective mentioned above, other experiences must be planned. Some suggestions follow.

Bring in some children's authors to talk to the children and to tell stories in small groups and at the general entertainment.

Encourage the upper grades to conduct a poll among the children to help determine who these favorite authors might be.

Arrange a special booth where the guest author's books may be sold. Ask him if he will appear to autograph books.

Find out, through a poll, who are the children's favorite illustrators. Bring one to the fair and have him give demonstrations and talks to the children.

Solicit help from local writers and illustrators—ask them to appear at a special place for "Chats with Real Authors and Illustrators," etc.

These experiences will need to be developed for each objective. All of them provide the learnings and the creative challenges in the form of open-ended problem-solving which can come from such a project.

In addition to inappropriate displays, the one way to destroy a fair is to have a *dead* one. The many activities above make the fair alive: patrons become involved with books or sensitive to the fair long before they come to the fair. Experiences planned to involve all people will take a great deal of planning but are well worth the time spent. If you do not plan to have such experiences waiting for your patrons, do not try to fool them by advertising the function as a fair. To most people a *fair* means excitement, color, and action. If this is not what you plan, say so; call it an exhibit or whatever, but do not advertise falsely.

There are other ways to keep the fair lively.

Appoint child hosts and hostesses and train them to meet people at the door and conduct them around the fair in small groups. Such an activity has the additional advantage of keeping people moving and thus eliminating traffic jams.

Establish an information booth at the entrance to the fair and be sure that the people in the booth really know how to answer the questions of the patrons or where to send them to find answers.

Provide maps showing the locations of various activities of the fair and the time schedule for each.

Do not overlook the possibility of using the outdoors if your school is located in a place where the weather is predictable.

Be sure to glamorize the fair with interesting activities, such as a ribbon-cutting opening, afternoon teas, opening ceremonies or demonstrations by the school band or orchestra, a short welcome speech by someone who can explain the purposes of the fair, etc.

Evaluating the School Book Fair

A school book fair can be rich in cultural, educational, social, and creative outcomes. But is it? Do some people become so involved that it results in activity for activity's sake and neglects the original objectives completely? All during the preparation for the fair, the head committee (often called the Steering Committee) should see to it that each experience, activity, or exhibit contributes to the fulfillment of at least one or more of the objectives of the fair. Some activity should also be planned to obtain a reaction from teachers, children, and parents as to whether the objectives of the fair have been met. These activities should be outlined at the beginning of the fair as part of the general planning, rather than as an afterthought, tacked on after the fair is over.

Sometimes a short questionnaire can be included in the program booklet which patrons are asked to check and drop in a box supplied for

FIGURE 16–8. One group of children prepares to set up exhibits of favorite Japanese books from which their unit originated.

the purpose near all the exits at the fair. Such a questionnaire may ask patrons to check certain boxes that will indicate whether each of the objectives has been met. For example: Did you learn something about local folklore at this fair?—yes—no deals with the *content* of the fair. Another section of the questionnaire may deal with the *arrangement* of the fair, such as: Were you able to view the demonstrations and exhibits easily? —yes —no. Still another section may deal with the *feeling* of the fair, such as: Were you well received and taken care of at the fair? —yes —no. Even though there will be many questions the Steering Committee will want to ask, they must keep the questionnaire short. No one will want to fill out a lengthy form while having a good time, but almost everyone will gladly fill in a few checks on a sheet. The committee will not receive *all* returns in any event, but a good sampling will serve its purposes.

At one fair the Steering Committee worked out a simple punch board system—at the fair's exit each patron went through a booth with a turnstile effect and punched the cards if he wished. It was all done in good fun by students dressed as clowns and added to the merriment of the fair.

Another way of evaluating the fair is to have persons assigned who drift in and out among the visitors listening to what they say and getting general impressions and reactions.

A follow-up on the fair can be a preplanned questionnaire given to teachers and students on the day following the closing of the fair and a questionnaire sent home to parents.

Other ways to evaluate the fair (providing a conscientious attempt is made ahead of time to observe these activities) is to note specifically how much the books are handled, how much information is distributed, how well the individual functions are attended, the general "feeling" about the fair, and the reactions of patrons to people serving as hosts, hostesses, and those stationed as guides or helpers in the information booth.

An evaluation of any function is of little importance unless it is used. Although school book fairs are not an annual event in many schools, the evaluations should be recorded and tabulated to be filed, so that they may become the springboard for the steering committee formed to plan the next book fair. A great deal of time and energy can be more positively directed when the weaknesses and pitfalls of one activity are avoided through forewarning.

Evaluations not only help groups identify the weak spots of any function, but also bring groups together in an emotional sense of warmth and well-being when their successes are noted. Success in the case of the school book fair means: (1) meeting the objectives planned for the fair, and (2) feeling *good* about it!

SUMMARY

The hub of the literature program is the school library. Modern concepts see it as the center of all school programs and a resource center for school activities. A modern school library provides book displays, listening centers, story-telling centers, and conference centers. The librarian of today is a member of the faculty team and can keep each teacher informed of the new materials available, as well as of the children's books that are newly published. Modern librarians direct their energies towards helping individuals. They have a definite place in developing an instructional program in library usage.

The librarian is responsible for many activities, chief among them being the planning and promoting of the school book fair.

TO THE COLLEGE STUDENT

1. Do you feel you were adequately trained in the use of library skills? If not, is this because the teaching of these skills was neglected or because library skills have changed considerably with the coming of microfilm, tapes, and other paraphernalia?

2. Would the ideas for presenting the book fair described in this chapter be applicable to a book fair at the college level?

3. Take any group of library skills that children should learn and brainstorm ways to teach these skills creatively.

4. You walk into a school to teach next fall and are told that your community has been working on developing an understanding of the open-school concept. Furthermore, you are told that you may set up your classroom according to this concept. What would you plan for the reading and literature center?

5. View some of the audiovisual materials now being prepared to aid the teacher in the teaching of library skills.

TO THE CLASSROOM TEACHER

1. Many audiovisual aids currently exist for the purpose of helping children learn library skills. See the list on pp. 485–91 for some suggestions for filmstrips, films,

and phonodiscs.

2. How does your library program stack up with the Glendale program? If your program is not as helpful to you, what constructive steps can you take to get a more effective program under way?

3. Do the children in your classroom have the library skills described in this chapter? If not, why not? Who in your school is responsible for developing these skills? If no one teaches these skills, design a program whereby they may be taught creatively.

4. Try the mini-course plan in your own classroom with a variety of topics and whatever help is available. Start by offering a few options and by giving the course for the last half-hour each day. Use high school students, special teachers, parents, and older children as possible resources. What would be the objectives in offering such a program?

5. How do you feel appreciation and taste for literature can be developed through the library program?

TO THE COLLEGE STUDENT
AND THE CLASSROOM TEACHER

1. Visit an elementary school library and quietly observe the behavior of the children. Notice whether or not they appear to have the attitudes and skills being taught in the library program described in this chapter. Do they have better library usage skills than you had when you were their age? Design a creative instructional program to teach these skills in a meaningful manner to any group of children.

2. If you have not been able to visit an open-school situation, do so. Note how the library and the resource center form the hub of the school. Discuss the total library program with the librarian.

3. There are many resources currently available to assist the teacher and the librarian in teaching library skills. See Appendixes B and D and the following bibliography for some of these resources. If you have time, it will be worthwhile to preview some of them and plan how to use them with children.

SELECTED BIBLIOGRAPHY

American Library Association. *Recipe for a Book Fair*. Chicago: American Library Association, Children's Book Council, 1970.

Beck, Margaret V., and Vera M. Pace. *A Guidebook for Teaching Library Skills*. Minneapolis: T. S. Denison, 1965.

Buchheimer, Naomi. *Let's Go to the Library*. New York: G. P. Putnam, 1957.

Davies, Ruth Ann. *The School Library Media Center: A Force for Educational Excellence*, 2nd ed. New York: R. R. Bowker, 1973.

Hodges, Elizabeth D., ed. *Books for Elementary School Libraries: An Initial Collection*. Chicago: American Library Association, 1969.

Hokanson, Naomi E. "A School Library Plans for Individualized Instruction." In *Readings in the Language Arts in the Elementary School*, edited by James C. MacCampbell. Boston: D. C. Heath, 1964.

Lowrie, Jean E. *Elementary School Libraries*, 2nd ed. New York: Scarecrow Press, 1970.

Palovic, Lora, and Elizabeth B. Goodman. *The Elementary School Library in Action*. Englewood Cliffs, N.J.: Prentice-Hall, 1968.

Pilgrim, Geneva H., and Mariana McAllister. *Books, Young People and Reading Guidance*, 2nd ed. New York: Harper Brothers, 1968.

School Library Association of California. *Library Skills*. Belmont, Calif.: Fearon, 1970.

Viquers, Ruth Hill. *Margin for Surprise: About Books, Children and Librarians*. Boston: Little, Brown, 1964.

PART IV

Resources for Teaching Children's Literature

CHAPTER 17

Resources for the Classroom Teacher

AN OVERVIEW

This book has been about strategies for the creative development of a knowledge and appreciation of children's literature. We have attempted to show how literature can be an integral part of the life of every child, how it can become the stimulant for their play activities, the basis for their reading enjoyment, the core of much of their learning, and a stimulant for creative development.

There is much to learn about children's literature which cannot be contained between the pages of any one book without making it too expensive and too cumbersome to use. Consequently, this chapter has been dedicated to a presentation of the types of resources available to teachers, students, and children who feel they must know more about the fascinating topic of books for children.

Under no circumstances should the reader conclude that the material presented here is exhaustive. We have been forced to eliminate many precious volumes because of space limitations. We have omitted: (1) those to which the average teacher does not have easy access, and (2)

---

1. John Updike, "My Children at the Dump," *Midpoint and Other Poems* (New York: Alfred A. Knopf, 1969). By permission.

those older volumes that have been supplanted by a more recent publication date. We have included: (1) those containing the references made in this volume, (2) those we have used successfully with children, (3) those that offer a unique strategy to the teacher or will serve well to supplement a strategy of her own, and (4) a sample of one from many publications to indicate types of material available.

The topics on the following pages are under these headings:

Environmental Resources
Anthologies
Bibliographies and Special Book Lists
Catalogues
Films
   Film Classics Worth Viewing
   Educational Films
   Films on Creativity
   Film Distributors
   Filmstrips
   Filmstrips and Films of Children's Literature
Multimedia
Book Clubs for Children
Recordings
Magazines
   Magazines for Children
   Magazines for Teachers
Other Resources
   Poetry
   Biography
   Social Studies
   Book Fairs and Exhibits
   Selected Bibliographies

Environmental Resources

A glance through the pages of this book will show how skillful teachers are in utilizing materials in the environment for setting conditions for the creative teaching of literature. Most of these teachers were creative because they used whatever materials were at hand. They did not despair at the lack of expensive equipment and all the latest teaching hardware. They put to use whatever they happened to have. Miss Briggs, who had a moving picture projector, used it, but Mrs. Carr, who did not have this elaborate equipment, used the black light, the overhead projector, garbage bags, and grocery bags to create a beautiful interpretation of *Where the Wild Things Are*—a real sample of creative teaching, since it involved taking unrelated objects and putting them together into new relationships.

The school and home environment is rich in material that may be used to develop an interest and appreciation in books. These materials range from the books themselves to the bits of realia that make them understandable, such as a coal scuttle, a button fastener, an apple corer, and a Franklin stove.

The following list of suggestions as to where teachers might look in their environment for material has been gleaned largely from the examples of teachers at work in this volume.

Use parents with special hobbies that form the core of a good book, such as one who makes patchwork quilts.

Foreign-born parents are often excellent at telling folktales.

Regional-born parents are also excellent for this, especially if they can talk in dialect. (No one has really heard Uncle Remus until he has heard it in Southern dialect.)

Parents who have special occupations can often be used to develop deep interest in a book. Miss Fenton lived in a town where umbrellas were made and asked a parent to tell about umbrellas; this provided a natural lead into the reading of *Mary Poppins*.

Field trips into the community can be readily correlated with social studies projects and can lead to reading many exciting stories. In one town where Nestle's has a chocolate-making factory, the teacher took the children on a trip through the chocolate factory and there followed many days of reading books about chocolate, such as *Hooray for Chocolate* by Jimmy Hymes and *Charlie and the Chocolate Factory* by Ronald Dahl.

Special shops and other places can become the center of attention to explain settings in children's books: an old general store, an antique shop, an old blacksmith shop, or a visit to an old churchyard. Such trips often help children to better understand the people in books such as *Little Women, Ginger Pye,* and *Prairie School.*

Antiquated objects about town also provide a point of interest for children: an old hitching post (remember the important part the hitching post played in Eleanor Estes's *The Moffats?*), a watering trough, an old mansion, some buried trolley tracks, or (again) an old cemetery.

Every town and city has a local historian who can be an invaluable aid in spinning yarns that begin with "When I was a boy . . . "

The link between generations can often be bridged by asking grandmothers and grandfathers to come to school to tell about life in their youth.

The town librarian is a "must" as a resource. Even though the school may have an excellent children's library, the teacher should solicit the help and friendship of the town librarian. Town librarians are oriented to their work differently from school librarians and can provide the service of finding materials for adults that are also suitable for children. They can also furnish many valuable resources for the teacher.

Museums are invaluable resources for explaining historical settings, costumes, artifacts, etc. The museum itself was the setting for *From the Mixed-Up Files of Mrs. Basil Frankweiler* by E. L. Konigsburg.

Historical sites are marvelous resources for stimulating interest in historical novels. After a visit to General Herkimer's homestead near Herkimer, New York, an entire class wanted to read *The Matchlock Gun* and follow the activity of the Revolutionary War across German Flats. Historical sites do more to reestablish a setting than any other resource. Old homes, forts, toll houses, and monuments can bring many stories to life.

Local history can also lead into many experiences with literature. Almost every community has a history and someone who has written about it. If no one has, the children can have a great time writing about it themselves.

The local airport should be mentioned specifically. So many modern books deal with airplanes and trips to places far away that a trip to the local airport can provide stimulation for many units of study.

Ruins have a mysterious quality that intrigues children. "What happened here?" they ask. "Why was this place left behind? What happened to the people who lived here?" In many places in New York state, ruins of the old Erie canal still stand. These ruins can become the springboard for reading such books as *Lock 'er Through* by Eric Berry Best, *Mostly Canallers* and *Rome Haul* by Walter Edmonds, and a host of others. Former boom towns in the West can serve the same purpose, as can the ruins of forts, highways, old homes, and old public buildings.

Natural native folklore has most always been recorded by someone in the distant past or used by a current author to create a modern best seller. Rosemary Nesbitt's *The Great Rope* is one example of such a legend put into a good story. Children can gather collections of local writers and use these books to learn a great deal about their own region.

Local industries will provide many aids to working with literature. When Mr. Carr wanted materials to make a large frame for the Robin Hood book, he visited the father of one of the boys in his class who ran a lumberyard and told him about the project. The lumber was donated to the class. Later a trip to the lumberyard led to an interest in wood and how it is marketed, and, of course, an exploration of the stories about *Paul Bunyan*.

Artifacts were mentioned as a means of introducing or developing a story. Every community is rich in artifacts. Every year some children and their parents go traveling. Many go abroad. People who travel almost always bring back souvenirs to show to friends, so will be delighted to loan them to the school or to bring them to school to talk about them. With a little planning, the teacher can supplement these materials with pictures and maps and can generally introduce relevant literature for the children. When Mrs. Fry returned from South America with a Peruvian necklace of authentic Inca designs, the teacher introduced Ann Nolan Clark's *The Secret of the Andes,* and the children were delighted with Mrs. Fry as well as the book.

The other members of the school faculty can be an invaluable help at times in planning experiences with literature. The librarian and/or the reading specialist can help find good stories on the reading level of all the children. After a trip to the local airport by an ungraded group, one small child was observed reading Lois Lenski's *Little Airplane* and an older child was engrossed in *The Spirit of St. Louis* by Charles Lindbergh.

Art teachers can be of special help when plays, puppet shows, and light shows result from interest in a piece of literature.

The industrial arts teacher can show children how to make flats or other construction work.

Music is almost always needed in making productions of any kind, and the music teacher can be encouraged to build her teaching around the literature being enjoyed. Had Mr. Carr not been able to handle the music for the Robin Hood production, a music teacher could have been brought in to help. Notice how the music teacher helped in the presentation of the opera *The Emperor's New Clothes*.

Some teachers are fortunate enough to have other faculty from whom they may receive help: a dramatics teacher, a dance or physical education teacher, an art teacher, and even a science specialist. All of these people can make valuable contributions to the study of children's litera-

a

b

c

FIGURE 17–1. Children's literature as a community project: An entire community thrilled to a dramatization of The Great Rope by Rosemary Nesbitt, an historical book about the children's hometown that
they dramatized to open the community's bicentennial celebration. An Oswego frontier cabin (a); the
militia set out to fight the British fleet (b); the men begin the march through the wilderness to Sackett's
Harbor bearing the great rope on their shoulders (c).

ture when these contributions are carefully correlated with any unit under way.

Also, some faculty members travel a great deal or spend their summers studying at distant universities. Their experiences can often be shared with groups of children interested in the literature of the particular region.

Anthologies

An anthology has been defined as a collection of poems or prose selections, usually from various authors, and especially of a particular type, period, or country. Anthologies of children's literature usually go far beyond this definition, however. They often cover the following topics:

A point of view about children's literature by the author.
An exposition of the importance of children's literature in the life of the child.
Criteria for choosing books and poems for children.
A classification of the various forms of children's literature.
A historical development of each of the forms of children's literature.
Samples of the actual writing from various authors and poets to illustrate the various forms of children's literature being discussed.
A listing of the various characteristics of each form of children's literature.
A discussion of the artists who illustrate children's books, with actual samples of their works taken from the books they have illustrated.
Extensive bibliographies of each form of children's literature.
Suggestions for using literature and poetry with children.
Suggestions for the reader on telling stories and reading poems.
Suggestions to the classroom teacher for the use of children's literature with the subject-matter areas.
A discussion of good books in the subject-matter fields.
A discussion of the functional school library.
A discussion of literature as it relates to reading.
A discussion of literature and mass media.
Lists of Caldecott and Newbery Award winners.
Lists of resources for the teacher: publishing house addresses, children's books in each of the categories, other anthologies, and books on the *use* of children's literature.

Some anthologies are not this broad in scope, inasmuch as they are limited to *one* aspect of children's literature. *The Illustrated Treasury of Children's Literature* edited by Margaret E. Montignoni is rich in illustrations and text extractions from the first editions of the books she discusses. The bulk of the book is devoted to excerpts from great books and poems for children and does not cover the topics mentioned above.

Other books deal entirely with poetry or with some specific phase of children's literature such as illustrations or authors.

Every teacher will find her work easier if she has at least one anthology at her fingertips. If she is to buy one so she can whip out a story or a poem at a moment's notice, certain anthologies provide this material, such as Montignoni's book mentioned above. If she needs one that will provide her with a great deal of information as well as illustrative material for classroom uses, she will want to carefully consider the Arbuthnot and Sutherland Anthologies, which contain all the above and more, and which are regularly brought up to date.

Having an anthology handy is a must for any teacher, but she will want to examine many before she decides which will best meet her needs. The following list of anthologies and other similar types of books is suggested for her examination. Most school libraries contain many of these selections.

ANTHOLOGIES AND REFERENCES OF CHILDREN'S LITERATURE

Arbuthnot, May Hill. *Time for Fairy Tales.* Glenview, Ill.: Scott, Foresman, 1961.

Arbuthnot, May Hill. *Time for True Tales and Almost True,* rev. ed. Glenview, Ill.: Scott, Foresman, 1961.

Arbuthnot, May Hill. *Children's Reading in the Home.* Glenview, Ill.: Scott, Foresman, 1969.

Arbuthnot, May Hill, and Dorothy M. Broderick. *Time for Stories of the Past and Present.* Glenview, Ill.: Scott, Foresman, 1968.

Arbuthnot, May Hill, and Dorothy M. Broderick. *Time for Stories.* Glenview, Ill.: Scott, Foresman, 1968.

Arbuthnot, May Hill, and Dorothy M. Broderick. *Time for Biography.* Glenview, Ill.: Scott, Foresman, 1969.

Arbuthnot, May Hill, and Mark Taylor. *Time for Old Magic.* Glenview, Ill.: Scott, Foresman, 1970.

Arbuthnot, May Hill, and Mark Taylor. *Time for New Magic.* Glenview, Ill.: Scott, Foresman, 1971.

Arbuthnot, May Hill, and Zena Sutherland. *Children and Books,* 4th ed. Glenview, Ill.: Scott, Foresman, 1972.

Arbuthnot, May Hill, et al. *The Arbuthnot Anthology of Children's Literature,* 3rd ed. Glenview, Ill.: Scott, Foresman, 1971.

Bowker Company, R. R. *Issues in Children's Book Selections: A Library Journal—School Library Anthology.* New York: R. R. Bowker, 1973.

Corrigan, Adeline, comp. *Holiday Ring: An Anthology of Holiday Stories and Poems.* Chicago: Albert Whitman, 1976.

Cott, Jonathan; Francella Butler; Robert Bator; and Robert Lee Wolff, eds. *Masterworks of English Children's Literature,* *1550–1900.* 5 vols. New York: George Braziller, 1976.

de Vries, Leonard, ed. *Flowers of Delight: An Agreeable Garland of Prose and Poetry.* New York: Pantheon, 1965.

Doyle, Brian, ed. *The Who's Who of Children's Literature.* New York: Schocken, 1969.

Ernest, Edward, ed. *The Kate Greenaway Treasury: An Anthology of the Illustrations and Writings of Kate Greenaway.* New York: World, 1967.

Hopkins, Lee Bennett. *Books Are by People: Interviews with 104 Authors and Illustrators of Books for Young Children.* New York: Citation Press, 1969.

Hopkins, Lee Bennett. *More Books by More People: Interviews with 65 Authors of Books for Children.* New York: Citation Press, 1974.

Huber, Miriam Blanton. *Story and Verse for Children,* 3rd ed. New York: Macmillan, 1965.

Huck, Charlotte S. *Children's Literature in the Elementary School,* 3rd ed. New York: Holt, Rinehart and Winston, 1976.

Johnson, Edna; Evelyn R. Sickels; and Frances Clarke Sayers. *Anthology of Children's Literature,* 4th ed. Boston: Houghton Mifflin, 1970.

Martignoni, Margaret, ed. *The Illustrated Treasury of Children's Literature.* New York: Grosset and Dunlop, 1955.

Sebasta, Sam Leaton, and William J. Iverson. *Literature for Thursday's Child.* Chicago: Science Research Associates, 1975.

Sutherland, Zena. *The Arbuthnot Anthology of Children's Literature,* 4th ed. Glenview, Ill.: Scott, Foresman, 1976.

Bibliographies and Special Book Lists

In addition to anthologies, many books are available to help the teacher in selecting and locating material for her instructional program. These books, among other things, categorize books by subject matter, bring the teacher up-to-date on recent publications, index stories, poems, and writing, indicate book costs, offer teachers suggestions for book usage, exploit the works of one selected author, annotate books, dwell on books of a certain type or period in history, select the best books for any one year, classify books for various uses, and on and on.

We have selected from the available books those we feel will be of special help to the classroom teacher and have listed them in Appendix B.

Catalogs

Some catalogs are available that will help the teacher in ordering books for children as well as books on children's literature.

A teacher should send cards to some of the publishing houses listed below and ask to be put on their mailing lists. This will ensure her of material on all the latest publications, including revisions. Also, some of the advertising distributed by the book companies contains valuable material she can use for bulletin boards, for leaflets, or for book reports.

Other sources of help are listed below. Most school libraries stock several of these books and catalogs. The most popular ones are starred.

*Allen, Patricia H., comp. *A Catalogue of 3300 of the Best Books for Children.* New York: R. R. Bowker, 1972.

American Friends Service Committee and Anti-Defamation League of B'nai B'rith. *Books Are Bridges.* New York: American Friends and League of B'nai B'rith, 1957.

American Institute of Graphic Arts. *Children's Books, 1958–60.* New York: The Institute, 1965.

*American Library Association. *A Basic Book Collection for Elementary Grades.* Chicago: The Association, published yearly.

*American Library Association. *Books for Children, 1960–1965.* Chicago: The Association, 1965 (revised periodically).

*American Library Association. *The Booklist: A Guide to Current Books.* Chicago: The Association, semi-monthly.

American Library Association. *Booklist and Subscription Books Bulletin.* Chicago: The Association, semi-monthly.

American Library Association, Young Adult Series Division. *Doors to More Mature Reading: Detailed Notes on Adult Books to Use with Young People.* Chicago: The Association, 1964.

American Library Association. *For Storytellers and Storytelling: Bibliographies, Materials and Resource Aids.* Chicago: The Association, 1968.

American Library Association. *Inexpensive Books for Boys and Girls.* Chicago: The Association.

*American Library Association Committee on Notable Children's Books, ed. *Notable Children's Books of 1974.* Chicago: The Association. (List appears in April issue of *ALA Bulletin.*)

*American Library Association. *Subject and Title Index to Short Stories for Children.* Chicago: The Association, 1955.

American Library Association. "1973 Notable Children's Books," *Publishers Weekly* 205 (Feb. 25, 1974): 59–60.

Association for Childhood Education. *Bibliography of Books for Children,* rev. ed. Washington, D. C.: The Association, 1971.

*Bowker Company, R. R. *Best Books for*

Children. New York: R. R. Bowker, revised annually.

Bowker Company, R. R. *The Best of the Best.* 2 vols. New York: R. R. Bowker, 1976.

*Bowker Company, R. R. *Children's Books in Print.* New York: R. R. Bowker, published annually.

*Bowker Company, R. R. *Paperbound Book Guide for Elementary Schools.* New York: R. R. Bowker, 1966.

Cavanagh, Gladys. *Subject Index to Children's Magazines.* 2223 Chamberlain Ave., Madison, Wisconsin. Semiannual.

Children's Catalog and Supplements. New York: H. W. Wilson, 1973.

*Colbert, Margaret, ed. *Children's Books, Awards and Prizes,* rev. ed. New York: Children's Book Council, 1971.

The Creative Thinker. Towson, Md.: Think Products, monthly.

Eakin, Mary K., ed. *Good Books for Children, 1960–1965,* 3rd ed. Chicago: University of Chicago Press, 1966.

Elementary School Library Collection. New Brunswick, N.J.: Bro-Dart Foundation, published annually.

*Fidell, Rachel, and Estell A. Fidell. *Children's Catalogue.* New York: H. W. Wilson, 1966. Supplement, 1972–75.

*Gaver, Mary V., ed. *The Elementary School Library Collection,* 7th ed. Newark: N. J. Bro-Dart Foundation, 1972. Supplements yearly.

Guilfoile, Elizabeth, ed. *Adventuring with Books: A Book List for Elementary Schools.* American Council of Teachers of English. New York: New American Library, 1966. Supplemental printings.

Haviland, Virginia, ed. *Children's Literature: A Guide to Reference Sources.* Washington, D. C.: Library of Congress, 1972.

Kurian, George. *Children's Literary Almanac.* Pelham, N.Y.: George Kurian (Box 154), 1973. Biennial.

Learning Resource Centers. *1973–1974 Catalog of Learning Things.* Portland, Ore.: Learning Resource Centers, 1974.

Roos, Jean Carolyn. *Patterns in Reading: An Annotated Book List for Young Adults.* Chicago: American Library Association, 1961.

*Root, Shelton L., Jr. *Adventuring with Books: 2400 Titles for Pre-Kindergarten– Grade 8,* 2nd ed. Compiled by the NCTE Committee on Adventuring with Books. New York: Citation Press, 1973.

Sayers, Frances Clarke. *A Bounty of Books.* Chicago: Compton, 1965.

*Simmons, Beatrice, ed. *Paperback Books for Children.* Compiled by Committee of the American Association of School Librarians. Chicago: American Association of School Librarians, 1972.

Sutherland, Zena. *The Best in Children's Books. University of Chicago Press, Guide to Children's Literature, 1966–1972.* Chicago: University of Chicago Press, 1973.

Films

There is a great deal of controversy about the use of mass media with children. Films, filmstrips, television shows, magazines, newspapers, comic strips, radio programs, moving pictures—all can and do have a decided effect on the attitudes and thinking of children, just as they do with adults. The primary purpose of most mass media today is to make money through one device or another. Therefore, much of the content is of a sensational nature and deals with topics that will sell, so that the producer will make money. Often the beautiful and the commonplace are ignored. Children viewing mass media may interpret the sensational as being the commonplace, and the commonplace as being irrelevant.

The mass media are a propaganda device. In the hands of unscrupulous people, they can be used for the purpose of altering opinions or coloring attitudes because they do not provide a thorough two-sided presentation of a problem.

A teacher has the responsibility, as part of her social studies program, to help children differentiate between fact and propaganda, even at a very early age. This critical attitude will be part of her program in developing an appreciation of good literature. She will help the children determine whether or not a moving picture, for instance, has been made because some producer really has a deep appreciation and love for a topic or a story, or whether he is out to make money and irresponsible as to what he does in transferring the story to the screen.

Writers publish children's books to make money just as producers produce films to make money. The writers of children's books, however, write for a select audience consisting of two factions. One faction is the children themselves, who can quickly determine whether a book appeals to them and can thus determine its success. The other faction is made up of the students of children's literature, who study, among other things, those qualities that appeal to children. Books written for these two groups that do not fulfill the criteria of appeal are generally economic failures.

Films, however, are made for everyone. A small portion of the total population has made a study of the qualities that appeal to children. Some poor films survive for reasons other than quality. Many survive because they appeal to sentiment and are actually oversentimentalized versions of the story of a book, though they do not catch the flavor of the story or the style of the author. Others are not really films for children, but records of what an adult *thinks* childhood is like and therefore very unrealistic and again overly sentimental. Many of Walt Disney's films fall into this category. They do not pay homage to the style of the author nor do they remain true to the text. Disney takes many liberties with stories. He has brought animated cartoons to the peak of perfection as an entertainment medium, but he has also distorted the children's concepts of original folktales and legends by changing stories to suit his needs and to appeal to adults as much as to children. Disney's films become an escape from modern daily toil and strife to lands where all problems are generally resolved with cute animals and beautiful people fluttering and dancing around.

Disney's music and art have, however, contributed enormously to the appreciation of children's literature. His original feature-length cartoon *Snow White and the Seven Dwarfs* was probably the best, because it remains more true to the fairy tale than many of those that followed. Scenes in this film, however, placed children in situations where they were very frightened and deeply troubled. Many Disney critics have condemned the frequent use of frightening scenes in these films. But others are less concerned. They state that the original fairy tales and many of the adventure stories are filled with crimes of passion and accounts of wicked and violent actions and that a child who can take this fare in his reading can take it in his viewing. There may be a great deal of truth in this statement. Perhaps this is the way children learn how to recognize and cope with their own emotions—by having them exhibited in the books and films for children.

One thing is certain. If we accept the assumption that children are capable of evaluating their own literature, then we must also accept the fact that they are capable of evaluating their own films. In that case, the Disney films are successful.

Perhaps the greatest criticism against all films is that, to a great degree, they destroy the pictures that reading allows the child to generate in his own imagination. The film is, after all, one person's concept of a story and to glamorize this concept in picture, movement, and sound, and to impose it on someone else is to deprive that individual of the joy of conjuring up the scenes that the words dictate in his own imagination.

If films are properly used, however, this fault can be turned into a valuable learning asset. The teacher will need to explain to the children that the film *is* one person's version of the story and that she is interested in knowing if it is like their version. As long as she does not impose her own values on the children, and allows the children to honestly disagree (or agree) with the producer's interpretation of the story and style of the author, she is helping the children in their development of appreciation through comparisons.

The teacher will not be so naive as to believe that a film will ruin a child's concept of a story and deaden his imagination, when at the same time she exposes him to book reports, pictures, and even to her own telling of a story. All of these presentations are biased according to the persons giving them. It is a healthy activity to expose children to many interpretations of the same story, so their imaginations can take flight and not be restricted.

Mr. Jackson read *Lentil* by Robert McCloskey to his middle schoolers. They were then divided into four groups, and each group was challenged to produce the story of Lentil in a manner different from the others. After a brainstorming session was held, the chairman of each group met with Mr. Jackson to relay the plans of the group so no duplicate ideas would be presented. One group presented the story through a shadow play, one group dramatized parts of the story, another group used paper bag puppets to give a presentation, and the fourth group gave it through pantomime and choral speaking.

Reading a story by yourself can be a great challenge to the imagination, but practice in using the imagination for affiliated purposes enhances the ability to use it at all times. In developing appreciation for good literature in a child, the ultimate goal is not to have the child say, "I don't like that movie—it is no good. That's not the way I imagined the story at all." The goal is to have the child say, "That was certainly an unusual interpretation of the story. It isn't at all like I imagined it. I didn't like it very much, really, but it was well done and was an interesting idea."

Teachers and parents constantly seek the ideal film made by the artist who not only has a sensitivity to the style and plot of the story but manages to also capture the emotional tone and style of the author. Such a film generally hits most people in the heart; they leave feeling much as they do when they put down a good book or come away from the inspiring narration of a good story. They experience a sense of well-being, a feeling of empathy and projection, a satisfaction that the author has been true, that the characters are old friends they have known from somewhere else, and that the settings are as they always imagined them. They have been moved completely away from the reality of their own lives into the imagery of the film. They are caught up in it and live the story through the emotions of the hero or heroine. A great film is a great human experience.

In translating a book to the screen, adjustments must always be made. In a good film, the viewer is not aware of those adjustments.

In recent years, many local television stations have brought back great film classics to show on Saturday morning or at some other time appropriate to children's viewing. A teacher can watch her local paper or consult her TV guide and can encourage children to view such films, especially on days when the weather is nasty and the children have little else to do.

Critics condemn television for the time it takes children away from other activities, particularly reading. These studies are really not very valid, for they do not present an account of the activities for which the television viewing is a substitute. A child might, for instance, rather be watching television than be engaged in a street fight, in trying drugs, or hanging out at the corner bar. As far as reading goes, any experience children have, be it direct or vicarious, helps them to develop oral vocabulary that can be used in forming a visual vocabulary in the teaching of reading. In Chapter 15 we saw that the teacher of reading must use the speaking vocabulary of the children to develop a reading vocabulary. What better way than through the common viewing of children's literature? Teachers can motivate children to view these programs by means of assignments.

Film Classics Worth Viewing

In Appendix C is a list of commercial film classics worth seeing and now showing on various television stations around the country. Consult your TV guide so viewing these films may be assignments for children and may form a basis for appreciative discussions in the classroom. Many of these films have been cut and edited for classroom use and are available through film-distributing houses. Some of these films, however, have been so poorly edited as to be mutilated and practically worthless. No teacher would hang a mutilated painting in her classroom. She should show a film artist the same respect.

Educational Films

Film companies have made many excellent films for use in the pursuit of children's literature. Once again the total list is too exhaustive to contain in a book of this nature. Teachers are advised to consult catalogues for help in choosing films. Each film distributor publishes a catalogue of the films available in his library. Teachers and librarians may ask to be placed on the various mailing lists.

Some commonly used films are indicated in Appendix C as samples of the type of materials available for classroom use. An excellent reference is Hannah Miller's "Feature Films for Children," *Wilson Library Bulletin* 45 (February 1971): 560–571.

Films on Creativity

Many excellent films have recently been designed to put children into open-ended, creative, problem-solving situations. These films may be used to develop divergent thinking in general. We have listed them in Appendix C.

Film Distributors

Addresses of film distributors for all films mentioned in this book will also be found in Appendix C.

Filmstrips

Filmstrips have the advantage over films that they may be discussed frame by frame and they are not closed-ended to the point that the child's imagination cannot be brought into play. They call upon the imagination, in fact, to fill in the missing parts between the pictures.

The same criticism can be leveled against the use of filmstrips as is often used against films, and the same responses can be made to these criticisms. Filmstrips do tend to follow a story closely, however; many of them now have accompanying records on which a storyteller narrates the story that goes with the pictures.

Some teachers question the value of filmstrips for telling children's stories. There are certainly many logical criticisms of their use. Once again, the teacher will need to determine *why* she wants to use the filmstrip and whether it will serve the purpose better than telling the story or allowing the children to read the story themselves.

Filmstrips seem to be most valuable in children's literature when they are used: (1) to help slow or non-readers, (2) to provide research on the costumes or setting of the story when this knowledge is necessary for the presentation of a puppet show or a play, (3) for individual study, especially with slow readers or slow-learning children who can get off in a dark corner and view them alone, especially those with accompanying records that tell the story (see Multimedia), (4) to promote lessons in good listening and perception training, and (5) for enjoyment.

Filmstrips of Children's Literature

Most famous of all filmstrips are the Weston Woods Filmstrips, which come from the Weston Woods Studios in Connecticut. These filmstrips are unique because for many of them the stories are told on an accompanying record by a good storyteller. The style and emotional tone of the book is kept by the addition of appropriate, unobtrusive background music, and the entire filmstrip is made of the illustrations taken from the original text.

The Weston Woods Filmstrips come with a booklet from which the story is read easily by a child, even in the semidarkness of the room, due to the large, heavy type in which the story is printed.

In the Weston Woods Films, the original illustrations are also used. The camera moves about the page and pans in and out to give the illusion of movement. Certain sound effects often contribute to this illusion. The entire production is an extension of the experience of the book.

The Weston Woods *Story Parade of Books* consists of many major picture books published for children in the past several years:

> *Andy and the Lion* by James Daugherty (P)
> *Blueberries for Sal* by Robert McCloskey (A)
> *The Camel Who Took a Walk* by Tworkov and Duvoisin (A)

Caps for Sale by Esphyr Slobodkina (P)
The Circus Baby by the Petershams (P)
Curious George Rides a Bike by H. A. Rey (P)
The Five Chinese Brothers by Bishop and Wiese (A)
Frog Went a Courtin' by Langstaff and Rojankovsky (P)
Georgie by Robert Bright (P)
Hercules by Hardie Gramatky (A)
In the Forest by Marie Hall Ets (P)
Jenny's Birthday by Esther Averill (P)
Lentil by Robert McCloskey (I)
The Little Red Lighthouse by Swift and Ward (P)
The Loudest Noise in the World by Elkin and Daugherty (A)
Magic Michael by Slobodkin (P)
Mike Mulligan and His Steam Shovel by Virginia Burton (P)
Millions of Cats by Wanda Gag (P)
Norman the Doorman by Don Freeman (A)
The Owl and the Pussycat by Lear and Cooney (A)
Pancho by Berta and Elmer Hader (P)
The Red Carpet by Rex Parkin (A)
The Snowy Day by Ezra Jack Keats (P)
The Sorcerer's Apprentice by Weill (A)
Stone Soup by Marcia Brown (A)
The Story about Ping by Flack and Wiese (P)
The Tale of Custard the Dragon by Ogden Nash (A)
This Is Ireland by M. Sasek (A)
This Is Israel by M. Sasek (A)
Time of Wonder by Robert McCloskey (I)
Wheel on the Chimney by Brown and Gergely (I)
Wynken, Blynken and Nod by Field and Cooney (P)
The Doughnuts (Homer Price) by Robert McCloskey (I)

For samples of filmstrips available for adventuring in children's literature, see Appendix D. For addresses of all the companies that distribute the filmstrips mentioned in this book, see the second part of Appendix D.

Multimedia

In the list of recommended filmstrips, there are many that have accompanying records or cassette tapes to supply an audio sound track. Most of the filmstrip, film, record and cassette tape distributing companies now deal with multimedia in presenting materials for use in the classroom.

They not only provide the content in multimedia but the hardware and machinery as well. Hardware includes carrel equipment, viewfinders, slide viewers, microscopes, enlargers, show-and-tell devices, audio light units, cassette tapes, recordings, phonodiscs, and the like. Machinery includes language machines, record players with trunk lines so many children may listen without disturbing other children, record players with accompanying visual equipment, cards with parts of tapes so voices speak when the card is pushed through a machine, games that include book characters who speak to children when a looped string attachment is pulled, and so on. It is an adventure these days to look through magazines and catalogues or to walk through a toy store and study the many gimmicks available to encourage and enrich learning.

Because of the vast number of multimedia resources, some attention must be afforded them here, but the list is by no means exhaustive. It is included as representative of the type of multimedia material available to assist the teacher with children's literature. (See Appendix F.)

One resource that will be especially helpful to the classroom teacher is *New Educational Materials, 1970: A Classified Guide to Books, Films, Recordings, Multi-Media Kits, Transparencies, Film Loops, Teaching-Learning Games, and Professional Guides* by the Evaluation Panels of *Scholastic Teacher Magazine* (New York: Citation Press, 1970).

Scholastic Teacher Magazine also publishes a read-along series that includes every type of children's literature, published separately in small books with a record to accompany each book. And in addition, Scholastic Book Services (904 Sylvan Avenue, Englewood Cliffs, New Jersey 07632) puts out a multimedia language arts–reading cassette-book companion series. Scholastic's materials are especially valuable because some are planned for summer reading through the Scholastic Book Club.

Book Clubs for Children

Many teachers initiate book clubs in their classrooms. Once a book club is under way, status and motivation can be supplied by joining a commercial or national book club. Children may write for materials to the various book clubs sponsored by publishers. They may weigh the advantages of belonging to one book club over another and decide on the one they would like to join. Book clubs keep children informed of new books being published; they often supply them with display material or with materials for keeping reading records, and many have a reduced rate plan for members. They are also aimed at various age levels and reading abilities. One of the greatest advantages of book clubs is that most of them sponsor summer reading programs.

A list of the current popular book clubs follows, as a resource for the teacher:

Arrow Book Club, Scholastic Book Services, 904 Sylvan Ave., Englewood Cliffs, N.J. 07632.

Best-in-Children's Books, Division of Doubleday, Garden City, N.Y. 11530.

Best Loved Girls' Books, Doubleday & Co., Garden City, N.Y. 11530.

The Book Plan, 921 Washington Ave., Brooklyn, N.Y. 11238.

Campus Book Club, Scholastic Book Services, 904 Sylvan Ave., Englewood Cliffs, N.J. 07632.

Junior Deluxe Editions Club, Garden City, N.Y. 11530.

Junior Literary Guild, 177 Park Avenue, New York, N.Y. 10017.

Lucky Book Club, Scholastic Book Services, 904 Sylvan Ave., Englewood Cliffs, N.J. 07632.

Parents' Magazine Read-Aloud Book Club For Little Listeners and Beginning Readers, Division of Parents' Magazine Enterprises, 52 Vanderbilt Avenue, New York, N.Y. 10017.

See-Saw Program, Scholastic Book Services, 904 Sylvan Ave., Englewood Cliffs, N.J. 07632.

Weekly Reader Book Club, 1250 Fairwood Avenue, Columbus, Ohio 43216.

Young America Book Club, 1250 Fairwood Ave., Columbus, Ohio 43216.

Young People's Book Club, 225 North Cass Avenue, Westmont, Ill. 60559.

Recordings

Since the basis of the literature program is listening (followed closely by the ability to read), the greatest resources for the use of children's literature lie in the manufacture of recordings and cassette tapes that effectively tell stories to children through a variety of different techniques. Sound effects and music have often been skillfully used on these recordings to better transmit the tone of a story. Often, tapes and recordings can bring the author directly into the classroom to talk to the children, as was the case with the children who developed the unit on Lois Lenski under Miss Murphy.

The number of tapes available is limitless and the best-known resource for them is in the following article: Johnson, Donald W. "National Tape Repository," *Educational Screen and Audiovisual Guide,* April, 1963, p. 204. This publication tells teachers how to find out about tapes and how to keep up-to-date with titles.

A selected list of recordings is reported in Appendix E to give the teacher an idea of the variety of resources available in this category. A list of the addresses of distributors of records for children will also be found in Appendix E. At this printing, we know of no one catalogue that publishes *all* the children's titles for tapes and records. Each company has its own catalogue, and teachers or librarians will benefit by sending a postcard asking to be placed on a mailing list.

Magazines

Magazines for Children

Children's interest in literature is greatly enhanced when the school library supplies them with contemporary information on literature through the medium of magazines. Some teachers feel that a magazine on children's literature that comes into the classroom each month gives the literature program a "periodical shot in the arm." Often when children raise money by some worthy activity, they use it to subscribe to a magazine on children's literature. This action certainly is one way to invest funds so that each child receives enjoyment from the investment.

Magazines currently popular with children are listed below. Not all of these are magazines on children's literature, but all do contain material on it from time to time. The ones preceded by an asterisk are literature magazines.

American Girl, 155 E. 44th St., New York, N.Y.

American Junior Red Cross, American National Red Cross, Washington, D.C.

Boy's Life, 2 Park Avenue, New York, N.Y.

Child Life, William S. Hawks, 30 Federal St., Boston, Mass. 02110.

Children's Activities, Child Training Association, Inc., 1111 S. Wabash Ave., Chicago, Ill. 60605.

Children's Digest, Parents' Institute, 80 Newbridge Rd., Bergenfield, N.J. 07621.

Cricket, Open Court Publishing Co., 1058 Eighth St., La Salle, Ill. 61301.

Highlights for Children, 968 Main St., Honesdale, Pa. 18431.

Humpty Dumpty's Magazine, Parents' Institute, 80 Newbridge Rd., Bergenfield, N.J. 07621.

Jack and Jill, Curtis Publishing Co., Independence Square, Philadelphia, Pa. 19106.

Junior Natural History, American Museum of Natural History, Central Park West at 79th St., New York, N.Y. 10025.

Popular Mechanics, 200 Ontario St., Chicago, Ill. 60611.

Popular Science, 353 Fourth Ave., New York, N.Y. 10003.

Seasame Street Magazine, Children's Television Workshop, One Lincoln Plaza, New York, N.Y. 10023.

Young Wings, Junior Literary Guild, Garden City, N.Y. 11530.

Magazines for Teachers

Magazines on children's literature can be of great service to the teacher. Some are not devoted entirely to children's literature, but most of them present material on the effective use of children's literature in the classroom. Many of these magazines contain a page each month of addresses to which teachers may write for free classroom materials. A list of magazines for teachers will be found in Appendix G. The ones preceded by an asterisk deal specifically with children's literature.

Other Resources

Poetry

Other resources have already been discussed in various portions of this book. In Chapter 5, reference was made to the many books of poetry available for children today. A bibliography of poetry books for children will be found in Appendix H.

Biography

In Chapter 2, reference was made to the many books available on biographies for children. A list of these books is available in Appendix I.

Social Studies

In Chapter 8, the reader was referred to Appendix J for a sample list of books for children that deal with social studies topics.

Book Fairs and Exhibits

Resources for helping teachers plan and stage book fairs are listed in Appendix K.

In connection with book fairs, teachers will want to know that the Children's Book Council maintains a *Speakers List* of authors and illustrators who will speak to school personnel, children, and professional community groups. These speakers are available for each region of the United States. Write to the following address:

Children's Book Council, Inc., *Speakers List,*
175 Fifth Ave., New York, N.Y. 10010

Selected Bibliographies

We would like to draw the reader's attention to the selected bibliographies at the end of each chapter of this book. Every book listed has been carefully selected as an excellent resource for the college student and/or the classroom teacher.

SUMMARY

Resources for adventuring with children's literature abound, and the limits for use are set only by the imagination of the teacher. In this chapter we have attempted to make the student and teacher aware of the many environmental resources available. We have provided selected samples of other resources including anthologies, bibliographies, selected book lists, catalogues, commercial films, educational films, films for developing creativity, and addresses of film distributors. We have also suggested uses for filmstrips and have provided appendixes of filmstrips to be used in the classroom along with multimedia equipment, recordings, magazines for children and teachers, poetry books, books on biography, books for use in the social studies, and material on book fairs and exhibits.

All of these materials are effective if they serve one major purpose: to bring children and books together in a love affair.

APPENDIXES

APPENDIX A

Addresses of Publishers

This list is an attempt to include every publishing house mentioned in this book. It also contains the publishers of books recognized in text footnotes, as well as those listed in the bibliographies at the end of each chapter.

Abelard-Schuman
666 Fifth Avenue
New York, NY 10019

Abingdon Press
Hastings House
151 E. 50th Street
New York, NY 10022

Harry N. Abrams
110 E. 59th Street
New York, NY 10022

Allyn and Bacon
470 Atlantic Avenue
Boston, MA 02210

American Association for the
Advancement of Science
1515 Massachusetts Avenue, NW
Washington, DC 20036

American Association of
Elementary Kindergarten,
Nursery Education
1201 Sixteenth Street, NW
Washington, DC 20036

American Book Company
450 W. 33rd Street
New York, NY 10001

American Council on Education
1 Dupont Circle, NW
Washington, DC 20036

American Friends Service
Committee
160 North 15th Street
Philadelphia, PA 19102

American Heritage Publishing
Company
1221 Avenue of the Americas
New York, NY 10020

American Institute of Graphic Arts
1059 Third Avenue
New York, NY 10021

American Library Association
50 E. Huron Street
Chicago, IL 60611

Antioch Press
Yellow Springs, OH 45389

Appleton-Century-Crofts
292 Madison Avenue
New York, NY 10017

Association for Childhood
Education International
3615 Wisconsin Avenue, NW
Washington, DC 20016

Atheneum Publishers
122 E. 42nd Street
New York, NY 10017

Atherton Press
70 Fifth Avenue
New York, NY 10011

Ballantine Books
101 Fifth Avenue
New York, NY 10003

Bantam Books
School and College Division
666 Fifth Avenue
New York, NY 10019

Barnes and Noble Books
10 E. 53rd Street
New York, NY 10022

Beacon Press
25 Beacon Street
Boston, MA 02108

Beckley-Cardy Company
1900 N. Narragansett
Chicago, IL 60611

Behavioral Publications
72 Fifth Avenue
New York, NY 10011

W. S. Benson and Company
P.O. Box 1866
Austin, TX 78767

Blaisdell Publishing Company
Division of Ginn and Company
275 Wyman Street
Waltham, MA 02154

Benjamin Blom, Inc., Publishers
2521 Broadway
New York, NY 10010

B'nai B'rith
1640 Rhode Island Avenue, NW
Washington, DC 20036

Bobbs-Merrill Company
4300 W. 62nd Street
Indianapolis, IN 46206

Bodley Head Ltd.
9 Bow Street
London, England WC2E7AL

R. R. Bowker Company
1180 Avenue of the Americas
New York, NY 10036

Bradbury Press
Scarsdale, NY 10583

George Braziller, Inc.
1 Park Avenue
New York, NY 10016

Broadman Press
127 Ninth Avenue, North
Nashville, TN 37234

William C. Brown Company
2460 Kerper Boulevard
Dubuque, IA 52001

Burgess Publishing Company
7108 Ohms Lane
Minneapolis, MN 55435

Cambridge University Press
32 E. 57th Street
New York, NY 10022

Center for Applied Research
  in Education
70 Fifth Avenue
New York, NY 10011

Center for Urban Education
345 Park Avenue
New York, NY 10022

Century House
Watkins Glen, NY 14891

Chandler Publishing Company
124 Spear Street
San Francisco, CA 94105

Children's Book Council
175 Fifth Avenue
New York, NY 10010

Children's Press
1224 W. Van Buren Street
Chicago, IL 60607

Chilton Book Company
Chilton Way
Radnor, PA 19089

Christopher Publishing House
53 Billings Road
North Quincy, MA 02171

Citation Press
50 W. 44th Street
New York, NY 10036

Clarkson-Potter
419 Park Avenue, South
New York, NY 10016

F. E. Compton Company
425 N. Michigan Avenue
Chicago, IL 60611

Coward, McCann & Geoghegan
200 Madison Avenue
New York, NY 10016

Cowles Book Company
488 Madison Avenue
New York, NY 10022

Creative Education Foundation
1300 Elmwood Avenue
Buffalo, NY 14222

Criterion Books
666 Fifth Avenue
New York, NY 10019

Thomas Y. Crowell Company
666 Fifth Avenue
New York, NY 10019

Crown Publishers
419 Park Avenue, South
New York, NY 10016

John Day Company
257 Park Avenue, South
New York, NY 10010

Dell Publishing Company
750 Third Avenue
New York, NY 10017

T. S. Dennison and Company
5100 W. 82nd Street
Minneapolis, MN 55431

Dial Press
245 E. 47th Street
New York, NY 10017

Dillon Press
106 Washington Avenue, North
Minneapolis, MN 55401

Dodd, Mead and Company
79 Madison Avenue
New York, NY 10016

D. O. K. Publishers
Buffalo, NY 14214

Doubleday and Company
245 Park Avenue
New York, NY 10017

Dover Publications
180 Varick Street
New York, NY 10014

Drier Educational Systems
320 Raritan Avenue
Highland Park, NJ 08904

Gerald Duckworth &
  Company, Ltd.
436 Glouster Crescent
London NW 170V, England

Duell, Sloan and Pearce
250 Park Avenue
New York, NY 10010

E. P. Dutton & Company
201 Park Avenue, South
New York, NY 10003

Educational Service
Benton Harbor, MI 49022

Educational Technology
  Publications
140 Sylvan Avenue
Englewood Cliffs, NJ 07632

Encyclopaedia Britannica
425 N. Michigan Avenue
Chicago, IL 60611

M. Evans & Company
216 East 49th Street
New York, NY 10017

Eye Gate House
146–01 Archer Avenue
Jamaica, NY 11426

Faber and Faber Ltd.
3 Queen Square
London, England WCIN3AV

Farrar, Straus and Giroux
19 Union Square, West
New York, NY 10003

F. W. Faxon Company
83 Francis Street
Boston, MA 02115

Fearon Publishers
6 Davis Street
Belmont, CA 94002

Field Enterprises Educational
  Corp.
510 Merchandise Mart Plaza
Chicago, IL 60654

Follett Corp.
1010 W. Washington Blvd.
Chicago, IL 60607

Four Winds Press
906 Sylvan Avenue
Englewood Cliffs, NJ 07632

Franklin Publishing Company
2047 Locust Street
Philadelphia, PA 19103

The Free Press
866 Third Avenue
New York, NY 10022

Friendship Press
475 Riverside Drive
New York, NY 10027

Funk and Wagnalls Publishing
  Company
665 Fifth Avenue
New York, NY 10019

Gale Research Company
1400 Book Tower
Detroit, MI 48226

Garrard Publishing Company
1607 N. Market Street
Champaign, IL 61820

Ginn and Company
191 Spring Street
Lexington, MA 02173

Golden Press
Educational Division
150 Parish Drive
Wayne, NJ 07470

Grade Teacher
P.O. Box 225
Cortland, NY 13045

Grosset and Dunlap
51 Madison Avenue
New York, NY 10010

Grossman Publishers
44 W. 56th Street
New York, NY 10019

Hammond Company
Maplewood, NJ 07040

Harcourt Brace Jovanovich
757 Third Avenue
New York, NY 10017

Harper & Row
10. E. 53rd Street
New York, NY 10022

Hastings House Publishers
10 E. 40th Street
New York, NY 10016

Hawthorne Books
70 Fifth Avenue
New York, NY 10011

D. C. Heath and Company
125 Spring Street
Lexington, MA 02173

Heinemann Publishers
15–16 Queen Street
London, WIX8BE

Holbrook Press
470 Atlantic Avenue
Boston, MA 02210

Holiday House
18 E. 56th Street
New York, NY 10022

Holt, Rinehart and Winston
383 Madison Avenue
New York, NY 10017

Horn Book
585 Boylston Street
Boston, MA 02159

Houghton Mifflin Company
1 Beacon Street
Boston, MA 02107

Institute of Human Relations
106 E. 56th Street
New York, NY 10019

International Reading Association
P.O. Box 695
Newark, DE 19711

Jossey-Bass Publishers
615 Montgomery Street
San Francisco, CA 94111

R. R. Knapp
P.O. Box 7234
San Diego, CA 92107

Alfred A. Knopf
201 E. 50th Street
New York, NY 10022

Library Association
7 Ridgemount Street
London, England WCIE7AE

Library of Congress
Washington, DC 20540

J. B. Lippincott Company
East Washington Square
Philadelphia, PA 19105

Little, Brown and Company
34 Beacon Street
Boston, MA 02106

Liveright Publishing Corp.
386 Park Avenue, South
New York, NY 10016

Longmans, Green and Company
55 Fifth Avenue
New York, NY 10003

Lothrop, Lee and Shepard
  Company
105 Madison Avenue
New York, NY 10016

McCutchan Publishing Corp.
2526 Grove Street
Berkeley, CA 94704

McGraw-Hill Book Company
330 W. 42nd Street
New York, NY 10036

David McKay Company
750 Third Avenue
New York, NY 10017

McKinley Publishing Company
P.O. Box 77
Ocean City, NJ 08226

Macmillan Company
866 Third Avenue
New York, NY 10022

Marquis Who's Who, Inc.
200 East Ohio Street
Chicago, IL 60611

Maxton Publishing Corp.
1012 W. Washington Blvd.
Chicago, IL.

Mentor Press (New American
  Library)
1301 Avenue of the Americas
New York, NY 10019

Meredith Corporation
1716 Locust Street
Des Moines, IA 50503

G. and C. Merriam Company
47 Federal Street
Springfield, MA 01101

Charles E. Merrill Publishing Co.
1300 Alum Creek Drive
Columbus, OH 43216

Jullian Messner
1 W. 39th Street
New York, NY 10018

William Morrow and Company
105 Madison Avenue
New York, NY 10016

National Conference of Christians
  and Jews
105 Court Street
Brooklyn, NY 11201

National Council of Teachers
  of English
111 Kenyon Road
Urbana, IL 61801

National Association for the
  Education of Young People
1834 Connecticut Avenue, NW
Washington, DC 20009

National Association Independent
  Schools
Committee on Junior Booklist
4 Liberty Square
Boston, MA 02190

National Education Association
1201 Sixteenth Street, NW
Washington, DC 20036

Thomas Nelson and Sons
Copewood and Davis Streets
Camden, NJ 08103

New American Library
1301 Avenue of the Americas
New York, NY 10019

New York Graphic Society Books
11 Beacon Street
Boston, MA 02108

New York Public Library
Fifth Avenue and 42nd Street
New York, NY 10018

W. W. Norton and Company
500 Fifth Avenue
New York, NY 10036

Oddo Publishing Company
201 S. Second Street
Mankato, MN 56001

Odyssey Press
4300 W. 62nd Street
Indianapolis, IN 46268

F. A. Owen Publishing Company
Dansville, NY 14437

Oxford University Press
200 Madison Avenue
New York, NY 10016

Paddington Press
30 E. 42nd Street
New York, NY 10017

Palo Verde Publishing Company
609 N. Fourth Avenue
Tucson, AR 85716

Pantheon Books
201 E. 50th Street
New York, NY 10022

Parnassus Press
4080 Halleck Street
Emeryville, CA 94608

Parents' Magazine Press
52 Vanderbilt Avenue
New York, NY 10017

Penguin Books
75 Fifth Avenue
New York, NY 10011

Pergamon Press
Maxwell House
Fairview Park
Elmsford, NY 10523

Personalized Reading Center
Xerox Education Center
Columbus, OH 43216

Personnel Press
191 Spring Street
Lexington, MA 02173

Peter Pauper Press
629 N. MacQuesten Parkway
Mt. Vernon, NY 10552

Pitman Publishing Corp.
6 Davis Drive
Belmont, CA 94002

Platt and Munk Company
1055 Bronx River Avenue
Bronx, NY 10472

Pocket Books
630 Fifth Avenue
New York, NY 10020

Frederick A. Praeger
111 Park Avenue, South
New York, NY 10003

Prentice-Hall
Englewood Cliffs, NJ 07632

G. P. Putnam's Sons
200 Madison Avenue
New York, NY 10016

Rand McNally & Company
P.O. Box 7600
Chicago, IL 60680

Random House
201 E. 50th Street
New York, NY 10022

Reilly and Lee Company
114 W. Illinois Street
Chicago, IL 60610

Rinehart and Company
79 Madison Avenue
New York, NY 10016

Ronald Press Company
79 Madison Avenue
New York, NY 10016

Row, Peterson and Company
1911 Ridge Avenue
Evanston, IL 60660

St. Martin's Press
175 Fifth Avenue
New York, NY 10010

W. B. Saunders Company
West Washington Square
Philadelphia, PA 19105

Scarecrow Press
52 Liberty Street
Box 656
Metuchen, NJ 08840

Schloat Productions
Pleasantville, NY 10570

Schocken Books
200 Madison Avenue
New York, NY 10016

Scholastic Book Services
Scholastic Magazines
50 W. 44th Street
New York, NY 10036

Science Research Associates
259 E. Erie Street
Chicago, IL 60611

William R. Scott
33 Avenue of the Americas
New York, NY 10014

Scott, Foresman and Company
1900 E. Lake Avenue
Glenview, IL 60025

Charles Scribner's Sons
597 Fifth Avenue
New York, NY 10017

Sheed and Ward
6700 Squibb Road
Mission, KA 66202

Silver-Burdett
250 James Street
Morristown, NJ 07960

Signet Books
New American Library
P.O. Box 2310
Grand Central Station
New York, NY 10017

Simon and Schuster
630 Fifth Avenue
New York, NY 10020

Sterling Publishing Company
419 Park Avenue, South
New York, NY 10016

Studio Vista Publishers
35 Red Lion Square
London, England SWIP3RB

Alan Swallow
1138 S. Wabash Avenue
Chicago, IL 60605

Taplinger Publishing Company
200 Park Avenue, South
New York, NY 10003

Teachers College Press
Columbia University
1234 Amsterdam Avenue
New York, NY 10027

Think Products
1209 Robin Hood Circle
Towson, MD 21204

Time-Life Books
Time-Life Building
New York, NY 10020

U. S. Government Printing Office
Washington, DC 20401

Vanguard Press
424 Madison Avenue
New York, NY 10017

Van Nostrand Reinhold Company
450 W. 33rd Street
New York, NY 10001

Viking Press
625 Madison Avenue
New York, NY 10022

Wadsworth Publishing Company
10 Davis Drive
Belmont, CA 94002

Wake-Brook House
303a N. Federal Highway
Fort Lauderdale, FL 33306

Henry Z. Walck
750 Third Avenue
New York, NY 10017

Walker and Company
720 Fifth Avenue
New York, NY 10019

Frederick Warne and Company
101 Fifth Avenue
New York, NY 10003

Watson-Guptill Publications
165 W. 46th Street
New York, NY 10036

Franklin Watts
730 Fifth Avenue
New York, NY 10019

Westminster Press
Witherspoon Building
Walnut and Juniper Streets
Philadelphia, PA 19107

Albert Whitman and Company
560 W. Lake Street
Chicago, IL 60606

John Wiley & Sons
605 Third Avenue
New York, NY 10016

H. W. Wilson Company
950 University Avenue
Bronx, NY 10452

World Publishing Company
110 E. 59th Street
New York, NY 10022

Writer Incorporated
8 Arlington Street
Boston, MA 02116

Xerox Education Group
1200 High Ridge Road
Stamford, CT 06903

Note: University presses may be contacted through their respective universities.

APPENDIX B

Bibliographies and Special Book Lists

American Library Association. *Subject and Title Index to Short Stories for Children.* New York: The Association, Editorial Committee, 1955.

Andersen, Hans Christian. *The Complete Andersen.* Translated by Jean Hersholt. New York: American Heritage Publishing Co., 1952.

Association for Childhood Education International. *Bibliography of Books for Children.* Washington, D. C.: The Association, 1965.

Association for Childhood Education International. *Children's Books for $1.25 or Less,* rev. ed. Washington, D.C.: The Association, 1965.

Association for Childhood Education Literature Committee. *Told Under the Green American.* New York: Macmillan, 1930.

Baker, Augusta, *Once upon a Time.* New York; New York Public Library, 1960.

Barchilon, Jacques, and Pettit, Henry. *The Authentic Mother Goose: Tales and Nursery Rhymes.* Chicago: Alan Swallow, 1960.

Baring-Gould, William, and Baring-Gould, Ceil, eds. *The Annotated Mother Goose.* New York: Crown, 1962.

Bechtel, Louise (Seaman). *Books in Search of Children: Speeches and Essays.* New York: Macmillan, 1969.

Benet, William Rose. *Mother Goose: A Comprehensive Collection of the Rhymes.* New York: American Heritage Publishing Co., 1936.

R. R. Bowker Company. *Growing Up with Books,* rev. ed. New York: R. R. Bowker, 1966.

R. R. Bowker Company. *Recommended Children's Books of 1972.* (Reprinted from *School Library Journal,* published annually.) New York: R. R. Bowker, 1972.

R. R Bowker Company, *Children's Books in Print.* New York: R. R. Bowker, annual.

Brean, Herbert, and Editors of *Life. The Life Treasury of American Folklore.* New York: Time–Life, 1961.

Brown, George I. "Literature in the Elementary School." *Review of Educational Research* 34 (April 1960): 187–93.

Butler, Franconia. *The Great Excluded: Critical Essays on Children's Literature,* vols. I and II. Storrs: University of Connecticut, 1973.

Child Study Association of America, ed. *Books of the Year for Children.* New York: The Association, 1965.

Child Study Association of America. *The Children's Bookshelf.* New York: Bantam Books, 1962.

Children's Book Council, *Children's Books: Awards and Prizes.* New York: The Council, revised annually.

Commire, Anne, ed. *Something about the Author,* vol. 1. Detroit: Gale Research, 1971.

Committee on Junior Booklist, National Association of Independent Schools. *Current Books: Junior Booklist.* Boston: The Association, 1972.

Committee of National Congress of Parents and Teachers and Children's Division, American Library Association. *Let's Read Together: Books for Family Enjoyment.* Chicago: The Association, 1964.

Currah, Ann, ed. *Best Books for Children.* New York: R. R. Bowker, 1967.

DeMontreville, Doris, and Hill, Donna. *Third Book of Junior Authors.* New York: H. W. Wilson, 1972.

Doyle, Brian, ed. *The Who's Who of Children's Literature,* rev. ed. New York: Schocken, 1971.

Eakin, Mary K., comp. *Good Books for Children 1948–1961.* Chicago: University of Chicago Press, 1962.

Eakin, Mary K., comp. *Subject Index to Books for Intermediate Grades,* 3rd ed. Chicago: American Library Association, 1963.

Eakin, Mary K., comp. *Subject Index to Books for Primary Grades,* 3rd ed. Chicago: American Library Association, 1967.

Eakin, Mary K., and Merritt, Eleanor. *Subject Index to Books for Primary Grades,* 2nd ed. Chicago: American Library Association, 1961.

Eastman, Mary, comp. *Index to Fairy Tales, Myths and Legends.* Boston: F. W. Faxon, 1952.

Egoff, Sheila; Stubbs, G. T.; and Ashley, L. F., eds. *Only Connect: Readings on Children's Literature.* New York: Oxford University Press, 1969.

Emrich, Marion V. *The Child's Book of Folklore.* New York: Dial Press, 1947.

Ferris, Helen, ed. *Writing Books for Boys and Girls.* New York: Doubleday, 1952.

Field, Elinor Whitney, comp. *Horn Book Reflections on Children's Books and Reading.* Boston: Horn Book, 1969.

Fryatt, Norma R. *A Horn Book Sampler.* Boston: Horn Book, 1959.

Fuller, Muriel, ed. *More Junior Authors.* New York: H. W. Wilson, 1963.

Gillespie, John, and Lembo, Diana. *Introducing Books: A Guide for Middle Grades.* New York: R. R. Bowker, 1970.

Green, Edward J., and O'Connell, Joan, eds. *An Annotated Bibliography of Visual Discrimination Learning.* New York: Teachers College Press, 1969.

Guilfoile, Elizabeth. *Books for Beginning Readers.* Champaign, Ill.: National Council of Teachers of English, 1964.

Guilfoile, Elizabeth, and Veatch, Jeanette. *Adventuring with Books: A Book List for Elementary Schools.* New York: National Council of Teachers of English, Signet Books, 1966.

Haviland, Virginia, comp. *Children's Literature: A Guide to Reference Sources.* Washington, D. C.: Library of Congress, 1966.

Haviland, Virginia, ed. *Children's Books of International Interest.* Chicago: American Library Association, 1972.

Haviland, Virginia, and Watts, Lois, eds. *Children's Books, 1972.* Washington, D.C.: U. S. Government Printing Office, 1972.

Hopkins, Lee Bennett. *Books Are by People.* New York: Citation Press, 1969.

Hopkins, Lee Bennett. *More Books by More People: Interviews with 65 Authors of Books for Children.* New York: Citation Press, 1974.

Horn Book Committee, ed. *Fanfare: The Horn Book's Honor List, 1961–1965.* Boston: Horn Book, 1967.

Jacoby, Susan. "Movies with Zip That Make Kids Flip," *Scholastic Teacher* 91 (October 1967): 5–6.

Johnson, Siddie Joe, ed. *Children's Books for $1.25 or Less.* Washington, D. C.: Association for Childhood Education International, 1965.

Jones, Milbrey L. *Book Selection Aids for Children and Teachers in Elementary and Secondary Schools.* Washington, D. C.: U. S. Government Printing Office, 1966.

Jordan, Alice Mabel. *Children's Classics,* 4th ed. Boston: Horn Book, 1967.

Jordan, Alice Mabel. *From Rollo to Tom Sawyer and Other Papers*. Boston: Horn Book, 1975.

Karl, Jean. *From Childhood to Childhood*. New York: John Day, 1970.

Kircher, Clara J. *Behavior Patterns in Children's Books: A Bibliography*. Washington, D. C.: Catholic University Press, 1966.

Library Association. *Chosen for Children*. (Carnegie Medal Books) London: The Association, 1967.

Marantz, Kenneth. *A Bibliography of Children's Art Literature*. Washington, D. C.: National Education Association, 1965.

Mahony, Bertha E.; Latimer, Louise P.; and Folmsbee, Beulah. *Illustrators of Children's Books, 1744–1945*. Boston: Horn Book, 1947.

Mahony, Bertha E., and Field, Elinor Whitney, eds. *Newbery Medal Books, 1922–1955*. Boston: Horn Book, 1955.

National Council of Teachers of English. *Books for You*. New York: Washington Square Press, Pocket Books, 1964.

Reid, Virginia M. *Children's Literature— Old and New*. Champaign, Ill.: National Council of Teachers of English, 1964.

Rollins, Charlemae, ed. *We Build Together: A Reader's Guide to Negro Life and Literature for Elementary and High School Use*, 3rd rev. ed. Champaign, Ill.: National Council of Teachers of English, 1967.

Roos, Jean. *Patterns in Reading: An Annotated Book List for Young People*, 2nd ed. Chicago: American Library Association, 1961.

Smith, Dora V. *Fifty Years of Children's Books, 1916–1960: Trends, Backgrounds, Influences*. Champaign, Ill.: National Council of Teachers of English, 1963.

Smith, Lillian. *The Unreluctant Years*. Chicago: American Library Association, 1953.

Snow, Miriam, et al., eds. *A Basic Book Collection for Elementary Grades*. Chicago: American Library Association, 1960.

Steckler, Phyllis, ed. *Children's Books for Schools and Libraries*. New York: R. R. Bowker, 1967.

Ward, Martha Eads, and Marquandt, Dorothy A. *Illustrators of Books for Young People*. New York: Scarecrow Press, 1970.

H. W. Wilson Company. *Children's Catalogue*. New York: H. W. Wilson Company, annual.

Withers, Carl, comp. *A Rocket in My Pocket*. New York: Holt, Rinehart & Winston, 1948.

Wolfe, Ann G. *About 100 Books: A Gateway to Better Inter-Group Understanding*, 5th ed. New York: American Jewish Committee, Institute of Human Relations, 1965.

APPENDIX C

Film Media

FEATURE FILMS

These are listed by name of film, date, and the stars of the film.

Adventures of Robin Hood. 1938. Errol Flynn, Basil Rathbone, Olivia de Haviland.

Adventures of Tom Sawyer. 1972. Jane Wyatt, Buddy Ebsen. (Television production.)

Adventures of Tom Sawyer. 1973. Johnny Whittaker, Jeff East, Celeste Holm, Jodie Foster.

Alice in Wonderland. 1933. W. C. Fields and others.

Bambi. 1948. Walt Disney animation.

Captains Courageous. 1936. Spencer Tracy, Freddie Bartholomew, Lionel Barrymore.

Charlotte's Web. 1974. Animation.

A Christmas Carol. 1938. Reginald Owen, Gene Lockhart.

Cinderella. 1957. Mary Martin. (Television production.)

A Connecticut Yankee in King Arthur's Court. 1949. Bing Crosby, Rhonda Fleming, Cedric Hartwicke.

David Copperfield. 1935. W. C. Fields, Lionel Barrymore, Maureen O'Sullivan, Freddie Bartholomew.

A Dog of Flanders. 1959. Donald Crisp, David Ladd, Theodore Bikel.

Drums Along the Mohawk. 1939. Claudette Colbert, Henry Fonda.

Ferdinand the Bull. 1938. Walt Disney animation.

Gulliver's Travels. 1939. Walt Disney animation.

Hans Brinker, or The Silver Skates. 1952. Danny Kaye, Jeanmarie, Farley Granger.

Heidi. 1937. Shirley Temple, Jean Hersholt.

The Hoober-Bloob Highway. 1975. Animation (Dr. Seuss).

Journey to the Center of the Earth. 1960. Pat Boone, James Mason, Arlene Dahl.

Lassie Come Home. 1943. Roddy MacDowell, Donald Crisp, Lassie.

Little Women. 1933. Katherine Hepburn, Joan Bennett, Frances Dee, Jean Parker.

Mary Poppins. 1964. Julie Andrews, Dick Van Dyke.

Moby Dick. 1956. Gregory Peck, Orson Welles, Richard Basehart, Leo Genn.

My Friend Flicka. 1943. Roddy MacDowell, Preston Foster.

Oliver Twist. 1948. Alec Guiness, John Howard Davies.

Peter Pan. 1953. Mary Martin, Cyril Ritchard. (Television production.)

The Pied Piper of Hamelin. 1957. Van Johnson, Claude Rains, Kay Starr. (Television production.)

Pinocchio. 1940. Walt Disney animation.

Pippi Longstocking. 1970. Foreign production.

The Prince and the Pauper. 1937. Errol Flynn, Claude Rains, Mauch Twins.

Really Rosie, Starring the Nutshell Kids. 1975. Animation (Maurice Sendak).

Rebecca of Sunnybrook Farm. 1938. Shirley Temple, Randolph Scott.

The Red Shoes. 1948. Moira Shearer, Anton Walbrook.

Robin Hood. 1973. Walt Disney animation.

Robinson Crusoe. 1953. Dan O'Herlihy.

The Secret Garden. 1949. Margaret O'Brien, Dean Stockwell, Herbert Marshall.

Snow White and the Seven Dwarfs. 1937. Walt Disney animation.

Song of the South (Uncle Remus tales). 1946. Walt Disney animation.

Sounder. 1973. Cicely Tyson.

The Swiss Family Robinson. 1940. Thomas Mitchell, Freddie Bartholomew, Tim Holt.

The Sword and the Stone. 1953. Walt Disney animation.

Thunderhead. 1945. Roddy MacDowell, Preston Foster.

Treasure Island. 1934. Wallace Beery, Jackie Cooper.

Wee Willie Winkie. 1937. Shirley Temple, Victor Maclaglen.

Winnie the Pooh and Tigger Too. 1974. Walt Disney animation.

The Wizard of Oz. 1939. Judy Garland, Jack Haley, Bert Lahr, Ray Bolger, Billie Burke, Margaret Hamilton, Frank Morgan.

The Yearling. 1946. Gregory Peck, Jane Wyman, Claude Jarman, Jr.

FILMS OF CHILDREN'S LITERATURE

These are listed by film, black and white (B&W) or color (C), running time, source, and levels: primary grades (P), intermediate grades (I), and any age group (A). Addresses of film distributors are given at the end of this appendix.

Andy and the Grasshopper. B&W. 11 min. Coronet. P.

A Book Is to Care For. B&W. 11 min. Coronet. I.

A Christmas Carol. C. 24 min. Coronet. A.

The Country Mouse and the City Mouse. C. 8 min. Coronet. P.

Goldilocks and the Three Bears. C. 11 min. Coronet. P.

King Midas and the Golden Touch. C. 11 min. Coronet. P.

The Little Engine That Could. B&W. 11 min. Coronet. P.

The Little Red Hen. B&W. 11 min. Coronet P.

The Littlest Angel. C. 13 min. Coronet. A.

The Lively Art of Picture Books. John Langstaff, host and narrator. C. 20 min. Weston Woods. A.

The Midnight of Paul Revere. B&W. 11 min. Coronet I.

Poems Are Fun C. 11 min. Coronet. I.

Poetry for Beginners. C. 11 min. Coronet. P.

Robert McCloskey. C. 11 min. Weston Woods. A.

Rumpelstiltskin. B&W. 11 min. Coronet. P.

Shadows, Shadows Everywhere. C. 11. min. Coronet. P.

The Shoemaker and the Elves. C. 13 min. Coronet. P.

The Sleeping Beauty. B&W. 13 min. Coronet. P.

The Sorcerer's Apprentice. 13 min. Coronet. P.

Storyacting Is Fun. B&W. 15 min. Indiana University. I.

Thumbelina. B&W. 11 min. Coronet. P.

NOTE: Children will enjoy a recent information book on animating films: The

Young Animators by the Young Filmmakers Foundation (New York: Frederick A. Praeger, 1973).

FILMS ON CREATIVITY FOR CHILDREN

Blinkity Blank. C. 6 min. International Film Bureau. *A.*

A Chairy Tale. B&W. 10 min. International Film Bureau. *I.*

Creativity. C. 10 min. Think Products. *I.*

Dance Squared. C. 4 min. International Film Bureau. *I.*

The Dot and the Line. C. 9 min. Creative Education Foundation. *A.*

The Face. C. 3 min. Brandon Films. *I.*

Fiddle Dee Dee. C. 4 min. International Film Bureau. *A.*

A Matter of Survival. C. 10 min. McGraw-Hill. *I.*

The Problem. C. 13 min. Brandon Films. *I.*

Where Does My Street Go? C. 20 min. Three Prong Television Productions. *I.*

Whose Garden Was This? C. 10 min. McGraw-Hill. *I.*

Why Man Creates. C. 25 min. Pyramid A.

ADDRESSES OF FILM DISTRIBUTORS

AIMS Instructional Media Service
P.O. Box 1010
Hollywood, CA 90028

American Library Association
50 E. Huron Street
Chicago, IL 60611

BNA Films
Bureau of National Affairs
5615 Fishers Lane
Rockville, MD 20852

Brandon Films
221 W. 57th Street
New York, NY 10019

British Information Services
30 Rockefeller Plaza
New York, NY 10020

Churchill Films
662 N. Robertson Blvd.
Los Angeles, CA 90069

Communications Group West
6335 Homewood Avenue
Hollywood, CA 90028

Contemporary Films
267 W. 25th Street
New York, NY 10001

Coronet Instructional Films
65 E. South Water Street
Chicago, IL 60601

Creative Education Foundation
State University College
Chase Hall
1300 Elmwood Avenue
Buffalo, NY 14222

Charles and Ray Eames
901 Washington Blvd.
Venice, CA 90291

Educational Film Library Assn.
250 W. 57th Street
New York, NY 10019

Encyclopaedia Britannica Films
1150 Wilmette Avenue
Wilmette, IL 60611

Film Associates of California
11014 Santa Monica Blvd.
Los Angeles, CA 90025

Film Center
189 North Wheeler Street
Orange, CA 92669

Filmmakers Library
290 West End Avenue
New York, NY 10023

Films Incorporated
733 Green Bay Road
Wilmette, IL 60091

Ford Film Library
American Road
Dearborn, MI 48121

GMC Film Library
General Motors Building
Detroit, MI 48202

Grover Film Productions
P.O. Box 303
Monterey, CA 93942

Hallmark Films and Recordings
1511 E. North Avenue
Baltimore, MD 21213

Hartley Productions
279 E. 44th Street
New York, NY 10017

Henk Newenhouse
1825 Willow Road
Northfield, IL 60093

IBM Film Library
c/o Modern Talking Picture
  Service
1212 Avenue of the Americas
New York, NY 10036

I/D/E/A's Informational Services
P.O. Box 446
Melbourne, FL 32991

Industrial Education Films
65 Pondfield Road
Bronxville, NY 10708

Innovation Group
254 Madison Avenue
New York, NY 10016

Instructional Media Center
Michigan State University
East Lansing, MI 48823

International Film Bureau
332 S. Michigan Avenue
Chicago, IL 60604

Jam Handy Organization
2821 E. Grand Blvd.
Detroit, MI 42811

Learning Corporation of America
711 Fifth Avenue
New York, NY 10022

McGraw-Hill Contemporary Films
330 W. 42nd Street
New York, NY 10036

Merit Film Productions
P.O. Box 5005
Mission Hills, CA 91340

Michigan State University
East Lansing, MI 48823

Modern Talking Picture Services
c/o Buchan Pictures
122 W. Chippewa Street
Buffalo, NY 14202

National Educational Television
  Film Library
Indiana University
Bloomington, IN 47401

National Film Board
680 Fifth Avenue
New York, NY 10019

Odeon Films
51 W. 86th Street
New York, NY 10024

Psychological Films
205 W. 20th Street
Santa Ana, CA 92706

Pyramid Films
P.O. Box 1048
Santa Monica, CA 90406

Peter M. Robeck & Co.
230 Park Avenue
New York, NY 10017

Roundtable Films
321 S. Beverly Drive
Beverly Hills, CA 90212

Seminar Films
8-12 Broadwick Street
London, W1, England

Seminar Films
Jay Hoffman Presentations
325 E. 57th Street
New York, NY 10022

Short Films Group
P.O. Box 4NE
London, W1, England

Society for Visual Education
1345 Diversay Parkway
Chicago, IL 60614

Sterling Educational Films
316 W. 57th Street
New York, NY 10019

Stuart Reynolds Productions
9465 Wilshire Blvd.
Beverly Hills, CA 90212

Syracuse University Film Library
1455 E. Colvin Street
Syracuse, NY 13210

Television Center
Delta College
University Center, MI 48710

Three Prong Television
  Productions
1525 E. 53rd Street
Chicago, IL 60615

United Nations Film and Visual
  Information
United Nations Plaza
New York, NY 10017

U. S. Dept. of Agriculture
Office of Information
Motion Picture Service
Washington, DC 20250

United World Films
1445 Park Avenue
New York, NY 10029

University of California
Extensions Media Center
Berkeley, CA 94720

University of Georgia
College of Education
Dept. of Educational Psychology
Athens, GA 30601

University of Michigan
  Television Center
310 Maynard Street
Ann Arbor, MI 48108

University of Southern California
Dept. of Cinema
Los Angeles, CA 90007

Walt Disney Productions
Educational Film Division
2400 W. Alameda Avenue
Burbank, CA 91500

Well-Springs
11667 Alba Road
Ben Lomond, CA 95005

Weston Woods Studios
Weston, CN 06880

Sy Wexler Film Productions
801 Seward
Los Angeles, CA 90038

Young America Films
McGraw-Hill Co.
330 W. 42nd Street
New York, NY 10036

APPENDIX D

Filmstrips for Teaching Children's Literature

These are listed by title, with other information, distributing company, and levels: primary grades (P), intermediate grades (I), and any age group (A). Addresses of film distributors are given at the end of this appendix.

Adventures of Paul Bunyan: An American Folktale. Phonodisc & tape. Guidance Associates. *I.*

Andy and the Lion. Weston Woods. *P.*

American Negro Pathfinders. Six filmstrips Bailey. *I.*

American Poets. Six filmstrips. Encyclopaedia Britannica. *I.*

Angus and the Ducks. M. Flack. Weston Woods. *P.*

Arabian Nights. Phonodisc. Imperial.

Basic Intermediate Science, Group I. Seven filmstrips. Society for Visual Education. *I.*

Basic Primary Science, Group I. Six filmstrips. Society for Visual Education. *P.*

Big Snow. Hader. Weston Woods. *A.*

The Biggest Bear. L. Ward. Weston Woods.. *P.*

Blueberries for Sal. McCloskey. Weston Woods. *A.*

Bottles, Boxes, Cups and Cans. On perception. Educational Reading Service. *I.*

The Camel Who Took a Walk. Weston Woods. *P.*

Caps for Sale. Slobodkin. Weston Woods. *P.*

Caterpillar and the Wild Animals. Phonodisc. Universal Education & Visual Arts. *P.*

Chanticleer and the Fox. B. Cooney. Weston Woods. *A.*

Charlotte and the White Horse. Krauss & Sendak. Weston Woods. *P.*

Children's Read Aloud Classics. 3 filmstrips. M & B. *A.*

Christmas in the Stable. Weston Woods. *A.*

Christmas Stories. 6 filmstrips, color. Encyclopaedia Britannica. *A.*

The Circus Baby. Petershams. Weston Woods. *P.*

The Cow Who Fell in the Canal. T. Yashima. Weston Woods. *P.*

Curious George Rides a Bike. H. Rey. Weston Woods. *P.*

Danny and the Dinosaur. Sid Hoff. Weston Woods. *P.*

Don't Count Your Chicks. Aulaire. Weston Woods. *P.*

The Door in the Wall. deAngeli. M & B. *P.*

Encyclopedias. 2 filmstrips, phonodisc. Library Filmstrip Center. *I.*

Fairy Tale Classics. 6 filmstrips. M & B. *A.*

Fairy Tales. 6 filmstrips, color. In Spanish: Goldilocks, Three Billygoats Gruff, Gingerbread Boy, Little Red Hen, and others. M & B. *P.*

Finders Keepers. Lipkind & Mordrinoff. Weston Woods. *P.*

Fish in the Air. K. Wiese. Weston Woods. *P.*

Five Senses. Senses, sensation. Jam Handy. *I.*

Folktales from Many Lands. McGraw-Hill. *A.*

Fun in the City: Libraries. McGraw-Hill. *A.*

Fun in the City: Museums. McGraw-Hill. *A.*

Getting to Know Books, rev. ed. With record. Society for Visual Education. *A.*

Golden Boy. With phonodisc. Universal Education & Visual Arts. *A.*

The Happy Owls. C. Piatti. Weston Woods. *A.*

Harold and the Purple Crayon. C. Johnson. Weston Woods. *P.*

Hey Diddle Diddle and Baby Bunting: The Milkmaid. R. Caldecott. Weston Woods. *P.*

A Hole Is to Dig. Krauss & Sendak. Weston Woods. *P.*

How to Use the Card Catalog, rev. ed. Record. Society for Visual Education. *A.*

How to Use the Enclopedia, rev. ed. Record. Society for Visual Education. *I.*

Humbatz the Wizard and the Two Brothers. Phonodisc. Joshua Tree. *A.*

Interpretations: The Me Nobody Knows. Stephen Joseph, ed. Record. New York Times. *I.*

An Introduction to the Library. With records. Warren Schloat. *A.*

John Henry. Godfrey Cambridge, narrator. Phonodisc. Look, Listen & Learn. *A.*

Johnny Crow's Garden. Weston Woods. *P.*

Journey Cake Ho. Ruth Sawyer. Cassette tape. Weston Woods. *A.*

Kantzil the Mouse Deer. Asian tale. Phonodisc. Look, Listen & Learn. *A.*

Let's Go to the Library. Earl Murphy, illus. Phonodisc. Putnam. *A.*

Little Bear's Visit. Weston Woods. *P.*

The Magic Drum. African tale. Phonodisc. Look, Listen & Learn. *A.*

The Magic Grocery Store. Phonodisc. Joshua Tree. *A.*

The Magic Leaf. Asian tale. Phonodisc. Look, Listen & Learn. *A.*

The Man Who Cut the Cinnamon Tree. Chinese tale. Phonodisc. Look, Listen & Learn. *A.*

The One-Inch Fellow. Japanese folktale. Phonodisc. Look, Listen & Learn. *A.*

Paul Bunyan. Phonodisc; teacher's guide. Look, Listen & Learn. *A.*

Pecos Bill. Phonodisc. Look, Listen & Learn. *A.*

Salt. Phonodisc. Weston Woods. (*P-I*)

Skills in Gathering Facts, rev. ed. Record. Society for Visual Education. *I.*

Spoken Arts Treasury of Fairy Tales, a Language Arts Kit for Pre-School, Kindergarten, Primary Grades. 10 filmstrips, 5 phonodiscs. Spoken Arts. *P.*

Stories from Other Lands. 6 filmstrips. Encyclopaedia Britannica.

The Strong Man Who Boasted Too Much. African tale. Phonodisc.

Taking a Trip with a Book. Educational Reading Service. *A.*

The Three Billygoats Gruff. Phonodisc. Weston Woods.

A Visit to the Library. Joanne Ireland, Beverly Gersti, illus. Troll. *A.*

Water Spirit. African tale. Phonodisc. Universal Education & Visual Arts. *P-I.*

What Do You Say, Dear? Joslin & Sendak. Weston Woods. *P.*

What's in a Dictionary, rev. ed. Record. Society for Visual Education. *A.*

Whistle for Willie. Weston Woods. *P.*

Wild Rose: A Cherokee Legend. Phonodisc. Encyclopaedia Britannica. *P-I*

Bailey Film Associates
11559 Santa Monica Blvd.
Los Angeles, CA 90025

Stanley Bowmar Company
4 Broadway
Valhalla, NY 10595

Carnegie-Mellon University
College of Fine Arts
Schenley Park
Pittsburgh, PA 15213

Curriculum Filmstrips
1319 Vine Street
Philadelphia, PA 19107

Educational Reading Service
320 Route 17
Rahwah, NJ 07430

Educational Technology
  Publications
2224 Hewlett Avenue
Merrick, NY 11566

Encyclopaedia Britannica Films
1150 Wilmette Avenue
Wilmette, IL 60091

Eye Gate House
146–01 Archer Avenue
Jamaica, NY 11431

Filmstrip House
432 Park Avenue South
New York, NY 10003

Grolier Educational Corp.
845 Third Avenue
New York, NY 10022

Guidance Associates
41 Washington Avenue
Pleasantville, NY 10570

Imperial
(Learning Resource Division)
202 Lake Miriam Drive
Lakeland, FL 33803

Jam Handy Organization
2821 E. Grand Blvd.
Detroit, MI 48211

Joshua Tree Productions
15 W. 46th Street
New York, NY 10038

Library Filmstrip Center
3033 Aloma
Wichita, KS 67211

Life Magazine Filmstrips
Rockefeller Plaza
New York, NY 10020

Look, Listen and Learn
825 Third Avenue
New York, NY 10022

McGraw-Hill Filmstrips
330 W. 42nd Street
New York, NY 10036

Miller-Brody Productions
342 Madison Avenue
New York, NY 10017

Phonovisual Products
12216 Parklawn Drive
Rockville, MD 20852

G. P. Putnam's Sons
210 Madison Avenue
New York, NY 10016

Scholastic Kindle Filmstrips
902 Sylvan Avenue
Englewood Cliffs, NJ 07632

Scott-Foresman Company
1900 E. Lake Avenue
Glenview, IL 60025

Society for Visual Education
1345 Diversey Parkway
Chicago, IL 60614

Spoken Arts
6920 Sunset Blvd.
Los Angeles, CA 90028

Troll Associates
320 Route 17
Nahwah, NJ 07430

United States Publishers Assoc.
386 Park Avenue
New York, NY 10022

Universal Education and
  Visual Arts
Division of Universal City Studios
100 Universal City Plaza
Universal City, CA 91608

University of Indiana
Communications Center
Bloomington, IN 47401

Warren Schloat Productions
Pleasantville, NY 10570

Weston Woods Studios
Weston, CT 06880

APPENDIX E

Recordings for Use with Children's Literature

These are listed by record title, story reader, distributor, and level: primary grades (P), intermediate grades (I), and any age group (A). Addresses of distributors are listed at the end of this appendix.

Adventures of Robin Hood. Retold by Paul Creswick. Read by Anthony Quayle. Caedmon. *I.*

Aesop's Fables. Columbia. *P.*

African Folk Tales, vol. I. Retold by Bertha Parker. CMS. *A.*

African Folk Tales, vol. II. Retold by Bertha Parker. CMS. *A.*

African Village Folktales, vol. I. Read by Brock Peters and Diana Sands. Caedmon. *A.*

African Village Folktales, vol. II. Read by Brock Peters and Diana Sands. Caedmon. *A.*

African Village Folktales, vol. III. Read by Brock Peters and Diana Sands. Caedmon. *A.*

Aladdin and His Lamp. Retold by Annabel Williams-Ellis. Read by Anthony Quayle. Caedmon. *A.*

Ali Baba and the Forty Thieves. Read by Anthony Quayle. Caedmon. *A.*

Ali Baba and the Forty Thieves; Sinbad the Sailor. Dramatized by a British cast. Riverside Wonderland Records. *A.*

Alice in Wonderland. By Lewis Carroll. Read by Joan Greenwood, Stanley Holloway, et al. Caedmon. *A.*

All About Dragons. Puff, The Magic Dragon; The Reluctant Dragon. Walt Disney Records. *A.*

America the Beautiful. Disneyland. *A.*

American Indian Tales for Children. Miller-Brody. *A.*

American Patriotism in Poems and Prose. Ed Begley, Julie Harris, and Frederick O'Neal. Caedmon. *A.*

American Tall Tales, vols. 1–4. Read by Ed Begley. Caedmon. *A.*

Andy and the Lion. Columbia. *A.*

Andy and the Lion (with book). Read by Daniel Ocko. SBS. *A.*

Andy and the Lion. By James Daugherty. Weston Woods. *P.*

Angus and the Ducks. By Marjorie Flack. Weston Woods. *P.*

Animals on the Farm. Columbia. *P.*

Arabian Nights. Read by Marian Carr. Libraphone. *A.*

Ballads of the British Isles. Sung by Robert Smith. Rhythms Prod. *A.*

Bambi. Disney Records. *A.*

Bayou Suzette. By Lois Lenski. Sound Book Press Society. *I.*

Beauty and the Beast and Other Stories. Read by Douglas Fairbanks. Caedmon. *A.*

Bertie's Little Brother. Columbia. *P.*

Best Loved Fairy Tales. Retold by Charles Perrault. *P.*

The Big Green Thing. Columbia. *P.*

The Big Snow. By Bert and Elmer Hader. Weston Woods. *A.*

The Biggest Bear. Columbia. *A.*

The Biggest Bear. Read by Darrell Sandeen. SBS. *P.*

Black Beauty. Miller-Brody. *I.*

Black Pearl. By Scott O'Dell. Miller-Brody. *I.*

Blueberries For Sal. By Robert McCloskey. Weston Woods. *A.*

The Boy, The Cat and the Magic Fiddle. Columbia. *A.*

Bread And Jam for Frances. Read by Anita Klever. SBS. *P.*

Brer Mud Turtle's Trickery. By Armstrong Sperry. Miller-Brody. *I.*

Bronze Bow. Elizabeth Speare. Miller-Brody.

Caddie Woodlawn. By Carol Ryrie Brink. Miller-Brody. *I.*

Call It Courage. By Armstrong Sperry. Miller-Brody. *I.*

The Camel Who Took a Walk. By Tworkow & Duvoisin. Weston Woods. *A.*

Caps for Sale. By Esphyr Slobodkin. Weston Woods. *P.*

Caps for Sale (with book). Read by Daniel Ocko. SBS. *P.*

Captain Kidd's Cow. By Phil Strong. Stokes Sound Book Press Society. *P.*

Carl Sandburg's Poems for Children. Discussion by Carl Sandburg. Caedmon. *I.*

Carry On, Mr. Bowditch. By Jean Lee Lathan. Miller-Brody. *I.*

The Cat That Walked by Herself and Other Just So Stories. Read by Boris Karloff. Caedmon. *P.*

The Cat Who Went to Heaven. Elizabeth Coatsworth. Miller-Brody. *P.*

Catch a Little Rhyme. Read by Eve Merriam. Caedmon. *P.*

Chanticleer and the Fox. By Barbara Cooney. Weston Woods. *A.*

Charlotte and the White Horse. By Krauss and Sendak. Weston Woods. *P.*

Charlotte's Web. Read by E. B. White. Miller-Brody. *A.*

The Children's Bible. Columbia. *A.*

A Child's Garden of Verses. Disney Records. *P.*

Chinese Folk Tales. Told by Anne Pellowski. CMS. *I.*

A Christmas Carol. By Charles Dickens. Read by Dan O'Herlihy. Audio Books. *A.*

A Christmas Carol. By Charles Dickens. Retold by Basil Rathbone. Columbia. *I.*

Christmas in the Stable. By Lindgren & Wiberg. Weston Woods. *A.*

Cinderella. Columbia. *A.*

Cinderella. Mary Martin TV Show. RCA Victor. *A.*

Cinderella and Other Fairy Tales. Retold by Walter de la Mare. Read by Claire Bloom. Caedmon. *A.*

Congo Boy (with book). Read by Bob Chapman. SBS. *P.*

Copper-Toed Boots. By Marguerite de Angeli. SBS. *P.*

Coven of Witches Tales. Told by Vincent Price. Caedmon. *I.*

The Cricket in Times Square. By George Selden. Miller-Brody. *I.*

Curious George and Other Stories. By H. A. Rey. Read by Julie Harris. Caedmon. *P.*

Curious George Rides a Bike. By. H. A. Rey. Weston Woods. *P.*

Curious George Rides a Bike. Read by Gilbert Mack. SBS. *P.*

Dark Frigate. By Charles Boardman Hawes. Miller-Brody. *I.*

Don Quixote. Read by George Rose. Miller-Brody. *I.*

Door in the Wall. By Marguerite de Angeli. Miller-Brody. *P-I.*

Downright Dencey. By Caroline D. Snedeker. SBS. *I.*

East of the Sun and West of the Moon (The Sheep and the Pig Who Set Up Housekeeping). By Gudrun Thorne-Thomsen. RCA Victor. *A.*

The Elephant's Child. By Rudyard Kipling. Read by Norman Rose. Columbia. *A.*

The Elephant's Child and Selections from Lewis Carroll. Miller-Brody. *A.*

The Emperor's New Clothes and Other Tales. By Hans Christian Andersen. Read by Michael Redgrave. Caedmon. *A.*

European Folk and Fairy Tales. Told by Anne Pellowski. CMS. *A.*

Fables. By Aesop. Read by Boris Karloff. Caedmon. *A.*

Fables from Aesop. Retold and read by Ennis Rees. McGraw-Hill. *A.*

Fables from Aesop. Retold by Ennis Rees. Miller-Brody. *P.*

Fairy Tale Favorites. Miller-Brody. *P.*

Fairy Tales of Hans Christian Andersen. Narrated by Danny Kaye. Golden Records. *A.*

Fairy Tales and Rhymes. Spoken Arts. *A.*

Fairy Tales for a Winter's Night. Miller-Brody. *A.*

Favorite American Poems. Read by Ed Begley. *I.*

Ferdinand. Columbia. *A.*

Fisherman and His Wife. By Wanda Gag. Weston Woods. *A.*

Fisherman and His Wife. By Brothers Grimm. Weston Woods. *A.*

Folk and Fairy Tales (from ten countries). Miller-Brody. *I.*

Folk Tales and Legends from Great Britain. Told by Lee Montague (English tales), Maureen Potter (Irish tales), Magnus Magnusson (Scottish tales), and Ray Smith (Welsh tales). CMS. *I.*

Folk Tales of the Tribes of Africa. Read by Eartha Kitt. Caedmon. *I.*

Forest Patrol. By Jim Kjelgaard. Sound Book Press Society.

The Frog. By Ruth Sawyer. *A.*

From the Mixed-Up Files of Mrs. Basil E. Frankweiler. By E. L. Konigsburg. Miller-Brody. *I.*

Gift of the Forest. By Eloise Lownsbery and H. L. Singh. Stokes Sound Book Press Society. *I.*

Ginger Pye. By Eleanor Estes. Miller-Brody. *I.*

Goldilocks and the Three Bears. Narrated by David Allen. Columbia. *P.*

Goldilocks and the Three Bears and Other Stories. Read by Claire Bloom. Caedmon. *P.*

Great Treasury of Classic Fairy Tales. Golden Records. *A.*

Grimms' Fairy Tales. Read by Eve Watkinson and Christopher Cassen. Spoken Arts. *A.*

Gudrun Thorne-Thomsen Recordings. American Library Association. *A.*

Gulliver's Travels. Read by Denis Johnston. Miller-Brody. *I.*

Gulliver's Travels. By Jonathan Swift. Read by Michael Redgrave. Caedmon. *I.*

Gulliver's Travels. By Jonathan Swift. Read by Hal Gerard. Audio Books. *I.*

Gwendolyn Brooks Reading Her Poetry. Caedmon. *I.*

Hans Christian Andersen. Columbia. *A.*

Hans Christian Andersen Fairy Tales, vols. 1–7. Read by Eve Watkinson and Christopher Casson. Spoken Arts. *A.*

Hans Christian Andersen Tales. Miller-Brody. *A.*

Hansel and Gretel and Others by the Grimm Brothers. Retold by Annabel Williams-Ellis. Read by Claire Bloom. Caedmon. *A.*

The Happy Prince. By Oscar Wilde. *A.*

Harold and the Purple Crayon. Columbia. *P.*

Harold and the Purple Crayon. Read by Anita Klever. SBS. *P.*

Harriet Tubman. Scott-Foresman. *I.*

Heroes, Gods and Monsters of the Greek Myths, vols. 1–6. Read by Julie Harris and Richard Kiley. Miller-Brody. Stokes. *I.*

Homer Price. By Robert McCloskey. Stokes Sound Book Press Society. *I.*

House at Pooh Corner. By A. A. Milne. Played by Jan Carmichael and Dick Bentley. Riverside-Wonderland. *P.*

House of Sixty Fathers. By Meindert De-Long. Miller-Brody. P-I.

I Know an Old Lady. Bonne, Mills & Graboff. Weston Woods. P.

I Met a Man. Written and read by John Ciardi. Pathways of Sound. P.

I'd Rather Be My Size. Columbia. A.

In the Beginning. Narrated and sung by Rod McKuen. Sunset. A.

In Clean Hay. By Erik P. Kelly. Sound Book Press Society.

Invincible Louisa. By Cornelia Meigs. Miller-Brody.

Jack and the Beanstalk (with book). Read by Owen Jordan. SBS. A.

Johnny Tremain. By Esther Forbes. Miller-Brody. I.

Joy to the World: Christmas Legends. Ruth Sawyer. Weston Woods. A.

Jungle Animals. Columbia. P.

Just So Stories. By Rudyard Kipling. Told by Gene Lockhart. Audio Books. I.

King of the Golden River. By John Ruskin. Read by Anthony Quayle. Caedmon. I.

King of the Wind. By Marguerite Henry. Miller-Brody. I.

The Legend of Sleepy Hollow. By Washington Irving. Read by Hurd Hatfield. Miller-Brody. I.

Legend of Sleepy Hollow. By Washington Irving. Read by Ed Begley. Caedmon. I.

Lentil. Read by Owen Jordan. SBS. I.

Lentil. Columbia. I.

Leonard Wibberly Reads His Poetry for Children. Miller-Brody. A.

Little Match Girl and Other Fairy Tales. Read by Boris Karloff. Caedmon. A.

The Little Mermaid. Read by Cathleen Nesbitt. Caedmon. P.

Little Red Riding Hood and Others. Walter de la Mare. Caedmon. P.

Little Women. By Louisa May Alcott. Read by Elinor Basescu. Miller-Brody. I.

The Lobster Quadrille. The Simon Sisters. Columbia Children's Library of Recorded Books. A.

Love Is a Hug. Columbia. P.

Madeline and the Gypsies and Other Stories. By Ludwig Bemelmans. Read by Carol Channing. Caedmon. P.

Madeline and Other Bemelmans. By Ludwig Bemelmans. Read by Carol Channing. Caedmon. P.

Madeline's Rescue. By Ludwig Bemelmans. Columbia. P.

Madeline's Rescue (with book). Read by Carole Danell. SBS. P.

Magic Ball and Other Tales from Silver Lands. Retold by Lawson Zerbe. N.A.C. A.

Make Way for Ducklings. By Robert McCloskey. Columbia. A.

Many Moons. By James Thurber. Read by Peter Ustinov. Caedmon. A.

Mark Twain Library. Read by Hiram Sherman. Miller-Brody. I.

Mary Poppins. Songs by original cast. Disney Records. I.

Mary Poppins. By P. L. Travers. Dramatized by Maggie Smith, Robert Stephens, et al. Caedmon. I.

Mike Mulligan. Columbia. A.

Mike's Magic Glasses. Columbia. P.

Miracles: Poems Written by Children. Collected by Richard Lewis. Caedmon. A.

Mischief in Fez. By Eleanor Hoffman. Stokes Sound Book Press Society. I.

Mocha the Djuka. By Frances Fullerton Neilson. Stokes Sound Book Press Society. I.

More Folk and Fairy Tales From Other Lands. Miller-Brody. A.

More Stories from the Arabian Nights. Miller-Brody. I.

Mother Goose. Columbia. P.

Norse Folk and Fairy Tales. Told by Anne Pellowski. CMS. A.

Nursery Rhymes. Columbia. P.

Oinks Are for Pigs. Columbia. P.

The Old Man and the Tiger. Columbia. A.

Oliver Twist. Columbia. I.

On the Dark of the Moon. By Don Lang. Sound Book Press Society. A.

Oscar Wilde Fairy Tales. Miller-Brody. A.

Paul Bunyan and Other Tall Tales of America. Read by Will Rogers. Riverside-Wonderland. *I.*

A Paul Bunyan Yarn. Told by Jack Lester. A.L.A. *I.*

A Pecos Bill Tale. By J. C. Bowman. Told by Jack Lester. A.L.A. *I.*

Penny Whistle. By Eric Berry. Young People's Records. *A.*

Peter Pan. Disney Records. *I.*

Peter Rabbit. By Beatrix Potter. Adapted by Nancy Sokoloff. Read by Gene Kelly. Columbia. *P.*

Peter Rabbit and Other Tales. Read by Frank Luther. Decca. *P.*

The Pickety Fence and Other Poems. By David McCord. Miller-Brody. *A.*

The Pied Piper and Other Stories. Read by Keith Baxter. Caedmon. *I.*

Ping. Columbia. *P.*

Pinocchio. Read by Cyril Ritchard. Caedmon. *A.*

Pinocchio. Columbia. *A.*

Pinocchio. Songs from original sound track. Disney Records. *A.*

Puss in Boots. Gilbert Mack and Jean Richards. SBS. *P.*

Railroad Rhythms. Rhythmic Prod. *A.*

The Rain God's Daughter and Other African Folktales. Collected and edited by Annabel Williams-Ellis and Clem Abiaziem Okafor. Caedmon. *I.*

The Red Pony. By John Steinbeck. Read by Eli Wallach. Caedmon. *I.*

Red Riding Hood; Goldilocks; The Water Babies. Read by Jean Metcalfe and Ann Todd. Riverside-Wonderland. *P.*

The Reluctant Dragon. By Kenneth Grahame. Read by Boris Karloff. Caedmon. *P.*

Rifles for Watie. By Harold Keith. Miller-Brody. *I.*

Rip Van Winkle. By Washington Irving. Read by Ed Begley. Caedmon. *I.*

Rip Van Winkle and the Legend of Sleepy Hollow. Read by Elinor Gene Hoffman. Literary Records. *I.*

Robin Hood Ballads. Sung by Wallace House with guitar. Folkways. *A.*

Rumpelstiltskin. Read by Roland Winters. RCA. *A.*

Schnitzle, Schnotzle, Schnootzle. By Ruth Sawyer. Viking. *P.*

Selections from the Arrow Book of Poetry (with book). Jean Richards and Jordan Charney. SBS. *A.*

The Seventh Princess and Other Fairy Tales. Miller-Brody. *A.*

Singing Games from Many Lands. Rhythms Prod. *P.*

The Singing Tree. By Kate Seredy. Sound Book Press Society. *A.*

Six Folk Tales. Columbia. *A.*

Sleeping Beauty. With music from sound track. Disney Records. *A.*

Smoky Bay. Steingumur Arason. Sound Book Press Society. *P.*

Snow Queen. Read by Cathleen Nesbitt. Caedmon. *A.*

Snow White and Others. Retold by Annabel Williams-Ellis. Read by Claire Bloom. Caedmon. *A.*

Songs from Dr. Doolittle. Disneyland Records. *A.*

Sounder. By William Armstrong. Miller-Brody. *I.*

Sounds of a City. Columbia. *P.*

Stories from the Arabian Nights. Miller-Brody. *I.*

Story of Ferdinand. Read by Juan Nazario. SBS. *A.*

Story of Peter Pan. Told by Glynis Johns. Caedmon. *I.*

The Story about Ping. Read by Anita Klever. SBS. *P.*

Strawberry Girl. By Lois Lenski. Miller-Brody. *I.*

Strawberry Girl. By Lois Lenski. Stokes Sound Book Press Society. *I.*

Stuart Little. Miller-Brody. *I.*

The Tailor of Gloucester and Other Stories. By Beatrix Potter. Read by Claire Bloom. Caedmon. *P.*

Tale of Little Pig Robinson. By Beatrix Potter. Read by Claire Bloom. Caedmon. *P.*

The Tale of Peter Rabbit and Others. By Beatrix Potter. Read by Claire Bloom. Caedmon. *P.*

Tales of Witches, Ghosts and Goblins. Told by Vincent Price. Caedmon. *A.*

Thimble Summer. By Elizabeth Enright. Miller-Brody. *I.*

The Thirteen Clocks. By James Thurber. Miller-Brody. *A.*

Three Billygoats Gruff; The Gingerbread Man. SBS. *P.*

Tom Sawyer. By Mark Twain. Read by Ed Begley. Caedmon. *I.*

Tom Sawyer; Adventures with Injun Joe. By Mark Twain. Read by Ed Begley. Caedmon. *I.*

Tom Thumb, Rumpelstiltskin, and Other Fairy Tales by the Grimm Brothers. Read by Joseph Schildkraut. Caedmon. *A.*

Too Much Noise. Read by Ralph Curtis. SBS. *P.*

Trap Lines North. By Stephen Meader. Sound Book Press Society. *I.*

Treasure Island. By Robert Louis Stevenson. Adapted by Ralph Rose. Columbia. *I.*

Treasure Island. By Robert Louis Stevenson. Dramatization. Decca. *I.*

The Trumpeter of Krakow. Eric P. Kelly. Miller-Brody. *I.*

The Ugly Duckling. Told by Frank Luther. Luther Records. *P.*

The Ugly Duckling and Other Tales. Read by Cathleen Nesbitt. Caedmon. *P.*

Uncle Remus Stories. By Joel Chandler Harris. Narrated by Morris Mitchell. Pathways of Sound. *I.*

Uncle Remus: The Wonderful Tar Baby Story. Narrated by Calder Crane. Allegro Music. *A.*

A Walk in the Forest. Young People's Records. *P.*

Who's Polite? Columbia. *P.*

The Wind in the Willows. By Kenneth Grahame. Narrated by Patricia Wymore and cast. London Records. *A.*

The Wind in the Willows. By Kenneth Grahame. Miller-Brody. *I.*

Winnie-The-Pooh. By A. A. Milne. Read by Carol Channing. Caedmon. *P.*

Winnie-The-Pooh. Miller-Brody. *P.*

The Witch of Blackbird Pond. By Elizabeth George Speare. Miller-Brody. *I.*

The Wizard of Oz. By Frank Baum. Read by Marvin Miller and Jane Webb. Audio Books. *A.*

Wynken, Blynken and Nod, and Other Poems by Eugene Field. Read by Julie Harris. Caedmon. *P.*

You Know Who, Fiddler Dan and John J. Plenty, and Other Poems. Read by John Ciardi. Miller-Brody. *P.*

You Read To Me, I'll Read To You. Read by John Ciardi and his children. Miller-Brody. *P.*

ADDRESSES OF DISTRIBUTORS OF RECORDS

American Library Association
50 E. Huron Street
Chicago, IL 60611

Angel Records
Division of Capitol Records
317 W. 44th Street
New York, NY 10036

Argo Record Company, Ltd.
113 Fulham Road
London S. W., England

Audio Book Company
501 Main Street
St. Joseph, MI 49085

Bartok Guild
154 W. 14th Street
New York, NY 10019

Bowmar Records
12 Cleveland Street
Valhalla, NY 10595

Caedmon Records
505 Eighth Avenue
New York, NY 10018

Capitol Records
Education Dept.
1750 N. Vine Street
Hollywood, CA 90028

Carillon Records
520 Fifth Avenue
New York, NY 10036

Children's Record Guild
1376 Coney Island Avenue
Brooklyn, NY 11230

CMS Records
14 Warren Street
New York, NY 10007

Columbia Records
799 Seventh Avenue
New York, NY 10019

Command Records
1501 Broadway
New York, NY 10036

Creative Associates
176 Newbury Street
Boston, MA 02116

Decca Records
445 Park Avenue
New York, NY 10022

Disneyland Records P.O.
Box 760
Great Neck, NY 11021

Elektra Records
51 W. 51st Street
New York, NY 10019

Enrichment Teaching Materials
246 Fifth Avenue
New York, NY 10001

Folkways Records
Record, Book and Film Sales
121 W. 47th Street
New York, NY 10036

Golden Records
Rockefeller Center
New York, NY 10020

Harcourt Brace Jovanovich
757 Third Avenue
New York, NY 10017

Libraphone Listening Library
18 W. Putnam Avenue
Greenwich, CT 06830

Living Literature
100 Avenue of the Americas
New York, NY 10013

London Records
539 E. 25th Street
New York, NY 10001

McGraw-Hill Records
330 W. 42nd Street
New York, NY 10036

Mentor Records
New American Library
501 Madison Avenue
New York, NY 10022

MGM Records
Division of Lowe's, Inc.
1540 Broadway
New York, NY 10036

National Council of Teachers
of English
Committee on Annotated
Recording List
508 S. Sixth Street
Champaign, IL 61822

Newbery Award Records
936 E. 10th Street
Brooklyn, NY 11230

Pathways of Sound
10 Mount Auburn Street
Cambridge, MA 02114

Poetry Records
c/o David Ross
475 Fifth Avenue
New York, NY 10017

Prestige-Lively Arts Records
203 S. Washington Avenue
Bergenfield, NJ 07621

RCA Victor Record Division
115 E. 24th Street
New York, NY 10010

Rhythms Productions Records
9844 Everest Street
Downey, CA 90242

Riverside Records
235 W. 46th Street
New York, NY 10036

Scholastic Magazine
AV Department
50 W. 44th Street
New York, NY 10036

Scott-Foresman Company
1900 E. Lake Avenue
Glenview, IL 60025

Sound Book Series
36 Garth Road
Scarsdale, NY 10583

Spoken Arts Records
1150 Wilmette Avenue
Wilmette, IL 60091

Sunset Records
6920 Sunset Blvd.
Los Angeles, CA 90028

Theatre Masterworks
20 Rockefeller Plaza
New York, NY 10020

Tradition Records
80 E. 11th Street
New York, NY 10011

Vanguard Record Sales Corp.
154 W. 14th Street
New York, NY 10011

Weston Woods Studios
Weston, CT 06880

Young People's Record Club
1376 Coney Island Avenue
Brooklyn, NY 11230

APPENDIX F

Selected Multimedia Components

These are listed by title, type of media included in each set, distributor and level: primary grades (P), intermediate grades (I), and any age group (A). Addresses are provided at the end of this appendix.

Aesop's Fables. 4 filmstrips, 2 records. Coronet. *P.*

African Folktales. Filmstrip, record, tape. Coronet. *A.*

American Folklore. Filmstrip, record, tape. Coronet. *A.*

Amos Fortune, Free Man. Record, filmstrip, cassette. Miller-Brody. *I.*

Andersen's Fairy Tales. 8 filmstrips, 4 records, tape. Coronet. *A.*

Baldur; Brer Mud Turtle's Trickery; The Frog; Gudbrand on the Hillside; A Paul Bunyan Yarn; A Pecos Bill Tale; Schnitzle, Schnotzle and Schnootzle; Sleeping Beauty; Tales from Volsunga Saga. 9 cassettes. Miller-Brody. *A.*

Caddie Woodlawn. By Carol R. Brink. Filmstrip, record, cassette. Miller-Brody. *I.*

Call It Courage. By Armstrong Sperry. Filmstrip, record, cassette. Miller-Brody. *I.*

The Cat Who Went to Heaven. Filmstrip, record, cassette. Miller-Brody. *I.*

Children of Courage (Amer. Ethnic Tales). 5 cassettes. Miller-Brody. *I.*

A Child's Garden of Verses. Records, 2 cassettes. Miller-Brody. *P.*

Classic Fairy Tales. 4 filmstrips, 4 records. Miller-Brody. *A.*

Creativity Program Kit for Individualizing and Humanizing the Learning Process. By Dr. Frank E. Williams. Books, records, pictures, etc. Educational Technology Publications. *I.*

Dream Keeper and Other Poems of Langston Hughes. Book, record. Folkways. *P–I.*

Famous Children's Stories. Filmstrips, record, tape. Coronet. *A.*

Favorite Children's Books. Filmstrips, cassettes. Coronet. *A.*

First Men on the Moon. Record and book. Scholastic. *I.*

Folk Tales from West Africa. Read by Harold Counlander. Record and book. Folkway Records. *I.*

Grimm Brothers' Favorites. 4 records, 8 filmstrips. Coronet. *A.*

Grimms' Fairy Tales. 4 filmstrips. 2 records or tape. Coronet. *A.*

Grimms' Fairy Tales. 5 cassettes. Miller-Brody. *A.*

It's Like This, Cat. By Emily Neville. Record, cassette. Miller-Brody. I.

Jungle Books. 4 filmstrips, 4 records. Miller-Brody. I.

Just So Stories. 2 cassettes. Miller-Brody. I.

Just So Stories. Filmstrip, record, tape. Coronet. I.

The Magic Ball and Other Tales from Silver Lands. Based on book by Charles J. Finger. Filmstrip, record, cassette. Miller-Brody. I.

The Matchlock Gun. By Walter D. Edmonds. Filmstrip, record, cassette. Miller-Brody. I.

Millions of Cats; Mike Mulligan; Make Way for Ducklings; Hercules. 4 filmstrips, 4 related text booklets, record. Weston Woods.

More Hans Christian Andersen Tales. 4 cassettes. Miller-Brody. A.

Peter Pan Book and Record Library. 20 records and books. Miller-Brody. A.

Peter Rabbit Look and Listen Collection. Told by Claire Bloom. Records, books, pictures. Frederick Warne & Co. P.

Pick a Peck o' Poems. 6 filmstrips, 6 records. Miller-Brody. A.

Pippi Longstocking. Records or cassettes. Miller-Brody. A.

Poetry Programs for Children. 3 vols. 3 records or cassettes. Miller-Brody. A.

Queeny Peavy. Cassette. Miller-Brody. P.

Stories For Joining In. 3 records, 3 filmstrips. Coronet. P.

Tales from Japan. Filmstrip, record, tape. Coronet. A.

Treasury of Fairy Tales. 10 filmstrips, 5 records. Miller-Brody. A.

Treasury of Lewis Carroll. Record or cassette. Miller-Brody. A.

A Treasury of Modern Tales for Children. 4 filmstrips, 4 records. Miller-Brody. A.

What Is Poetry? Narrator, Claire Bloom. Teacher, Carl Sandburg. 10 color filmstrips, 10 records, teacher's guide with duplicating masters. Caedmon. A.

The Wheel on the School. By Meindert de Jong. Filmstrip, record, cassette. Miller-Brody. I.

Why Do We Need Creative Thinking? Slides plus script. Think Products. I.

Note: Most popular children's books are now available in the Scholastic Record and Book Companion Series. Write Scholastic Audio-Visual Materials, 906 Sylvan Avenue, Englewood Cliffs, NJ 07632.

ADDRESSES OF POPULAR MULTIMEDIA COMPANIES

Bailey-Film Associates
11559 Santa Monica Blvd.
Los Angeles, CA 90025

Stanley Bowmar Company
4 Broadway
New York, NY 10595

Caedman Records
505 Eighth Avenue
New York, NY 10018

Carnegie-Mellon University
College of Fine Arts
Schenley Park
Pittsburgh, PA 15213

CMS Records
14 Warren Street
New York, NY 10001

Coronet Instructional Films
65 E. South Water Street
Chicago, IL 60601

Educational Technology
  Publications
2224 Hewlett Avenue
Merrick, NY 11566

Encyclopaedia Britannica Films
1150 Wilmette Avenue
Wilmette, IL 60091

Eye Gate House
146–01 Archer Avenue
Jamaica, NY 11431

Filmstrip House
432 Park Avenue South
New York, NY 10016

Folkway Records
117 W. 46th Street
New York, NY 10011

Frederick Warne & Company
161 Fifth Avenue
New York, NY 10003

Grolier Educational Corp.
845 Third Avenue
New York, NY 10022

Innovative Resources
P.O. Box 26655
El Paso, TX 79926

Jam Handy Organization
2821 E. Grand Blvd.
Detroit, MI 48211

Learning Education Today Center
530 University Avenue
Palo Alto, CA 94301

Life Magazine Filmstrips
Rockefeller Plaza
New York, NY 10020

McGraw-Hill Filmstrips
330 W. 42nd Street
New York, NY 10036

Miller-Brody Productions
342 Madison Avenue
New York, NY 10017

Scholastic Audio-Visual Center
904 Sylvan Avenue
Englewood Cliffs, NJ 07632

Warren Schloat Productions
Pleasantville, NY 10570

Spoken Arts
6926 Sunset Blvd.
Los Angeles, CA 90028

Weston Woods Studios
Weston Woods, CT 06883

APPENDIX G

Magazines on Children's Literature for Teachers

Asterisks denote magazines that deal exclusively with children's literature.

A Basic Collection for Elementary Grades. Chicago: American Library Association, 1960.

Bookbird. International Board on Books for Young People. 119 Fifth Avenue, New York, NY. Quarterly.

The Booklist and Subscription Books Bulletin. American Library Association. Semimonthly.

The Bookmark. New York State Library. Five times a year.

Book Review Digest. New York: H. W. Wilson Company.

Book Week (Supplement to *Washington Post* and *Chicago Sun Times.*) 125 Barclay Street, New York, NY.

Book World (Supplement to *Chicago Sunday Tribune.*) 230 W. 41st Street, New York, NY 10036.

The Bulletin of the Center for Children's Books. Graduate Library School, University of Chicago, 5750 Ellis Avenue, Chicago, IL 60637.

Bulletin of Teaching Ideas and Materials. P.O. Box 495, West Nyack, NY 10994.

Calendar. Children's Book Council, 175 Fifth Avenue, New York, NY 10010. Quarterly.

Cavanaugh, Gladys. *Subject Index to Children's Magazines.* 2223 Chamberlain Avenue, Madison, WI. Monthly—August to May; semi-annual cumulations in February and August.

Childhood Education. Association for Childhood Education International, 3615 Wisconsin Avenue, NW, Washington, DC 20016.

Children's Literature in Education. Dept. H, APS Publications, Inc., 150 Fifth Avenue, New York, NY 10011. Three issues annually.

Cricket. Open Court Publishing Company, 1058 Eighth Street, La Salle, IL. Monthly.

Dobler, Lavinia, and Fuller, Muriel. *The Dobler World Directory of Youth Periodicals.* 3rd ed. New York: Citation Press, 1970.

Early Learning. Riverside, NJ 08075.

Early Years. Allen Raymond, P.O. Box

1223, Darien, Conn. 06820. Published September through May. (Pre-school through grade 3.)

Educating Children: Early and Middle Years. 1201–16th Street NW, Washington, DC 20036.

Elementary English. National Council of Teachers of English. Monthly.

The Grade Teacher. Teachers' Publishing Corp., 23 Leroy Avenue, Darien, CT. 06820. Monthly.

Horn Book. Johnson Associates, P.O. Box 1017, Greenwich, CT 06830. Available in microfiche from 1924–1975.

*Horn Book Magazine. Horn Book. Six times annually.

The Instructor. F. A. Owen Publishing Company. Ten issues annually.

Journal of Creative Behavior. The Creative Education Foundation, State University College, 1300 Elmwood Avenue, Buffalo, NY 14222.

Kirkus Reviews. Kirkus Service, 60 W. 13th Street, New York, NY 10011.

Learning, The Magazine for Creative Teaching. 1255 Portland Place, Boulder, Colo. 80302.

*Library Journal. R. R. Bowker Co., Monthly.

Monographs for Elementary Teachers. Row-Peterson Company. Monographs distributed free of charge, often containing material on children's literature.

New York Early Education Reporter. 33 Kellogg Street, Clinton, NY.

*The New York Times Book Review. Weekly.

Primary Activities. Scott, Foresman & Company. A free service for teachers.

*Publishers Weekly. R. R. Bowker Company.

Saturday Review World. 25 W. 45th Street, New York, NY 10036. Weekly.

*Science Books. American Association for the Advancement of Science, 1515 Massachusetts Avenue, NW, Washington, DC 20005. Quarterly review.

Science and Children. National Science Teachers Association, 1201 16th Street, NW, Washington, DC 20036. Eight issues annually.

*Subject Index to Children's Magazines. Monthly, August to May.

Today's Education. The Journal of the National Education Association.

*Wilson Library Bulletin. H. W. Wilson Company. Monthly.

*Young Readers Review. Box 137, Wall Street Station, New York, NY 10005.

APPENDIX H

Poetry Books for Children

These are listed by author and distinguished by level: primary grades (P), intermediate grades (I), and any age group (A). Addresses of publishers are listed in Appendix A.

Adoff, Arnold. *City in All Directions.* Toronto: Macmillan Co., 1969. *I.*

Adoff, Arnold. *My Black Me: A Beginning Book of Black Poetry.* New York: E. P. Dutton, 1974. *P–I.*

Agree, Rose H., Peggy Wilson, illus. *How to Eat a Poem and Other Morsels: Food Poems for Children.* New York: Macmillan, 1969. *P–I.*

Aldis, Dorothy. Peggy Westphal, illus. *Quick as a Wink.* New York: G. P. Putnam's Sons, 1960. *A.*

Arbuthnot, May Hill, and Root, Shelton L., Jr. *Time for Poetry.* Palo Alto, Calif.: Scott, Foresman, 1968. *A.*

Arnstein, Flora J. *Poetry in the Elementary Classroom.* New York: Appleton-Century-Crofts, 1962. *A.*

Association of Childhood Education. Dorothy Lathrop, illus. *Sung Under the Golden Umbrella.* New York: Macmillan. *A.*

Beatty, Jerome, Jr. Gahan Wilson, illus. *Matthew Looney's Voyage to the Earth.* New York: W. R. Scott, 1961. *A.*

Behn, Harry, author and illustrator. *The Little Hill.* New York: Harcourt, Brace & World, 1953. *A.*

Behn, Harry, author and illustrator. *The Wizard in the Well.* New York: Harcourt, Brace & World, 1956. *A.*

Behn, Harry. *Chrysalis: Concerning Children and Poetry.* New York: Harcourt, Brace & World, 1968. *A.*

Beirhorst, John. Joe Servello, illus. *Songs of the Chippewa.* New York: Farrar, Straus, and Giroux, 1974. *A.*

Betting, Natalie, comp. *Our Fathers Had Powerful Songs.* New York: E. P. Dutton, 1974. *A.*

Blake, William. Thomas Stothard, illus. *Songs of Innocence and Experience.* New York: Peter Pauper, 1938. *A.*

Bissett, Donald J., comp. *Poems and Verses to Begin On.* San Francisco: Chandler, 1967. *P.*

Bly, Robert. *The Sea and the Honeycomb.* Boston: Beacon Press, 1972. *A.*

Brandon, William. *The Magic World: American Indian Poems and Songs.* New York: William Morrow, 1971. *I–A.*

Brewerton, Sara, and Brewerton, John. Vera Bock, illus. *Birthday Candles Burning Bright.* New York: Macmillan, 1960. *A.*

Brooks, Gwendolyn. Ronni Solbert, illus. *Bronzeville Boys and Girls*. New York: Harper & Row, 1956. A.

Browning, Robert. Harold Jones, illus. *The Pied Piper of Hamlin*. New York: Franklin Watts, 1962. I.

Ciardi, John. Robert Osborn, illus. *I Met A Man*. Boston: Houghton Mifflin, 1961. P.

Ciardi, John. Edward Gorey, illus. *The Man Who Sang the Sillies*. Phila.: J. B. Lippincott Co., 1961. P.

Ciardi, John. Madeline Gekiere, illus. *The Reason for the Pelican*. Phila.: J. B. Lippincott Co., 1959. A.

Ciardi, John. Jane Miller, illus. *Scrappy the Pup*. Phila.: J. B. Lippincott Co., 1960. P.

Coatsworth, Elizabeth. Genevieve Valguan-Jackson, illus. *Mouse Chorus*. New York: Pantheon Books, 1955. P.

Coatsworth, Elizabeth, author and illustrator. *The Peaceable Kingdom*. New York: Macmillan. A.

Coatsworth, Elizabeth. *The Sparrow Bush*. New York: W. W. Norton, 1966. P.

Cole, William, ed. *Pick Me Up: A Book of Short, Short Poems*. Boston: Little, Brown and Co., 1972. P.

Cole, William. Tomi Ungerer, illus. *Oh, How Silly!* New York: Viking Press, 1970. P.

Cole, William. Charles Keeping, illus. *Poet's Tales: A New Book of Story Poems*. New York: World Publishing Co., 1971. I.

Daugherty, James. *Walt Whitman's America*. New York: World Publishing Co., 1964. I.

De la Mare, Walter. Barbara Cooney, illus. *Peacock Pie*. New York: Alfred A. Knopf, 1961. A.

De la Mare, Walter. Margery Gill, illus. *Tom Tiddler's Ground*. London: Bodley Head, 1961. A.

de Regniers, Beatrice Schenk. Paul Galdone, illus. *It Does Not Say Meow*. New York: Seabury, 1972. P.

Downie, Mary Alice. Barbara Robertson, comp. Elizabeth Cleaver, illus. *The Wind Has Wings: Poems from Canada*. New York: Henry Z. Walck, 1968. A.

Dunning, Stephen, et al. *Reflections on a Gift of Watermelon Pickle*. New York: Lothrop, Lee & Shepard, 1972. A.

Dunning, Stephen, et al. *Some Haystacks Don't Even Have Needles*. New York: Lothrop, Lee & Shepard, 1969. A.

Ferris, Helen. *Favorite Poems Old and New*. Garden City, NY.: Doubleday, 1957. A.

Giovanni, Nikki. George Ford and Lawrence Hill. illus. *Ego-Tripping and Other Poems for Young People*. New York: Farrar, Straus, & Giroux, 1973. I.

Gregory, Horace, and Zaturenska, Marya. Diana Bloomfield, illus. *The Crystal Cabinet*. New York: Holt, Rinehart and Winston, 1962. I.

Hannum, Sara, and Reed, Gwendolyn. *Lean Out of the Window*. New York: Atheneum, 1965. A.

Hillyer, Robert. *In Pursuit of Poetry*. New York: McGraw-Hill, 1960. A.

Hoberman, Mary. Norman Hoberman, illus. *Hello and Good-Bye*. Boston: Little, Brown and Co., 1959. A.

Houston, James, editor and illustrator. *Songs of the Dream People*. New York: Atheneum, 1972. I.

Hubbell, Patricia. *Catch Me a Wind*. New York: Atheneum. 1968. P–I.

Huber, Miriam Blanton. *Story and Verse for Children*. New York: Macmillan, 1965. A.

Huffard, Grace T. Willy Pogany, illus. *My Poetry Book*, rev. ed. New York: Holt, Rinehart and Winston, 1956. A.

Hughes, Rosalind, and Edwards, G. N. *Let's Enjoy Poetry*. Boston: Houghton Mifflin, 1958. A.

Hymes, James, and Hymes, Lucia. L. Kessler, illus. *Hooray for Chocolate*. New York: Wm. R. Scott, 1965. P.

Jacobs, Leland. Joann Storer, illus. *Poetry for Summer*. Champaign, Ill.: Garrard, 1970. P–I.

Jacobs, Leland. Frank Aloise, illus. *Poetry for Space*. Champaign, Ill.: Garrard, 1971. I.

Johnson, Hannah Lyons. Tony Chen, illus. *Hello, Small Sparrow*. New York: Lothrop, Lee & Shepard, 1971. A.

Kuskin, Karla. *Any Me I Want To Be*. New York: Harper & Row, 1972. *P*.

Kuskin, Karla, author and illustrator. *The Bear Who Saw the Spring*. New York: Harper & Row, 1961. *A*.

Kuskin, Karla. *In the Middle of the Trees*. New York: Harper & Row, 1958. *A*.

Kuskin, Karla. *James and the Rain*. New York: Harper & Row, 1957. *A*.

Kuskin, Karla. *The Rose on My Cake*. New York: Harper & Row, 1964. *A*.

Lear, Edward. Lady Strachey, ed. *The Complete Nonsense Book*. New York: Dodd, Mead & Co., 1942. *A*.

Lear, Edward. Tony Palazzo, ed. and illus. *Nonsense Book*. New York: Doubleday, 1956. *A*.

Lear, Edward. William Pené du Bois, illus. *The Owl and the Pussy Cat*. New York: Doubleday, 1962. *I*.

Lewis, Richard. *There Are Two Lives*. New York: Simon and Schuster, 1970. *I*.

Livingston, Myrna Cohn, ed. *A Tune Beyond Us*. New York: Harcourt, Brace & World, 1968. *A*.

Livingston, Myra Cohn. Jacqueline Chwast, illus. *Whispers and Other Poems*. New York: Harcourt, Brace, & World, 1958. *A*.

Longfellow, Henry Wadsworth. Paul Galdone, illus. *Paul Revere's Ride*. New York: Thomas Y. Crowell, 1963. *I*.

McCord, David. Henry B. Kane, illus. *Far And Few: Rhymes of the Never Was and Always Is*. Boston: Little, Brown and Co., 1952. *A*.

McGinley, Phyllis. *The Love Letters of Phyllis McGinley*. New York: Viking Press, 1954. *A*.

McGinley, Phyllis. Kurt Werth, illus. *The Year Without Santa Claus*. Phila.: J. B. Lippincott, 1957. *A*.

McGinley, Phyllis. John Alcorn, illus. *Wonderful Time*. Phila.: J. B. Lippincott Co., 1966. *A*.

McGovern, Ann. *Arrow Book of Poetry*. New York: Scholastic Book Service, 1965. *A*.

Merriam, Eve, author and illustrator. *Catch a Little Rhyme*. New York: Atheneum, 1966. *P*.

Merriam, Eve, author and illustrator. *Out Loud*. New York: Atheneum, 1973. *P–I*.

Merriam, Eve. Joseph Schindelman, illus. *There Is No Rhyme for Silver*. New York: Atheneum, 1962. *A*.

Mezey, Robert, ed. Moishe Smith, illus. *Poems from the Hebrew*. New York: Crowell, 1973. *I*.

Miller, Mary Britton. Julia Kepes, illus. *Give a Guess*. New York: Pantheon Books, 1957. *A*.

Milne, A. A. Ernest Shepard, illus. *Now We Are Six*. New York: E. P. Dutton & Co., 1927. *P*.

Milne, A. A. Ernest Shepard, illus. *When We Were Very Young*. New York: E. P. Dutton & Co., 1924. *A*.

Milne, A. A. Ernest Shepard, illus. *The World of Christopher Robin*. New York: E. P. Dutton & Co., 1958. *P*.

Moore, Lillian, and Thurman, Judith. *To See the World Afresh*. New York: Atheneum, 1974. *P–I*.

Nash, Ogden, *Versus*. Boston: Little, Brown, and Co., 1949. *A*.

Newcomb, Covelle. Addison Burbank, illus. *The Secret Door: The Story of Kate*. New York: Dodd, Mead & Co., 1946. *A*.

Noyes, Alfred. Kritz Kredel, illus. *Daddy Fell into the Pond, and Other Poems for Children*. New York: Sheed & Ward, 1952. *A*.

O'Neill, Mary. Leonard Weissgard, illus. *Hailstones and Halibut Bones*. New York: Doubleday & Co., 1961. *A*.

O'Neill, Mary. James Barkley, illus. *Winds*. New York: Doubleday, 1970. *P–I*.

Parker, Elinor. Clare Leighton, illus. *The Singing and the Gold*. New York: Thomas Y. Crowell, 1962. *A*.

Poe, Edgar Allan. Paul Galdone, illus. *Three Poems of Edgar Allan Poe*. New York: McGraw-Hill, 1966. *I*.

Rasmussen, Knud, comp. Guy Mary Rousseliere, illus. *Beyond the High Hills: A Book of Eskimo Poems*. Cleveland: World Publishing Co., 1961. *A*.

Read, Herbert. Juliet Kepes, illus. *This Way, Delight*. New York: Pantheon Books, 1956. *A*.

Reed, Gwendolyn. *Songs the Sandman Sings*. New York: Atheneum, 1969. *P–I*.

Reeves, James. Edward Ardizzone, illus. *Prefabulous Animals*. New York: E. P. Dutton, 1960. *A*.

Richards, Laura E. Marguerite Davis, illus. *Tirra Lirra: Rhymes Old and New*. Boston: Little, Brown, and Co., 1955. *A*.

Rieu, E. V. E. H. Shepard, illus. *The Flattered Flying Fish*. New York: E. P. Dutton, 1962. *A*.

Ross, David, ed. B. Burris et al., illus. *Illustrated Treasury of Poetry for Children*. New York: Grosset & Dunlap, 1970. *A*.

Sandburg, Carl. Paul Bacon, illus. *Sandburg Treasury: Prose and Poetry for Young People*. New York: Harcourt, Brace Jovanovich, 1970. *P*.

Shakespeare, William. Bernice Grohskopf, comp. Kelly Oechsli, illus. *Seeds of Time*. New York: Atheneum, 1963. *A*.

Smith, Janet Adam. *The Faber Book of Children's Verse*. London: Faber and Faber, Ltd., 1953. *A*.

Smith, William Jay. Juliet Kepes, illus. *Boy Blue's Book of Beasts*. Boston: Little, Brown, & Co., 1957. *A*.

Smith, William Jay. Juliet Kepes, illus. *Laughing Time*. Boston: Little, Brown, and Co., 1955. *A*.

Starbird, Kaye. Rita Dava, illus. *Speaking of Cows*. Phila.: J. B. Lippincott Co., 1960. *P*.

Stearns, Monroe. Adolph Zabransky, illus. *Ring-a-Ling*. Phila.: J. B. Lippincott Co., 1959. *A*.

APPENDIX I

Biography for Children

These are listed by author and level: primary grades (P), intermediate grades (I), and any age group (A), Addresses of publishers are listed in Appendix A.

Appel, Benjamin. *Hitler: From Power to Ruin.* New York: Grosset & Dunlap, 1964. *I.*

Bailey, Bernadine. Howard Simon, illus. *Abe Lincoln's Mother: The Story of Sarah Bush Lincoln.* New York: J. Messner, 1941. *I.*

Bakeless, Katherine. *Story-Lives of American Composers.* Phila.: J. B. Lippincott, 1953. *I.*

Baker, Nina Brown. Paul Valentino, illus. *Amerigo Vespucci.* New York: Alfred A. Knopf, 1956. *I.*

Baker, Nina Brown. Alan Moyler, illus. *Texas Yankee: The Story of Gail Borden.* New York: Harcourt, Brace and World, 1955. *I.*

Bell, Margaret E. Harry Daugherty, illus. *Kit Carson: Mountain Man.* New York: William Morrow, 1952. *I.*

Blackstock, Josephine. Maurice Bower, illus. *Songs For Sixpence: A Story about John Newberry.* Chicago: Follett Publishing Co., 1955. *A.*

Brown, Slater. William Moyers, illus. *Ethan Allen and the Green Mountain Boys.* New York: Random House, 1956. *I.*

Brownmiller, Susan. *Shirley Chisholm: A Biography.* New York: Doubleday Co., 1970. *I.*

Bulla, Clyde. Peter Burchard, illus. *John Bullington: Friend of Squanto.* New York: Thomas Y. Crowell, 1956. *A.*

Bulla, Clyde. Peter Burchard, illus. *Squanto: Friend of the White Man.* New York: Thomas Y. Crowell, 1954. *A.*

Commager, Henry Steele. Lynn Ward, illus. *America's Robert E. Lee.* Boston: Houghton Mifflin, 1951. *I.*

Crouse, Anna Erskine, and Crouse, Russel. Walter Buehr, illus. *Alexander Hamilton And Aaron Burr: Their Lives, Their Times, Their Duel.* New York: Random House, 1958. *I.*

Dalgliesh, Alice. Leo Politi, illus. *The Columbus Story.* New York: Charles Scribner's Sons, 1955. *A.*

Daugherty, Charles Michael. Kurt Werth, illus. *Samuel Clemens.* New York: Thomas Y. Crowell, 1970. *I.*

Daugherty, James, author and illustrator. *Of Courage Undaunted: Across the Continent with Lewis and Clark.* New York: Viking Press, 1951. *I.*

Daugherty, Sonia. James Daugherty. illus. *Ten Brave Men.* Phila.: J. B. Lippincott Co., 1953. I.

David, Jay, and Green, Catherine J. *Black Roots: An Anthology.* New York: Lothrop, Lee & Shepard, 1971. I.

DeGering, Etta. Emil Weiss, illus. *Seeing Fingers.* New York: David McKay Co., 1962. I.

DeLeeuw, Adele. *Marie Curie: Woman of Genius.* Champaign, Ill.: Garrard, 1970. I.

Eaton, Jeanette. Harve Stein, illus. *Jean d'Arc: The Warrior Saint.* New York: Harper & Row, 1931. I.

Eaton, Jeanette. Henry C. Pitz, illus. *That Lively Man, Ben Franklin.* New York: William Morrow, 1948. I.

Epstein, Sam, and Epstein, Beryl. R. Burns, illus. *Enrico Fermi: Father of Atomic Power.* Champaign, Ill.: Garrard, 1970. I.

Epstein, Sam, and Epstein, Beryl. *Winston Churchill: Lion of Britain.* Champaign, Ill.: Garrard, 1971. I.

Ewen, David. *Leonard Bernstein: A Biography for Young People,* rev. ed. Phila.: Chilton, 1967. I.

Fisher, Aileen. L. Vosburgh, illus. *My Cousin Abe.* New York: Thomas Nelson & Sons, 1950. I.

Fisher, Dorothy Canfield. Norman Price, illus. *Paul Revere and the Minute Men.* New York: Random House, 1950. I.

Forbes, Esther. Lynn Ward, illus. *America's Paul Revere.* Boston: Houghton Mifflin, 1946. I.

Foster, Genevieve, author and illustrator. *Abraham Lincoln: An Initial Biography.* New York: Charles Scribner's Sons, 1950. I.

Foster, Genevieve, author and illustrator. *Andrew Jackson.* New York: Charles Scribner's Sons, 1951. I.

Foster, Genevieve, author and illustrator. *George Washington.* New York: Charles Scribner's Sons, 1949. I.

Foster, Genevieve, author and illustrator. *Theodore Roosevelt.* New York: Charles Scribner's Sons, 1954. I.

Freeman, Douglas Southall. *Lee of Virginia.* New York: Charles Scribner's Sons, 1958. I.

Gelman, Steve. *Young Baseball Champions.* New York: W. W. Norton & Co., 1966. I.

Gersh, Harry. Mel Silverman, illus. *Women Who Made America Great.* Phila.: J. B. Lippincott Co., 1962. I.

Glines, Carroll V. *Wright Brothers: Pioneers of Power Flight.* New York: Franklin Watts, 1968. I.

Gowdy, George. Howard Simon, illus. *Young Buffalo Bill.* New York: Lothrop, Lee & Shepard, 1955. I.

Graham, Shirley, and Lipscomb, George. Elton C. Fax, illus. *Dr. George Washington Carver: Scientist.* New York: Julian Messner, 1944. I.

Grant, Neil. Gerald McCann, illus. *English Explorers of North America.* New York: Julian Messner, 1970. I.

Heiderstadt, Dorothy. Carl Kidwell, illus. *Stolen by the Indians.* New York: David McKay, 1968. I.

Higdon, Hal. Paul Frame, illus. *Heroes of the Olympics.* New York: Prentice-Hall, 1965. I.

Hirshberg, Al. *Basketball's Greatest Stars.* New York: G. P. Putnam's Sons, 1963. I.

Holbrook, Stewart. Lynd Ward, illus. *America's Ethan Allen.* Boston: Houghton Mifflin, 1949. I.

Hollander, Zander, ed. *Great American Athletes of the 20th Century.* New York: Random House, 1966. I.

Holst, Imogen. *Bach.* New York: Thomas Y. Crowell, 1965. I.

Hoyt, Mary Finch. *American Women of the Space Age.* New York: Atheneum, 1966. I.

Hughes, Langston. *Famous American Negroes.* New York: Dodd, Mead & Co., 1964. I.

Hume, Ruth Fox. Robert Frankenberg, illus. *Great Men of Medicine.* New York: Random House, 1961. I.

Judson, Clara Ingram. *Abraham Lincoln: Friend of the People.* Chicago: Follett, 1958. I.

Judson, Clara Ingram. *Andrew Carnegie.* Chicago: Follett, 1964. I.

Judson, Clara Ingram. *Andrew Jackson: Frontier Statesman.* Chicago: Follett, 1954. I.

Judson, Clara Ingram. *Boat Builder: The Story of Robert Fulton.* New York: Charles Scribner's Sons, 1940. *I.*

Judson, Clara Ingram. *City Neighbor: The Story of Jane Addams.* New York: Charles Scribner's Sons, 1951. *I.*

Judson, Clara Ingram. *George Washington: Leader of the People.* Chicago: Follett, 1951. *I.*

Judson, Clara Ingram. *James Jerome Hill.* New York: Row, Peterson & Co., 1950. *I.*

Kelsey, Vera. *Young Men So Daring.* Indianapolis: Bobbs, Merrill Co., 1956. *I.*

Kielty, Bernadette. Douglas Gorsline, illus. *Marie Antoinette.* New York: Random House, 1955. *I.*

Knightly, Philip. *Lawrence of Arabia.* Camden, N.J.: Landmark, 1976. *I.*

Latham, Jean Lee. John O'Hara, illus. *Carry On, Mr. Bowditch.* Boston: Houghton Mifflin, 1955. *I.*

Lawson, Don. Elizabeth Donald, illus. *Young People in the White House.* New York: Abelard-Schuman, 1970. *I.*

Leighton, Margaret. Corinne Dillon, illus. *The Story of Florence Nightingale.* New York: Grosset & Dunlap, 1952. *I.*

Le Sueur, Meridel. Aldren Watson, illus. *Chanticleer of Wilderness Road: A Story of Davy Crockett.* New York: Alfred A. Knopf, 1951. *I.*

McDearman, Kay. *Mahalia: Gospel Singer.* New York: Dodd, Mead, and Co. *I.*

McNeer, May, and Ward, Lynd. Lynd Ward, illus. *Armed With Courage.* Nashville, Tenn.: Abingdon, 1957. *I.*

Meadowcroft, Enid. William Reusswig, illus. *The Story of Crazy Horse.* New York: Grosset & Dunlap, 1954. *I.*

Meigs, Elizabeth. Dorothy B. Morse, illus. *Candle in the Sky.* New York: E. P. Dutton & Co., 1953. *I.*

Meltzer, Milton. *Langston Hughes: A Biography.* New York: Thomas Y. Crowell, 1968. *I.*

Meyer, Edith Patterson. Eric von Schmidt, illus. *Champions of Peace.* Boston: Little, Brown, and Co., 1959. *I.*

Mill, Lois. William Moyers, illus. *Three Together: The Story of the Wright Brothers and Their Sister.* Chicago: Follett, 1955. *I.*

Monjo, Ferdinand. *The One Bad Thing about Father.* New York: Harper & Row, 1970. *P–I.*

Montgomery, Elizabeth. William Hutchinson, illus. *Albert Schweitzer: Great Humanitarian.* Champaign, Ill.: Garrard, 1971. *I.*

Montgomery, Elizabeth. Vic Mays, illus. *Walt Disney: Master of Make Believe.* Champaign, Ill.: Garrard, 1971. *P–I.*

North, Sterling. Lee Ames, illus. *Abe Lincoln: Log Cabin to White House.* New York: Random House, 1956. *I.*

North, Sterling. Lee Ames, illus. *George Washington: Frontier Colonel.* New York: Random House, 1957. *I.*

North, Sterling. William Barss, illus. *Young Thomas Edison.* Boston: Houghton Mifflin, 1958. *I.*

Pace, Mildred. Robert Ball, illus. *Clara Barton.* New York: Charles Scribner's Sons, 1941. *I.*

Petersham, Maud. *Story of Presidents of the United States of America.* New York: Macmillan, 1966. *I.*

Peterson, Helen S. Paul Frame, illus. *Susan B. Anthony: Pioneer in Women's Rights.* Champaign, Ill.: Garrard, 1971. *I.*

Richards, Kenneth G. *Charles Lindbergh.* Chicago: Children's Press, 1968. *I.*

Robinson, Ray. *Baseball's Most Colorful Managers.* New York: G. P. Putnam's Sons, 1969. *I.*

Rudeen, Kenneth. Frank Mullins, illus. *Wilt Chamberlain.* New York: Thomas Y. Crowell, 1970. *I.*

Sandburg, Carl. Richard Hoethe, illus. *Mr. Bell Invents the Telephone.* New York: Random House, 1952. *I.*

Shirer, William. *The Rise and Fall of Adolph Hitler.* New York: Random House, 1961. *I.*

Sickels, Eleanor. Ilse Bischoff, illus. *In Calico and Crinoline: True Stories of American Women, 1608–1865.* New York: Viking Press, 1935. *I.*

Signature Books. *Biography Series.* New York: Grosset and Dunlap. *A.*

Smith, Margaret Chase, and Jeffers, H. Paul. Paul Giovanopoulas, illus. *Gallant Women.* New York: McGraw-Hill, 1968. *I.*

Sperry, Armstrong. *John Paul Jones: Fighting Sailor*. New York: Random House, 1953. *I.*

Sullivan, Navin. *Pioneer Germ Fighters*. New York: Atheneum, 1962. *I.*

Sutton, Felix. *Master of Ballyhoo: The Story of P. T. Barnum*. New York: G. P. Putnam's Sons, 1968.

Syme, Ronald. William Stobbs, illus. *Balboa: Finder of the Pacific*. New York: William Morrow, 1956. *I.*

Yates, Elizabeth. Nora S. Unwin, illus. *Amos Fortune: Free Man*. New York: E. P. Dutton, 1950. *I.*

APPENDIX J

Children's Literature for Social Studies

These are listed by author and level: primary grades (P), intermediate grades (I), and any age group (A). Addresses of publishers are listed in Appendix A.

Alexander, Ann. *ABC of Cars and Trucks.* New York: Dodd, Mead, & Co., 1956. P.

Allen, Jerry. *The Adventures of Jimmy Poole.* Minneapolis: Dillon, 1976.

American Heritage. *Discoverers of the New World.* New York: American Heritage Co., 1960. I.

American Heritage. *The Pilgrims and Plymouth Colony.* New York: American Heritage Co., 1961. I.

Ames, Gerald, and Wyler, Rose. L. Weisgard, illus. *First People in the World.* New York: Harper & Row, 1958. I.

Armstrong, Louise. *A Child's Guide to Economics.* New York: Harcourt, Brace Jovanovich, 1976. I.

Asimov, Isaac. *ABC's of Ecology.* New York: Walker, 1972. P–I.

Batchelor, Julie. C. D. Batchelor, illus. *Communication: From Cave Writing to Television.* New York: Harcourt, Brace & World, 1953. I.

Bendick, Jeanne, author and illustrator. *The First Book of Airplanes.* New York: Franklin Watts, 1958. I.

Bendick, Jeanne, author and illustrator. *The First Book of Automobiles.* New York: Franklin Watts, 1955, I.

Bendick, Jeanne, author and illustrator. *The First Book of Ships.* New York: Franklin Watts, 1959. I.

Bendick, Jeanne, and Bendick, Robert. *Television Works Like.* New York: McGraw-Hill, 1959. I.

Bierhorst, John. *Black Rainbow* (ancient Peru). New York: Farrar, Straus, Giroux, 1976. I.

Bierhorst, John, ed. *Songs of the Chippewa.* New York: Farrar, Straus, & Giroux, 1974. A.

Bleeker, Sonia. *Indians of the Longhouse: Story of the Iroquois.* New York: William Morrow, 1950. I.

Blue, Rose. *Seven Years from Home.* Chicago: Children's Press, 1976. I.

Branley, Franklyn. Victor G. Ambrus, illus. *The Mystery of Stonehenge.* New York: Thomas Y. Crowell, 1969. I.

Breetveld, Jim. Don Lambo, illus. *Getting to Know Alaska.* New York: Coward-McCann, 1958. I.

Buchheimer, Naomi. Barbara Corrigan, illus. *Let's Go to the Telephone Company.* New York: G. P. Putnam's Sons, 1958. *I.*

Buehr, Walter, author and illustrator. *Knights and Castles and Feudal Life.* New York: G. P. Putnam's Sons, 1957. *I.*

Caldwell, John C. *Let's Visit Argentina.* New York: Viking Press, 1961. *I.* Photos, maps, illus.

Caldwell, John C. *Let's Visit Brazil.* New York: John Day Co., 1961. *I.* Photos, maps, illus.

Carmer, Carl. Rafaelo Busoni, illus. *The Hudson River.* New York: Holt, Rinehart and Winston, 1962. *I.*

Cooke, Donald. *Marvels of American Industry.* Maplewood, N.J.: Hammond Co., 1962. *I.*

Dalgliesh, Alice. Lois Maloy, illus. *America Begins: The Story of the Finding of the New World,* rev. ed. New York: Charles Scribner's Sons, 1958. *I.*

Dalgliesh, Alice. Marie Nonnast, illus. *The Fourth of July Story.* New York: Charles Scribner's Sons, 1956. *P.*

de Garza, Patricia. *Chicanos: The Story of Mexican Americans.* New York: Messner, 1973. *I.*

Ditzel, Paul C. *Fire Alarm.* New York: Van Nostrand, 1969. *P.*

Drotning, Phillip T., and Smith, Wesley. *Up from the Ghetto.* New York: Cowles, 1970. *I.*

Edwards, Patricia. Richard Lebenson, illus. *Patriots in Petticoats.* New York: Dodd, Mead & Co., 1976. *I.*

Elliot, Paul Michael. *Eskimos of the World.* New York: Messner, 1976. *I.*

Epstein, Edna. *The First Book of the United Nations,* rev. ed. New York: Franklin Watts, 1961. *I.*

Euller, John. *Arctic World.* New York: Abelard-Schuman, 1958. *I.* Photos, maps, illus.

Evans, Eva Knox. Ursula Koering, illus. *Why We Live and Where We Live.* Boston: Little, Brown and Co., 1953. *I.*

Evans, J. A., author and illustrator. *I Know a Telephone Operator.* New York: G. P. Putnam's Sons, 1971. *A.*

Feelings, Tom. *Black Pilgrimage.* New York: Lothrop, Lee, Shepard, 1972. *P–I.*

Felton, Harold W. Gordon Laite, illus. *Big Mose, Hero Fireman.* Champaign, Ill.: Garrard Press, 1969. *P.*

Foreman, Michael. *Dinosaurs and All That Rubbish.* New York: Thomas Y. Crowell, 1973. *P.*

Foster, Genevieve. *Birthdays of Freedom.* New York: Charles Scribner's Sons, 1952. *I.*

Foster, Genevieve, author and illustrator. *The World of Columbus and Sons.* New York: Charles Scribner's Sons, 1965. *I.*

Foster, Genevieve. *Year of Independence: 1776.* New York: Charles Scribner's Sons, 1970. *I.*

Foster, Genevieve. *Year of Lincoln.* New York: Charles Scribner's Sons, 1970. *I.*

Fritz, Jean. Trina Schart Hyman, illus. *Will You Sign Here, John Hancock?* New York: Coward, McCann and Geoghegan, 1976. *I.*

Gatti, Ellen, and Gatti, Attilio. Rafael Palacois, illus. *The New Africa.* New York: Charles Scribner's Sons, 1960. *I.*

Glubok, Shirley. *The Art of Ancient Egypt.* New York: Atheneum Press, 1962. *I.*

Gregor, Arthur. W. T. Mars, illus. *How the World's First Cities Began.* New York: E. P. Dutton, 1967. *I.*

Gridley, Marion E. *American Indian Women.* New York: Hawthorn, 1974. *I.*

Gunther, John, with Sam and Beryl Epstein. *Meet North Africa.* New York: Harper & Row, 1958. *I.*

Haeberle, Billie. *Looking Forward to a Career: Radio and Television.* Minneapolis: Dillon Press, 1970. *I.*

Harnan, Terry. *African Rhythm: African Dance.* New York: Alfred A. Knopf, 1974. *I.*

Hesselberg, Erik, author and illustrator. *Kon-Tiki and I.* Englewood Cliffs, N.J.: Prentice-Hall, 1970. *I.*

Hofsinde, Robert, author and illustrator. *Indian Picture Writing.* New York: William Morrow, 1959. *I.*

Holbrook, Sabra. *The French Founders of North America and Their Heritage.* New York: Atheneum, 1976. *A.*

Holling, Holling C., author and illustrator. *Paddle-to-the-Sea*. Boston: Houghton Mifflin, 1942. I.

Hoyt, Edwin P., Charles Greer, illus. *From the Turtle to the Nautilus: The Story of Submarines*. Boston: Little, Brown, and Co., 1963. I.

Hoyt, Olga. *American Indians Today*. New York: Abelard-Schuman, 1973. I.

Hughes, Langston. Robert Burce, illus. *The First Book of the West Indies*. New York: Franklin Watts, 1956. I.

Jackson, Florence. *The Black Man in America*, 2 vols. New York: Watts, 1972–73. I.

Johnson, Gerald W. Leonard Fisher, illus. *The Congress*. New York: William Morrow, 1963. I.

Johnson, Gerald W. Leonard E. Fisher, illus. *The Presidency*. New York: William Morrow, 1962. I.

Kaufman, Michael. *Rooftops and Alleys: Adventures with a City Kid*. New York: Alfred A. Knopf, 1973. I.

Kirk, Ruth. *Oldest Men in America: An Adventure in Archaeology*. New York: Harcourt, Brace Jovanovich, 1970. I.

Klien, Norma. *Girls Can Be Anything*. New York: E. P. Dutton, 1973. P.

Leaf, Munro, author and illustrator. *Geography Can Be Fun*. Phila.: J. B. Lippincott, 1962. P.

Macaulay, David. *Cathedral*. Boston: Houghton Mifflin, 1973. I.

McNeer, May. Lynd Ward, illus. *The Canadian Story*. New York: Farrar, Straus & Giroux, 1958. I.

Madison, Arnold. *Drugs and You*. New York: J. Messner, 1971. I.

Manning, Jack, author and illustrator. *Young Puerto Rico*. New York: Dodd, Mead, & Co., 1962. I.

Marr, John S. Lynn Sweat, illus. *Good Drug and the Bad Drug*. Evans, 1970. I.

Martel, Cruz. *Yagua Days*. New York: Dial Press, 1976. P.

Mead, Margaret. W. T. Mars and Jan Fairservis, illus. *People And Places*. New York: World Publishing Co., 1959. I.

Meyer, Carolyn. *Lots and Lots of Candy* New York: Harcourt, Brace Jovanovich, 1976. P–I. (Economics).

Morgan, Edmund S. *So What About History?* New York: Atheneum, 1969. I.

Phelan, May Kay. *Story of the Boston Massacre*. New York: Thomas Y. Crowell, 1976. I.

Reeder, Red. Frederick Chapman, illus. *The Story of the Civil War*. New York: Duell, Sloan & Pearce, 1958. I.

Rich, Louise Dickinson. Cary Dickinson, illus. *The First Book of New World Explorers*. New York: Franklin Watts, 1960. I.

Robinson, Charles. John Mackey, illus. *The First Book of Ancient Rome*. New York: Franklin Watts, 1960. I.

Ross, George E. Seymour Fleischman, illus. *Know Your Government*. New York: Rand McNally, 1959. I.

Rounds, Glen. *The Prairie Schooners*. New York: Holiday House, 1968. I.

Sasek, Miroslav, author and illustrator. *This Is Israel*. New York: Macmillan, 1962. I.

Sasek, Miroslav, author and illustrator. *This Is Munich*. New York: Macmillan, 1961. I.

Sasek, Miroslav, author and illustrator. *This Is New York*. New York: Macmillan, 1960. I.

Sasek, Miroslav, author and illustrator. *This Is Paris*. New York: Macmillan, 1959. I.

Sasek, Miroslav, author and illustrator. *This Is Rome*. New York: Macmillan, 1960. I.

Sasek, Miroslav, author and illustrator. *This Is San Francisco*. New York: Macmillan, 1962. I.

Sasek, Miroslav, author and illustrator. *This Is Venice*. New York: Macmillan, 1961. I.

Schick, Alia, and Allen, Marjorie. *The Remarkable Ride of Israel Bissell as Related by Molly the Crow*. Phila.: J. B. Lippincott, 1976. P.

Schlein, Miriam. Leonard Kessler, illus. *It's about Time*. New York: W. R. Scott, 1955. I.

Schneider, Herman, and Schneider, Nina. *Let's Look under the City*. New York: W. R. Scott, 1954. *I.*

Sheppard, Sally. *The First Book of Brazil*. New York: Franklin Watts, 1962. *I.* (Photos, illus.).

Shippen, Katherine B. *Miracle in Motion: The Story of America's Industry*. New York: Harper & Row, 1955. *I.*

Smith, Bradford. *The Islands of Hawaii*. Phila.: J. B. Lippincott, 1957. *I.* (Photos, illus.

Sootin, Laura. *Let's Go to the Airport*. New York: G. P. Putnam's Sons, 1958. *I.*

Sperry, Armstrong, author and illustrator. *All about the Arctic and Antarctic*. New York: Random House, 1957. *I.*

Sperry, Armstrong, author and illustrator. *Pacific Islands Speaking*. New York: Macmillan, 1955. *I.*

Steele, William O. *The Man with the Silver Eyes*. New York: Harcourt, Brace Jovanovich, 1976. *I.*

Stefansson, Evelyn. *Here Is Alaska*. New York: Charles Scribner's Sons, 1959. *I.* (Photos, illus.)

Sterling, Dorothy. *United Nations*. New York: Charles Scribner's Sons, 1961. *I.*

Stevens, Carla. Eve Rice, illus. *Stories from a Snowy Meadow*. New York: Seabury, 1976. *I.* (Deals with death)

Stockton, Frank. *Buccaneers and Pirates of Our Coast*. New York: Macmillan, 1967. *I.*

Taylor, Mildred. *Song of the Trees*. New York: Dell, 1976. *I.*

Tor, Regina, author and illustrator. *Getting to Know Canada*. New York: Coward-McCann, 1956. *I.*

Tudor, Tasha, author and illustrator. *Around the Year*. New York: Henry Z. Walck, 1957, *P.*

Tunis, Edwin, author and illustrator. *Colonial Livings*. New York: Henry Z. Walck, 1957. *I.*

Watson, Jane W. Cornelius DeWitt, illus. *The Golden History of the World*. New York: Golden Press, 1955. *I.*

Weisgard, Leonard, author and illustrator. *The Beginnings of Cities*. New York: Coward-McCann, 1968. *I.*

Werner, Elsa Jane. Cornelius DeWitt, illus. *The Golden Geography*. New York: Golden Press, 1952. *I.*

White, Anne Terry. Tom O'Sullivan, photog. & illus. *All about Archaeology*. New York: Random House, 1959. *I.*

Winn, Marie, author and illustrator. *The Sick Book*. New York: Four Winds, 1976. *P.*

Wise, William. T. dePaola, illus. *Monsters of the Middle Ages*. New York: G. P. Putnam's Sons, 1971. *I.*

Yadin, Yigael. *The Story of Masada*. New York: Random House, 1969. *I.*

Zemach, Harre. *Salt*. New York: Farar, Straus and Giroux, 1976. *P.*

Ziner, Feenie, and Thompson, Elizabeth. Katherine Evans, illus. *The True Book of Time*. Chicago: The Children's Press, 1956. *P.*

APPENDIX K

Book Fairs and Exhibits

Teachers may write to the following organizations, publishers, and individuals for information concerning when book fairs are held and what materials will be exhibited.

American Publishers Corporation
1024 W. Washington Blvd.
Chicago, IL 60607

Book Fairs, Inc.
162 Atlantic Avenue
Lynbrook, NY 11563

Book Fair Associates
1200 No. Branch Street
Chicago, IL 60622

Book Fair Distributors
Mear Road
Holbrook, MA 02343

Book Mail Service
8229 164 Street
Jamaica, NY 11432

Books on Exhibit
No. Bedford Road
Mount Kisco, NY 10549

Coleman Book Service
23 E. 22nd Street
New York, NY 10010

The Combined Paperback Exhibit
  in Schools
Albany Post Road
Briarcliff Manor, NY 10510

Conference Book Services, Inc.
201 S. Washington Street
Alexandria, VA 22313

Cosmo Book Distributing Co.
Institutional Division
Whelan Road,
East Rutherford, NY 07073

Educational Reading Service
64 East Midland Avenue
Paramus, NJ 07073

Follett Library Book Company
1018 W. Washington Blvd.
Chicago, IL 60607

H. R. Hunting Company
Burnett Road and First Avenue
Chicopee Falls, MA 01020

Jean Karr and Company
5656 Third Street NE
Washington, D.C. 20011

Lord Associates
115 E. 92nd Street
New York, NY 10028

A. C. McClurg and Company
2121 Landmeier Road
Elk Grove Village, IL 60007

Marco Book Company
577 Albany Avenue
Brooklyn, NY 11203

Materials for Learning
1376 Coney Island Avenue
Brooklyn, NY 11230

Melton Book Company
1901 Levee Street
Dallas, TX 76207

New England Mobile Book Fair
1980 Centre Street
West Roxbury, MA 02132

New Method Book Bindery
W. Morton Road
Jacksonville, IL 62650

Newton, Mary Griffin
4095 W. Buena Vista
Detroit, MI 48238

North Shore Book Fairs
814 Glenwood Lane
Glenview, IL 60025

Perc B. Sapsis, Inc.
1795 Del Monte Blvd.
Seaside, CA 93955

Pilgrim Book Society, Inc.
83 Pembroke Road
Akron, OH 44313

Sather Gate Book Shop
6355 Hollis Street
Emeryville, CA 94608

Scholastic Book Service
900 Sylvan Avenue
Englewood Cliffs, NJ 07632

Tooze, Ruth
Santa Coloma Farm, Route #1
Chapel Hill, NC 27514

The Day of the Bubble

by
Jᴀᴍᴇs A. Sᴍɪᴛʜ

The following story (introduced to the reader on page 388) is reprinted for the teacher in hopes that he or she will find many creative ways to use it with students.

Once there was a boy named Homer. He lived on the top of a hill over-looking the town of Sleepy Hollow. He lived with his Uncle Henry in an old, ramshackle house.

Children design a cover for The Day of the Bubble.

All day long Homer helped his Uncle Henry with the chores on their small farm. But, as soon as supper was over, Homer sat with his Uncle Henry on the front porch and played at his favorite hobby.

His hobby was blowing bubbles. Now Homer's bubbles were not just *ordinary bubbles*. No, sir! Homer had worked for years on making extra big bubbles. And, his bubbles lasted and lasted. The reason that they lasted was that Homer used a special kind of mixture to make them. He didn't use just water and soap like most people did. Homer was a scientist. He experimented with the mixture to try to make bubbles that would last.

First to the water and soap he added a little glue, but that was too thick. So one night he got the idea that maybe he could thin the glue with kerosene. That was better. Then, another night he tried adding soap powder. That night he made a bubble three feet across that floated five minutes before it hit Uncle Henry on the nose and burst!

Homer was excited. He thought a little shampoo might help. It did. Then he added rubber cement and a little molasses. And the bubbles got bigger and bigger and lasted longer and longer.

Uncle Henry, who was always getting hit by Homer's bubbles would say, "Homer, some day you're going to get into trouble with those big bubbles! It just ain't natural for bubbles to be so big and to last so long!"

Children's illustrations for The Day of the Bubble: *(1) the old, ram-shackle house; (2) one night Homer made a bubble that was three feet across; (3) Uncle Henry always said, "Homer, someday you're going to get into trouble"; (4) the bubble grew and grew.*

But Homer was a scientist. He couldn't help it. He went on experimenting and experimenting!

One night after supper, Homer and Uncle Henry were sitting on the porch on the house on the hill. Homer had just mixed up a batch of his bubble mix. This time he added just a wee bit of tar which he had found on the newly paved road.

Uncle Henry looked up from lighting his pipe. "Homer," he said, "some day you're going to get into trouble with those big bubbles! It ain't natural for bubbles to be so big and to last so long!"

But Homer was a scientist. He had to experiment. So he ran into the house and got his old faithful bubble pipe and began to blow.

It was hard to blow at first. But then the bubble began to come, and blowing became easier and easier. Homer took a deep breath and blew and blew and the bubble got bigger and bigger. Soon it was the biggest bubble he had ever blown. And it was still getting bigger and bigger! Homer could no longer see the town, or the yard, or even Uncle Henry.

More children's illustrations for The Day of the Bubble: *(5) and kept on growing . . . ; (6) with an enormous POP the bubble broke away from the bubble pipe; (7) Homer was off, chasing the bubble; (8) the bubble rolled on; (9) coming up the hill was old Bessie, the cow.*

Somewhere in the background he heard Uncle Henry saying, "Now, Homer, you watch it there! Some day you're going to get into trouble—it just ain't natural—"

But Homer couldn't hear any more. The bubble was so big he had to keep it from scraping the ground. Slowly he blew and blew! He was all out of breath from blowing! But still the bubble grew and grew!

Homer moved carefully to the edge of the porch so the bubble could hang over. Ten feet, eleven feet, twelve feet—and still the bubble grew. Thirteen feet, fourteen feet—and all Homer could hear was Uncle Henry saying, "Holy Mackerel!"

Just about then there was an enormous POP, and the bubble broke away from the bubble pipe. For a moment it shook and quivered. But it did not break. Instead it began to roll, slowly at first, and then faster and faster down the hill. Uncle Henry was on his feet. "Homer," he said, "didn't I tell you that someday—" But Homer heard no more. He was off down the hill chasing his enormous bubble.

Coming up the hill was old Bessie, the cow. She looked up from the grass she was chewing and bellowed, "Moo," and then the bubble hit! It was so sticky it just picked up Bessie and on it rolled.

Clem Thompson was bringing Uncle Henry some eggs when he looked up and saw the bubble. Before he could even holler "Help," the bubble had picked him up and he was rolling back down the hill towards Sleepy Hollow.

Prissy, the cat, was following old Clem. In a second's time she was in the bubble, rolling on toward the town. After it ran Homer, and after him came Uncle Henry crying, "Homer, I told you——"

Before long the bubble came to the highway. Mr. Arnold, the grocer, was driving his horse toward Sleepy Hollow at a slow, easy pace. He was almost asleep. Daisy, his horse, knew how to get home without his help. Before he knew what had happened to him, the bubble hit, and the horse, carriage, and groceries and Mr. Arnold went rolling down toward Main Street.

By now the horse was neighing, the cat was meowing, the cow was mooing, Clem Thompson was screaming, and Mr. Arnold was hollering, "Help!"

Everyone on Main Street turned to see what was making such a racket. They stopped in amazement to see an enormous bubble start down the street with arms, legs and animals sticking out of it. Before they could run for shelter, the bubble hit!

First, it picked up an automobile that was parked outside Dr. Parsons's office. Then it gathered up old Miss Annie Jones who was sitting on a park bench knitting. A group of girls who were playing hopscotch disappeared right off the sidewalk.

Two dogs who were chasing each other were scooped up in no time at all. Everybody and everything that was on Main Street that wasn't fastened down was rolled up into that enormous, sticky bubble.

By now Homer and Uncle Henry were entering Main Street. They stood horrified as they watched the bubble roll through the town, picking up everything in its path.

"Uncle Henry, Uncle Henry," cried Homer, "How will I stop it—what will I do?"

And all Uncle Henry could say was, "Homer, I told you someday——"

At the end of Main Street stood the church. It was a pretty little church, and the people in Sleepy Hollow were very proud of it because it had a tall, pointed steeple. Now, as the bubble rolled on down Main Street, full of people and animals and things, it was headed directly for the little old church.

"Oh, dear," cried Homer, "everyone will be killed and it's all my fault!"

By now the bubble was going so fast that it was bouncing. And what a noise! Everyone was screaming and crying and the animals were all bellowing. Just before the bubble hit the church it gave one big bounce —and landed smack up against the steeple! For a minute it stood still, and then with a great sigh and a sissing noise which was all of Homer's breath escaping, the bubble died!

More children's illustrations for The Day of the Bubble: *(10) a group of girls played hopscotch; (11) the bubble picked up Miss Annie Jones who was sitting on a park bench, knitting; (12) everything and everybody that was on Main Street was rolled into that enormous, sticky bubble.*

Such a mess! It spilled people, cars, animals, carts, benches, and groceries all over the end of Main Street—all sitting there in a gooey, sticky mess.

It took four weeks to clean up the town after Homer's bubble broke There had never been anything like it! For a year after, people were cleaning Homer's scientific experiment out of their clothes and hair. No one in Sleepy Hollow ever forgot the day of the bubble.

As for Homer, they took up a collection and sent him off to college where he could continue his scientific experiments without damaging the whole town.

Uncle Henry missed Homer. Every night after supper he would sit on the porch, and light his pipe. "That Homer," he would say, "I knew some day he'd make good with all those scientific experiments!"

More children's illustrations for The Day of the Bubble: *(15) with a great hiss, the bubble died; (16) it spilled people, cars, animals, carts, benches, and groceries all over Main Street.*

More children's illustrations for The Day of the Bubble: *(17) it took four weeks to clean up the town; (18) they sent Homer off to college to work on his scientific experiments.*

The Day of the Bubble

Index of Names and Titles

Book," 328n, 332
Metric Measure (Zim and
    Skelly), 442
Meyer, Carolyn, 331
Michael Is Brave (Buckley), 62,
    81, 205, 444
*Michael Strogoff: A Courier of the
    Czar* (Verne), 231–232
Michelangelo, 349–350
Michelangelo (Ripley), 350
*Michelangelo Buonarroti,
    1475–1564: Five Sons of Italy*
    (Acker), 350
Middle Moffat, The (Estes),
    200, 201
Middle Sister, The (Mason), 79
Midsummer-Night's Dream, A
    (Shakespeare), 227
*Mighty Men from Achilles to
    Caesar* (Farjeon), 303
*Mighty Men from Beowulf to
    William the Conqueror*
    (Farjeon), 303
*Mike Mulligan and His Steam
    Shovel* (Burton), 251–252
Milhous, Katherine, 94, 408
Millay, Edna St. Vincent, 47
Miller, Hannah, 488
Miller, Helen Markley, 78
Millions of Cats (Gag), 36,
    90, 246–247
Mills of God, The (Armstrong), 35
Milne, A. A., 34, 80, *187*, 229–230,
    245, 303
Milne, Christopher Robin, 187
Minarik, Else Holmelund, 29, 210
Minori, Bruno, 28, 33
Miracles on Maple Hill
    (Sorenson), 88
Miranda the Great (Estes), 200, 201
Miss Alcott of Concord
    (Worthington), 177n
Miss Hickory (Bailey), 55, 88
Miss Pickerell Goes to Mars
    (MacGregor), 57
Mitch and Amy (Cleary), 203
Mitchell, Lucy Sprague, 204
Mitchell, Margaret, 435, 437
Modest Proposal, A (Swift), 163
Moffats, The (Estes), 78, 200,
    201, 479
*Moja Means One: The Swahili
    Counting Book* (Feelings), 263
Molesworth, Mrs., 223
Moll Flanders (Defoe), 163
*Monkey and the Crocodile,
    The,* 256
Monsieur Racine and the Beast
    (Ungerer), 261
Monson, Dianne L., 86n
Montignoni, Margaret E., 483
Montresor, Beni, 33, 94
Montreville, Doris de, 208n
Moods (Alcott), 178
Moon in My Room, The
    (Shulevitz), 263
Moore, Noel, 228
Mordvinoff, Nicholas, 94, 95
More Junior Authors (Fuller, ed.),
    197n, 198n
*More Nursery Rhymes of London
    Town* (Farjeon), 303

More Tales from Grimm (Gag), 248
Morgan, Roy, 46
Morris, William, 223
Mostly Canallers (Edmonds), 480
Mother Goose, 87
Mother Goose (Greenaway),
    33, 225
Mother Goose (puppet show), 31
Mother Goose (Wildsmith), 33
Mother Goose Lost (Tucker), 33
Mother Goose in Prose
    (Baum), 182
Mother Goose Treasury
    (Brigg), 33
*Mother Goose's Melody or
    Sonnets for the Cradle*
    (Newbery), 31, 87
Motivation and Personality
    (Maslow), 75n
Mouse and His Child, The
    (Hoban), 206
Mouse and the Motorcycle, The
    (Cleary), 203
Moy Loy (Politi), 244, 251
Mr. Popper's Penguins (Atwater
    and Atwater), 10, 35
Mrs. Frisby and the Rats of Nimh
    (O'Brien), 57, 63, 89
Muffel and Plums (Fromm), 28
Muhammad Ali (Rudeen), 445
My Animals (Armstrong), 35
*My Cat Has Eyes of Sapphire
    Blue* (Fisher), 446
"My Country Calls" (Wyss), 166
My Friend Flicka (O'Hara), 80
My Friend John (Zolotow), 202
My Grandson Lew (Zolotow), 59,
    150, 202, 257
My Mother's House (Clark), 78
My Peaceable Paints
    (Weisgard), 259
My Sister and I (Buckley), 80, 205
My Special Best Words
    (Steptoe), 264
My Twin Sister Erika (Vogel), 437
"Mysterious Cat, The"
    (Lindsay), 303
Mysterious Island, The
    (Verne), 173
*Mystery of the Missing Red
    Mitten, The* (Kellogg), 54–55
Mystery in the Museum, The
    (Cavanna), 350
Mystery of the Pirate's Ghost
    (Honness), 53

Names, Sets and Numbers
    (Bendick), 33
Nancy Drew Cookbook, 442
Napoleon I, 167
Nash, Ogden, 304
Nassiet, Claude, 442
"National Tape Repository"
    (Johnson), 492
Nesbitt, Rosemary, 480, 481
Ness, Evaline, 41, 80, 94,
    243, *253*–254
*Neurotic Distortion of the Creative
    Process* (Kubie), 118n
Neville, Emily Cheney, 58, 79,
    82, 89
New Education Materials 1970: A

*Classified Guide to Books,
    Films, Recordings, Multi-
    Media Kits, Transparencies,
    Film Loops, Teaching-
    Learning Games, and
    Professional Guides,* 491
Newbery, John, 31, 87, 351
Newbitt, Rosemary, 81
*New Forest, Its History and
    Scenery, The* (Wise), 222
New Friend (Zolotow), 202
New Pet, The (Flack), 80
Newell, Hope, 380
*Newsmakers: The Press and the
    President* (Smith and
    Norris), 442
"Night Before Christmas,
    The," 364
Night Fall (Aiken), 53, 54
Night Wind, The (Allan), 54
Nikki (Blue), 444
Nine Days to Christmas (Etts and
    Labastida), 94
Noble Gases, The (Asimov), 66
*Nobody's Family Is Going to
    Change* (Fitzhugh), 209
Noisy Book (Brown), 203
Nonsense Songs and Stories
    (Lear), 303
Norris, Gunilla B., 81, 431
Norris, Lorraine, 442
Norse Gods and Giants (D'Aulaire
    and D'Aulaire), 46
North, Sterling, 34
Norton, Mary, 55
*Nothing Ever Happens on My
    Block* (Raskin), 36, 84
Now It's Fall (Lenski), 327
Now We Are Six (Milne), 229–230
Nowell, George W., 86n
Nursery and Household Tales
    (Brothers Grimm), 167–168
Nursery Rhymes of London Town
    (Farjeon), 303
Nutshell Library (Sendak), 97, 211

O'Brien, Robert C., 57, 63, 89
Ocean-Born Mary (Lenski), 330
O'Dell, Scott, 82, 89, 400
Odyssey (Homer), 45
Oh, The Thinks You Can Think
    (Seuss), 200
O'Hara, Mary, 80
Olaf Reads (Lexau), 213, 214
Old Christmas (Irving), 224
Old Fashioned Girl, An
    (Alcott), 178
*Old Mother Hubbard and Her
    Dog* (Ness), 254
On a Summer Day (Lenski), 327
Once a Mouse (Brown), 94,
    259, 260
Once on a Time (Milne), 187
Once We Went on a Picnic
    (Chen), 241
One, Two, Where's My Shoe?
    (Ungerer), 33
One Bite at a Time (Irwin), 444
One Fine Day (Hogrogian), 94
100 Hamburgers (Solot), 256
*120 Questions and Answers about
    the Birds* (Angell), 446

Witheridge, Elizabeth, 79
Witty, Paul, 86n
Wizard of Oz, The (film), 417
Wizard in the Well, The (Behn), 302
Wojciechowska, Maia, 89, 192,
   206–208
Wonder Book for Girls and Boys
   (Hawthorne), 223, 227
Wonder Clock, The (Pyle), 231
Wonder of Seasons, The
   (Parker), 85
Wonderful Little Boy, The
   (Buckley), 205
Wonderful Wizard of Oz, The
   (Baum), 182–184, 357
*Wondrous World of Seedless
   Plants, The* (Grimm and
   Craig), 446

Wood, Ray, 33
Work (Alcott), 179
Worlds to Come (Knight), 446
Worthington, Marjorie, 177n
Wreath of Christmas Legends, A
   (McGinley), 259
Wrinkle in Time, A (L'Engle), 27,
   57, 83, 89, 399, 446
Wurmfeld, Hope, 244
Wyeth, Andrew, 231
Wyeth, Jamie, 231
Wyeth, N. C., 186, *231–232*
Wyndham, Lee, 59
"Wynken, Blynken and Nod"
   (Field), 304, 364, 375
Wyss, Johann David, 165–166, 173
Wyss, Johann Emmanuel, 165
Wyss, Johann Rudolf, *165–166,* 173

Yates, Elizabeth, 65, 88
Yearling, The (Rawlings), 58
Yeats, William Butler, 395
Yeck Eck (Ness), 254
*Yo-Yo Kid, The (*Blue), 437

Zaffo, George, 97
Zamani Goes to Market
   (Feelings), 263
Zemach, Harve, 37, 94
Zim, Herbert, 442, 446
Zimmerman, Dianne I., 268
Zolotow, Charlotte, 59, 150,
   201–202, 257, 258, 259
Zolotow, Maurice, 201

Subject Index

Adventure strategies, 352–413
   artifacts, use of, 383–386
   the book fair, 375, 394
   book reports, 373–374
   booklets, 397–398
   box theaters, 374–375
   bulletin-boards, 367–373
   choral speaking, 396–397
   clay modeling, 408–410
   contact with authors, 392
   creating ballads, 407
   dance interpretations, 410–411
   dioramas, 392–393
   displays and exhibits, 394
   dramatizations, 352–360
   felt-o-grams, 364–365
   field trips, 402
   film-making, 365–367
   filmstrips, 395–396
   finger plays, 389
   flannel boards, 364–365
   games, 391–392
   impersonations, 411–412
   lap stories, 404–406
   mobiles, 407–408
   murals, 390–391
   peep shows, 400–402
   peg board displays, 394–395
   pictorial maps, 406–407
   puppets, 360–364
   radio programs, 399
   reading stories, 383
   realia, use of, 383–386
   recordings, 395–396
   roll movies, 399
   shadow boxes, 399–400
   shadow plays, 402–404
   sound stories, 386–389
   television programs, 399
   telling stories, 379–383
Adventure tales, 50–52, 160
Alphabet books, 33
American folktales, 40–41
American Library Association,
   87, 250
Analogy, development of, 341–344
Animal stories, 34–36

Anthologies, resources for,
   482–483
Appreciation for literature,
   developing, 333–346
   adventures and experiences, 335
   analogies, 341–344
   creative writing and, 344–345
   empathy, 335–336
   evaluative discussions, 336
   experiencing contrasts,
      333–334
   metaphors, 341–344
   perception development,
      338–341
   relevance, 337
   sensory experiences, 337–338
   similes, 341–344
Art, literature and, 430–431
Artifacts, 383–386
Authors:
   classical, 159–191
   contact with, as adventure
      strategy, 392
   modern, 192–218

Ballads, 46–49, 407
Baseball Hall of Fame, 351
Bibliographies, 484, 494
Bibliotherapy, 149–151
Biography, 63–65
   resources for, 493
Book clubs, 491
Book fairs, 465–472
   as adventure strategy, 375, 394
   evaluation of, 470–472
   objectives of, 465–466, 469–470
   planning for, 466–469
   resources for the teacher, 493
Book reports, as adventure
   strategy, 373–374
Booklets, as adventure strategy,
   397–398
Bookmobiles, 465
Box theaters, 374–375
Brainstorming, 124–128
Bulletin boards, as adventure
   strategy, 367–373

Caldecott Medal, 43, 93, 103, 203,
   210, 225, 243, 249, 250, 252,
   254, 256, 258, 259, 263, 369
   list of winning books, 93–94
Catalogs, resources for, 484–485
Chapbooks, 221
Character development, 61–63
Chicago Show Window, 182
Chicago Tribune, 465
Child Study Association, 208, 445
Choral speaking, 396–397
Christian Science Monitor, 465
Classical authors, 159–191
Classical illustrators, 219–235
   first illustrated children's
      book, 221
Classics, the, 159–162
   defined, 159
   four genres of, 160–162
   universality of, 159–160
Classifications of children's
   literature, 25–67
   adventure tales, 50–52
   alphabet books, 33
   animal stories, 34–36
   concept books, 33–34
   counting books, 33
   fantasy tales, 55–57
   folklore, 38–50
   humor, 36–38
   illustrated books, 28–30
   Mother Goose rhymes, 30–33
   mystery stories, 52–54
   nonfiction, 63–67
   picture books, 28–30
   picture-story books, 28–30
   poetry, 38
   realistic fiction, 57–63
   romance, 54–55
   science fiction, 55–57
Classroom library, 463–465
Clay modeling, 408–410
Concept books, 33–34
Con-Sociate Society, 177
Counting books, 33
Creative communication, literature
   as, 4–18